Reports to the 74th General Convention

Otherwise Known as THE BLUE BOOK

ENGAGE
GOD'S MISSION
2|0
0|3

Reports of the Committees, Commissions, Boards and Agencies of
The General Convention of the Episcopal Church
Seventy-Fourth General Convention, Minneapolis, Minnesota, July 30-August 8, 2003

 CHURCH

Church Publishing, New York

Letter to Bishops and Deputies from the
Secretarty of the 74th General Convention

Dear Friends,

It is a privilege to present to you the Report of the Commissions, Committees, Agencies and Boards to the 74th General Convention in what has become known as *The Blue Book.*

The hard work and best thinking of more than 500 members of our Church generates these reports. The General Convention Office has collaborated with these groups to make the material as accessible as possible. There is significant information to digest in these documents. The content will inform the decision making of the Bishops and Deputies to the 74th General Convention.

The Blue Book will be available online at http://www.dfms.org/gc/gc2003 and http://www.churchpublishing.org. You will also receive a CD-ROM as part of this publication.

On behalf of the Church, I wish to gratefully acknowledge the work of the many persons who have contributed to this volume. In particular, I want to recognize Anne Karoly, Publications Manager for the General Convention Office and the staff of Church Publishing.

The staff of the General Convention Office and I look forward to greeting you in Minneapolis at the 74th General Convention.

Faithfully yours in Christ,

The Rev. Rosemari G. Sullivan
Secretary of the General Convention

In Memoriam
JOHN KEMPER CANNON
1932-2002

For a quarter of a century, John Kemper Cannon served the House of
Deputies as Parliamentarian, Chancellor to the President, and a
member of the President's Council of Advice. He served the local
and national Church in many capacities, including the Executive
Council. He chaired the Boards of Directors of the Church Pension
Fund and The Archives of the Episcopal Church. We thank God for
his life and service.

CONTENTS

AGENCIES

AND

BOARDS

THE BOARD OF THE ARCHIVES OF THE EPISCOPAL CHURCH
www.episcopalarchives.org

MEMBERSHIP

Mr. John K. Cannon, *Chair**	Southwest Florida, 2003, (deceased Dec. 15, 2002)
The Right Reverend Larry E. Maze, *Vice- Chair*	Arkansas, 2003
The Reverend Dr. Robert G. Carroon, *Secretary**	Connecticut, 2003
Mr. R.P.M. Bowden	Atlanta, 2006
Mr. Mark J. Duffy*	*Canonical Archivist, ex officio*
Ms. Michelle A. Francis*	Western North Carolina, 2006
The Right Reverend Richard F. Grein*	New York, 2006
The Reverend John Kitagawa*	Maryland, 2003
Ms. Margaret D. Lewis	Washington, 2006
The Very Reverend Titus Presler	*Dean of ETSS, ex officio*
The Right Reverend James H. Ottley	Panama, 2003
The Reverend Canon Edward W. Rodman	Massachusetts, 2006
Mr. Newland F. Smith	Chicago, 2006

WORK SUMMARY

The purpose of the Board is to provide general direction for the Church Archives and to establish policies for its care and management. The Board oversees the work of the Canonical Archivist and represents the interests of the Archives in other venues of Church life. As of the publication of this report, the full Board will have held two meetings at the Archives in Austin. In addition, a meeting was held in Chicago of the full Archives Site Selection Committee, which includes several members of the Board and other representatives.

In this triennium the committee continued to work with the Archivist to resolve the space issue, to tie the development of a future Friends group to fundraising for a new archival building, to develop policies and guidelines for the archival preservation and management of electronic records, and to conduct its regular review of archival operations and planning. As a result of new funding in this triennium, the Board was able to receive new reports on the records management program, which is working to improve management of the paper and electronic records of the Episcopal Church Center, and to examine several innovative databases that have been launched on the Internet as part of the Board's priority to make institutional records available for education and mission.

The Board gave considerable time and attention to the task of locating new quarters for the Archives. This effort was supplemented by the work of the Archives Site Selection Committee, which included the members whose names above are given an asterisk (*) as well as the following representatives:

> Ms. Judy Dailey (National Archives and Records Administration)
> The Reverend Kenneth Kesselus (Executive Council)
> Ms. Patricia Mordecai (Executive for Administration, DFMS)
> Russell Palmore, Jr., Esq. (Executive Council)

A smaller executive committee headed by Mr. John Cannon conducted numerous conversations with potential partners. Several locations were examined with the strongest interest coming from the New Haven, New York, and Philadelphia areas. As of this report, however, no conclusive settlement on a future site has been reached. The delay in progress reflects our reluctance to act without regard to coincidental discussions that emerged in Executive Council on the relocation of the Episcopal Church Center and the possibility of a fund-raising effort. Either of these events would have a profound impact on the direction or resources open to the Archives. The settlement of the headquarters issue in favor of remaining at 815 Second Avenue in late 2002 leaves the Board to consider raising funds in conjunction with a similar prospect that may yet arise from the Executive Council. In addition, new leadership at our current host institution, the Episcopal Theological

Seminary of the Southwest, has led to renewed interest in retaining the Archives in Austin and blending programs of mission and education.

The untimely death of the Board's Chair in the midst of these negotiations brought sadness to all of us who have taken an interest in the mission of the Church Archives. John Kemper Cannon served as a member of the Board of the Archives since 1997. He immediately assumed leadership by crafting the Board's discussions and policies in several areas that strengthened the Archives' holdings. He negotiated with other Church agencies to try to reduce overlap in mission and stewardship of the Church's historical documentation. He pursued various promising partnerships for the Archives even as the unpredictability of events held the rest of us in abeyance. His counsel, wisdom, fairness, and humor were valuable gifts that he freely gave in many Church venues. The Board and the staff of the Archives feel his loss acutely. We are ever grateful for the time he gave us and for his devotion to the Church's spiritual and cultural heritage.

Financial Report for the 2001 – 2003 Triennium
Archives/Records Management Expenses

	2001	2002 Projected	2003 Projected	Total Projected
Salaries and Benefits (estimated)	$424,022	$511,369	$501,298	$1,436,689
Rent, Facilities, Storage	46,825	45,000	53,990	145,815
Operations	49,662	50,836	75,201	175,699
Information Services	35,919	61,976	48,860	146,755
Total	$556,428	$669,181	$679,349	$1,904,958

Board of the Archives Expenses

	2001	2002 Projected	2003 Projected	Total Projected
Non-Staff/Consultants	$ 0	$ 0	$ 0	$ 0
Administrative	0	128	500	628
Full Board Meetings	12,316	3,618	18,500	34,434
	$12,316	$3,746	$19,000	$35,062

Goals and Objectives for the 2001-2003 Triennium
The Board understands its mission as the education of Church and society about The Episcopal Church's place in the shaping of a reflective, historical community. The specific goals for the coming triennium are to extend the content and reach of the digital archives of contemporary Church communications, but to add to these more description of the historical archives. The Board will work with the Archivist to find approaches to the difficult task of preserving access to non-current electronic records (including many of our diocesan journals) that are now being created by Church agencies exclusively as databases. Finally, the Board will continue to pursue plans for a permanent and adequate repository for the national Church Archives. The following budget was presented by the Executive Council.

BUDGET APPROPRIATION
Archives and Records Management

	2004	2005	2006	Total
Salaries and Benefits	$512,069	$530,317	$549,364	$1,591,750
Rent, Facilities, Storage	53,990	53,990	53,990	161,970
Operations	70,201	70,201	70,201	210,603
Information Services	30,160	30,160	30,660	90,980
Total	$666,420	$684,668	$704,215	$2,055,303

Board of the Archives

	2004	2005	2006	Total
Non-Staff/Consultants	$ 7,500	$ 7,500	$ 0	$15,000
Administrative	1,000	1,000	1,000	3,000
Full Board Meetings	12,000	12,000	9,000	33,000
Executive Committee	4,500	4,500	5,000	14,000
	$25,000	$25,000	$15,000	$65,000

Report of the Archivist

Archives, Mission and Memory

The stereotypical description of the church-going Episcopalian of the previous century was a person more interested in ritual than revelry. On any Sunday morning one could observe a service celebrated at either the traditional east end of the altar or a traditional high altar. The variation speaks to the local re-interpretations of a common liturgy, wherein a familiar sacramental re-enactment mysteriously invokes a corporate memory that each individual can, in time, tap into as part of an Anglican identity. As with the worship service, institutions sustain memories through the communication of texts, which are themselves the product of mundane but vital rituals. Prayer books, canons, pastoral documents, newsletters and magazines, and even websites are among the many ways that we collectively create a common spiritual home and individually re-enact our faith in and through the community.

The Church's archival holdings are among the substantive historical objects that both manifest the story of our journey and propagate that story back into the mission of the Church today. Archivists of religion around the world were gratified when the Roman Catholic Church's pontifical commission on the Church's cultural heritage recently issued a formal call for preservation and opening of archives as a vital source for a "new evangelism." We are reminded not only of the mission priorities that have found momentum in this triennium, but also of the 'rootedness' of the specific appeal in a history of domestic and foreign missionary activity. The Church Archives is part of the connectivity that sustains the institutional memory through the rituals of documenting, researching, managing, and communicating information into the system in anticipation of changing priorities. The increased use of the Archives in recent years by parish priests and educators, diocesan chancellors and committee members, church administrators, publishers, and seminary students gives us reason to believe that the Archives is contributing to a more knowledgeable discourse.

Several projects in this triennium have gone beyond everyday archival practice and have added qualitatively to the shoring up of our institutional memory. The Archives rose to the occasion of a sudden loss of key General Convention staff who were responsible for publishing the *Journal of Convention*. Being familiar with the *Journal's* overall structure and design from repeated use in our historical research, the Archives could also bring to the task its knowledge of the legislative process by virtue of its on-site legislative support. The staff assumed the task in August 2001 and produced a finished volume by year's end. It is by far the most accurate record of Convention proceedings to be produced in some time and demonstrates the value of redundant layers of knowledge in an organizational system.

The Archives faces the dual challenge of trying to make stored institutional knowledge available through electronic communication and managing new electronic assets so that they are available in the future. In 2003 the Archives published a re-designed website that included several keyword-searchable databases of resolutions and news stories. These digital archives were carefully edited and coded with an eye to delivering accurate and reliable data that can be easily migrated to future Internet operating environments. Related to this venture, and in response to *GC Resolution 2000-A016*, the Archives drafted a proposal for the evaluation, retention, and preservation of electronic records of the DFMS (i.e., principally the Episcopal Church Center offices). The policy proposal was delivered to the administration for review early in 2003. The proposal includes discussion points for clarifying the community's assumptions and values, and recommendations for an ongoing involvement by the Archives in managing electronic records for future access. The outcome of this work hinges on the will of the Church Center staff to coordinate the separate activities of current databases, legacy files, website publications, and related online communications.

In almost every programmatic aspect of its work, the Archives is limited by the space it currently occupies. While our investigation of alternatives continues, however, we celebrate the many expressions of trust that our private donors make in the stewardship of their personal papers and organizational records. The Archives will not relinquish its commitment to documenting and interpreting the Church's history in its full diversity. Among the highlights of this triennium was the opening of a major exhibit, *The Church Awakens,* an examination of the civil rights movement within The Episcopal Church. While it covered the whole of the twentieth century, special emphasis was placed on the central role of the Episcopal Society for Cultural and Racial Unity (ESCRU). Over 88 document boxes of records of ESCRU have been donated to the Archives in recent years and, under terms of the transfer, were opened to researchers in 2000. The exhibit of photographs and documents covers over 500 square feet of wall space in the ETSS library. Eventually, the exhibit will make its way to the Archives' website where it can support curricula and serve as a reminder of the dynamic and multi-dimensional nature of mission.

Research Services

The Archives' research and reference services have responded to an increasingly eclectic mix of historical and contemporary information requests. The proportion of purely *historical* inquiries declined to 49 percent of the total in 2002; more individuals seemed to turn to the Archives for information on fairly recent (i.e., roughly the last 3 to 5 years) events and programs of the national and local church. That we are successful in helping people with their short-term memory in this way only adds to a reputation as a reliable and helpful source. As one of our Province IV cathedral deans commented after the staff hunted down a document he knew only vaguely by topic, "I was told *the* Archives is the place to go if you want to find an answer – quickly." In this sense, the Archives is not unlike The Episcopal Church's own research library of primary sources. The relative drop in historical inquiries may also reflect our ability to provide answers about General Convention resolutions through new online databases, although it is too early to tell, as the Internet can also create new interest and inquiry. The following table summarizes the number of assisted (i.e., substantive) research inquiries as well as other minor information requests and consultations.

	2000	2001	2002
Assisted Research			
Historical	858	890	658
Administrative	132	97	83
Contemporary	478	507	525
Total – Assisted Research	1,468	1,494	1,266
Total – All Research and Archives Inquiries	1,866	1,814	1,583

Extended research in support of administrative and program initiatives is now a common expectation of the Archives. In the past triennium, we reported for Church agencies and offices on such areas as the establishment and history of HIV/AIDS ministries, the gathering of parochial reports, the national ethnic desks, the Episcopal Church's involvement in Native-American tribal re-settlement, the foreign missionary budget in perspective, the Church in Cuba and Liberia, and as well as numerous diocesan inquiries on bioethics, human sexuality, and war and peace. The Archives gave close to 30 consultations to parishes and dioceses in each year of the triennium. It should be noted that a range of 60-67 percent of our patrons in any recent year identified themselves as being Episcopalians.

The Archives also serves scholarly research of religion. The following list is a sample of works produced in the past three years based on research in the Archives.

> Article, Chinese University of Hong Kong. The Rev. H. N. Woo in the American Civil War
> Article, Episcopal Women's History Project. Cynthia Wedel
> Dissertation, SUNY– Binghamton. Christian Socialism in the Episcopal Church
> Dissertation, Princeton Theological Seminary. Episcopal Mission to the Philippines
> Dissertation, Yale University. American Religion in the 1960s
> Dissertation, Princeton University. Deaconess Movement in Protestant Churches

Dissertation, General Theological Seminary. Baptism and Confirmation in the 1979 Prayer Book Revision
Monograph, Zhongshan University, Guangdong. Mary Elizabeth Wood and the Modern Library in China
Monograph, Nashotah House. Bishop Robert E. Terwilliger
Monograph, American University. Cathedral Films and the Development of Religious Film Making
Monograph, Independent. Civil Rights Movement in the United States
Monograph, University of Western Australia. Joseph Jeffrey Walters and the Episcopal Mission to Liberia
Monograph, Salem State College. The Reverend Samuel Farmar Jarvis
Monograph, University of San Diego. St. Hilda's School for Girls, Wuchang, China
Monograph, Church Divinity School of the Pacific. St. Margaret's House
Monograph, Episcopal Divinity School. Windham House and Lay Women's Vocations
Monograph, Independent. U.S. Grant's "Peace Policy" and the Episcopal Church's Indian Agents
Monograph, Episcopal Divinity School. Episcopal Women and Christian Education
Monograph, Independent. Revision of White & Dykman's Annotated Canons
Monograph, Independent. Annie Craig Farthing, Missionary to Alaska
Play, Independent. Juliet Thompson and the Reverend Percy Stickney Grant

Acquisition of Archives

The Archives acquired 339 cubic feet (representing 360 accessions) of historical records to the Austin repository in the three-year period 2000-2002; an additional 858 cubic feet of archives and records were accessioned into an enlarged records center in the Episcopal Church Center. The Archives now sends to warehouse storage at least as much as it takes into the Austin repository, where papers of individuals, organizational records, and special collections are principally housed. In the same period, 422 cubic feet of records were transferred to a privately owned, offsite facility. We have exhausted our supply of security copies and less important materials and are beginning to store valuable historical records in space that is not environmentally protected or conducive to research. This situation will have to change in the coming triennium.

A number of remarkable collections have been added to the Archives' holdings. Special mention is made of several collections that offer considerable insight into the Church's changing identity and its voice in the public forum. In the first case, the Church's development of Hispanic ministry is documented by the Records of the Instituto Pastoral Hispano, c.1977-1998. The struggle for parity in the treatment of women is captured in the papers of Wyndham House dean and educator, Dr. Helen Turnbull (papers 1939-1990), and the collections of Sally Mitchell Bucklee (papers 1974-2001), a prominent lay leader in the transition to greater access for women to ministerial leadership. An important collection of ecumenical reports and work papers, particularly relating to ARCIC, were donated by Bishop Arthur Vogel. Foreign mission is well documented in the Papers of Charles Henry Long, Jr., 1947-1998, who was a locus of communication among former missionaries and who recognized the centrality of foreign mission to the Church's domestic health. In the area of social ministry, the Archives was chosen as the repository for two key collections that document advocacy for human rights from a Christian standpoint: the Records of the Episcopal Appalachian (People's) Ministries, 1960-1997, and the Papers of the Reverend Seiichi Michael Yasutake, c.1964-2000. We are grateful for these and for the gifts of all our donors. A list of the significant acquisitions of personal papers, organizational records, and special collections since 2000 can be found on the Archives' website (episcopalarchives.org).

The Archives began a preservation project in 2000 to acquire through microfilm or other means copies of diocesan newspapers. These primary records are the principal source of news on parish beginnings, diocesan events, outreach programs and ministries; indeed, the Church's response to all forms of human need and community building can be found in these pages. As of this report, the following diocesan newspapers, most of which were filmed at little or no cost to the diocese, have been added to the national Church Archives.

California	*Pacific Church News*, 1861-2000
Central Pennsylvania	*The Churchman*, 1911-2000
Connecticut	*Connecticut Churchman/The Good News*, 1906-2002
El Camino Real	*The Mission Bell*, 1981-1992
Iowa	*Iowa Churchman*, 1877-1973
Minnesota	*The Minnesota Missionary*, 1879-1967

Missouri	*The Interim*, 1870-1989
Oklahoma	*The Oklahoma Churchman*, 1891-1964
Quincy	*The Light/The Harvest Plain*, 1935-1998
Texas	*The Mission Record/Texas Churchman*, 1873-1988
West Texas	*Church News*, 1883-1976

Processing and Preservation of Holdings

The organization of archival records, including the preparation of inventories, finding aids, and indexes, is a labor-intensive process, without which the knowledge contained in the records cannot be tapped. The Archives benefits from the availability of nearby University of Texas students who assist the curatorial staff in arranging, describing, and caring for the physical record. Several of the foreign mission collections – remarkably important research collections to the Church as well as for students of the humanities and social sciences – were re-organized as a result of a multi-year effort to replace decaying paper documents and to re-house the material in archival folders and containers.

A total of 438 cubic feet of records were processed at some level of detail in the three-year period. Finding aids were created for 336 cubic feet of new material, which is very close to the volume of records received into the Archives in the same period (339 cu.ft.). As a result of the processing, the Archives was able to discard over 115 cubic feet of obsolete records, thus recovering valuable storage space. Of special note is our attempt to capture, inventory, and preserve a complete run of all diocesan convention journals as required by the Canons. These annual reports are an invaluable source of information and statistical data that are gradually (and without much thought about future access) being issued only as electronic web versions. The following archival collections have been newly processed and opened for research.

Alexander Boyd Andrews Prayer Book Collection, 1710-1929, 382 vols.
Prayer Book and Liturgy Collection of the Church Archives, 1667-1989, 597 vols.
The Records of the North Conway Institute, 1950-1999, 72 cu.ft.
DFMS. Missionary Personnel and Correspondence Files, c.1890-1970, 49 cu.ft.
Diocesan Convention Journals, Canonical Deposit Collection, 1790-2000, 896 volumes
Records of the Episcopal Church Mission in China, 1839-1954, 49 cu.ft.
Records of the Episcopal Mission in the Philippines, 1898-1963, 12 cu.ft.
Records of the Girls' Friendly Society of the USA, 1860-1986, 12 cu.ft.
Records of the Board of Foreign Parishes, 1859-1992, 10 cu.ft.
Papers of Emeline Bowne, Missionary to China, 1902-1986, 4.3 cu.ft.
Papers of the Right Reverend Daniel N. Corrigan, 1931-1989, 1.0 cubic foot

Digital Archives and Records Management

The records management program at the Episcopal Church Center was staffed with a professional archivist beginning in March 2000. As a result, significant progress has been made to regularize the flow of records from Church Center offices. The archivist in New York has been able to work with office staff to improve information systems and record-keeping in general, and to make a large dent in years of backlogged records stored throughout the building. The Archives inventoried over 270 cubic feet of records held in storage and isolated several hundred cubic feet of records for destruction, and completed 15 records retention schedules that will guide us in the future disposition of noncurrent records. A notable development is the creation of a manual to aid the record keeping processes of the General Convention in 2003. The New York office was instrumental in creating the electronic records policy proposal that could become the basis for managing the growing accumulation of database records.

A special source of satisfaction in this triennium is the creation of several innovative and promising applications for online access to vital information of the national Church. The conversion of paper documents to a digital archive requires careful, quality-controlled attention to re-producing accurate, authentic data, and, where possible, offering more complete data than is currently available in any one place in paper form. Searchable databases of digital archives have been created for the following resources on the web:

> The Acts of Convention, 1976-2000
> The Resolves of Executive Council, 1976-2000
> The Living Church Archives, 1995-2000
> Episcopal Press and News, 1976-2000

A primary concern for the Archives is to create a digital record that is not only faithful to the original, but can also be easily migrated to new operating environments that may yet emerge through the Internet. In the final year of the triennium, the Archives will turn to publishing descriptions of its historical holdings.

Acknowledgment
The Director wishes to acknowledge the contribution of the professional staff, whose talents have made the Archives a welcoming place for our constituents and a more valuable resource to the Church than it has ever been: Sylvia Baker (Technical Archivist), Jennifer Dunbar (Administrative Deputy), Maribeth Betton (Archivist for Access and Collection Management), Caroline Higgins (Records Management and Information Services Archivist), and Jennifer Peters (Research and Public Services Archivist). Several part-time employees, especially Amy FitzGerald, Enrique Parada, Yogi Patel, and Melany Tovar, have worked for several years in the Archives and have enriched us by their intelligence and good spirit.

Mark J. Duffy
Canonical Archivist and Director
January 17, 2003

Resolution A001 Budget Appropriation for the Archives of the Episcopal Church

1   *Resolved,* and in accordance with Title I, Canon 5, Section 4, That the 74th General Convention
2   appropriate approximately $1,591,750 for salaries and benefits for the staff of The Archives of the
3   Episcopal Church for the triennium 2004-2006; the allocation of these funds within the Canonical budget
4   shall be determined by the Joint Standing Committee on Program, Budget and Finance; and be it further
5   *Resolved*, in accordance with Title I, Canon 5, Section 4, That the 74th General Convention appropriate
6    $463,553 for operations, site and facility, and information services expenses of The Archives of the
7   Episcopal Church for the triennium 2004-2006; the allocation of these funds within the Canonical budget
8   shall be determined by the Joint Standing Committee on Program, Budget and Finance; and be it further
9   *Resolved,* That there be appropriated from the Canonical budget of General Convention $65,000 for
10   meetings and expenses of the Board of the Archives of the Episcopal Church for the triennium 2004-2006.

THE BOARD FOR CHURCH DEPLOYMENT
www.episcopalchurch.org/cdo

MEMBERSHIP

The Rt. Rev. Clifton Daniel, III, *Chair*	East Carolina, *2003*
Canon Roberta Fairman, *Vice-Chair*	New Hampshire, *2006*
The Rt. Rev. Richard S. O. Chang	Hawaii, *2006*
Canon Betsy H. Greenman	Olympia, *2003*
The Very Rev. Jorge Gutierrez	Rochester, *2003*
The Rev. David W. Kent	Kansas, *2006*
The Rev. John F. Koepke, III	Southern Ohio, *2006*
Mr. Jesse Milan, Jr.	Maryland, *2003*
Ms. Jean Mulligan	Maine, *2003*
The Rt. Rev. F. Neff Powell	Southwestern Virginia, *2006*
The Rt. Rev. Creighton L. Robertson	South Dakota, *2003*
The Rev. Janice M. Robinson	Washington, *2006*

Board Representatives at General Convention

Bishop Clifton Daniel and Deputy Roberta Fairman are authorized to receive non-substantive amendments to the report.

WORK SUMMARY

During the triennium 2001-2003, the Church Deployment Office (CDO) completed a series of major staff transitions that began during the previous triennium. These transitions were occasioned by three retirements, the hiring of several new staff members, and the reassignment of others. With the development of new office technology, staff roles have changed dramatically in recent years. CDO staff has been developing the more sophisticated technical knowledge necessary to work on a person-to-person basis with CDO users in the delivery of services. All staff have demonstrated the requisite "people skills" and communications skills to function optimally in this new environment.

In April 2002 the new CDO On Line system was launched, greatly enhancing the accessibility of CDO services in real time over the internet. A period of debugging and correcting some design flaws followed the system's introduction. By late 2002 the development of program enhancements, to further improve performance and user-friendliness, was well under way. Some of the important features of the new system:

- Registrants (clergy and lay professionals) are now able to access and update their profiles on line and to print them locally.
- Diocesan deployment officers have access to all active and retired personal profiles, and can print profiles locally. They are able to update a personal profile with the user's permission.
- Deployment officers can create and edit position profiles and list them on the *Positions Open Bulletin* in real time.
- Subscribers can search the *Positions Open Bulletin*, access position profiles on line and print them.
- Deployment officers can search the personnel database for qualified candidates for positions.
- Manuals and forms can be downloaded and printed directly from the site.

CDO has launched a training program for diocesan deployment officers (DDO) and bishops, designed to give them hands-on training in the operation of the new system. This program has been greatly enhanced by the development and upgrading of a high tech computer lab at the Episcopal Church Center by our Management Information Systems (MIS) department. The standard training seminars that are offered three times a year are being supplemented by a series of one-day technical training events and demonstrations at deployment officers' regional gatherings.

CDO collaborated with the Office for Ministry Development (OMD), Cornerstone, diocesan representatives, and others to create the Fresh Start Program, an important new resource for congregations and clergy in transition. The initiative for development of this program came from the National Deployment Officers' gathering in 1998 that was facilitated by the Board for Church Deployment (BCD). The primary goal of the program is to build stronger relationships among clergy, between clergy and congregations, and between clergy/congregations and their dioceses. As of the Fall 2002 over 50 dioceses are participating at some level in the Fresh Start Program. The participation of 70% of dioceses is projected by the 2003 General Convention. CDO is also participating in a major spinoff of the Fresh Start program: a working group that is developing new resources for Mutual Ministry Review. As of Fall 2002, ten pilot dioceses are testing draft materials. It is anticipated that the Mutual Ministry Review materials will be in circulation by the end of 2003.

In mid-2001, the Board began a visioning process to develop a strategic plan for the future of the Board and the Office. After the Fall 2001 meeting, the Rev. Robert Gallagher was engaged as a consultant to further this process. In Spring 2002, a Working Group of the Board was created to help bring this work forward. Issues that give rise to this initiative included the changing deployment needs of dioceses and congregations; changing ministry settings; and changing technology. The consultant and the Working Group are helping the Board and the Office to gather insights from around the church as they move to engage these new realities.

As has been the case for many conventions, the Board will have a booth at the General Convention in Minneapolis staffed by Board members and CDO staff. This convention we expect to have computers with Internet access to enable users to update their Personal Profiles and to access other CDO services.

The Board adopted these objectives for the triennium 2001-2003:

1. **Implement and perfect the web-based CDO system**
   New CDO On Line Services introduced to the Church in April 2002.[1]
   - Redesign the CDO system
     Major redesign completed April 2002. Improvements continue in consultation with DDO's and other CDO users.**[2]
   - Make accessible a web-based Personal Profile database for use of DDOs
     Deployment officers can now search the personnel database, view and print individual personal profiles. *
   - Collaborate interdepartmentally on the website
     Worked closely with Media Services and MIS to develop web-site services. *
   - Train DDOs in the use of the new system
     Training program in place and scheduled for May 2002. **
   - Redesign and distribute supportive materials
     Initial redesign completed April 2002. Documents available on web-site as electronic documents or in downloadable, printable format. *
   - Maintain the Internet *Positions Open Bulletin.*
     New improved version introduced April 2002. Database is accessible in real time and can be edited in real time by authorized diocesan personnel. **
   - Maintain a national DDO List Service
     This service is continued with the cooperation of our Media Services department. The list is maintained by CDO staff. **

2. **Promote compliance in deployment with the canonical requirement of non-discrimination.**
   Board members have participated in anti-racism training as mandated by General Convention. **
   - CDO will implement the Board policy: "The CDO will search its records without regard to age, sex, race, or marital status, except to further by positive action the deployment of women and minorities."
     Board policy incorporated into design of new CDO On Line Services and particularly into search engine for personnel database. **

---

[1] * indicates an objective has been achieved.
[2] ** indicates the objective is an on-going concern.

- The Church Deployment Board will distribute a document on inclusivity
  Initial draft of a booklet developed in 2001. Consulting funds became available in Fall 2002. Contracted with consultant to edit and perfect booklet for publication in Spring 2003. **
- Establish a national program to assist DDOs in raising awareness of inclusivity, providing materials and procedures to work with parishes in the search process
  The development of the resource above is a first step in this direction. **

3. **Register all clergy and lay professionals and promote updating of all records.**
   As of November 2002, new registrants added since the beginning of the triennium is 786. ** *Direct contact by CDO staff with lay professionals has elicited new registrations from same.* ** *As of November 2002, the number of updated profiles has increased by 33% since introduction of On Line Services in April 2002, providing users with Internet access to their profiles.* **

4. **Continue to work with diocesan deployment officers to strengthen their ministries through:**
   a) Facilitating a triennial National Deployment Officers Conference.
       The fourth national conference held in San Francisco in April 2001 was attended by 75 persons and regarded as a great success. * *Some concerns addressed:*
       - *Training for New CDO Computer System*
       - *Fresh Start (for Clergy and Congregations in Transition)*
       - *Mutual Ministry Reviews and Letters of Agreement*
       - *Background Checks*
       - *DDO Standards*
       - *Inclusivity Issues*
       - *Interim Training, Using an Appreciative Inquiry Model*
       - *FOCUS – Working with*
       - *Orderly Exchange of Ministers with ELCA*
       - *Dialogue between the Board for Church Deployment and Diocesan Deployment Officers*
       - *Deployment Officers and Emotional Labor*
   b) Orienting, networking, and training of deployment officers. Encouraging development of provincial and regional networks of diocesan deployment officers and bishops.
       Basic DDO Training offered three times a year. Enhanced by hands-on training in upgraded ECC computer lab. Supplemented by On Line Services training events (four offered May 2002 - Feb 2003); Online demos at DDO regional gatherings; and individual training consultations. **
   c) Facilitating the establishment of principles and standards for role and operations of deployment officers. **
   d) Encouraging diocesan deployment officers in training, networking, and utilization of Interim Search Consultants. **

5. **Work with other professional ministry development bodies to identify and address areas of common concern, as opportunity permits.** **
   CDO collaborated with OMD, Cornerstone, and others in developing the Fresh Start program, a major new resource for clergy and congregations in transition. This collaboration is continuing with the development of transition resources for lay leaders and a comprehensive initiative in developing resources for Mutual Ministry Review.
   CDO has been one of the agencies that assisted in the development of Families of Clergy United in Support (FOCUS). CDO also assisted in the creation and continues supporting Colloquium of Episcopal Professional and Vocational Associations (CEPVA).
   CDO has worked with numerous agencies of the national church, the Church Pension Group, and many others in addressing issues around data-gathering and research in the Episcopal Church.

6. **Continue to explore ways to work with the ELCA on deployment issues.** **
   CDO collaborated with the ELCA Division for Ministries, ECUSA's Office for Ministry Development, the Presiding Bishop's Office, the Church Pension Group, and others in the publication and distribution of standards and procedures for the Orderly Exchange of Pastors and Priests. The CDO Executive Director

demonstrated the new CDO On Line Services to the ELCA national ministries staff. CDO has begun to register Lutheran pastors on the CDO system, pursuant to "Called to Common Mission." CDO has listed and conducted searches for a number of shared Lutheran-Episcopal Ministries and the Positions Open Bulletin is available for ECLA positions. At least one Episcopal diocese is conducting its Fresh Start program jointly with the local ELCA synod.

OBJECTIVES FOR TRIENNIUM 2004-2007

1. **Oversee the leadership transition after the retirement of the current Executive Director of the Church Deployment Office.**
   - In collaboration with diocesan deployment officers, bishops, church center staff and others, develop a vision for the future direction of the Board and the Office.
   - In collaboration with the Presiding Bishop's Office develop a position description and a search process for the Executive Director.
   - Build a working relationship and common vision between the Executive Director and Board.

2. **Refine and enhance the CDO On Line system.**
   - Continue interdepartmental collaboration.
   - Maintain *Positions Open Bulletin* and diocesan deployment officers' email list serve.
   - Solicit, evaluate and implement feedback from constituents to augment "user-friendly" qualities on the system.
   - Provide ongoing training for bishops and diocesan deployment officers in the use of the On Line system.

3. **Promote compliance with the canonical requirement of non-discrimination in deployment.**
   - CDO will continue to implement the long-standing Board policy: "The CDO will search its records without regard to age, sex, race, or marital status, except to further by positive action the deployment of women and minorities."
   - Assist diocesan deployment officers in raising awareness of inclusivity issues, providing materials and procedures to work with parishes in the calling process.

4. **Register all clergy and lay professionals and promote updating of all records.**

5. **Continue to work with diocesan deployment officers to strengthen their ministries**
   - Facilitate a National Deployment Officers' Conference in 2004.
   - Provide orientation and training for diocesan deployment officers.
   - Encourage formation and development of provincial and regional networks of deployment officers and bishops.
   - Encourage the establishment of principles and standards for role and conduct of deployment officers.
   - Encourage diocesan deployment officers in the identification, training, and utilization of consultants in transition and calling process(es).

6. **Work with other professional ministry development bodies to identify and address areas of common concern. Develop resources for lay leaders, clergy, and congregations in leadership transition, as opportunity permits.**

7. **Continue to explore ways to work with the ELCA on deployment issues, including sharing of materials and resources and the development of collegial relationships.**

Resolution A002 Budget Appropriation for the Board for Church Deployment

1 *Resolved,* the House of _____ concurring, That there be appropriated from the Assessment Budget of the
2 General Convention the sum of $90,000 during the triennium 2004-2007 for the expenses of the Board for
3 Church Deployment.

EXPLANATION
The Board for Church Deployment will meet approximately six times during the triennium. This will require at least $30,000 per year for a total of $90,000. There will also be several meetings of a four-person Working Group on Strategic Visioning in 2004 and early 2005, perhaps five meetings in all.

This page is intentionally blank.

THE CHURCH PENSION FUND AND AFFILIATES
www.cpg.org

OVERVIEW

The Church Pension Fund (CPF), an independent agency of the Episcopal Church incorporated by a special act of the New York State legislature in 1914, is currently responsible for over $6 billion of the church's assets. Through its pension-related and wellness work, the Church Pension Fund affects all clergy and most lay people of the church. Further, its subsidiaries, which offer services in retirement planning, pension and investment services, life and disability insurance, health benefits, property and casualty insurance and book publishing, affect almost every organization of the church.

At each General Convention, the House of Deputies elects at least 12 of the Church Pension Fund's 25-member Board of Trustees, selecting from 24 or more nominees proposed by General Convention's Nominating Committee. The CPF board is then responsible for all important CPF decisions.

At General Convention, CPF works closely with the Pension Fund Committee, a permanent committee of General Convention. Resolutions considered by the Pension Fund Committee are presented to both the House of Bishops and the House of Deputies, meaning that there are times when the entire General Convention is considering matters pertaining to the pension fund.

Because of the wide-ranging responsibilities of the Church Pension Group (CPG), it is essential that those responsible for guiding the Church Pension Fund – its board of trustees and senior management – be in constant dialogue with church leaders about how CPG can serve the church. To further this objective, CPG traditionally publishes a comprehensive Report to General Convention, mailed to each member of the House of Deputies and House of Bishops along with our Annual Report. Usually, that Report to General Convention is formally accepted by General Convention and ordered published with the official Report of the General Convention.

This year, as a supplement to our comprehensive report, we are presenting this executive summary on five vital topics, each of which will be expanded upon in our Report to General Convention. We also discuss in this report the most critical responsibility General Convention has in regard to CPF – the election of our trustees.

Specifically, the following pages cover six important topics:

- Investment Management
- $1 Billion in Clergy Benefit Enhancements
- The CREDO Program
- Services to Lay Employees
- CPF's Affiliated Companies
- The Election of CPF Trustees

INVESTMENT MANAGEMENT

Successful investment management is the foundation for CPF's most essential tasks. We take great pride both in our investment results and our investment process. As discussed in detail in our recent annual reports, CPF now has a widely diversified investment portfolio, consisting of more than 100 portfolios and investment partnerships. We have investment managers in nine investment categories, an outstanding internal investment management staff, and a wide range of expert outside advisors including Cambridge Associates, Buck Consultants, Inc., Winklevoss Technologies, Inc., and Davis Polk & Wardwell.

The two charts below illustrate our success in recent years, a period encompassing both ebullient and difficult markets. As shown in Exhibit 1, we kept pace with the market in two of three "up" years, and performed spectacularly in the third. In the two difficult years, we have done considerably better than a benchmark portfolio. As a consequence, our portfolio experienced cumulative investment gains of 60% over this 4½-year period compared with a benchmark portfolio which would have decreased by .7%.

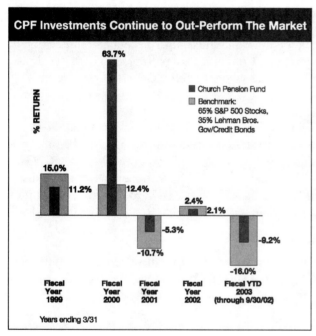

Exhibit 1

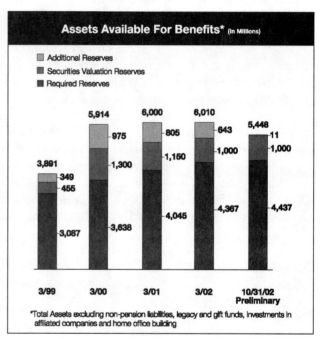

Exhibit 2

Exhibit 2 shows the impact of this investment success on our assets available for clergy benefits. Available assets rose by more than $2 billion in fiscal 2000. Despite the difficult markets with which we have had to contend since then, available assets have declined by only about $466 million, 7.9% of the total value. "Additional reserves," the amount available after setting aside the amount actuaries say we need today to fund future commitments, have declined by over $900 million dollars. Some of this decline is due to the overall portfolio decline in value. A far larger factor is the tremendous increase in "required reserves" stemming from our benefit enhancements and predictable growth.

$1 BILLION IN CLERGY BENEFIT ENHANCEMENTS

Without doubt, CPF's most important news is the extensive and varied benefit enhancements which excellent investment performance has made possible. Crafted with much input from trustees, staff and advisors, these enhancements have been widely discussed with the church. Exhibit 3 illustrates the depth and complexity of the enhancements made to the clergy pension plan since 1994. Nearly $1 billion in benefit enhancements have been implemented for clergy not-yet-retired, retired clergy, and surviving spouses – and that figure excludes $292 million for "normal" cost-of-living increases. Parishes and dioceses have benefited significantly from this enhancement program, as well. Our stewardship of the fund's resources is an ongoing process.

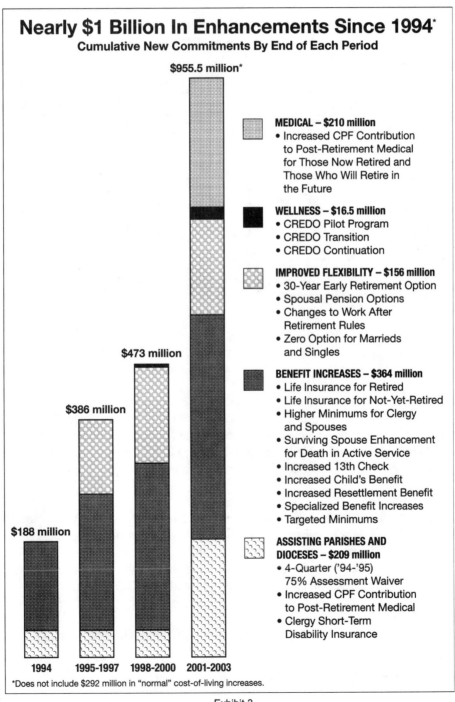

Exhibit 3

THE CREDO PROGRAM

CREDO – an eight-day reflection and discernment experience for clergy – is one of CPF's most successful benefit innovations of the last decade. CREDO's goal is to provide opportunities for clergy to examine significant areas of their lives and to discern prayerfully the direction of their vocation as they respond to God's call in a lifelong process of practice and transformation.

Each eight-day conference includes about thirty clergy participants, who are randomly selected from the Church Pension Fund participant database. As Exhibit 4 illustrates, over 2,600 clergy will have attended a CREDO conference by the end of 2005.

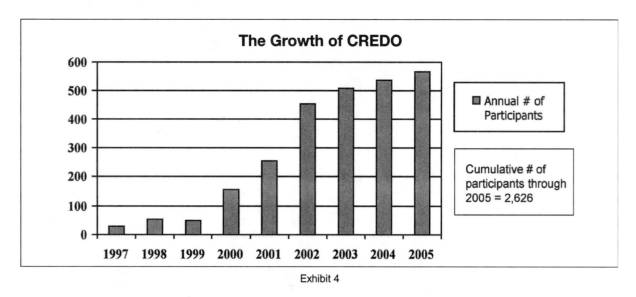

Exhibit 4

Over the past three years, the Church Pension Fund has significantly increased funding of this valuable wellness program. Our goal is to make the CREDO conference experience available to clergy every ten years during their careers. Alternative approaches to funding CREDO, or initiatives like it, are under discussion.

In January 2001, CREDO Institute, Inc. was established as a freestanding 501(c)3 corporation with the task of oversight and continued development of CREDO. Primarily funded by the Church Pension Fund, CREDO Institute, Inc. also receives contributions from the Episcopal Church Foundation and the Office of Pastoral Development of the Episcopal Church. In addition to managing CREDO conferences, the Institute seeks avenues for educational and leadership-based alliances between the Episcopal Church and ecumenical partners.

CREDO is more than a conference. Through a holistic approach to wellness, clergy are invited to examine mind, body, spirit, and heart. Literally translated, the Latin word *credo* means, "I give my heart." CREDO provides clergy a profound opportunity to renew, reaffirm, and recommit their core belief in the saving power of Jesus Christ as expressed in the baptismal covenant. An extensive evaluation process, including both quantitative and qualitative analyses, has conclusively determined that CREDO has made a statistically significant difference in the personal and professional lives of those who have participated.

A full report by CREDO Institute, Inc. will be included in our Report to General Convention.

SERVICES TO LAY EMPLOYEES

The Church Pension Group's lay retirement programs have grown significantly in this triennium. As shown in Exhibit 5, the number of employees participating in our defined contribution and defined benefit plans now exceeds 7,800. Likewise, the number of employers participating in the plans has increased to an all-time high of 2,250. In addition, as shown in Exhibit 6, employer and participant contributions to the plans have grown by approximately 23% to an annual total of almost $21 million.

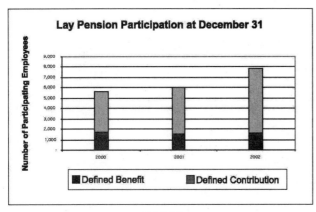

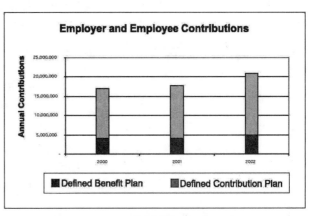

Exhibit 5   Exhibit 6

During the triennium, the defined contribution plan saw two major enhancements:

- In spring 2002, six investment vehicles became available.
- By accessing their accounts either through our website (www.cpg.org) or our toll-free telephone number (877-208-0092), participants in the Episcopal Church Lay Employees' Defined Contribution Retirement Plan can determine their current account balance, transfer funds between investment options, change the way future contributions are invested and even apply for a loan virtually 24 hours a day, 7 days a week.

The defined benefit plan was also improved. Participants received:

- Cost-of-living increases at rates that exceed the benchmark Social Security Administration increase;
- A compensation-based lump sum death benefit for active participants under age 72;
- An enhanced early retirement provision that significantly increases the retirement benefit for qualified early retirees;
- An enhanced disability provision that reduces the benefit eligibility waiting period for a participant who is rendered permanently and totally disabled.

There was no cost increase for either participants or employers as a result of these enhancements.

CPF'S AFFILIATED COMPANIES

Over the past three years, the Church Pension Fund and its affiliated companies have continued to expand and improve the services and products we provide to individuals and institutions of the Episcopal Church. Exhibit 7 provides a brief summary of the clients served and services provided by each of the CPF major affiliates.

CPG Services and Clients

Church Pension Fund	Clergy	Not-Yet-Retired	7,796*
		Retired	5,658*
	Surviving Spouses		2,468* ⎫ 24,602
	Lay Employees	Not-Yet-Retired	7,831
		Retired	849
Church Publishing Incorporated	Titles in Print		202
	Individual Customers		16,977
	Institutional Customers		10,249
Church Life Insurance Corporation	Group Insurance Policies		14,716
	Individual Insurance Policies		2,884
	Annuities		4,323
	Disability Insureds		4,396
The Church Insurance Companies	Total Churches Insured Through CIAC		7,767
	Total Churches Protected by CIC P&C Policies		5,625
The Episcopal Church Medical Trust	Clergy		5,776 ⎫
	Lay Employees		7,136 ⎬ 24,538
	Dependents		11,626 ⎭

* As of March 31, 2002

Exhibit 7

Church Publishing Incorporated (CPI) has produced the official worship materials of the Episcopal Church since 1918. In addition to basic and gift editions of prayer books and hymnals, and the Episcopal Clerical Directory, CPI has a growing title list in the areas of liturgy, music and recordings, church history, Anglican spirituality, including the JourneyBook line of personal meditation books, and the company now also offers the Rite Series software for parishes and new online services.

Since 1922, Church Life Insurance Corporation (CLIC) has provided life insurance protection and retirement savings plans to clergy, laity, and their families. Products offered include annuities and IRAs, as well as individual and group life insurance. Additionally, CLIC administers pension plans for lay employees of the Episcopal Church. Since 2000, CLIC has successfully introduced major new products such as short- and long-term disability insurance, and has added to its client base by expanding investment options for participants in the Episcopal Church Lay Employees' Defined Contribution Retirement Plan.

The Church Insurance Companies consist of the Church Insurance Company (CIC), the Church Insurance Agency Corporation (CIAC), and the Church Insurance Company of Vermont (CIC-VT). CIC has provided property and liability coverage for church institutions since 1929. Today, 82% of Episcopal dioceses and over

74% of parishes rely on CIC for their commercial package coverage. CIAC offers a broad range of coverages, tailored to the special needs of Episcopal institutions, from its sister underwriting companies and third-party product partner companies. Six regional service offices serve CIC clients. CIC-VT is a single-parent captive insurance company incorporated in 1999 to allow church institutions to benefit from the coverage flexibility and potential cost advantages of this risk-financing approach. Thanks to the enthusiastic reception of the CIC-VT program, CIC has increased its market share dramatically over the past several years. While the company experienced losses due to the settlement of several very large claims, these losses were incurred in our mission – to protect the people and property of the Episcopal Church.

The Episcopal Church Medical Trust, now in its 25th year, provides the clergy and laity of the Episcopal Church with a broad array of health plan options, offering a wide variety of self-funded preferred provider, managed care, and indemnity plans, as well as mental health, vision, and dental care plans. For retired participants, the Medical Trust offers Medicare supplement plans, as well as Medicare HMOs in select regions of the country. Over the past three years, the Medical Trust has increased the percentage of dioceses it serves from 54% to 61%, as it introduced national plans and improved the competitiveness of its pricing and client service.

Current CPF Board of Trustees
Lay Persons (15)

Exhibit 8

THE ELECTION OF CPF TRUSTEES

At the 74th General Convention, 14 Church Pension Fund Trustees will be elected: 12 for full 6-year terms and 2 for unexpired 3-year terms. The election of outstanding church persons to these important positions is essential to CPF carrying out its responsibilities.

The Work of the CPF Board

The trustees of the Church Pension Fund play a vital role in the governance and management of CPG's complex affairs. They make significant policy decisions affecting, for example, investment policy, pension benefits, and Church Pension Group services; they regularly address complex issues, often balancing sometimes conflicting social and fiduciary responsibilities.

The trustees also provide governance and oversight to the management of a large and varied consortium of businesses. They are responsible for the oversight of assets worth over $6 billion, and a combination of companies that typically has revenues and cash flow of over $400 million a year. Of the many aspects to the Church Pension Group organization, investment management, medical benefits provision, and property and casualty insurance are among the most complicated – and, in the last two cases, the most troubled – business areas in America today. It would be difficult to overstate the importance of bringing to our deliberations the most expert and thoughtful advice available in our Episcopal world.

The Current Board and the Election Process

We believe the election process has historically resulted in outstanding leadership for CPF, as shown by the current board in Exhibit 8. Fifteen of CPF's current 25 trustees are lay leaders, generally with strong business experience. The current board includes individuals with significant experience in four critical specialties: investment management, accounting, health care, and the law. Each of these areas of expertise is essential to board deliberations. In addition, the current board includes seven individuals with general business and/or management experience. The ten clergy trustees are evenly split between bishops and priests. The ordained group represents a diverse mix of geographic location, as well as a variety of parish, diocesan, and national staff experience.

Church canons require the election, at each General Convention, of trustees to fill 12 seats scheduled to expire. They also require elections to fill any "unexpired terms," seats that have become vacant since the last General Convention and have been temporarily filled by an interim election conducted by the sitting trustees.

Currently, there are two such unexpired seats to be filled. This means that only 11 incumbent CPF Trustees continue their terms beyond the General Convention: the President, elected by and serving at the pleasure of the CPF Board, and ten trustees elected by General Convention in 2000 to serve terms which expire in 2006.

Exhibit 9 identifies and categorizes the 11 continuing trustees. **Note that no lay persons with primary experience in accounting, health care, or the law are in this group.** Further, the balance between lay and clergy is changed significantly, with the number of continuing clergy trustees almost the same as the number of lay trustees.

Continuing CPF Board Members*

Lay Persons (6)		Clergy (5)
Investment Management (2)	*Law (0)*	*Priests (2)*
Amy L. Domini	- - - -	**A. Thomas Blackmon**
Quintin E. Primo III		**Randall Chase, Jr.**
	Financial & General Business (4)	
Accounting (0)	**Alan F. Blanchard**	*Bishops (3)*
- - - -	**Deborah Harmon Hines, Ph.D.**	**Chilton R. Knudsen**
Health Care (0)	**Arthur K. Kusumoto**	**Peter J. Lee, D.D.**
- - - -	**Katherine Tyler Scott**	**Claude E. Payne, D.D.**

*The President plus 10 Trustees elected in 2000 to serve until 2006

Exhibit 9

THE ELECTION OF 12 TRUSTEES TO 6-YEAR TERMS

Exhibit 10 identifies the 24 candidates nominated by the Joint Standing Committee on Nominations for six-year terms. Candidates are grouped by their primary area of experience. Incumbent trustees, the nine current trustees eligible for re-election, are shown in bold. Among the 15 new nominees are eight priests, four bishops, and three lay leaders, grouped in areas of expertise that our limited knowledge suggests are most appropriate.

In general, the continuing trustees and staff of the Church Pension Fund strongly support the re-election of all incumbent trustees. We hope the General Convention deputies will recognize the value of accumulated experience, continuity, and wisdom, especially during this time of financial market volatility.

Beyond endorsing our incumbents, we welcome all new trustees, noting that a balance of business skills is essential. **We urge particular consideration of lay leaders with experience in critical sub-areas: investment management, health care, and the law.**

Candidates For Election To A 6-Year Term*

(12 to be elected)

Lay Persons		Clergy	
Investment Management	*Finance & General Business*	*Priests*	*Bishops*
James E. Bayne	**Joon D. Matsumura**	**M. L. Agnew, Jr.**	**Gayle E. Harris**
David L. Brigham	**Virginia A. Norman**	**Carlson Gerdau**	
	Jon B. Boss	Samuel G. Candler	David C. Bane, Jr.
		Peter F. Casparian	Robert H. Johnson
Accounting	*Law*	Donald A. Fishburne	Henry N. Parsley, Jr.
Sheridan C. Biggs	Theresa M. Brion	Scott B. Hayashi	Wayne P. Wright
		Lynn Jay	
Health Care		Caryl A. Marsh	
David R. Pitts		V. Gene Robinson	
		Robert Sessum	
Carla M. Cooper			

*Names shown in bold are incumbent Trustees

Exhibit 10

THE ELECTION OF 2 TRUSTEES TO 3-YEAR TERMS

Exhibit 11 identifies the four candidates nominated for three-year terms by the Joint Standing Committee on Nominations. **Two are incumbent trustees. Note that the two incumbents nominated here are the only nominated attorneys with experience on the CPG Board.** We believe that this fact, combined with the complexity of our work and the increased incidence of litigation against churches, give special importance to their candidacy.

Candidates For Election To A 3-Year Term*

(2 to be elected)

Lay Persons		Clergy	
Finance & General Business	*Law*	*Priests*	*Bishops*
Theodore B. Sloan	**Barbara B. Creed**	Mark S. Nestlehutt	
	Cecil Wray		

*Names shown in bold are incumbent Trustees

Exhibit 11

* * *

The Joint Standing Committee on Nominations, chaired by former CPF Trustee Matthew Chew, has assembled an outstanding list of nominees. We thank them for their work. Now it is time for us to ask that the House of Deputies give thoughtful, prayerful attention to this important task.

THE ASSOCIATION OF EPISCOPAL COLLEGES
THE UNITED STATES CHAPTER OF THE
COLLEGES AND UNIVERSITIES OF THE ANGLICAN COMMUNION
AND

THREE HISTORICALLY BLACK COLLEGES SUPPORTED BY THE EPISCOPAL CHURCH

SAINT AUGUSTINE'S COLLEGE (1867) RALEIGH, NC
SAINT PAUL'S COLLEGE (1888) LAWRENCEVILLE, VR
VOORHEES COLLEGE (1897) DENMARK, SC

MEMBERSHIP
Officers
The Most Rev. Frank T. Griswold III, *Presiding Bishop*, *Honorary Chair, ex officio*
Dr. Joel Cunningham, *Chair*, Tennessee
The Rt. Rev. Douglas Theuner, *Vice-Chair*, New Hampshire
Mr. Seth Edwards, *Treasurer*, New York
Mr. Nevin Brown, *Secretary*, Washington
The Rev. Canon Dr. Donald F. Thompson, *General Secretary*, Connecticut

Institutional Members - Presidents of the Institutional Member Colleges
Dr. Mark Gearan, *Hobart College*, Central New York
Dr. Dianne Boardley Suber, *St. Augustine's College* (NC), North Carolina
Dr. Leon Botstein, *Bard College*, C. New York (and rep. Dr. Stuart Levine)
Dr. John Waddell, *St. Paul's College*, Southern Virginia
Dr. S. Georgia Nugent, *Kenyon College*, Ohio
Dr. Lee Monroe, Jr., *Voorhees College*, South Carolina
Dr. Clara Brennan, *St. Augustine College (IL)*, Chicago
Dr. Henrique Tokpa, *Cuttington University College*, Liberia
Dr. Jay Upright, *Clarkson College*, Nebraska
Dr. Josefina Sumaya, *Trinity College, Quezon City*, Central Philippines
Dr. Joel Cunningham, *University of the South*, Tennessee

Associate Members
The Rev. Dr. Stephen White, New Jersey
Ms. Katherine Adamson, Connecticut
The Rt. Rev. Neil Alexander, Atlanta
The Rt. Rev. Herbert Donovan, Jr., New York
Dr. Perry Lentz, Ohio
Dr. Debora Guthrie, Washington

The Association of Episcopal Colleges approved this report at its Board Meeting of January 9th, 2003.

Representatives at General Convention
The Rt. Rev. Douglas Theuner and the Rt. Rev. Neil Alexander are authorized to receive non-substantive amendments to the report.

OVERVIEW
www.cuac.org

The three historically black colleges (HBC) founded by The Episcopal Church continue their important contribution to education in a Christian context for African-American students and for the development of African-American leadership in The Episcopal Church.

The mission of these colleges is directly related to the goals of the Church's 20/20 initiative since leaders of the Church in 20/20 are in college right now. The three historically Black Episcopal colleges are in a unique position to raise up lay and ordained leaders from the African-American community.

The purposes of these institutions are on the one hand particular to The Episcopal Church's special relationship with the African-American community, but are also similar to the role which Episcopal Colleges nationwide (Association of Episcopal Colleges -AEC) and Anglican colleges worldwide play in providing a high standard of post-secondary education in a Christian setting.

These three colleges have evolved into fully accredited post-secondary institutions with the on-going support of The Episcopal Church. They all are accredited by the Southern Association of Colleges and Schools, are members of the United Negro College Fund, and offer baccalaureate degrees. With a rich heritage in African-American culture and identity, these Colleges now also serve students of all races and backgrounds. Their missions and goals have grown over time to reflect the changes in society and educational patterns expected of private liberal arts institutions.

As private, church-related, co-educational institutions with a Christian heritage, these institutions of The Episcopal Church mandate is to focus on undergraduate liberal arts and sciences, pre-professional programs, business, and teacher education. To meet these challenges, the colleges have undertaken initiatives to improve their undergraduate education and improve accessibility and response to community needs.

Although the proportion of the Episcopal population of these colleges is generally under 10% of enrollment, these campuses remain one of the central places where African-Americans encounter and are welcomed into an Episcopal Christian community. There is consistently a higher proportion of Episcopalians among the graduates than among first year students, precisely because of the welcome students discover at an Episcopal College.

Over the years, the colleges have collectively graduated over 100 clergy, Episcopal and other. Among the important new initiatives the colleges wish to make are programs that directly recruit students for ministry in The Episcopal Church.

Under Domestic Appropriations in the 2000-2003 General Convention Budget, support was given "which demonstrates the Church's commitment to our historic mission for higher education for African-Americans". An appropriation of $4,050,000 was made as a block grant.

These Colleges affirm their partnership with The Episcopal Church to achieve collaboratively a joint Christian and educational mission. This commitment is demonstrated by the continuous relationship of each administration in having Diocesan representation on the institution's board. All three institutions have an Episcopal Chaplain as a paid member of college to promote Christian faith in academic life on campus and to provide Sunday and weekly chapel services utilizing the Book of Common Prayer and an Episcopal liturgical tradition. The colleges work together in areas such as student and faculty exchanges and training.

WORK SUMMARY
Programs of the Colleges and Impact of Past Funding

Saint Augustine's College
Saint Augustine's enrollment stands at 1502, of which approximately 10% are Episcopalian. There were 209 graduates in 2002. The College's annual operating budget is over $20,000,000.

Over the past three years, Saint Augustine's College has been faced with the challenge of declining enrollment, fiscal uncertainty and restoring facilities left too long without a maintenance plan. In January 2000, the College with new leadership established a five-year plan that aggressively addressed many of these issues. A new chief financial officer instituted a fiscal plan that restructured debt; developed a ten-year deferred maintenance plan; renovated residence halls, the student center, and the college athletic facility; and revised and implemented fiscal policies and practices consistent with sound accounting practices.

In addressing accreditation requirements relative to institutional effectiveness, the College developed and implemented a planning cycle which requires that all units – academic, administration and service–complete performance assessments, use outcomes to establish goals and objectives, and evaluate - until the cycle is complete. This process has resulted in systemic changes across the College that have significantly enhanced and/or improved the institution's overall effectiveness.

A new initiative that the college has undertaken congruent to the past three-year grant of The Episcopal Church, is the "Transitional, Traditional, Accelerated Approach to Learning" program (TTAAL). This program applies a three-tier approach to education, allowing students to enroll in a 3, 4 or 5-year plan of study. The 4-year plan, which encompasses the majority of the student body, is targeted at the traditional college student; the 5-year plan targets students who may have struggled in high school or who did not perform well on the College's entrance exams, but have demonstrated potential to achieve both by attitude and hard work. Students enrolled in a 5-year plan of study spend their first year developing the skills and knowledge base necessary to successfully compete in college. The uniqueness of this program is that it allows for financial aid during the entire 5 years of study.

Saint Paul's College

Saint Paul's enrollment is currently 701 of which approximately 8% are Episcopalian. There were 114 graduates in 2002. The College's annual operating budget is over $10,000,000.

During the past three years, enrollment and retention figures have increased. In addition, St. Paul's has upgraded campus facilities. These include basic deferred maintenance projects, upgrades in student housing, the cafeterias and other academic and administrative buildings.

St. Paul's evaluates and measures the success of its mission through the following indicators:
- Student application inquiries
- Student enrollment growth
- A successful ten year reaffirmation of accreditation by SACS
- Retention and Graduation ratios
- Career and graduate school placement
- Feedback from Internal/External Constituents of the college.

Within the next five years, St. Paul's projects growth in:
- Faculty, staff, and student surveys
- Enrollment growth to 1,000 students
- Increased federal and private contracts and grants
- New library
- Multi-purpose Residence halls
- New gymnasium
- Major capital campaign.

St. Paul's has also enhanced the academic support and residential life aspect of its Single Parent program, initiated with the support of The Episcopal Church grant. The Single Parent Support System (SPSS) offers three interrelated systems of support:
- Academic: Single parents are given the opportunity to obtain a bachelor's degree in three intensive calendar years of study by attending fall, spring and summer sessions
- Economic: This assistance includes on-campus year-round housing, work-study, in-house computers, books and supplies and a limited amount of food and medical care during a family crisis
- Child-care: High-quality child care is provided for the children of single parents who are enrolled in the SPSS as full-time students, thereby enabling them to remain full-time parents.

Voorhees College

Voorhees College's enrollment stands at 738 students, of which 5% are Episcopalian. There were 155 graduates in 2002. The College's annual operating budget is over $15,000,000.

Voorhees College has been a good steward of the funding received from the General Convention budget of The Episcopal Church. The allocations received in the past have had a direct impact on the College's ability to fulfill its mission of educating the heart, mind, and spirit of young men and women.

Voorhees measures its performance through the comprehensive planning and evaluation system. The Strategic Planning Council, which drives all planning activities, along with the Institutional Effectiveness Planning Committee, is responsible for reporting all planning activities and mission attainment results.

The Board of Trustees has adopted a new mission statement, "Partners in Mission: An Agenda for Excellence," which will be the college's driving theme for the next five years. Under this new mission, the college renews its historical partnership with The Episcopal Church. This partnership was based on the church and school proclamation that the Rule of God is at hand, to nourish Christ's people from the riches of his grace and to strengthen them to glorify God in this life and in the life to come. The church alone cannot provide effective teaching and learning that help its learners to proclaim the rule of God, the church/school partnership is an integral part of the new mission.

Voorhees used the Episcopal Church support to begin the Single Mothers Achieving Re-education through Training for Self-Sufficiency (SMARTS) Program, a specific initiative of the last General Convention initiative, with two young women and their children. The program has grown considerably since then to include 15 single parents and 20 children who live in a campus residential building (Menafee Hall) that was refurbished into single apartments with a federal grant. There is a waiting list of over 100 female heads-of-household, between the ages of 18 and 30 with one or more dependent children. All SMARTS participants receive support services to assist in the successful completion of their degree program including career, academic and personal counseling, job placement referrals, and personal development workshops.

BUDGET

The General Convention support is unrestricted and used by each College to provide institutional aid to a variety of students from diverse backgrounds. The Audited Financial Statements of the three institutions are available from the Association of Episcopal Colleges table at General Convention. All institutions are self-supporting, but depend on a variety of funding sources above and beyond tuition, of which the General Convention appropriation is one.

The appropriation for the 2000-2003 Triennium was $1,350,000 a year for a total of $4,050,000. Each college used the increase in funding from the last Triennium to develop programs for special populations of students. These initiatives were in part a response to General Convention's approval of a Single Parent/Mother Support Program.

GOALS AND OBJECTIVES FOR THE NEXT TRIENNIUM/NEW INITIATIVES

20/20 Initiative

The three historically black colleges founded by The Episcopal Church are strategically positioned to make an important contribution to education in a Christian context for African-American students and to develop African-American leadership in The Episcopal Church. They are central places where African-Americans encounter and are welcomed into an Episcopal Christian community.

Called to Serve

As part of the overall Association of Episcopal Colleges initiative, "Called to Serve," the HBCs intend to create new initiatives through their Chaplaincies and other campus programs to recruit membership in The Episcopal Church and to promote vocations to ordained ministry. This will call for enhanced staffing of the Chaplaincies, and also program costs for gatherings and Conferences to foster and support student vocations.

College	2004	2005	2006	Total
St Augustine's	$30,000	$30,000	$30,000	$90,000
St Paul's	$30,000	$30,000	$30,000	$90,000
Voorhees	$30,000	$30,000	$30,000	$90,000
Totals	$90,000	$90,000	$90,000	$270,000

The Goal of "Called to Serve" is to provoke and stimulate awareness of Christian (Episcopalian) vocations (secular and ordained) that serve church and world through personal, professional and occupational explorations, decisions and choices during the post-secondary educational years. This is an initiative to enhance membership, leadership and commitment in and beyond The Episcopal Church communities.

The HBCs can take leadership in this program in African-American communities, both on their own campuses and nationally. Hopefully the result will be significant recruitment to vocations to Episcopalian leadership and ministry.

REQUESTED BUDGET FOR 2004-2006

	2004	2005	2006	Total
Prior Grant	$1,350,000	$1,350,000	$1,350,000	$4,050,000
"Called to Serve"	90,000	90,000	90,000	$270,000
	$1,440,000	$1,440,000	$1,440,000	$4,320,000

The Rev. Canon Dr. Don F. Thompson
General Secretary

THE EPISCOPAL CHURCH BUILDING FUND
www.ecbf.org

MEMBERSHIP

The Rt. Rev. Gethin B. Hughes, *Chair*	San Diego
Mr. Stanley I. Garnett, *Vice-Chair*	Southwest Florida
The Rev. Charles N. Fulton III, *President*	New York
Ms. Sarah Dresser, *Vice-President*	Non-trustee staff
Mr. Thomas D. Haines, *Treasurer*	Connecticut
Robert Royce, Esq., *Legal Counsel*	Virgin Islands
The Rev. Christoph Keller, *Secretary*	New York
Mr. William M. Barnum	Rhode Island
Mr. Brewster Caesar	Colorado
Mrs. Marion Carr	Connecticut
Mrs. Marina Carrott	Chicago
Mr. Melvin W. Ellis	Oregon
Lawrence M. Knapp, Esq.	Pittsburgh
The Rev. Eliza M. Linley	California
Ms. Barbara Losse	Utah
The Ven. Richard F. Milwee	Arkansas
The Rev. Richard Petranek	Texas
The Rev. Ralph R. Warren, Jr.	Southeast Florida

MISSION STATEMENT   *"Helping Build the Church and Helping the Church to Build"*

In faithfulness to our baptismal covenant and our mission as the church to restore all people to unity with God and each other in Christ and in recognition of the importance of place and space for worship, proclamation and service, the mission of the Episcopal Church Building Fund is to aid in the building, improvement, and repair of churches, rectories, parochial, and diocesan buildings by providing assistance in planning and loans, and to aid in the development of congregations through providing training, education, and resources.

WORK SUMMARY

The Episcopal Church Building Fund (ECBF) was established by the General Convention in 1880 as the American Church Building Fund Commission, a self-supporting agency.

In addition to its own funds, the ECBF manages the General Loan Fund portfolio of the DFMS. The ECBF assists congregations with the process of planning for a building project. The goal of these services is to provide the church with buildings that are tools for ministry. The ECBF helps congregations to address to issues of congregational health and growth.

TO THIS END, THE ECBF PROVIDES

I.   FINANCIAL ASSISTANCE

Fixed rate, non-mortgage loans of up to $200,000 are available to qualifying congregations and organizations of the Episcopal Church, through the diocese, within the domestic United States. Loans of up to $100,000 are available to dioceses throughout the Anglican Communion. Loans are issued to a diocese for the applying congregation and are awarded based on evidence of the ability to repay. These monies are available from the ECBF's revolving loan fund. As loan demand increases, additional monies are secured through a Debenture investment program with Episcopal parishes, diocese and organizations.

II.   EDUCATIONAL RESOURCES

The ECBF has recently updated its primary printed resource for congregations, *A Congregational Planning Process*, which outlines a planning and decision-making process designed to minimize conflict, set a manageable budget, and clarify the architectural implications of the ministries which the building must support. Also published is *The Church for Common Prayer: A Statement on Worship Space for the Episcopal Church*, which sets forth the theological principals for worship space. A video, *Churches for Common Prayer: Buildings for the Liturgical Assembly*, provides a tour through two church buildings, one new and one traditional building which has been renovated. The video depicts the benefits of flexible space and ways to make church buildings inviting to the newcomer. The Congregational Builder newsletter focuses on practical issues for parishes concerned with how their buildings serve as tools for ministry, and on issues of congregational health and growth. The Congregational Builder is mailed to every active ordained person and others upon request; all other resources are available at a nominal cost.

III.   DIOCESAN WORKSHOPS

The ECBF conducts free daylong workshops for congregations planning a new building, repair, renovation, or expansion. Topics include congregational life cycle, building support for change, decision making as a community, determining a realistic budget, the congruence between the ministries and building, and a slide show depicting the principles of liturgical design.

IV.   START UP! START OVER! CONGREGATIONAL DEVELOPMENT SEMINAR

The ECBF coordinates the Start Up! Start Over! Congregational Development Seminar, now in its 18th year, for the Office of Congregational Development. The five-day seminar provides basic congregational development and growth training for new and existing congregations seeking revitalization. Topics include: congregational life cycle, dealing with conflict and resistance to change, marketing the church, new member incorporation, reaching the unchurched, and the use of multi-media in worship and ministry.

GOALS AND OBJECTIVES FOR THE COMING TRIEUNNIUM

Consultation   To provide services of education and support to dioceses in their efforts to develop congregations.

Resources   To expand the written and video resources available to the church for building, congregational health and development.

Financial   To increase the capacity to make loans which meet the variety of needs of dioceses and congregations.

EPISCOPAL RELIEF AND DEVELOPMENT
www.er-d.org

BOARD OF DIRECTORS

The Most Rev. Frank T. Griswold, Presiding Bishop and Primate, Honorary Chair
The Rt. Rev. Robert G. Tharp, Chair (East Tennessee), The Rev. Dr. W. Robert Abstein II, (Tennessee), The Rt. Rev. Harry B. Bainbridge III, (Idaho), Ms. Margaret Boeth (New York), Mr. Jacob F. Bryan IV, (Florida), The Rev. Gwen Buehrens (Massachusetts), Mr. Edwin K. Hall, Vice-chair (Washington), Mr. Gerald W. Harner (El Camino Real), The Rev. Dr. J. Barney Hawkins (Maryland), Dr. Lawrence Howard (Pittsburgh), Dr. Bessie Lyman (Massachusetts), Ms. Patricia Mordecai, Treasurer (New York), Mr. Ralph O'Hara (Chicago), The Rev. Canon David W. Perry, Secretary (Oregon), The Rev. Douglass Ray (Colorado), Ms. Rita Redfield (Maine), Mr. Witney Schneidman (Virginia), Dr. Stan Shaffer (West Missouri), Ms. Sandra S. Swan, ERD President (Connecticut), Ms. Gilda Wray (New York).

ADMINISTRATORS

Sandra S. Swan, President; Donald Hammond, Vice President; Mary Becchi, Deputy Director, Program and Program Planning; Patricia Carter, Grants Operations Manager; Ayana Davis, Public Relations Associate; Xerxes Eclipse, Donor Associate; J. Coe Economou, Program Associate; Teresa Franco, Donor Associate; Linda Gulla, Executive Assistant; Joyce Hogg, Director, Networks and Special Projects; Malaika Kamunanwire, Director, Development and Public Relations; Dawn Murray, Grants Associate; Abagail Nelson, Director, Latin American Programs; Janette O'Neill, Senior Program Advisor; Linwood Parsons, Regional HIV/AIDS Project Coordinator; Chris Rodriguez, Administrative Assistant; Judy Rose, Director, Domestic Grants; Brian Sellers-Petersen, Director, West Coast Operations; Mark Spina, Director, Overseas Grants; Allison Taylor, Administrative Assistant.

WORK SUMMARY

Episcopal Relief and Development (ERD) works on behalf of the Episcopal Church to provide emergency relief in times of crises, rebuild devastated communities after disasters, and support long-term solutions to challenging problems. For 62 years, ERD has served people in more than 100 countries.

In the past three years, ERD has helped individuals, families, and communities in the following ways:

ERD Provided Emergency Relief

ERD responded to natural disasters, war, civil unrest, and other catastrophes that shattered lives, destroyed property, and tore apart communities and families. ERD supplied food, water, shelter, and other basic necessities in the immediate aftermath of crises.

During 2000 to 2002, ERD assisted more than 75 communities around the world affected by natural disasters such as hurricanes, floods, tornadoes, typhoons, drought, famine, and fires. ERD was there to help when devastating earthquakes killed thousands and caused unprecedented damage in Turkey, El Salvador, India, and Afghanistan. When fierce Caribbean hurricanes struck Belize two years in a row, ERD was there to provide immediate assistance. ERD supplied desperately needed food to victims of famine in Malawi.

ERD also reached people suffering because of man-made disasters. ERD provided emergency assistance to dioceses in several areas facing civil unrest, such as Liberia, Colombia, Burundi, and the Middle East. We provided care to refugees fleeing war in Afghanistan, Sierra Leone, Ethiopia, and Sudan.

ERD responded immediately to the terrorist attacks of September 11, 2001, with support for rescue and recovery workers at Ground Zero. We gave emergency assistance to victims' families and unemployed survivors, including financial support, grief and trauma counseling, and job training.

ERD Helped Rebuild After Disasters

Natural disasters or wars often destroy entire communities, leaving people without homes, schools, churches, or medical facilities. Disasters can ruin crops, kill livestock, and shut down businesses, making families economically vulnerable.

During 2000 to 2002, ERD helped rebuild several disaster-devastated communities across the globe. ERD constructed the *Faith, Hope, and Joy* community in San Pedro Sula, Honduras after several areas in the country were destroyed by Hurricane Mitch. The new community includes 200 homes, a school, church, community center, and medical clinic. ERD also completed 109 new houses for families who lost their homes in Turkey's massive earthquake of 1999.

ERD rebuilt 122 small shops in Gjakove, in war-torn Kosovo, so that merchants could get back on their feet. ERD also helped 90 small business owners rebuild their shops destroyed in the Mesa Redonda fire in Lima, Peru.

ERD launched two major reconstruction projects that will continue for the next few years. In El Salvador, ERD is partnering with the Diocese of El Salvador and Fundación Cristosal, a non-profit Episcopal agency. Along with the diocese and Cristosal, ERD is constructing homes as well as a medical clinic, school, and church in four villages affected by the earthquakes of 2001. After hurricanes in Belize, ERD is also rebuilding houses, schools, and church and community properties in two communities hit by Hurricanes Keith and Iris.

ERD Developed Long-term Solutions to Challenging Problems

ERD continued its work with churches and partner organizations to find long-term solutions that make lives safer, healthier, and more fulfilling in communities both here in the U.S. and around the world.

Continuing to fight the spread of HIV/AIDS, ERD launched a new partnership to bring much-needed HIV/AIDS education to four Anglican seminaries in some of the hardest-hit countries in Africa. ERD is providing HIV/AIDS education and care for people affected by the disease in areas such as South Africa, the United States, Kenya, Uganda, Zambia, Haiti, and Brazil.

ERD helped struggling communities become economically self-sufficient. In Uganda, ERD supported community-based development projects to help farmers move into the economic mainstream. In Honduras, El Salvador, and Belize, ERD began micro-credit and agricultural development programs so that people affected by disasters can regain economic security.

ERD provided educational opportunities so that people can thrive. In partnership with the Diocese of Haiti, ERD developed plans and curricula for the Episcopal Business and Technology Institute that will train young people in Les Cayes for good-paying jobs. ERD worked with the Church of Bangladesh to improve primary schools and enable disabled children to attend school. ERD supported after-school enrichment programs for children in low-income communities around the United States, as well as English as a Second Language (ESL) classes for newly arrived immigrants.

ERD worked with the Diocese of Liberia to rebuild several war-ravaged elementary and high schools in Liberia. ERD has also supported Cuttington University College by rebuilding damaged campus buildings and restoring services. Along with a number of partners, ERD also restored electricity to Cuttington and installed a generator to supply power to the student dormitories, classrooms, and staff and faculty houses.

As part of a multi-faceted and long-term response to September 11, 2001, ERD launched the Interfaith Education Initiative (IEI) in partnership with the Office of Ecumenical and Interfaith Relations of the ECUSA. IEI will provide resources and training to help Episcopalians build positive relationships among religious groups in communities across the United States.

From 2000 to 2002, ERD provided $26.6 million for crisis relief, rehabilitation, and long-term development assistance for people in need across the world.

GOALS AND OBJECTIVES FOR THE COMING TRIENNIUM

Episcopal Relief and Development will continue to increase its capacity to assist the Anglican Communion in meeting the needs of people worldwide by providing emergency assistance in times of natural or human-made disasters; helping communities rebuild after the immediate crisis is over; and offering opportunities for individuals, families, and communities to strive for self-sufficiency.

THE GENERAL BOARD OF EXAMINING CHAPLAINS

MEMBERSHIP
Bishops
The Rt. Rev. Robert L. Ladehoff, *Chair*	Oregon, 2003
The Rt. Rev. Edward L. Lee, Jr.	Western Michigan, 2006
The Rt. Rev. John B. Lipscomb	Southwest Florida, 2006, *resigned*
The Rt. Rev. Arthur E. Walmsley	Connecticut, Retired, 2003

Clergy with Pastoral Responsibilities
The Rev. Katharine C. Black	Massachusetts, 2006
The Rev. Mark Taylor Crawford	Texas, 2003
The Rev. Rev. Philip M. Duncan, II	Dallas, 2003
The Rev. F. Scott Hennessy	Virginia, 2006
The Rev. John H. Loving	Northwest Texas, 2006
The Rev. Canon Anne W. Robbins	Southern Ohio, 2003

Members of Faculties
The Rev. Thomas E. Breidenthal	General, 2003, *resigned*
The Rev. Lloyd A. Lewis, Jr.	Virginia, 2006
The Very Rev. Guy Lytle	Sewanee, 2003
The Rev. Leonel L. Mitchell	Seabury-Western, 2006
The Rev. Harmon L. Smith	Duke, 2006
The Rev. Ellen K. Wondra	Bexley Hall, 2003, *resigned*

Lay Persons
Dr. Mary C. Callaway	New York, 2003
Mr. Philip Clark	Northern California, 2006
Mrs. Josephine R. Giannini	Indianapolis, 2006
Dr. Leonard W. Johnson, *Vice-Chair*	California, 2003
Dr. Susan Hill Lindley	Minnesota, 2006
Dr. Peter W. Williams	Southern Ohio, 2006

Administrator
The Rev. Richard F. Tombaugh, 920 Farmington Avenue, #202, West Hartford CT 06107

Board representatives at General Convention
Bishop Robert L. Ladehoff and the Rev. Canon Anne W. Robbins are authorized to receive non-substantive amendments to this report.

WORK SUMMARY

During the triennium 2000-2003, the General Board of Examining Chaplains (GBEC) made a major change in the way in which examinations were read and evaluated. In the past, the papers had been sent to several reading stations, in various parts of the country. The Board found that this process led to inconsistencies in the evaluations. On the advice of experts in testing, the Board in 2000 set up a single reading session at Camp Allen in Texas, at which all papers were read and evaluated. As a result, there was greater consistency in the evaluations. It also became possible for the results to be distributed in a more timely fashion. The response to this change was so positive that we continue to go to Camp Allen each year in February, to read all of the examinations. In carrying out its canonical responsibilities, the Board:

- Convened at the College of Preachers in October of each year to prepare the General Ordination Examination (GOE) to be administered the following January, and produced background material for the guidance of readers who would evaluate the candidates' papers.
- Arranged for the administration of the GOE annually in thirty-five to forty locations throughout the United States and abroad.

- Recruited, supervised and assisted readers in the evaluation process (270 - 292 candidates per year).
- Reported the examination results and recommendations to candidates, their diocesan authorities, and seminary deans.
- Attended diocesan and provincial meetings, and a meeting of the Council of Seminary Deans, to explain and interpret the work of the GBEC, and to solicit advice.
- Informed seminary deans concerning how their candidates compared with those from other seminaries; in this comparison seminaries were not identified by name but by an arbitrary alphabetical designation.
- Through a Planning Committee evaluated each year's GOE, its administration and results; adapted and altered subsequent years' exams and procedures in response to feedback solicited from candidates, readers, diocesan authorities, and others.
- Greeted the Rev. Susan Dolan-Henderson and the Rev. Dr. Robert D. Hughes, III, as replacement members of the GBEC, elected by the House of Bishops; and greeted the Rev. Mary C. Sulerud, appointed by the Presiding Bishop.
- Accepted with sadness the retirement of the Rev. Locke E. Bowman, Jr., who served as Administrator for the GBEC from 1996 until 2002 with wisdom and creativity and dedication; and accepted with sadness the retirement of the Rev. Thomas N. Rightmyer, who had served well and faithfully as Assistant to Dr. Bowman and to Bishop Charlton, his predecessor.
- Welcomed the Rev. Richard F. Tombaugh, Retired Canon to the Ordinary of the Diocese of Connecticut, as Administrator.
- Moved the GBEC office from Chapel Hill, NC, to West Hartford CT.
- Reorganized its administrative structure, resulting in lower asking from the General Convention budget: $391,712 in 2000, $335,169 in 2003.
- Reported through its chair to the interim meetings of the House of Bishops, as required by Canon.

FINANCIAL REPORT FOR THE 2000-2003 TRIENNIUM

	2001 Actual	2002 Actual	2003 Actual	Total
Income				
Exam fees (1)	94,500	67,500	96,600	258,600
Gen. Conv. Budget	130,042	130,042	130,042	390,126
Total	224,542	197,542	226,642	648,726
Expenses				
Salaries and benefits (2)	80,639	67,114	40,613	188,366
Board meetings	25,000	25,450	26,000	76,450
Readers' meetings	102,249	101,400	106,000	309,649
Office expense	17,932	27,000	36,300	81,232
Total	225,820	220,964	208,913	655,697

Notes

(1) These figures represent $300 x the number of candidates taking the exam.

(2) Benefits include health insurance, pension payments, and 50 percent of Social Security.

GOALS AND OBJECTIVES FOR THE COMING TRIENNIUM

Title III, Canon 31.1 defines the responsibilities of the General Board of Examining Chaplains. The Board is to develop annually a General Ordination Examination; to administer it to certified candidates; and to evaluate the results and report them to the candidates, their diocesan authorities, and their seminary deans. The principle objectives of the Board and its executive during the next triennium will be to continue accomplishing those tasks in as fair and efficient a manner as possible.

Three years ago a major change was made in the Board's process. Instead of having the papers read and evaluated at several reading stations, all papers are now being evaluated at one central place and at one time. We have received enthusiastic responses to this change from bishops and dioceses, from students and from the seminaries. At the same time, we are grateful to all of these groups for offering helpful recommendations. During the next triennium we plan to continue to refine this process.

The Board is grateful that the Administrator has made changes in his office that make it possible for us to ask a lesser amount from the General Convention budget than we did in 2000. We will watch this operation carefully, so be sure that these changes will not affect the efficiency or the quality of the work of this office.

The Board will continue to work to create examinations and background material that are both measuring instruments and stimuli for learning.

The Board looks forward to working with other groups involved in theological education, such as the Council of Seminary Deans and the Presiding Bishop's Task Force on Seminary and Diocesan Relations, so that we will better serve bishops, students and their dioceses.

The Board will continue its ongoing effort to help diocesan authorities to make proper and full use of the GOE results. These results ought not to be regarded on a "pass or fail" basis; on the contrary, they provide potentially useful data of a diagnostic or analytic nature. The GOE results should not be the sole or final determination of a candidates's readiness for ordination, but they do provide a view, not otherwise available, to be given due weight along with seminary reports and other data. The GOE advises diocesan authorities about a candidate's examination results as compared with other candidates seeking ordination at the same time. To make these points clear may be the GBEC's greatest challenge, because the manner in which its products are used is beyond the Board's control except by persuasion. The value of the entire GOE effort depends upon the use of its information by diocesan authorities in the ways intended.

BUDGET APPROPRIATION

	2003	2004	2005	Total
Income				
Exam fees (1)	105,000	105,000	105.000	315,000
Gen. Conv. Budget (2)	108,181	111,746	115,242	335,169
Total	213,181	216.746	220.242	650,169
Expenses				
Salaries and benefits (3)	41,681	42,746	43,842	128,269
Board Meetings	26,000	28,000	29,000	84,000
Readers' meetings	108,000	108,000	108,000	324,000
Office expense	36,500	38,000	39,400	113,900
Total	213,181	216,746	220,242	650,169

Notes
(1) This figure represents a fee of $350 x estimates of 300 candidates each year.
(2) This figure represents the amount necessary to balance estimated expenses.
(3) Benefits include health insurance, pension payments, and 50 percent of Social Security.

Resolution A003 Budget Appropriation for the General Board of Examining Chaplains

1   *Resolved,* the House of _____ concurring, That the following amount be appropriated from the
2   General Convention budget for the General Board of Examining Chaplains: $108,181 in 2003, 111,746 in
3   2004, and $115,242 in 2005. This totals $335,169 for the triennium.

Resolution A004 General Ordination Exam Fee

1   *Resolved,* the House of _____ concurring, That the authorization for the General Board of
2   Examining Chaplains to charge a fee for the General Ordination Examination be continued for the next
3   triennium, such fee not to exceed $350.00 per candidate; this authorization is granted with the proviso that
4   fees shall be reduced or waived, at the Administrator's discretion, for qualified candidates who are unable
5   to obtain funds for the stated fee.

FORWARD MOVEMENT PUBLICATIONS
www.forwardmovement.org

MEMBERSHIP

Forward Movement Publications (FMP), an official, non-profit agency of The Episcopal Church, established by the General Convention under the direction of the Presiding Bishop, is sustained through sales and non-profit contributions of its readers. An outgrowth of the 1934 Joint Commission on the Forward Movement of the Church, it has been governed since 1940 by an *Executive Committee*:

Ms. Margaret Graham Beers, *Chair*	Washington
The Rt. Rev. J. Clark Grew II, *Vice Chair*	Ohio
Mr. Addison Lanier II, Treasurer	Southern Ohio
The Rev. Edward Stone Gleason, *Secretary*	Southern Ohio
The Rt. Rev. Edward W. Jones	Indianapolis
The Rt. Rev. Stacy F. Sauls	Lexington
Ms. Naomi Tucker Stoehr	Southern Ohio
Ms. Phyllis Alexander Tickle	West Tennessee
The Ven. Lorentho Wooden	Southern Ohio

The Executive Committee meets yearly with the Advisory Board for consultation and recommendation. The *Advisory Board* includes:

Mr. Sam McDonald (Ohio), Ms. Cynthia Logan Shattuck (Rhode Island), Mr. David K. Urion, MD (Massachusetts), Mr. N. Beverley Tucker (Southern Ohio), The Rev. Robert Harold Thompson (New Hampshire), The Rev. Richard Joseph Aguilar (Southern Ohio), The Rev. Marcia Miller Lockwood (El Camino Real), The Rev. William P. Billow, Jr. (Washington), The Rev. Jonathan T. Glass (Los Angeles), Ms. Derby Quin Hirst (Maryland), The Rev. Jonathon Jensen (Kansas), Ms. Allene Russell Pierson (Maryland), Mr. Warren Cummings Cook (Maine), Mr. Joel Wilson Motley III (New York)

The Rev. Edward S. Gleason is editor and director with general oversight for the editorial and business office. Jane Lyman Paraskevopoulos is business manager. The Rev. George Curwood Allen II is assistant editor. Carolyn Kent Searle is Director of Marketing. Carole Jean Miller is Director of Production.

The Rt. Rev. Henry Wise Hobson, Bishop of Southern Ohio, the founder of FMP, led the Executive Committee until succeeded by The Rt. Rev John M. Krumm, Southern Ohio, who was Chair until 1991, when he was succeeded by Bishop Jones of Indianapolis. Bishop Krumm continued as Honorary Chairman until his death in 1995. Bishop Jones was succeeded as Chair in 2002 by Margaret Graham Beers of Washington.

WORK SUMMARY

Forward Movement (FMP) was established in 1934 "to help reinvigorate the life of the church," and it was determined that this mission would best be furthered by supporting persons in their lives of prayer and faith. Our devotional quarterly, Forward Day by Day, was first published in 1935. Quarterly distribution (regular print, large print and Spanish editions) has increased from 1,468,305 in 1999 to 1,490,358 in 2002. Forward Day by Day is also available in Braille, audio cassette, by e-mail subscription and on line. Several retreats for readers of Forward Day by Day have been well received.

The Anglican Cycle of Prayer has been published by FMP for more than twenty-five years. It is offered thanks to the support and close cooperation of the Anglican Consultative Council and the understanding that the Anglican Communion exists because we pray with and for one another.

As the mission of FMP has unfolded, it has been further fulfilled through the publication of more than four hundred other publications, varying in length from two to two hundred pages, interpreting, describing and explicating aspects of the faith and life of Christians and members of the Episcopal Church. The clear traditions of FMP that continue to define our publications are brevity, clarity and quality. 584,089 books and tracts were sold in the year 2002.

One annual catalogue describes each book published by FMP and a second annual catalogue describes each of our pamphlets. Each quarter FMP publishes one or two books or booklets, and four to six pamphlets, while often re-issuing well-used, time-tested materials that serve the church. Our all-time best-sellers include: Prayers for All Occasions, For Those Who Mourn, Discovering the Episcopal Church, Brother Lawrence. The total number of new titles offered in this Triennium is115. FMP's website first appeared in 1996 and was extensively re-designed in 2002. It receives an average of 9000 visits a week.

FMP is deeply grateful for the many authors who have contributed their work, often anonymously and with modest financial compensation. FMP has always been a fellowship of Christian writers whose words are offered as a gift for the benefit of the entire church. These contributors work appeared in the past Triennium: *Bishops*: C. Fitzsimmons Allison, Frank T. Griswold, Edward W. Jones, Gerald N. McAllister, Stacy F. Sauls, M. Thomas Shaw SSJE, Richard L. Shimpfky, Herbert Thompson, Jr.

Clergy: Curtis Almquist, James A. Belcher, Lee Hastings Bristol III, Charles F. Brumbaugh, James L. Burns, Elizabeth Canham, Peter Chase, Daniel G. Conklin, Pamela Lee Cranston, Gilbert Crosby, William L. Dols, Jr., Travis Talmadge Du Priest, Thomas L. Ehrich, William Tate Elliott, Randloph L. Frew, Edward S. Gleason, Joseph W. Goetz, Peter J. Gomes, Holt H. Graham, Margaret B. Gunness, Harvey H. Gutherie, Jr., John Hall, James A. Hanisian, Bert H. Hatch, Robert B. Horine, Jr., Margaret Bullitt-Jonas, Raymond F. Kasch, Jr., Jason E. Leo, Samuel Thames Lloyd III, Heyward H. Macdonald, Beth Maynard, Michael T. McEwen, Mary Rose McGeady, R. Charles Meyer, Robert C. Morris, Murray L. Newman, Joseph L. Pace, Sam A. Portaro, Jr., Richard Reid, Isaías A. Rodríguez, Joseph P. Russell, Richard H. Schmidt, Robert Boak Slocum, Carroll Simcox, Peter Stebinger, Sylvia Sweeney, John Throop, Francis H. Wade, Edward Waldron, Christopher L. Webber, Nancy G. Westerfield, John Westerhoff, J. Robert Wright.

Laity: Melanie Ashworth, Mary Barwell, Michael Barwell, Margaret Graham Beers, Pamela P. Chinnis, Christopher Cleveland, Nan Cobbey, Peter Cooley, Bo Don Cox, David S. Cunningham, Philip Dean, Deborah Smith Douglas, Alison Gibson, William W. Graham, Barbara Hall, Hobey Hinchman, Roland S. Homet, Jr., Kristen J. Ingram, Janet Irwin, Anne Shelburne Jones, Candy McMillan, Judith Newman, Allan Mitchell Parrent, Frederick Osborn, Sally B. Sedgwick, Betty Streett, David K. Urion, Sydney vom Lehn.

FINANCIAL REPORT FOR THE 2000-2003 TRIENNIUM

FMP is self-supporting, sustained by the consistently low fees set for our literature. The support FMP receives through the purchases of these materials continues to increase. Gross sales at the end of the last fiscal year (June 2002) were $1,804,020 as compared with June 1999, when they were $1,637,470, an increase of 10%.

Some of the work of FMP is further sustained by three special funds established by the gifts and bequests of readers:

1. The Braille Fund provides Braille editions of Forward Day by Day (free) and the Prayer Book (at nominal cost) to any blind person and subsidizes large print editions of Day by Day and other works. The FMP investment account stands at $1,310,810 ($372,554 is designated as the Braille Fund).

2. The Henry Wise Hobson Fund was established in honor of the founder of FMP, who served as chairman for forty years. The Hobson Fund now totals $887,663. The income is used to provide free literature for use in prisons and hospitals for those unable to pay. The increase of this fund continues to strengthen the work and mission of FMP.

3. The Mamie and Edgar Woolard Fund was established in 1999 to provide FMP materials free for hospital patients. The Woolard Fund was established by Edgar S. Woolard, Jr., and currently totals $123,298.

GOALS AND OBJECTIVES FOR THE 2004 – 2006 TRIENNIUM

FMP Publications is presently involved in the initial stages of **The Forward Fund,** a capital campaign to raise $2.75 million to establish *A New Day* by achieving three important goals:

4. Increase and improve our spaces better to serve the larger numbers of persons who desire support in their lives of prayer and faith.
5. Extend our outreach through new marketing efforts, new initiatives to reach more Episcopalians, younger readers, Hispanic readers and those in crisis.
6. Strengthen our endowment to provide additional materials for those who otherwise are unable to afford them especially those in institutions.

Resolution A005 Continue Forward Movement Publications

1   *Resolved,* the House of _____ concurring, That the Presiding Bishop be authorized to continue
2   Forward Movement Publications under his supervision and to appoint such staff members and commission
3   as may be required to maintain its work.

THE GENERAL THEOLOGICAL SEMINARY OF THE EPISCOPAL CHURCH
www.gts.edu

BOARD OF TRUSTEES

Officers

The Very Rev. Robert Giannini, *Chairman of the Board of Trustees*
Ms. Juli S. Towell, *Vice Chairman*
Mr. Frederick W. Gerbracht, Jr., *Treasurer*
Miss Gwendolyn Simmons, *Secretary*

Ex-Officio Members

The Very Rev. Ward B. Ewing, *Dean and President*
The Most Rev. Frank T. Griswold III, *Presiding Bishop*
The Rt. Rev. Mark S. Sisk, *Bishop of New York*

Elected Members

The Rev. Lauren Ackland
The Rt. Rev. J. Neil Alexander
The Rt. Rev. G. P. Mellick Belshaw
Ms. Pamela P. Chinnis
Ms. Marjorie L. Christie
The Rev. Paul C. Christopherson
The Rt. Rev. John Palmer
   Croneberger
Duncan N. Darrow, Esq.
Mr. Joseph A. Davenport III
Gabrielle Porter Dennison, Esq.
Mr. William B. Eagleson, Jr.
The Rev. Deena M. Galantowicz

Mr. Michael F. Gilligan
Mr. Warren F. Ilchman
Mr. Gary Johnson
Mrs. Patricia B. Kilpatrick
The Rev. Dr. William C. Lutz
The Rev. Dr. Daniel Paul Matthews
The Rev. Denis M. O'Pray
Mr. Richard Pivirotto
Ms. Diane Pollard
Ms. Diane M. Porter
The Rt. Rev. Wilfrido Ramos-Orench
The Rev. James C. Ransom
The Rev. Douglas E. Remer

The Rev. Canon V. Gene Robinson
The Rev. Canon Nancy A. Roosevelt
The Rt. Rev. Catherine S. Roskam
Ms. Cynthia H. Schwab
The Rev. Alfred R. Shands
The Rt. Rev. Douglas E. Theuner
The Rev. Jeffrey H. Walker
The Rev. Canon Frederick B.
   Williams
Mrs. Caroline K. Winter
Mr. Robert E. Wright

Retired Trustees

2001
Ms. Sally M. Bucklee
The Rev. T. Mark Dunnam
Mr. Delbert Glover
The Rt. Rev. Richard Grein, *Ex Officio*
The Rt. Rev. Samuel B. Hulsey
Mr. Charles C. Lee
Ms. Sarah Mauger-Veil
Mr. Gary Shilling
The Rev. William M. Tully

2002
The Rt. Rev. Leopold Frade
The Rt. Rev. James L. Jelinek
The Rev. Steven Woolley

2003
The Rev. Robert W. Cromey
The Rev. C. Hugh Hildesley

WORK SUMMARY

The General Theological Seminary (GTS) stands on the threshold of a new era. The Board of Trustees elected a new Chairman in January 2001, the Very Rev. Robert Giannini, Dean and Rector of Christ Church Cathedral in Indianapolis. Dean Giannini, GTS class of 1967, leads an institution invigorated by hope and creativity, collaborating with committed trustees, faculty, students, and staff. New and revitalized programs, fresh ideas, and a willingness to explore bold initiatives contribute to the vibrant atmosphere of growth.

Founded in 1817 by General Convention, the Seminary is not content to rest on its history and unique position within the Episcopal Church. GTS has begun planning for the creation of a dynamic education center and inn to serve as a hub for conferences, institutes and new programs. Through an enhanced M.A. program, General will provide a flexible, academically rigorous path for continuing and lay education. In all, General aims to become the seminary of the whole church not merely in name, but through engagement with the wider church and the formation and education of future leaders of the church.

PROGRAMS AND THEOLOGICAL EDUCATION

Enrollment in the Masters of Divinity Program at GTS has nearly doubled in the last three years. In the 2002-03 academic year, General welcomed students from 41 dioceses and 3 Lutheran Synods, and 30% of the junior class was under age 30. GTS continues its long tradition of supporting theological education through significant financial aid expenditures; last year the GTS scholarship fund provided 48% of tuition and fees for all programs, including the Center for Christian Spirituality and the College for Bishops. Approximately two-thirds of all M.Div. students receive aid.

In the fall of 2001, the first students of the *Programa Hispano/Latino de Teologia y Pastoral*—a fully accredited M.Div. program for primary speakers of Spanish—started taking classes in Spanish at GTS. The program, directed by the Rev. Canon Juan M.C. Oliver, Ph.D., now enrolls 17 postulants or aspirants for ordination. There is an urgent need in the Episcopal church for Hispanic clergy, especially in urban areas, and it is part of the GTS mission, located as it is in the heart of the largest urban area in the United States, to respond to that need. This program is supported through partnerships with the Episcopal dioceses of New York, New Jersey, Newark, Connecticut and Long Island, as well the Metropolitan New York and New Jersey Synods of the ECLA.

In 2001, the Rev. Jonathan Linman, Ph.D., was appointed Director of the Center for Christian Spirituality. Dr. Linman, a Lutheran pastor with twelve years experience in parish ministry, has focused on clarifying the Center's mission. He says, "We hope the Center will provide leaven for spiritual growth among the Church's future generations of leaders through its presence in this community." The Center received a three-year grant from the Henry Luce Foundation to expand and gain self-sufficiency as a ministry of General Seminary. To achieve these goals, the Center has increased its course offerings, encouraged greater participation among M.Div. students, and begun more targeted publicity. In February 2003, Sandra Schneiders, I.H.M., S.T.D., gave the first annual lecture in Christian Spirituality sponsored by the Center, *Embodying the Word: The Role of Interpretation in Biblical Spirituality.*

Beginning in September 2003, GTS will extend the part-time Masters degree programs in Christian Spirituality, Biblical Studies, and Anglican Studies. The courses are shaped to meet the needs of both M.Div. and M.A. students and are scheduled at times convenient for both constituencies. The focus on lay ministry reflects values deeply cherished by the Seminary: community, hospitality, accessibility, and the centrality of worship. The program will invite part-time students to share all the resources of the seminary and flows naturally from our mission to form leaders for the Church in a changing world.

THE REDEVELOPMENT OF CHELSEA SQUARE

During the last three years, the Seminary has planned the redevelopment of its historic Close on Chelsea Square. General has seized on its mission of educating and forming church leaders to guide these plans. The concept of an education center on the Close remains central to the vision of General in the 21st century. Outside feasibility studies and internal investigation have confirmed that:

- An education center will provide much-needed conference space at or below market rates for church-related organizations in the heart of New York City, a crossroads of the international Anglican Communion.
- Millions of dollars of deferred maintenance will be addressed through facilities renovation.
- The Seminary gains a permanent income stream to support theological education.

The education center facility is slated to contain numerous programs and institutes. One possibility is a center focused on peace and justice whose internationally oriented activities, conferences and lectures would be based at General. In addition, GTS would play host to a wide range of academic and church-related events, made possible by the ability to house and feed participants on-site at reasonable rates.

LEADERS FOR THE CHURCH

In 2001, General's Board of Trustees approved the largest capital-funds drive in the Seminary's history. The $21-million Leaders for the Church campaign will seek $10 million for the education center and improvements to other academic spaces; $6 million for our endowment; and $5 million for annual operations.

The GTS Board—whose members will conduct a retreat on trusteeship and governance in October 2003—are profoundly committed to the health and future of the Seminary. Their expertise and generosity are integral to the success of the campaign, and they are largely responsible for the good work already underway.

As part of the fund-raising effort, General Seminary has sought and received more major grants from philanthropic organizations and individuals than in any other three-year period in its history. A grant from the Lilly Endowment allowed the creation of two "smart classrooms" and a computer lab; a strategic planning grant from the Arthur Vining Davis Foundations supported four feasibility studies; dual grants from the Teagle Foundation strengthened the leadership and management of the institution; a grant from the H. Boone Porter Charitable Trust endowed a chair in liturgics; several anonymous grants provide the footing for the redevelopment of Chelsea Square; and the Henry Luce Foundation grant helped revitalize the Center for Christian Spirituality. All testify to a strong belief that the Seminary is a place worthy of significant investment.

APPOINTMENTS

In faculty appointments—in addition to Dr. Linman's—the Rev. Robert J. Owens, Ph.D., joined General Seminary as Professor of Old Testament in 2001. The Rev. James W. Farwell, Ph.D., a 1987 GTS alumnus, arrived for the Michaelmas Term 2002 as Assistant Professor of Liturgics in the H. Boone Porter Chair. Both Professors Owens and Farwell cite the integration of academic study with the life of faith as a motivation for accepting their respective positions. As Dr. Owens writes in our 2003 catalog, "I have been delighted to discover the seriousness and depth of faith of our students.…The rich experience of our students gives special meaning to the description of GTS as a community of Christian learning. Both faculty and students actively share our common adult life in Christ, as we engage in rigorous theological study."

Three other senior appointments were made in late 2002. J. Frederick Rogers, the great-great-grandson of a member of the Class of 1858, began service as Vice President for Institutional Advancement and Alumni/ae Relations in November. Maureen Burnley was appointed Vice President for Finance and Operations in December. The Rev. Andrew G. Kadel began his duties as Director of The St. Mark's Library in January 2003.

In other recent news, Dr. Robert Bruce Mullin, Sub-Dean for Academic Affairs, and Professor of History and World Mission, and Modern Anglican Studies, published his latest book, *The Puritan as Yankee: A Life of Horace Bushnell*, in November 2002. In 2001, Professor of Ecclesiastical History, the Rev. Dr. J. Robert Wright, published a beautifully illustrated and very well received history of Saint Thomas Church, Fifth Avenue.

The General Theological Seminary is a vibrant community of faith in New York City, grounded in scholarship, academic study, and worship. All postulants for ordination write spiritual autobiographies as part of their discernment process. Much of the process of formation revolves around this concept. The Seminary has its own spiritual autobiography to write. It would be the history of all those who have passed beyond its walls, into the service of Christ. It would be a history of the walls themselves, as they record the theological arguments of eras past that still echo down the corridors. And it would be a history of the discussions of the future among trustees, students, faculty and staff that create the place anew with every generation. Beloved, historic, and modern all at once, General Seminary has the will and the resources to thrive in the 21st century.

Respectfully submitted,

The Very Rev. Ward B. Ewing
Dean and President

HISTORICAL SOCIETY OF THE EPISCOPAL CHURCH
www.hsec-usa.org/

MEMBERSHIP
Officers
Dr. Thad W. Tate, *President*, Southern Virginia
The Rev. Dr. Alfred A. Moss, Jr., *First Vice President*, Virginia
The Rev. Dr. Eugene Y. Lowe, Jr., *Second Vice President*, Illinois
The Rev. William M. Bennett, *Treasurer*, Texas
Dr. Thomas A. Mason, *Secretary*, Indiana

Ex Officio Members
Dr. Mary Sudman Donovan, *Past President*
The Most Rev. Frank T. Griswold III, *Presiding Bishop*
The Rt. Rev. Bennett J. Sims, *Past President*
The Very Rev. George L. W. Werner, *President of the House of Deputies*
Mr. Ralph O'Hara, *Treasurer of The Episcopal Church*
The Rt. Rev. Richard S. O. Chang, *Secretary of the House of Bishops*
The Rev. Rosemari Sullivan, *Secretary of the General Convention*

Board Members
Dr. Henry Warner Bowden, NJ
Dr. James E. Bradley, Los Angeles
Dr. Pamela W. Darling, PA
Mr. Mark J. Duffy, TX
Rev. Dr. N. Brooks Graebner, NC
Ms. Alexandra S. Gressitt, VA

Dr. Allen C. Guelzo, PA
Dr. David L. Holmes, S. VA
The Rt. Rev. David B. Joslin, NJ
Mr. Grant LeMarquand, Pittsburgh
The Rev. J. Patrick Mauney, RI
The Rev. J. Barrett Miller, VA

Dr. Alda Marsh Morgan, CA
Dr. Fredrica Harris Thompsett, MA
Dr. Peter W. Williams, S. Ohio
The Rev. Dr. John F. Woolverton, ME
The Rev. Canon J. Robert Wright, NY

SOCIETY REPRESENTATIVES AT GENERAL CONVENTION
The Society authorizes the Rt. Rev. David B. Joslin, House of Bishops, and Mr. Russell Randle, Diocese of Virginia, to receive non-substantive amendments to the report.

SUMMARY OF THE SOCIETY'S WORK

The Historical Society of the Episcopal Church, by General Convention Resolutions, is the designated publisher of the Church's quarterly historical journal, *Anglican and Episcopal History* (formerly the *Historical Magazine of the Protestant Episcopal Church*). Although publication of the journal remains a major part of its activities, the Society now undertakes a number of other programs as part of its recently redefined mission "to encourage scholarship and to generate and sustain greater interest in Anglican and Episcopal history among the widest possible audience."

In the time since the report to the 73rd General Convention in 2000, the Rev. Dr. John F. Woolverton has continued to serve as editor of *Anglican and Episcopal History*. The journal has published a wide range of articles not only relating to the Anglican Church in America and Great Britain but also extending to the history of the Church in many other parts of the world. An especially pertinent example is the issue of June 2002, devoted to "Essays on the Anglican Church in the Sudan" with an introductory editorial and a review of recent work by Grant LeMarquand, the International Editor of the journal. The timeliness and breadth of coverage of this special issue attracted an unusually large number of orders from non-subscribers. In the succeeding issue of September 2002 Dr. Woolverton compiled under the title "New Frontiers in American Episcopal History" a collection of statements by fifteen Church historians that offer a rich and challenging agenda for fresh areas of investigation. The section of the journal devoted to book reviews and church reviews of the conduct of worship services in a variety of churches also continues to attract the interest of readers.

A second publishing activity of the Society is its book series, *Studies in Anglican History*. Under the editorship of Dr. Peter W. Williams six titles have been published, two of them within the past two years (Michael T. Beary, *Black Bishop: Edward T. Demby and the Struggle for Racial Equality in the Episcopal Church* and David Hein, *Noble Powell and the Episcopal Establishment in the Twentieth Century*). One additional title is in press, and three others are undergoing revision. While the Board of Directors has been impressed with the quality of scholarship that the series has achieved, members reluctantly reached a decision at the 2002 annual meeting that rapidly increasing costs of publication will necessitate termination of the series in its present form after the four remaining titles have been published. The Board also voted, however, to explore possible alternative ways of encouraging book publication at less cost. The Society also continues to award small grants annually to support research in progress. Seven such awards have been made in the past three years, five to individual scholars and two to aid the preparation of parish histories.

Four years ago the Society embarked upon an ambitious new undertaking—the establishment of the African American Historical Collection of the Episcopal Church that would seek to collect and preserve archival materials relating to the history of African Americans in the Church. With initial financial support from the Society and from outside grants, a special standing committee drawn from present and former members of the Board of Directors has worked diligently to develop a sound and workable plan, including partnership with an institution able to provide professional archival management of the materials received. Those efforts reached a successful end on December 11, 2002, when the Historical Society and the Virginia Theological Seminary signed an agreement whereby the Bishop Payne Library at the Seminary will receive and administer the Collection while the two institutions will work together in the effort to build the Collection and find the necessary financial support to maintain the archive. Both parties recognize that this undertaking may well present a daunting challenge but those within the Society and at Virginia Seminary who have worked very hard to come this far are excited by the prospect of what may be achieved in preserving and making available to researchers this often neglected but vital part of the history of the Episcopal Church.

The Society also works closely with other organizations concerned with the history of the Church, especially The National Episcopal Historians and Archivists (NEHA) and the Episcopal Women's History Project (EWHP). *The Historiographer*, founded as the NEHA newsletter, now carries news of all three organizations and receives partial support of the costs of publication from the Historical Society. The major cooperative activity of the three organizations is, however, sponsorship every third year of a "Tri-Conference" for Church historians. The most recent gathering in June 2001 became, in fact, a "Quad-Conference" when the Canadian Church Historical Society joined in sponsoring "(Re)Making Anglican Tradition(s) in North America: A Conference for Historians and Archivists Commemorating the Tercentenary of the Society for the Propagation of the Gospel in Foreign Parts," held at Trinity College, Toronto. It proved to be the largest and best attended of the conferences that have been held.

The Historical Society likewise values its working relationship with the Archivist of the Church, Mark J. Duffy, and the Historiographer, the Rev. Canon J. Robert Wright. Both serve as voting members of the Board of Directors of the Society. The report of Canon Wright, appointed as Historiographer in 2000 following the retirement of the Rev. Dr. John E. Booty, appears in a succeeding section of this report.

The Board of Directors of the Society meets annually. In 2000 members convened at Denver during the General Convention. Its now traditional General Convention dinner featured as its speaker, the Hon. John T. Noonan, Jr., Judge of the Ninth U.S. Circuit Court of Appeals and author of *The Lustre of Our Country: The American Experience of Religious Freedom* (1998). His address, "Lights of the Law: Madison, Key, Jackson," subsequently appeared in the December 2000 issue of *Anglican and Episcopal History*. The 2001 meeting took place in conjunction with the Toronto Conference, and in 2002 the Board met at the College of Preachers at Washington National Cathedral. The 2003 meeting will take place on August 1-2 at Minneapolis. The speaker for the Convention dinner will be the Rev. Dr. Bruce B. Lawrence, an Episcopal priest and the Nancy and Jeffrey Marcus Professor of Religion at Duke University. A specialist in Islamic and other Asian religious traditions, Dr. Lawrence will address the topic "Muslims, Christians, Terrorists: The Crescent and the Crisis, At Home and Abroad, After 9/11."

REPORT OF THE HISTORIOGRAPHER OF THE EPISCOPAL CHURCH

In the summer of 2000, I was pleased to be nominated by the Presiding Bishop and elected by both houses of General Convention as Historiographer of the Episcopal Church in succession to my distinguished predecessor the Rev. Dr. John E. Booty. I stated in my letter of acceptance that in a general way I took my assignment to "promote throughout the Episcopal Church the serious study and intelligent use of the history of the church in every place and from every century of its existence." I added, "This is something I already try to do, and now I shall be pleased to do it in a more formal and official way." Further role definition of the position of Historiographer is clearly "a work in progress," and I have already published a preliminary sketch of the development and possibilities of this office in the spring 2002 issue of *The Historiographer*.

During the past triennium, I have sought to work as closely as possible with the Historical Society of the Episcopal Church, the Episcopal Church Archives, the National Episcopal Historians and Archivists, the Episcopal Women's History Project, the Conference of Anglican Church Historians, and the journal *Anglican and Episcopal History*. I have traveled to attend a few major conferences, sometimes giving presentations of a historical nature. I have published two major books, one on the history of *Saint Thomas Church Fifth Avenue* (Eerdmans, 2001; 344 pages and 659 footnotes) which has already sold over four thousand copies and is a selection of the Episcopal Book Club, and the other an annotated, limited reprint edition of *Russo-Greek Papers 1863–1874* (Norman Ross Publishing, 2001, 389 pp). To accompany the latter, I published, with Edward Kasinec, "Charles Hale and the Russian Church: The Biography of Innokentii" in the March 2002 issue of *Anglican and Episcopal History,* Hale having been the secretary of this landmark committee of General Convention and later Bishop of Cairo Illinois (a see that never existed). My personal collection of 226 historical portrait-engravings of Anglican Divines from the 16th to the 19th centuries I have recently presented to the Episcopal Archives in Austin. My latest honorary doctorate is from the University of Bern in Switzerland, and I have been inducted as a life fellow of the Society of Antiquaries of London.

In addition to publishing the usual round of historical articles and papers, I have also fielded various historical enquiries that now come to me from the office of the Presiding Bishop. These have included gathering of evidence at the request of his chancellor for court cases challenging the hierarchical nature of the Episcopal Church and its related jurisdiction of church property based on that principle, as well as preparation of a major legal affidavit of historical, theological, and sacramental testimony for the lawsuit over the church and property of All Saints, Waccamaw, Pawleys Island, SC. Another paper I prepared for the House of Bishops at the PB's request reviewed the historical and theological basis for "supplemental episcopal pastoral care," concluding that we do not need to have "flying bishops" as in the Church of England. This paper was published in *The Anglican* for July 2002 and also distributed by him to the Primates of the Anglican Communion.

Just after "9/11" I delivered a full-day seminar of four two-hour lectures on 22 September 2001 on "The Church of England and the Anglican Tradition" at the Smithsonian Institution, which was attended by an audience well in excess of one hundred. I also presented a series of six public lectures on "The Anglican Tradition" for the Church Club of New York, and then served as historical coordinator for a subsequent pilgrimage to Canterbury in June 2002. In September of 2002 I represented the Historical Society of the Episcopal Church by an address given in the Great Hall of Lambeth Palace at the publication of *The Bibliography of the Book of Common Prayer 1549-1999* by David Griffiths, for which I served as the principal American consultant. I also sponsored and arranged a day's visit for the Board of the Historical Society to the Archives of the Episcopal Diocese of New York in October of the same year.

Respectfully submitted,
J. Robert Wright

FINANCIAL REPORT

The Historical Society financial support comes from endowment, memberships, and donations and does not request funds from the General Convention. In past reports the Society has requested funding for the Historiographer's office and travel expenses. The Society does not need to submit a funding resolution to the General Convention because the Office of the Presiding Bishop's budget shall provide this funding in the future.

GOALS AND OBJECTIVES FOR THE COMING TRIENNIUM

The Historical Society remains committed to its existing programmatic activities such as publication of *Anglican and Episcopal History* and the award of research grants. It will work, however, to replace *Studies in Anglican History* in its present form with a less expensive alternative.

The new African American Historical Collection will constitute a new and extremely important activity for the Society. Over the next several months Virginia Seminary will complete an expansion of its archival space in the Bishop Payne Library while the Society will seek from its members and friends the necessary support for the first-year salary of a part-time archivist. When we have met that goal, we will initiate a more active search for documentary materials to enlarge the Collection and for financial support from outside sources.

The Society, the National Episcopal Historians and Archivists, the Episcopal Women's History Project, and representatives of Canadian Lutherans and Anglicans are actively planning and organizing the "Tri-Conference," titled "Anglicans and Lutherans: The North American Experience of Two European Traditions," to be held in Chicago, June 20–23, 2004. We have already held a first round of discussions with Lutheran historians, who are enthusiastic about joining with us in this effort.

The Historical Society at the same time recognizes that it is significantly enlarging its activities at a time when its membership and financial resources are at best static. The Board of Directors began to address the problem at the 2002 annual meeting by appointing a special committee to conduct a full-scale review of finances, membership, and programs and to make recommendations for the future. The Society has since begun to take steps to implement those recommendations, and a further review will take place at the 2003 Board meeting.

Thad W. Tate, President
Thomas A. Mason, Secretary

EXECUTIVE
COUNCIL

EXECUTIVE COUNCIL
CONTENTS

THE EXECUTIVE COUNCIL
www.episcopalchurch.org/gc/ec/default.html

Membership

Ex-Officio Members
The Most Rev. Frank T. Griswold III, D.D.,
Presiding Bishop, DFMS President and Chair
The Very Rev. George L.W. Werner,
House of Deputies President, DFMS Vice President
and Vice Chair
Mrs. Patricia C. Mordecai, Vice President
The Rev. Rosemari G. Sullivan, Secretary
Mr. Stephen Duggan, Treasurer, until 11/2001,
replaced by Mr. Ralph L. O'Hara, 1/2002

Elected by General Convention
until General Convention 2003
The Rt. Rev. Keith L. Ackerman, (Quincy, V)
Dr. Thomas R. Bates, (Central Florida, IV)
The Hon. James E. Bradberry,(Southern Virginia, III)
The Very Rev. David T. Chee, (Los Angeles, VIII)
The Rt. Rev. Robert H. Johnson,(WNorth Carolina, IV)
Ms. Carole Jan Lee, (California, VIII)
Ms. Barbara G. Mann, (South Carolina, IV)
The Rev. Barnum McCarty, (Florida, IV)
Mr. Richard E. Miller, (Southeast Florida, IV)
Dr. Warren C. Ramshaw, (Central New York, II)

Elected by Province
until General Convention 2003
I	Ms. Rita Tams Redfield, (Maine)
II	Mr. Alfred D. Price, (Western New York)
III	Ms. Iris E. Harris, (Washington)
IV	The Rev. Robert L. Sessum, (Lexington)
V	Mrs. Constance Ott, (Milwaukee)
VI	Mr. Don Betts, (Nebraska)
VII	Ms. Shelly Vescovo, (Dallas)
VIII	Mrs. Nancy T. Salmon, (San Joaquin)
IX	The Rt. Rev. Francisco Duque, (Colombia)

Elected by General Convention
until General Convention 2006
The Very Rev. Cynthia L. Black, (Western Michigan, V)
Dr. Louie Crew, (Newark, II)
The Rt. Rev. Theodore A. Daniels, (Virgin Islands, II)
The Rev. J. Anthony Guillen, (Los Angeles, VIII)
Ms. Sarah T. Harte, (New York, II)
Mr. Frank L. Oberly, (Oklahoma, VII)
Mr. Russell V. Palmore Jr., (Virginia, III)
Ms. Diane B. Pollard, (New York, II)
The Rt. Rev. Catherine S. Roskam, (New York, II)
Ms. D. Rebecca Snow, (Alaska, VIII)

Elected by Province
until General Convention 2006
I	The Rev. Ann S. Coburn, (Rhode Island)
II	The Rev. Canon Stephen T. Lane, (Rochester)
III	The Rev. Edward E. Godden, (Delaware)
IV	Dr. Lillian E. Yeager, (Kentucky)
V	The Rev. Kwasi A. Thornell, (Southern Ohio)
VI	The Rev. Canon Tim E. Vann, (Nebraska)
VII	The Rev. Kenneth W. Kesselus, (Texas)
VIII	The Rev. Brian N. Prior, (Spokane)
IX	Mrs. Carmen Brooks, (Honduras)

By Invitation
Mr. Vincent C. Currie Jr.,
House of Deputies Vice President
The Rev. Arthur Anderson (past rep.); The Ven.
James B. Boyles; Ms. Dorothy Davies-Flindall (past
rep.); The Rev. Helena Rose Houldcroft; Mr. Todd
Russell; Partners, Anglican Church of Canada
The Rev. Dan Martensen (past rep.); The Rev. Karen
Parker; Partner, Evangelical Lutheran Church of
America

Meeting Dates and Sites

Delavan, Wisconsin, October 24-27, 2000
Parsippany, New Jersey, February 5-8, 2001
Salt Lake City, Utah, June 8-11, 2001
Jacksonville, Florida, October 15-18, 2001
San Antonio, Texas, February 22-25, 2001

Durham, New Hampshire, June 10-13, 2002
Jackson, Wyoming, October 11-14, 2002
Santo Domingo, Dominican Republic
January 27-30, 2003
Ellicott, Maryland, April 28-May 1, 2003

Introduction

The Executive Council (Council) was established by the Canons of the Episcopal Church in 1919 to work with the Presiding Bishop between Conventions, implementing and monitoring the policies and programs authorized by the Convention including budget oversight.[1] It serves as the Board of Directors for the Domestic and Foreign Missionary Society (DFMS) and is charged with making a full published report to General Convention each triennium.[2] The Executive Council may initiate and develop new works as necessary between General Conventions.[3]

The Executive Council is comprised of forty voting members including 20 members elected by General Convention, 18 members elected by the nine provinces, the Presiding Bishop who serves as Chair and the President of the House of Deputies who serves as Vice Chair. There are three additional non-voting positions: the Secretary of General Convention who serves as Secretary of the Council, the Treasurer of DFMS and the Assistant to the Presiding Bishop for Administration who serves as Vice-President. The life of Council is enriched by the presence of representatives from two partner churches, the Anglican Church of Canada and the Evangelical Lutheran Church in America (ECLA).

During each year of the triennium the Executive Council meets three times. Daily worship, bible study, and reflection provide the framework for each meeting's deliberations and decision making. The committees of Executive Council are Administration and Finance (A&F), International Concerns (INC), National Concerns (NAT) and Congregations in Ministry (CIM). Each committee studies matters brought before them and reports to the Council which acts on them by resolution as appropriate. Reports of these committees and those from the other entities that report to the General Convention through the Executive Council follow this summary of the Executive Council's function and work.

Summary of Work

The Executive Council addressed many issues during the triennium. The General Convention web-site (http://www.episcopalchurch.org/gc/ec/default.html) has more details about its work including meeting minutes and resolutions passed by Council. Key issues considered this triennium include:

- Peace efforts in the Middle East
- The Episcopal Church's response to the events of September 11th and its aftermath
- Work accomplished on Resolution A033, "20/20 A Clear Vision" and Resolution AO34, "Rebuilding the Church"
- Response to the irregular ordinations to the Episcopate in light of Anglican Provinces polity
- Anti-Racism Training for Executive Council
- Consideration of a possible re-location of the Episcopal Church Center to the General Theological Seminary and facility sharing with them
- Development of a mission-driven budget with clear priorities
- Production of church documents in languages other than English
- Implementation of Resolution A045, "Monitoring Ordination of Women"

---

[1] Canon 1.4.1(a) and 2(e)
[2] Canon 1.4.1 (b)
[3] Canon 1.4.2 (e)

73RD GENERAL CONVENTION RESOLUTIONS

This is a summary of actions on Convention resolutions referred to the Executive Council and the Commissions, Committees, Agencies and Boards (CCAB's) reporting to General Convention through Executive Council.

NUMBER	TITLE	REFERRED TO	BRIEF SUMMARY
A001	International Education, Advocacy, and Development	INC Dioceses	Council approved an annual diocesan report to measure progress in meeting resolution goals, especially funding for international development programs.
A009	Identification of "Safe Spaces"	CIM	Developed a method for congregations to identify themselves as welcoming sexual minorities. Recommended three curricula for parish use.
A012	Assistance for Haiti	INC	Several initiatives are in development.
A014	A Modern Archival Facility	A&F Archives	Council appointed committee. Draft Request for Proposal sent to potential sites, spring, 2002. Recommendations scheduled for Dec. Archives mtg. It was cancelled due to Chair's death.
A028	Disciplinary Policy & Procedure	COSE Title IV	Task Force established. Writing a theology paper.
A033	20/20 A Clear Vision	20/20	SCDME responding to General Convention on Task Force recommendations.
A034	Rebuilding the Church	SCDME	
A045	Monitoring Ordination of Women	A045	Collection of data from diocesan survey. Visitations to three dioceses.
A047	Extend Anti-Racism Commitment	NAT AR	NAT recommended to Council to extend its own commitment to Anti-Racism work. AR provided training and developed materials.
A050	HIV/AIDS Prevention Education	HIV/AIDS	2 curricula developed by NEAC.
A051	HIV/AIDS Availability of AIDS Medications	HIV/AIDS	Office of Government Relations (OGR) successfully lobbied for US to urge companies to make drugs affordable in Africa by limiting royalty claims.
A052	HIV/AIDS Justice issues related to HIV/AIDS	HIV/AIDS	Episcopal Life covered subject. ERD provided assistance.
A057	Trafficking of Women, Girls, and Boys	CSW	CSW monitors trafficking. OGR alerted about US legislation to increase law enforcement effectiveness.
A128	Partnership for Global Mission	INC	Council approved "Standards for Sending Long Term Missionaries" composed by Episcopal Partnership for Global Mission (EPGM).
A129	World Mission: Overseas Diocese and Covenants	INC	Reviewed periodic agreements with overseas dioceses. Revised Liberia's agreement due to urgent priorities. Tightened monitoring of all covenants.
A133	Research and Information Management	A&F	Communication Office implementing a single entry system for church and clergy data.
A134	An Episcopal Service Corp	INC	Established Young Adult Service Corps (YASC). Nine people deployed initially; as of Jan. 31, 2003 eleven deployed.

73ʀᴅ GENERAL CONVENTION RESOLUTIONS

This is a summary of actions on Convention resolutions referred to the Executive Council and the Commissions, Committees, Agencies and Boards (CCAB's) reporting to General Convention through Executive Council.

NUMBER	TITLE	REFERRED TO	BRIEF SUMMARY
B012	Endowment Fund for Philippines	INC A&F	Council passed resolution supporting the fund.
B037	Economic Justice Loan Committee Funds	A&F EJLC	Chose external administrator. Structure in place to increase base of seven million dollars.
B041	Evaluation of Contracts with Vendors	A&F	DFMS participates in the validation process administered by Project Equality (PE) to verify vendors are represented in PE's *Buyer's Guide*.
B049	Required Anti-Racism Training:	AR, NAT, Dioceses	Council committed itself to Anti-Racism Training in the Church and to participate itself. AR provided training for church leaders.
C006	Implement Urbanization Resolution	NAT	
C012	Indigenous Training Institute Funding	ECIM	Council approved the Indigenous Theological Training Institute (ITTI) as the scholarship review committee for DFMS indigenous people trust funds.
C039	On Church Pension Fund Investments	SRI	SRI and CPF co-sponsored workshops.
C042	Maternity/Paternity Leave for Clergy	A&F Dioceses	Benefits include sick and vacation leave. DFMS complies with the Family Medical Leave Act.
C044	Gambling	NAT	NAT discharged from action due to a 1994 study and no funds budgeted for Task Force.
D005	Environmental Racism	SRI, NAT	Council asked OGR to track legislation protecting the ecology of low income communities. SRI developed a share holder resolution.
D011	Science and Faith Curriculum	STF	Materials developed.
D012	Support of Ministry on Aging	CIM	Consultation on Aging proposed a Church Center desk. CIM recommended, Council approved 74ᵗʰ GC Resolution for a Task Force to analyze church program and policy options and report to them for action.
D015	Church Workplace Justice	CIM	Surveyed diocesan personnel policies and practices in collaboration with CPF. CIM recommended a 74ᵗʰ GC Resolution to establish a Task Force to study issue.
D022	Decade for a Culture of Nonviolence	NAT	NAT recommended Church Center, especially the Social Justice Office, continue its work for justice and non-violence.
D023	Reconciliation and Accountability	CIM	Study committee not funded.
D049	Abstinence to Prevent STDs	HIV/AIDS	Refer to A050, curricula include subject.
D050	Communication Strategy	A&F	New Communication Director gathered all communication into one Church Center department including new web-site design, electronic newsletter to the church, video, publications and research functions.

ADMINISTRATION AND FINANCE

Membership: Richard Miller, Chair; Russell Palmore, Vice Chair; Ann Coburn; Kenneth Kesselus; Barbara Mann; Barnum McCarty; Diane Pollard; Nancy Salmon; Tim Vann; **Ex-officio:** Frank Griswold; George Werner; Patricia Mordecai; Rosemari Sullivan; Stephen Duggan until 11/2001, replaced by Ralph O'Hara.

Committee Goal

Administration and Finance (A&F) facilitates the ministry of the Episcopal Church by supporting the Assistant to the Presiding Bishop for Administration and the Office of the Treasurer while overseeing the Domestic and Foreign Missionary Society (DFMS). A&F works closely with the Joint Standing Committee on Program, Budget and Finance (PB&F). A&F met in New York City in April 2001, January 2002, September 2002 and December 2002, and at every regular EC meeting.

SUMMARY OF WORK

- Reviewed financial statements, audit reports, year-end budgets, and statements of operation for DFMS.
- Recommended establishment of various trust funds in accordance with established procedures.
- Discussed diocesan commitments to the National Church's Budget.
- Recommended approval of exploring the Episcopal Church Center move and joint venture facilities with General Theological Seminary.
- Implemented a survey of the church which provided a basis for establishing budget priorities.
- Recommended approval of new priorities for the triennial budget development.
- Developed and recommended to Executive Council next triennium's budget.

- Recommended presentations on endowments and charitable funds.
- Recommended revisions to Church travel guidelines and travel agents.
- Reviewed changes for Church Center staff positions.
- Recommended approval of the Principal Group to manage the lay employees pension plan (conversion from the Church Pension Fund) and additional funding to alleviate potential inequities caused by the previous conversion from a defined benefit to a defined contribution plan.
- Recommended approval of Episcopal Relief And Development becoming a separate 501 (c)(3) entity.
- Council reaffirmed the Episcopal Church Foundation as the arm for planned giving in the Episcopal Church.

CONGREGATIONS IN MINISTRY COMMITTEE

Membership: Shelly Vescovo, Chair; Cynthia Black, Vice Chair; Don Betts; David Chee; Sarah Harte; Stephen Lane, Secretary; Constance Ott; Alfred Price; Catherine Roskam; **Ex-officio:** Frank Griswold; George Werner

Committee Goal

The Congregations in Ministry Committee (CIM) is a link with Church Center programs and the Standing Committees and Commissions of General Convention concerned with congregations and their ministries. CIM monitors related General Convention resolutions.

SUMMARY OF WORK

- 73rd General Convention Resolution A009: Identification of "Safe Spaces". CIM developed a method for congregations to identify themselves as welcoming sexual minorities. Council adopted a resolution encouraging parishes to welcome sexual minorities. Three curricula were recommended for parish use: "Room for Grace Dialogue"; "All Love Is of God" and "Claiming the Promise". The resolution asked our Anglican Consultative Council representatives to advocate in the Anglican Communion for sexual minorities.

- 73rd General Convention Resolution A045: Monitoring Ordination of Women. Work was completed in two parts: a survey of all dioceses on the ministry of ordained women, and visitations to the Fort Worth, Quincy, and San Joaquin dioceses. All domestic dioceses responded to the survey. Council unanimously approved a Council resolution requiring 1) the continuation of the statistical work done in the survey so that the church is informed about the ministries of ordained women; 2) coordination of data-gathering with the Church Pension Fund and other appropriate bodies; and 3) commendation of dioceses where at least one out of three priests is a woman while urging those dioceses with a lower ratio to improve their percentage.

- 73rd General Convention Resolution D015 Church Workplace Justice. CIM surveyed dioceses on their personnel policies and practices. Fifty dioceses responded. We encourage a discussion of the Colloquium of Episcopal Professional and Vocational Associations (CEPVA) principles. It was clear more work is needed in addressing workplace inequity. Council approved a resolution for an Employment Policies Task Group to be coordinated with Church Pension Fund.

- Council by resolution reaffirmed the Episcopal Council on Indigenous Ministries (ECIM) as a committee reporting to Council and established policies for indigenous ministries. ECIM advocates for funding but may not disburse funds. The Indigenous Ministries Office oversees the distribution of allocated funds.

- Council by resolution authorized the Indigenous Theological Training Institute (ITTI) as the scholarship review committee for the disbursement of DFMS trust funds held for indigenous peoples.

- The 20/20 Task Force reported to Council. Council referred the report to Standing Commission on Domestic Mission and Evangelism (SCDME) and took steps to expand the number of persons involved with SCDME's implementation of the report. Council's charge to SCDME included: 1) recommend implementation steps of the 20/20 Task Force vision; 2) invite committees and commissions and Church Center staff to consider the initiative in their work and 3) ensure the church includes social justice and marginalized populations in its mission and evangelism work.

INTERNATIONAL CONCERNS COMMITTEE

Membership: Robert Sessum, Chair; Anthony Guillen, Vice Chair; Keith Ackerman; Thomas Bates; Carmen Brooks; Louie Crew; Theodore Daniels; Francisco Duque; Edward Godden; Carole Jan Lee; Rita Redfield; **Ex-officio:** Frank Griswold; George Werner. (Ms. Cheryl Dawkins, Secretary)

Committee Goal
The International Concerns Committee (INC) monitors international policies and programs of the Episcopal Church, especially in these places: Africa, the Middle East, Central America, the Caribbean, Mexico, Canada, the Philippines, Eastern Europe and Russia. Discussions include environmental concerns, AIDS in developing countries and issues in Zimbabwe, Uganda, Colombia and Haiti. Meetings were translated for Spanish-speaking members.

SUMMARY OF WORK

- We recognized missionaries appointed by the Presiding Bishop. As of Fall 2002, there were 126 current and 66 returned missionaries, including for the first time missionaries from three voluntary Episcopal missionary societies.

- Anglican and Global Relations (AGR), Episcopal Relief and Development (ERD), Episcopal Migration Ministries (EMM), and Peace and Justice Ministries, Office of Government Relations, Ecumenical and Interfaith Relations, Office for the Bishop for the Armed Services, and Episcopal Partnership for Global Mission (EPGM) representatives shared their work with INC. EMM reported on the current refugee crisis. EPGM composed "Standards for Sending Long Term Missionaries" for missionary agencies. It was approved to have one agency to report each year to Council. ERD reported its response to the African AIDS crisis.

- Support was expressed for the Episcopal College of the Iglesia Anglicana de Mexico as they work to remedy the Northern Mexico and Western Mexico situation.

- Council approved resolutions supporting the Church's global peacemaking efforts, including the Middle East, Colombia and Iraq.

- Council passed two resolutions after a report on Sudan by the Standing Commission on Anglican and International Peace with Justice Concerns. One condemned the Khartoum authorities' 4/11/2001 actions against Christians. The second urged Episcopalians and Episcopal organizations to divest shares in entities supporting the current Sudanese government.

- Council resolution approved use of the Diocese of Liberia trust monies for reconstructing the Episcopal School system and Cuttington College.

- Council approved translating the 20/20 report into Spanish and considered releasing announcements and documents concurrently in different languages.

- Council resolution passed to translate into Spanish all Episcopal Church Center materials by 2006.

NATIONAL CONCERNS

Membership: Robert Johnson, Chair; D. Rebecca Snow, Vice-Chair; James Bradberry; Iris Harris; Frank Oberly; Brian Prior; Warren Ramshaw, Secretary; Kwasi Thornell; Lillian Yeager; **Ex-officio:** Frank Griswold; George Werner

Committee Goal

In this triennium, the previous National and International Concerns committee of the Executive Council was divided into two committees. Each committee has been able to focus more attention on issues which concern the church. The National Concerns Committee (NAT) mission included acting on referred 73rd General Convention resolutions; generating policy statements for Council adoption; considering legislation for the 74th General Convention while mindful of our ecumenical partnerships and interfaith cooperation and working closely with Episcopal Church staff. NAT is committed to addressing conditions, needs and social issues of this nation as a major mission of our church.

SUMMARY OF WORK

- Reviewed government Faith-Based Initiatives especially public funding concerns for Faith-Based social services.

- Authorized an "Ethics and the New Genetics Task Force," $68,000 budget for triennium.

- Supported anti-racism training programs for Provinces.

- Held anti-Racism training for Council.

- Expressed a continuing commitment to the abolishment of capital punishment.

- Recommended to fund two videos: one informed the Church on Episcopal Migration Ministries (EMM) and the second shared the Church's hearings on racism. Monies from the Constable Fund.

- Recommended EMM receive an additional $150,000 this triennium and recommended an additional $300,000 in the next triennium to permit advocacy.

- Recommended adoption of a disinvestment policy for companies with direct operations in Sudan.

- Expressed, with INC, condolences to those who lost loved ones in the attacks of September 11, 2001, and commended parishes, agencies and services of those contributing bravely and faithfully in this tragedy.

- Council resolution encouraged bishops to permit use of "the Sacrament of the Lord's Supper, 1984", and the Inaugural Liturgy of "Churches Uniting in Christ" in their dioceses with other CUIC partner churches, using the "Guidelines for Eucharistic Sharing."

- Asked the U.S. Congress and Administration to pass conservation-based energy legislation and refrain from drilling or mining lands important to indigenous people and animal life such as the Alaska National Wildlife Refuge and the Gwich'in people in Alaska.

- Called on U.S. Congress and Administration to reduce domestic poverty by assisting needy families.

- Received the Committee on Science, Technology and Faith report on Genetically Modified Food and other American food supply issues.

- Approved nine diocesan partnerships between American and overseas dioceses.

- Approved 207 new Jubilee Centers as of January 31, 2003.

RESOLUTIONS APPROVED BY EXECUTIVE COUNCIL
FOR
PRESENTATION TO THE 74TH GENERAL CONVENTION

Resolution A006 Employment Policies Task Group

1   *Resolved,* the House of _____ concurring, That the 74th General Convention authorize the Executive
2   Council to appoint a Task Group in consultation with the Church Pension Fund to study employment
3   policies and practices in the dioceses and parishes of the church and consider policy recommendations to
4   the 75th General Convention that address issues of equity and justice for church employees working in
5   circumstances of both affluence and poverty; and be it further
6   *Resolved,* That $10,000 be allocated for this purpose.

Resolution A007 Aging Task Force

1   *Resolved,* the House of _____ concurring That the 74th General Convention authorize the creation of a six-
2   person Task Force of the Executive Council, coordinated through the Office of Ministry Development and
3   the Office of the Bishop of the Armed Services, Health Care and Prison Ministries, to assess ministry
4   opportunities with and for an aging population both within and outside the church; and be it further
5   *Resolved,* That $10,000 be allocated for this purpose.

Resolution A008 Repeal Mandatory Federal Sentencing Guidelines

1   *Resolved,* the House of _____ concurring That the 74th General Convention urges the Congress of the
2   United States to repeal the mandatory Federal sentencing guidelines used in federal criminal matters, and
3   restore the discretion of federal trial judges.

EXPLANATION

Federal sentencing guidelines now in place are mandatory and sentences must be imposed within the guideline range, with extremely narrow exceptions. As a result, young offenders, defendants not playing a major role in a criminal activity, and defendants with minimal criminal records are all forced into long-term confinement, devoid of any socially rehabilitative behavior. There is only the most minimal rehabilitative presence in the Federal correctional system and inmates have no reasonable chance to return to their families and their private lives. Not all prisoners are beyond rehabilitation; not all defendants deserve long-term imprisonment; not all inmates should be written off as beyond salvation. Until the guidelines are made more discretionary, as opposed to mandatory, no sense of rehabilitation and restoration will be restored to the Federal prison system.

Resolution A009 Amend Canon I.4.2(b)

1   *Resolved,* the House of _____ concurring That Canon I.4.2(b) be amended to read as follows:
2   (b) Except in the case of members initially elected for shorter terms in order to achieve rotation of terms,
3   the terms of office of the members of the Council (other than *ex officio* members) shall be equal to twice
4   the interval between regular meetings of the General Convention. The terms of office of all members shall
5   commence immediately upon the adjournment of the General Convention at which they were elected or, in
6   the case of election by a Synod, upon adjournment of the first regular meeting of General Convention
7   following such election. <u>The term of a member shall become vacant in the event of two absences from</u>
8   <u>meetings of the Council in the interval between successive regular meetings of the General Convention</u>
9   <u>unless excused by the Chair for good cause.</u> Members shall remain in office until their successors are
10   elected and qualified. No person who has served at least three successive years on the Executive Council
11   shall be eligible for immediate re-election for a term of more than three years. After any person has served
12   six consecutive years on the Executive Council, a period of three years shall elapse before such person
13   shall be eligible for re-election to the Council.

GENERAL CONVENTION DIOCESAN REPORTS AND RESOLUTION TRACKING

Diocesan Compliance

Eighty-percent of dioceses have submitted their canonically required diocesan reports during the 2000 – 2003 triennium.

2000 General Convention Resolutions Referred to Dioceses for Action or Consideration

The diocesan response ---from 54 dioceses of 113 reporting jurisdictions ---to referred resolutions for action or consideration after the 73rd General Convention is recorded below.

	Title	Completed	Ongoing	Considered	No Action
A001	International Education, Advocacy, and Development	2	15	11	27
A074	Continuing Education for Clergy & Lay Professionals	9	28	9	10
A077	Study of End-of-Life Issues	2	12	8	33
A080	Dialogue on Fidelity in Human Relationships	2	17	9	22
A081	Implementation of a Just Wage	8	16	9	21
A083	Educational Materials related to the Death Penalty	4	14	8	29
B049	Required Anti-Racism Training	3	37	5	7
C025	Sexual and Domestic Violence Awareness	4	22	7	21
C030	Adopt NCC Policy Statement	5	11	5	32
C031	Boy Scouts of America Policy on Homosexuals	8	8	9	28
C032	Mental Illness and Their Families Referred to Congregations)				
C042	Maternity/Paternity Leave for Clergy	12	12	7	23
D001	All Episcopal Property As "Tobacco-free Zones"	15	12	5	22
D008	Suicide Prevention	7	9	6	32
D009	Hate Crimes	8	18	4	24
D014	Funding by One-Percent Formula	4	19	12	19
D033	Economic Development: Micro-Credit Programs	6	9	11	34
D073	Domestic Violence – Enact State Statutes	7	12	6	30
D082	Concern for Growing Practice of Infanticide	6	3	9	36
D083	Men and Women Suffering From Post Abortive Stress	2	3	9	40

First Reading Resolutions

The total dioceses ---of the 54 reporting ---who completed the first reading of these 73rd General Convention resolutions is as follows:

A025	Constitution: Amend Article IX	46
A087	Constitution: Amend Article II	46
A132	Constitution: Amend Article X	46

Reports from Bodies created by Executive Council, Reporting to Council and through Council to General Convention

COMMITTEE ON ANTI-RACISM
www.episcopalchurch.org/peace-justice/antiracism.asp

Membership

The Rev. Dr. Sheryl A. Kujawa-Holbrook, *Chair*	Massachusetts
Mr. Hilario Albert	New York
Mr. Don Betts, *Member as well as EC Liaison*	Nebraska
The Rt. Rev. Carol Joy Gallagher	Southern Virginia
Dr. Anita George	Mississippi
The Rev. Canon John E. Kitagawa	Maryland
Ms. Harriet Kollin	Pennsylvania
The Rt. Rev. Edwin M. Leidel Jr.	Eastern Michigan
The Rt. Rev. John L. Rabb	Maryland
The Rev. Albert R. Rodriguez	Texas
The Rev. William H. Stokes	Southeast Florida
The Rev. Jayne Oasin	*Staff Consultant*

WORK SUMMARY

The Episcopal Church recommitted itself to eradicating the sin of racism in our churches and society at the 73rd General Convention. This report highlights the Anti-Racism Committee's work during this triennium. Jayne Oasin's dedicated work has been key in improving the anti-racism training programs. Her interaction on the provincial level and ecumenically has further encouraged dialogue in this arena. In today's post 9/11 society, this work has become more important. We are grateful for the continued support of the Presiding Bishop and the Executive Council.

Our present work begins at the 1991 General Convention when the Church committed itself to a three-triennial effort to overcome the "sin of racism." Little was accomplished in the initial six years because no specific group was given the task. Exceptions are the *racial audit* at the General Convention in 1991 and the House of Bishops' pastoral letter, "The Sin of Racism," in 1994. An ad hoc committee was formed to develop an effective training program for combating racism at all Church levels in 1996. Some of the results were:

- Publication of the Martin Luther King Day Dialogues Manual and initial training event.
- Training for the Executive Council, House of Bishops and Episcopal Church Center Staff.
- The then new Presiding Bishop shared his theological insights on this issue at the 1998 Episcopal Urban Caucus Assembly.
- Dioceses of Maryland, Massachusetts, Newark, Ohio and West Virginia took leadership in this first phase. Massachusetts assisted in the development of two videos, *"Eracism"* and *"In the Name of God."*
- Church Divinity School of the Pacific and the Episcopal Divinity School hosted trainer events.

While no formal review of these first nine years exists, sufficient momentum was generated for the 2000 General Convention to renew the mandate for anti-racism work during the next three Triennia. The Executive Council established a committee with clear oversight, a budget and a staff position. Our work has been refined through the learnings of the last six years, including:

- Most people "get it" while finding the early training stages fun and instructive.
- A cadre of remarkable people desire further training for certification. We hope this group will become a network, responding to the needs of provinces, dioceses and other church organizations.
- Resistance increases with the deepening of the exposure to the evil of racism and its relationship to other oppressive systems.
- Trainers need greater skills to overcome heightened resistance existing when training is "mandated."

- Many potential trainers drop out at Level Three when the institutional reality of racism is confronted.
- Confusion exists around the relationship between class, culture and race, fueling confusion on the definitions of diversity and multiculturalism and their relation to race and class prejudice.

The balance of this report describes the committee's work in progress. A new manual and curriculum incorporating these will debut at the General Convention in Minneapolis.

By the fall of 2002, 61 dioceses have anti-racism committees while holding at least one training event. Other dioceses will begin the process by presenting training at clergy conferences. Most participating dioceses have sent committee members to national training events. Every province has a coordinator and are establishing their own network. By the end of the triennium every province will hold a training event. Training for national church boards has included the Executive Council, the Church Pension Fund and Program, Budget and Finance (PB&F).

We estimate 1,500 people have taken some type of anti-racism training. People trained at the parish level and in affiliated organizations are not included in this number. Fifty trainers will be certified by the time of General Convention.

The committee identified and established the following criteria for effective Anti-Racism Training programs for dioceses and other agencies that comply with the anti-racism mandate:

Anti-Racism Training Program Elements
- Scriptural, doctrinal and Episcopal/Anglican foundations naming racism as sin.
- Training with didactic and experiential modules including:
  - Clear definition of racism as prejudice plus power, bias, discrimination and other forms of exclusion.
  - Culture and ethnicity discussions with explicit connects between racism, exclusion and oppression.
  - Activities focusing on individual, institutional and systematic racism.
- Strategies for implementing a comprehensive antiracism program.
- An approach which encourages an understanding of the Anglican Communion, ecumenism, interfaith connections, and the civil society beyond the church.

Compliance Standards
By the end of an anti-racism training, attendees should:
- Be aware and appreciate cultural differences.
- Understand one's own ethnocentrism.
- Be empowered as an agent of change individually and corporately.
- Know resistance to change is normal and it is easier for most people to deny cultural, ethnic and racial differences.
- Be comfortable in presenting their understanding of race, culture, prejudice and racism including those with differing opinions.
- Define racism as prejudice plus power, and state the inter-relationships between racism and other types of oppression.
- Willingly participate in a visionary planning for a comprehensive anti-racism program with goals and objectives.

New Initiatives
1. National Hearings on racism were conducted in conjunction with the Rev. Carmen Guerrero, Jubilee Ministries Staff Officer. A video with special film clips will be presented at General Convention. It will be a promotional tool during the next triennium with an accompanying curriculum. These themes emerged offering guidance in the Church's life:

- The Church must stand as a witness against racial injustice and hate instead of mirroring society's racism. Its ministry includes recognizing and eliminating all forms of stereotyping.
- All are constantly called to live the Gospel by respecting those who have been traditionally marginalized and by recognizing the skills and contributions offered by people of color.

- Cultural and historical barriers exist to the recruitment, training and deployment of people of color for ordained and lay professional ministries.
- The Church must set leadership models for people of color that are non-traditional and reflect liturgical, cultural, racial and ethic diversity and remember that tokenism is not a substitute for diversity.
- The National Church's anti-oppression work deserves increased support, especially for new immigrants and the rural poor of all races.

2. A new **One-day** Training model (six hour) focusing on multi-cultural competence in today's church and society was developed.

3. A study of racism in the ordination process has been initiated with the Anti-Racism Committee of the House of Bishops under the leadership of Bishop Rabb. He will survey commissions on ministry and other church offices on the call, discernment, ordination and deployment of persons of color. This report will be presented to the 2006 General Convention.

4. 20/20 Initiative Conversations. We are hoping to have complimentary and not redundant resolutions for action that respect the focus of each group.

5. Follow up on the hearings leading toward a dialogue among the various peoples of color in the Episcopal Church. This is especially important in light of the key themes that emerged from the hearings and relate to the obstacles that this training has encountered.

Recommendations and Next Steps

Although much has been accomplished in the last three years the Committee feels strongly, that we enter the Second Triennium of our three triennial mandate with much more to do, such as:

- Developing a coherent and effective network of anti-racism trainers in the Provinces and Dioceses who provide prompt response to training requests.
- Recognition that while the spirit of "mandating this training" gives it appropriate status it sets up a deeper resistance. Further, the purpose of the training is not to get a piece of paper, but rather, to identify targets for change leading to a Church without racism and inclusive of all people.
- Reconciliation of the any methodologies, not all compatible, available for engaging this issue. Even with established criteria for training programs, we find no common language. For example, differing definitions tax our untangling of the matrix of race, class, religion and other oppressive systems.
- Developing appropriate evaluation tools for measuring our progress in eradicating racism.
- Holding hearings, like those recently concluded, dramatize the need for training in dioceses, agencies, seminaries and urban areas.

Our work has assumed enhanced significance because of September 11, 2001 and the developing internal and external situation. There is an increased emphasis on internal security and proactive military action. Pre-existing prejudices, stereotypes and bigotry based on race, religion, and national identity have been exacerbated by this reality. Racial profiling, abuse of police powers, abridgment of human rights and resorting to rhetoric rather than reason make the work of anti-racism increasingly difficult.

A principal reason for oppressive systems is the combination of ignorance and fear of the "*Other*." This in turn is compounded by the primary obstacle to overcoming racism: unearned white skin privilege. This last year has been a tendency to revert to classic nationalism, both at home and abroad, which has been inherently racist and detrimental to the welfare of the "two-thirds world." The "*Other*" has born the consequences of decisions which advantaged the few at the expense of the many. The question "why do they hate us?" masks the deeper fear of these historic inequities. Asking such questions may help those who wish to understand the implications of racism in its broadest terms. They gain a clearer understanding of what must be given up by those who have reaped the benefits of these inequities. This is the place where true anti-racism work begins and ends.

Resolution A010 Continue Anti-Racism Mandate

1   *Resolved,* the House of _____ concurring, That the Executive Council continue the anti-racism program
2   with appropriate staffing and budget, under the mandate as defined by the committee recommendation
3   regarding compliance; and be it further
4   *Resolved,* That the emerging provincial network of anti-racism trainers be recognized as an important
5   resource, its utilization commended to the several provinces, dioceses and affiliated organizations of the
6   Church; and be it further
7   *Resolved,* That the 74th General Convention extend its appreciation to the organizers and participants of the
8   anti-racism hearings and calls upon the anti-racism committee to implement a program that responds to the
9   issues raised at the hearings, as appropriate; and be it further
10   *Resolved,* That all persons seeking election or appointment to the several standing commissions, other
11   committees of Executive Council, related boards and auxiliary organizations should have had the
12   mandated anti-racism training as prescribed by this General Convention; and be it further
13   *Resolved,* That the the Office of Peace and Justice be commended for its "Stop the Hate" Campaign and
14   encourage it to develop similar programs that address the issues of racial profiling and other abuses of the
15   criminal justice system that have emerged in this post 9/11 environment; and be it further
16   *Resolved,* That the Anti-Racism Committee of Executive Council be directed to prepare a report for the
17   other standing committees and commissions of the Church that inform them of the several issues emerging
18   from the anti-racism hearings and specify what actions each might take to ameliorate the impact of racism
19   in their area of concern.

ECONOMIC JUSTICE LOAN COMMITTEE

Membership

W. B. McKeown, Esq., *Chair*	New York
Mrs. Joyce Phillips Austin	New York
Mr. Alfred C. Jones III	*Investment Committee Representative*
Mrs. Toni H. McGauley	East Tennessee
Ms. Lindsey W. Parsons	Massachusetts
Ms. Iris E. Harris	*Council Liaison*

WORK SUMMARY

In 1998 the Executive Council created the Economic Justice Loan Committee (EJLC) to combine and oversee two predecessor programs. EJLC meets twice yearly and several times by telephone conference to consider loan applications and conduct other business.

Seven million dollars of investment assets of DFMS had been set aside by separate actions of the General Convention in 1988 and Executive Council in 1989. These assets are loaned by DFMS to support greater economic justice. "Economic justice" refers to enhancing peoples' ability to improve their economic well being and empowering the powerless and oppressed.

DFMS loans its loan fund assets to community development financial intermediaries. They re-lend the assets to groups with appropriate economic justice development programs. Many intermediaries operate in the United States and globally making loans to organizations involved in community economic development, affordable housing, micro-enterprise lending, job creation, and the provision of social services.

The 2000 General Convention passed a resolution (B037) with the intent of increasing the DFMS loan fund to $24 million in the future. This triennium, in addition to continuing to make loans, EJLC has focused on improving the administration of the program to support possible expansion. EJLC searched for an organization to assist DFMS with 1) evaluation and due diligence of new loan applications; 2) monitoring loans in the portfolio; and 3) assessment of the portfolio's impact. DFMS and the National Community Capital Association (NCCA), the leading industry group for community development financial intermediaries, signed an agreement in May 2002. NCCA has helped EJLC find new loan applicants while improving its ability to assess applicants and its whole program.

During the triennium, EJLC reviewed and acted on loan applications. Six loans totaling $1.4 million were dispersed, including one to the Diocese of Atlanta for affordable housing. Another two loans totaling $550,000 have been approved but not yet dispersed, and a number of other loan applications are in the pipeline. The entire economic justice loan portfolio includes $5.6 million in loans outstanding to 25 different institutions, with an additional $1.5 million available as of January 1, 2003 for investment.

During the remainder of the current and into the next triennium, EJLC hopes to improve communication with parishes, dioceses and Church institutions to increase the effectiveness of its work, as it seeks increased Episcopal Church involvement in this important ministry.

ETHICS AND THE NEW GENETICS TASK FORCE
http://www.episcopalchurch.org/gc/ec/ccs/eceng/default.html

Membership

Mr. David H. Smith, PhD, *Chair*	Indianapolis
The Rev. David Ames	Rhode Island
Ms. Mary Anderlik, JD, PhD	Kentucky
Ms. Cynthia Cohen, PhD, JD	Washington
The Rt. Rev. Theodore Daniels	Virgin Islands
The Rev. Lindon Eaves, PhD	Virginia
Ms. Elizabeth Heitman, PhD	Texas
The Rev. Jan Heller, PhD	Olympia
Mr. Bruce Jennings, MA	New York
The Very Rev. James Lemler	Chicago
Mr. Timothy Sedgwick, PhD	Virginia
Mr. LeRoy Walters, PhD	Washington
Ms Mary White, PhD	Southern Ohio
Dr. Ellen Wright Clayton, JD	Tennessee

WORK SUMMARY

The Task Force on Ethics and the New Genetics was created by the Executive Council after General Convention 2000 to address concerns raised by the new genetics. Its work, *A Christian Response to our Genetic Powers*, will be distributed at General Convention. Rowman and Littlefield will publish and *Anglican Theological Review* will receive royalties. Possibilities that get us started include:

- Genetic information can inform decisions on whether to have children.
- Genetic testing on adults or children may reveal surprising information on the individual and others.
- Embryos and fetuses may be tested for specific genetic traits.
- Genes of humans or embryos may possibly be "improved," thus shaping the individual's biology.
- Genetic knowledge may be used to deny employment or health insurance.

These possibilities raise concerns for the whole Church. Moral teaching is a first concern. The church must listen, study and share its wisdom. The second concern is pastoral. Improving human lives is balanced by the possibility of abuse and injustice. Anticipating problems may enable thoughtful preparation but still tax counseling and liturgical resources.

New genetic knowledge raises theological issues. For example, the roles of fate and choice seem to be changing, as phenomena once deemed beyond human control become controllable. A genetic misfortune once seen as bad luck may now be considered someone's fault. For example, a parent or a physician who did not run a test might be blamed.

No Task Force can give definitive answers to these ethical and theological issues. Our goal is to encourage a continuing dialogue as we draw on our Anglican tradition in addressing them.

Theological Perspectives

Genetic research should be celebrated. Awe and wonder increases the more we know about God's creation. Genetic knowledge lets us help each other when things go awry. Alas, our knowledge may be used incorrectly. Three metaphors in scripture and tradition structure our use of genetic knowledge.

First, is the metaphor that humans are made in God's image. We work with God to bring about good. Theological traditions have diversely interpreted this metaphor. For us, being made in God's image suggests responsibility for God's creation as we treat humans with something like the respect due God.

Life as a gift from God is the second metaphor; it is gratuitous that we exist. This metaphor is misused when it implies that all misfortunes, including genetic ones, are simply crosses to bear. Yes, God's handiwork is in all things; the mistake is thinking that acceptance is the only response. If this is true no medical care is ever appropriate! Our stewardship of God's creation is to prayerfully discern what to celebrate, let go or change.

A third metaphor refers to family life. We speak of the "household of God" and "children of God." These suggest the importance of virtues such as love, hope and thankfulness. Attention shifts from "What is OK for me to do?" to the needs of others.

These convictions lead us to three basic points. "Playing God" is a criticism often made of using our new genetic powers. We reject this charge. Yet we live in a world too broken to allow us to assume that using genetic knowledge or technology will always come out right.

A second important issue is suffering and God's love. The genetic lottery is unfair. Genetic problems are not the fault of ill or troubled persons, their parents, or any identifiable human group. Guilt or blame has no place in the distribution of genetic abnormalities. Misfortune may offer spiritual growth but there is no correlation between it and a human's spiritual needs. We can find help in trusting God and in Christ's identification with us in suffering and death.

Genetic Testing

Since our understanding of genetics is still in its relative infancy, what we know is constantly changing. As a result, the diagnostic or predictive value of many genetic tests is uncertain. Further, genetic test results have implications for the blood relatives of the person tested, which raises new questions of responsibility and confidentiality within families.

Prenatal testing is offered to women at high risk of having a child with abnormalities such as trisomy 21 or Down syndrome. No therapy exists for these defects. Prenatal testing is ethically controversial since a parent may terminate a pregnancy because of test results. This can invoke, for example, the abortion debate, the disability critique, "playing God," commodification of children, new parental responsibilities, and eugenics.

Postnatal testing, which comes in many forms, including newborn screening (the most common form of genetic testing), testing of children and adolescents, and adult testing, raises questions about *when* testing is appropriate. Other issues include whether individuals have a duty to be tested, a right to refuse testing and a right not to have test results disclosed to third parties including relatives.

The history of eugenic practices and policies of the last century, and the problem of abuse of power are serious causes for worry. The problems are different, however in a culture that focuses on the liberty of the individual. Additional knowledge may be liberating. It also may become a basis of ill informed discrimination in employment, a ground for loss of health insurance, and an occasion for conflict within families. We defend human dignity in the face of social pressures and stress increased attention to informed counsel and communal support.

Gene Transfer for Therapy or Enhancement

Our growing capacity to introduce, delete, and change genes in human's promises to impact our lives and our descendants. The prevention of gene-linked disease is one possible goal of treatment and another may be to improve humans. Two sorts of interventions might be possible because of our new genetic powers. These interventions are:

- Somatic cell interventions that introduce genes into the non-reproductive cells of the human body.
- Germline interventions that target genes in the early embryo.

We conclude that somatic cell gene therapy, if rendered safe and effective, would be morally acceptable to use in humans. Research into somatic cell therapy must be governed by strict adherence to ethical standards of research. Germline gene therapy would also be morally acceptable, in principle, but research into such interventions should not be undertaken until safety precautions are developed that account for the welfare of future generations, and until there has been greater public discussion of the ethical and social issues that they raise. We urge that a public body be appointed to oversee all research and clinical use of these genetic interventions.

Creating and Shaping Children

We turn to the union of new genetic capabilities with new reproductive technologies, exploring the historic and contemporary meanings of procreation and of parenthood. We stress both the companionate and procreative ends of our God-given sexuality. We continue a persuasive historic bias for describing children as a gift. Christian parents are called to rear children with love and care, mindful of the integrity, dignity and value of each child. We note the tension between accepting children as they come to us and seeking to alter them for their good or our own.

In this context, we consider interventions that raise ethical and theological concerns:

- *In vitro* fertilization (IVF) is needed for several of them, and we conclude that it is a morally acceptable way to overcome fertility barriers if parents and health professionals are mindful of its dangers.
- Three procreative interventions dependent on IVF can be used to avoid serious genetic disease in children: gamete donation, pre-implantation genetic diagnosis (PGD), and germline interventions. Gamete donation is use of sperm or egg from someone other than the couple to have a child. Pre-implantation genetic diagnosis (PGD) involves the selection of some embryos for implantation and the discard of others with genes associated with serious disease. Germline interventions involve repairing or changing genes in early embryos that would then be transferred to a woman's body to develop into children.
- We argue that both gamete donation and PGD are morally acceptable ways of averting genetic disease in future children even as they raise a need for moral caution. We are uneasy ethically about using germline interventions to overcome genetic disease in future children both because of serious risk to the future child and the further risk of excessive parental control or manipulation to specify the characteristics of their future children.
- Reproductive cloning, a fourth intervention that might be used to address serious disease in future children, is not morally acceptable at this time as it endangers the safety of children who might be conceived and threatens their dignity as unique individuals. Its use departs from accepted social and ethical values.

We are convinced that using new technology to avert genetic disease in children should be guided by the purpose of seeking good for them in a responsible and just manner. A commitment to the good of children may lead to public policies that limit choices for adults.

The Moral Status of Human Embryos and the New Genetics

We consider the question of the moral status of the early embryo in light of scripture, the Christian tradition, recent discoveries in embryology, and contemporary thought. Although scripture provides no explicit discussion of this question, it deeply values human life as it is being made. The Church Fathers distinguished between "unformed" and "formed" human life, viewing the latter, but not the former as potentially human. To end "unformed" embryonic life was considered to violate the procreative end of sexual relations; to end "formed" embryonic or fetal life was considered morally more serious and akin to homicide.

We conclude that early embryos before 14 days do not have the same moral status as living humans but that they are owed moral consideration since approximately 20 percent of them might avoid miscarriage (80% of them are lost before implantation) and go on to become humans. Moreover, the best work in embryology suggests that the embryo isn't a stable individual until approximately 14 days after fertilization. The question of using these embryos is different from the issue in abortion: the earliest embryo is a different *kind* of entity than the later fetus, and poses no risks to its genetic mother since it has not implanted. "Moral consideration" means that early embryos are owed appropriate care, respect and protection, but that there can be moral justification for not transferring an early embryo to a woman's body.

Our view, in principle, would allow pre-implantation genetic diagnosis to be used to implement decisions against transferring affected early embryos in order to avoid serious genetic disease in future children. Since germline interventions would be employed to treat early embryos with disease-linked genes, the use of these interventions, if safe and efficacious, would show moral consideration for the early embryo and future children.

Economics and Politics of the New Genetics

We return to the economics and politics shaping the choices offered by the new genetics. Science is prompting individuals, families, and health professionals and legislators to raise questions about the uses, patenting, and sale of genetically altered genes and DNA sequences. We weigh the contention that existing law and policy endanger respect for life by treating it simply as a commodity to be bought or sold.

Morally adequate answers are elusive but the metaphor of stewardship illuminates debate over appropriate paths for development of products and services based on genetic research. This perspective links the patenting debate to a larger discussion concerning the norms of science versus commerce, the relationship between public and private genetic endeavors, and the sufficiency of oversight of controversial areas of research. The question of who should benefit from investment in research needs to be informed by considerations of justice, and by attention to those on the margins of society and who lack basic health care.

Church action

How can the Church participate in the dialogue while providing appropriate leadership and raising critical questions about genetic issues? The Episcopal Church's role includes education, pastoral care and advocacy for those who suffer from genetic and other disease. To be effective ministers we need a solid education about genetic issues and we must speak for a just allocation of resources in health care.

Christian education programs, including those for children and teens, should share how we differ due to our genetic make-up while emphasizing that all are loved by God and each is a child of God. Adult education programs should engage questions about genetics so that people can: 1) gain current and useful information about genetics; 2) relate compassionately to people with a genetic disease, or who are struggling with genetic testing and diagnosis decisions; and 3) identify and refer anyone who would benefit from genetics counseling and services.

Education programs at the diocesan, provincial, or seminary levels might develop collaborative relationships with other disciplines, institutions and communities of faith to further their expertise in offering pastoral care for families and individuals with genetic disease.

Pastoral care related to genetics begins with pre-marital counseling and continues with a child's birth until death. Conditions related to genetics can occur at any time in a life. Some pastoral care topics are:
- Questions about conception, carrier testing prior to pregnancy, prenatal care and diagnosis.
- Problems with infertility, including in-vitro fertilization, adoption, surrogate parenting.
- The possible need for neonatal intensive care, support for the "new" family and child care.

Finally, the Church has an advocacy role. Public policy issues of justice, equality and access to appropriate health care and adequate insurance are paramount in assuring the safety and well-being of every person. Christians, along with other religious bodies and secular organizations, can support legislation to assure high quality care for individuals and families through genetic screening, testing, and disease management.

Resolution A011 Ethical Guidelines for Gene Transfer and Germline Interventions

1   *Resolved*, the House of _____ concurring, That the 74th General Convention recognizes that God has
2   entrusted us to use our medical and other capabilities to work toward healing and restoring creation where
3   it has gone awry. Therefore, this General Convention sets forth the following guidelines for genetic
4   research and interventions:
5   • It is morally acceptable, in principle, to engage in experimental <u>somatic cell</u> human gene transfer for
6   therapeutic purposes, in an effort to treat or prevent disease.
7   • All <u>experimental</u> genetic interventions in <u>human beings</u> must meet ethical standards of research, which
8   require that investigators demonstrate the scientific merit of their research, protect the health and
9   welfare of human volunteers, while ensuring their voluntary choice to participate.
10   • Until there is strong scientific evidence that the use of <u>germline</u> procedures is safe, effective, and
11   stable across generations and that guidelines have been established for their use before they are
12   employed, we should not consider the use of germline interventions in human beings.
13   • Ongoing public oversight of research into both somatic cell and germline interventions, in both the
14   public and private sectors, is essential. Members of a federally appointed interdisciplinary review body
15   should be chosen by publicly accountable methods.

EXPLANATION

As stewards of creation, we are called to help mend and renew the world in many ways. It is in keeping with God's loving and healing purposes to carry out research into the use of somatic cell (non-reproductive) genetic interventions that might treat and prevent serious disease. However, such gene transfer has not yet been proven safe and effective for general use in human beings Likewise, we are not at a point where it would be safe to engage in research into germline interventions, nor have we given adequate public reflection to the ethical and social import of doing so.

The need for careful oversight of research into both somatic cell and germline interventions and for public discussion of the ethical, theological, and policy issues raised by the possibility of using germline interventions in humans is currently being addressed only to a limited degree. Until recently, the Recombinant DNA Advisory Committee (RAC) of the National Institutes of Health, had authority to review federally funded research protocols involving recombinant DNA, as well as private sector protocols sent to it voluntarily. We recommend that the re-empowered RAC be placed under the aegis of a federal agency, such as the Department of Health and Human Services, that is independent of those federal agencies that directly fund biomedical research.

Resolution A012 Caring for Children in the Face of the New Genetics

1   *Resolved*, the House of _____ concurring, That the 74th General Convention reaffirms the church's
2   traditional teaching about parenting and that children are trusts and gifts from God to be nurtured toward
3   maturity. Therefore:
4   • Genetic testing of children can be an important part of parental responsibility, and may be carried out
5   if it is clearly in the child's best interests to be tested.
6   • Parents should make responsible use of medical services, including treatment for genetic diseases and
7   the use of somatic gene transfer therapies if they should be proven safe and effective.
8   • New genetic techniques may be used in conjunction with *in vitro* fertilization to avoid procreation of
9   human beings with clearly serious disorders of their DNA or chromosomes.
10   • It is not morally acceptable to use reproductive cloning at this time for any reason, because the
11   technique constitutes an unsafe form of experimentation on children. It is therefore morally
12   irresponsible for physicians, scientists, and prospective parents to engage in it.

EXPLANATION

Our rapidly expanding genetic capabilities and our highly sophisticated new technologies for reproduction offer parents and medical providers powerful tools with which to address genetically based problems in our children. This novel genetic and reproductive power is a gift from God to be used for the benefit of children with the intent of healing. It should not be used to fashion children according to their parents' unique personal ambitions or in ways that unduly deny children freedom of choice when they mature.

The hope of becoming parents of children who are free of disease-linked genes should not be fulfilled by using novel reproductive measures that endanger the safety of the resulting children. Germline genetic alteration is not intrinsically wrong, but attempts genetically to modify our children when carried out solely to give parents great control over the biological properties and personality traits of their offspring, are morally questionable, for they challenge the individual integrity, dignity, and value of the child. Reproductive cloning endangers the safety of the resulting children and puts important ethical and social values at risk. Those who hope to be parents but who are at risk of having children with serious genetic disease should consider using other measures, such as adoption, to have children.

Resolution A013 The Church's Role in Counseling and Education on Biomedical Ethics

1 *Resolved*, the House of _____ concurring, That the 74th General Convention, recognizing the changing world
2 in which we live, continue a program of sustained study in bioethics to inform and educate members of
3 congregations and clergy about the expanding range of issues and choices they and their children will face
4 throughout life. To this end, we commend study of *A Christian Response to our New Genetic Powers*; and be
5 it further
6 *Resolved,* That the Church:
7 • Call on Provinces and Dioceses to work with congregations to encourage local education and to provide
8   resource teams.
9 • Devise a way to sustain initiative and development of expertise in biomedical ethics in the national church
10   through the continued work of an Executive Council Task Force with a budget of $36,000 for the
11   triennium.
12 • Stress the importance of basic education about science and biomedicine among the people of God and
13   encourage and support the teaching of biomedical ethics in its seminaries.
14 • Commit itself to ecumenical and interfaith discussion of questions of biomedical ethics and be prepared to
15   join with other groups in such interfaith educational ventures.

EXPLANATION

Bioethics is the study of the social, ethical and spiritual questions arising from expanding knowledge and technological possibilities in medicine and the life sciences. It addresses issues of and professional practice in health care, public policy regarding the uses of biotechnology, business enterprise in the area of health care, and many other areas of importance to our life together. The questions of biomedical ethics directly impact on issues of life and death, birth and aging that human beings face. Education is essential if the church as a whole is to be prepared to offer informed counsel. Church leaders must know when to consult with or refer to persons with relevant expertise when dealing with issues of genetic testing and intervention, uses of new reproductive technologies, and the prospect or reality of death. We should use or develop liturgical forms that will help patients and professionals who are rejoicing, worried or sorrowful.

Resolution A014 Approve Research on Human Stem Cells

1 *Resolved,* the House of _____ concurring, That the 74th General Convention supports the choice of those
2 who wish to donate their early embryos, remaining after *in vitro* fertilization (IVF) procedures have ended,
3 for embryonic stem cell research, and urges the United States Congress to pass legislation that would
4 authorize federally funded research for the derivation and use of human stem cells from early embryos that
5 have been donated for such research by those who have completed IVF procedures, provided that:
6 • these early embryos are no longer required for procreation by those donating them;
7 • those donating early embryos have given their prior informed consent to their use in stem cell
8   research;

9 • directors of fertility clinics from which early embryos are obtained certify that they were not
10 deliberately created for research; and
11 • directors of fertility clinics and stem cell investigators certify that such early embryos have not been
12 obtained through sale or purchase; and be it further
13 *Resolved*, That the 74th General Convention urge the Secretary of Health and Human Services to establish
14 an interdisciplinary oversight body for all research in both the public and private sectors that involves stem
15 cells from human embryos, parthenotes, sperm cells, or egg cells and have this body in place within six
16 months of passing such legislation.

EXPLANATION

In recent years, biomedical investigators have explored the possibility that the use of human stem cells might be effective in treating such diseases as Alzheimer's, Parkinson's, stroke, cardiovascular disease, diabetes, and spinal cord injuries. The use of these cells might also provide an alternative to organ transplantation. Stem cell investigators have therefore begun to carry out research involving both adult human stem cells and early human embryonic stem cells at the blastocyst stage (five days after fertilization).

Ethical concerns have been raised about whether this research should use stem cells that have been derived from early human embryos. Episcopalians generally recognize that early embryos are owed special moral consideration. For some this is because they are already persons in the eyes of God; for others the fact that embryos may mature and be born as children makes them special.

Even before stem cell research became a scientific possibility, the use of the new reproductive technologies required the creation of early human embryos. Early embryos have been developed at fertility clinics in conjunction with the use of *in vitro* fertilization (IVF) to assist persons who face physical barriers to procreation. At most infertility clinics, several embryos are created at one time during the IVF procedure to ensure that there will be a sufficient number available for later attempts at implantation should the first try prove unsuccessful. We have acknowledged and accepted this as a society and as a church body. Two resolutions of the General Convention have also approved the use of IVF by those who experience difficulties in having children *(GC Resolution -1982-A067 Approve the Use of "In Vitro" Fertilization and GC Resolution-1991-A101 Reaffirm the Recommendation Considering External Fertilization)*.

Early embryos remaining after IVF procedures have ended could morally be donated for embryonic stem cell research. The alternatives for couples who have completed their reproduction are to donate the embryos for research, to donate the embryos to other couples, to discard the embryos, or to preserve them as long as possible. Most couples prefer not to donate remaining embryos to other couples, and indefinite preservation simply postpones the inevitable. Thus the two remaining alternatives are to discard the embryos or to donate them for research. If these embryos are donated for stem cell investigations, they could assist promising research that might enable those who are seriously ill with little hope of recovery to be healed.

EPISCOPAL COUNCIL OF INDIGENOUS MINISTRIES

Membership

Mr. Frank L. Oberly, *Chair*	Oklahoma
The Rt. Rev. Carol Joy Gallagher, *Secretary*	Southern Virginia
Mr. Malcolm N. Chun	Hawaii
The Rt. Rev. Andrew H. Fairfield	North Dakota
The Rt. Rev. Mark L. MacDonald	Alaska
Mr. Robert McGhee	Alabama
The Rt. Rev. Steven T. Plummer	Navajoland Area Mission
The Rt. Rev. Creighton L. Robertson	South Dakota
The Rev. Canon Michael Smith	Minnesota
The Rev. Robert Two Bulls Jr.	Los Angeles

WORK SUMMARY

A special gathering of about 100 Native American Anglicans and representatives from dioceses involved in Native American work met in July 2001. The Rt. Rev. Steven Charleston convened the meeting with the Assistant to the Presiding Bishop for Program, Ms. Sonia Francis who provided logistical support. Clarity, understanding, and a better working relationship among Native American Anglicans, the Episcopal Council on Indigenous Ministries (ECIM), and the Episcopal Church Center was the meeting's purpose.

This prayer offered guidance. "O God, help me to get ready to meet with my brothers and sisters in Denver. Clear my mind of past hurts. Calm my spirit so that I may reach out to them with an open heart. Show me the path to new relationship. Forgive me for my mistakes as I forgive others for theirs. And bless the ministry with our Native American people that it may grow and serve them for years to come, through Jesus Christ, in whose Name I pray. Amen."

From this historic gathering on Native American ministry and the clarity it provided, the consensus was that ECIM has been the voice for Native American Anglicans and it should continue in this role. ECIM was directed to meet to do work given by General Conventions since 1991.

At the November 2001 meeting, convened by the Chair, work accomplished included: a by-laws revision; grant approvals for programs in dioceses with indigenous ministries; reviewing scholarship programs and studying ECIM's relationship with Council and the Episcopal Church.

In February 2002, ECIM became a committee reporting to Council. In June 2002, the Indigenous Theological Training Institute (ITTI) was approved to administer scholarship funds for indigenous peoples, held in trust by DFMS. ITTI is an independent 501(c)(3) corporation which provides theological education training for indigenous communities in the Anglican Church.

ECIM involvement continues in programs that are meaningful for indigenous peoples, including:

- Decade of Remembrance, Recognition and Reconciliation (1997-2007): In November 1997 the Native American communities and the Episcopal Church in Jamestown, VA, signed a "new" Jamestown Covenant. ECIM continues its support of this decade's importance.
- Wintertalk: annual gathering of Anglican lay workers, priests, bishops, youth, elders, academics and national church staff working with indigenous groups in the United States and Canada. At it, concerns and issues are shared while the program, social and religious needs of indigenous peoples are identified.
- Mountains and Deserts Regional Ministries: Nevada, Utah, Wyoming, and North California network.
- Paths Crossing Anglicans: indigenous and non-indigenous congregation reps. meet to form partnerships.
- Strong Heart Ministries: national native youth organization and Urban Indian Coalition.

JUBILEE MINISTRIES ADVISORY COMMITTEE
http://www.episcopalchurch.org/jubilee/

Membership

Mr. Phillip Mantle, *Chair*	Chicago
Mrs. Linda Bemis	Kansas
The Ven. Michael Kendall	New York
Mrs. Priscilla Murguia	West Texas
Mr. Peter Ng	New York
Dr. Jack Plimpton	Los Angeles
Mrs. Carol Robertson, resigned, 2002	South Dakota
replaced by Mrs. Debra Hubbard	West Tennessee
The Rt. Rev. Charles vonRosenberg	East Tennessee
Mr. Frank Oberly	*Executive Council liaison*
The Rev. Canon Carmen B. Guerrero	*Staff*

WORK SUMMARY

Jubilee Ministry's (JM) mission is to make a direct and dynamic link between our theology and our ethics – said another way – the **talk** of our faith and the **walk** of our faith.

The Standing Commission on the Church in Metropolitan Areas (SCCM), created by the 1979 General Convention, was to make recommendations for "new patterns of mission and ministry." The 1982 report to Convention included a program for "mission and evangelism in urban and other deprived areas, with … focus on the local congregations." JM was called a "celebrative ministry…, in partnership with the poor, the powerless" and so at the same Convention with Resolution A80a, JM was born over 20 years ago.

JM centers have almost tripled this triennium with a quality assurance component now in place. At the three training events for new Jubilee Centers directors, over 400 attended. Two national Jubilee Gatherings strengthened the Diocesan Jubilee Officers and Program Directors network. Ministry workshops and a presentation on anti-racism were provided while connections between evangelism and justice were concretized. Three training events for new Diocesan Jubilee Officers were held, at each, a session on site visits for re-confirmation and potential Jubilee Centers was held.

The Jubilee Ministry Advisory Committee (JMAC) met six times. JMAC recommended to Council a plan for its own restructuring and that centers be reaffirmed every seven years. JMAC created a new Jubilee ministry category, "Affiliation," for 40 Jubilee Ministry Centers in Latin America and the Caribbean.

Other JM work this triennium: 1) A consultation with the Hispanic Ministry Office; 67 congregations learned about JM. 2) Jubilee Center site visits by the Presiding Bishop. 3) Anti-racism hearings (Social Justice Office, co-sponsor), held at Jubilee Centers in five dioceses; 50 African American, Hispanic American, Native American, and Asian American Episcopalians shared their stories. 4) A Justice, Peace and Integrity of Creation consultation (JPIC) were sixteen justice ministries presented. Members from the Council's Committee on National Concerns, the House of Deputies president, and Church Center staff attended.

The Office of Jubilee Ministry work included:
- Five Volumes of "Jubilee Centers" books highlighting their ministry.
- A small book on the Jubilee story from a legislative perspective in the church.
- Yearly calendars with Jubilee Center photos and lessons from the daily office.
- The "2000 Jubilee" video translated into Spanish. Distribution: English, 700 and Spanish, 100.
- Developed and revised the application, site visit and reaffirmation forms.
- Web-site implemented http://www.episcopalchurch.org/jubilee/

Resolution A015 Jubilee Ministry Thanksgiving

1   *Resolved,* the House of _____ concurring, That the 74th General Convention acknowledge with thanks to
2   God the ministry of Jubilee on its 21st anniversary; and be it further
3   *Resolved,* That this ministry of "joint discipleship in Christ with poor and oppressed people, wherever they
4   are found, to meet basic human needs and to build a just society," continue to be "at the heart of the
5   mission of the Church…;" and be it further
6   *Resolved,* That Jubilee Ministry be reaffirmed and commended to the whole Church.

COMMITTEE ON SCIENCE, TECHNOLOGY AND FAITH
www.episcopalchurch.org/gc/ec/ccs/ecstf/default.html

Membership (2000-2003)

Mr. Milton Coleman, *acting Co-Chair*	Central New York
The Rev. Barbara Smith-Moran, S.O.Sc., *Co-Chair*	Massachusetts
The Rev. Dr. Norman Faramelli	Massachusetts
The Rev. Dr. Kendall Harmon	South Carolina
Dr. Neil James	Florida (appointed 10/02)
The Rt. Rev. Robert H. Johnson	*Council Liaison*
Dr. Robert Schneider	Western North Carolina
Chaplain Lt. Mark Winward, USN, *Co-Chair*	Assigned to Olympia (resigned 10/02)
Ms. Susan Youmans	Massachusetts

WORK SUMMARY

The redemption of Christ brings healing and restoration, not simply to men and women in creation, but to the whole created order. The God who makes the world comes to that world to redeem a holy people *in* and *for* the world. With this understanding, the Committee on Science, Technology and Faith (ST&F) strives to bring before the Church concerns resulting from science and technology that bear upon the redeemed life of God's people and their relationship with the whole of creation.

Toward this end, ST&F reports the following initiatives undertaken during the 2000 – 2003 Triennium:

- 1/01 national 3-day conference, "Genetic Engineering and Food for the World," at the Cathedral of St. John the Divine, New York City.
- 2/01 public forum with speaker Bill Joy of Sun Microsystems: "Genomics, Robotics, and Nanotechnology," at Grace Cathedral, San Francisco.
- 11/01 launch of the new electronic ST&F network newsletter: at <http://home.earthlink.net/~smithmoran/>.
- 4/02 program for the Ecumenical Roundtable on Science, Technology and the Church in Canada and the US. A practicum on effective educational writing in science and religion, with Jim DeLa, Director of Communications, Diocese of Southwest Florida.
- 4/03 Ecumenical Roundtable hosted by ST&F at Roslyn Conference Center, Diocese of Virginia.

To implement its work, ST&F chose four study areas in the current triennium because of their immediate importance for the beliefs and communal life of faith. Four subcommittees were formed:

The **Subcommittee on Creation** received endorsement for its Mission Statement at the June 2002 Executive Council meeting <http://www.episcopalchurch.org/gc/ec/ccs/ecstf/minutes/default.html>. Its educational agenda assists the Church corporately and Episcopalians individually in acquiring a thorough knowledge of and appreciation for the Christian doctrine of creation, particularly in its Anglican expression. Subcommittee chair Robert Schneider is writing a set of essays on critical issues in science and religion for the Berea College web site at <http://www.berea.edu>. These will serve as preliminary studies for materials for distribution to the Church via the web.

The **Subcommittee on the Ecumenical Roundtable** with similar committees from other churches and denominations plans the annual meeting of the Ecumenical Roundtable on Science, Technology and the Church in Canada and the U.S. Before ST&F was appointed by the 1997 General Convention, several members were founders of the Roundtable in the mid 1980s.

Subcommittee chair Barbara Smith-Moran is the convener of the Steering Board of the Episcopal Church Network for Science, Technology and Faith (ECNSTF). This membership organization, with about 140 members, serves as a church-wide pool of expertise, available to provide technical and scientific information and advice to our Church. Consultants-at-large to the four subcommittees are drawn from ECNSTF.

The **Subcommittee on Genetically Modified Foods** has been considering such issues as the environmental and social impact of genetically modified crops, including their safety and efficacy in alleviating world hunger. These topics were addressed in the national conference, "Genetic Engineering and Food for the World," held in January 2001 at the Cathedral of St. John the Divine in New York City. An edited volume of essays from that conference will be available on the web. Beyond these topics, the subcommittee has uncovered a network of related concerns, all the more pressing since the 9/11 terrorist attacks. Subcommittee chair Susan Youmans made a presentation on food security to the Executive Council Committee on National Concerns in June 2002. This presentation is the basis for the Food Security resolution submitted by ST&F.

The **Subcommittee on Robotics and Nanotechnology** was formed after a public talk by computer technologist Bill Joy in February 2001 on "Genomics, Robotics, & Nanotechnology," co-sponsored by ST&F, at Grace Cathedral, San Francisco. His concerns about the rapid technological development, and society's slowness to regulate it, prompted ST&F to monitor these areas. Under chair Mark Winward, the subcommittee has been considering changes in the nature and understanding of life and death as computer-assisted replacement organs become available, purporting to considerably extend an individual's life.

Restructured Approach for the 2004-2006 Triennium

Having been a working group of The Executive Council, ST&F was authorized by resolution D011 of the 2000 General Convention. Following Convention, a petition to give special emphasis to the new concern about stem cell research resulted in an Ethics and the New Genetics Task Force (ENGTF), for one triennium. Funding was drawn from ST&F's budget plus augmentation from Council, and ST&F had a reduced membership of seven persons. For the upcoming triennium, an ongoing, restructured approach should obviate the need to split ST&F in the future.

ST&F formed The Episcopal Church Network for Science, Technology and Faith (ECNSTF), consisting of about 140 respected members of the scientific community, who offer expertise to ST&F in fields such as biomedical ethics, human genetic research and gene therapy, but it receives no General Convention funding. This resource will help ST&F offer web based education programs in such disciplines as bioengineering and genetic science. Human genetic research is a subject in which the Church's application of moral theology is of immediate concern. Provisions for education and guidance in matters of genetic testing, stem cell applications, and gene therapy are important to equip the leadership of the church.

ST&F's restructuring and its utilization of ECNSTF can offer a sound interface between science and religion for the Episcopal Church. This country and other countries receive misinformation on food security, the stewardship of our world and attempts to divorce the natural world from God's creation. The Doctrine of Creation is the theological context for ST&F's mission and its membership should include theologians, ethicists, and scholars of culture to maintain this interface.

- ST&F has been restructured and will include theologically sensitive Episcopalians with scientific or technical training in a wider range of fields than the current seven members can represent, including knowledge in food systems science, environmental science/engineering, genetics/cell biology, astronomy/cosmology, medicine/healthcare, computer science/technology, materials science/technology and neuroscience/neuropharmacology.

- The ST&F mandate is to act as a clearing-house for articles, monographs, scientific papers, commentaries, books and other works by scientists and researchers, drawn from ECNSTF and other sources, relating to issues which can inform the faith of Episcopalians.
- ST&F will check each author's reputation and their work's reliability. It will assess the work for suitability for an Episcopal audience while making editorial suggestions for understanding.
- ST&F will share its findings with the Director of Communication at the Episcopal Church Center who will arrange for a web library of informative and timely articles. These will educate the Church without a need for the General Convention to take a theological or ethical policy position on developments that are always changing. The Director of Communication is considering a regularly published feature on challenging topics for information, but not doctrinal mandate, for the whole church. Articles by ST&F or ECNSTF could be reprinted by Forward Movement.
- ST&F's work will include representation at meetings, conferences, and consultations with other churches and professional organizations. ST&F members will participate in discussions, interact with leaders in various fields, learn about the theological and ethical ramifications of cutting-edge developments in science and technology, and build ECNSTF. Possible meetings are the American Association for the Advancement of Science (ST&F contributes to a resource table); the American Public Health Association; the American Academy of Religion; and consultations of the Society of Ordained Scientists and the Church of Scotland's Society, Religion and Technology Project, which has done benchmark work in communicating matters of scientific and ethical interest to church constituents.
- ST&F will be comprised of 12 members. They will meet twice a year: in April, to coincide with the Ecumenical Roundtable on Science, Technology & the Church in Canada and the U.S., and in the fall. This will require $87,000 for the six meetings and attendance at other meetings during the triennium.

Resolution A016 Food Security

1 *Resolved,* the House of _____ concurring, That the mind of this 74th General Convention reflect the
2 conclusions of the Executive Council Committee on Science, Technology and Faith (ST&F) in its capacity
3 of providing to the Church informed conclusions concerning the intersection of science and technology
4 with the faith life of Episcopalians. Christians are called by God to be stewards of and delighters in God's
5 world, and to protect the diversity of God's Creation. We urge Episcopalians in their corporate,
6 community and individual action to integrate national and international food security into their
7 understanding of Christian responsibility; and be it further
8 *Resolved,* That in their understanding of Christian responsibility all Episcopalians support public policy
9 and actions that foster research and development of the types of science and technology that preserve
10 "biodiversity in food production", which refers to the maintenance of a healthy relationship among
11 varieties of food crops and species on which they depend; and be it further
12 *Resolved,* That Episcopalians become informed about trade conditions and intellectual property practices
13 that exacerbate the tendency of genetic modification technologies to reduce biodiversity in food
14 production; and be it further
15 *Resolved,* That Episcopalians support and participate in programs that protect farming and farmlands and
16 promote intentional purchases of food produced locally

EXPLANATION

Since 2000, ST&F has examined the validity of claims for genetic engineering to alleviate world hunger. Its position is that:

1. The limited time frame and context for the research conducted has produced insufficient data for full agreement on the environmental and biosafety implications of genetically modified plants and food.
2. The burden of responsibility should be with technology producers to assure consumer and environmental safety, rather than with consumers to prove harm.
3. Genetically modified seeds usage can lock farmers into a food production approach that reduces the need for human stewardship skills and requires more expensive seeds and increased, costly chemical inputs.

4. For impoverished nations, this worsens the trend in which food diversity produced for local consumption is replaced by monoculture crop production (the practice of planting a single genetic variant of a crop species, rather than multiple varieties and species) for export. Food producers' ability to buy food for themselves becomes dependent on their success in exporting crops internationally.

ST&F is aware of the cumulative effects of changes affecting production, distribution and consumption of food in the U.S. and globally. What was once called a "farm crisis" is now called a "food revolution".

For decades in the U.S., industrialized food production and a decreasing amount of the food dollar returned to food producers has caused serious secular and faith community concern. A small number of corporations have increased their market share in owning and cultivating resources to produce, manufacture, process, and market food. Countless farmers, ranchers, and fishermen and communities have been dislocated. Food producers' independence has diminished. Fewer and fewer corporations control seed development and patents, utilizing arrangements in which seed or stock, chemicals, and plant technology are included in contracts.

In the last decade, food producers as suppliers of raw materials have been denied a fair share in the value-added economic activity of the food system that extends from the grower to the consumer. Less food is being produced and consumed locally; domestic food products are directed at international markets; and domestic infrastructures to support production aimed at regional markets have been reduced. The rate of agribusiness corporate mergers has accelerated, and corporate consolidation has virtually eliminated competition among food product buyers, leaving many producers unable to bargain over prices they receive.

The 9/11 terrorist attacks generate additional concern for national food security. Domestic food systems are vulnerable due to reliance on long-distance crop shipments. A clash over use and protection of knowledge between developing and developed countries reinforces perceptions of unbridgeable differences between the interests of rich and poor nations.

ST&F asserts that biodiversity in food production manifests the variety in God's Creation and the roles of caring and relatedness within God's Kingdom. Humans steward local varieties of seeds and pass them down over generations. In millions of microclimates women and men use their knowledge of local conditions to feed their families. Finally, Jesus' preference for the poor is a compelling argument against domination of countries' seed and food production by large commercial interests.

ST&F rejects claims that treating plants and animals as food production units and eliminating their cultivation as a value-added human process ultimately alleviate hunger. ST&F believes that, in impoverished countries, changing over from food production for local use to crop production for export substitutes trade conditions for food sustainability and causes hungry people to be losers in international markets.

ST&F believes that monoculture food production practices require increased use of synthetic fertilizers, herbicides and pesticides that adversely affect microorganisms and surrounding plant and animal species. ST&F believes subsidized transportation to bring food to distant markets has hidden environmental costs of greenhouse-gas emissions and soil, air, and water contamination harmful to diverse ecosystems. ST&F questions whether genetically modified seed cultivation reduces the need for pesticides and herbicides.

The science and technology predominant in industrial food production have resulted in the reduction of diversity in ecosystems, habitats, and species, as well as in genetic variation within species. This trend has been accelerated by the energy-intensive agriculture introduced by the Green Revolution's new seeds, fertilizers, pesticides and herbicides. Today, interdependence of regional ecosystems enforced by political and economic structures makes this trend a matter of urgent concern. Science and technology must be directed toward promoting sustainability in long-term food production.

SOCIAL RESPONSIBILITY IN INVESTMENTS COMMITTEE

Membership

Mrs. Joyce Phillips Austin, *Chair* New York
Mr. Larry J. Bingham Kansas
The Rev. Peter T. Elvin Western Massachusetts
The Rev. Elizabeth McWhorter Washington
Mr. Paul M. Neuhauser Iowa
Ms. Lindsey W. Parsons Massachusetts
The Rt. Rev. Orris G. Walker Jr. Long Island
Mr. Warren J. Wong California
Mr. Richard E. Miller *Council liaison*
Mr. Harry Van Buren *Staff Consultant*

WORK SUMMARY

The Social Responsibility in Investments Committee (SRI) is charged by Council to research the social records of companies in DFMS portfolios and recommend action, including filing shareholder resolutions. Since 1971, when the Episcopal Church filed a shareholder resolution with General Motors asking that company to withdraw from South Africa, SRI has sought to identify key issues related to corporate social responsibility and work for changes in corporate behavior. The Episcopal Church is a member of the Interfaith Center on Corporate Responsibility, a coalition of 300 religious institutions engaged in shareholder activism. The Episcopal Church leads about eight shareholder actions annually and supports another half-dozen led by other religious institutions.

There are successes to report for this triennium. SRI engages in dialogue with companies and withdraws shareholder resolutions when an agreement is reached. Several companies with all white-male boards of directors, for example, have adopted policy statements on board diversity. Some have acted to increase their board diversity. SRI has had several successful dialogues about predatory lending. Other concerns are global warming, military contracting activities, equal employment opportunity, and ethical standards for a company's international operations.

Two principles guide SRI: 1) more corporate disclosure about social performance is better than less and 2) ethical minimums exist for all corporate activities. SRI is pleased to report its work with the Church Pension Fund (CPF). DFMS and CPF co-filed several resolutions. SRI and CPF co-sponsored a successful pilot conference in Williamstown with the Diocese of Western Massachusetts and the Diocese of Vermont for its neighboring parishes. Our partnership has much promise for the future.

SRI has done significant research for General Convention resolution D005 on environmental racism. A shareholder resolution on community consultation mechanisms was drafted and will be filed with some companies. A key issue related to environmental justice, namely, the lack of power that poor communities (including communities of color) have in affecting corporate behavior is addressed by asking companies to share their consulting methods with communities when seeking new facility locations.

During its thirty-one years, SRI has furthered the Episcopal Church's social witness. In so doing, the Episcopal Church has impacted societal expectations of corporate behaviors and corporate responses to greater demands for social responsibility.

Reports from Bodies created by General Convention, reporting to Executive Council and through Council to General Convention

20/20 TASK FORCE
www.episcopalchurch.org/congdev/2020home.html

Membership

The Rt. Rev. Gethin B. Hughes, *Chair*	San Diego
The Rt. Rev. Leopoldo J. Alard	Texas
The Rev. Richard Kew	Tennessee
The Very Rev. James B. Lemler	Chicago
The Rev. Canon Kevin E. Martin	Texas
Mr. Albert T. Mollegen Jr.	Connecticut
Ms. Deborah Robayo	Virginia
Mrs. Cecil P. Williamson	Alabama
The Very Rev. Sandra A. Wilson	Minnesota

WORK SUMMARY

Resolution A033, "20/20: A Clear Vision," established evangelism as an important priority for the Episcopal Church and made a commitment to doubling the baptized membership by the year 2020. *GC Resolution 2000-A034*, "Rebuilding the Church," authorized the establishment of the 2020 Task Force. Its charge was to develop a strategic plan for achieving the evangelistic vision of A033 including: creative strategies for evangelism; prayer and spiritual development; recruiting and equipping innovative leaders; strengthening congregational life; focusing on children, youth, and campus ministries.

During 2001, the nine member Task Force, under the leadership of Bishop Hughes, gathered data and considered the best methods for meeting the resolution's goals. In October 2001 the Task Force shared its report with the Executive Council. The report, *Doubling by 2020 Report: Building A Church of disciples who make disciples* and a *Summary of Recommendations and Action Areas* is the outcome of their work. Each report is available at http://www.episcopalchurch.org/2020TF/downloads.htm.

The final report offered actions in these areas: Celebrating the 20/20 Movement; Spirituality, Prayer and Worship; Research and Analysis; New Church Development, Congregation Development and Diocesan Development; Identifying, Recruiting and Training 20/20 Leaders; The Next Generations and Funding and Communicating the 20/20 Vision. Council referred the report and the further work on the 20/20 Vision to the Standing Commission on Domestic Mission and Evangelism. SCDME's report includes the final 20/20 report.

A045 TASK FORCE

Membership

Ms. Sarah Taylor Harte, *Co-Chair*	New York
The Rt. Rev. Peter James Lee, *Co-Chair*	Virginia
The Very Rev. David T. Chee	Los Angeles
The Rev. Ann Coburn	Rhode Island
Mrs. Pauline Getz	San Diego
The Very Rev. Scott H. Kirby	Eau Claire
The Rt. Rev. John Lipscomb	Southwest Florida
Ms. Diane B. Pollard	New York
The Rt. Rev. Catherine Roskam	New York

WORK SUMMARY

The *73rd General Convention's Resolution A045* directed the Executive Council to establish a Task Force "to visit, interview, assess and assist" the bishops, leaders, and people of the Dioceses of Fort Worth, Quincy and San Joaquin in plans for full compliance with the canons regarding the ordination of women.

These are the A045 reports from the teams who visited each diocese. We accomplished the first three of our tasks: to visit, interview and assess. We found that the intrusion of an unwelcome and uninvited group made it impossible "to assist."[4] We are a diverse church, committed to inclusivity, but some of our behavior sends to self-described traditionalists a message of unwelcome.

Report of the Fort Worth Team

On October 9, 2001, team members, The Very Rev. David T. Chee, Ms. Sarah Harte and The Rt. Rev. Peter James Lee, met with The Rt. Rev. Jack Iker and diocesan leaders at the Diocesan Center for Ministry in Fort Worth. Representatives from the Commission on Ministry, World Mission Committee, the Standing Committee, Bishop Iker's Canon to the Ordinary and a diocesan vice chancellor were present.

Bishop Iker, in his opening remarks, made clear that he viewed the presence of the A045 Committee as "An unwelcome intrusion into the life of the Diocese…interfering with the internal affairs of the Diocese." He said, "We think that A045 is headed towards punitive action" to the three dioceses named in the resolution. Bishop Iker declared that, "We don't have any trust in the Executive Council, the General Convention, and the Presiding Bishop…we feel abused and unappreciated and now under attack."

Task Force representatives were impressed by the diocese's vitality in mission. We saw a short video, heard about congregational growth, and a successful capital drive, and were assured by a Standing Committee female member that "women are full partners in the ministry of this diocese." We were told that over half of the diocesan convention delegates are women, two of the three lay Standing Committee members are women, and virtually every parish has women vestry members while many have women wardens.

The Dallas/Fort Worth Plan lets women with a vocation to priesthood have access to the ordination process. A woman in this plan is interviewed by Bishop Iker and, if approved, is referred to the Diocese of Dallas for the ordination process. Three women priests from the Diocese of Fort Worth, whom we met at our next meeting, are now serving in the Diocese of Dallas. The Bishop has made it clear that any Fort Worth parish who wishes to call a woman as an assistant or rector could ask for Episcopal oversight from the Bishop of Dallas. No parish has taken advantage of this plan.

We returned on March 6, 2002 meeting at Trinity Church, Fort Worth. In our October meeting, we had told the Bishop and the diocesan leaders that the General Convention resolution required us to meet with "the

---

[4] The report prepared by the entire Task Force included a second part to this sentence. It reads, " and we encourage the Executive Council and General Convention to avoid such intrusive policies in the future."

people" of the Diocese. We wanted to identify a cross section of lay and clergy who might have different views than the leadership community we met in October. A letter dated February 5, 2002, from Bishop Lee, informed Bishop Iker of our plan to return. He had already heard of our intentions from people we had invited to our meeting. He, with the Standing Committee of Fort Worth, objected strongly to our presence. When we arrived at Trinity Church, Fort Worth, on March 6, 2002, we found the Diocesan Standing Committee present with a Pastoral Direction from the Bishop. It directed the Trinity Church Rector to make it possible for the Standing Committee to attend our meetings.

We met with three groups. The first was a randomly selected group who served on the Diocesan Executive Committee representing various views. One lay woman read a written statement which expressed her loyalty to the Episcopal Church. She said, "What a wonderful church, holding Jesus in his proper place, apostolic succession of our bishops, women under the covering of their husband and/or their priest moved freely in their activities." Her opposition to the ordination of women was held by a number of the leaders we met. Another woman, however, described her participation in a strategic planning process for her parish. None of the parish focus groups had any objection to the ordination of women or to an ordained woman serving in their parish.

The second group was composed of clergy and lay persons we had invited on suggestions from others and from email requests asking they be heard. Support for the ordination of women was much more widespread in this group than among diocesan elected leaders.

The third group included three women priests originally from the Diocese of Forth Worth serving in the Diocese of Dallas. Each was positive about Bishop Iker's encouragement as she moved through the ordination process. Each also said that she could not imagine serving as a woman priest in the Diocese of Fort Worth because of the widespread opposition to women's ordination.

In summary, we witnessed much vitality and strong mission work in the Diocese of Fort Worth. We recognized that much of the diocesan leadership opposes the ordination of women. They also share the Bishop's opinion that people in the Diocese of Fort Worth are marginalized by the Episcopal Church because of their traditional views.

We encourage the people in the Diocese of Fort Worth to expand their experience of the wider church so that they might see the value of women in ordained leadership, a value now widely rejected in the diocese. We do sympathize with the feeling of marginalization that seemed evident in the Diocese. Those for the ordination of women and self-described traditionalists both feel marginalized by the wider church.

Report of the Quincy Team
Team members, The Rev. Ann Coburn, the Rt. Rev. John B. Lipscomb and Ms. Diane Pollard, traveled to St. Louis, Missouri and met with Diocese of Quincy representatives on October 1, 2001 at the Diocese of Springfield offices. The sub-committee outlined some of the issues after introductions. We stressed that this was an initial visit and we hoped to schedule a follow-up visit. Everyone agreed to a second visit.

A second visit was made on August 29, 2002. The conversations were to be held at the Diocese of Springfield offices. Instead they were held at St. John's Church, Quincy. Bishop Ackerman and Father Herrmann had to be present at the church because of a fire. It seemed best to have the conversations even with the distractions and the reduced participants from Quincy.

We continued the past year's conversation after Morning Prayer and Eucharist with Bishop Ackerman and Father Herrmann, the diocesan Chancellor and the Commission on Ministry Chair. The diocesan representatives present expressed a willingness and expectation to observe the canons of the church by providing equal access to the ordination process for women and men. Currently, the diocese has several women postulants preparing for the vocational diaconate.

When the question was raised regarding ordination to the priesthood, the response was the diocese intends to follow the canons with equal access to the ordination process even though to date no woman has presented herself for discernment. Bishop Ackerman has chosen not to develop a policy such as Fort Worth's because he wants the freedom to deal with each individual as a unique person and as a moment for discernment. There are no plans for a third conversation.

Report of the San Joaquin Team

Team members, Mrs. Pauline Getz, The Very Rev. H. Scott Kirby and The Rt. Rev. Catherine Roskam , visited the Rt. Rev. John David Schofield in the Diocese of San Joaquin on July 12, 2001. Bishop Schofield arranged for us to meet at ECCO, the diocesan camp and conference center. He had invited a dozen people to meet with us, including himself.

We were greeted with what might be described as gracious hostility. It was very clear that the bishop and most of the clergy were convinced we had come to dig up information to bring charges against him. Bishop Schofield and most of the clergy present were defensive and often angry, even though we reiterated several times that we had come to listen. Our articulated position was that we cannot fulfill the General Convention charge until we know what is going on in their diocese. It was clear that many clergy do not share the bishop's position on the ordination of women, although it was equally clear that they support him.

We learned that Bishop Schofield has been supportive of women pursuing ordination. Several women are currently in the process. When asked what will happen when they are ready for ordination, he said, "They will be ordained." He would not address the future, but made it clear that, if it were today, it is not likely he would ordain them. In the past, he arranged for a woman who became a deacon in his diocese to be ordained in the Diocese of California. He indicated one woman serves in the diocese with his permission, but he will not license her.

Bishop Schofield's position seems to be that, while he is open to the movement of the Holy Spirit in this matter, he is not convinced that the General Convention, in revising the Canons, was in fact reflective of the will of the Holy Spirit. Therefore he is not convinced that women who go through ordination are truly ordained. He is concerned they are "make believe" priests, and that any person who believes they receiving a sacrament from such a woman is actually being barred from grace.

Instead of another diocesan visit, we felt it would be more helpful to offer Bishop Schofield an opportunity to personally experience the ordained ministry of women in different circumstances and in an environment where their ministry is a given. Bishop Schofield has been invited by Bishop Roskam to visit the Diocese of New York. He and a priest, who is the past president of the diocesan Standing Committee, will spend time with her in October 2002.

They will have three different experiences: being present at ordinary events in the Diocese of New York in which ordained women are an integral part, observing the particular ministries of ordained women, and participating in a theological discussion on women's ordination. It is hoped that this visit will give everyone a deeper understanding and offer the Holy Spirit a welcome environment to move and touch hearts.

Conclusion

We expect all dioceses to respect people of different convictions. We rejoice in the gifts of ordained women and encourage a conversation throughout this church that will enable people of differing convictions to learn from one another. We believe the way forward is one of inclusion and respect. We offer the following resolutions as a process to strengthen the church's unity.

Resolution A017 National Conversation on Women's Ordination

1   *Resolved,* the House of _____ concurring, That the 74th General Convention receive with thanks the report
2   of the visitors representing the Executive Council in the implementation of Resolution A045 of the 73rd
3   General Convention; and be it further
4   *Resolved,* That we give thanks for the work of the Holy Spirit within our communion through the life-
5   giving ministry of ordained women; and be it further

6   *Resolved*, That, inasmuch as the 72nd General Convention in resolution A052 clarified that the canons
7   regarding the ordination of women are mandatory, we engage in a national conversation drawing on the
8   best theological resources available to assist the whole church to promote, explore and develop ways to
9   facilitate the ordination of women in every diocese and their full and equal deployment throughout the
10   church; and be it further
11   *Resolved,* That such conversations be sponsored by the Executive Council of this Church and begin in the
12   year following this General Convention in preparation for a day of dialogue and reflection to be held at the
13   75th General Convention in 2006; and be it further
14   *Resolved*, That the 2004-2006 Triennium budget include $50,000 for this national conversation.

STANDING COMMITTEE ON HIV/AIDS
http://www.episcopalchurch.org/gc/ec/ccs/echa/default.html

Membership

The Rev. Richard F. Brewer, *Co-Chair*	Long Island
The Rt. Rev. Rodney R. Michel, *Co-Chair*	Long Island
The Rev. Billy J. Alford	Georgia
The Rev. Gordon Chastain	Indianapolis
Mr. E. Bruce Garner	Atlanta
Ms. Lyn Headley-Moore	Newark
Ms. Mary Ellen Honsaker	Wyoming
Ms. Elizabethe Payne	Texas
The Rev. Valerie B. Thomas	Florida

WORK SUMMARY

The Executive Council Standing Committee on HIV/AIDS (the Committee or HIV/AIDS), first established in 1994, is charged with monitoring the HIV/AIDS pandemic. The Committee met four times during the triennium and has been asked to recommend how to increase other Commissions, Committees, Agencies and Boards' response to the pandemic. HIV/AIDS participated in a Justice, Peace, and the Integrity of Creation (JPIC) consultation resulting in a proposal to collaborate with other CCABs in addressing the societal issues related to HIV/AIDS prevention and education. HIV/AIDS encourages more consultations so that CCABs may collaborate further.

Continuing the work assigned, the Committee responded to these General Convention resolutions: *GC Resolution 2000-A050* called for more training in prevention, education materials, and that these ministries expand to young adults by adapting materials or developing new resources. This was a timely resolution because of new infection statistics but the $40,000 was not allocated.

The National Episcopal AIDS Coalition (NEAC) utilized support from the United Thank Offering, the Centers for Disease Control, and its own budget for a revision of the **Youth in the Age of AIDS** materials. This is a joint project with the Youth Ministries cluster at the Episcopal Church Center. NEAC is also revising the **Teen Aids Prevention** (TAP) curriculum to be more accessible for parish use. The Committee applauds the NEAC in seeking funding other than the National Church's program budget. Ministry is hindered without needed funding.

GC Resolution 2000-A051 asked the US government to make drugs affordable and to continue research. The USA has urged companies to make drugs affordable in Africa by limiting their royalty claims because many in and outside the USA do not receive life-extending drug therapies.

GC Resolution 2000-A052 called the church to recognize justice issues which hinder an effective response to the HIV/AIDS pandemic. It asked that prevention and pastoral needs be addressed. The Committee is heartened by Episcopal Life's increased coverage of the world wide AIDS pandemic and the assistance given by organizations such as ERD this triennium. There is a tendency to focus on the HIV/AIDS pandemic in

Africa while ignoring the epidemic demands on the Episcopal Church in the USA. This excerpt from, "The New Scarlet Letter: A for AIDS: *Fighting the Shame and the Silence*" shares the statistics on the rising epidemic in the USA. It is available at http://www.episcopalchurch.org/gc/ec/ccs/echa/default.html or http://www.neac.org/.

HIV/AIDS Pandemic in the United States

HIV and AIDS have not moved to Africa and Asia. There is new evidence of rising HIV infection rates in North America especially among vulnerable and forgotten populations. HIV and AIDS are more than health problems. There are economic and human rights problems associated with the disease. Our refusal, in and outside the Episcopal Church, to deal honestly with the causes of these problems and their prevention is a concern. UN AIDS Executive Director, Peter Piot raises the major question confronting this Committee: "Why, 20 years into the epidemic, are people with HIV still the targets of hate?"[5]

Men have sex with men (MSM). Intravenous drug users are both genders and all colors. These people and their sexual partners are at high risk of contracting HIV. We are all at risk until we confront our discomfort about their sexual behavior and talk honestly about safe sexual behavior. As Dr. Coates states, "AIDS is a disease that holds a magnifying glass to some of America's ugliest social problems."[6]

Sex and Drugs

- A Center for Disease Control (CDC) survey of men 15 to 29 revealed 60 percent of infected white MSM and 70 percent of infected Hispanic men did not know they were infected and saw themselves as low risk.
- Although MSMs' HIV infection rate is nine times higher, heterosexual transmission is rising faster. One reason is some MSMs have sex with women. Another reason is minority MSMs are reluctant to identify as gay because homophobia is strong in minority communities.
- Very few people especially in the federal government want to deal with the fact that HIV and AIDS are spread among injection drugs users (IDU). In ten years the rate of infected drug injectors fell from fifty to twenty percent in New York City because of a clean needle program.[7]
- Gay and bisexual men with psychosocial health factors, such as childhood sexual abuse, are five times more likely to engage in high-risk sex. Women with chronic sexual abuse are seven times more likely to engage in risky sexual behaviors than women without abuse histories.

People of Color

- In 1982, less than a third of all AIDS cases were people of color. Today 62 percent of those with AIDS are people of color even though they are about 30% of the US population. AIDS is the leading killer of Latinos aged 24 to 44. Almost half of all new AIDS cases are African-Americans. Communities of color receive substandard AIDS care compared with whites.[8]
- A Native American group reports: a) many infected are not treated because of the stigma; b) poverty, isolation, and poor medical care contribute and c) there may be no access to testing or drugs for treatment.[9]
- For Asian Americans and Pacific Islanders, former Surgeon General David Satcher believes "There is a great under-representation of the incidence of HIV/AIDS…," due to "linguistic isolation": with 40 cultures and 100 languages, they lack information about HIV transmission and are more likely to believe myths about who is at risk.[10]

---

[5] Peter Piot, "Keeping the Promise," Keynote Speech, XIV International AIDS Conference, July 2002

[6] Thomas Coates, M.D., professor of medicine, University of California, San Francisco

[7] "Lesson for AIDS Fighters: Syringe Swaps Work," *Newsday (New York),* August 16, 2001.

[8] Ceci Connolly, "Report Says U.S. Minorities Get Lower-Quality Health Care: Moral Implications of Widespread Pattern Noted," *Washington Post*, March 21, 2002; report issued by the Institute of Medicine.

[9] Nicholas K. Geranios, "Native American Group Says Stigma Surrounding AIDS Prevents Many from Receiving Treatment," Associated Press, November 27, 2001.

[10] David Satcher, M.D., www.surgeongeneral.gov/aids/tlcapage1.html (May, 2001).

Seniors
- HIV and AIDS rates are rising twice as fast among people aged 50 and over. The epidemic does not respect income: 17% of the AIDS cases in Palm Beach County, Florida, are over 50.
- Non-whites over 50 with AIDS die more quickly than whites. For people over 65, the disease tends to lead twice as fast to death, perhaps due to impaired health.
- Condoms are thought to prevent pregnancy, not disease. Doctors may not talk about safe sex with older patients and may not test for HIV even with related symptoms, instead linking them to age instead.

Youth
- Half of those with HIV became infected before the age of 25. Most teens in the U.S. lack information on protection. Many do not know that HIV is sexually transmitted. This is a concern because young people are sexually active at a younger age.
- It is estimated that 26 percent of gay teens are forced from home because of their sexual orientation. On the street, they are subject to physical violence, rape, drug and alcohol abuse and prostitution.
- Race and gender matter. In Houston in 1999, 78 percent of the cases among 13–19 year-olds were African-American females.

Gender
- Rates of infection are rising faster for women than men. AIDS is a leading cause of death for all U.S. women aged 25 – 44. It is the third leading cause for African-American women in this age group.
- Male sexual partners pose the greatest risk factor for American women.
- Although the AIDS case rate for Latino men is almost three times that for white non-Hispanic men, for Latino women the rate is six times higher. For Latino men, heterosexual contact accounts for approximately seven percent of HIV cases, but for Latino women it accounts for 44 percent.
- Women tend to get diagnosed later than men. If a gay man has chest pains, a doctor thinks of AIDS related pneumonia; but a woman has the flu.

Prisons and the Rural Areas
- AIDS is six times higher in the US correctional system than the general public. Many ex-offenders do not know if they are HIV infected. Unlike outside, incarcerated women are three times as likely to have AIDS. Outside, men are four times more likely to be infected.
- Although peer-led HIV education programs have proved highly effective, they are offered in only 13 percent of state and federal facilities and 3 percent of city and county facilities.
- Only about six jails nationwide distribute condoms. Canadian federal prisons have given out condoms for ten years. European prison systems providing condoms is up to 81 percent, from 53 percent in 1989.
- People with HIV who live in rural areas are imprisoned by distance, community ignorance, unprepared health providers, and loneliness.
- In rural areas there are practically no public health HIV prevention efforts and no mandatory HIV education in the schools. Health providers do not recognize the symptoms.

Conclusion
In conclusion, the HIV/AIDS pandemic has not left the United States for Africa or Asia. The Episcopal Church has a ministry stateside by ministering to persons infected with HIV/AIDS, including their families and by educating its members on prevention and the social issues that accompanies the pandemic. HIV/AIDS is committed to assisting the Church in this fight by telling the story of HIV/AIDS to the Church and offering ways the CCABs can collaborate on prevention programs and those addressing societal ills. The Committee offers these standards that congregations, dioceses and other church related organizations may use in their HIV/AIDS ministries.

The Committee on HIV/AIDS calls on the Episcopal Church and each member to:
- Recognize that condemning people infected with HIV and AIDS breaches social justice.
- Speak against governmental policies placing personal prejudices above health care priorities.
- Speak honestly, no matter how uncomfortable, about HIV's transmission and prevention.
- Understand that the HIV/AID epidemic includes an index of social and economic injustices.

- Incorporate HIV/AIDS education in confirmation preparation, marital counseling, counseling for blessing of same sex unions, in seminaries and nursing homes.
- Learn who lives with HIV and AIDS in their church, especially rural churches, and offer help and hope.
- Live the Gospel's call to love and healing.
- And finally, realize that courageous, resilient, and resourceful peoples on the margins, those who are left out, or put out, do not need imposed solutions as much as assistance in discovering their own answers.[11]

Budget for 2003–2006 Triennium

The Executive Council Standing Committee on HIV/AIDS will meet approximately 4 times during the next triennium. This will require $14,000 for 2004; $14,000 for 2005 and $16,000 for 2006 for a total of $44,000 for the triennium.

Resolution A018 HIV/AIDS Drugs Full Inclusion

1   *Resolved,* the House of _____ concurring, That the Episcopal Church, through the General Convention,
2   urge American pharmaceutical companies and the United States Food and Drug Administration to increase
3   their inclusion of women, African-Americans and members of other communities of color in both the
4   clinical drug trials for new HIV medications and the studies of the efficacy of new HIV medications to
5   help insure that the medications perform effectively in all populations.

EXPLANATION

Women, African-Americans and members of other communities of color have traditionally been under-represented in the clinical trials for new HIV medications. Consequently, the efficacy and the side effects of those medications on members of those communities have not always been known.

Resolution A019 Continue Standing Committee on HIV/AIDS

1   *Resolved,* the House of _____ concurring, That the 74th General Convention authorize the continuation of
2   the Executive Council Standing Committee on HIV/AIDS for the 2003-2006 Triennium; and be it further
3   *Resolved,* That the Standing Committee on HIV/AIDS for the next triennium focus on the "quiet voices of
4   AIDS" in our church and in our nation, those whom we are called to serve but may overlook; and be it
5   further
6   *Resolved,* That the Standing Committee undertake a survey of HIV/AIDS ministries at all levels of the
7   church; and be it further
8   *Resolved,* That the Standing Committee on HIV/AIDS report at least annually to the Executive Council of
9   the General Convention on the state of the church's response to the HIV/AIDS pandemic, with particular
10   attention to the implementation of pertinent resolutions of General Convention.

EXPLANATION

Many of those infected by HIV/AIDS remain effectively hidden from view in the epidemic. They endure their infection and affliction silently due to such factors as racism, cultural stigma, and homophobia. Their stories are not told publicly and much can be learned from them to help others.

Resolution A020 HIV Medications Availability

1   *Resolved,* the House of _____ concurring, That the Episcopal Church, through its General Convention,
2   urge American pharmaceutical companies, the United States Food and Drug Administration and the
3   United States Patent Office to relinquish patent rights to pharmaceutical companies in developing
4   countries to allow for the development of HIV medications and the creation of generic versions of those
5   medications with the purpose of making those medications available to those who need them in those
6   developing countries.

EXPLANATION

Virtually all HIV medications currently in use have been patented by major pharmaceutical companies. Their costs are very high by United States health care standards and are too expensive for those who need

---

[11] Rader, note 3.

them in developing countries around the world. Allowing the development of generic versions would make those medications available to thousands who desperately need them.

Resolution A021 Broadening HIV Prevention Methods

1   *Resolved,* the House of _____concurring, That the Episcopal Church, through its General Convention, call
2   upon its African-American members and its congregations with larger populations of African-Americans
3   to take the lead in insuring that *all* methods used to prevent the spread of HIV are taught in school
4   curricula, Church School curricula and in other educational settings. Educational efforts shall be
5   intentionally directed toward the prevention of HIV among men who have sex with other men.

EXPLANATION

HIV infection continues to rise at alarming rates in the African-American community. The most prevalent route of transmission of HIV in women is from men who have sex with men to their female sexual partners. There is great reluctance in the African-American community to discuss this phenomenon. It is referred to by such code names as "on the down low" or "on the DL" reflecting the unwillingness to discuss the subject openly and honestly. The stigma associated with AIDS and the reluctance to discuss matters of human sexuality greatly hinder prevention education efforts.

COMMITTEE ON SEXUAL EXPLOITATION

Membership

The Rev. Virginia N. Herring, *Chair*	North Carolina
Mr. Les Alvis	Mississippi
The Rev. Dr. Lee Alison Crawford	Vermont
The Rt. Rev. Duncan Montgomery Gray III	Mississippi
The Rev. Dena A. Harrison	Texas
Mr. William A.G. Hogg	Long Island
The Rt. Rev. George E. Packard	New York
The Rev. Dr. Virginia M. Sheay	New Jersey
The Rev. Debra L. Trakel	Milwaukee

WORK SUMMARY

Created by the 70th General Convention, the Committee on Sexual Exploitation (COSE) has been renewed each triennium as the work has expanded beyond the original intent. COSE worked diligently to open dialogue with victims, with other churches and institutions, with bishops, and with clergy. Sample policies and procedures and educational materials have been produced. Training events have been held to support diocesan response. The work has been difficult because historically sexual misconduct by clergy or church employees has been kept quiet, and suppressed. Confidentiality has been in tension with the need to provide adequate information for congregations and clergy groups to heal. Denial has existed at all levels.

COSE's work in this triennium has centered on the recommendations from a survey of all dioceses from the last triennium. Media attention to sexual misconduct in religious bodies, particularly through child abuse has brought new urgency to our work, as well as new cases. Procedures vary widely across the church, and education is still needed.

1999 Survey of Diocesan Policies Regarding Sexual Misconduct Response

The survey itself was an educational tool for many. Our follow-up has included:

National Conference on Pastoral Standards
In June 2001, the first national Pastoral Standards Conference was held. One hundred twenty-five people represented 70 dioceses; an extraordinary gathering of bishops, chancellors, and clergy and laity. Honored at the opening worship service were: The Rt. Rev. Robert Anderson, Mrs. Marge Burke, The Rt. Rev. Harold Hopkins, Mrs. Nancy Hopkins, The Rt. Rev. Chilton Knudsen, The Rev. Margo Maris, and Mrs. Mary

Meader for their pioneering efforts in this work. Education and networking was the focus of the conference with an overwhelming request for more conferences.

Develop a National Network
Those working with sexual misconduct need to be in regular communication with others in the field. Much is gained by shared stories and information, and connection in a wider community helps ease the burden of pain. After studying, NNECA, CODE, and BEST,[12] COSE brought together a representative group from the June conference in September 2002. The "Nathan Network" was formed.

Strengthen collaboration between COSE, the Office of Pastoral Ministry Development, the Standing Commissions on Constitution and Canon,s and Ministry Development
Resolution A028 of the 73rd General Convention created a Task Force to study and evaluate the disciplinary canons (Title IV). Its membership includes persons from these groups.

Assist the Office of Pastoral Development as it implements prevention programs while articulating professional standards
The Bishop from the Office of Pastoral Development and COSE worked jointly on training sessions at the national conference and at two events for bishops. An evaluative, comprehensive report of the policies, procedure manuals and training materials from 70 dioceses was shared with the AO28 Task Force and CPG. New professional standard models by CPG will be available in the next triennium.

Conclusion
COSE's work helped the Episcopal Church face squarely the problem of sexual misconduct in church settings. COSE has completed its charge, but the work is not finished. Our commitment to repentance, healing and reconciliation implicit in the baptismal covenant requires that we continue to struggle. We must provide a mindful presence to the risks inherent in human relationship and thereby encourage health in our institution. We must work with greater wisdom for prevention and institutional accountability as we move from crisis mode to the deeper work of response and responsibility.

A resolution for a full-time staff position in the Office of Pastoral Development at a cost of $309,000 per triennium was created by the Province VIII bishops' gathering in January, 2002, and subsequently approved by the Province IV bishops. Such a person would provide the on-going necessary oversight, consultation, education, and management of the work.

COSE believes this is the most expeditious and efficacious way to continue the work. However, if funding constraints prevent the establishment of the office, then we propose the establishment of a Task Force on Institutional Wellness and the Prevention of Sexual Misconduct. This group will work with the Church Pension Group and others to establish standards of ethical behavior and codes of conduct, especially for those working with children. It would meet six times in the next triennium and require $50,000 in funding.

The primary locus of authority in these matters is the diocesan bishop's office. COSE urges the House of Bishops to appoint a Task Force to help bishops share information and work across diocesan lines. A more holistic response across the Church can only strengthen our identity as the Body of Christ.

Finally, we are mindful of the budget priorities guiding the Church in stewardship of its resources. We have learned that education and prevention costs less than "handling cases." We see these connections between our work and the Administration and Finance Committee's "Ordered Priorities for Program and Budget Development" as presented to the Executive Council:
- Reaching out to youth means their protection and safety is a primary concern.
- Proclaiming the Gospel means we are a place of safety, healing, reconciliation, and love.

---

[12] National Network of Episcopal Clergy Associations, Conference of Diocesan Executives and Bishop's Executive Secretaries Together

- Congregations wounded by sexual misconduct and not given the opportunity for healing become dysfunctional and continue the wounding to future generations. Learning better ways to offer healing will enable congregations to be "revitalized and transformed."
- Hearing the "voiceless needy," the long-silenced victims of clergy sexual abuse, began the COSE goal to "promote justice and peace for all of God's creation" and all persons.

Resolution A022 Nathan Network Funding

1 *Resolved,* the House of _____ concurring, That the sum of $49,000 be appropriated for the next triennium
2 to provide start-up funding for a national network of diocesan personnel working with sexual misconduct
3 in the Church.

Resolution A023 Establish Institutional Wellness and the Prevention of Sexual Misconduct Task Force

1 *Resolved,* the House of _____ concurring, That General Convention establish, pursuant to Joint Rule 23, a
2 Task Force of not less than ten nor more than fifteen persons. These persons should be laity, bishops,
3 priests, and deacons with experience and expertise in dealing with sexual misconduct in church settings.
4 Membership should include, but not be limited to representatives from the Standing Commission on
5 Ministry Development, the Council of Seminary Deans, the Nathan Network, the Committee on Sexual
6 Exploitation, the National Network of Episcopal Clergy Associations, the A028 Task Force, and the
7 National Network of Lay Professionals; and be it further
8 *Resolved,* That the Task Force shall study and gather information concerning matters of institutional
9 wellness for the prevention of sexual misconduct. Its study shall include such concerns as screening,
10 selection and training of clergy, lay employees and volunteers; monitoring and supervision; behavior
11 management; incident investigation; and the articulation of pastoral standards and codes of ethical
12 behavior; and be it further
13 *Resolved,* That each body named shall recommend Task Force members from its own membership, and
14 the appointments shall be overseen by the Bishop of the Office of Pastoral Development. Additional
15 members shall then be appointed by the Bishop of the Office of Pastoral Development, and the entire Task
16 Force shall include at least two bishops, two clergy, and two laity. The Task Force shall have the services
17 of the Office of Pastoral Development and a Church Pension staff person; and be it further
18 *Resolved,* That $50,000 be appropriated for the work of this Task Force for the next triennium.

EXECUTIVE COUNCIL COMMITTEE ON THE STATUS OF WOMEN
www.episcopalchurch.org/women

Membership

Sally Bucklee, *Chair*	Washington
Cynthia Bartol	Virginia
Jon Bruno	Los Angeles
Marjorie Burke	New Hampshire
Jennifer Baskerville	Newark, *resigned 2001*
Debra Cavanaugh	San Joaquin
Robert Cowperthwaite	Tennessee
Guadelupe Guillen	Los Angeles
Sheila Nelson-McJilton	Easton
Virginia Paul	Western Louisiana
Barbara Schlachter	Southern Ohio
Marge Christie	*Consultant*
Sally Sedgwick	*Staff*

WORK SUMMARY

Despite limited resources, the Committee on the Status of Women (CSW) addressed its mission to investigate and advocate for women's full participation in the Episcopal Church and to advise the church on theological, educational, health and socioeconomic factors determining women's lives in the Church and wider community. CSW is grateful for the Executive Council's financial support for the 21st Century Survey, which compared Episcopal women's status today with women in 1987, when a similar survey was conducted.

1. The 21st Century Survey: Reaching Toward Wholeness II

Designed by Dr. Adair Lummis of the Hartford Seminary in consultation with CSW, the survey was distributed by local committees in 18 dioceses participating at the Presiding Bishop's invitation. These were Bethlehem, Maine, Massachusetts, New York, Washington, Indianapolis, Iowa, Kentucky, Southern Ohio, Central Gulf Coast, South Carolina, Virginia, Western Louisiana, Los Angeles, South Dakota, Texas and Wyoming. Half participated in 1987. In each diocese, 200 women, 100 men and 50 leaders received the survey. Participation by Church Center staff and the CCAB chairs provided national, diocesan and congregational comparisons. The entire report will be sent to dioceses and the Executive Council. A summary of the findings will be available for bishops and deputies at General Convention.

Major highlights included:
- Increased support among women and men for inclusive/expansive language when referring to humans.
- The highest acceptance of inclusive/expansive language for God was among female clergy.
- Ordained women's presence at the altar and in the pulpit engenders approval of lay women as leaders.
- Respondents saw themselves as more open to women's leadership than their congregations.
- There is an obvious need for educational materials related to women's issues and ministries.
- The larger the congregation the less the acceptance of a woman as rector.

While the data found that women still lack parity in church governance in many dioceses and congregations, there has been an increase in the past 15 years in lay and clergy women in leadership positions. Using survey results, CSW will continue to
- mobilize women to act boldly on their faith.
- focus attention on unjust societies and the ugly conditions in which many women live.
- encourage secular and religious leaders to make the world a better place, especially for children.
- look for reasons why women hold more leadership positions in some regions of the country than others.
- explore ways to overcome resistance to female rectors in large congregations.

2. Celebrating Women and Ordination

September 16, 2001, was the 25th anniversary of General Convention's decision to clarify that the ordination canons apply equally to women and men. CSW brought this to the Church's attention. Joyous celebrations took place across the country. Local statistics and history were collected.

3. The United Nations and Gender Justice

The UN has become a strong advocate for women's rights as human rights and a major worldwide force for gender equality. There is need for increased support by the Episcopal Church of women's concerns globally and locally and closer ties with the UN. CSW members have participated in UN events in this triennium and will do so in the coming triennium.

CSW recommends the Beijing+5 Declaration and Platform for adoption as social policy of the Episcopal Church, particularly by Peace and Justice Ministries, Ethnic Ministries and Women's Ministries in setting budget and legislative priorities. The Platform's priorities are a) overcoming poverty, b) ensuring access to quality education and health care, c) elimination of violence and d) economic self-reliance for women.

CSW urges the Office of Government Relations to place top priority on working with other religious bodies to build support for 1) the UN Convention for the Elimination of all Forms of Discrimination Against Women, finally released in 2002 by the Senate Foreign Relations Committee, after 20 years, and for 2) the Equal Rights Amendment. Both have been approved by previous Conventions.

Sex (and the corresponding terms "female" and "male") refers to the biologically determined characteristics of men and women, such as the ability to bear children. *Gender* refers to socially-constructed roles (what it means to be masculine or feminine), and is usually defined along sex lines. Gender roles, differing by culture, can change but often become stereotypes that limit an individual's opportunities, whether male or female. Work to advance the status of women aims at expanding men's and women's gender roles so that neither is the basis for discrimination, for example, to propose leave with pay for both parents to care for a new baby.

4. Violence Against Women

The status of women and violence against women are tightly interlocked. CSW has repeatedly brought this issue to the General Convention and does again. *Now That the Silence is Broken: The Next Step* is a new CSW publication for congregations and dioceses. Containing hot line numbers, guidelines for recognizing victims and predators, litanies, prayers and scripture passages, it can be a first step in "making a congregation a safe place." With financial support from the Women's Ministries office, this one-dollar booklet is available in English or Spanish from Forward Movement. CSW approached *The Witness* editor and the April 2002 issue presented key issues related to violence against women with sensitivity and insight.

5. Trafficking and Sex Tourism

These are two of the most hideous forms of violence, with the prime target girls ages 13 to 18. One to two million women, girls and boys are "trafficked" each year from less developed to industrialized countries, primarily for sex use but also slave labor for manufacturing, housekeeping and child care. Several legislative steps to increase the effectiveness of United States law enforcement would reduce American men's sex tour participation. CSW has alerted the Government Relations Office to its concern about these issues and recommends joining the "vital voices alert" meeting, www.ecpatusa.org, for additional information.

6. The Power of Language

The 21st Century Survey data show a high correlation between the acceptance of women in leadership positions and the use of inclusive language in liturgy and music. Healthy churches fully incorporate women in their ministry, leadership and language and this contributes to church growth spiritually and numerically. It also has a positive effect on men's participation.

Words, and their images, have enormous power; they seem objective but they convey hidden messages. Words hurt and oppress; they heal and liberate. According to Susan Thistlewaite, Chicago Theological Seminary professor, "words like 'he' and 'men' are supposed to mean 'people' or 'humans' but silently shape our thinking and world view by making women and girls 'linguistically invisible.' Since children think in concrete terms until ten, childhood words form images and symbols that remain throughout life.

The term "laymen" for years meant white males only, thus denying baptismal parity to men of color and women. This prevented either from seeking ordination, election or appointed office in the Episcopal Church. At the same time, the term "who for us men and our salvation" in the Nicene Creed was said to include women and men of color even though they were linguistically invisible. Outdated English grammar rules and the English language's lack of a common gender, third person singular pronoun created much of the current linguistic problem.

CSW has shared its concern with SCLM. A committee member prepared a paper that emphasizes the importance of linguistic visibility for females as well as males in education, music, the lections and liturgy. It is available on the CSW web site and at the Episcopal Women's Caucus booth in Minneapolis.

Given the high correlation between the acceptance of women in leadership positions and expansive language, the 20/20 Task Force's goal to "make disciples of Jesus" will be more readily achieved as materials such as those listed are put into use in the Church.

Enriching Our Worship
The Revised Common Lectionary [1969, revised 1981] preferred globally by many English speaking denominations
The Access Bible, New Revised Standard Version with Apocrypha, Oxford University Press, Inc., 1999

7. The Rise of Fundamentalism–and its Effect on Women and Girls

Theologian Karen Armstrong has described fundamentalism, evident in faiths globally, as "representing a kind of revolt or rebellion against the secular hegemony of the modern world...a widespread dislike and disenchantment with modernity." The Presbyterian, Methodist and Episcopal Churches are confronted with vigorous efforts from within and without to reshape their historic, vital role as the nation's conscience; dismember agencies committed to social justice; take over the governance and leadership of church bodies, and gain control of their fiduciary assets. Religion can liberate or be a tool for oppression.

Elizabeth Proctor-Smith is convinced that authority is the issue. She asks, "who decides how things are supposed to be? Who decides what is orthodox?" In a patriarchal culture "men are allowed to represent everybody...women are not." A cultural war is being waged in which women are exhorted to forego leadership roles and submit to men as the leaders of family, church and society. Fearful of change, fundamentalist groups, religious and secular, target women. Girls and women today stand at a crossroad between the promise of unprecedented advances and deeply entrenched, well-financed barriers to equality. A paper on fundamentalism is available on the CSW web-site or in Minneapolis at the Episcopal Women's Caucus booth.

8. Talking Together as the People of God
The International Anglican Conversations on Human Sexuality final report recommended that "there be opportunities throughout the Communion for ongoing structured conversations regarding difficult issues." The Archbishop of Canterbury commented that the conversations demonstrated that "another way is possible...for working together through difficult issues we face as churches."

CSW commends to the Executive Council the processes developed by the Evangelical Lutheran Church in America (ELCA), the Episcopal Peace Fellowship and the Union of Black Episcopalians, for dialogue models on social and ethical issues including racism, globalization, full baptismal parity and U.S. militarism. The Council should commit itself to prepare a body of trainers who facilitate conversations on the national, diocesan and local levels.

9. Women and Health Care
The Episcopal Church has endorsed the U.S. House of Representatives Resolution 99. It would require Congress by October 2004 to enact legislation to guarantee everyone in the US affordable, cost efficient, comprehensive and easily accessible health care. Dioceses and congregations can join in the effort; for information: www.uhcan.org or www.healthtogether.org.

10. Multiculturism
The United States is increasingly more multiracial and multicultural. Congregations need guidance in ways to warmly welcome those who connect with "Anglican" more than "Episcopal." CSW urges funding for the 20/20 Task Force and the Peace and Justice Ministries Office for materials and training on welcoming immigrants. The Church has long depended on immigration to expand its membership and such an opportunity is present again.

Objectives for the 2003-2006 Triennium
1. Continue to serve in an advisory capacity to the Presiding Bishop, Executive Council and Women's Ministries office on issues affecting women.
2. With women still lacking parity in many dioceses and congregations as well as whole nations, CSW will continue to mobilize women.
3. Monitor the development of resources for meeting the UN Beijing+5 Platform for Action goals.
4. Use a modified version of the *Reaching Toward Wholeness II* survey to study the attitudes and participation of Episcopalians ages 15-30. This will require special funding and will provide valuable information to the 20/20 Task Force.
5. Based on the 2002 Survey, address regional differences in accepting women in leadership. Participate in developing models for leadership training and raising up leaders for the 21st century; promote and work with the "Dialogue Committee" to develop open and inclusive processes of discussion.
6. Partner with Peace and Justice Ministries to:
   - Overcome fundamentalism in the Episcopal Church, the American culture and government at every level.

- Monitor justice issues, such as trafficking, reproductive rights, violence and abuse against women and girls.
- Develop the capacity to respond quickly and competently on key issues that affect women in proposed federal legislation, as well as issues that arise in the United Nations.
- Encourage leaders, religious and secular, to make the world a better place for all, but especially children.

7. Develop educational materials on the trafficking of women, girls and boys.
8. Develop education materials on sex tourism.

Budget for the 2003–2006 Triennium

The Executive Council Committee on the Status of Women will meet approximately 6 times during the next triennium. This will require two meetings per year during the triennium for a total of $45,000.

Resolution A024 Support for CEDAW

1 *Resolved,* the House of _____ concurring, That the 74th General Convention deputies and bishops convey
2 to their senators their strong support for ratification of the United Nations Convention on the Elimination
3 of all Forms of Discrimination against Women (CEDAW).

EXPLANATION
The 1979 United Nations Convention for the Elimination of All Forms of Discrimination Against Women, ratified by over 110 nations, offers hope for raising the status of women universally. The United States is the only industrialized nation that has not ratified CEDAW but the General Convention has long supported it.

Resolution A025 Trafficking of Women, Girls and Boys

1 *Resolved,* the House of _____ concurring, That the 74th General Convention recommends that every
2 diocese bring to the attention of its members the domestic and international problem of trafficking in
3 women, girls and boys as well as any known local connections to trafficking; and be it further
4 *Resolved,* That the Executive Council provide $4,000 to the Committee on the Status of Women to enable
5 identification and development of resource materials to be used by congregations and dioceses to address
6 this problem; and be it further
7 *Resolved,* That the Office of Government Relations put trafficking–especially the sexual abuse of women
8 and young girls---among its top priorities, including working with other denominations and alerting the
9 Public Policy Network of opportunities to address trafficking in their home communities.

Resolution A026 Baptismal Parity

1 *Resolved,* the House of _____ concurring, That the 74th General Convention commit itself to baptismal
2 parity for all members of all ages; and be it further
3 *Resolved,* That the 74th General Convention direct the Executive Council to appoint a special task force for
4 1)interpreting our biblical and theological language and heritage about God and people in ways that
5 include all those created in God's image, 2) offer guidelines to assure linguistic visibility, and 3) introduce
6 same in the everyday worship, music, education, preaching, written materials, and clip art used at the
7 congregational, diocesan and national levels of the Episcopal Church; and be it further
8 *Resolved,* That the task force include theologians, members of the Standing Commission on Liturgy and
9 Music, the Committee on the Status of Women, the House of Bishops' Theology Committee, the
10 Executive Council Anti-Racism Committee, and the Episcopal News Service; and be it further
11 *Resolved,* That the task force publish by 2006 those principles and guidelines with recommendations for
12 introducing them to congregations, the Episcopal Church Center, church-related organizations, staff and
13 media. Many Protestant denominations have such guidelines and stated commitments to linguistic
14 inclusion, which encompass art work as well as language; and be it further
15 *Resolved,* That Baptismal parity is the welcoming of all baptized persons into the Body of Christ, where all
16 are included equally and the grace and gifts bestowed by God are recognized and fully utilized; and be it
17 further

18 *Resolved,* That the Executive Council provide $34,000 for two meetings of the Task Force and $1,500 for
19 publication of the principles and guidelines.

EXPLANATION
Inclusivity and equality are the common denominators in all of Jesus' parables about the household
(kingdom) of God. Today the Church is challenged to look at what it means to receive someone through
baptism into the household of God and to include them fully into its life and ministry.

Resolution A027 Use of Titles

1 *Resolved,* the House of _____ concurring, That the 74th General Convention direct all bodies of ECUSA to
2 respect the baptismal parity of women and men in the church by consistently using language and titles that
3 equally identify women (lay and ordained) with their male counterparts.

EXPLANATION
In conversation, introductions and written documents, the titles or terms of address which are used for
women and men should be consistent but they are often different: For example, introducing a male priest
to someone with a title while introducing a female priest by first name, or sending a letter to all priests in a
diocese addressed to, "Dear Brothers," when there are female clergy in the diocese.

Resolution A028 Palestinian and Afghani Women Support

1 *Resolved,* the House of _____ concurring, That the bishops and deputies of the 74th General Convention
2 convey to their dioceses to reach out to Palestinian and Afghani women and children by using web-sites,
3 such as, http://www.vitalvoices.org/programs/afghan_women/ or www.pcwf.org or earmarking
4 contributions to Jerusalem 2000 or Episcopal Relief and Development.

Resolution A029 Open Dialogue on Difficult Issues

1 *Resolved,* the House of _____ concurring, That the 74th General Convention of the Episcopal Church
2 commits itself to foster moral deliberation on social questions, seeking to be a community where open,
3 passionate, and respectful deliberation of challenging, contemporary issues is expected and encouraged;
4 engage those of diverse classes, genders, ages, races, cultures and perspectives in the deliberation process
5 so that our limited horizons might be expanded and our witness in the world enhanced; address the issues
6 faced by the people of God, in order to equip them for their discipleship and citizenship in the world; and
7 be it further
8 *Resolved,* That the 74th General Convention direct the Peace and Justice Ministries Office and Ethnic and
9 Women's Ministries to collaborate in developing models and trainers, lay and ordained, across the Church
10 to guide conversations on difficult issues facing Americans today; and be it further
11 *Resolved,* That up to $28,000 be allocated from the Program Budget for this work including $6,000 for
12 planning the process and printing materials; $20,000 to bring trainers from dioceses and provinces together
13 to learn the process and $2,000 to sustain the process.

EXPLANATION
The success of the International Anglican Conversations on Human Sexuality, chaired by The Most Rev.
Frank Griswold, offers a model for structured discourse to work through opposing ideas. The Evangelical
Lutheran Church in America has also developed an excellent process. The major expense would be to
prepare a cadre of trainers across the Church to provide skills and structure for the conversations and train
others for an on-going dialogue. Using Church Center staff and trainers already in dioceses or provinces
will keep costs low.

Resolution A030 21st Century Survey Resources

1 *Resolved,* the House of _____ concurring, That the 74th General Convention direct the Episcopal Church
2 Center staff to use data from the 21st Century Survey and other sources to develop educational resources
3 on issues of violence, poverty, justice and inclusion, particularly as these issues pertain to women; and be
4 it further
5 *Resolved,* That $8,000 be allocated from the Program Budget for this work.

EXPLANATION

The Executive Council and its Committee on the Status of Women over the past two triennia have invested considerable energy and funding in researching the current status of women in the Episcopal Church. A next step is to develop and distribute educational resources and programs on inclusion, justice, and violence as these pertain to women in the church and community. Using Church Center staff primarily, the costs could be kept to $4,000 for writers and printing and $4,000 to develop workshop designs.

Resolution A031 A Multicultural, Multiracial Church

1 *Resolved,* the House of _____ concurring, That the 74th General Convention direct the 20/20 Committee,
2 the Executive Council Anti-Racism Committee, the Peace and Justice Ministries, the Ethnic Ministries and
3 Women's Ministries to jointly develop materials and training for diocesan and congregational use on ways
4 to becoming an inclusive, multi-racial and multi-cultural diocese and congregation; and be it further
5 *Resolved,* That $20,000 be allocated from the Program Budget for this purpose.

EXPLANATION

The United States is increasingly more multi-racial and multi-cultural. Congregations need guidance and multi-cultural competence in how to welcome and warmly include those who connect more with "Anglican" than "Episcopal." The Episcopal Church has historically depended on immigration to expand its membership. Costs would be kept at a minimum if the Ethnic, Women's and Peace and Justice Ministry Offices collaborate on this task. The initial cost of defining the needs and developing training models for clergy, local newcomer committees and parish organizations would be $15,000. Developing and printing multilingual training materials for use by dioceses and congregations, $5,000.

Resolution A032 Youth Study

1 *Resolved,* the House of _____ concurring, That the 74th General Convention direct the Committee on the
2 Status of Women, in cooperation with the 20/20 Committee and using a modified version of the 21st
3 Century Survey, to study the attitudes, participation and worship preferences of Episcopalians ages 15-30;
4 and be it further
5 *Resolved,* That $10,000 for the survey and $1,500 for printing be allocated from the Program Budget for
6 this work.

Committee on the Status of Women Endorsements

1. Health Care for all Americans. The Episcopal Church has endorsed the US House of Representatives' Resolution 99 that would require Congress to enact legislation to guarantee everyone in the United States access to affordable, high quality health care by October 2004. Massive grassroots support is needed for its enactment. Contact www.uhcan.org or www.healthtogether.org. to join this effort.
2. Improving Access to and Health Care for Children resolution, submitted by the SCNC.
3. Establishment of a Living Wage resolution, submitted by the SCNC. It will upgrade the status of millions of women and their children in the US, especially those in lower pay scales.
4. SCLM resolutions to include the Rev. Florence Li Tim Oi, first female priest in the Anglican Communion and Florence Nightingale (second reading) in the Lesser Feasts and Fasts Calendar; the continued use of Enriching Our Worship Volumes I and II and SCLM's charge to develop expansive language liturgies for pastoral offices and other rites; authorize these rites to be available in print and electronic media and authorization of the *Revised Common Lectionary.*

This page is intentionally blank.

STANDING
COMMISSIONS

STANDING COMMISSION ON ANGLICAN AND INTERNATIONAL PEACE WITH JUSTICE CONCERNS

www.episcopalchurch.org/gc/ccab/scaipjc/default.html

Membership

The Rt. Rev. Richard L. Shimpfky, *Chair*	El Camino Real, 2003
Ms. Jacqueline B. Scott, *Secretary*	Colorado, 2006
Ms. Mayra Arguelles	Honduras, 2006
Mrs. Jackie B. Batjer	Northwest Texas, 2003
The Rev. Theodora N. Brooks	New York, 2006
The Rt. Rev. Steven Charleston	Massachusetts, 2006, *resigned and not replaced*
Dr. Louie Crew	Newark, 2003, *Member as well as Executive Council liaison*
The Rev. Randolph K. Dales	New Hampshire, 2006
Mr. Fred H. Ellis	Dallas, 2003
The Rt. Rev. J. Gary Gloster	North Carolina, 2006
The Rev. Herbert J. McMullan	Virginia, 2006
Ms. Mary H. Miller	Maryland, 2006
The Rev. Canon Benjamin Musoke-Lubega	Michigan, 2003, *resigned and replaced by*
The Rev. Nancy A.G. Vogele	Vermont
The Rt. Rev. E. Don Taylor	New York, 2003

The Commission extends its sincere thanks to the Rt. Rev. Richard L. Shimpfky for his leadership and his extraordinary gift of himself, his time and his faithfulness. The Commission is also grateful for the professional assistance so freely given it by the Rev. Canon Brian J. Grieves, Director, Peace and Justice Ministries Program, and to Mr. Thomas Hart, Director, Office of Government Relations, Peace and Justice Ministries Program.

COMMISSION REPRESENTATIVES AT GENERAL CONVENTION

Bishop Gary Gloster and Deputy Jacqueline B. Scott are authorized to receive non-substantive amendments to this report.

WORK SUMMARY

The duty of the Standing Commission on Anglican and International Peace with Justice Concerns (SCAIPJC or the Commission) is to develop recommendations and strategies regarding ministry opportunities and concerns shared with other Provinces of the Anglican Communion as to the work of this Church and the Anglican Communion on issues of international peace with justice and to make recommendations to the Presiding Bishop, the Executive Council and the General Convention.

The Commission reaffirmed the Guidelines established by its predecessor Commissions to determine areas of involvement including: a) a significant Anglican presence; b) systemic injustice as evidenced by racism; use of violence as a matter of policy, domination or control; or human suffering; c) availability of adequate and verifiable information with resources for decision-making, including the possibility for consultation with affected parties; d) significant U.S. involvement—political, economic, or military; e) potential for large-scale impact and f) an invitation from the concerned parties.

The Executive Council referred *GC Resolution 2000-A057 Trafficking in Women, Girls and Boys* to SCAIPJC. The issues were examined in two site visits and addressed in the United Nations Millennium Development Goals, Resolution A002. Additionally, in each site visit the commission witnessed examples of the worldwide persecution of gay and lesbian Christians and the need for the conversations called for by Lambeth resolutions.

The Commission met four times, carrying out its work between meetings by site visits, extensive use of email, and internet and other research. The Commission received the written report from the Anglican Peace and Justice Network meeting of November 2001.

Speakers/experts who addressed the AIPJC:
- The Rt. Rev. Arthur Walmsley, former Bishop of Connecticut
- The Very Rev. George L.W. Werner, President of the House of Deputies
- Dr. Douglas Huber, Epidemiologist, Anglican Conference on AIDS in South Africa
- The Rev. Leon Spencer, Washington Office on Africa
- The Rt. Rev. Daniel Deng Bul of Renk Diocese in the Upper Nile of Sudan,
     Chairman, Peace and Justice Committee, House of Bishops of Sudan
- Mr. Adam Isacson, Center for International Policy, Columbia Project
- Ms. Yuki Tatsumi, Center for Strategic and International Studies
- The Rev. Canon Tony Jewiss, Deputy Executive Officer, Office of General Convention
- The Rev. Canon Brian Grieves, Director, Peace and Justice Ministries Program
- Mr. Tom Hart, Director, Episcopal Office of Government Relations, Peace and Justice Ministries Program
- Ms. Jere Skipper, International Policy Analyst, Episcopal Office of Government Relations
- Confidential reports from various U.S. State Department officials

Sub-committees visited:
- Uganda, Kenya and Sudanese bishops (Crew, Dales, McMullan, Scott, Shimpfky),
- Japan and Korea (Crew, Miller, Shimpfky)
- Colombia and Brazil (Batjer, Brooks, Ellis, Gloster)

The Commission sent four resolutions to Executive Council:
- Funding for the Episcopal Dioceses of Colombia
- Opposition to pre-emptive attack by the United States on Iraq
- Interim Report on Sudan
- September 11, 2001 attacks on Washington, D.C. and New York City

The Commission has its own Web site, http://newark.rutgers.edu/~lcrew/scaai.html, established in 1997 by Dr. Louie Crew. Site visit reports and reports from the previous triennium are posted on the web site. It may also be reached through the General Convention web site for the Commission.

Waging Peace in the Midst of War
The Commission's work this triennium was conducted in the context of heightened conflict and increased civilian casualties in Israel and Palestine, the September 11, 2001 attack on the United States, the US military action in Afghanistan, the build-up to war with Iraq, and the threat of nuclear weapons in North Korea, as well as continuing conflicts in other regions of the world.

As civilian and religious leaders use the terminology of traditional Just War principles either to support or to reject the morality of a "war on terror," the SCAIPJC realizes that many people remain unaware of the religious concept of Just War or the clear Anglican and Episcopal teaching on war. The Commission proposes a resolution to put before Episcopalians these traditional resources about the waging of peace and the waging of war, with the hope that widespread discussion and discernment may continue within our household of faith as the Episcopal Church and its members "seek peace and pursue it."

Resolution A033 Just and Unjust Wars
1   *Resolved,* the House of _____ concurring, That the 74th General Convention, recalling the longstanding
2   Episcopal Church view, originally adopted by the 1930 Lambeth Conference and by the 1931 General
3   Convention, that "war as a method of settling international disputes is incompatible with the teaching and
4   example of our Lord Jesus Christ," calls upon all members of the Episcopal Church, in discussions about
5   war and especially the strategy of preemptive strikes, to seriously consider and utilize the Just War criteria
6   developed over the centuries and generally expressed as follows:

7　First, whether lethal force may be used is governed by the following criteria:

8 • Just cause: Force may be used only to correct a grave, public evil, i.e., aggression or massive violation
9　　of the basic rights of whole populations.
10 • Comparative justice: While there may be rights and wrongs on all sides of a conflict, to override the
11　　presumption against the use of force, the injustice suffered by one part must significantly outweigh
12　　that suffered by the other.
13 • Legitimate authority: Only duly constituted public authorities may use deadly force or wage war.
14 • Right intention: Force may be used only in a truly just cause and solely for that purpose.
15 • Probability of success: Arms may not be used in a futile cause or in a case where disproportionate
16　　measures are required to achieve success.
17 • Proportionality: The overall destruction expected from the use of force must be outweighed by the
18　　good to be achieved.
19 • Last resort: Force may be used only after all peaceful alternatives have been seriously tried and
20　　exhausted.
21　These criteria taken as a whole must be satisfied in order to override the strong presumption against the
22　use of force.
23　　Second, the just war tradition seeks also to curb the violence of war through restraint on armed combat
24　between the contending parties by imposing the following moral standards for the conduct of armed conflict:

25 • Noncombatant immunity: Civilians may not be the objects of direct attack, and military personnel
26　　must take due care to avoid and minimize indirect harm to civilians.
27 • Proportionality: In the conduct of hostilities, efforts must be made to attain military objectives with no
28　　more force than is militarily necessary and to avoid disproportionate collateral damage to civilian life
29　　and property.
30 • Right intention: Even in the midst of conflict, the aim of political and military leaders must be peace
31　　with justice, so that acts of vengeance and indiscriminate violence, whether by individuals, military
32　　units or governments, are forbidden; and be it further
33　*Resolved,* That when legitimate civilian authority determines that war is justified, members of the
34　Episcopal Church recall our Lord's teaching to love our enemies, counsel that participation in or refusal to
35　participate in any war is a discernment process requiring deep reflection and prayer with humility, and
36　acknowledge that one participates in war with great reluctance, always seeking God's mercy and
37　forgiveness.

Development Goals

It is the Commission's experience, reinforced throughout the triennium, that, despite the existence of phenomenal abundance in wealth and technology, much of humankind continues to labor under the seemingly intractable problems related to poverty, a dearth of educational opportunities, grossly excessive rates of malnutrition and disease, the continuing oppression of women and the scandalously abusive squandering of the gift of millions of children, many of whom are seriously at risk and subject to cruel and early death. This specter was evident in all areas where we traveled as guests of the local Church.

In the face of this juggernaut of carnage, the Commission's hopes were buoyed by the United Nations' Millennium Development Goals. It is our conviction that these Development Goals provide a relevant framework for the church to live out the Gospel of Jesus Christ through and with our Church partners around globally. All 189 United Nation member states have pledged to meet its goals by the year 2015.

Resolution A034 United Nations Millennium Development Goals

1　*Resolved,* the House of _____ concurring, That the 74th General Convention endorse and embrace the
2　United Nations Millennium Development Goals, and urge the Episcopal Church to use the goals as an
3　effective framework in its development efforts; and be it further
4　*Resolved,* That the United States government, as one of the 189 national signatories to the United Nations
5　Millennium Development Goals, be encouraged to provide appropriate leadership and resources toward
6　international efforts to implement these goals through strategies to include, but not limited to, debt relief,

7   development assistance and trade policy.
8   These goals are:
9   1.   Eradicate extreme poverty and hunger
10   • Reduce by half the proportion of people living on less than a dollar a day.
11   • Reduce by half the proportion of people who suffer from hunger.
12   2.   Achieve universal primary education
13   • Ensure that all boys and girls complete a full course of primary schooling.
14   3.   Promote gender equality and empower women
15   • Eliminate gender disparity in primary and secondary education preferably by 2005 and at all
16   levels by 2015.
17   4.   Reduce child mortality
18   • Reduce by two-thirds the mortality rate among children under 5.
19   5.   Improve maternal health
20   • Reduce by two-thirds the maternal mortality ratio.
21   6.   Combat HIV/AIDS, malaria and other diseases
22   • Halt and begin to reverse the spread of HIV/AIDS
23   • Halt and begin to reverse the incidence of malaria and other major diseases.
24   7.   Ensure environmental sustainability
25   • Integrate the principles of sustainable development into country policies and programs;
26   reverse loss of environmental resources.
27   • Reduce by half the proportion of people without sustainable access to safe drinking water.
28   • Achieve significant improvement in lives of at least 100 million slum dwellers, by 2020.
29   8.   Develop a global partnership for development
30   • Develop further an open trading and financial system that is rule-based, predictable and non-
31   discriminatory. Includes a commitment to good governance, development and poverty
32   reduction – nationally and internationally.
33   • Address the least developed countries' special needs. This includes tariff- and quota-free
34   access for their exports, enhances debt relief for heavily indebted poor countries, cancellation
35   of official bilateral debt, and more generous official development assistance for countries
36   committed to poverty reduction.
37   • Address the special needs of landlocked and small island developing States.
38   • Deal comprehensively with developing countries' debt problems through national and
39   international measures to make debt sustainable in the long term.
40   • In cooperation with the developing countries, develop decent and productive work for youth.
41   • In cooperation with pharmaceutical companies, provide access to affordable essential drugs in
42   developing countries.
43   • In cooperation with the private sector, make available the benefits of new technologies –
44   especially information and communications technologies.

Africa
Africa is a continent of extreme contrasts, a place of widespread desperation mixed with great hope. One of its greatest hopes is the Anglican Church in Africa, often the most effective vehicle for change and assistance, whether dealing with AIDS, orphans, education, civil unrest, or religious and territorial clashes. The Commission vigorously supports the adoption by the Episcopal Church of the United Nations Millennium Development Goals (Resolution A034) to be used as a framework for efforts in support of our African sisters and brothers.

Great Lakes Region – AIDS, Poverty and Injustice
The Great Lakes African nations of Congo, Uganda, Kenya, Tanzania, Burundi and Rwanda, along with the war-ravaged country of Sudan, comprise one of three areas worldwide studied by SCAIPJC this triennium. Five commission members traveled to Uganda in 2001, where they met with Archbishop Livingstone

Mpalanyi-Nkoyoyo of Uganda and provincial leaders. In addition, the team spent two days with 21 of the 24 bishops of the Episcopal Church of Sudan, gathered for a Provincial meeting in Kampala, Uganda. One commission member went to Kenya to meet with Archbishop David Gitari.

Commission members went to the Great Lakes Region with four goals: to learn more about AIDS and the Church's efforts to combat it; to give attention to the role of education and the plight of women and children; to witness the effects of globalization and urbanization on this part of Africa; and to understand more about Christian-Islamic tensions and regional conflicts.

The astounding numbers associated with AIDS in Africa are almost beyond comprehension. In Uganda, the Anglican Church is a leading force in the effort to educate people about AIDS and to respond to its scourge. Uganda has a population of some 20 million people, nearly 8 million of whom are Anglicans. Almost 1.5 million people are living with AIDS in that country. There are already 1.7 million AIDS orphans in Uganda. And that is only one country. In Africa, there are already 10 million children orphaned by AIDS, and researchers predict that by the year 2010 the number will grow to 44 million – equal to the total of all the elementary school children living in the United States east of the Mississippi River.

AIDS in Africa has been the subject of previous General Convention resolutions, and more resolutions are not needed. AIDS is Africa's 21st century plague. Medicine, clinics, education and pastoral care are urgently needed, but politics, profits and poverty impede the good work being done by the churches in these countries. Africa desperately needs the continuous attention of our churches, while Americans need to be challenged to act out of our abundance to generate much larger financial contributions.

Resolution A035 Implement Humanitarian Goals in Africa

1   *Resolved,* the House of _____ concurring, That the 74th General Convention, in response to widespread
2   humanitarian needs in Africa, commend those churches in Africa fighting AIDS, poverty and injustice,
3   and calls on the Episcopal Church at all levels to partner with the Anglican Churches in Africa and other
4   agencies to implement the United Nations Millennium Development Goals in Africa; and be it further
5   *Resolved*, That this convention commit $100,000 per year for three years through the Partnership Office
6   for Africa to support a church-wide campaign to implement humanitarian development goals in Africa.

War-ravaged Sudan

Sudan is suffering the longest uninterrupted civil war in the world. The current conflict has persisted for 20 years, but the country has been embroiled in civil war for 36 of the past 47 years since independence in 1956. People all over Sudan are suffering as a consequence.

More than 2 million Sudanese are estimated to have died of causes directly or indirectly linked to war and repressive Sudanese government policies. In addition, according to the best available estimates, more than 300 people die per day in Sudan because of war-related causes. Sudan's death toll is larger than the combined fatalities in Bosnia, Kosovo, Afghanistan, Chechnya, Somalia and Algeria. Twice as many Sudanese have perished in the past two decades as have perished in all the war-related deaths of Americans in the past 200 years.

The civil war that has raged in Sudan since the country gained independence from Britain is a complicated conflict. It pits a predominantly Arab population in the north against a mostly African population in the south. It involves an Islamic government, backed by the National Islamic Front, which pushes for the radical implementation of Islamic law called Sharia, against the mostly Christian communities in the west and south. But it is even more complicated. In the south there are at least two factions, one of predominantly Dinka tribes seeking reform and the other based in the Nuer tribes which seek full independence.

In our meetings, the Sudanese bishops did not ask for military support or for weapons. They want the world to find a way to stop the war. As Bishop Daniel Deng Bul put it, "I was born in the war, and I am getting old in the war. Many of our children for generations have had no schooling. We are losing our language, our culture, because we have been at war for almost half a century. When is the world going to come and rescue us?"

The 73rd General Convention of the Episcopal Church in 2000 adopted Resolution A130: Human Rights: Solidarity with Persecuted Christians in the Sudan. It called on the United States government to assign the highest priority to advancing a just peace in Sudan.

In 2001, the Commission reported to the Executive Council, and the Council adopted a resolution condemning the discrimination against Christians and again calling on the U.S. government to assign the highest priority to advancing a just peace in Sudan.

North-East Asia

Relations among the countries of North-East Asia[1] are delicate, especially between Korea and Japan. The long history of Japanese occupation of Korea and oppression of Korean people is still a source of great pain, but the churches are giving priority to reconciliation. The Koreans speak of the Korean Peninsula, rather than of South and North Korea. The commitment to reunification is very strong and something not widely understood in the United States. The Episcopal Church needs to advocate U.S. policies and practices which foster reconciliation.

The Cold War has not ended. The damage done by President Bush's "axis of evil" rhetoric is extensive and regrettable. The people we met view their neighbors differently. They are realistic about the north and its leaders, but they do not demonize them and do not ordinarily feel threatened by them. Diplomacy is the way to handle ongoing tensions and concerns in North-East Asia. Confrontation, patronizing and demonizing do not solve any existing problems but rather exacerbate them.

Japan is host to 47,000 U.S. troops. The U.S. Seventh Fleet is based at Yokosuka, and the U.S. occupies 75% of Okinawa. For many years the U.S. has exerted pressure on Japan to re-arm, to take a fuller share of responsibility for its own defense, and currently to join more fully in "the war on terrorism." This directly contradicts the Japanese Constitution and its Article 9 "pacifist clause," which limits military power to self-defense. This does not mean that Japan's defense force is small; indeed it is substantial. But the continued pressure exerted by the U.S. diminishes hopes for peace and disarmament and is a source of conflict in Japan.

In Korea, 37,000 U.S. troops in 96 installations join the troops of the Republic of Korea in a standoff with the troops to the North. There are numerous instances of rape and other abuses of Korean citizens by U.S. soldiers. The United States needs to revise the Status of Forces Agreement (SOFA) with the Republic of Korea. The Korean people must be able to trust the justice rendered under either U.S. military or Korean courts in cases of abuse by U.S. troops. The current SOFA does not adequately address these injustices.

Economic and social dislocation can be expected if the United States moves to reduce the land used by U.S. military bases and return it to the Korea and Japan peoples. Sectors of society have become dependent on the U.S., for example for jobs. In addition, the land and waters will inevitably be littered with munitions and toxins. The U.S. must commit to safe and complete cleanup.

Signs of Hope

Doors can open which have long been assumed locked forever. Japan and the Republic of Korea co-hosted the World Cup soccer matches in Spring 2002. The flags of both countries were posted on poles in both capital cities. This was astonishing, knowing the history of Korea-Japan relationships. If it can happen once it can happen again.

It is critical that the Episcopal Church remain in dialogue and a working partnership with the Nippon Sei Ko Kai and the Anglican Church of Korea and, whenever possible, to include the China Christian Council. While in Seoul, we participated in the Anglican International Conference for the Peaceful Reunification of Korea and Peace in North-East Asia. This conference inaugurates a closer relationship among partner churches.

---

[1] "North-East Asia" is the usage in all papers received from Korea.

Reconciliation has its political difficulties but progress towards it seems to be broader than in the past. Whatever we can do to encourage our national leaders to respect these efforts will be welcomed by our partners in North-East Asia. U.S. policy too often interrupts and destabilizes regional relationships and aspirations. The churches can make a difference in fostering people-to-people diplomacy, in supporting nonviolent peace activism, and in urging citizen action with our own elected leadership in the United States.

SungKongHoe University, the international conference site, is a sign of hope. No other university has a concentration in non-governmental organizations (NGO) studies, preparing new leadership for civil society. SungKongHoe University's program is a commendable example of what a church-related academic institution can accomplish in the ongoing effort to shape a peaceful world.

Resolution A036 Korean Peninsula and the Democratic Peoples Republic of Korea

1   *Resolved,* the House of _____ concurring, That the 74th General Convention of the Episcopal Church in
2   the United States of America support the Anglican Church of Korea in its advocacy for the peaceful
3   reunification of the Korean peninsula; and be it further
4   *Resolved,* That the Episcopal Church through its own offices and agencies and by appeal to the United
5   States Government urge special attention and aid to the relief of humanitarian needs and development of
6   the Democratic Peoples Republic of Korea (North Korea) including poverty alleviation, food aid, energy
7   development, transportation, education and protection of human rights and the environment; and be it
8   further
9   *Resolved,* That the Church urge the end of political demonization and militaristic rhetoric toward the
10   Democratic Peoples Republic of Korea and its leaders in an effort to establish a more peaceful climate in
11   the community of nations.

Resolution A037 Status of Forces Agreement with Korea

1   *Resolved,* the House of _____ concurring, That the 74th General Convention of the Episcopal Church in
2   the United States of America urge the United States Government in its renegotiation of the Status of
3   Forces Agreement (SOFA) with the Republic of Korea to give special attention to:
4   1. The rights of Korean citizens to equal treatment and legal redress of grievances and adequate
5   compensation to victims of weapons practice and testing; pollution of the environment; personal abuse,
6   especially of a violent or sexual nature; and other deleterious effects of U.S. military presence and activity;
7   and
8   2. U.S. accountability for troops' misconduct and the right of victims to have U.S. troops tried in local
9   courts, including the right to extradite personnel who have been removed from the host country; and be it
10   further
11   *Resolved,* That the Episcopal Church urge the U.S. government in all SOFA negotiations to recognize the
12   rights of local people and assure their access to all mechanisms for redress of their grievances against U.S.
13   military personnel; and be it further
14   *Resolved,* That the eventual goal be the phasing out of U.S. military bases in Korea.

Resolution A038 Peace and Justice Studies and Training

1   *Resolved,* the House of _____ concurring, That the 74th General Convention of the Episcopal Church
2   commend to Episcopal colleges and schools the inclusion in their curriculum of peace and justice studies
3   and education and training for service and careers in non-governmental organizations and civil society.

Colombia and Brazil

Repeatedly discussed during the visit to Columbia was the daily reality of survival in the midst of more than 40 years of conflict between various groups, including the government, the guerilla groups, and para-military groups. The conflict has resulted in the forced acquisition/abandonment of land, displacement of the civilian population (estimated at 1,000 people per day) including women and children, kidnapping, and forced use of child combatants. Of every 100 people displaced, 55 are estimated to be women and children and 65 are under the age of 18. In 2001 over 3,000 people were reported to have been kidnapped.

After worship at the Diocesan Cathedral in Bogota and meeting its congregation, our group proceeded to discussions with non-governmental and governmental agencies. The focus of these agencies was on human rights, displaced persons, criminal and political activity associated with the civil unrest, and the involvement of the United States government through Plan Colombia. Our visit included meeting local Colombian agencies, the United Nations High Commissioner for Human Rights, and the United States Ambassador.

The group then traveled to Quibdo, a city in northwest Colombia, to meet with members of the Church and visit several settlements of displaced people. Colombia is second only to Sudan in the number of internally displaced people in the world. This visit reinforced the human tragedy that is a daily fact of life for the people of Colombia. Bishop Francisco Duque gave the most meaningful description of life for people in the church: "The Episcopal Church in Colombia is living between the cross and the rifle."

Subsequent to our visit, recommendations were made to, and a resolution passed by Executive Council, recognizing the suffering of the people of Colombia and the efforts of the Episcopal Church in Colombia to make a significant contribution to bringing peace and stability to this country.

The group continued to Brazil, which has the world's eighth largest economy, yet over 32 million people live on less than $1.00 a day. In our meeting with Brazilian Congressman Dr. Marcos Rolim, the Rt. Rev. Orlando Santos de Oliveira, and the Rt. Rev. Luiz Prado, six items were identified in Brazil's human rights agenda. These are violence and crime, abandoned/abused children, homes for the elderly, psychiatric care, police violence, and discrimination against minorities (including blacks, indigenous people, homosexuals). The unbalanced concentration of wealth in Brazil creates extreme poverty.

The Episcopal Anglican Church in Brazil is working with the National Movement of Landless/Jobless People. The people of this organization have lost their land and jobs and understand first-hand the social mechanisms that produce injustice and misery. One of the methods being used by this organization, with government support, is progressive land reform. Their activism has set in motion political alternatives to end these inequities. In the visit to the landless/jobless settlements, the SCAIPJC representatives witnessed the integrity and resolve of the people to survive and improve their situation.

As a result of this visit, we commend the Southern Diocese of the Episcopal Anglican Church of Brazil in its support of impoverished, landless, jobless people, and for building ecumenical relationships in the fight for justice. We also commend Brazil manufacture of eight of the 15 drugs used to fight HIV/AIDS.

Goals and Objectives for the Coming Triennium
We recommend that the Standing Commission on Anglican and International Peace with Justice Concerns continue to work on policy recommendations including strategies for common ministry opportunities with the Anglican Communion. Because the world is changing so rapidly, we are reluctant, in January 2003, to suggest priorities for the next triennium. We urge that SCAIPJC continue to use the stated Guidelines established in 1995.

Financial Report
The Commission was budgeted for $57,000 for the 2000-2003 Triennium. At the time of this report, SCAICJP had expended $56,357 of its budget.

The Standing Commission on Anglican and International Peace with Justice Concerns will meet approximately four times and make three site visits during the next triennium. This will require $20,000 in 2004, $40,000 in 2005 and $12,000 in 2006 for a total of $72,000.

STANDING COMMISSION ON CONSTITUTION AND CANONS
www.episcopalchurch.org/gc/ccab/sccc/default.html

Membership

The Rev. Canon George W. Brandt Jr., *Chair*	New York, 2003
Mr. Paul Cooney, *Secretary*	Washington, 2003
Ms. Rosalie Simmonds Ballentine	Virgin Islands, 2006
Mr. Duncan A. Bayne	Olympia, 2006
Mr. William Fleener	Western Michigan, 2006
Mr. Richard J. Hoskins	Chicago, 2003
The Rev. Gregory A. Jacobs	Ohio, 2006
The Rev. Stan Runnels	Mississippi, 2006
The Rt. Rev. Stacy Fred Sauls	Lexington, 2006
The Rt. Rev. Catherine M. Waynick	Indianapolis, 2003
Ms. D. Rebecca Snow	Alaska, 2003 Member as well as *Executive Council liaison*

The Right Rev. Charles E. Jenkins (Louisiana) was appointed to a six year term in 2000 but resigned from the Commission in February 2002 and took no part in any subsequent deliberations of the SCCC.

COMMISSION REPRESENTATIVES AT GENERAL CONVENTION
Bishop Stacy Fred Sauls and Deputy Duncan A. Bayne are authorized to receive non-substantive amendments to this report.

SUMMARY OF THE COMMISSION'S WORK

The Standing Commission on Constitution and Canons ("the Commission" or "SCCC") met in Atlanta, Georgia in February 2001, Bethesda, Maryland in February, 2002, and in Chicago, Illinois in September and December 2002. It also met in two conference calls. At its organizational meeting the Commission elected the Rev. Canon George W. Brandt Jr. as its Chair and Paul E. Cooney as its Secretary. At its initial meeting and in subsequent meetings the Commission received comment and took action as reflected in this report.

Revisions to Title III Pursuant to Resolution A073 of the 73rd General Convention
The 73rd General Convention, sitting in Denver in 2000, adopted **Resolution A073**, as follows:
Resolved, the House of Deputies concurring, that in implementation of the priority of the Episcopal Church to make disciples and apostles at all levels of the Church, the Standing Commission on Ministry Development be requested, in consultation with the Standing Commission on Constitution and Canons, to undertake a full review of the Title III Canons, said review to be informed by the report entitled, "Toward a Theology of Ministry," as well as other reports and papers on the subject of the theology of Ministry; and be it further
Resolved, that the Standing Commission on Ministry Development prepare and present to the 74th General Convention any proposed revisions to the Title III Canons…..

In furtherance of its charge under this resolution, SCCC appointed four of its members to work throughout the triennium with SCMD in its preparation of proposed changes toTitle III. These were the Right Reverend Stacy Fred Sauls, Ms. Rosalie Simmonds Ballentine, Mr. William Fleener and Ms. D. Rebecca Snow, all of whom spent time with SCMD during its meetings, or in reviewing material outside of meetings. In addition, the entire SCCC devoted the bulk of its meeting in December, 2002 in Chicago to reviewing the package of changes the SCMD advised it was going to propose, and suggesting editorial corrections to assist internal consistency and with other Canons. The Commission's suggested revisions were presented to SCMD, which met to review those revisions and finalize its own report to the General Convention after SCCC's last meeting. Therefore, the final proposal of SCMD has not been reviewed or approved by SCCC.

Study of Disciplinary Canons

The 73rd General Convention, in response to comments from SCCC from the prior triennium and other commentary, adopted **Resolution A028**, as follows:

Resolved, The House of Bishops concurring, That the General Convention establish, pursuant to Joint Rule 23, a Task Force of not less than 6 or more than 12 persons, of whom one-half shall be appointed by the Standing Commission on Ministry Development and one-half shall be appointed by the Standing Commission on Constitution and Canons; and, that in light of the Church's theology and the Church's experience, the Task Force: (1) assess the present models of church discipline, as reflected both in the policies and procedures addressing allegations of clergy misconduct and in Title IV of the national canons of the Episcopal Church; (2) study and explore other models for addressing misconduct, such as the disciplinary models used by physicians, professors, lawyers and other professionals; and (3) at or before the 74th General Convention, deliver a report of its findings and recommendations to the Standing Commission on Ministry Development, The Standing Commission on Constitution and Canons, and the Committee on Sexual Exploitation, and the 74th General Convention: and (4) at or before the 75th General Convention, deliver its final report of such findings and recommendations to the same bodies;....

At its initial meeting in February, 2001, the Commission appointed the Right Reverend Catherine M. Waynick, Duncan A. Bayne and Steven Hutchinson to represent SCCC on the Task Force. The Rev. Canon George Brandt, Jr. subsequently also joined the Task Force on behalf of SCCC. The Commission further agreed that in addition to appointments to be made by the Standing Commission on Ministry Development, several appointments should be allocated to be made by the Committee on Sexual Exploitation. The Task Force has met on several occasions and offers a report in this Blue Book .

On the subject of Title IV, it has been noted by SCCC that a number of Dioceses have failed to conform their diocesan canons to the requirements of Title IV. The Commission is concerned about the risk non-conforming dioceses pose to the rights of both complainants and accused, points out that it is a requirement of the canons that each diocese be in conformity with Title IV, and urges each diocese to make necessary amendments at the earliest possible moment.

The Commission also received a number of comments regarding the absence of recommended forms and procedures for application of Title IV in a consistent fashion, and is exploring with others the potential for generating a procedures manual to assist those who participate in Title IV proceedings on an infrequent basis. Regardless, SCCC urges each diocese to educate all responsible parties on the procedures to be followed.

Finally, concern has been raised over the absence of any compilations of prior opinions issued under Title IV, and of the desire for some office in which to record and retrieve such opinions for the guidance of others attempting to apply Title IV principles, or to learn from their prior application to others.

Update Concerning Preparation of Supplement to White & Dykman

The Commission has expressed concerns over several triennia about the need for a comprehensive supplement to the 1981 edition of the *Annotated Constitution and Canons for the Government of the Protestant Episcopal Church of the United States of America, otherwise known as the Episcopal Church,* commonly referred to as "White and Dykman." Major canonical and constitutional changes have occurred in 1994, 1997, and 2000, none of which are reflected in White and Dykman. The Commission has been advised that the drafting of the Supplement is nearing completion, and publication may occur as funding is identified.

Compliance with Canon 1.2.2.(n)(2)

The Commission continues to refrain from judicial interpretation of the body of church law in accordance with the limitations expressed in its authority and duties assigned by Canon 1.2.2.(n)(2).

RESOLUTIONS
Resolution A039 Amend Article II, Section 2 of the Constitution, First Reading
1   *Resolved,* the House of _____ concurring, That the second sentence of Article II, Section 2 of the
2   Constitution be amended to read as follows:
3   Section 2. ....But if the election shall have taken place within ~~three months next~~ 120 days before the
4   meeting of General Convention, the consent of the House of Deputies shall be required in place of that of a
5   majority of the Standing Committees.
  EXPLANATION
The proposed amendment picks up a time limit changed in most other applicable places in 1997. The Church's experience is that it often takes more than three months to obtain all the required consents to the election of a Bishop.

Resolution A40 Amend Canon l.l.2(n)
1   *Resolved,* the House of _____ concurring, That Canon I.1.2(n) be amended by adding this subsection:
2   (6) A Standing Commission on **Liturgy and Music** consisting of 16 members (4 Bishops, 4 Priests and/or
3   Deacons and 8 Lay Persons). In addition, the Custodian of the Book of Common Prayer shall be a member
4   *ex officio* with voice, but without vote. The Standing Commission shall:
5   (i)   Discharge such duties as shall be assigned to it by the General Convention as to policies and
6   strategies concerning the common worship of this Church.
7   (ii) Collect, collate and catalogue material bearing upon possible future revisions of The Book of
8   Common Prayer.
9   (iii) Cause to be prepared and to present to the General Convention recommendations concerning the
10   Lectionary, Psalter, and offices for special occasions as authorized or directed by the General
11   Convention or House of Bishops.
12   (iv) Recommend to the General Convention authorized translations of the Holy Scripture from which the
13   Lessons prescribed in the Book of Common Prayer are to be read.
14   (v) Receive and evaluate requests for consideration of individuals or groups to be included in the
15   Calendar of the Church year and make recommendations thereon to the General Convention for
16   acceptance or rejection.
17   (vi) Collect, collate and catalogue material bearing upon possible future revisions of The Hymnal 1982
18   and other musical publications regularly in use in this Church and encourage the composition of new
19   musical materials.
20   (vii) Cause to be prepared and present to the General Convention recommendations concerning the
21   musical settings of liturgical texts and rubrics, and norms as to liturgical music and the manner of its
22   rendition.
23   (viii)At the direction of General Convention, serve the Church in matters pertaining to policies and
24   strategies concerning Church music.
  EXPLANATION
The 72nd General Convention, convened in Philadelphia, July, 1997, adopted a revised structure for many of the Church's Standing Commissions, including the Standing Commission on Liturgy and Music. The legislation was adopted by the House of Deputies with the title of "Standing Commission on Common Worship," but the title was amended in the House of Bishops to "Liturgy and Music". This amendment was not placed on the calendar of the House of Deputies for concurrence in the amendment. This matter was never challenged but was discovered during the revision process for the 2000 edition of Constitution & Canons. See also, "Editors Note", page 18, Constitution & Canons 2000.

Resolution A041 Ratify Actions of Standing Commission on Liturgy and Music
1   *Resolved,* the House of _____ concurring, That all actions taken by and in the name of the Standing
2   Commission on Liturgy and Music since the adjournment sine die of the 72nd General Convention, be and
3   the same hereby are ratified in all respects.

Resolution A042 Amend Canon I.1.9

1 *Resolved,* the House of _____ concurring, That Canon I.1.9 be amended as follows:
2 Sec.9. The Treasurer <u>of the General Convention</u> shall have authority to borrow, in behalf and in the name
3 of the General Convention, such a sum as may be judged by the Treasurer to be necessary to help defray
4 the expense of the General Convention, with the approval of the Presiding Bishop and the Executive
5 Council.

EXPLANATION

This resolution amends a 1994 Canon (Canon 1.1.9) which begins with the phrase "The Treasurer of the General Convention." The words "of the General Convention" were omitted, however, from the original text when it was printed in both the Blue Book and the Journal. The phrase should have been printed with an overstrike in the original and final text of the Journal if the General Convention's intention was to delete the phrase. The phrase was not included in the Constitution & Canons 1997, page 23. As there is more than one Treasurer referenced in the Canons, it is useful to maintain the qualifier as to which Treasurer was being granted the authority to borrow.

SCCC NOTE: Certain proposed canonical changes were referred in draft form by the Standing Commission on Stewardship and Development to SCCC for review at its December, 2002, meeting. The following resolution is the product of that review by SCCC. It is being printed here in the SCCC report as an accommodation to the Standing Commission on Stewardship and Development (SCSD). Any comments or inquiries regarding the substance of these proposed changes should be directed to the SCSD.

Resolution A043 Amend Canon I.6.1

1 *Resolved,* the House of _____ concurring, That Canon I.6.1 be amended to read as follows:
2 Sec. 1. A report of every Parish and other Congregation of this Church shall be prepared annually for the
3 year ending December 31 preceding, in the form authorized by the Executive Council and approved by the
4 Committee on the State of the Church, and shall be filed not later than March 1 with the Bishop of the
5 Diocese, or, where there is no Bishop, with the ecclesiastical authority of the Diocese. The Bishop or the
6 ecclesiastical authority, as the case may be, shall keep a copy and submit the report to the Executive
7 Council not later than May 1. In every Parish <u>or other Congregation</u> the preparation and filing of this
8 report shall be the joint duty of the Rector ~~and Vestry; and in every other Congregation~~ the duty of the
9 Member of the Clergy in charge thereof <u>and the lay leadership. Before the filing thereof the report shall be</u>
10 <u>approved by the Vestry or bishop's committee or mission council.</u> This report shall include the following
11 information:
12 (1) (unchanged) and (2) (unchanged)
13 (3) such other relevant information as is needed to secure an accurate view of the state of this Church, as
14 required by the approved form<u>, including: the average Sunday attendance, total plate and pledge income,</u>
15 <u>total plate and pledge income divided by average Sunday attendance, total operating revenues, operating</u>
16 <u>revenues divided by average Sunday attendance, total number of pledging units, total amount pledged, and</u>
17 <u>average annual pledge derived by divided by the number of pledging units.</u>

EXPLANATION

The information supplied in the parochial report is essential to planning by the diocese and national churches, but it is even more vital that the leadership of congregations be fully engaged in the process and annually review the statistical data associated with the congregation. Since compilations of past data will now be provided to congregations, review of new data will help assure greater understanding and awareness of historical data and trend.

Resolution A044 Amend Canon I.17.1(c)

1 *Resolved,* the House of _____ concurring, That Canon I.17.1(c) be amended to read as follows:
2 (c) It is expected that all adult members of this Church, after appropriate instruction, will have made a
3 mature public affirmation of their faith and commitment to the responsibilities of their Baptism and will
4 have been confirmed or received <u>by the laying on of hands</u> by a Bishop of this Church or by a Bishop of a

5   Church in communion with this Church. Those who have previously made a mature public commitment in
6   another Church may be received <u>by the laying on of hands by a Bishop of this Church</u>, not confirmed.
    EXPLANATION
    This added language makes the intent of I.17.1(c) clearer and by stipulating reception is by a Bishop with
    the laying on of hands brings the language of this section into consistency with 1.17.1.d. It in not intended
    to in any way alter the substance of the provision.

Resolution A045 Amend Canon I.17.2

1   *Resolved,* the House of _____ concurring, That Canon 1.17.2 be amended to read as follows:
2   <u>(a) All members of this Church who have received Holy Communion in this Church at least three times</u>
3   <u>during the preceding year are to be considered communicants of this Church.</u>
4   <u>(b)</u> For the purposes of statistical consistency throughout the Church, communicants sixteen years of age
5   and over are to be considered adult communicants.

    EXPLANATION
    The definition of "communicants" was deleted from Canon I.17.2 by action of the last General
    Convention, in connection with amendments to statistical reporting requirements. The Commission
    believes that this deletion was unfortunate, as "communicant" is a term used throughout the Canons, and
    should be defined to give consistency in its use. This restores the definition of "communicant" to the
    Canons.

Title III

As noted earlier in this report, a number of changes to Title III are proposed by the Standing Commission on
Ministry Development. Although the SCCC has reviewed these changes in draft form, it has not reviewed the
final form and can offer no opinion on them. A corrective resolution is necessary, however, for Canon
III.22.1(e).

Resolution A046 Amend Canon III.22.1(e)

1   *Resolved,* the House of _____ concurring, That Canon III.22.1(e) be amended as follows:
2   (e) The Secretary of the <u>body</u> (Convention) electing a Bishop Diocesan, Bishop Coadjutor, or Bishop
3   Suffragan, shall inform the Presiding Bishop promptly of the name of the person elected. It shall be the
4   duty of the Bishop-elect to notify the Presiding Bishop of his acceptance or declination of the election, at
5   the same time as the Bishop-elect notifies the electing diocese.

    EXPLANATION
    The word "Convention" that appears in the text of Canon III. 22. 1 (e) is a change from the word "body"
    which was the usage in the Constitution & Canons 1994. The replacement word "Convention" was not
    italicized, nor the word "body" struck out, as required by Canon and legislative form. The word "body" is
    significant in the context of this Canon, as Bishops may be elected by other than Convention.

Resolution A047 Amend Canon IV.14.13

1   *Resolved,* the House of _____ concurring, That Canon IV.14.13be amended to add "<u>(a)</u>" to the title of the
2   existing section, and add a new subparagraph (b) to read as follows:
3   <u>(b) Any Bishop exercising authority as provided in this Title (i) who is related by blood or marriage to the</u>
4   <u>Respondent or any alleged victim, or (ii) who reasonably believes himself or herself unable to render a fair</u>
5   <u>and independent sentence, shall be disqualified and excused from service in connection with the matter.</u>

    EXPLANATION
    Canon IV.12.4.(a) assumes there might be circumstances in which a Bishop would be disqualified in a
    Title IV proceeding. However, the Canon does not describe the circumstances under which such
    disqualification might occur. This amendment provides clarity relative to the phrase "... or in case that
    Bishop is disqualified..." in IV.12.4.(a)

Resolution A048 Amend Canon IV.4.16(d)

1 *Resolved,* the House of _____ concurring, That Canon IV.4.16(d) be amended to read as follows:
2 (d) If the Respondent fails or refuses to answer or otherwise enter an appearance, except for reasonable
3 cause to be allowed by the Court, the Church Attorney may, no sooner than thirty days after the answer is
4 due, move for Summary Judgment in accordance with the Rules of Procedure. If the motion is granted <u>the</u>
5 <u>Bishop shall be notified</u>, and the Respondent shall be given notice that Sentence of Admonition,
6 Suspension or Deposition will be adjudged and pronounced by <u>the Bishop</u> at the expiration of thirty days
7 after the Notice of Sentence, or at such convenient time thereafter as the Bishop shall determine.

EXPLANATION

The canon as originally adopted is in conflict with the Constitution, Article IX, which provides that only a Bishop may pronounce a Sentence

Resolution A049 Amend Canon IV.2(A)(2)

1 *Resolved,* the House of _____ concurring, That Canon IV.2(A)(2) be amended to read as follows:
2 Sec.2. The Waiver and Voluntary Submission shall be evidenced by a written instrument, which shall
3 contain: (i) the name of the Priest or Deacon, (ii) a reference to the Canon specifying the Offense, (iii)
4 general information sufficient to identify the Offense, and (iv) a statement that the Priest or Deacon is
5 aware of the Sentence to be imposed and the effect thereof, and shall be signed and Acknowledged by the
6 Priest or Deacon, after opportunity to consult with and obtain advice from independent legal counsel of the
7 Priest or Deacon's choosing. If the Priest or Deacon has so consulted with legal counsel, that counsel shall
8 also be identified in the Waiver and Voluntary Submission. Legal counsel shall not be a Chancellor, a
9 Vice Chancellor, the Church Attorney or a Lay Assessor in that Diocese. The Waiver and Voluntary
10 Submission may be withdrawn by the Priest or Deacon within three days of execution by the Priest or
11 Deacon and thereafter shall be effective and irrevocable. The Church Attorney, each Complainant and
12 Victim shall be given an opportunity to be heard <u>on the Sentence</u> by the Bishop who is to impose and
13 pronounce Sentence prior to the execution of the Waiver and Voluntary Submission.

EXPLANATION

This amendment merely clarifies the right of the Church Attorney, the Complainant and Victim to be heard by the Bishop on the substance of the Sentence to be pronounced.

Resolution A050 Amend IV.2(A)(10)

1 *Resolved,* the House of _____ concurring, That Canon IV.2(A)(10) be amended to read as follows:
2 Sec.10. The Waiver and Voluntary Submission shall be evidenced by a written instrument, which shall
3 contain (i) the name of the Bishop, (ii) a reference to the Canon specifying the Offense, (iii) general
4 information sufficient to identify the Offense, and (iv) a statement that the Bishop is aware of the Sentence
5 to be imposed and the effect thereof, and shall be signed and Acknowledged by the Bishop, after
6 opportunity to consult with and obtain advice from independent legal counsel of the Bishop's choosing. If
7 the Bishop has so consulted with legal counsel, that counsel shall also be identified in the Waiver and
8 Voluntary Submission. Legal counsel shall not be the Presiding Bishop's Chancellor. The Waiver and
9 Voluntary Submission may be withdrawn by the Bishop within three days of execution by the Bishop and
10 thereafter shall be effective and irrevocable. The Church Attorney, each Complainant and Victim shall be
11 given an opportunity to be heard <u>on the Sentence</u> by the presiding Bishop who is to impose and pronounce
12 Sentence prior to the execution of the Waiver and Voluntary Submission.

EXPLANATION

This amendment accomplishes the same result in the provision regarding Bishops as the above resolution did with respects to Priests and Deacons.

Title IV Record Keeping

Title IV was essentially silent on the requirements of record keeping and access to the records of proceedings. Instances were cited to the Commission where the trial record was virtually non-existent, and had to be reconstructed virtually from scratch. The resolutions making up the balance of our report all relate to record-keeping requirements under Title IV.

Resolution A051 Amend Canon IV.4.14

1   *Resolved,* the House of _____ concurring, That Canon IV.4.14 be amended by numbering the existing
2   section as (a), and adding a new section (b) as follows:
3   (b) The record shall be in the custody of the Clerk and kept in the depository of the Registrar of the
4   General Convention, and in the Archives of the Episcopal Church.

Resolution A052 Amend Canon IV.4.48

1   *Resolved,* the House of _____ concurring, That Canon IV.4.48 be amended as follows:
2   (a) The Court of Review shall keep a record of all proceedings in each case brought before it and the
3   record shall be certified by the Presiding Officer of the Court. If the record cannot be authenticated by the
4   presiding Officer by reason of the presiding Officer's death, disability or absence, it shall be authenticated
5   by a member of the Court designated for that purpose by majority vote of the Court.
6   (b) The record shall be in the custody of the Clerk and kept in the depository of the Registrar of the
7   General Convention, and in the Archives of the Episcopal Church.

EXPLANATION

This amendment accomplishes the same result in the provision regarding Bishops as the above resolution did with respects to Priests and Deacons.

Resolution A053 Amend Canon IV.5.29

1   *Resolved,* the House of _____ concurring, That Canon IV.5.29 be amended to read as follows:
2   (a) The Court shall keep a record of all proceedings in each case brought before it and the record shall be
3   certified by the Presiding Judge of the Court. If the record cannot be authenticated by the Presiding Judge
4   by reason of the Presiding Judge's death, disability or absence, it shall be authenticated by a member of the
5   Court designated for that purpose by majority vote of the Court.
6   (b) ~~The record shall be kept by the Clerk, inserted in a book and be attested by the signature of the~~
7   ~~Presiding Judge and Clerk.~~ The record shall be in the custody of the Clerk and kept in the depository of the
8   Registrar of the General Convention, and in the Archives of the Episcopal Church. ~~and shall be open to the~~
9   ~~inspection of every member of this church.~~

Resolution A054 Amend Canon IV.6

1   *Resolved,* the House of _____ concurring, That a new section be added to Canon IV.6 numbered 22 as
2   follows and that the existing Section 22 of Canon IV.6 be renumbered Section 23,
3   Sec.22. (a) The Court of Review of the Trial of a Bishop shall keep a record of all proceedings in each
4   case brought before it and the record shall be certified by the Presiding Judge of the Court. If the record
5   cannot be authenticated by the Presiding Judge by reason of the Presiding Judge's death, disability or
6   absence, it shall be authenticated by a member of the Court designated for that purpose by majority vote of
7   the Court.
8   (b) The record shall be in the custody of the Clerk and kept in the depository of the Registrar of the
9   General Convention, and in the Archives of the Episcopal Church.
10   Sec. 23 When the Court is not in session,...

Resolution A055 Amend Canon IV.12.9

1   *Resolved,* the House of _____ concurring, That Canon IV.12.9 be amended by numbering the existing
2   section as (a), adding language, and adding a new subsection (b) to read as follows:
3   (b) The record of Sentence, whether Admonition, Suspension or Deposition, shall specify under what
4   Canon the action is being taken and be kept in the depository of the Registrar of the General Convention,
5   and in the Archives of the Episcopal Church.

Resolution 056 Amend Canon IV.12.11

1   *Resolved,* the House of _____ concurring, That Canon IV.12.11 be amended by numbering the existing
2   section (a), adding to (a) and inserting a new (b) to read as follows:
3   Sec.11. (a) In the case of the suspension or deposition of a Bishop, it shall be the duty of the Presiding
4   Bishop to give notice of the Sentence to the Ecclesiastical Authority of every Diocese of this Church, to

5   the Recorder, to the Church Deployment Office, and to the Secretary of the House of Bishops, and to all
6   Archbishops and Metropolitans, and to all Presiding Bishops of Churches in communion with this Church.
7   The notice shall specify under what Canon the Bishop has been suspended or deposed.
8   (b) The record of the Sentence, whether Admonition, Suspension or Deposition, shall specify under what
9   Canon action is being taken, and be kept in the depository of the registrar of the General Convention, and
10 in the Archives of the Episcopal Church.

Resolution A057 Amend Canon IV.13.1

1   *Resolved,* the House of _____ concurring, That Canon IV.13.1 be amended to read as follows:
2   Sec. 1. The House of Bishops may remit and terminate any judicial Sentence which may have been
3   imposed upon a Bishop, or modify the same so far as to designate a precise period of time, or other
4   specific contingency, on the occurrence of which the Sentence shall utterly cease, and be of no further
5   force or effect; Provided, that no such Remission or modification shall be made except at a meeting of the
6   House of Bishops, during the. session of some General Convention, or at a special meeting of the House of
7   Bishops, which shall be convened by the Presiding Bishop on the application of any five Bishops, after
8   three months' notice in writing of the time, place, and object of the meeting being given to each Bishop;
9   Provided, also, that the Remission or modification be assented to by not less than a majority of the
10 Bishops; And provided, that nothing herein shall be construed to repeal or alter the provisions of Canon
11 IV.12. A record of any action of remission or modification of a sentence shall be submitted by the
12 Presiding Bishop to the Archives of the Episcopal Church and kept in the depository of the Registrar of the
13 General Convention.

Resolution A058 Amend Canon IV.13.5

1   *Resolved,* the House of _____ concurring, That Canon IV.13.5 be amended to read as follows:
2   Sec. 5. A Bishop who shall grant Remission for any Sentence of Removal or Deposition shall, without
3   delay, give due notice thereof under the Bishop's own hand sending the notice in a sealed envelope to
4   every Member of the Clergy, each Vestry, the Secretary of the Convention and the Standing Committee. of
5   the Diocese, which shall be added to the official records of the Diocese; to the Presiding Bishop, to all
6   other Bishops of this Church, and where there is no Bishop, to the Ecclesiastical Authority of each Diocese
7   of this Church; to the Recorder; to the Church Deployment Office; and to the Secretary of the House of
8   Bishops and Secretary of the House of Deputies, who shall deposit and preserve the notice among the
9   archives of those Houses giving, with the full name of the person restored, the date of the Removal or
10 Deposition, and the Order of the Ministry to which that person is restored. A record of any action of
11 remission or modification of a sentence shall be submitted by the Bishop to the Archives of the Episcopal
12 Church and kept in the depository of the Registrar of the General Convention. Submission.

EXPLANATION

These amendments are intended to provide internal consistency and clarity to the matter of record-keeping in Title IV actions throughout the Church. These amendments involve no substantive alteration of any canonical provisions. These amendments are technically desirable and will provide an important repository of information for those responsible for the exercise of the Title IV (disciplinary) canons.

FINANCIAL RECAP AND BUDGET APPROPRIATION REQUEST

The Commission met four times during the Triennium as a body, and several of its members met at other times with SCMD and the Title IV Revisions Task Force. Out of a budget through 2002 of $30,000, the Commission has spent $22,514, with a few expenses still to be recorded. It appears that SCCC has accomplished its work well within the established budget. No further meetings are scheduled during 2003.

The Standing Commission on Constitution and Canons expects to meet six times during the next triennium, the first meeting being scheduled for February, 2004. SCCC requests a budget of $19,000 per year, for a total of $57,000 for the triennium.

STANDING COMMISSION ON DOMESTIC MISSION AND EVANGELISM
www.episcopalchurch.org/gc/ccab/scdme/default.html
20/20 STRATEGY GROUP

Membership

The Rev. John A.M. Guernsey, *Chair*	Virginia, 2003
Ms. Sarah E. Lawton, V*ice Chair*	California, 2006
Edgar K. Byham, Esq., S*ecretary*	Newark, 2006
The Rev. Dr. James H. Cooper	Florida, 2006
The Rt. Rev. Michael W. Creighton	Central Pennsylvania, 2003
Dr. Scott E. Evenbeck	Indianapolis, 2003
The Rt. Rev. Daniel W. Herzog	Albany, 2006
The Rev. Colenzo Hubbard	West Tennessee, 2006
Mr. David H. Keller	Upper South Carolina, 2006
Mr. Albert T. Mollegen, Jr.	Connecticut, 2003
Mr. Robert Schoeck	Massachusetts, 2006
The Rev. Canon David L. Seger	Northern Indiana, 2003
The Rev. Gary Steele	Alaska, 2006
Mr. Howard M. Tischler	Rio Grande, 2003
Dr. Shirleen S. Wait	Florida, 2003
The Rev. LeeAnne Watkins	Minnesota, 2003
The Rev. Kwasi A. Thornell	*Executive Council Liaison*

20/20 Strategy Group Membership

Ms. Sarah E. Lawton, *Chair*	The Very Rev. James Lemler	The Rev. Kwasi A. Thornell
The Rev. Dr. James Cooper, V.*Chair*	The Rev. Canon Kevin E. Martin	The Rev. Winnie Varghese
The Rt. Rev. Leopoldo Alard	The Rev. Bonnie A. Perry	Ms. Shelley Vescovo
The Rev. Anthony J. Guillen	The Rt. Rev. Katharine Jefferts Schori	The Very Rev. Sandra A. Wilson
Ms. Kate Hays		

SCDME Charge: Canon I.1.2(n)

(4) A Standing Commission on Domestic Mission and Evangelism consisting of 16 members (2 Bishops, 6 Priests and/or Deacons and 8 Lay Persons). It shall be the duty of the Commission to identify, study and consider major general policies, priorities and concerns as to the domestic mission of this Church. This shall include a review of the shaping of new patterns and directions for evangelism particularly in rural and metropolitan areas. The Commission shall develop and recommend to the General Convention comprehensive and coordinated policies and strategies to restore all people to unity with God and each other in Christ.

Meetings

The Standing Commission on Domestic Mission and Evangelism (SCDME) met three times during this triennium: February 19-22, 2001, at Virginia Theological Seminary in Alexandria, Virginia; January 28-31, 2002, at Camp Allen in Texas with 20/20 Strategy Group and Program Teams; November 21-23, 2002, at Camp Allen in Texas with 20/20 Strategy Group. The 20/20 Strategy Group met separately on April 29-30, 2002, in Houston, Texas.

WORK SUMMARY

The story of 20/20 begins with a renewed fire for mission moving through the Episcopal Church. In March 1998, the Standing Commission on Domestic Mission and Evangelism—holding its very first meeting as a newly created interim body—conceived the 20/20 vision for the Episcopal Church in response to news of renewed interest in mission initiatives at the grassroots level. After wide consultation during the triennium, the Commission issued a bold challenge to the Episcopal Church to be a healthy, dynamic, inviting church, reflective of the diversity of our society, with the goal of doubling the baptized membership of the Church by the year 2020. The 73rd General Convention embraced this mission priority by adopting A033:

Resolved, That the 73rd General Convention joyfully embrace as its priority the following domestic mission imperative: Called to restore all people to unity with God and each other in Christ, we commit to being a healthy, dynamic, inviting church, reflective of the diversity of our society, deeply rooted in faith and the gospel, so that we live out our baptismal promise to be disciples who make disciples of Jesus Christ. We will do this through: *Creative strategies for evangelism; Prayer and spiritual development; Recruiting and equipping innovative leaders; Strengthening congregational life; Focusing on children, youth, and campus ministries.* In response to this commitment we intend with God's help, to double our baptized membership by the year 2020.

The 73rd General Convention also established, through Executive Council, the 20/20 Task Force. The Task Force, under the leadership of Bishop Gethin Hughes, was charged to prepare—in just a year—a report on this vision to Executive Council. The Task Force worked intensively and presented its creative and visionary report to Council in October 2001, the main text of which follows. The report's full text, including appendices, endnotes, and charts, can be found at: http://www.episcopalchurch.org/2020TF/downloads.htm.

20/20 Task Report: Building a church of disciples who make disciples

Respectfully submitted to the Executive Council of the Episcopal Church of the United States of America, by the 20/20 Task Force, October 15, 2001.

Contents
Task Force members
Resolution
20/20 Movement and Vision
A Changing American Demographic
Spiritual Hunger and Curiosity
Disciples
A Transformational Church
Time Line and Accountability
Recommendations

Task Force
The Rt. Rev. Gethin B. Hughes, Chair
The Rt. Rev. Leopoldo J. Alard
The Rev. Richard Kew
The Very Rev. James B. Lemler
The Rev. Canon Kevin E. Martin
Mr. Albert T. Mollegen, Jr., Secretary
Ms. Deborah Robayo
Mrs. Cecil P. Williamson
The Very Rev. Sandra A. Wilson

The 20/20 Charge and Mandate—GC Resolution 2000-A034

Resolved, the House of Deputies concurring, That in order to be a healthy, dynamic and inviting church and to achieve the goal of doubling our baptized membership by the year 2020, the 73rd General Convention directs the Executive Council to set as a priority the appointment of a task force on "2020, A Clear Vision," with the advice of the Standing Commission on Domestic Mission and Evangelism.

The task force shall prepare a plan to implement the vision, to include:

•*Creative strategies for evangelism; Prayer and spiritual development; Recruiting and equipping innovative leaders*
•*Strengthening congregational life; Focusing on children, youth and campus ministries.*

Special emphasis shall be given to: *Recruiting, educating, and training evangelists and church planters who were born after 1964 and/or people of color; Training of lay and ordained leaders in second language skills and cross-cultural sensitivity;*

The plan shall include a detailed system for evaluation, review, and accountability; and be it further

Resolved, That the task force shall include substantive and creative means of financing this evangelistic vision as an investment in the future of Christ's Church, utilizing such sources as:

The Alleluia Fund (A036); •*The General Church budget;* •*Unrestricted investment return;* •*Matching funds.*

It is the expectation of the 73rd General Convention that the aggregate of funds from these and other sources will equal at least 10% of the aggregate income of the Domestic and Foreign Missionary Society derived from diocesan and investment income; and be it further

Resolved, That the task force will present a detailed plan by July 1, 2001, to the Executive Council, which shall begin implementation of the plan and report on its progress to the 74th General Convention; and be it further

Resolved, That the 73rd General Convention directs that the sum of $75,000 shall be appropriated from the general budget, for the expense of the task force.

THE 20/20 MOVEMENT AND VISION
20/20 is about tomorrow

20/20 is bold and visionary. It is about how the Episcopal Church faces the new century. The 20/20 Vision is an affirmation of confidence in the faithfulness of God. It provides a framework around which the next chapter of the Episcopal Church's story can be organized and written, as we seek to be wholehearted in our obedience to Jesus Christ in the 21st century.

The 20/20 Vision calls on Episcopalians to look at themselves, their world, and their church, and consider the following questions:

- From where have we come?
- Who are we now?
- Where are we going?
- Who are we going to be in this new century?
- What is different and what is changing about our context?
- What is our mission to our society?
- What is our responsibility to those who do not know Christ?

Our Spiritual Journey in a Changing World

20/20 is daring and extravagant. Grounded in the Missio Dei—God's mission to this world with ourselves as partners—the 20/20 Vision dares us to be a church of disciples who in turn are equipped to intentionally make new disciples. 20/20 challenges the Episcopal Church to reconsider its spiritual journey, looking at itself in terms that face tomorrow's opportunity while remaining deeply rooted in the Gospel message as understood by our Anglican heritage.

As the 20th century waned, the speed with which change enveloped our culture accelerated. Only those who are blind or stubbornly determined not to recognize what is happening will deny that the world being born is not the one in which most of us were nurtured and grew. The "old" America with which we were familiar is rapidly taking on a different face, mind and heart. Amidst so much cultural and social soul-searching and transition, we are being challenged to ask afresh what it means to be faithful as we find our way forward. As challenging and bewildering as this emerging society can sometimes be, it has enormous opportunities for Christian service and witness—not least because millions are starting to ask life's ultimate questions with both honesty and intense curiosity.

Yet, paradoxically, even as American society has launched itself into an intense spiritual odyssey, it has simultaneously been busily detaching itself from its Judeo-Christian roots, loosening the hold of 1,500 years of Christian heritage; as yet neither the United States nor the rest of the Western world is sure of the long-term implications of this decisive shift.

Because of America's boundless energy and creativity, it is even more of a magnet than ever, attracting millions of both documented and undocumented immigrants from all over the world. Inward migration has further reshaped our understanding of the Judeo-Christian heritage, loosening America's identification with its predominantly Anglo-Saxon and northern European roots. The arrival of such a diversity of newcomers merely intensifies the magnitude of the journey upon which we in this country now find ourselves. When people of several dozen nationalities or ethnic groups might live on the same street, interacting with one another, soul-searching and creativity are obligatory if we as a church are to respond effectively. This infusion of new life, coupled with the growing self-confidence of the historic and more established social and ethnic "minorities" within our culture, is altering perceptions and values in far-reaching ways.

We are now a highly technical, multicultural, multiethnic, multi-religious society whose diversity is unprecedented. Today's Americans come from many places, speak many languages and adhere to many customs, while being caught up in a knowledge revolution every bit as profound as the explosion of learning that accompanied the invention of movable type 500 years ago.

This remarkable mingling of peoples and ideas has made the United States one of the most ingenious societies on earth. Such radically changing demographics should encourage the church to be courageous and resourceful, passionate and enthusiastic in its response to these new circumstances. We have to decide whether our church will embrace the opportunities of changing times with excitement and zeal or whether we will defensively retreat from all the opportunities being presented, thereby rendering ourselves increasingly marginal.

A CHANGING AMERICAN DEMOGRAPHIC: *How is America changing?*

M.I.T. professor, consultant and writer, Peter Senge writes, "The next ten to twenty years will bring more change than the last ten or twenty years. We live in a really epic time of change. These are fundamental changes, and it's not so much predicting the specifics but trying to understand the forces that are at play."

The table below is a "snapshot" of how things have changed in the last twenty years and of some of the changes that are likely to happen in the next twenty. These few examples are a sample of the alterations that will be taking place in the setting in which we are called to minister in the next twenty years.

1980	*2000*	*2020*
PC invented	PC 1000x more powerful	Computers near human intelligence
Touch tone phones	Cell phones	Virtual Reality
Internet for scientists	Internet in adolescence	Internet ubiquitous
230 million Americans	282 million Americans	340 million Americans
12 million Hispanics	35 million Hispanics	70 million Hispanics
Median age: 30	Median age: 35.3	Median age: 38-39
Chrysler bailed out	Global auto companies	Cars run on hydrogen batteries
Challenger disaster	Manned Space Station	First mission to Mars
S & L crisis brewing	Banking v. financial services	Most banking online
Cold War	US only superpower	China reaches superpower status
Christendom dying	Christendom dead	New kind of religious culture
Sexual experiment	Sexual confusion	Unpredictable
AIDS identified	AIDS - global epidemic	AIDS under control or pandemic
US perceived as past it	US economically dominant	Integrated global economy

SPIRITUAL HUNGER AND CURIOSITY

Despite unprecedented wealth and materialism, those around us today are showing symptoms of a persistent and far deeper yearning. Having discovered that life is more than enjoying physical comfort and material contentment, huge numbers of women and men, young and old, are on a spiritual quest. "The fact that people so often speak of spirituality as something to 'find' suggests that in popular understanding it is seen as requiring some degree of scouting around, and very much depends on how a person goes about trying to find it and how much the person succeeds."

Searching is one of the motifs of our age. Whatever their origins, in the midst of this complex interplay of forces, many whose lives are soaked in the fluidity of our culture are asking ultimate questions about identity and where they belong. Those who are on this spiritual journey are not just strangers and those who are far off:—the unchurched or formerly churched—include our friends, neighbors, families—even our own children. It is inevitable that their thoughts will eventually center on the divine—even if they do not know or use theological words or spiritual terms to describe their longing. A recent survey commissioned by the United Methodist Church identifies two out of five American adults in the 25-54-year-old age range as serious seekers after spiritual truth.

It would appear that God has gone before us through a troubled and disturbing era. Now, could it be that God is in the process of preparing the Episcopal Church to play a significant missional role at a moment such as this? God has given us both passion and resources to be agents of transformation in obedience to Jesus Christ, in this changing situation.

What Jesus told his disciples as he looked at his own first century world are words that apply equally well to our own: "the harvest truly is plentiful..."

A MOVEMENT ALREADY UNDERWAY

The 20/20 Vision is neither a program nor even a series of programs. 20/20 has not just been invented but is a movement that is already underway, has been quietly building and is now converging with increased urgency from every corner of the church. It is celebratory and expectant, believing God has begun something new in our midst—and yet this new thing returns us to our roots, integrating tomorrow's challenge with the Gospel message, our history and our heritage.

The 20/20 Vision is to reclaim and re-energize our missional identity, breathing new life into what it means to be the Domestic and Foreign Missionary Society. 20/20 focuses a vision that has depth as well as dynamic and transforming power. God has been preparing the soil and now challenges us to live into our Baptismal Covenant with renewed energy and ardor. The heart of the 20/20 Vision is our commitment to be effective and enthusiastic as we proclaim "by word and example the Good News of God in Christ."

The 20/20 movement found formal expression at the 73rd General Convention in Resolutions A033 and A034. In these the church "joyfully embrace(d) as its priority... being a healthy, dynamic, inviting church... so that we live out our baptismal promise to be disciples who make disciples of Jesus Christ." Furthermore, the Episcopal Church pledged itself "in response to this commitment... with God's help to double our baptized membership by the year 2020." This breathtaking declaration is catching the imagination of Episcopalians, generating enthusiasm and excitement, for they see it as a way to reverse significantly our thirty-year numerical decline.

The 20/20 Vision is the Episcopal expression of the emerging ecumenical discipleship movement that is influencing Christians across the United States and around the world.

The vigor of 20/20 stems from its passion to mobilize Episcopal Christians, bringing them to maturity in Christ, so that ours might be a church where transformed lives bring transformation to other lives, and to our whole society.

The statistical component of 20/20 is important not because of numbers for numbers' sake, but because it challenges us to be intentional, requiring accountability for the policies pursued and the actions taken. The accurate accumulation of data demands regular and constructive evaluation—and mechanisms for review are built into this proposal.

Numbers are important to the 20/20 Movement and are a yardstick that helps measure our passion to form faithful, holy and obedient disciples and disciple-makers. Viewing 20/20 from this disciple-making perspective, the Task Force recommends that the General Convention resolutions be modified from a commitment to doubling membership to a commitment to doubling Average Sunday Attendance (ASA). The Task Force believes Sunday attendance is a much more accurate gauge of our effectiveness as disciple-makers and disciple-multipliers; it also moves us away from the increasingly fuzzy notion of membership. In addition, attendance figures are more reliable, better measuring Christian commitment than the number of the baptized.

DISCIPLES

Disciples are enrolled by baptism and, thereby, committed to a lifetime involvement with the missionary imperative of making new disciples. The baptized are taught all that Jesus imparted to his apostles. In place of his presence among them, Jesus Christ sent the Holy Spirit to superintend, direct and apply his teaching among the baptized. The definition of a Christian is therefore a lifelong committed learner, a disciple under permanent instruction by the Holy Spirit. A local church consists of the group of disciples gathered for teaching by the Holy Spirit in that place.

This definition of discipleship is adapted from one given by Rev. Robert Brow in his book *Go Make Learners*. Brow is a priest of the Diocese of Kingston, Ontario.

The 20/20 Vision, as it focuses the church's attention on Jesus Christ, requires coordination of the primary components for effective mission, while calling Episcopalians to far greater levels of cooperation, collaboration and partnership, both within our church and with Christians of other backgrounds and traditions. Obedience to the Missio Dei invites us to become a transformational church, a vocation with far-reaching spiritual and numerical implications. One of our major priorities must be to raise the profile of evangelism in the life of our church and equip Episcopalians for evangelistic ministries and lifestyles.

It will be through sharing in mission together that we will learn afresh how to work together, drawing upon the insights and the gifts of each Episcopalian, ministry, parish, diocese and ethnic group. A further corollary is that we are not alone in this endeavor. 20/20 is part of a trans-denominational movement, as Christians from every background seek to respond creatively and without delay to the opportunities being birthed by this different kind of world: the United Methodist Church's "Igniting Ministry" campaign is an example of this from another denominational tradition. This requires that we build ecumenical bridges in new and determined ways, linking with believers across the whole Christian spectrum.

A TRANSFORMATIONAL CHURCH

Transformational churches are themselves already being transformed by the love of Christ, God's grace being prevenient. Transformational churches are vision-driven, never quite satisfied by their own performance, but constantly assessing and reassessing, striving with their mission priorities and their ministry performance. Transformational churches take seriously their relationship with and dependence upon God, giving precedence to prayer and intercession. Furthermore, transformational churches are aware of the implications of the rapid changes taking place in the culture and respond with both urgency and drive. The Episcopal Church is in the process of learning what these factors mean and how to live into their implications.

We reiterate the seriousness with which we should take the nation's ethnic and multicultural diversity. It is imperative, if we are to be a transformational church, that we grapple with the missional implications of the massive demographic changes taking place all around us. The clock cannot be set back; the United States is on an irreversible course from its European-shaped past toward being a thoroughly multicultural society. Such massive varieties of peoples cannot be ignored and must figure prominently in plans we make, the goals we seek to accomplish and the manner in which we use our resources. The changing face of America presents us with a much clearer vision of the richness of God's Kingdom. With such diversity comes abundance, and the diversity is to be celebrated as a source of renewal and vision.

For example, Hispanic people in the United States no longer cluster along the Mexican border or in a handful of major cities, but are from all over the Latin world and are to be found in increasing numbers everywhere. The Spanish-speaking, Latino bishops of the Episcopal Church have drawn our attention to the challenges and opportunities of the growth of Hispanics in the United States: "We cannot ignore any longer the presence of the Hispanic people in our midst. As a church with the obligation to carry on the Divine Commission (Mt. 28:19-20), we cannot present defensive excuses of language or of any other kind, to avoid being involved in this mission and ministry. When the primitive church started spreading the gospel of our Lord, it faced similar circumstances, and yet, they were able to cover the whole Roman Empire."

Meanwhile, the historic African-American population is being augmented by African-descended immigrants from an array of different cultures from all over that continent and from the Caribbean. Some come seeking economic opportunity, others who arrive are refugees—many are devout and committed Anglicans when they reach these shores, eager to serve God wholeheartedly in this new land. As numbers coming from Europe have slowed to a trickle, those from the rest of the world have turned into a flood. Their presence in our midst offers not only extraordinary opportunities for making known the Good News, but also exceptional challenges as to how we interpret Christ to people of diverse ethnic, religious and cultural backgrounds. Mission to these communities requires intentionality, focus, resources, and zeal, the local initiative resting upon dioceses and congregations.

A Lost Boy is called

Stephen is in his early twenties. He was chased from his village in Sudan when very young and spent his early years wandering the face of Africa with other "Lost Boys." A deeply committed Christian, he was formed in his faith by Anglican bishops, priests, catechists and evangelists in refugee camps in Kenya. Now a resident of the United States and part of the Episcopal Church of the United States of America, he believes that God is calling him to the priesthood.

Yet as we look at the demographics of the Episcopal Church, not only do we remain a predominantly white and Anglo-Saxon church, but many of the presuppositions that shape our mission and ministry will require radical reappraisal if we are faithfully to respond to the reshaping of America that is going on around us.

In addition to the ethnic diversification of the population, there are other changing demographics that need to be taken into account. We are still primarily a confederation of small churches organized to reach out to nuclear families at a time when 44% of the U.S. adult population is single. Also, for a quarter of a century our membership has been aging even more rapidly than the median age of the United States. In common with the other formerly mainline denominations, our median age has risen so that it is now more than twenty years higher than the median age of the general population.

The 20/20 Vision will not be fulfilled unless we reverse this trend, recognizing afresh that the church is renewed each generation: as the old saw has it, "God has no grandchildren." While it is of utmost importance that we take seriously the challenge of reaching with Christ's love the aging segments of the population, an urgent key component of the 20/20 Movement must be renewed attention to work among children, ministry by and among youth and teenagers, and the multiplication and support of effective Episcopal campus ministry.

Not only do those on a spiritual search respond to the Good News more enthusiastically when young, but also these young disciples then become the pool from which tomorrow's leadership, both lay and ordained, is drawn. The future health and growth of the Episcopal Church are dependent upon the identification, recruiting and training of significant numbers of transformational leaders, entrepreneurs and risk-takers, both lay and ordained.

Tomorrow's leadership needs to be made up of women and men who see societal change as an extraordinary opportunity, not a terrifying threat.

A Spiritual Movement, Not a Statistical One

While statistics are an important element of the 20/20 challenge, we need to remind ourselves that first and foremost this is a spiritual movement. Within the "quest culture" that is in the process of swamping most other approaches to believing, we are being challenged to reassess our habitual approaches toward the exercise of ministry and to discover fresh ways that we might make disciples: introducing to Jesus Christ males and females, young and old, rich and poor, married and single, from every conceivable social and ethnic background, and then forming and deepening them in their new-found faith. As in the first century, so now, the church is a multifaceted coalescing of people.

However, if 20/20 is to achieve lasting, cumulative results, it must be rooted and grounded in a biblical theology, as well as the prayers and intercessions of all God's people, led by their bishops, clergy, lay leaders and religious. It is our heartfelt belief that the 20/20 Movement is not merely an opportunity to grow the church, but a challenge to all of us to deepen our spirituality and dependence upon the God of truth to whom we lift our praises, prayers and intercessions.

TIME LINE, STEPS AND ACCOUNTABILITY FOR THE 20/20 MOVEMENT

The 20/20 Task Force recognizes that searching for the shape of tomorrow's ministry is fraught with hazards that can easily divert us, but we urge that the church never lose sight of our overall objective of doubling the Average Sunday Attendance (ASA) by the end of the year 2020. All our efforts should be projected and organized toward this goal. However, given all the uncertainties the further out we project, the 20/20 Movement is best guided toward its goal a step at a time. We, therefore, recommend that, although we continue to use broad brushstrokes to paint the 20/20 picture further out, the following time line should be used to direct the first few steps of the movement:

11/2000 – 10/2001	Preparation: Defining the task
10/2001 – GC2003	Step One: Laying the foundations
2003 – 2006	Step Two: Gathering momentum
2006 – 2009	Step Three: Completed by GC2009

The 20/20 Movement should figure prominently in the substance and agenda of the Minneapolis General Convention. This in an occasion at which the eyes of the church can be focused on the task to which we have committed ourselves, and every effort be made for 20/20 to be acclaimed and celebrated on that occasion by the whole church.

During the period leading to 2003, the scene needs to be set, and our strategy should be concentrated on certain identified areas of success that parishes, dioceses and ministries have had around the country. These will draw the attention of the Episcopal Church to the multiplication of such possibilities as the 20/20 Movement continues to gather momentum.

The progress being made must be kept under close scrutiny, and as a result changes in trajectory will be both recognized and made. We recommend that the Presiding Officers call a gathering on an annual basis that is open to the whole church to celebrate progress made and consult together, while honestly asking and seeking to answer the following questions:

- What have we achieved in the last twelve months?
- What have we forgotten, pushed to one side or overlooked?
- What is new in the equation requiring reassessment of our goals and direction?

All this will play a part in keeping the 20/20 Vision before the church, discovering where the energy is and allowing both the structures and the fringes to be involved in the conversation, while refocusing our commitment for the years ahead.

RECOMMENDATIONS
Celebrating the 20/20 Movement

Recommendations—
- That a relatively small 20/20 Task Force Work Group be appointed by November 15 for the 20/20 Movement, to guide the movement, to serve as an accountable body and to be the review committee for the movement
- That the 20/20 Vision provide a framework and focus for the General Convention 2003
- That there be an annual gathering open to all that celebrates progress, links, guides, and holds accountable the whole church to the fulfilling of the 20/20 task
- That the chair of the continuing 20/20 Task Force Work Group report progress to the presiding officers every two months

20/20 is a movement to be celebrated, not programming to be implemented. 20/20 is the church reclaiming, reinterpreting and reinvigorating what it means to be a missionary society that is both domestic and foreign. We cannot emphasize strongly enough how radically and rapidly our domestic circumstances are changing, creating perhaps the most multicultural society in human history. As complicating as this might be, the energy that the emerging culture generates is palpable. Each of the following components of 20/20 gives substance to the transition that is necessary from a primarily pastoral to a primarily missional approach to ministry.

The parameters laid out in this document having been identified, the 20/20 Task Force now believes it necessary for a 20/20 Network to begin to focus itself around a reconstituted 20/20 Task Force Work Group. We ask the Presiding Officers of the Episcopal Church to form this by November 15, 2001, in order to guide the 20/20 Movement so that it might reach out into the whole church. The reorganized 20/20 Task Force Work Group should function as the hub of the 20/20 Network, stimulating interaction and linkage between those who are involved in creative and constructive evangelism and mission ministry within all the formal structures of the church, as well as in its various organizations, mission agencies and voluntary ministries.

The nine members of the present 20/20 Task Force are ready to continue involvement in this vision should they be invited, but request that the reconfigured 20/20 Task Force remain small enough to function effectively—we recommend a number in the region of no more than twelve members. The new 20/20 Task Force will need direct and significant access to a wide range of other Episcopalians, to means of communication and to the existing and the rising leadership of the church.

It is vital that the following be involved with the Task Force in the development of the 20/20 process: communicators, representatives of the Standing Commission on Stewardship and Development, the Treasurer or the Treasurer's representative, Generation X leaders, Millennial Generation leaders, missioners and church planters, youth ministers and youth ministry developers, those involved in ethnic and urban ministry, representatives of the Standing Commission on Domestic Mission and Evangelism, voluntary bodies involved in mission and evangelism.

If the 20/20 Vision is to have any chance of success, it must be given substantial exposure at the General Convention 2003 as the church focuses upon the Missio Dei. We perceive that the 20/20 Movement has been called into being by God to leaven the life of the church as it seeks fresh ways to be obedient to its Lord'scommands, helping us collectively to live into our baptismal covenant.

Spirituality, Prayer and Worship

Recommendations—

- That the Presiding Bishop, working with a cross-section of the church's theologians, give theological articulation to the 20/20 imperatives and the Great Commission of Jesus Christ
- That the bishops of the church, led by the Presiding Bishop, call the church to prayer and intercession that God's grace may blossom through the 20/20 Movement. We ask especially that the Anglican Fellowship of Prayer, the Daughters of the King, the Brotherhood of St. Andrew, devotional fellowships and the religious communities in the church be challenged to be the core around which the national intercessory component of the 20/20 Movement is allowed to coalesce
- That liturgical resources be developed to enable the church as a whole to celebrate its mission as a 20/20 people
- That 20/20 discipleship—being disciples who make disciples—be an integral part of our teaching around the Baptismal Covenant

What the 20/20 Movement is seeking to accomplish cannot begin to be achieved through our own efforts. The transformation we envision and are seeking will not come about merely through adding programs, reconfiguring structures, planting new congregations, training a fresh cadre of leaders or raising huge sums of money, no matter how effectively these ends are pursued. At its heart, 20/20 is a spiritual pursuit, dependent upon God's grace, inspired by Christ's love and empowered by the Holy Spirit. To have any chance of succeeding, it must be rooted in biblically-based theology, sustained by intercession and reflected in the worship of God's people.

The theological undergirding of the 20/20 endeavor needs to be centered in a scriptural understanding of the Kingdom of God—a realm of grace and growth, of truth and transformation. We note that the parables of the Kingdom that Jesus taught are always stories of abundance and not scarcity, of generosity rather than withholding. These are the heart of the Missio Dei, God's work in the world, his continual miraculous intervention in the lives and affairs of humankind. As we respond to our own Baptismal Covenant, we affirm that "the duty of the Christian is to follow Christ; to come together week by week for corporate worship; and to work, pray, and give for the spread of the Kingdom of God."

At the heart of the 20/20 Vision must be a cascade of prayer continually rising to God. We, therefore, encourage the Presiding Bishop to lead us as a people constantly in prayer for the church's mission, and we urge that religious communities, devotional and prayer ministries of the church focus their efforts upon the 20/20 Vision.

The emerging 20/20 Movement reflects a yearning for faithful and effective Christian discipleship in the power of the Holy Spirit. It demands self-examination, personal piety and a fullness of discipleship beyond what is normally lived out, preached and taught in so many of our churches. Crucial to our discipleship is the life of worship, and we recognize that by God's grace we tend to grow into what we profess in worship. Our liturgy reflects our spiritual yearnings and influences how we act out all that our Baptismal Covenant entails as we live out our discipleship in the world. The 20/20 Vision needs to be integrated into the weekly worship of our churches. Growing out of the 20/20 Movement should be prayers, specific intercessions, special liturgies to celebrate what the Holy Spirit is doing in our midst, providing grace-filled vehicles for personal transformation and institutional change.

None of this is new. It is as we have recommitted ourselves to the scriptural imperatives that these things have always found fresh expression in Anglican theology, spirituality and worship. The 20/20 Vision is calling the church to grow more fully into what we profess and what God is calling us to be.

Research and Analysis

Recommendations—

- That the Episcopal Church establish a Research and Analysis Unit under the direction of a skilled statistician and researcher. This unit should collect appropriate data, analyze and interpret it on a consistent and long-term basis.
- That the base figure of worshipers in Episcopal churches in 2000 be identified.
- That the parochial report be thoroughly overhauled and redesigned in order that we collect data appropriate to the fulfilling of the 20/20 Vision

In commissioning the 20/20 Task Force to develop plans to double the church's size, the church has drawn attention to the glaring inadequacy of the Episcopal Church's collection and interpretation of data. It will be impossible for us to measure where we are going, if we do not start with an accurate assessment of where we are now or where we have been.

If the 20/20 process is to have a precise starting point, and the 20/20 Movement is to be statistically honest, then the Episcopal Church will need to improve its statistical record keeping, making better use of parochial report information and demographic information using sources such as the Percept Company. As cities grow and as the population shifts, it is essential that we have at our fingertips the facts to guide efforts to focus our ministry in the right locations, as well as data about the church that tells us how we are responding to these changing circumstances.

These challenges alone demonstrate the need that the Episcopal Church has for an effective research and analysis arm, and this is a task that would be appropriately undertaken by the Episcopal Church Center or an agency attached to it. The task force supports and endorses efforts now underway to fill this gap.

In addition, local dioceses require data-informed assistance as they target areas for new congregation development. Accurate information will also allow for a coordinated strategy for revitalization of present congregations and effective response to new ethnic groups in a community. This should also be coordinated with ecumenical partners such as the ELCA. This developing database should be made widely available for research, and tools such as the World Wide Web should encourage such research. Correcting the shortcomings in our collection and interpretation of data should be given the highest priority.

New Church, Congregational and Diocesan Development

Recommendations—

- Establish a strong national strategy and approach to new church development to go alongside regional, diocesan and local efforts
- Empower and enhance the ministry of new church development by coordinating and developing resources on a national and regional level to support local diocese's initiatives through congregations
- Begin the process that will result in the establishment of 300 new missional congregations by 2006, in addition to suburban congregations adding urban and inner city plants that are sensitive to the multicultural demands of an ethnically diverse society and culture
- Identify and provide the expertise, resources and funding to assist dioceses in every facet of new church development.
- Establish a strategy and identify the expertise and resources to revitalize midsize and transitional-level congregations
- Identify and showcase ten 20/20 models that are already in existence in the Episcopal Church at General Convention 2003

If we are to double attendance in Episcopal churches by 2020, it is essential that we radically reassess our approach to new church development and the revitalization and development of existing congregations. The 20/20 Vision is a call for the church to consider a wide array of new, imaginative and creative approaches to "doing church." While accepting that not every congregation has the potential for significant numerical growth, especially those in areas of sparse or declining population, almost every parish or mission is able to form Christians, to further develop itself and to move forward deepening its discipleship, obedience and servant ministry.

Research within the American religious context strongly suggests that the largest proportion of any numerical expansion is likely to take place in new congregations, which means that every effort should be made to make new church development a major priority of the church as a whole, and of dioceses in particular, during the next two decades. At the same time, considerable growth and increased effectiveness are possible as the process of congregational development is applied to existing parishes, as is being seen in dioceses that are committing to that task.

The accompanying time line suggests that, if we are to meet the 20/20 target, it will be necessary to establish a significant number of new congregations between now and 2020. While the Episcopal Church is rediscovering the adventure of developing and launching new congregations, considerable effort and resources will be necessary if we are to succeed in meeting our goal. It is possible in the early stages of 20/20 that, if we are to find the necessary missioners for new church development, we will have to look to the laity and even outside the United States.

While we expect that dioceses and existing parishes will be the primary sponsors of new congregations, we recognize that there are significant areas of population growth in the United States that are beyond the resources of the local diocese, especially in the West. Two examples to which we have given thought are the Las Vegas metropolitan area in the numerically small and resource-limited Diocese of Nevada and the Boise area in the Diocese of Idaho. A national strategy and national sources of funding for new church development will be required. Such an initiative will require significant funding for seed money, consulting, training, mentoring, prayer support and tools that enable accountability.

It has been the experience of those both within and beyond the Episcopal Church who are seriously committed to congregational development that, properly resourced, it is midsize, transitional level congregations of 100-200 Average Sunday Attendance located in well-populated areas which have the most potential for growth. In addition to New Church Development, we recommend that a strategy be framed and resources be developed to support and revitalize such congregations, monitoring their progress.

Congregations that fall within this range need to be identified and then assisted with consulting, mentoring, resources, etc., to move beyond their present plateau, responding effectively to the opportunities in their locality. This, again, will require significant funding and expertise.

It is the intention of the 20/20 Task Force that we find ten outstanding existing models of the 20/20 Movement at work in our church and to showcase these at the General Convention 2003: these will be new congregations, revitalized congregations, congregations doing exciting missional things in difficult and demanding circumstances, etc.

Projected Targets to Reach the 20/20 Goal   (see http://members.aol.com/ENE2024/model071301.htm)

	2001	2002	2003	2004	2005
ASA	830,000	853,240	877,131	901,690	926,938
Number of plants	46	48	49	50	52
Dollars needed	27,888,000	28,668,864	29,471,592	30,296,797	31,145,107
Dollars per ASA	33.60	33.60	33.60	33.60	33.60
Cumulative plants	46	94	143	194	246

2006	2007	2008	2009	2010
952,892	991,961	1,032,631	1,074,969	1,119,043
53	102	106	110	115
32,017,170	61,005,573	63,506,802	66,110,580	68,821,114
33.60	61.50	61.50	61.50	61.50
299	401	507	617	732

2011	2012	2013	2014	2015
1,164,923	1,212,685	1,262,405	1,314,164	1,368,045
119	124	129	135	140
71,642,780	74,580,134	77,637,919	80,821,074	84,134,738
61.50	61.50	61.50	61.50	61.50

2016	2017	2018	2019	2020
1,424,134	1,482,524	1,543,307	1,606,583	1,672,453
146	152	158	165	171
87,584,262	91,175,217	94,913,401	98,804,850	102,855,849
61.50	61.50	61.50	61.50	61.50
1,526	1,678	1,836	2,000	2,172

Assumptions
2.80% Initial Growth Rate
4.70% Growth Rate 2007-2020
60% Initial Growth Rate from New Congregations
75% Growth Rate from New Congregations 2007-2020
Average Sunday Attendance (ASA) per New Congregation = 300

Identifying, Recruiting and Training 20/20 Leaders

The 20/20 dynamic assumes that at this critical moment God is raising up the kind of leadership necessary for visionary movements to reshape the life of the church. Dynamic, transforming leadership is central to effective mission and the growth of the church, and the development of that leadership must be a primary component of our present and future.

Recommendations—

- That the Episcopal Church recognize the gravity of our leadership imbalances and commit to act to recruit the kind of leaders and add the diversity we need in the 21st century
- That in 2002 the Domestic and Foreign Missionary Society begin identifying the best practices in our own and other denominations and then in 2003 begin searching for and recruiting transformational leaders whose backgrounds reflect a diversity of cultures, generations and other social groupings
- That the church as a whole be prepared to learn from successful approaches to the identification and recruiting of young leaders and those from a variety of ethnic groups
- That the church offer on a continuing basis a variety of much-increased regional training for dioceses, parishes and other ministries, so that a growing number of Episcopalians might catch the vision of what is happening and the wonderful possibilities that are part of these changing circumstances
- That there be carefully planned follow-up, with established but flexible procedures for accountability built into the process, as dioceses and congregations reconfigure themselves for more effective mission and ministry.

The good news is that God has given great gifts for leadership by virtue of the Spirit's grace, and through human obedience to our own baptismal identity in Jesus Christ. The challenging news is that we must recruit and equip more leaders for mission, if we are to prosper in that mission, and fulfill the 20/20 Vision. This latter is important not just because of the 20/20 challenge, but because it is looking increasingly likely that the Episcopal Church is facing a shortfall of ordained leadership. Church Pension Fund statistics demonstrate that "the Episcopal Church certainly has a parish clergy that is top-heavy age wise," and although cautious because of the variables to make too many far-reaching predictions, researchers at the Pension Fund recognize that as older clergy are retiring there are far smaller cohorts of younger leaders to take their place. Independent observers are less sanguine and cautious, with some projecting a significant loss of ordained leadership in parishes during the coming two decades. However the realities pan out, it is crucial that we give significant attention to ordained and lay leadership needs during a period in which existing parishes will require creative direction, while new congregations are being launched to meet the pressing needs of a shifting and growing population.

In addition, we as a church need to review and revise our approach to leadership selection so that we are able to identify, recruit, and equip lay and ordained leaders who are entrepreneurial, self-starting, and not averse to taking risks. These are some of the skills necessary if leaders are to be agents of transformation, and we will only find them with careful recruiting. The 20/20 Vision holds that as the new century progresses, both laity and clergy alike need to be shaped and educated for vital missional leadership in local communities of faith, in the wider church, and into society and the world.

A further ingredient of the leadership challenge will be to raise vigorous leaders who reflect the diversity of the multilingual, multicultural society to which we now belong. Given the position in which we find ourselves now, this is going to be a huge challenge. Significant resources and creativity need to be applied to the development of Hispanic, African-American, Asian and other ethnic leaders, providing them opportunities within a church that has hitherto consciously or unconsciously relegated them to the position of "second class citizens."

An equally large challenge is to address our pressing shortage of young leaders. With a mere 4% of our ordained leadership under the age of 35, and declining numbers of the next generations involved in the life of the Episcopal Church, there is much to be done to redress this imbalance. Only the Roman Catholic Church is faced with a greater leadership challenge than the Episcopal Church, although other mainline denominations are not far behind us. We are only just beginning to give attention to raising up young lay and ordained leadership. Our past shortsightedness in this area could mean that leadership for mission will be inhibited into the future as we seek to grow, unless we are prepared to think and work outside the box.

There are many exciting possibilities for leadership development in the life of the church. Creative and innovative approaches to theological education and leadership training are fundamental to any vision for the future. Dioceses, congregations, organizations and seminaries are looking at leadership in new ways, and there is an increasing realization that leadership development and leadership education are a fundamental part of the work of all of these entities. However, there is far too little focus and coordination of these efforts. There is still a sentiment that leaders will somehow appear, and the Episcopal Church is not devoting sufficient attention or resources to identifying and development of leaders—especially in an environment where other denominations, career paths and secular organizations are aggressively pursuing the brightest and best of Generation X and the Millennial Generation.

The Next Generations

Recommendations—

- That significant resources and personnel be trained and deployed to enrich youth ministry in parishes and dioceses
- That the Episcopal Church reengage in ministry upon college and university campuses and that this ministry be both multicultural and multiethnic
- That there be a continual focus on, and bringing together for idea exchange and strategizing, those committed to working among the next generations
- That the Episcopal Church enable youth and campus ministries to take a lead in developing innovative and creative ways to reach out to the rising generations
- That we redouble our efforts for identifying, recruiting and training youth and young adults in ministry leadership, both lay and ordained: such efforts have to be at the grass roots

At the heart of our priorities, and interwoven into each of the components outlined in this Report, must be work among the next generations—that is, continuing work among:

- *Generation X (those born between the mid-sixties and mid-eighties)*
- *The Millennial Generation (those born between the mid-eighties and the early years of this new century)*
- *The generation that will follow them.*

It is vital for any organization to give concentrated thought and energy to the succession of leadership: in addition, we should also recognize that ministry among the young is of vital importance because the overwhelming majority of those who make a lifetime Christian commitment do so before they reach the age of twenty.

We have seen already that ours is an aging church: few of our leaders belong to tomorrow's generations. Following a quarter century during which the median age of ordinations has risen from the twenties to the mid- or late forties, the time is long overdue for the Episcopal Church to reach out intentionally for energetic leadership in the rising generations.

This task will not be easy because so many other institutions and corporations are also looking for "the brightest and the best" and are more aggressive in their recruitment than the church; in addition, they have access to an abundance of resources and blandishments. Furthermore, many of the other caring and serving professions are facing the same chronic shortages as ourselves: teaching, nursing and the civil service are three examples. Yet, as those who have deliberately sought to recruit young leaders for Christian ministry have discovered, the young will respond when offered the opportunity of sacrificial Christian service.

It is imperative that we paint the big picture, casting a vision that will catch the imagination of the next generations: the younger cohorts of Generation X and the earliest cohorts of the Millennial Generation. Dioceses urgently need to consider significantly revising their ordination processes, which in many places have selected out the young rather than recruiting them in. Some dioceses have begun working in this direction and can provide models for others which have yet to begin this task.

In addition to concentrating considerable effort and energy upon ministry among the young, it is vital that the young be given every opportunity to play a leading role in ministry. Every opportunity should be taken to enable them to lead, take initiatives and present Christ in a manner that is culturally appropriate. The next generations best understand the post-Christendom culture in which they and their contemporaries live, and can best reach them. It is imperative that we encourage, enable and provide the freedom and framework for them to minister effectively. Neither should we be surprised how the life of these young churches will spill over onto the Web. The role of older generations of leaders is to be there as mentors for these rising leaders—and they both seek and yearn for mentors who will walk with them as they explore the challenges of ministry.

A further observation regarding ministry among the young and the raising of young leaders is that the next generations are less hampered by preconceived cultural and ethnic stereotypes which have distorted some of the perceptions of those who are older. This means that their presence and input will inevitably work to change the dynamics that will enable the Episcopal Church to better reflect the diversity of the United States.

There are some extraordinary advances in culturally appropriate ministry among the young in various other parts of the Anglican Communion—especially within the Church of England and parts of the Anglican Church in Australia. In a global culture where the young are the first truly global generation, it is imperative that the Episcopal Church be prepared to "go to school" on successful ministries among the young elsewhere in the world.

Funding

The 20/20 Vision will require significant financial resources if it is to be successful. If the 20/20 Vision is to be fulfilled, initiatives will be funded from a variety of sources: local, regional and national. To establish a viable financial plan for the funding of the 20/20 Movement, it is necessary that the ongoing 20/20 Task Force Work Group have immediate and direct access to the Treasurer of the Domestic and Foreign Missionary Society to help identify national funding that will "prime the pump" as we begin to move from a maintenance to a mission-driven vision. A number of significant financial decisions will need to be made prior to and during General Convention 2003.

It is essential for the 20/20 Movement to have a strong financial development component because the success of the vision depends heavily upon the raising of new dollars to sustain this advance. Funding will be necessary for many components of the vision, but especially leadership training, the purchase of real estate and assisting smaller dioceses facing large challenges in new church development, to name just a handful of examples.

This development arm will seek major gifts, planned gifts, challenge funds, etc. It would also enable the 20/20 Vision to become a significant stimulus for giving as the massive transfer of capital funds that is occurring in the United States at the moment continues. The monies necessary for the fulfillment of the 20/20 Vision are an investment in the future, and there are many Episcopalians out there willing to make such investments—if their imagination can be caught. There are various models upon which a 20/20 organization could be based to enable ownership of the movement by the whole church and also to allow both designated funds from church budgets and especially the raising of new dollars.

> **Recommendations—**
> - The development of a strong relationship between the Treasurer, the Treasurer's Office and the 20/20 Movement so that funds might be identified and committed to the development of this work
> - The establishment of a close-working relationship with the Standing Commission on Stewardship to explore and make decisions about the implication of the 20/20 vision
> - The establishment of a strong development component for 20/20 to raise the funds needed for the success of the initiative, and that 20/20 and the Treasurer have a plan to accomplish the goals identified by the middle of 2002
> - The establishment of a working relationship with the Executive Council's Administration and Finance Committee, and the General Convention's Standing Committee on Program, Finance, and Budget to focus energies around the 20/20 vision
> - The consideration of approaches to raise funds for the extension of the 20/20 Vision, bringing recommendations to the General Convention in 2003

A key component of the financial aspects of the 20/20 challenge will be the mobilization of those with skills in the whole area of resource development. The Episcopal Church is rich in undeveloped economic resources, and much is possible if we can learn ways to best leverage our assets. At both local and national levels the church needs advice on how we might creatively use our assets to underwrite and enable the vision. This may mean the development of a 20/20 Fund and/or for 20/20 to have significant access to funds that already exist or are planned, like the Alleluia Fund.

Communicating the 20/20 Vision

This is a major turning point—truly a kairos moment. To accomplish our goal of doubling the Average Sunday Attendance in the Episcopal Church by 2020, we must clearly and with intention communicate that the true mission of the church is to make disciples who can make disciples. This message must be constantly and consistently communicated to our own membership as well as to the world around us.

Communicating the 20/20 Vision to Episcopalians in an

> **Recommendations—**
> - Extend the work of the network of communicators enthusiastic about the possibilities of the 20/20 Movement and prepared to use their skills and insights in the service of the Good News in this way.
> - Give the 20/20 Vision and Movement a high profile in all church publications. One suggestion that can begin almost immediately is the launching of a monthly 20/20 page in *Episcopal Life*
> - The establishment of a lively 20/20 site with plenty of cross-linkages, especially accessible through the www.episcopalchurch.org home page
> - The establishment of networks both traditional and electronic that can publicize information of resources, both within and beyond Anglicanism, that are able to advance the 20/20 Vision.

effective and winning way is essential if we are to build up the 20/20 Movement within the church. This will require that we make more effective use of both traditional and electronic media, at local and at national levels, getting the message of 20/20 into every corner of the church and making sure it is at the top of congregational, diocesan and national church priorities. In addition, we need to be constantly open to newly developing modes of communication to improve our ability to share news and ideas as widely as possible.

It will be of paramount importance to broadcast to a wide audience the message that God and God's church are doing something new. There is intense spiritual hunger within our society, and there are segments of our culture whose curiosity about things spiritual can best be addressed by the approach of a historic liturgical church like our own. We need to be gathering and celebrating in both print and electronic media the success stories that come from our dioceses, congregations and other ministries. Now is the time to take the initiative by telling the good news of the Episcopal Church rather than allowing the press to shape public perceptions of what this church is like. Perhaps the time has come to consider how to shape the image of the Episcopal Church to serve our commitment to being a church that makes disciples who make disciples, thereby fulfilling the 20/20 Vision.

In terms of communicating the message about what God is doing in and through the Episcopal Church, we have been slow to develop an effective presence on the World Wide Web. Given that the generations we are seeking to reach intermingle meaningfully and naturally both in real time and online, significant opportunities are being lost. It is vital that the church encourage the development and multiplication of the finest interactive web sites at the local level, but also that diocesan and national sites be upgraded in both content and presentation rather than being mere electronic versions of newsletters, organizational directories, catalogues of church publications, traditional magazines or church bulletin boards. The production of engaging web sites, web-delivered educational content and web-delivered training is certainly an area in which young Christians must take a lead.

Conclusion

It is our dream that, during the next twenty years, the Episcopal Church will have come to terms with the fact that Christianity is no longer dominant in our culture. We recognize that the formerly mainline churches may have a much more modest place in the scheme of things than has historically been the case. We further recognize that we will be living in a society where a multiplicity of faith groups and religions are in aggressive competition with us, and that we are called to answer the challenge with both grace and enthusiasm.

The 20/20 Vision is built around a dream—that our church, the Episcopal Church, is willing to make the necessary changes, becoming a church of disciples eager to proclaim and live out the Good News of God in Christ Jesus in the fast-changing world in which it now finds itself. It is built around the assumption that our church is prepared to reconfigure itself where necessary in order to be faithful to our Lord. It is our hope that by 2020 we will have moved toward updating our church's understanding of Christian discipleship.

It is our dream that, when 2020 arrives, as many as 25% of our congregations will be less than 20 years old and that, while our worshiping numbers will have doubled from our present 830,000 each Sunday, the median age of our parishes will be considerably younger. It is also our fervent hope that those who are Episcopalians in 2020 will socially and ethnically "look more like America" as a whole than we do today.

We dream that the Episcopal Church of 2020 will be a vibrant fellowship of God's people, a significant proportion of its membership living into their Baptismal Covenant with enthusiasm and in sacrificial Christian service. This Episcopal Church will be bubbling over with possibilities, hopeful, upbeat and committed unflinchingly to the Gospel message of Jesus Christ. We dream that, as the 20/20 Vision has taken hold in the intervening years, gathering momentum and bringing about transformation, that more and more Episcopalians, touched by the Spirit of God, will be taking the message into the rest of the world, while others will be eagerly living Christ's love in the hearts of our urban centers, and among the marginalized and least fortunate.

The 20/20 Task Force dreams and yearns that by 2020 Episcopal Christians will have a fresh, new understanding of what it means to be a follower of Jesus Christ, a disciple and a member of the Episcopal Church.

AFTER THE 20/20 TASK FORCE REPORT: 20/20 STRATEGY GROUP

The 20/20 Task Force presented the above report to Executive Council in October 2001. The Executive Council received the report and then handed responsibility for developing strategies to implement the vision back to the Standing Commission on Domestic Mission and Evangelism. The Presiding Bishop, the President of the House of Deputies, and SCDME officers created a 20/20 Strategy Group and nine Program Teams in order to assist the SCDME with its mid-triennium charge from Executive Council to articulate specific strategies to support, encourage, and implement the vision of 20/20.

The 20/20 Strategy Group and SCDME understood in taking on this charge that no group or groups could own 20/20 and that it will be on the grassroots level that 20/20 will catch fire, a level not easily "programmed"or "legislated." Additionally, we understood that the charge was to address the missional energy of the whole church in its tremendous diversity to turn outward to an even more diverse society, understanding that any group or sub-group could easily say, "for us it is different." We sought not to offer so many right answers but to offer support to mission that is defined and generated from the context of local conditions. The following strategies and resolutions are offered in the spirit of that understanding.

In turn, the 20/20 Strategy Group was assisted by the ideas and energy of the following Program Team members, who were convened a large and diverse gathering of committed people in Camp Allen in January 2002 to propose strategies in the following areas: Leaders, Spirituality, Prayer, and Worship, Research, New Congregation Development, Congregational Revitalization, Next Generations, Communication and Funding.

CAMP ALLEN PROGRAM TEAMS

General Convention 2003
Edgar Kim Byham, Esq., Newark, II
The Rev. John A.M. Guernsey, Virginia, III
Ms. Nina Meigs, Conv. American Churches in Europe

Spirituality, Prayer, and Worship
The Rev. Paige Blair, Chair, Maine, I
The Rt. Rev. Michael Creighton, Central Pennsylvania, III
The Rev. J. Anthony Guillen, Los Angeles, VIII
The Rev. Timothy Jones, Tennessee, IV
Ms. Jessica Marth, Alaska, VIII
Ms. Heather York, Southern Virginia, III

Research
Mrs. C.J. Ditzenberger, Chair, Upper South Carolina, IV
The Rev. Kwasi Thornell, Southern Ohio, V
Mr. Howard M. Tischler, Rio Grande, VII
The Rev. Thomas Hansen, Nebraska, VI

New Congregation Development
The Rev. David Jones, Chair, Virginia, III
Ms. S. Dylan Breuer, Maryland, III
The Rt. Rev. Katharine Jefferts Schori, Nevada, VIII
Mr. David Keller, Upper South Carolina, IV
The Rev. Canon Kevin Martin, Texas, VII
The Rev. Uriel Osnaya-Jimenez, Texas, VII
The Rev. David H. Roseberry, Dallas, VII
Ms. Laura Russell, Esq., Newark, II
The Rev. George S. Sotelo, California, VIII

Congregational Revitalization
The Rev. Susanne Watson, Chair, Iowa, VI
The Rev. Stacy Alan, Western Michigan, V
The Rev. Anita Braden, Milwaukee, V
The Rev. Dr. James Cooper, Florida, IV
The Ven. William Coyne, Western Mass, I

The Rev. Colenzo Hubbard, West Tennessee, IV
The Very Rev. Sandra Wilson, Minnesota, VI

Leaders
The Rev. Bonnie Perry, Chair, Chicago, V
Ms. Latosha Collins, Western New York, II
The Rev. Carolyn Jones, Missouri, V
The Very Rev. James Lemler, Chicago, V
The Rev. Gary Steele, Alaska, VIII
The Rev. Winnie Varghese, Los Angeles, VIII
The Rev. LeeAnne Watkins, Minnesota, VI

Funding
The Rev. George Conger, Chair, Central Florida, IV
Mr. Albert T. Mollegen, Connecticut, I
Ms. Jessica Osaki, Los Angeles, VIII
Ms. Shelley Vescovo, Dallas, VII

Communication
Ms. Susan T. Erdey, Chair, New York, II
Ms. Carol Barnwell, Texas, VII
Mr. David Code, New York, II
Mrs. Nell Gibson, New York, II
Ms. Sarah Lawton, California, VIII
Canon Lydia Lopez, Los Angeles, VIII
The Rev. Canon David Seger, Northern Indiana, V

Next Generations
The Rev. Charlie Dupree, Chair, East Carolina, IV
The Rt. Rev. Leopoldo Alard, Texas, VII
Ms. Kate Hays, Virginia, III
The Rev. Michael Hopkins, Washington, III
Mr. Robert Schoeck, Massachusetts, I
Dr. Shirleen S. Wait, Florida, IV
Ms. Amber Stancliffe, California, VIII
The Rev. Sylvia Vasquez, Delaware, III

20/20 is already generating an enormous amount of spirit and enthusiasm for mission on the local level, reinforcing the reality that 20/20 is not a program, nor an initiative, but a *movement* that is spreading at the grassroots level across our church.

Now, even more than when the 20/20 initiative was first embraced by General Convention, the Episcopal Church faces variables of international scope that affect our approach to mission, including an ongoing worldwide war on terrorism, a globalized economic uncertainty, and scandals pointing to deficiencies of accountability in the wider Body of Christ. We also face the challenge of speaking the diverse languages of the communities we serve—including idioms of generation, culture, and place. A major theme throughout the program areas is a call to offer a broad range of resources appropriate to this new time.

Thus, the work of the 20/20 has and will, of necessity, follow an iterative, spiral model of constant reevaluation and retooling to meet new challenges as they emerge.

Much evidence points to 20/20 having been integrated and woven into the fabric of existing programs at the Episcopal Church Center, redirecting existing work and driving new initiatives. It is important to note that the program groups have not met physically since January 2002—instead, modeling the best use of technology tools available to them, the groups have convened around Internet discussion groups.

The following resolutions are presented by the SCDME with the support of the 20/20 Group:

1. LEADERSHIP
Strong leadership in all the orders of ministry is vital for the success of the work of 20/20 to be accomplished. We must identify, recruit, cultivate, and educate the leadership we need for the twenty-first century, including:
- individuals with multilingual and intercultural skills to serve the emerging majority population that is not primarily of European descent;
- individuals who speak the language of the "next generations" who can embody and proclaim the Gospel in a postmodern context and use appropriate appealing methods to spread the Gospel;
- Individuals with skill and temperaments to revitalize existing congregations and plant new congregations.

Resolution A059 Design New Resources
1   *Resolved,* the House of _____ concurring, That the seminaries and diocesan schools for ministry of the
2   Episcopal Church be urged to review curriculum resources and design new resources that focus on:
3   - intercultural leadership
4   - contemporary foreign language courses
5   - anti-racism education
6   - church planting
7   - congregational revitalization
8   - evangelism
9   - management of change
10 - negotiation of conflict

Resolution A060 Contemporary Language Competency
1   *Resolved,* the House of _____ concurring, That this 74th General Convention direct the Standing
2   Commission on Ministry Development to prepare revisions of the ordination canons to require
3   competency in a contemporary language other than English or a culture other than the candidate's native
4   culture, and require intercultural field education experience of all candidates.

Resolution A061 Continuing Education Scholarships
1   *Resolved,* the House of _____ concurring, That this 74th General Convention allocate $250,000 towards
2   scholarships for clergy and congregational leaders for continuing education in areas of change, decision
3   making, conflict resolution, and congregational renewal.

Resolution A062 Diversity in Leadership Recruitment

1   *Resolved,* the House of _____ concurring, That the Episcopal Church recruit leadership that reflects the
2   diversity of our society and create multiple discernment options reflecting the variety of places from which
3   individuals hear a call to ministry, and that the canons be altered to allow sponsorships:
4   • by campus ministries
5   • by internship programs for ordination in "home" or "away" dioceses
6   • by seminaries with intentional vocational discernment programs for undergraduate and graduate
7   students.

Resolution A063 Ethnic Specific Discernment Committees

1   *Resolved,* the House of _____ concurring, That this 74th General Convention encourage bishops and
2   commissions on ministry to designate ethnic-specific discernment committees to identify, support, and
3   retain individuals for ministry from communities not well represented within a diocese's current
4   leadership.

Resolution A064 Seminarian Expenses

1   *Resolved,* the House of _____ concurring, That the Episcopal Church as a national body move towards
2   paying for seminarians' expenses in preparation for ministry; and be it further
3   *Resolved,* That the Church Pension Fund be urged to examine the feasibility of a program to underwrite
4   the loan costs for seminarians of the church exploring such possibilities as:
5   • determining the feasibility of amortizing seminary loan payments over the course of a cleric's career;
6   • including seminary debt in the pension premium of parochial/institutional clergy, distributed over the
7   course of a cleric's career; and be it further
8   *Resolved,* That dioceses and congregations commit a greater proportion of income to the support of
9   candidates preparing for ordination and lay professionals; and be it further
10   *Resolved,* That the Episcopal Church seek funding support for the debt reduction of newly ordained
11   persons who serve in priority mission areas that are under-served and under-funded, including new church
12   plants, multi-cultural and specialized cultural ministries and rural areas; and be it further
13   *Resolved,* That the Episcopal Church encourage the development of a fund to defray the educational
14   expenses of seminarians through a partnership with the Episcopal Church Foundation, Society for the
15   Increase of the Ministry, Episcopal Evangelical Education Society, and the Church Pension Fund.

Resolution A065 Leadership Programs for 18-25 Year-Olds

1   *Resolved,* the House of _____ concurring, That the Episcopal Church encourage dioceses to explore and
2   develop exciting internships and leadership development programs aimed at 18-25 year-olds, with a focus
3   on social justice, discipleship, simple living, intentional community, spiritual formation, theological
4   reflection, and vocational discernment.

Resolution A066 Campus Ministry Allocation

1   *Resolved,* the House of _____ concurring, That the 74th General Convention call upon all dioceses of the
2   Episcopal Church to allocate a meaningful proportion of budgeted income to campus ministry as a form of
3   mission to the next generation.

Resolution A067 Fund for Theological Education

1   *Resolved,* the House of _____ concurring, That the Episcopal Church allocate $300,000 to be matched by
2   the Lilly Endowment's $2.3 million to be a full partner and participant in the Fund for Theological
3   Education's pastoral leadership search effort (Pulse Project) which will identify, cultivate, and recruit
4   exceptional candidates under age 35 for ordination by developing materials, a database, and a web site,
5   this project being in conjunction with the Presbyterian Church (USA), the United Methodist Church, and
6   the Evangelical Lutheran Church in America.

2. Spirituality, Prayer, and Worship

"It is not necessary that Traditions and Ceremonies be in all places one, or utterly like; for at all times they
have been divers, and may be changed according to the diversity of countries, times, and men's manners, so
that nothing be ordained against God's Word" (Article XXXIV of the Articles of Religion, *Book of Common*

Prayer, p. 874). In keeping with this spirit of Anglicanism, it is clear that in order for us to fulfill the 20/20 call, our worship must be relevant to the times, languages, and cultures of our people. However, it is not enough to mandate new liturgies, but rather our worship of God must be relational, transformational, and leading to an encounter with the Risen Christ, thus compelling us to share our experience with others.

Resolution A068 Episcopal Church Web-Site

1   *Resolved,* the House of _____ concurring, That the 74th General Convention direct the Episcopal Church
2   Center staff to collect and post on the Episcopal Church website a variety of resources related to faith
3   formation, ongoing spiritual growth, and education of both children and adults. This should include
4   resources that are oriented to seekers from outside the Episcopal Church, and that assist in making
5   disciples oriented to mission for the local context.

Resolution A069 Spanish Music Resources

1   *Resolved,* the House of _____ concurring, That the 74th General Convention direct the Standing
2   Commission on Liturgy and Music, in cooperation with the Office of Hispanic Ministries, to collect,
3   create, and publish music resources in the Spanish language that are reflective of and appropriate to Latino
4   cultures in the United States, and that $100,000 be approved for this purpose.

Resolution A070 Creative Worship Resources

1   *Resolved,* the House of _____ concurring, That the 74th General Convention direct the Office of Liturgy,
2   in cooperation with the Offices of Congregational Development and the Standing Commission on Liturgy
3   and Music, to cooperate with our ecumenical partners in sponsoring and promoting conferences on music
4   and liturgy which teach and promote fresh resources for creative, multisensory worship that is done well,
5   and that includes a mix of multicultural and multilingual music and a variety of musical styles and sounds.

Resolution A071 Mission-based Prayers

1   *Resolved,* the House of _____ concurring, That the 74th General Convention direct the Office of
2   Liturgy and the Offices of Congregational Development to compile and post on the Episcopal
3   Church website mission-based prayers of the people and other liturgical resources that support the
4   20/20 vision, and post links to other 20/20–related liturgical resources that have been developed
5   throughout the Church.

3. Research

Current, accurate, and thorough demographic data on Episcopal parishes and membership is a pressing need. Improvements in the parochial reporting system have been made in recent years but more and different kinds of data need to be collected. One important change has been in the hiring of a qualified and experienced director of research at the Episcopal Church Center. Dr. C. Kirk Hadaway began work in 2002. Additional resources for this critically important task will be required.

As we are targeting research questions and projects, we raise several areas in which additional knowledge would be helpful. Include in the parochial report requests for information we seek to support 20/20 goals, including:

- Ethnicity/race, language, sex, and age information on congregations and their leadership, recognizing that such information will be somewhat subjective;
- Baptisms, categorized by child and adult;
- Confirmations and Receptions, categorized by child and adult;
- Annually varying topical questions such as average family income in the parish, outreach projects being undertaken, etc.

Annual reports are now being sent to congregations with a ten-year history of attendance and stewardship together with projections out three to five years. These should be included with the parochial report forms to encourage the clergy and lay leadership to provide thorough and accurate information.

Accuracy in data is vitally important, especially with respect to Average Sunday Attendance ("ASA"), which is widely regarded as the most reliable statistical measure of congregational health. There are significant advantages to software versions of parish registers. These should be downloadable and moderate in cost or free. Such programs could minimize mathematical errors and allow for ongoing statistical analyses, such as doing a review of Easter services over the period for which data is available. Ideally, there could be software usable on handheld devices which can be located in the sacristy and the information downloaded on other computers for compilation.

Percept continues to be a very useful tool in evangelism by providing pertinent demographic data. The costs of such useful services have been significant for some dioceses; thus, dioceses are encouraged to work together, especially through provinces, to negotiate with Percept for affordable fees.

Make the parochial report more useful by assuring that more of the church leadership has an opportunity to review it. To that end, we propose the following amendment to the canons:

Resolution A072 Amend Canon I.6.2

1 *Resolved,* the House of _____ concurring, That Canon I.6.2 be amended to read as follows:
2 A report of every Parish and other Congregation of this Church shall be prepared annually for the year
3 ending December 31 preceding, in the form authorized by the Executive Council and approved by the
4 Committee on the State of the Church, and shall be filed not later than March 1 with the Bishop of the
5 Diocese, or, where there is no Bishop, with the ecclesiastical authority of the Diocese. The Bishop or the
6 ecclesiastical authority, as the case may be, shall keep a copy and submit the report to the Executive
7 Council not later than May 1. In every Parish and other Congregation the preparation and filing of this
8 report shall be the joint duty of the Rector or Member of the Clergy and ~~Vestry; and in every other~~
9 ~~Congregation the duty of the Member of the Clergy in charge thereof.~~ the lay leadership; and before the
10 filing thereof the report shall be approved by the Vestry or bishop's committee or mission council. This
11 report shall include the following information…

EXPLANATION

The information supplied in the parochial report is essential to planning by the dioceses and national church, but it is even more vital that the leadership of congregations be fully engaged in the process and annually review the statistical data associated with the congregation. Since compilations of past data will now be provided to congregations, review of new data will help assure greater understanding and awareness of historical data and trends.

4. New Congregation Development

A large percentage of the Episcopal congregations in the United States were planted in the early years of the last century. Research within the American religious context strongly suggests that the largest proportion of any numerical expansion is likely to take place in new congregations, which means that every effort should be made to make new church development a major priority of the church as a whole, and of dioceses in particular, during the next two decades.

This is an area in which the Episcopal Church has not traditionally excelled, and so major education efforts will be necessary in order to meet the challenges of having every diocese plant new congregations by 2020.

Resolution A073 Plant New Churches

1 *Resolved,* the House of _____ concurring, That the 74th General Convention direct the Congregational
2 Development Unit of the Episcopal Church Center to:
3 • develop a system for identifying persons with the skills and temperament to plant new churches and/or
4   revitalize existing congregations;
5 • develop and carry out events to include an annual national conference of church planters to share
6   stories and resources;
7 • develop training and mentoring programs for laypersons involved in church planting;
8 • through the office of the Director of Research at the Episcopal Church Center, conduct and fund
9   research into how other denominations plant and sustain new churches, with special emphasis on
10   learning best practices for planting churches in less affluent areas or areas with negative population
11   growth;
12 • develop a 20/20 Resource Bank to support new church plants by creating a grassroots network that
13   matches resources of all types with those that need them.

EXPLANATION

Since we have committed to double attendance in Episcopal Churches by 2020, it is essential that we radically reassess our approach to new church development. If we are to meet the 2020 target, it will be necessary to establish a significant number of new churches. While the Episcopal Church is rediscovering the adventure of launching new congregations, considerable effort and resources will be necessary to succeed.

Church planters are often isolated because of their unique ministry. Further, those interested in the process of church planting often do not have or know where to find resources to assist them. If the goal of 2020 is to be reached, new church planting will be the major component. Therefore, the Standing Commission on Domestic Mission and Evangelism and the 2020 Strategy Group recommend that the Congregational Development Unit and the Director of Research take charge of ensuring that information on church planting is compiled and shared in an easily accessible format. Further, the Standing Commission and Task Force recommend the Congregational Development Unit coordinate conferences and events for the sharing of information among diocesan leaders and ordained and lay church planters.

5. Vital Congregations

A vital mission-minded congregation is called to restore all people to unity with God and each other in Christ and will be a healthy, dynamic, and inviting church, reflective of the diversity of our society, deeply rooted in faith and the gospel, so that its members live out their baptismal covenant to be disciples who make disciples and extend the Reign of God in the world.

Although average Sunday attendance (ASA) is certainly not the sole indicator of a congregation's health and vitality, it is an important baseline measure to consider. Over half of the 7,500 parishes in the Episcopal Church have an ASA of under 100 people. In many cases, this is due to geography and demographics—rural parishes, for example, may be alive and vibrant while only attracting 50 or 60 to Sunday services.

Often enough, however, the low ASA is due to parishes losing their mission focus and concentrating on mere maintenance and survival.

Resolution A074 Congregational Annual Study

1 *Resolved,* the House of _____ concurring, That every congregation of the Episcopal Church be strongly
2 encouraged to engage in annual (regular) study and review of its common life.

EXPLANATION

This is a dynamic and ongoing process that seeks God's longing, as well as opportunities to engage in the mission of reconciling the world. This is a primary route to truth-telling, and might include questions such as:

- Who are we? Who are we called to be?
- Who is our neighbor? Are we meeting and learning about our neighbor?
- What is our mission in this place? What ought it to be?
- How are lives and communities being transformed?
- How are people being equipped for Christ's ministry of reconciliation?
- How is this community and congregation different from a year ago? 5 years ago? 10 years ago?
- How is leadership recognized, affirmed, and shared here?

Resolution A075 Diocese Mission Perspective

1 *Resolved,* the House of _____ concurring, That every diocese in the Episcopal Church be strongly
2 encouraged to:
3 - foster a missional perspective or culture;
4 - foster a culture of partnering with others (congregations, denominations, etc.) for mission and ministry;
5 - equip people to facilitate congregational self-study;
6 - foster a culture in which transformation, death, and resurrection are the normal perspective on
7   congregational life.

Resolution A076 Transformation Resources

1   *Resolved,* the House of _____ concurring, That Episcopal Church Center staff be charged to:

2   • continue to develop strategic resources for transformation, such as: Transformation and Renewal
3   (vitalization in Black congregations) and Start Up, Start Over (theory and best practices for
4   congregational renewal)
5   • continue to hold up paradigmatic examples of transformation and resurrection, including those in
6   multicultural congregations, via *Episcopal Life*, the national church website, etc.
7   • continue to develop and offer multicultural and multilingual resources for transforming congregations
8   • develop a national consultancy/gathering for leaders in multicultural congregations, for the purpose of
9   networking, learning, and resource sharing
10 • continue to develop educational resources for transformation, such as Bible studies and small group
11   resources for hospitality, mission, evangelism, and how to tell our own stories; resources that make
12   liturgy more accessible, e.g., the Rite series; resources for learning about culture and change
13 • continue to maintain awareness of opportunities for learning and transformation in congregational life
14   (Congregational Development office).

EXPLANATION (for all three resolutions)

Principles:

- The gifts needed for ministry in a particular place are present in the local worshiping community.
- The apostolic task is to give the scriptures and sacraments to a faith community, that they may then proceed to live their Christian life of mission.
- Maturity in the faith develops in an atmosphere of prayer, biblical literacy, reflection, and witness.
- Vital congregations may be of any size, but they invite and encourage diversity.

Characteristics of a vital (revitalized) congregation—which transcend those stylistic things which have traditionally divided us:

- transforms lives within the congregation so that lives beyond the congregation may also be transformed;
- invites others into its life and mission, and is open to being changed by those who respond;
- knows the gospel gives courage and strength to live in a world of chaos and change, even within the church;
- intentionally transcends social boundaries;
- offers liturgy which is transformative, and points the way to Jesus;
- exhibits a graced confidence in its common life;
- provides a setting in which everyone's story is heard, everyone's gifts are discovered, and the community blesses and affirms their use in the world;
- gives discipleship and leadership development a central role;
- offers pastoral care which is more than adequate, and is a ministry of the whole body
- ensures effective administration;
- demonstrates a willingness to learn from the larger church, and to share our learning with others.

6. Next Generations

The numbers are all too familiar: demographically, we are an aging church with aging clergy, in a world where most people make a commitment to follow Christ by their early adult years. Our congregants' median age is 57.9 years old, which is more than 20 years older than the 36.4 years median age of the general American population.

As serious a picture as this paints for the future of our church, what is more serious is the vast spiritual hunger present in the world in which we live. Lives will be transformed by the love of God, and some will be best able to hear the Good News in the particular way we as Anglicans articulate it. Ultimately what is at stake is the transformation of the world into a more just, more peaceful place that mirrors the Reign of God.

The intention is to challenge the next generations (a term generally referring to GenX, GenY/Millennials, and children) to live into their baptismal covenants in the contexts in which they live so that all will come to know the love God has for them and the hope God has for the world.

Resolution A077 Trained Leadership

1   *Resolved,* the House of _____ concurring, That the 74th General Convention adopt a vision of a trained
2   children's minister, a trained youth minister, and a trained young adult minister in every congregation; and
3   an Episcopal ministry on every college campus; and be it further
4   *Resolved,* That the 74th General Convention authorize $4,000,000 for the next triennium to be dispersed
5   among the provinces for the training and mentoring of those who minister with children, youth, young
6   adults, and on college campuses; and be it further
7   *Resolved,* That provinces and dioceses be encouraged to match these funds.

EXPLANATION

We believe in communicating the Gospel to the next generations because we believe a relationship with Christ to be vital in navigating the changes and chances of every stage in life. When we encounter the living God, our lives are transformed, and patterning our lives after Christ's will ultimately transform the world around us to more fully resemble the Reign of God.

Our experience teaches us that we are more likely to hear the Good News when it is offered to us in the context of trusted relationship and in a language and culture similar to our own. Therefore it is the next generations themselves who will be most effective in proclaiming the reconciling love of God in Christ. What we most need at this time in our church's life is to mentor those in the next generations who will share their experience of God so that lives will be transformed. In doing so, our church will not only be faithful to its mission, it will in turn be transformed.

Better decisions are often made by the people most affected by them. Therefore we call on the provincial networks to allocate resources as they deem to be most appropriate for their province.

Resolution A078 Next Generation Mentoring

1   *Resolved,* the House of _____ concurring, That the 74th General Convention call the Office of
2   Communications and the Ministries with Young People Cluster to devote a portion of the Episcopal
3   Church website to mentoring and relationship building among those who work with the next generations,
4   including campus ministries, young adult ministries, youth ministries, and children's ministries.

EXPLANATION

Ministry is all about relationships and the web can be an essential tool for building relationships. We imagine such communication would be especially helpful to rural or isolated congregations.

Resolution A079 General Convention Deputies

1   *Resolved,* the House of _____ concurring, That the 74th General Convention recommend that diocesan
2   conventions elect deputations to General Convention that represent the next generations, and also the
3   multilingual, multicultural character of our churches and communities, so that deputations reflect the
4   vision we have for the church we would like to be in 2020.

EXPLANATION

Real transformation of our church will only happen when all people are welcome at the table. Presently the younger generations and the new cultural majority are severely underrepresented among General Convention deputations.

7. Communication

The highly networked nature of the 20/20 movement means that communication is a key component to its success. Without a comprehensive national communication strategy for 20/20, the work of the other eight program areas cannot become known and replicated across the church.

Resolution A080 Episcopal Church Website

1   *Resolved,* the House of _____ concurring, That the 74th General Convention direct the Episcopal Church
2   Center staff to develop and maintain a highly visual, dynamic, interactive, and constantly updated website
3   that is professional in appearance and easy to navigate; to deploy user-profiling tools to deliver website
4   material according to user preferences (such as seeker, lay, clergy, deputy, standing commission member);
5   to include multilingual and next generations resources in all areas of the website; and to develop software
6   and freeware resources for downloading.

Resolution A081 National Ad Campaign

1   *Resolved,* the House of _____ concurring, That the 74th General Convention direct the Office of
2   Communication to develop a national advertising campaign, with radio and television ads; and that the
3   General Convention urge congregations and dioceses to offer training in welcoming and incorporating
4   newcomers who may come in response to the advertising campaign; and that $750,000 be approved for
5   this purpose.

Resolution A082 Multi-Lingual Publications

1   *Resolved,* the House of _____ concurring, That the 74th General Convention, consistent with the
2   Executive Council's June 2002 mandate that materials issued by the Church Center be multilingual, invest
3   in additional linguistically and culturally skilled staff at the Church Center, the initial step being the
4   employment of translation services; and that the General Convention direct the Church Center Staff to
5   develop a strategy for multilingual publications and communication and report to Executive Council; and
6   that $85,000 per year for the triennium be approved for this purpose.

Resolution A083 Articulate Faith Story

1   *Resolved,* the House of _____ concurring, That the 74th General Convention urge every Episcopalian to be
2   able to articulate his or her faith story beginning with Epiphany 2004; and urge dioceses and congregations
3   to create opportunities for these stories to be told.

8. Funding

Funding will be necessary for many components of the 20/20 vision to be realized. The programs and
initiatives outlined in this proposal cannot be funded from the current structure of General Convention
budgets. Significant fundraising, in the form of a capital campaign for national 20/20 mission, among other
efforts, must be undertaken on a national level.

The Episcopal Church is rich in undeveloped economic resources. At both local and national levels the church
needs advice on how we might creatively use our assets to underwrite and enable the vision. A new
development arm must be established to seek major gifts, planned gifts, challenge funds, and other funding
devices to leverage the massive intergenerational transfer of capital funds that is now occurring in the United
States.

We support the work of the Standing Commission on Stewardship and Development and their resolutions [A-
140 and A-134] which urge the establishment of an Office of Mission Funding and Development, and which
urge implementation of the Alleluia Fund in each diocese and its use as one source of funding for 20/20
initiatives.

9. Reporting

Resolution A084 20/20 Vision Reporting

1   *Resolved,* the House of _____ concurring, That the 74th General Convention direct the SCDME:
2   • to report regularly to the Executive Council and the Episcopal Church at large on how the whole
3   church is living into the missional vision of 20/20;
4   • to facilitate communication among different agencies of the church that are carrying out parts of the
5   20/20 vision.

EXPLANATION

The 20/20 vision and movement cannot be directed or contained by any one agency of the church, but a body
is needed to be a central coordinating and reporting agency. The SCDME will hold hearings, gather and
dispense information, facilitate networking, evaluate progress, and celebrate successes along the way.

BUDGET

The Standing Commission on Domestic Mission and Evangelism will meet approximately five times during
the next triennium. This will require $40,000 for 2004, $41,000 for 2005 and $26,000 for 2006 for a total of
$107,000 for the triennium.

STANDING COMMISSION ON ECUMENICAL RELATIONS

www.episcopalchurch.org/gc/ccab/scer/default.html
For the full text of this report, go to
www.episcopalchurch.org/ecumenism/bbreport

Membership

The Rt. Rev. William O. Gregg, *Chair*	Eastern Oregon, 2003
The Very Rev. Donald D. Brown, *Vice-Chair*	Northern California, 2006
Ms. Margaret J. Faulk, *Secretary*	New Hampshire, 2003
Mr. James R. Foster	Eastern Oregon, 2006
The Rt. Rev. Leo Frade	Southeast Florida, 2003
Mr. John L. Harrison, Jr.	New Hampshire, 2003
The Rt. Rev. Carolyn T. Irish	Utah, 2003
The Rt. Rev. Stephen H. Jecko	Florida, 2006
Mrs. Diane Knippers	Virginia, 2006
The Rev. Charles D. Krutz	Louisiana, 2003
Ms. Donna McNiel	West Missouri, 2003
The Rt. Rev. William D. Persell	Chicago, 2006
The Rev. Canon Ephraim Radner	Colorado, 2006
The Rev. Canon Saundra Richardson	Michigan, 2003
The Rt. Rev. Douglas E. Theuner	New Hampshire, 2006
The Rev. Chris Rankin-Williams	Los Angeles, 2003
Ms. Alice Roberta Webley	Western Michigan, 2006
The Rev. Ellen K. Wondra	Rochester, 2006

Staff

The Rt. Rev. C. Christopher Epting, Deputy for Ecumenical and Interfaith Relations
Dr. Thomas C. Ferguson, Associate Deputy for the Ecumenical and Interfaith Relations
The Rev. Canon J. Robert Wright, Consultant to the Ecumenical Office

Adjunct

The Rev. Canon Robert Miner, *EDEO Liaison*
The Rev. Randall Lee, *ELCA Liaison*

Contents

I. INTRODUCTION

The Standing Commission on Ecumenical Relations (SCER) is charged with recommending to General Convention "a comprehensive and coordinated policy and strategy on relations between this Church and other Churches" and "to make recommendations to General Convention concerning interchurch cooperation and unity." In addition the SCER is responsible for coordinating this Church's participation in "governing bodies of ecumenical organizations to which this Church belongs by action of the General Convention." (Title I, Canon 1.2.(n)(5). Thus the SCER works closely with the Office of Ecumenical and Interfaith Relations and the Presiding Bishop as chief Ecumenical Officer to monitor this Church's Full Communion partners, to develop and sustain a variety of dialogues with the Roman Catholic, Eastern Orthodox, Moravian, United Methodist, and Presbyterian Churches, and to coordinate this Church's participation in the National Council of Churches of Christ in the USA and the World Council of Churches. The SCER met five times during the triennium and remained in close contact in between meetings.

Reports to the 74th General Convention

II. LEGISLATIVE MATTERS FOR GENERAL CONVENTION

Evangelical Lutheran Church in America

The passage of *Called To Common Mission* by the 73rd Convention of the Episcopal Church inaugurated a full communion relationship between the Episcopal Church and the Evangelical Lutheran Church in America. The new Presiding Bishop of the ELCA, the Rev. Mark Hanson, was installed in October of 2001 according to the provisions of *Called to Common Mission*, which included three bishops in the historic succession participating in the laying on of hands, including Presiding Bishop Griswold. For examples of practical cooperation and joint mission between the churches, please consult the website of the Office of Ecumenical and Interfaith Relations, **www.episcopalchurch.org/ecumenism/elca/cooperation.**

Paragraphs 23 and 24 of CCM mandated the creation of a joint commission. The Lutheran-Episcopal Coordinating Committee (LECC) meets twice each year to identify issues pertaining to the "full communion" relationship between our two churches and refer them to appropriate national staff or program units of the two church bodies to address. The Coordinating Committee is not a decision making body for either church. The sole area in which the Committee is a decision making body is in the matter of putting forth a commentary on the text of CCM. This commentary is available from the website of the Office of Ecumenical and Interfaith Relations of the Episcopal Church, **www.episcopalchurch.org/ecumenism/elca/ccmcommentary.**

One of the matters that received extensive consideration was the matter of how to receive individuals from either church that are transferring membership to the other. The LECC asked the SCER, which also had considerable discussion on this issue, to submit the following resolution to the 74th General Convention:

Resolution A085 ELCA Member Reception

1   *Resolved,* the House of _____ concurring, That the rubrics concerning Confirmation with forms for
2   Reception and the Reaffirmation of Baptismal Vows (BCP, 412) allow such reception of members of the
3   Evangelical Lutheran Church in America.

EXPLANATION

In both our traditions, Holy Baptism "by water and the Holy Spirit" establishes full membership in Christ's body, the Church (LBW, p. 121; BCP, p. 298). Baptism is the sacramental basis for mission and ministry of the whole church and all its members.

At its 2001 Churchwide Assembly, the Evangelical Lutheran Church in America passed an ordination bylaw, allowing exceptions to be granted for pastors to preside at the ordination of pastors. There have been three such exceptions granted, and these persons are not eligible for transfer for service in the Episcopal Church. Both the SCER and the International Anglican Standing Commission on Ecumenical Relations (an internationally representative group established to monitor all Anglican ecumenical relations which may give advice, but its purpose is neither prescriptive nor compulsory) have considered this matter.

In the belief that wider rather than minimal discussion is appropriate to this situation, the SCER hereby offers the following resolution:

Resolution A086 Lutheran Ordination Bylaw

1   *Resolved,* the House of _____ concurring, That the House of Bishops is hereby requested to establish a
2   committee to monitor the ways and extent to which the ELCA ordination bylaw exception may cause any
3   additional limitations upon the full communion that has been jointly established and to report their
4   findings and any recommendations to the next General Convention.

EXPLANATION

At its 2001 Churchwide Assembly, the Evangelical Lutheran Church in America passed a bylaw to Called to Common Mission which allows the ordination of ELCA pastors by other than bishops in unusual circumstances contrary to Called to Common Mission paragraph 20. It is the hope that this bylaw will not impair or hinder the relationship of full communion between our two churches. However we are mindful also of the difficulty that this development poses for Anglican relations with certain other ecumenical partners, especially as this further limitation upon the interchangeability of pastors/presbyters has been questioned by the Inter Anglican Standing Commission on Ecumenical Relations.

Moravian-Episcopal Dialogue

The Moravian-Episcopal dialogue was authorized by the 1997 General Convention and met five times during the triennium. The Moravian Church in America is part of the worldwide church called the Unity of the Brethren who trace their origin to the Hussite movement in 15th century Bohemia. The Moravian Church in the United Kingdom has engaged in significant dialogue with the Church of England, producing the *Fetter Lane Common Statement* in 1995. In the USA, the Episcopal Church-Moravian Church dialogue emerged from a local North Carolina dialogue.

Significant progress has been made in discussion of the interchangeability of ministries and for establishing a relationship of Interim Eucharistic Sharing. The following resolution to establish Interim Eucharistic Sharing was drafted by the dialogue team and was approved by the SCER to be brought to the 2003 General Convention. An identical resolution was passed by the Provincial Synods of the Moravian Church in America, Northern and Southern Provinces, which met in the summer of 2002.

Resolution A087 Interim Eucharistic Sharing with the Moravian Church in America, Northern and Southern Provinces

1 *Resolved,* the House of _____ and the Synods of the Moravian Church in America (Northern and Southern
2 Provinces) concurring, That the 74th General Convention meeting in Minneapolis, MN, July 30-August 8,
3 2003, authorize continuing dialogue with the Moravian Church in America (Northern and Southern
4 Provinces) which may lead to a future proposal of Full Communion including interchangeability of clergy
5 for ministry of Word and Sacrament; and be it further
6 *Resolved*, the House of _____ and the synods of the Moravian Church in America (Northern and Southern
7 Provinces) concurring, That the 74th General Convention of the Episcopal Church, meeting in
8 Minneapolis, MN, July 30-August 8, 2003, establishes Interim Eucharistic Sharing between the Episcopal
9 Church and the Moravian Church under the following guidelines:
10 **1.** Moravian Provincial Elders' Conferences and Episcopal diocesan authorities are hereby encouraged to
11 authorize joint celebrations of the Eucharist.
12 **2.** An authorized liturgy of the host church must be used, with ordained ministers of both churches
13 standing at the Communion Table for the Great Thanksgiving.
14 **3.** The Preacher may be from either church.

EXPLANATION

1. We welcome and rejoice in the substantial progress of the dialogue between the Episcopal Church and the Moravian Church in America (Northern and Southern Provinces), authorized in 1997 and meeting 1999-2002, and of the progress of the initial North Carolina Moravian-Episcopal dialogue, which met from 1994-1997. Similar progress has been made in other Moravian-Anglican dialogues, including the dialogue between the Moravian Church in Great Britain and Ireland and the Church of England that resulted in the Fetter Lane Declaration of May 19, 1995. We share the hope of the *Fetter Lane Declaration*: "We look forward to the day when full communion in faith and life for the sake of our common mission is recognized by our churches."

2. We acknowledge with thanksgiving the dialogue between the Moravian Church in America and the Evangelical Lutheran Church in America which resulted in a full communion agreement in 1999 on the basis of the document *Following Our Shepherd to Full Communion*.

3. We recognize in one another the faith of the one, holy, catholic, apostolic, and undivided church as it is witnessed in the Moravian Church in America in the *Moravian Book of Worship*, the *Ground of the Unity*, the *Moravian Covenant for Christian Living*, and the *Books of Order* of the Northern and Southern Provinces and the *Book of Common Prayer* and the *Constitution and Canons* of the Episcopal Church.

In addition we concur with the points of agreement in the *Fetter Lane Common Statement*:

"a We accept the authority of and read the Scriptures of the Old and New Testaments. Each church provides a lectionary, and in the course of the Church's year appropriate Scriptures are read to mark the festivals and seasons.

"b We accept the Niceno-Constantinopolitan and Apostles' Creeds and confess the basic trinitarian and christological dogmas to which these creeds testify. That is, we believe Jesus of Nazareth is true God and true Man, and that God is one God in three persons, Father, Son, and Holy Spirit.[17]

"c We celebrate the apostolic faith in worship, and centrally in liturgical worship, which is both a celebration of salvation through Christ and a significant factor in forming the *consensus fidelium* (the common mind of the faithful). We rejoice at the extent of 'our common tradition of spirituality, liturgy, and sacramental life,' which has given us similar forms of worship, common texts, hymns, canticles, and prayers. We are influenced by a common liturgical renewal. We also rejoice at the variety of expressions shown in different cultural settings.[18]

"d Baptism is both God's gift and our human response to that gift in repentance and faith.[19] It is a sign of God's gracious activity in the life of the person baptized. Baptism with water in the name of the Triune God is the sacrament of union with the death and resurrection of Jesus Christ, initiating the one baptized into the One, Holy, Catholic and Apostolic Church. Baptism is related not only to a momentary experience, but to life-long growth into Christ.[20] Both our churches offer baptism to adults and infants and regard it as unrepeatable. Since we practise and value infant baptism, we also take seriously our catechetical task for the nurture of baptized children to mature commitment to Christ.[21] The life of the Christian is necessarily one of continuing struggle yet also of continuing experience of grace.[22] In both our traditions infant baptism is followed by a rite of confirmation, which includes invocation of the Triune God, renewal of the baptismal profession of faith and a prayer that through renewal of the grace of baptism the candidate may be strengthened now and for ever.[23]

"e We believe that the celebration of the Eucharist (or the Lord's Supper or Holy Communion) is the feast of the new covenant instituted by Jesus Christ in which we set forth his life, death, and resurrection and look for his coming in glory. In the Eucharist the risen Christ gives his body and blood under the visible signs of bread and wine to the Christian community. 'In the action of the Eucharist Christ is truly present to share his risen life with us and unite us with himself in his self-offering to the Father, the one full, perfect, and sufficient sacrifice which he alone can offer and has offered once for all.'[24] In the Eucharist, through the power of the Holy Spirit, the Church experiences the love of God and the forgiveness of sins in Jesus Christ and proclaims his death and resurrection until he comes and brings his Kingdom to completion.[25]

"f We believe and proclaim the gospel, that in his great love God, through Christ, redeems the world. We 'share a common understanding of God's justifying grace, i.e. that we are accounted righteous and are made righteous before God only by grace through faith because of the merits of our Lord and Saviour Jesus Christ, and not on account of our works or merits…Both our traditions affirm that justification leads to "good works"; authentic faith issues in love'.[26]

"g We share a common hope in the final consummation of the Kingdom of God, and believe that in this eschatological perspective we are called to work now for the furtherance of justice and peace. Our life in the world and in the Church is governed by the obligations of the Kingdom. 'The Christian faith is that God has made peace through Jesus "by the blood of his cross" (Col. 1.20), so establishing the one valid centre for the unity of the whole human family.'[27]

"h We believe that the Church is constituted and sustained by the Triune God through God's saving action in word and sacraments, and is not the creation of individual believers. We believe that the Church is sent into the world as sign, instrument and foretaste of the Kingdom of God. But we also recognize that the Church, being at the same time a human organization, stands in constant need of reform and renewal.[28]

"i We believe that all members of the Church are called to participate in its apostolic mission. There are therefore various gifts of the Holy Spirit for the building up of the community and the fulfilment of its calling.[29] Within the community of the Church the ordained ministry exists to serve the ministry of the whole people of God. We hold the ordained ministry of word and sacrament to be a gift of God to his Church and therefore an office of divine instutition.[30]

"Both our churches have a threefold ministry of bishop, presbyter, and deacon and believe it to serve as an expression of the unity we seek and also a means of achieving it.[31] Within this threefold ministry the bishop signifies and focuses the continuity and unity of the whole Church. Apostolic continuity and unity in both our churches is expressed in the consecration and ordination of bishops in succession. The ordination of other ministers in both our churches is always by a bishop, with the assent of the community of the Church.[32] Integrally linked with the episcopal ordination is our common tradition that the bishop has a special pastoral care for the clergy as for the whole church.

"j A ministry of oversight (*episcope*) is a gift of God to the Church. In both our Churches it is exercised in personal, collegial and communal ways. It is necessary in order to witness and safeguard the unity and apostolicity of the Church.[33] In both our traditions in the course of history the exact structure and distribution of oversight functions have varied."

The extract from The Fetter Lane Common Statement is copyright © Peter Coleman and Geoffrey Birtill.

We find this agreement sufficient to hereby establish a relationship of interim eucharistic sharing.

4. We encourage development of common life throughout the Moravian and Episcopal Churches by such means as the following:
   a. Mutual prayer and mutual support, including covenants and agreements at all levels;
   b. Common study of the Holy Scriptures, the histories and theological traditions of each church, and the material prepared by the dialogue;
   c. Joint programs of worship, religious education, theological discussion, mission, evangelism, and social action;
   d. Joint use of facilities.

5. This resolution and experience of Interim Eucharistic Sharing will be communicated at regular intervals to the other Moravian provinces, to other churches of the Anglican Communion throughout the world, to other churches with whom this Church is in full communion, as well as to the ecumenical dialogues in which Moravians and Anglicans are engaged, in order that consultation may be fostered, similar experiences encouraged elsewhere, and already existing relationships of full communion strengthened.

[17] Cf. *Anglican Lutheran International Conversations: the Report of the Conversations 1970-1972, authorized by the Lambeth Conference and the Lutheran World Federation* (London, 1973) (*Pullach*), paras. 23-25.

[18] Cf. *Helsinki*, para. 31; *Baptism, Eucharist and Ministry* (WCC Faith and Order Paper No. 111, 1982) (*BEM*), *Baprism*, paras 17-23, *Eucharist* paras 27-33, *Ministry*, paras 41-44.

[19] Cf. *BEM, Baptism*, para. 8.

[20] Cf. *BEM, Baptism*, para. 9.

[21] Conversations between the British and Irish Anglican Churches and the Nordic and Baltic Lutheran Churches, *The Porvoo Common Statement* (CCU Occasional Paper No. 3, 1993) (*Porvoo*), para 32(g).

[22] Cf. *BEM, Baptism*, para. 9.

[23] Cf. *Porvoo*, para 32(g).

[24] *God's Reign and Our Unity*, para. 65.

[25] Cf. *BEM, Eucharist*, para. 1.

[26] *Helsinki*, para. 20; cf. paras 17-21.

[27] *God's Reign and Our Unity*, para. 18; cf. para 43 and *Pullach*, para. 59.

[28] Cf. para. 21 above.

[29] Cf. *BEM, Ministry*, para. 7.

[30] Cf. *Helsinki*, paras 32-43; *God's Reign and Our Unity*, paras. 91-97, *BEM, Ministry*, paras 4 and 12.

[31] Cf, *BEM, Ministry*, para. 22.

[32] Cf. 'The Office of Bishop in our Churches: Texts', appended to this Common Statement.

Response to ARCIC Document *Gift of Authority*

In May 1999, Anglican-Roman Catholic International Consultation (ARCIC) issued its third agreed statement on authority, *The Gift of Authority* (hereafter shortened to *GA*). This document explores further the nature and practice of authority in the two churches and makes concrete suggestions as to the challenges and issues each church faces in relationship to the other in this area. The Anglican Communion Office has requested official responses to *GA* from the Provinces. SCER's response is included as part of this report.

For further developments in Anglican-Roman Catholic dialogues, including the important establishment of the International Anglican-Roman Catholic Commission for Unity and Mission (IARCCUM, whose goal is to look at areas of practical cooperation for the two churches), the Anglican-Roman Catholic International Commission (ARCIC, chaired by Presiding Bishop Frank Griswold), and the Anglican-Roman Catholic dialogue in the USA (ARCUSA, which meets twice yearly), please consult **www.episcopalchurch.org/ecumenism/romancatholic/developments**.

The following response to *GA* was drafted and approved by the Standing Commission on Ecumenical Relations in consultation with the seminaries of the Episcopal Church and the Episcopal Diocesan Ecumenical Officers. The specific questions asked by the Anglican Communion Office are appended to the response.

RESPONSE TO THE GIFT OF AUTHORITY
BY THE EPISCOPAL CHURCH IN THE UNITED STATES
Formulated by the Standing Commission on Ecumenical Relations and the Office for Ecumenical and Interfaith Relations

Introduction

1. *The Gift of Authority* (1998; hereafter GA[1]) continues the substantial history of dialogues and formal documents of the Anglican-Roman Catholic International Commission (ARCIC). Since the time of Michael Ramsey, Archbishop of Canterbury, and Paul VI, Bishop of Rome, our Churches have diligently and officially sought to explore together the faith we hold in common. The ultimate goal of these explorations has been to promote and sustain mutual respect and understanding in order to build that consensus which would ultimately culminate in the restoration of full communion between us. This goal of unity both baptismally, which now exists, and ecclesiastically, which does not now exist, is grounded in our shared knowing of the truth that there is one Lord, one faith, one Baptism, one God and Father of us all.

2. While profound and important strides forward have been made in developing consensus around our theologies of ministry and ordination, and Eucharist,[2] ARCIC has consistently found the area of authority and ecclesiology to be difficult and, as yet, insoluble. GA is intended to take the conversation further, as it grows out of the responses and concerns that emerged from Authority in the Church I & II[3] and out of developments in the two Churches in the intervening years. In formulating GA, ARCIC has carefully and courageously addressed a number of complex and controversial issues between and within our Churches. We are grateful to ARCIC for its work, and we welcome GA as a contribution to the ongoing conversation that is needed as we continue to live more deeply into communion with each other.

3. When the eleventh meeting of the Anglican Consultative Council commended GA to the Provinces of the Anglican Communion for "careful and critical study," each Province was asked to consider particular questions. (See Appendix I) As the body authorized by the Constitution and Canons of the Episcopal Church in the U.S.A. "to make recommendations to General Convention concerning interchurch cooperation and unity,"[4] the Standing Commission on Ecumenical Relations has considered these questions carefully and prayerfully. We have also consulted with diocesan ecumenical officers and others involved in the Episcopal

---

[1] *The Gift of Authority.* London: Catholic Truth Society; Toronto, Canada, Anglican book Centre; and New York: Church Publishing, Incorporated, 1999. Chapter II (Reference hereafter will be by Chapter and section, *viz.*, I.7).

[2] See *The Final Report (Windsor, 1981).* Cincinnati, OH: Forward movement Publications and Washington, D.C.: Office of Publishing Services, U.S. Catholic Conference. 1982.

[3] *Authority in the Church I (1976), Elucidation (1981), Authority in the Church II (1981).* Hereafter, *AC I/II, or AC/E.*

[4] Canon I.1.2(n).5.

Church's ecumenical efforts. This response includes our careful consideration of these questions and what we have heard in response to them and to GA itself.

4. Our general response is this: GA contributes one articulation of a way to understand and embody authority and primacy institutionally. The document uses Scripture and some elements of tradition to build and support its argument. It is particularly helpful in uncovering some elements of Anglican lack of clarity on where authority does reside and might reside within the Anglican Communion. However, our general response to GA requires us to say that it falls short of its goal in several substantive ways. We conclude that it has not substantively furthered our relationship together or our movement toward our final goal.

5. At the same time, we do not believe that GA marks an end. Rather, precisely because of its contents, it raises important issues and questions that call for further conversation, thinking, and work by our Churches. GA challenges the Anglican Communion and the Episcopal Church to be more self-critical about our theology and praxis[5] of authority, be that the primary authority of Scripture, or the authority of various offices and structures within our church and between member churches of the Anglican Communion. These issues are difficult and will require a new level of honesty and risk within and from both Churches in order to embrace creatively and constructively God's call to us to move forward toward full communion.

6. With gratitude, we acknowledge and accept GA as a part of a conversation that is of serious content and nature, and is important to us in the Episcopal Church in the United States of America. We remain fully committed to the goals of full communion and unity, and entirely convinced of the necessity of continuing conversation and work toward those ends. It is only in our mutual steadfast commitment to continue in dialog that we have the possibility of bringing our Churches into deeper relationship, and ultimately into full communion with one another in that unity for which our Baptism calls and empowers us by the Spirit in our one Lord. To further our conversations, we believe that we must speak frankly and clearly, yet within the rubric of "speaking the truth in love" (Ephesians 4. 15).

The Response and Critique

IN GENERAL

7. The theology and praxis of authority within the Church is rightly recognized by ARCIC as an essential topic around which we must come to common understanding and theology if we are to move toward full communion and unity. How that common understanding and theology are embodied in our current praxis is a further question, one that GA does not address. Instead, until §58, GA gives an idealized view of the church with little reference to actual current or desired future practice.[6] Yet the issue of how authority is exercised in the concrete must be addressed as part of our movement toward full communion. GA's failure to do so contributes to the reluctance of many in both Churches to agree with ARCIC's claim that its work "has resulted in sufficient agreement on universal primacy as a gift to be shared, for us to propose that such a primacy could be offered and received even before our churches are in full communion."[7]

8. The experience of the Anglican Communion indicates that praxis is a matter in which we do not necessarily need uniformity.[8] We believe that this holds true between our two Churches as well as within each of them. GA does not appear to allow this possibility.

9. While GA seeks to address three areas of authority our Churches posed for further exploration,[9] the direction, argument, and conclusions do not represent a wide consensus either within the Episcopal Church (USA) or the Anglican Communion, though it is asserted that they do represent a consensus among members

---

[5] That is, the interplay of practice and reflection that is present in the church at every level.

[6] This continues the practice of the earlier ARCIC documents on authority. See *AE I*, Preface.

[7] GA §60

[8] Chicago-Lambeth Quadrilateral, 4.

[9] *GA*, Introduction, p. 10. These areas are: (1) the relationship of Scripture and Tradition to the exercise of authority, (2) collegiality, conciliarity, and the role of the laity, and (3) Petrine primacy in relationship to Scripture and Tradition. The 1988 Lambeth Conference also identified primatial jurisdiction as an area needing discussion. (1988 Lambeth Conference: Resolution 8 and Explanatory Note regarding ARCIC I) GA does not directly address this issue.

of ARCIC. In part, we believe this is because ARCIC has not taken adequately into account important theological developments in the Anglican Communion since AC II (1981). Of particular importance to the question of authority in the church is the theology of baptism and ministry found in The Book of Common Prayer 1979. Further, ARCIC has not been a body representing the breadth and riches of the Anglican Communion. We believe these two factors have negatively affected the approach of GA.

10. We agree with GA's position that the "root of all authority is through the activity of the Triune God, who authors life in its fullness," indeed "new life for all." [10] As ARCIC's Church as Communion states, "God's purpose is to bring all people into communion with himself within a transformed creation."[11] Yet, as the document moves into the institutional implementation of authority given in service of the divine purpose, there is an increasing emphasis on the power and decision-making that is claimed for the Office of Bishop. This is matched by an underdeveloped, vague treatment of the role, responsibilities, and authority of the laity, as well as a generally underdeveloped consideration of the importance and relationships of all the People of God to power, authority, and decision-making. This is at odds with the understanding and practice of authority of ECUSA and the Anglican Communion, in which all the baptized are given authority in the church.[12]

11. GA addresses the relationship between Scripture and authority in the church by beginning with an interpretation of 2 Cor. 1:18-20 ("God's 'Yes' to us and our 'Amen' to God") that provides a central model of authority as a gift that originates in God and is entrusted to the People of God. This model is intended to provide a clear and understandable theological and conceptual center for the document.[13] However, as the document develops, this model becomes ever less persuasive, and in some sections functions as a convenient literary device rather than an adequate support for the claims made.[14] Thus, GA does not provide an adequate view of the relationship between Scripture and authority in the church.

AUTHORITY

12. The fundamental understanding of the exercise of authority in the church given by GA is too juridical and narrow, equating authority with power and the exercise of power. This equation is contrary to GA's own interpretation of 2 Cor. 1:18-20[15] and to its various assertions that authority is properly exercised fundamentally as a form of servanthood.[16]

13. GA claims to develop a coherent argument or explication of authority by building on the work of AC I & II.[17] We note that while GA offers one possible and plausible development of these earlier ARCIC documents, it is one that does not take adequately into account concerns expressed by the Anglican Communion, including ECUSA, particularly regarding the role of the laity and the relation between universal primacy and collegiality.[18] Nor does it adequately into account important theological developments in the Anglican Communion in our theology of baptism.

14. The methodology of GA in developing its particular understanding and application of "authority" as well as the interpretation of its central biblical model is one of argument by assertion.[19] There is an assumption of large amounts of knowledge, and of the logic that connects the assertions being made. It is not prima facie

---

[10] *GA*, I.7

[11] *Church as Communion,* 16, quoted in *GA* I.7

[12] See, for example, BCP "Catechism" 855-856.

[13] GA, §7-10.

[14] E.g., §19-25, 43, 50.

[15] Cf. GA §7-9

[16] E.g., GA §§ 9, 12, 37, 42, 46, 47, 51, 52

[17] Both *AC I & II* contain more precise and coherent definitions and understandings of authority. It appears that in *GA*, there is a break, which is unexplained, from the development of the understanding of authority in these previous two documents of ARCIC.

[18] *The Emmaus Report (prepared for Anglican Consultative Council 7 [1987] and the Lambeth Conference [1988]),* 64-69.

[19] GA Preface para. 3

---

clear what either the logic or the connections are. Given the importance and sensitivity of the matters treated, this clarity is sorely needed.

15. Theologically, authority is a matter of relationships: between God the Father and Jesus the Son of God, between God and the Church, among members of the Church which is the People of God. God is the source or author of all authority, but authority is given to all the People of God so that all may freely and willingly participate in the fulfillment of God's promises, in communion with one another and with God. Thus authority is properly understood as dispersed among the People of God, regardless of their order of ministry,[20] but in a way that is conducive to Christian freedom and communion.

16. On the whole, GA fails to address adequately the Church's traditional practices of synodal, collegial, and conciliar discernment and decision-making over time, practices which involve the participation of laity, deacons, and priests as well as bishops. GA does not make it clear how and when there is broader participation in the decision-making of the Church by the priests, deacons, and laity. GA does indicate that decision-making involves "consultation" with all the baptized, but "consultation" is a vague term, vaguely used, and lacks a direct and serious commitment to the active role of members of the Church in addition to the Bishops. Further, to say that consultation ought to take place is not the same as saying that it will or must take place.[21]

17. In GA, the authority of priests, deacons, and laity of the Church along with bishops[22] is not effectively addressed or included as is their right by Baptism. GA does not address the particular authority proper to bishops, priests, deacons, and laity as distinguishable orders within the People of God. Instead, the active participation of laity, deacons, and priests is downplayed, thereby giving the impression that Bishops are, as a function of their Office, the primary (if not only) natural recipients of definitive revelation and the power to make definitive judgments for the Church. Further, GA's emphasis on authority as the legislative prerogative of Bishops fails to recognize the existence of and the need for adequate and appropriate lines of authority, responsibility, and accountability beyond legislative processes.

18. The principle of inclusion of all is not merely a political democratization of power, authority, or primacy. Rather it is a principle sacramentally grounded in Baptism and a related ecclesiology that makes the whole People of God responsible for the Church's life. This does not deny or abrogate the reality that within the Church, the various Orders of baptismal ministry carry different degrees of responsibility and accountability, as well as particular and different roles and ministries for the life of the Church in itself and in the world. The issue that is not adequately addressed in GA and needs more and further consideration is that of sustaining explicitly the whole context of each Order within the entire People of God, specifically in terms of authority, power, and decision-making.

19. The portrait presented by GA of the exercise of authority among the people of God is not consistent with an ecclesiology grounded in Baptism, such as that of ECUSA. Nor is it an adequate or accurate representation of the theology and praxis of the Anglican Communion or of the Episcopal Church, in which there are already a variety of expressions of synodality, collegiality, and conciliarity (as well as primacy). We note that a similar variety exists in theory in the Roman Catholic Church, though actual practice may be minimal and/or sporadic.[23] This is not to say that we believe that our own understanding or practice, as Anglicans or as Episcopalians, is adequate, or that we are convinced it must be the model for a united church; we are keenly aware of our own shortcomings in both theology and practice. However, we do believe that synodality, collegiality, and conciliarity are indispensable elements of the church's theology and praxis of authority, and need to be seen as such in relation to primacy.

PRIMACY

---

[20] BCP, "Catechism," 855-856.

[21] Cf. GA §57

[22] BCP 517-518

[23] SEE, E.G., ARCUSA'S AGREED REPORT ON THE LOCAL/UNIVERSAL CHURCH, NOVEMBER 15, 1999.

20. The definition of primacy, the theology growing from it, and the praxis of primacy set forth in GA are seriously problematic from our perspective in part because they contradict the praxis of primacy of the Episcopal Church USA; and of the Anglican Communion, in which primacy among the constituent Provinces is thought of and embodied in a variety of ways. It seems to us that the notion of primacy advocated in GA would require Anglicans to sacrifice the particularity of our heritage and identity and be subsumed under what is essentially the existing understanding and practice of primacy by the Bishop of Rome. The form of primacy articulated as acceptable in GA may reflect the membership of ARCIC, but it does not reflect a consensus on primacy within Anglicanism. Nor does GA reflect a consensus within the Episcopal Church in the USA.

21. Moreover, in a dialogue between equal partner Churches, it is inappropriate to make a case, even implicitly, for one partner to be subsumed into the theology and praxis of the other. It is neither reasonable nor appropriate to assert, implicitly or explicitly, that either church should relinquish its particular identity and tradition as a requirement for full communion. In this regard, GA goes well beyond the *subsistit in* of *Lumen gentium* and marks a return to earlier, pre-Vatican II thinking and practice.[24]

22. The issue here is GA's assertion of what ought to be (and implicitly what must be) the form and exercise of primacy theologically and in praxis. We make no claim that the Anglican Tradition has or claims to have all the answers or the only right way to embody primacy in and for the Church. We believe that a consensus on this matter within each Church and between our Churches is possible and desirable. We believe that the legitimate praxis of primacy can and ought to be broader rather than narrower, allowing an appropriate diversity without assuming that such diversity necessarily breeches the unity of the Church.[25] We would hope that our continued conversation and thinking may open the way for consensus on both the possibility and desirability of a form of primacy exercised in both Churches and specifically with regard to the Bishop of Rome.

23. GA reflects a rigid and detached hierarchical model of primacy that has historically demonstrated itself to be seriously problematic theologically, canonically, and practically. GA's task is made more difficult than it need be insofar as it approaches primacy and authority primarily from the perspective of structure and canons for the exercise of power. We urge a broadening of the context within which primacy in general, and specifically a special primacy for the Bishop of Rome, might be considered. The broader context would focus more intentionally on the relationship among the members of the Church and between a Bishop and the Church as a community of faith. Further, our understanding of primacy theologically and practically needs to be developed in relationship to the processes of decision-making within both our Churches, explicitly including all members of the Church as necessary participants.

24. GA does not explicitly address a particular instance of the exercise of authority that is of significant concern to Anglicans: the Bishop of Rome's exercise of direct, immediate, ordinary, universal jurisdiction. The exercise of such authority is incompatible with the understanding of authority in the Anglican Communion that we have highlighted throughout this response. Indeed, the manner in which universal primacy and direct, immediate jurisdiction have been exercised historically does not encourage us to receive this model. Nor does its exercise by the current Bishop of Rome subsequent to AC I and II and the encyclical *Ut Unum Sint*.

25. The theology and practice of primacy in GA inadequately addresses issues of accountability and responsibility. Here again, the issue is an evident disparity between structure and canons on the one hand and the relationships, formal and informal, which inhere in the life of the Church and are essential to its life and

---

[24] *Lumen gentium* I.8. The key sentence is, *"Hæc Ecclesia, in hoc mundo ut societas constituta et ordinata, subsistit in Ecclesia catholica, a successore Petri et Episcopis in eius communione gubernata, licet extra eius compaginem elementa plura sanctificationis et veritatis inveniantur, quæ ut dona Ecclesiæ Christi propria, ad unitatem catholicam impellunt."* ("This Church constituted and organized in the world as a society, *subsists in* the Catholic Church, which is governed by the successor of Peter and by the Bishops in communion with him, although many elements of sanctification and of truth are found outside of its visible structure. These elements, as gifts belonging to the Church of Christ, are forces impelling toward catholic unity." Italics added)

[25] See BCP, "The Chicago-Lambeth Quadrilateral," 876-877.

---

work. The relationship among the Orders of persons within the Church (Laity, Bishop, Priest, Deacon) as well as the personal relationships among the People of God are the context within which episcopacy, primacy, and authority are lived. Therefore, clear and reasonable lines of responsibility and accountability are essential for the good health of the People of God and the Church.

26. The matter of location of a universal primacy is a separate question. While it is historically correct to recognize the primacy of the See of Rome, and while (as GA says) the primatial ministry of the Bishop of Rome has been exercised for the benefit of both the whole church and the local church,[26] these are not the only relevant factors involved. The exercise of primacy of the Bishop of Rome has been and continues to be a source of controversy in our churches, controversy which has contributed to our unhappy divisions.[27] This historical legacy must be weighed along with the benefits of the exercise of primacy by this See.

27. We have concluded that the form of primacy advocated in GA does not reflect a consensus on primacy within the Episcopal Church USA or within Anglicanism. We have concluded that there is a need for further work that moves toward both greater theological depth and clarity as well as greater understanding of what constitutes good, reasonable, and faithful praxis. We hope that our continued conversation and thinking may open the way for consensus on both the possibility and desirability of a form of primacy exercised in both Churches and specifically with regard to the Bishop of Rome. The argument made in GA is, to us, too narrow and does not provide for a legitimate diversity of theology and praxis for primacy. We also believe that, for Anglicans, evident reform of the practice of primacy by the Bishop of Rome is necessary if a way to consensus is to be opened.

INDEFECTIBILITY AND INFALLIBILITY

28. The discussion of indefectibility and infallibility in the context of authority and primacy is inadequate, and crafted in a way that seems to us to conform to the understanding and practices of the Church of Rome (See par. 47). There is, as elsewhere in GA, a failure to distinguish clearly and precisely between the descriptive and ideal on the one hand, and the prescriptive and essential on the other hand. Everything is treated as of equal value and weight, and therefore of equal importance.[28] Yet ecclesiologically, everything is clearly not of the *esse* of the Church or of authority, primacy, and indefectibility.

29. The theology of infallibility within GA is presented as inherent to the Office of Bishop, but we do not find the argument persuasive, nor a significant advance on what has been said in AC II.[29] GA's position is problematic not only in terms of the definition and understanding of the episcopate within the Anglican Tradition, but also in terms of the episcopate's relationship to the authority of the baptized in our ecclesiology. There is a long-standing agreement among Anglicans that it is the church that is indefectible, and only because indefectibility is a gift given by God and guaranteed by grace. We are not persuaded that the same holds true of infallibility. Further, to say that the church is indefectible does not mean that the church can necessarily claim indefectibility at any given point or for any given statement.[30] For these reasons, we doubt that the concept of infallibility expressed in GA can be embraced by the Episcopal Church without a great deal more study and discussion. In the course of such study and discussion, the Episcopal church must continue to self-critical of its own limitations in both ecclesiology and praxis.

30. We would raise these questions for serious consideration: Is the doctrine of infallibility of the *esse* of episcopacy, in both theology and practice? Is it essential for a theology and praxis of authority? What is actually lost in these discussions if we were to emphasize indefectibility, while bracketing infallibility as something not necessary to full communion between our two Churches? If the essential issue is God's preservation of the church from error, in what other ways might this issue be addressed that will nurture and sustain the Church and promote unity and full communion between us?

---

[26] GA §46

[27] *Ut Unum Sint* (1995), §§ 88, 95.

[28] See *Unitatis redintegratio* III.11 regarding the concept of "hierarchy of truths."

[29] *AC II* §§ 23-22

[30] BCP, "The Articles of Religion," Article 21, 872.

THE TERMS OF FULL COMMUNION AND UNITY

31. Official Roman Catholic teaching claims that communion with the Bishop of Rome *understood as universal primate* is necessary to full communion with the Roman Catholic Church.[31] In this teaching, this is one of the essential or necessary "marks" of the true Church; any church not having it is regarded as deficient or defective. While this issue is not directly or explicitly addressed in GA, we believe such an understanding is implicit in this document.[32] The Anglican Communion has not found this understanding consonant with Scripture, nor with the Catholic tradition in which the Anglican Communion shares. Nor is it consonant with the Reformation tradition that is also part of our heritage and identity. For this understanding to be persuasive to Anglicans, what is needed is not a claim of necessity, but a clear and persuasive account of the benefits to the whole Church of universal primacy. GA presumes that earlier ARCIC work on authority has already provided such an account. We believe there are still important questions that must be addressed.

32. The question of the necessity to recognize the universal primacy of the Bishop of Rome raises a larger question: what constitutes unity in general, and what is the *esse* of that unity? This is a question that each Church must engage within itself, and in dialogue with the other. Our two Churches are committed to the unity of the Church as more than a theoretical proposition. We both agree that it is a Gospel mandate. We also agree that unity is not a matter of one Church conforming to what the other has traditionally determined to be "necessary."

33. Further, the Episcopal Church USA maintains that until and unless all churches come to full communion, we are all lacking in the fullness of the faith and of unity in Christ. In this light, we must ask what might be the appropriate symbols of real, organic unity. For example, if our two Churches agree that the See of Rome is the primary center of unity, in what sense do we understand that unity to be embodied in that symbol? Is it organic, historical, canonical, sacramental, or does it have some other basis? How does that symbol function within the Church and among the Churches as a symbol of our unity?[33]

34. We believe that further conversation is necessary about the essential nature of the Church. Specifically, the assertion of *Lumen gentium* that the "fullness of the Church subsists in" the Church of Rome must be addressed,[34] with attention not only to what this document was intended to say, but also to how is currently interpreted by the Roman Catholic Church. Herein lies a major theological question which has not been addressed by ARCIC. Yet it must be addressed: it is a profound part of how any resolution of the questions of primacy, authority, and the relationship between the Bishop of Rome and the Anglican Communion may be devised and implemented.

35. The Anglican tradition has always claimed to be part of the Catholic Church. The questions for Anglicans are, On what basis do we make this claim? Are there elements of the Catholic faith that are absent from the Anglican Tradition? What of catholic polity (bishops, priests, deacons, laity) that is essential for the support, nurture, and transmission of the Catholic faith is absent from Anglican Tradition? In what ways can the Anglican communion claim to meet *Lumen gentium*'s criterion[35] of governance "by the successor of Peter and by the Bishops" ("*a successore Petri et Episcopis*")? Does Anglican diversity of understanding and practice in the particular area of universal primacy undermine or prevent full communion? If, as we believe is the case, the Anglican Communion lacks none of the essentials of the Church except full communion with

---

[31] Note that the issue here is not communion with the Bishop of Rome *as bishop*. Clearly that is necessary to full communion. The issue, rather, is how the See of Rome is understood in distinction from all other Sees. See Joseph Ratzinger, *Principles of Catholic Theology: Building Stones for a Fundamental Theology*, trans. Mary Frances McCarthy (San Francisco: Ignatius, 1987), 246.

[32] E.g., GA §46-47, 52, 59-62; see also *Dominus Jesus* no. 16; Congregation for the Doctrine of the Faith, "Letter to the Bishops of the Catholic Church on Some Aspects of the Church Understood as Communion," *communionis notio* (1992). 10.

[33] *Ut Unum Sint* §88, 95-96

[34] See above, n. 24.

[35] See n. 24.

other churches, there is no necessary theological reason why "governance in communion" ("*ejus communione gubernata*") cannot become the real, logical, and necessary conclusion of these dialogues.

36. Both Churches have legitimate concerns and interest in the details of precisely how catholic faith is understood and how polity is structured and actually exercised. As GA notes, both Churches have equally hard questions to ask of themselves about their own ecclesiology and polity and the level of flexibility that they bring to the conversation. We have raised some additional questions and concerns here. Both Anglicans and Roman Catholics must be open to the possibility that the resolution will take a form not yet thought of or imagined, and that it will be a new thing for all of us.

Next Steps for the Dialog

37. To continue the work of ARCIC and to further the relationship between our two Churches, it seems to us that there are a number of important and weighty questions and issues that need to be addressed. We would propose the following topics, mindful that this list is not exhaustive, but indicates the major areas of concern needing further conversation and work.

38. The Anglican component of ARCIC must become more broadly representative of the Anglican Communion and its range of understandings and practices of authority, primacy, and the participation of all the Baptized in the life of the Church and its decision-making. The theology reflected in GA is not representative of either the Episcopal Church or other Provinces of the Anglican Communion, and in many places is inconsistent with our theological understandings and practices.

39. ARCIC can and should continue in conversation on the problems and issues that emerge from GA. This should also be a priority for national and regional dialogues between the two Churches.[36]

40. Further consideration is needed of the historical models of authority and primacy, as well as the ecclesiologies of the two Churches, with an eye to what new models of authority and primacy may emerge from such consideration.

41. Further consideration is needed of the relation of diversity and unity as these are related to the central issues of primacy, authority, and communion between our two Churches. Specifically, discussion is needed about the necessary extent of agreement and the range of acceptable diversity needed to preserve it. This discussion must take into account the actual practices of both Churches, as well as their theology.

42. Further work is needed to show how the central theological and biblical grounding for authority more clearly and directly applies to and connects with the issues at hand.

43. The ministry of the Bishop, in its totality and in particular relationship to authority, discernment, and decision-making must be set more firmly in the context of an explicit theology of the active participation of the whole People of God. Particular note needs to be taken of the role of all the Baptized together in the movement from *sensus fidei* to *consensus fidelium*.

44. Further work is needed to examine more deeply the nature of power and authority, the difference between them, and their relationship to and engagement within Catholic polity. For example, GA proposes that problems incapable of resolution be referred to a universal primate. On the other hand, the Lambeth Conference (1998) passed non-binding resolutions that such problems be referred to the Primates' Meeting for resolution.[37] What insights into the nature of power and authority do each of these proposals provide, both for ecclesiology and for praxis? On what grounds is one deemed preferable to the other?

45. The roles and relationships of the Churches to the Bishop of Rome must be discussed further with openness and straight-forwardness. Until a sound theological rationale is developed for the primacy of the

---

[36] Thus, we note ARCUSA's current study of authority, and commend to it these issues and concerns. We also hope that various Lutheran-Anglican-Roman Catholic dialogue groups discuss them as well.

[37] The proposal was that the Primates' Meeting, under the presidency of the Archbishop of Canterbury should have authority to intervene in such matters. Further, it was proposed that in very exceptional cases, the Archbishop of Canterbury exercise an extra-ordinary ministry of oversight in the affairs of a province not his own for the sake of maintaining communion. Lambeth Conference Resolutions III.6(b); IV.13(b).

See of Rome, and until reform of the practice of primacy is evidently underway, we do not believe the Anglican Communion may accept the universal primacy of the Bishop of Rome.

46. Further work is needed to develop the role of leadership and servanthood in the exercise of authority. We believe that emphasizing the various relationships involved is necessary to such work

47. We strongly recommend that the following actions take place within the United States at national, diocesan, and regional levels. These actions are consistent with the Action Plan of Communion in Mission from the meeting of Anglican and Roman Catholic Bishops at Mississauga in May, 2000, and with the work of IARCCUM.[38] The purpose of these actions is building mutual understanding, respect, and creative possibilities through intentionally developed relationships between Episcopal and Roman Catholic Bishops.

1. A joint meeting between the House of Bishops of the Episcopal Church and the U. S. National Conference of Catholic Bishops, with the clear understanding that each Church understands its Bishops to be bishops in historic succession.

2. Regular meetings of local Episcopal and Roman Catholic Bishops for study, reflection, conversation, and support; and for shared action insofar as that is possible

3. Collaboration in the various dioceses among parishes, especially in mission.

4. Concerted collaborative efforts to build greater awareness, knowledge, and joint activity at the local level.

5. A conference convened by the Episcopal Church of its ecumenical partners to examine the proposals of GA.

48. In conclusion, we reaffirm the unwavering commitment of the Episcopal Church to the restoration of full communion between the Anglican Communion and the Roman Catholic Church. We reaffirm that the Episcopal Church must be willing to examine and reform its own theology and praxis in order to live into this commitment. We welcome ARCIC'S document *The Gift of Authority* as a contribution to the ongoing conversation that is needed. We find GA helpful in indicating areas where Anglicans need greater clarity on the theology and praxis of authority both within our own Communion and between our Church and other Churches. At the same time, we find that GA falls short of its goal in several substantive ways. Further work is needed before it is appropriate or possible for the Episcopal Church and the Anglican Communion to accept GA's proposals. We have offered these comments in the hope that they will contribute to this work, and to that full communion which is God's will for us, and for which we continually pray.

Appendix I
Questions for Study by the Provinces
From the Office of Ecumenical Affairs and Studies
Anglican Communion Office

1 With regard to the relation between Scripture and Tradition and the exercise of teaching authority:
  a. To what extent does The Gift of Authority reflect the understanding and practice which the Anglican Communion has received?
  b. What fresh insights into, or challenges to that understanding are suggested in The Gift of Authority?
  c. What consequences does the understanding in The Gift of Authority have for deepening Anglican-Roman Catholic relations in the future?
2 With regard to collegiality, conciliarity and the role of laity in decision making:
  a. To what extent does The Gift of Authority reflect the understanding and practice which the Anglican Communion has received?
  b. What fresh insights into, or challenges to that understanding are suggested in The Gift of Authority?

---

[38] International Anglican-Roman Catholic Consultation for Unity and Mission.

> c. What consequences does the understanding in The Gift of Authority have for deepening Anglican-Roman Catholic relations in the future?

3 With regard to the Petrine ministry of universal primacy in relation to Scripture and Tradition:

> a. The Lambeth Conference of 1988 resolution III.8 (h) requested study "on whether effective communion, at all levels, does not require appropriate instruments, with due safeguards, not only for legislation, but also for oversight, as well as on the issue of a universal ministry in the service of Christian unity". What fresh insights into, or challenges to this area are suggested in The Gift of Authority?
>
> b. How can these insights or challenges be accepted into the life of the Anglican Communion?
>
> c. What consequences does the understanding in The Gift of Authority have for deepening Anglican-Roman Catholic relations in the future?

Resolution A088 Response to *Gift of Authority*

1 *Resolved,* the House of _____ concurring, That the affirmations noted and the questions raised in the
2 report of the Standing Commission on Ecumenical Relations be referred to ARCIC for further dialogue;
3 and be it further
4 *Resolved*, That the Report of the Standing Commission on Ecumenical Relations on the Gift of Authority
5 be transmitted to the Anglican Communion Office as the official response of this Church.

Resolution on "Open Communion"

At its October 2002 meeting, the Standing Commission on Ecumenical Relations discussed the increasingly common practice of open communion and its ecumenical implications. This practice is in conflict with Title I, Canon 17, Section 7 and the 1979 General Convention guidelines on eucharistic sharing. This conflict between official position and widespread practice raises questions and concerns in our ecumenical dialogues, in which agreement on the nature of Baptism and the Holy Eucharist is necessary to moving toward the full communion to which this church is committed. The SCER believes it is time for this matter to be addressed by the larger church. In order to maintain the integrity and credibility of the Episcopal Church in the ecumenical sphere, the Standing Commission on Ecumenical Relations urges the following resolution be adopted by the General Convention:

Resolution A089 "Open Communion"

1 *Resolved,* the House of _____ concurring, That the 74th General Convention of the Episcopal Church
2 establish a task force to study the matter of the increasingly common practice of open communion to
3 report back to the 2006 General Convention; and be it further
4 *Resolved*, that this task force shall be comprised of Bishops, Priests, Deacons, and lay persons with
5 representation from the Standing Commission on Ecumenical Relations, the Standing Commission on
6 Liturgy and Music, and the Standing Commission on Constitution and Canons, as proposed by the Chairs
7 of those Commissions.

EXPLANATION

It has become increasingly common for Episcopal clergy to invite all persons, whether baptized or not, to receive Holy Communion. The clear provision of Title I, Canon 17, Section 7 is this: "No unbaptized person shall be eligible to receive Holy Communion in this church." The Guidelines on Eucharistic Sharing endorsed by the 1979 General Convention state that "It is no service to the unity of Christ's Church when one group contributes to…undermining of discipline of another." (1979 Journal of the General Convention, AA-81.) The unauthorized practice of "open communion" is at apparent odds with the official teachings of this church on Baptism and the Holy Eucharist. In official dialogues between this church and others, our appointed members are to represent the official position of this church. In light of the increasingly widespread practice of "open communion," it is increasingly difficult for them to do so with credibility. Further, the practice appears to invite members of other churches to receive communion when to do so is contrary to their own church's eucharistic discipline.

At the same time, the practice may indicate a shift in our own consensus of the faith that is to be the basis of our official teachings. In such a situation, we believe it is time for the church to give due and careful consideration to the matter. Therefore, we are proposing the establishment of a task force with the expertise necessary to discuss a matter of this weight, complexity, and significance.

Resolution on Interfaith Relations

With the disbanding in the previous triennium of the Presiding Bishop's Advisory Committee on Interfaith Relations, a group appointed by the Presiding Bishop recommended that oversight of interfaith relations be lodged with the SCER. In 1999 this proposal was accepted by the SCER.

During the past triennium, the SCER has tried to assume its responsibilities for Interfaith relations, although it has confronted some obstacles. The SCER has recognized the authority of EIR office to oversee directly Interfaith Relations for ECUSA, in consultation with SCER, and has encouraged EIR to form a "taskforce" to help in Interfaith Relations. This taskforce has been organized, although for logistical reasons it has not yet met.

An important development has been the establishment of the Interfaith Education Initiative (IEI), a joint project between the Office of Ecumenical and Interfaith Relations and Episcopal Relief and Development. The goals of the IEI are to provide resources in Interfaith Education, to strengthen local networks to facilitate local interfaith dialogue, and to help identify resource persons and experts in the field of Interfaith Education. A comprehensive website is available at www.interfaitheducationinitiative.org. The SCER has maintained contact with the project through regular reports from the IEI's Coordinator.

Given the challenges facing Christian-Muslim efforts at mutual understanding in wake of current world conflicts and in the midst of Anglican struggles in Africa, we are committed to establishing our own sustained educational and dialogical work in this regard on foundations of equitable and realistic respect for human rights. Despite taking on, in good faith and as requested, the oversight of Interfaith Relations, SCER has had to face the fact that its on-going and substantive work in ecumenical affairs practically precludes its ability adequately to supervise the essential work of Interfaith relations, and that while it has been a tremendous resource, the funding for the IEI will only continue through 2004.

In light of the pressing world challenges that bear upon interfaith understanding, and the realities of supporting interfaith work in ways that sustain its energy and purpose, along with continuing to support the work of the IEI through 2004, this Commission intends to present a proposal for a full-time Associate Deputy for Interfaith Relations to the General Convention of 2006. We propose the following resolution:

Resolution A090 Christian-Muslim Dialogue

1 *Resolved,* the House of _____ concurring, That this 74th General Convention reaffirms Resolution 1997-
2 D069 on "Substantive Dialogue Between Christian and Muslim Communities", which calls for a "dialogue
3 that maintains the theological integrity of both faith communities and commitment to genuine human
4 rights and religious freedom as affirmed by the 71st General Convention (1994-D015)"; be it further
5 *Resolved,* That the General Convention directs current and future ECUSA efforts at Christian-Muslim
6 dialogue and education to embody and strengthen that resolution's commitments to dialogue founded on
7 "genuine human rights and religious freedom", as embodied in the United Nations Declaration on Human
8 Rights (1948), Article 18, which states that "everyone has the right to freedom of thought, conscience, and
9 religion; this right includes freedom to change his religion or belief, and freedom, either alone or in
10 community with others and in public or private, to manifest his religion or belief in teaching, practice,
11 worship, and observance"; and be it further
12 *Resolved,* That the General Convention directs that such efforts strengthen the peaceful and secure
13 religious witness of other Christians around the world in their ministry among Muslim neighbors,
14 particularly in areas of experienced religious oppression.

III.   ONGOING GENERAL CONVENTION MANDATES

United Methodist Church - Episcopal Church
The United Methodist-Episcopal Church bilateral authorized by the 2000 General Convention met twice during the triennium and is scheduled to meet six times during the 2003-2006 triennium. The dialogue set its goals as "full communion, including interchangeability of ministries, for the sake of common mission and

witness." The first meeting included presentations on our shared Anglican and American experiences, as well as divergences between the two churches, and the second began to explore questions of how authority is exercised in both our churches, examined the ecclesiology of our two communions, and studied the covenant documents proposed by the British Methodist Church and the Church of England and the final report of the Anglican-Methodist International Commission, *Sharing in the Apostolic Communion*.

Anglican-Oriental Orthodox

The Anglican-Oriental Orthodox International Commission met in the summer of 2001 and set an agenda to draft a common statement on Christology in time for the Lambeth Conference of 2008. The Inter-Anglican Standing Commission on Ecumenical Relations (IASCER), including its Episcopal Church representatives, has requested the Provinces of the Anglican Communion to submit the text of the Agreement for study by those who have responsibility for monitoring faith and order issues in their provinces requesting them to offer any comments they may have to IASCER by 30 October 2003.

Anglican-Orthodox Dialogue

The Standing Conference of Canonical Orthodox Bishops (SCOBA) and the 73rd General Convention of the Episcopal Church both agreed to resume an official dialogue. A Steering Committee consisting of representatives of both churches met during the triennium. The documents which were issued by the dialogue during the time period of 1976-1991 were researched and produced, and dialogue teams were appointed. Currently the Steering Committee is attempting to find a suitable date for the bilateral to take place.

Consultation on Church Union / Churches Uniting in Christ
Churches Uniting in Christ (CUIC)

For over forty years, the member churches of the Consultation on Church Union (COCU) have met together seeking ways to make full communion possible. The 73rd General Convention resolved that the Episcopal Church "commit itself to continuing participation in COCU and to a process of engagement and dialogue beginning in 2002 with the inauguration of Churches Uniting in Christ (CUIC)" and affirmed this Church's commitment to the Chicago-Lambeth Quadrilateral and commended it as the theological basis for a future reconciled ministry between the member churches.

In January of 2002, the CUIC inauguration was held in Memphis, TN, during the Week of Prayer for Christian Unity. Delegates from the nine member churches approved this new relationship on behalf of their respective Communions. CUIC identifies eight marks descriptive of this new relationship and calls for dialogue whose goal is full reconciliation of ministry by 2007, with approval of "A Call to Christian Commitment and Action to Combat Racism."

While enthusiastically supporting the anti-racism initiative, the Episcopal delegation made it clear that the Episcopal Church cannot enter into a relationship that includes the mutual recognition of ordained ministry, unless it has assurance that future reconciliation would include bishops in historic succession and a common and fully interchangeable three-fold ministry.

On Monday, January 21, 2002, the Episcopal Church's delegates to the Memphis Assembly participated in the march on Martin Luther King, Jr. Day to the National Civil Rights Museum where representatives of the nine member communions as well as the Evangelical Lutheran Church in America signed a proclamation condemning racism and pledging their commitment to overcome this insidious evil in our society, and issued an "Appeal to the Churches."

Before the close of the Memphis plenary the CUIC Coordinating Council had an organizational meeting. Each Communion has one member on the Council. Additionally, the Council has established three task forces to facilitate its work: Racial Justice, Ministry and a Local and Regional task force. All three task forces are active with full representation. For important information about these new developments in CUIC, please consult the website of the Office of Ecumenical and Interfaith Relations, **www.episcopalchurch.org/ecumenism/cuic**.

It should be noted that one of the ways in which CUIC asks member churches to inaugurate this new relationship is through joint prayer and celebration of the Eucharist. At its March 2002 meeting the SCER authorized the Office of Ecumenical and Interfaith Relations to update this Church's guidelines for

Eucharistic sharing within the context of CUIC. These guidelines are available from the Office of Ecumenical and Interfaith Relations at **www.episcopalchurch.org/ecumenism/guidelines**.

Presbyterian Church, U.S.A.-Episcopal Church Dialogue
The Episcopal Church-Presbyterian Church, USA dialogue, established by the 73rd General Convention met four times during the triennium. The group will continue to meet twice a year and coordinate its meetings with the CUIC Ministry Task Force. The Episcopal-Presbyterian dialogue will be critical for the future goal of reconciliation of ministries by 2007 within the context of CUIC. Four goals were established for the dialogue: Clarification of our common apostolicity, exploring how our churches see themselves as expressions of the one, holy, catholic, and apostolic church; reconciliation of Ministry, including the ministry of the baptized and the ordained ministry, with particular the focus on the two churches' understanding of how *episcope* is both shared and how it is focused in the historic episcopate as well as the place of the office of presbyter in both our traditions; to intentionally coordinate the work of the bilateral with the CUIC Ministry Task Force; and to discover ways for reception of the dialogue with our denominations.

Continuing Churches
In response to General Convention 2000 Resolution D047, the SCER invited the Rt. Rev. Keith Ackerman to its October 2001 to consult with the Commission on the most appropriate course of action in reaching out to non-ECUSA expressions of Anglicanism. The SCER commissioned the Ecumenical Relations Office to draft a letter inviting these "Continuing" Churches to dialogue. A letter was sent twenty-six different "Continuing" Anglican jurisdictions. As they were not in the same category as the "Continuing" Churches, a similar but slightly different letter was sent to the Reformed Episcopal Church and the Charismatic Episcopal Church. The letter regretted the divisions between Anglicans, and suggested agreeing to disagree on the issues which divide us in order to engage in a dialogue towards mutual understanding of one another. Twelve different groups responded favorably.

Accordingly, at its March 2002 meeting the SCER requested that a questionnaire be circulated to those churches which responded in order to determine which issues could be identified for discussion at a future meeting. The questionnaire was circulated and the responses were gathered.

The Office of Ecumenical and Interfaith Relations issued an invitation to the churches which responded, inviting them to an organizational meeting to discuss future goals for this dialogue. A plenary meeting was held in December, 2002, and chaired by Bishop Christopher Epting along with representatives from the Standing Commission, to discuss the feasibility of moving forward with such a dialogue. In the final analysis, the "Continuing" Churches were unable or unwilling to send a delegation. SCER will have to consider how to proceed, given this apparent lack of interest.

Reformed Episcopal-Anglican Province of America-Episcopal Church Trilateral
As part of the action taken in regard to Resolution D047, the Office of Ecumenical and Interfaith Relations invited the Reformed Episcopal Church and the Anglican Province in America into a trilateral dialogue with the Episcopal Church. This decision was made for two reasons. The first was due to the special relationship between the Episcopal Church and these two churches. The Episcopal Church has been involved in bilateral dialogues with both churches in the past: the Reformed Episcopal Church in the 1930s and 1990s, and the Anglican Province in America's predecessor body, the American Episcopal Church, in the 1980s. Second, it seemed to be the proper way to proceed given the forthcoming full, organic merger planned between these two churches. The first meeting of the trilateral was held in January, 2003 and examined previous dialogue between the churches, the issues which divide the churches, and the possibility of establishing a formal dialogue. By consensus, representatives of the churches agreed to proceed with the dialogue. The dialogue team is scheduled to meet regularly during the 2003-2006 triennium, and established the goal of full communion.

Evangelicals and Pentecostals
The SCER was given a mandate by the 1997 and 2000 General Conventions to seek open dialogue with Evangelicals and Pentecostals. SCER has taken initial steps to outline what the purpose and scope of these discussions might be. We invited an expert on evangelicalism in the United States to address our February

2003 meeting. SCER is also monitoring and encouraging the participation of Evangelicals and Pentecostals in the Global Christian Forum process (in part an outgrowth of the WCC) and the Christian Churches Together in the U.S.A.

National Council of Churches of Christ, USA

The Standing Commission on Ecumenical Relations continues to fulfill its canonical charge and to monitor this Church's involvement in the National Council of Churches. Dr. Thomas Ferguson presented a detailed report for SCER about the Episcopal Church's history and involvement with the venerable ecumenical organization over the years, and which recommended that the SCER return to its previous practice of having a standing subcommittee to monitor this church's participation in the NCCC and WCC. This proposal was adopted, and a Standing Subcommittee was appointed to monitor this church's participation in the World Council of Churches and the National Council of Churches. For more information on the programs which the NCCC supports, please consult their website, **www.ncccusa.org**

Dr. Robert Edgar, General Secretary, was able to report over the summer of 2002 that NCCCUSA ended its fiscal year June 30 with a balanced budget. The organization's programs include Christian education, economic and environmental justice efforts, and interfaith dialogue. The NCCCUSA was very active following the tragic events of September 11, 2001. The Rev. Canon Patrick Mauney serves as President of Church World Service and Witness, now separate from the NCCCUSA.

Christian Churches Together in the USA

Bishop Christopher Epting, Deputy for Ecumenical and Interfaith Relations, represents the Episcopal Church in a brainstorming effort known as "Churches Together in the USA" to look into the possibility of a successor organization to the NCCCUSA which might include Roman Catholic, Evangelical, and Pentecostal participation. A second meeting was held at Fuller Seminary in Los Angeles in January of 2003 to further explore the possible nature, scope, and shape of CCTUSA. This meeting witnessed significant involvement from a wide variety of Evangelical, Pentecostal, Roman Catholic, and Orthodox Churches. It is the hope that this organization could be launched in 2005. The SCER will continue to monitor the development of Christian Churches Together during the next triennium. For more information on Christian Churches Together, including news releases and documentation, please consult www.episcopalchurch.org/ecumenism/cct.

World Council of Churches

Questions on the future shape of the ecumenical movement and of the World Council of Churches dominated the 2002 WCC Central Committee meeting in Geneva and highlighted many of the concerns which have marked this conciliar fellowship during the triennium. An important step towards renewing the structure, style and ethos of the WCC was taken when the Central Committee received and endorsed with some procedural changes the Final Report of the Special Commission on Orthodox Participation in the WCC. Main themes of the report included ecclesiology, social and ethical issues, common prayer, a consensus-model of decision-making, and future membership and representation in the Council.

The 158-member Committee also reviewed the WCC's program plans for 2003-2005 with a view to strengthening the organization and charting a course for the future. The Central Committee made two more decisions affecting the future of the organization. It appointed an 18-person search committee that will seek candidates to succeed Dr. Konrad Raiser as General Secretary when he retires in 2003, and also selected Porto Alegre, Brazil, as the site for the next General Assembly in 2006.

The Episcopal Church continues to participate in the US Board of the World Council of Churches, which is comprised of representatives of member churches of the WCC. The WCC maintains a US Office consisting of several staff members. The role of the US Office has been to promote awareness of WCC programs in the US Churches, assist in fundraising and development for the churches, and to hold an annual meeting to promote ecumenical activities and cooperation among member churches.

In addition, in January of 2003 a meeting was held at the Episcopal Church Center to discuss this church's participation in the program work of conciliar ecumenical bodies. The Office of Ecumenical and Interfaith Relations invited members of the church's General Assembly delegation, Standing Commission on

Ecumenical Relations, and all Episcopalians serving on program or governance committees of the NCCC or WCC, in an effort to coordinate the church's work in conciliar ecumenism. Important progress was made in facilitating communication between a number of Episcopalians involved in a wide range of conciliar ecumenical work, as well as with the SCER.

IV.   ADDITIONAL ECUMENICAL COMMITMENTS

Episcopal Diocesan Ecumenical Officers
The Episcopal Diocesan Ecumenical Officers (EDEO) continue to fill the role as educators of clergy and laity, councils of advice to bishops, representatives of their bishops at ecumenical gatherings, and as grassroots initiators of ecumenical and interfaith dialogue and cooperation. During the triennium, a major focus of EDEO was continued participation in the National Workshops on Christian Unity. In addition, EDEO held annual Winter Meetings of the Executive Committee. The winter meeting serve as a time for planning, both for the Annual Meeting and for other actions and activities of EDEO. During the triennium the Executive Committee of the National Association of Diocesan Ecumenical Officers (NADEO), the Roman Catholic parallel body, and the Lutheran Ecumenical Representatives Network (LERN), met in conjunction with the EDEO Executive Board.

Episcopal - Russian Orthodox Church Joint Coordinating Committee
The Russian Orthodox Joint Coordinating Committee was established in 1989 by Presiding Bishop Edmond Browning and Patriarch Pimen, and first met in 1991. The goal of the Committee is to facilitate practical cooperation between the two churches. This has involved seminarian exchanges, theological dialogues, and collaboration in models of military and other chaplaincies. Representatives of the Episcopal Church traveled to Moscow in June, 2002, at the invitation of Metropolitan Kyrill of Smolensk, Chair of the Department of External Church Relations for the Moscow Patriarchate, to renew the work of the Committee. Fruitful discussions were held with Metropolitan Kyrill as well as with Metropolitan Sergei of Solnechnogorsk, the Chancellor of the Moscow Patriarchate and director of the Department of Charities. The meeting with Metropolitan Kyrill and the staff of the Department of External Church Relations highlighted the historic ties between our two churches, focused on the need for renewed theological dialogue, and explored possible areas of future cooperation. The visit with Metropolitan Sergei celebrated the warm and close relationship between the Russia Committee of the Diocese of New York and the Department of Charities, and explored how to transfer the work of Russia Committee within the context of the Office of Ecumenical and Interfaith Relations and other relevant departments at the Episcopal Church Center.

A meeting of the full Coordinating Committee is scheduled for the summer of 2003.

Inter-Anglican Standing Commission on Ecumenical Relations
The Inter Anglican Standing Commission on Ecumenical Relations held two meetings during the triennium. This group has been established to monitor all Anglican ecumenical relations and may also give advice where it thinks necessary, but its purpose is neither prescriptive nor compulsory.

Regarding the bylaw of the Evangelical Lutheran Church in America permitting planned exceptions in certain circumstances for ordinations by pastors, rather than bishops, in unilateral violation of the promise made by that church in the bilateral agreement that was voted, IASCER transmitted the following notice to the Presiding Bishop and other authorities of the Episcopal Church by a separate letter which the SCER feels bound to share in this report to the General Convention: "IASCER is concerned about unilaterally altering agreements after they are signed, in light of the developments in Anglican-Lutheran relations in the U.S.A., namely the implications of the ECLA bylaw concerning ordination 'in unusual circumstances,' which contradicts the agreement in 'Called to Common Mission.' Such a development seems to undermine ecumenical method and could potentially hinder progress in dialogue between Anglicans and Lutherans in other parts of the world. IASCER maintains that the ordination by pastors in Lutheran Churches which have entered binding agreements with Anglican Churches is an inconsistency which would be difficult to explain to other ecumenical partners, especially the Orthodox and Oriental Churches and the Roman Catholic Church. Anglicans do not consider ordination solely by pastors/presbyters to be an acceptable practice within an agreement of this nature which is intended to bring about a fully interchangeable ministry. IASCER has a similar concern about the continuing practice of ordination by Deans in the Church of Norway, which Anglicans had anticipated would be phased out in the light of the Porvoo agreement."

In response to this notification, the SCER has submitted a resolution which may be found in Section I.

Episcopal Church Representatives to Dialogues and Ecumenical Agencies
For the complete list of Episcopal Church representatives on all of our dialogue teams as well as the National Council of Churches and World Council of Churches, please go to www.episcopalchurch.org/ecumenism/representatives.

BUDGET

The Standing Commission on Ecumenical Relations will meet approximately five times during the next triennium. This will require $38,000 in 2004, $37,000 in 2005 and $38,000 in 2006 for a total of $113,000 for the 2004-2006 triennium.

STANDING COMMISSION ON LITURGY AND MUSIC
www.episcopalchurch.org/gc/ccab/sclm/default.html

Membership

The Rev. Bruce W.B. Jenneker, *Co-Chair*	Massachusetts, 2003
The Rt. Rev. Jeffery W. Rowthorn, *Co-Chair*	Connecticut, 2003
Dr. Mary Abrams	Kentucky, 2003
The Rev. Sr. Jean Campbell	New York, 2003
Ms. Judith Dodge	Washington, 2006
The Rt. Rev. Wendell N. Gibbs, Jr.	Michigan, 2006
The Rt. Rev. Barry R. Howe	West Missouri, 2006
Mrs. Paula MacLean	Southeast Florida, 2003
The Rev. Patrick Malloy	Bethlehem, 2006, *Consultant to A066*
The Rt. Rev. Paul V. Marshall	Bethlehem, 2003
Mr. Monte Mason	Minnesota, 2003
Mr. Gordon Panton	Georgia, 2006, *resigned, January 15, 2002, not replaced*
Miss Marcia S. Pruner	Northern Michigan, 2006
The Rev. John W. Ruder	Olympia, 2006
Mr. M. Milner Seifert	Chicago, 2003
The Rev. Susan Anslow Williams	Western New York, 2006
Mr. Ted M. Yumoto	San Joaquin, 2006, *appointed upon Patrick Malloy's ordination to the priesthood, to complete his term.*
The Rev. J. Anthony Guillén	*Executive Council liaison*
The Rev. Canon Gregory M. Howe	*Custodian of the Standard Book of Common Prayer*
The Rev. Dr. Clayton L. Morris	*Episcopal Church Center staff liaison*

Commission Representatives at General Convention
Bishop Jeffery Rowthorn and Deputy Sr. Jean Campbell, OSH are authorized to receive non-substantive amendments to this report.

COMMISSION MEETINGS DATES

January 29 – February 1, 2001, Flushing, New York	January 28 – 31, 2002, New Orleans, Louisiana
May 21 – 24, 2001, Los Angeles, California	May 20 – 23, 2002, Sioux Falls, South Dakota
August 27 – 30, 2001, Wilmington, North Carolina	October 7 – 11, 2002, Cupertino, California

GOALS AND OBJECTIVES FOR THE NEXT TRIENNIUM
Resolution A-104; the response to *GC Resolution 2000-A066*, expresses the specific goals and objectives of the Standing Commission on Liturgy and Music (SCLM). These derive from the mandate given to SCLM by General Convention and are informed by data gathered from the whole church during the past triennium. Along with this, there is the continuing goal of engaging in a profound way both liturgical and musical dimensions of worship in the execution of all the tasks referred to the SCLM.

COMMITTEE REPORTS AND RESOLUTIONS FOR CONVENTION ACTION

Enriching our Music Task Force
SCLM Members: Judy Dodge, Monte Mason, Ted Yumoto
Consultants: Jack Burnham, George Emblom, Sharon Harrington, Albert Melton
Meetings: April 11 – 13, 2002, Minnetonka Beach, Minnesota; June 12 – 15, 2002, Washington, DC; and November 14 – 16, 2002, Bloomington, Minnesota

The Enriching our Music project (EOM) was created from SCLM meeting discussions in the triennium 1995-1997, and reiterated by the commission of the same, 2001 – 2003. The triennium of 1995-1997 was the first for the newly formed commission, which combined the former Standing Liturgical Commission and the Standing Commission on Church Music.

Enriching Our Worship I includes texts of revised Eucharistic Prayers and many new canticles. The possibilities for musical accompaniment to these texts became readily apparent, and the SCLM accordingly identified some general areas of need in this regard. For the scope of the present triennium, two of these were within the means of immediate practicality: mass, and canticle settings. The mass settings were further divided into two categories: through-composed settings of a majority of the ordinary texts, and single settings of the ordinary texts. Others areas, such as music for children's worship, and new hymn settings have been rescheduled for development and publishing in the next triennium.

As justification for this and future projected collections of musical resource material, the SCLM has taken quite seriously the 71st General Convention resolution (easily accessed in the preface to *Wonder, Love, and Praise*), directing the SCLM to continue preparing supplements to the *Hymnal 1982*, featuring inclusive language and non-English texts; in addition to English and settings of texts written since the compiling of the present hymnal.

Invitations to submit materials for what has now been named *Enriching Our Music* (EOM) were sent to the Association of Anglican Musicians membership, other professional organizations, seminaries, etc. The Reading Committee has received well over 700 submissions for this project. In addition, the committee has examined many previously published resource, including those from the Lutheran, Roman Catholic, and Unitarian traditions.

Collecting musical resources relies heavily on those who are willing to share the fruits of their creativity or who have gained access to the submission process. Cultures like the Hispanic, for whom music is essentially a matter of only aural learning, are not as well represented in the first volume of *Enriching our Music* as the reading committee might have wished. This realization has led us to understand the difficulties of the current collection process. We would instead, and for the future, suggest that the reading process include groups from our largest constituencies - Hispanic, black, white, Asian, Native American, etc. and those knowledgeable within the broad spectrum of their own culture. It would be most appropriate for the SCLM to establish a means by which this would be possible in the next triennium. Such a process would articulate the broad diversity of this church, represent it musically, and do so in a much more authentic manner.

In other words, a conversation between a majority and minority culture tends to look like this: Anglo + Hispanic = Anglo. Anglo is the majority culture in this equation, and as information is gathered, it is quite naturally filtered, explained, or re-invented through the expectations and metaphors of the majority culture.

Yet this model is not equipped to handle the need for diversity that this Church considers to be so important. A different process is needed that will filter materials through more than the dominant culture, allowing minority cultures to speak to each other on some very basic levels, and without a primary "translation" through the culture of the majority.

As presented at this triennium's last SCLM meeting in Cupertino, California, another model is easily available. Picture, a hexagram, and at the points of this hexagram, place some dominant constituencies at separate points: Black (American), Hispanic, Native American, White, African and Pacific Rim. Now draw lines connecting each of these points.

The model looks something like this:

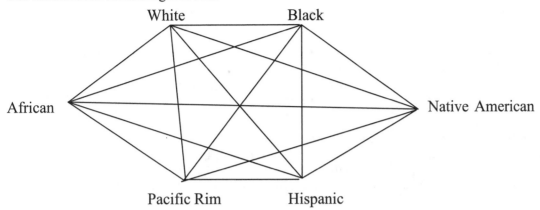

The greater possibilities for enriched conversations, etc., are too obvious to ignore - especially as the SCLM moves toward a greater understanding of its role of gathering new materials for future publications. Clearly, the above sets a new, non-linear standard of such materials, and one that is even more complicated than the more direct approach used now. Regardless, the SCLM has embraced this standard with enthusiasm, urging that its work now be informed through this new model.

With this caveat, the SCLM and the Reading Committee for Enriching Our Music is proud of its achievement. The new canticles in EOM are explored in ways that will be usefully spiritual, and the new eucharistic settings provide needed stylistic expansion of this repertoire.

Resolution A091 Continue use of *Enriching Our Worship 1 & 2*

1   *Resolved,* the House of _____ concurring, That this 74th General Convention authorize continuing use of
2   *Enriching our Worship Volume 1*: The Daily Office, Great Litany, and Eucharist and *Enriching our*
3   *Worship Volume 2*: Ministry with the Sick and Dying, and Burial of a Child during the 2003-2006
4   triennium, under the direction of the diocesan bishop or ecclesiastical authority.

EXPLANATION
Enriching our Worship 1 was first authorized for use by the 72nd. General Convention in 1997. *Enriching Our Worship 2* was first authorized at the 73rd Convention in 2000.This resolution permits continued use of these liturgies and texts.

Resolution A092 Reauthorize *Enriching our Worship* work

1   *Resolved,* the House of _____ concurring, That this 74th General Convention direct the Standing
2   Commission on Liturgy and Music to continue to develop expansive language liturgies for the Pastoral
3   Offices of the Book of Common Prayer 1979; and be it further
4   *Resolved,* That the Office for Liturgy and Music, in consultation with the Standing Commission on Liturgy
5   and Music, create a Task Force of six people to engage the work; and be it further
6   *Resolved,* that the sum of $14,400 be appropriated for the work of the Task Force.

EXPLANATION
The SCLM has produced *Enriching Our Worship 1 & 2* which have been authorized for use by the General Convention. Work is in progress to develop materials for the Burial of the Dead (of an adult) and the Celebration of a New Ministry. This will continue this work.

Committee on the Calendar
SCLM Members: Barry Howe, Gregory Howe, Jeffery Rowthorn. *Consultant*: Phoebe Pettingell. Meeting: April 23 – 25, 2002, St. Louis, Missouri.

The Committee on the Calendar of the Church Year has considered several of the resolutions adopted by the 73rd General Convention and then referred to the SCLM for appropriate action.

In addition, the Commission has given its support to the committee's recommendation that the ordination of Florence Li Tim-Oi, who became the first woman priest in the Anglican Communion on January 25, 1944, should be commemorated in the Calendar of the Church Year. If approved by General Convention, this commemoration would be observed for the first time on January 24, 2004, the day before the sixtieth anniversary of her ordination.

With the encouragement of the Presiding Bishop who served as Chair of the Commission during two triennia (1991 - 1997), the SCLM - and in particular the Committee on the Calendar - has embarked on a detailed evaluation of the scope and adequacy of the commemorations and accompanying liturgical propers contained in *Lesser Feasts and Fasts 2000*. This study has led the Commission to the conclusion that a thorough revision of the book should be begun in the coming triennium.

Resolution A093 Approve Liturgical Calendar Commemorations

1 *Resolved,* the House of _____ concurring, That the commemorations of Enmegahbowh, Florence
2 Nightingale, and Philip the Deacon, proposed by the 73rd General Convention (Journal, page 473) and
3 approved for trial use, be now finally approved and entered in the Calendar of the Church Year (Book of
4 Common Prayer, pages 15 - 30).

Resolution A094 Church Year Calendar Inclusions

1 *Resolved,* the House of _____ concurring, That this 74th General Convention propose additional
2 commemorations for inclusion in the Calendar of the Church Year and authorize trial use thereof for the
3 triennium 2004 - 2006, as follows:
4 February 17—Janani Luwum, Archbishop of Uganda, and Martyr, 1977
5 November 6—William Temple, Archbishop of Canterbury, 1944
6 November 22—Clive Staples Lewis, Apologist and Spiritual Writer, 1963

EXPLANATION

By concurrent action on Resolution B038 (Journal, p.641) the 73rd General Convention directed the Standing Commission on Liturgy and Music to add the names of C.S. Lewis, Janani Luwum and William Temple to the Calendar of the Church Year, together with appropriate liturgical propers. The name of Festo Kivengere, Bishop of Kigezi, Uganda, was also included in Resolution B038. It is the opinion of the SCLM that the inclusion of Bishop Kivengere at this time would not accord with the Guidelines approved by the 71st General Convention (see Lesser Feasts and Fasts 2000, pp.467- 472), and for that reason his name does not appear in the above resolution.

Resolution A095 Authorize Trial Use of Commemorations

1 *Resolved,* the House of _____ concurring, That this 74th General Convention authorize, for trial use until
2 the 2006 General Convention, the commemorations proposed by this Convention, with the following
3 propers:

4 ***February 17***
5 **Janani Luwum**
6 *Archbishop of Uganda, and Martyr, 1977*
7 I   O God, whose Son the Good Shepherd laid down his life for the sheep: We give thee thanks for thy
8 faithful shepherd, Janani Luwum, who after his Savior's example gave up his life for the people of
9 Uganda. Grant us to be so inspired by his witness that we make no peace with oppression, but live as those
10 who are sealed with the cross of Christ, who died and rose again, and now liveth and reigneth with thee
11 and the Holy Spirit, one God, for ever and ever. *Amen.*

12 II O God, whose Son the Good Shepherd laid down his life for the sheep: We give you thanks for your
13 faithful shepherd, Janani Luwum, who after his Savior's example gave up his life for the people of
14 Uganda. Grant us to be so inspired by his witness that we make no peace with oppression, but live as those
15 who are sealed with the cross of Christ, who died and rose again, and now lives and reigns with you and
16 the Holy Spirit, one God, for ever and ever. *Amen.*
17 Psalm - 119:41-48
18 Lesson - Ecclesiasticus 4:20-28
19 Gospel - John 12: 24-32
20 Preface of Holy Week

November 6
William Temple
Archbishop of Canterbury, 1944

I   O God of light and love, who illumined thy Church through the witness of thy servant William Temple: Inspire us, we pray, by his teaching and example, that we may rejoice with courage, confidence and faith in the Word made flesh, and may be led to establish that city which has justice for its foundation and love for its law; through Jesus Christ, the light of the world, who liveth and reigneth with thee and the Holy Spirit, one God, now and for ever. *Amen.*

II   O God of light and love, you illumined your Church through the witness of your servant William Temple: Inspire us, we pray, by his teaching and example, that we may rejoice with courage, confidence and faith in the Word made flesh, and may be led to establish that city which has justice for its foundation and love for its law; through Jesus Christ, the light of the world, who lives and reigns with you and the Holy Spirit, one God, now and for ever. *Amen.*

　　Psalm - 119: 97-104
　　Lesson - Ephesians 3:7-12
　　Gospel - John 1:9-18
　　Preface of the Epiphany

November 22
Clive Staples Lewis
Apologist and Spiritual Writer, 1963

I   O God of searing truth and surpassing beauty, we give thee thanks for Clive Staples Lewis whose sanctified imagination lighteth fires of faith in young and old alike; Surprise us also with thy joy and draw us into that new and abundant life which is ours in Christ Jesus, who liveth and reigneth with thee and the Holy Spirit, one God, now and for ever. *Amen.*

II   O God of searing truth and surpassing beauty, we give you thanks for Clive Staples Lewis whose sanctified imagination lights fires of faith in young and old alike; Surprise us also with your joy and draw us into that new and abundant life which is ours in Christ Jesus, who lives and reigns with you and the Holy Spirit, one God, now and for ever. *Amen.*

Psalm -139:1-9
Lesson - 1 Peter 1:3-9
Gospel - John 16:7-15
Preface of a Saint (3)

Resolution A096 Inclusion in the Church Year Calendar

Resolved, the House of _____ concurring, That this 74th General Convention propose an additional commemoration for inclusion in the Calendar of the Church Year and authorize trial use thereof for the triennium 2004 - 2006, as follows

　　September 22—Philander Chase, Bishop of Ohio, and of Illinois, 1852

EXPLANATION

By concurrent action on Resolution C014 (Journal, p.642), the 73rd General Convention encouraged the Standing Commission on Liturgy and Music to add the name of Philander Chase to the Calendar of the Church Year and to provide appropriate liturgical propers for his commemoration on September 22 (the first available free day in the Calendar following the anniversary of his death on September 20, 1852).

Resolution A097 Authorize Trial Use of Commemoration

Resolved, the House of _____ concurring, That this 74th General Convention authorize, for trial use until the General Convention of 2006, the commemoration proposed by this Convention, with the following propers:

　　September 22
　　Philander Chase
　　Bishop of Ohio, and of Illinois, 1852

6   I.   Almighty God, whose Son Jesus Christ is the pioneer and perfecter of our faith We give thee heartfelt
7   thanks for the pioneering spirit of thy servant Philander Chase, and for his zeal in opening new frontiers for
8   the ministry of thy Church. Grant us grace to minister in Christ's name in every place, led by bold witnesses
9   to the Gospel of the Prince of Peace, even Jesus Christ our Lord, who liveth and reigneth with thee and the
10 Holy Spirit, one God, for ever and ever. *Amen.*
11 II. Almighty God, whose Son Jesus Christ is the pioneer and perfecter of our faith: We give you heartfelt
12 thanks for the pioneering spirit of your servant Philander Chase, and for his zeal in opening new frontiers for
13 the ministry of your Church. Grant us grace to minister in Christ's name in every place, led by bold witnesses
14 to the Gospel of the Prince of Peace, Jesus Christ our Lord, who lives and reigns with you and the Holy Spirit,
15 one God, for ever and ever. *Amen.*
16   Psalm -108:1-6 or 16:5-11
17   Lesson-Isaiah 44:1-6, 8
18   Gospel-Luke 9:1-6
19   Preface of a Saint(1)

Resolution A098 Church Year Calendar Inclusion

1   *Resolved,* the House of _____ concurring, That this 74th General Convention propose an additional
2   commemoration for inclusion in the Calendar of the Church Year and authorize trial use for the triennium
3   2003 - 2006, as follows:
4   January 24—Ordination of Florence Li Tim-Oi, First Woman Priest in the Anglican Communion, 1944

EXPLANATION

January 25, 2004 will mark the 60th anniversary of the ordination of the first woman priest in the Anglican
Communion. On the Feast of the Conversion of St. Paul in 1944, Florence Li Tim-Oi was ordained in
Shaoqing on the Chinese mainland by Bishop Hall of Hong Kong. Two years after her death in 1992, the Li
Tim-Oi Foundation was established by the Archbishop of Canterbury and others. The Foundation has helped
women from more than 60 dioceses in eleven Anglican provinces as they have trained for a variety of
leadership roles in their own countries. The date of January 24 is proposed for her commemoration as it is the
eve of the anniversary of her ordination on the Feast of the Conversion of St. Paul in 1944.

Resolution A099 Authorize Trial Use of Commemoration

1   *Resolved,* the House of _____ concurring, That That this 74th General Convention authorize, for trial use
2   until the General Convention of 2006, the above-listed commemoration proposed by this Convention, with
3   the following propers:
4   **January 24**
5   **Ordination of Florence Li Tim-Oi**
6   *First Woman Priest in the Anglican Communion, 1944*
7   I   Gracious God, we thank thee for calling Florence Li Tim-Oi, much-beloved daughter, to be the first
8   woman to exercise the office of a priest in our Communion; By the grace of thy Spirit inspire us to follow
9   her example, serving thy people with patience and happiness all our days, and witnessing in every
10 circumstance to our Savior Jesus Christ, who liveth and reigneth with thee and the same Spirit, one God,
11 for ever and ever. *Amen.*
12 II   Gracious God, we thank you for calling Florence Li Tim-Oi, much-beloved daughter, to be the first
13 woman to exercise the office of a priest in our Communion; By the grace of your Spirit inspire us to
14 follow her example, serving your people with patience and happiness all our days, and witnessing in every
15 circumstance to our Savior Jesus Christ, who lives and reigns with you and the same Spirit, one God, for
16 ever and ever. *Amen.*
17   Psalm - 116:1-2
18   Lesson - Galatians 3:23-28
19   Gospel - Luke 10:1-9
20   Preface of a Saint(2)

Resolution A100 Revise Lesser Feasts and Fasts 2000

1   *Resolved,* the House of _____ concurring, That this 74th General Convention direct the Standing
2   Commission on Liturgy and Music to undertake a revision of *Lesser Feasts and Fasts 2000*, and to report
3   on the progress of this revision to the 75th General Convention; and be it further
4   *Resolved*, that the sum of $18,000.00 be appropriated for support of this undertaking during the triennium
5   2003 - 2006; this appropriation to be administered by the Office of Liturgy and Music.

EXPLANATION

The great changes which have taken place during the past half-century have made each of us more aware of all four orders of ministry, of the wider Anglican Communion and of our ecumenical partners. With this in mind, the SCLM has embarked on a careful evaluation of the scope and adequacy of the commemorations and accompanying propers contained in *Lesser Feasts and Fasts 2000*. The Commission believes it is time for a revision of this important aspect of the worship which the Church offers to God in the company of the saints of every time and place.

Committee on General Convention Resolution 2000-B039

Liturgies to Celebrate Church Planting

SCLM Member: Susan Anslow Williams. *Consultants*: Stacey Fussell, Victoria Heard, Jennifer Phillips, Frederick Richardson, Isaias Rodriguez, Anthony Vidal
Meeting Date: April 24 – 25, 2002, Ambridge, Pennsylvania.

INTRODUCTION

The SCLM assigned this work to a task group composed of members of the SCLM and church planters from four dioceses. The input of interested others, including bishops, planters, missioners and liturgists, was gratefully received and incorporated.

When the working group met, it became clear that more liturgies were needed than the two specified by Resolution B039. The members noted that a series of events typically takes place within planting dioceses or regions, as (a) the guidance of the Holy Spirit is sought, (b) a planter or team is chosen and sent forth, and (c) eventually a public launch or opening service is held. These three events were chosen for liturgical celebration.

Also observing that new congregations often meet in a "borrowed," secular location, at least for the beginning of their life together, a rite was developed to set aside and hallow such space for worship. For this rite the committee drew from the Lutheran (ELCA) Book of Occasional Services. Further materials include: a variety of new collects and other prayers, written by The Rev. Jennifer Phillips; a Litany for Mission, which is an adaptation of a litany created by the Diocese of Texas, previously made available by the Episcopal Church Center for World Mission Sunday; and a list of hymns especially appropriate for church planting and mission, referring to *The Hymnal 1982; Lift Every Voice and Sing II; Wonder, Love and Praise*; and *El Himnario*.

Mindful of the charge given by the 72nd General Convention (C021s) and reaffirmed by the 73rd Convention, to provide "forms of worship reflective of our multicultural, multiethnic, multilingual and multigenerational Church while providing rites and structures that ensure the unity of Common Prayer," all of these materials have been translated into Spanish for consideration at this 74th Convention. Adaptation is encouraged throughout the liturgies, since the anticipated circumstances of their use will vary widely. The collects and other texts employ a fresh diversity of images taken from Scripture, while seeking to avoid language that assumes prior church experience.

With the exceptions noted above, the texts consist primarily of newly written materials. References are made to the *1979 Book of Common Prayer*, its translation into Spanish (1989) and *Enriching Our Worship I* (1997).

The pages that follow are laid out in the form in which they will be published.

Concerning the Celebration

This service has been created to help congregations, dioceses or other church bodies who are considering a new church mission, to discern the will of the Holy Spirit. The service may also be used by a team preparing for a new church plant, and/or be incorporated into one or several Sunday services by supporting/sponsoring congregation(s). The service may be used to initiate a period of intentional discernment; and at points within that process.

The service encourages silence and stillness to listen to the movement of the Holy Spirit. It is not a Eucharistic liturgy.

Lo Concerniente a la Celebración

Este servicio se ha pensado para ayudar a las congregaciones, diócesis u otros cuerpos eclesiásticos, que están considerando fundar una iglesia-misión nueva, a discernir la voluntad del Espíritu Santo. El servicio lo puede usar el grupo que se prepara para fundar una iglesia. También puede ser incorporado en uno o varios servicios de la(s) congregación(es) que apoya(n) o patrocina(n) la misión. El servicio se puede usar para iniciar un período de discernimiento; y en varios otros momentos durante ese proceso.

El servicio invita al silencio y a la calma para escuchar el movimiento del Espíritu Santo. No es una liturgia eucarística.

Discernment for a New Church Mission

Officiant	Be still before the Lord,
People	And wait patiently for God's presence.

A period of silence is kept.

Officiant	O Holy Spirit, you are the seeker's resource and guide.
People	Come, create, renew and inspire.
Officiant	Teach us to hear, teach us to speak.
People	Show us your will that we may follow.

One or two Lessons are read.
A list of suggested lessons and psalms

I Kings 3:3-10 (The Lord asks Solomon, "Ask what I shall give you.")
Isaiah 49: 5-13 (I will give you as a light to the nations, that my salvation may reach…)
Ruth 1: 8-18. (Your people shall be my people, and your God my God…)
Hosea 6:1-6, 11-7:1a (For you also, O Judah, a harvest is appointed)

Psalms: 37, 46

Matthew 28:17-20 (Go therefore and make disciples of all nations…)
John 5:25-39 (I seek not my own will but the will of him who sent me.)
Ephesians 1:1-14. (For he has made known to us … the mystery of his will)

A significant period of silence is kept after each Scripture Reading. A sermon or homily is discouraged in favor of time to listen to the movement of the Holy Spirit.

After the [second] period of silence, a person appointed leads the Litany

Litany for the Mission of the Church

The Officiant then continues with one of the following, or some other suitable Collect.

A Collect for Parish-led Church Planting

O God, who inspired your apostles in Jerusalem to pray and fast to discern your will: send us your Spirit, that we may learn what you would have us do and the words and witness you would have us offer, that your Kingdom may come and your power be revealed in this *(diocese, deanery, town);* to the glory of your Name. *Amen.*

Discernimiento sobre la fundación de una iglesia-misión nueva

Oficiante   Estén tranquilos ante el Señor,
Pueblo   Y esperen pacientemente la presencia del Señor.

Se guarda un periodo de silencio.

Oficiante   Oh Santo Espíritu, que eres recurso y guía del que busca.
Pueblo   Ven, crea, renueva e inspira.
Oficiant   Enséñanos a escuchar, enséñanos a hablar.
Pueblo   Manifiéstanos tu voluntad para que la sigamos.

Se leen una o dos lecturas.
He aquí una lista de lecturas y salmos:

1 Reyes 3: 3-10 (El Señor dijo a Salomón: Pídeme lo que quieras que te dé.)
Isaías 49: 5-13 (Te voy a poner por luz de las gentes, para que mi salvación alcance…)
Rut 1: 8-19 (Tu pueblo será mi pueblo y tu Dios mi Dios…)
Oseas 6: 1-6, 11-7:1a (También para ti, Judá, hay preparada una cosecha)

Salmos: 37,46

Mateo 28: 17-20 (Id, haced discípulos a todas las gentes, bautizándolas…)
Juan 5: 25-39 (No busco mi voluntad sino la del que me ha enviado"
Efesios 1: 1-14 (Porque nos ha dado a conocer… el misterio de su voluntad)

Se guarda un significativo período de silencio después de cada lectura. No se aconseja sermón ni homilía en preferencia al silencio para sentir el movimiento del Espíritu Santo.

Después del [segundo] período de silencio, una persona indicada lee la letanía

Letanía por la misión de la Iglesia

Luego el oficiante continúa con una de las siguientes, o alguna otra colecta apropiada.

Coleta para la fundación de una iglesia, por iniciativa de una parroquia

Oh Dios, que inspiraste a los apóstoles en Jerusalén a que oraran y ayunaran para discernir tu voluntad: envíanos tu Espíritu para que aprendamos lo que te gustaría que hiciéramos y las palabras y testimonio que quieras que ofrezcamos, para que tu reino venga y tu poder se manifieste en esta *(diócesis, ciudad, etc)*. Para la gloria de tu Nombre. *Amén.*

A Collect for Apostolic-model Church Planting

Gracious Father, you sent your Son Jesus to proclaim to all the Good News of your Kingdom, and through him inspired individuals to sow the seeds of your church: Guide us as we continue this work; show us the next field in which to plant; and give us the gifts to accomplish your will; all of which we ask through Jesus our Savior. *Amen.*

A Collect for Regional Collaboration in Church Planting

O Holy God, you breathe your life-giving Spirit into the congregations of this *(region, deanery, ...),* calling us to join together in mission for the spreading of the Gospel: show us the people to whom we should go and the path we should travel; help us to understand the deep longings of their hearts, and enable us to feed them through the living presence of Jesus Christ our Savior, in whose power we set forth and in whose name we pray. *Amen.*

A Collect for Multicultural Church Planting

Eternal God, you have promised your salvation to all peoples, and have given us a vision of a great multitude around your throne, from all nations and tribes and languages: help us to bring this vision into our time and place; banish from us all prejudices and false presumptions; and enable us to hear and to speak new words of hope and praise; through Jesus Christ, the living Word. *Amen.*

A Collect for Regular Use during Sunday Worship by Congregations in Discernment

Lord Jesus, you commissioned us to make disciples of all the nations and promised that you would be with us always: so guide this congregation to see the peoples you would have us reach and empower us to be instruments of your saving work, for the glory of God. *Amen.*

or

Blessed God, you make all things new: Guide us as we seek your will for a new community of Word and Sacrament, that it may be leaven for the world's bread, and wine of delight for hearts in need; a gathering strong for service and glad in praise; and a people listening and responding to your presence in their midst; through Jesus our redeemer and steadfast companion. *Amen.*

A Collect for Raising Up of People with Skills Needed for a Church Planting

Holy Spirit, you delight to equip us with all the gifts of service *(especially ___)* and with power to establish the Realm of God: raise up among us those whom you have blessed for this new work, that the Body of Christ may grow in strength and health, for the transforming of the world; through Jesus Christ our Lord. *Amen.*

Para la fundación de una iglesia con modelo apostólico

Padre clemente, que enviaste a tu Hijo Jesús a proclamar las Buenas Nuevas del reino y por él inspiraste a otros a sembrar las semillas de tu Iglesia: guíanos para continuar este trabajo; manifiéstanos el próximo lugar donde fundar; y dános los dones para cumplir tu voluntad. Te lo pedimos por Jesucristo nuestro salvador. *Amén.*

Por la colaboración regional en la fundación de una iglesia

Oh Dios santísimo, que soplas tu Espíritu, dador de vida, en las congregaciones de esta *(región)*, llamándonos a reunirnos en espíritu misionero para difundir el evangelio: manifiéstanos a qué gentes hemos de ir y el camino que hemos de andar; ayúdanos a entender las profundas aspiraciones de sus corazones y capacítanos para alimentarlos mediante la viva presencia de Jesucristo nuestro salvador, en cuyo poder enseñamos y en cuyo nombre rezamos. *Amén.*

Por la fundación de una iglesia multicultural

Dios eterno, que has prometido la salvación a todos los pueblos y nos has ofrecido la visión de una gran multitud de gentes de todas las naciones y tribus y lenguas alrededor de tu trono, ayúdanos a traer esa visión a nuestro tiempo y lugar; disipa de nosotros todo prejuicio y arrogancia; capacítanos para que escuchemos y hablemos palabras nuevas de esperanza y alabanza. Por Jesucristo, la palabra viva. *Amén.*

Para ser usada en servicio del domingo por la congregación que está discerniendo

Señor Jesús, que nos encomendaste hacer discípulos a todas las naciones y prometiste que siempre estarías con nosotros, guía a esta congregación para que acierte a llegar a las gentes que deseas y capacítanos para ser instrumentos de tu obra salvadora, para la gloria de Dios. *Amén.*

O bien

Dios bendito, que creas todas las cosas nuevas: guíanos mientras descubrimos tu voluntad para fundar una comunidad nueva de la Palabra y del Sacramento, para que sea levadura para el pan del mundo y vino que alegra el corazón de los necesitados; una asamblea vigorosa para el servicio y alegre en la alabanza; y un pueblo que escucha y responde a tu presencia en medio de ellos. Por Jesucristo nuestro redentor y firme compañero. *Amén.*

Para escoger gente con la destreza necesaria para fundar una iglesia

Santo Espíritu, que te deleitas capacitándonos con dones para tu servicio (especialmente_____) y con poder para establecer el reino de Dios: escoge de entre nosotros aquellos que has seleccionado para esta obra nueva, para que el cuerpo de Cristo crezca en fortaleza y salud, para la transformación del mundo. Por Jesucristo nuestro Señor. *Amén.*

The Lord's Prayer

The Officiant introduces the prayer with this or some other sentence.

Gathering our prayers into one, as Jesus taught us we now pray:

Our Father…

A deacon, or the Officiant, dismisses the people using the following or some other suitable dismissal

Go forth now in the Name of Christ.
Go into the (*City, town, village, region…*) of _____.
Go into your own neighborhoods.
Go to unknown lands and places.
Go where God's name is well known and where it has yet to be known.
Go to those who welcome you and to those who reject you.
Go forth into the world and share the Good News of God's love. [Alleluia, Alleluia!]

The People respond   Thanks be to God. [Alleluia, Alleluia!]

In Lent the Alleluias are omitted. In Easter season they are included.

Padre Nuestro

Sigue la oración del Padrenuestro con esta u otra introducción

Aunando nuestras oraciones en ésta, oramos como Jesús nos enseñó:

Padre nuestro…

El diácono, o el oficiante, despide al pueblo usando las siguientes u otras despedidas apropiadas:

Salgan en el nombre de Cristo.:
Vayan a la (ciudad, pueblo, región…) de_____.
Vayan a sus propios barrios.
Vayan a tierras y lugares apartados.
Vayan donde el nombre de Dios es bien conocido y donde todavía no es conocido.
Vayan a quienes les dan la bienvenida y a quienes les rechazan.
Vayan al mundo y compartan la Buena Nueva del amor de Dios. [¡Aleluya, aleluya!]

Pueblo Demos gracias a Dios. [¡Aleluya, aleluya!]

En Cuaresma se omiten las aleluyas. En la época pascual se incluyen.

Concerning the Service

This liturgy is designed for use on the occasion when a selected and trained church planter, missioner and/or mission team is to be sent forth by a diocese (and sponsoring congregation), to a designated location/congregation. If the new church has been named, there are opportunities in the liturgy for that designation. The service should be adapted to the mission circumstances.

This is a Eucharistic liturgy. It presumes the participation of the diocesan bishop or bishop's representative; clergy and other members of any sponsoring congregation(s); and the church planter and his/her team, their supporters, and members of the new church.

The liturgy is rooted in the imagery and theology of Baptism, recognizing that the work of spreading the Gospel and building up of Christ's Body the Church is the work of all baptized persons. With that understanding, particular ministers are commissioned and their responsibilities recognized in this liturgy.

Lo Concerniente al Rito

Esta liturgia se ha pensado para cuando un fundador de iglesia, un misionero o un grupo misionero, seleccionado y entrenado, va a ser enviado por la diócesis (y por la congregación patrocinadora), a un lugar reservado para una congregación. Si la nueva iglesia ya tiene nombre, hay oportunidades en la liturgia para ese caso. El servicio se debe adaptar a las circunstancias de la misión.

Esta es una liturgia eucarística. Se da por entendido la participación del obispo o su representante, del clero y otros miembros de la(s) congregación(es) patrocinadora(s), del fundador de la iglesia y de su equipo, de los que han apoyado al equipo y de los miembros de la nueva iglesia.

Esta liturgia tiene sus raíces en los símbolos y teología del Bautismo, reconociendo que el trabajo de divulgar el evangelio y de edificar el cuerpo de Cristo, que es la Iglesia, es una tarea de todos los bautizados. Con ésto en mente, en esta liturgia, se comisionan a determinados ministros y se reconocen sus responsabilidades.

A Liturgy for Commissioning a Church Planter, Missioner or Mission Team

A hymn or anthem may be sung

An Opening Acclamation from the Book of Common Prayer (page 299) or Enriching our Worship I (page 50) is used

Then follows

Celebrant	There is one Body and one Spirit;
People	There is one hope in God's call to us;
Celebrant	One Lord, one Faith, one Baptism;
People	One God and Father of all.

A song of praise may be sung.

Celebrant	The Lord be with you.
People	And also with you.
Celebrant	Let us pray.

One of the following collects; or the Collect of the Day; or one of the collects for the Mission of the Church (BCP pages 257, 816) follows.

For Parish-led Church Planting

Lord Christ, you equipped and sent forth your friends to bring the Good News of salvation from Jerusalem into Judea and all the world: be present as we send forth these friends and companions in your service, that your Kingdom may come with power in _____ [*place or name of new church*]; to the glory of your Name. *Amen.*

For Apostolic-model Church Planting

Gracious Father, you sent your Son Jesus to proclaim to all the Good News of your Kingdom, and through him inspired individuals to sow the seeds of your church: help us as we continue this work. Empower N. your servant and all who support *her*, and give them the gifts to accomplish your will; all of which we ask through Jesus our Savior. Amen.

For Regional Collaboration in Church Planting

O Holy God, you breathe your life-giving Spirit into the congregations of this (*region, deanery, ...*), calling us to join together in mission for the spreading of the Gospel: bless us as we begin this new journey; go with those whom you have raised up for this work; and enable them to feed your people in _____ through the living presence of Jesus Christ our Savior, in whose power we set forth and in whose Name we pray. *Amen.*

Liturgia para comisionar a un fundador de iglesia, a un misionero o a un grupo misionero

Se puede cantar una canción o un himno.

Se usa una aclamación inicial, tomada del Libro de Oración Común (página 219) o Enriching Our Worship I (página 50).

Luego, sigue de esta manera

Celebrante	Hay un Cuerpo y un Espíritu.
Pueblo	Hay una esperanza en el llamado de Dios.
Celebrante	Un Señor, una Fe, un Bautismo.
Pueblo	Un Dios y Padre de todos.

Se puede cantar una canción de alabanza.

Celebrante	El Señor sea con ustedes.
Pueblo	Y con tu espíritu.
Celebrante	Oremos.

Sigue una de las colectas siguientes, o la colecta del día, o una de las colectas para la Misión de la Iglesia (LOC páginas 175 y 706).

Para la fundación de una iglesia por iniciativa de una parroquia

Señor Jesucristo, que proveíste a tus amigos y los enviaste a difundir las Buenas Nuevas de salvación de Jerusalén a Judea y a todo el mundo. Acompáñanos mientras enviamos a estos amigos y compañeros en tu servicio, para que tu reino pueda llegar con poder a _____(*lugar o nombre de la nueva iglesia*). Para la gloria de tu nombre. *Amén.*

Para la fundación de una iglesia con modelo apostólico

Padre clemente, que enviaste a tu Hijo Jesús a proclamar a todo el mundo las Buenas Nuevas de tu reino y que por él inspiraste a otros a sembrar las semillas de tu Iglesia, ayúdanos mientras continuamos tu obra. Da poder a tu siervo/a y a todos los que le apoyan y dale los dones para cumplir tu voluntad. Te lo pedimos por Jesucristo nuestro salvador. *Amén.*

Por la colaboración regional en la fundación de una iglesia

Oh Dios santísimo, que soplas tu Espíritu, dador de vida, en las congregaciones de esta (región…), llamándonos a reunirnos en espíritu misionero para difundir el evangelio, bendícenos al comenzar este nuevo viaje, acompaña a quienes hemos escogido para esta tarea y capacítalos para que alimenten a tu pueblo en _____ mediante la viva presencia de Jesucristo nuestro salvador, en cuyo poder enseñamos y en cuyo nombre rezamos. *Amén.*

A Collect for Multicultural Church Planting

Eternal God, you have promised your salvation to all peoples, and have given us a vision of a great multitude around your throne, from all nations and tribes and languages: help us as we bring this vision into our time and place; go with those who now undertake your work in ____; and enable them to hear and to speak new words of hope and praise; through Jesus Christ, the living Word. *Amen.*

For Any Church Planters

O Holy God, you raise up laborers for your harvest, sending them out as sowers of your Gospel and caretakers of new life: bless *these your servants* in *their* work of planting and tending your Church in ____; equip *them* for service, enliven *them* with your joy, and help *them* remember and trust that it is you who will bring in the harvest; through Jesus Christ, the Savior of souls. *Amen.*

or

Blessed God, you call forth light from darkness: send the power of your Spirit upon your servants *N. (and N.)* as *they* carry your Gospel to _____. May your light so fill *them* that *they* may shine with your radiance, drawing all to the brightness of your love and mercy; through Jesus, our Savior and true Light. *Amen.*

Then one or more of the following passages from Holy Scripture is read. Other passages particularly suited to the day may be substituted. If there is to be a Communion, a passage from the Gospel always concludes the readings.

Joshua 1:6-9 *(call of Joshua)*
Isaiah 6: 1-8 *(call of Isaiah)*
Jeremiah: 1:5-10 *(call of Jeremiah)*

Psalms: 65, 66; 100; 115; 147

Acts: 13:1-4 *(setting apart for church planting of Paul and Barnabas)*
Acts 16:6-10 *(The call of Paul to Macedonia)*
Acts: 18:1-4, 7-10 *(Paul's vision of Christ in Corinth: "I have many people in this city")*

Romans 15:13-21 *(May the God of hope fill you with all joy...)*
I Corinthians 3:5-12 *(Paul plants, Apollos watered, and God gives the increase)*
II Corinthians 5:16-6:2 *(We are ambassadors for Christ.)*
Ephesians 2:13-22 *(He preached peace to those who were far off...)*

A hymn, psalm or anthem may be sung.

Matthew 9: 36-38 *(Jesus has compassion on the people)*
Matthew 28:16-20 *(Go, make disciples of all nations, baptizing them...)*
Luke 10:1-9 *(Pray the Lord of the harvest to send laborers.)*
Luke 24:44-50 *(Forgiveness of sins will be preached to all peoples)*
John 4:34-38 *(Look at the fields, they are white with harvest)*

Por la fundación de una iglesia multicultural

Dios eterno, que has prometido la salvación a todos los pueblos y nos has ofrecido la visión de una gran multitud de gentes de todas las naciones y tribus y lenguas alrededor de tu trono, ayúdanos mientras traemos esa visión a nuestro tiempo y lugar; acompaña a quienes ahora emprenden tu labor en _____; y capacítalos para que escuchen y hablen palabras nuevas de esperanza y alabanza. Por Jesucristo, la palabra viva. *Amén.*

Por los fundadores de cualquier iglesia

Oh Dios santo, que escoges trabajadores para tu cosecha, enviándolos como sembradores de tu Evangelio y cuidadores de la nueva vida, bendice a *estos tus siervos* en *su* tarea de fundar y cuidar de tu Iglesia en _____; hazlos aptos para el servicio, anímalos con tu alegría, y ayúdalos a que se acuerden y confíen en que eres tú quien da la cosecha. Por Jesucristo, el salvador de las almas. *Amén.*

O bien

Bendito Dios, que sacas luz de las tinieblas: envía el poder de tu Espíritu sobre estos siervos *N. (y N.)* que se disponen a llevar tu evangelio a _____. Que vayan llenos de tu luz para que brillen con tu resplandor y atraigan a todo el mundo al deslumbre de tu amor y compasión. Por Jesús, nuestra luz y salvación. *Amén.*

Se lae uno o dos de los siguientes pasajes de las Sagradas Escrituras. Si se celebra la Comunió, las Lecturas concluyen siempre con un pasje del Evangelio.

Josué 1: 6-9 *(Vocación de Josué)*
Isaías 8: 1-8 *(Vocación de Isaías)*
Jeremías 1: 5-10 *(Vocación de Jeremías)*

Salmos: 65, 66; 100; 115; 147

Hechos 15: 13-21 *(Separación de Pablo y Bernabé para el trabajo misionero)*
Hechos 16: 6-10 *(Envío de Pablo a Macedonia)*
Hechos 18: 1-4, 7-10 *(Cristo dice a Pablo en una visión: "Tengo un pueblo numeroso en esta ciudad)*

Romanos 15: 13-21 *(El Dios de la esperanza os colme de todo gozo...).*
1 Corintios 3: 5-12 *(Pablo planta, Apolo riega, y Dios da el crecimiento)*
2 Corintios 5: 16-62 *(Somos embajadores de Cristo)*
Efesios 2: 13-22 *(Predicó la paz a los que estaban lejos...)*

(Se puede cantar un himno o una canción)

Mateo 9: 36-38 *(Jesús se compadece de la gente)*
Mateo 28: 16-20 *(Id, haced discípulos a todas las gentes, bautizándolas...)*
Lucas 10: 1-9 *(Rogad para que el Dueño de la mies envíe obreros)*
Lucas 24: 44-50 *(El perdón de los pecados se predicará a todos los pueblos)*
Juan 4: 34-38 *(Ved los campos, ya blanquean para la siega)*

The Sermon

The Commissioning

The church planter/team stands before the bishop or the bishop's representative and representatives of the diocese, sponsoring congregation(s), and others as appropriate. If there are members of the new congregation already identified, they should stand with the planting team

The Bishop or the Bishop's Representative says

> The *vicar (missioner, team...)* and members of the new congregation _____ will now be presented.

The rector of the sending parish, or a diocesan representative, says

> I present *N.* to be commissioned as a *church planter*, and to serve as *vicar* of _____ in the Diocese of ____.

The Bishop says

> Do you believe that *she* is well qualified and duly prepared for this ministry?

The Rector or Diocesan Representative responds   I do.

Bishop   N., do you, in the presence of this congregation,
    commit yourself to this new trust and responsibility?

Planter   I do.

Planter   I present these persons who represent all those who will serve with me
    in planting this new church.

Bishop   Will you who are committing yourselves to this new work do all in your
    power to support the life and mission of this new congregation?

Members of the team and/or new congregation   We will.

The Bishop then addresses the whole assembly

> Will you who witness this new beginning, support and uphold *N. (these persons)* and the community of ____ in this ministry?

People   We will.

Bishop   Let us join with those who are accepting this ministry of the Gospel,
    and renew our own baptismal covenant.

El sermón

La comisión

El fundador -y grupo misionero- de la iglesia está delante del obispo o de su representante y representantes de la diócesis, de la(s) congregación(es) patrocinadora(s) y de otras personas según sea apropiado. Si ya existen miembros de la nueva congregación, deben estar con el grupo fundador.

El obispo o representante del obispo dice

Que el *vicario (misionero, grupo misionero..)* y miembros de la nueva congregación _____ sean presentados ahora.

El rector de la parroquia misionera, o un representante de la diócesis, dice

Presento a *N.* para que sea comisionado como *fundador de una iglesia,* y para que sirva como *vicario* de _____ en la Diócesis de _____.

Obispo

¿Crees que está bien cualificado y debidamente preparado para este ministerio?

El rector o representante diocesano

Sí lo creo.

Obispo	¿*N.,* en la presencia de esta congregación, te comprometes a esta nueva confianza y responsabilidad?
Fundador	Me comprometo.
Fundador	Presento a estas personas que representan a todos los que servirán conmigo en la fundación de esta nueva iglesia.
Obispo	Ustedes que se están comprometiendo a este nuevo trabajo, ¿harán todo lo posible para apoyar la vida y misión de esta nueva congregación?

Los miembros del grupo misionero y/ o la nueva congregación   Así lo haremos.

Entonces el obispo se dirige a toda la asamblea

Ustedes, testigos de este nuevo inicio, ¿apoyarán y orarán por *N. (estas personas)* y por la comunidad de _____ en este ministerio?

El pueblo	Así lo haremos.
Obispo	Unámonos a estos que aceptan este ministerio del evangelio y renovemos nuestro pacto bautismal.

The Baptismal Covenant

Bishop	Do you believe in God the Father?
People	I believe in God, the Father almighty,
	creator of heaven and earth.
Bishop	Do you believe in Jesus Christ, the Son of God?
People	I believe in Jesus Christ, his only Son, our Lord.

        He was conceived by the power of the Holy Spirit
           and born of the Virgin Mary.
        He suffered under Pontius Pilate,
           was crucified, died, and was buried.
        He descended to the dead.
        On the third day he rose again.
        He ascended into heaven,
           and is seated at the right hand of the Father.
        He will come again to judge the living and the dead.

Bishop	Do you believe in God the Holy Spirit?
People	I believe in the Holy Spirit,

        the holy catholic Church,
        the communion of saints,
        the forgiveness of sins,
        the resurrection of the body,
        and the life everlasting.

Bishop	Will you continue in the apostles' teaching and fellowship, in the breaking of bread, and in the prayers ?
People	I will, with God's help.
Bishop	Will you persevere in resisting evil, and, whenever you fall into sin, repent and return to the Lord?
People	I will, with God's help.
Bishop	Will you proclaim by word and example the Good News of God in Christ?
People	I will, with God's help.
Bishop	Will you seek and serve Christ in all persons, loving your neighbor as yourself?
People	I will, with God's help.
Bishop	Will you strive for justice and peace among all people, and respect the dignity of every human being?
People	I will, with God's help.

El pacto bautismal

Obispo   ¿Crees en Dios Padre?
Pueblo   Creo en Dios Padre todopoderoso,
Creador del cielo y de la tierra.

Obispo   ¿Crees en Jesucristo, el Hijo de Dios?
Pueblo   Creo en Jesucristo, su único Hijo, nuestro Señor.
        Fue concebido por obra y gracia del Espíritu Santo
            y nació de la Virgen María.
    Padeció bajo el poder de Poncio Pilato.
    Fue crucificado, muerto y sepultado.
    Descendió a los infiernos.
    Al tercer día resucitó de entre los muertos.
    Subió a los cielos
        y está sentado a la diestra de Dios Padre.
    Desde allí ha de venir a juzgar a
        vivos y muertos.

Obispo   ¿Crees en Dios el Espíritu Santo?
Pueblo   Creo en el Espíritu Santo,
        la santa Iglesia católica,
        la comunión de los santos,
        el perdón de los pecados,
        la resurrección de los muertos,
        y la vida eterna.

Obispo   ¿Continuarás en la enseñanza y comunión de los apóstoles,
en la fracción del pan y en las oraciones?
Pueblo   Así lo haré con la ayuda de Dios.

Obispo   ¿Perseverarás en resistir al mal, y cuando caigas en pecado,
te arrepentirás y te volverás al Señor?
Pueblo   Así lo haré con la ayuda del Dios.

Obispo   ¿Proclamarás por medio de la palabra y el ejemplo
las Buenas Nuevas de Dios en Cristo?
Pueblo   Así lo haré con la ayuda de Dios.

Obispo   ¿Buscarás y servirás a Cristo en todas las personas,
amando a tu prójimo como a ti mismo?
Pueblo   Así lo haré con la ayuda de Dios.

Obispo   ¿Lucharás por la justicia y la paz entre todos los pueblos,
Y respetarás la dignidad de todo ser humano?
Pueblo   Así lo haré, con la ayuda de Dios.

Bishop Let us offer our prayers to God for all people and for this new congregation.

The Litany for the Mission of the Church (page 196) or the following Litany of Thanksgiving is led by a person appointed.

For the Church universal, of which you, O Christ, are the foundation and chief cornerstone,
We thank you, Lord.

For your presence whenever two or three have gathered together in your Name,
We thank you, Lord.

For making us your children by adoption and grace,
and refreshing us day by day with the bread of life.
We thank you, Lord.

For the knowledge of your will and the grace to perform it,
We thank you, Lord.

For the fulfilling of our desires and petitions as may be best for us,
We thank you, Lord.

For the pardoning of our sins, which restores us to the company of your faithful people,
We thank you, Lord.

For the blessing of lives with your goodness,
We thank you, Lord.

For the faith and perseverance of those who have gone before us,
We thank you, Lord.

For the fellowship of (Mary the God-bearer, the holy apostles, blessed N. and of) all the saints,
We thank you, Lord.

After a period of silent prayer, the Bishop concludes with the following

O God, we praise you for the redemption of the world through the death and resurrection of Jesus the Christ. We thank you for pouring out your Spirit upon us, making some apostles, some prophets, some evangelists, some pastors and teachers to equip your people for the building up of the Body of Christ. Bless this new work that we undertake, that your Name may be glorified, now and for ever. *Amen.*

The Peace

Obispo   Recemos a Dios por todo el mundo y por esta nueva congregación.

Una persona indicada dirige la letanía por la Misión de la Iglesia (página 197) o la siguiente letanía de acción de gracias.

Por la Iglesia universal, de la cual, oh Cristo, eres el fundamento y la piedra principal,
Gracias, Señor.

Por tu presencia dondequiera que dos o tres se reúnan en tu nombre,
Gracias, Señor.

Por hacernos hijos tuyos por adopción y gracia, y nutrirnos cada día con el pan de vida,
Gracias, Señor.

Por el conocimiento de tu voluntad y la gracia para cumplirla,
Gracias, Señor.

Por el cumplimiento de nuestros deseos y peticiones según sean para nuestro bien,
Gracias, Señor.

Por el perdón de nuestros pecados que nos restaura en la compañía de los fieles,
Gracias, Señor.

Por la bendición de la vida con tu bondad.
Gracias, Señor.

Por la fe y perseverancia de aquellos que han partido antes que nosotros,
Gracias, Señor.

Por la compañía de (María la portadora de Dios, los santos apóstoles, el bendito N. y de) todos los santos,
Gracias, Señor.

Después de un momento de oración en silencio, el obispo concluye de esta manera

Oh Dios, te alabamos por la redención del mundo mediante la muerte y resurrección de Jesucristo. Te damos gracias por derramar tu Espíritu sobre nosotros, haciendo apóstoles de unos, de otros profetas, de otros evangelistas, de otros pastores y maestros para capacitar a tu pueblo para la edificación del cuerpo de Cristo. Bendice esta obra que emprendemos, para que tu Nombre sea glorificado, ahora y por siempre. *Amén.*

La paz

The Eucharist continues with the Great Thanksgiving, the Bishop or Bishop's representative, or Rector of the sending parish, presiding at the table and the planters assisting according to their order.

Except for major feasts, the Preface is that of Pentecost.

Following Communion, the planter/ team (and members of the new congregation) come to the front of the assembly for the following prayer

In place of the usual postcommunion prayer, the following is said

Celebrant

Eternal Giver of love and life, you have nourished us with the Body and Blood of your Son Jesus Christ. Now send us into the world to preach your Good News, to do your justice, and to walk humbly in your way.

People

Glory to God, whose power working in us can do infinitely more than we can ask or imagine. Glory to God from generation to generation in the Church, and in Christ Jesus for ever and ever. Amen.

The Bishop or bishop's representative presents the team with a Bible and The Book of Common Prayer, saying

Receive this Bible. Go, proclaim the Word of God. *Amen.*

Receive this Book of Common Prayer. Go, lead a new community in the worship of God. *Amen.*

The following or another form of the Dismissal is used

| *Deacon* | Go forth into the world and share the Good News of God's love. [Alleluia, alleluia.] |
| *People* | In the Name of Christ we go. [Alleluia, alleluia.] |

The alleluias are omitted in Lent. They are used in the Easter Season.

La Eucaristía continúa con la Gran Plegaria Eucarística, el obispo o su representante, o rector de la parroquia misionera, presiden en el altar y los fundadores asisten de acuerdo a su orden.

Excepto en fiestas mayores, el prefacio es el de Pentecostés.

Después de la comunión, el fundador -y grupo misionero- (y miembros de la nueva congregación) vienen al frente de la asamblea, para rezar la siguiente oración

En lugar de la oración después de la comunión

Celebrante

Eterno Dios, dador de amor y vida, nos has nutrido con el cuerpo y la sangre de tu Hijo Jesucristo. Envíanos ahora al mundo para predicar las buenas nuevas, para hacer tu justicia y para caminar humildemente en tu camino.

Pueblo

Gloria sea dada a Dios, que puede obrar en nosotros infinitamente más de lo que podemos pedir o imaginarnos. Gloria sea dada a Dios, de generación en generación en la Iglesia y en Jesucristo por los siglos de los siglos. Amén.

El obispo o su representante ofrece al grupo una Biblia y un Libro de Oración Común, luego dice

Reciban esta Biblia. Vayan y proclamen la Palabra de Dios. *Amén.*
Reciban este Libro de Oración Común. Vayan, guíen en oración a Dios a la nueva comunidad. *Amén.*

Se puede usar la siguiente despedida u otra similar

Diácono	Vayan al mundo y compartan la Buena Nueva del amor de Dios. [¡Aleluya, aleluya!]
Pueblo	Vamos en el nombre de Cristo. [¡Aleluya, aleluya!]

En Cuaresma se omiten las aleluyas. En la época pascual se incluyen.

Concerning the Service

The opening service of a new congregation is a celebration for the members of the new community, but more importantly, an opportunity for them to show hospitality to those seeking a church home in the broader community.

It is important to choose a day appropriate for the culture surrounding the new mission – for example, the feast of The Epiphany is of particular significance in the Hispanic community and an effective date for a public launch. Days such as Palm Sunday, Easter, and Christmas are <u>not</u> recommended. Experience shows that dates between late August through the Last Sunday after Pentecost work well in most contexts.

The congregation is gathered to serve those coming for the first time, and should be mindful of the opportunities to proclaim the Gospel within the liturgy. The host members should be conscientious of the need for simplicity and clarity. It is important that a variety of persons participate in the leadership of the service.

This service assumes a Eucharistic context. It may be adapted to a service of the Word.

If appropriate the Liturgy for Setting Apart Secular Space for Sacred Use (page 194) may immediately precede the service.

Lo concerniente al servicio

El servicio de inauguración de una congregación es una celebración para los miembros de la nueva comunidad pero, todavía más importante, una oportunidad para mostrar hospitalidad a todos aquellos que buscan una iglesia a la cual asistir.

Es importante escoger un día apropiado dentro de la cultura que rodea a la nueva misión, por ejemplo, la fiesta de la Epifanía tiene significado especial en la comunidad hispana y es un día muy apto para captar la atención del pueblo. No se recomiendan días como el Domingo de Ramos, Pascua y Navidad. La experiencia demuestra que, en la mayoría de los ambientes, las mejores fechas van de finales de agosto al último domingo de Pentecostés.

La congregación se reúne para servir a los que vienen por vez primera y deben ser conscientes de la oportunidad de proclamar el evangelio en la liturgia. Los miembros anfitriones se han de dar cuenta de la necesidad de la claridad y simplicidad. Es importante que una variedad de personas participe en el liderazgo del servicio.

Este servicio da por entendido un contexto eucarístico. Se puede adaptar para un servicio de la Palabra.

Si es apropiado, puede preceder inmediatamente al servicio la Liturgia para reservar un espacio para el uso sagrado (página 195).

A Liturgy for the Opening of a New Congregation

The Gathering

One of the following, or an Opening Acclamation from the Book of Common Prayer (page 355) or Enriching Our Worship I (page 50), may be used

Officiant/Celebrant	Holy God, you have called for yourself a people.
People	Fill us with your presence, affirm us with your love.

or

Officiant/Celebrant	This is the day that the Lord has made.
People	Let us rejoice and be glad in it.

Opening Prayer *The following or the Collect of the Day may be used.*

Officiant/Celebrant	O God, the source of all beginnings: we thank you for bringing us to this new day.
People	Send us your Spirit as we begin our journey as the people of _____ *[name of congregation]*. Equip us to proclaim the Good News of Jesus, defend us from all evil, and give us the grace to live together in peace and common prayer. In your power, may we become a holy community that transforms the world around us.
Officiant/Celebrant	All this we ask through Jesus Christ our Savior, who lives and reigns with you and the Holy Spirit, one God, for ever and ever. *Amen.*

The Word

The Propers of the Day, or two or more of the following may be used.

From the Old Testament

Exodus 6:2-8 (I will take you as my people)
Ezekiel 11:17-20 (I will gather you from the peoples)
Ezekiel 36:23b-30 (the nations shall know that I am the Lord)

Between the readings, a Psalm, hymn, or canticle may be sung or said. Appropriate Psalms are 67 and 98.

Liturgia para la inauguración de una congregación

Reunión de asamblea comunitaria

Se puede usar una de las siguientes, o una aclamación del Libro de Oración Común (página 245) o Enriching Our Worship I (página 50)

Oficiante/celebrante	Dios santo, que has llamado para ti a un pueblo:
Pueblo	Llénanos de tu presencia, afírmanos en tu am*or*.

O bien

Oficiante/celebrante	Este es día que el Señor ha hecho;
Pueblo	Alegrémonos y gocémonos en él.

Oración de Entrada *La siguiente o se puede usar la colecta del día.*

Oficiante/celebrante	Oh Dios, fuente de todo principio*:*
	Te damos gracias por traernos a este nuevo día.

Pueblo	Envíanos tu Espíritu al comenzar este caminar
	como pueblo de_____[nombre de la congregación].
	Capacítanos para proclamar las Buenas Nuevas de Jesús,
	protégenos de todo mal,
	y danos la gracia de vivir juntos en paz y oración común.
	Que en tu poder, lleguemos a ser una comunidad santa
	que transforme el mundo alrededor nuestro.

Oficiante/celebrante	Te lo pedimos por Jesucristo, nuestro salvador, que vive y
	reina contigo y el Espíritu Santo, un Dios, ahora y por siempre.
	Amén.

La palabra

Lecturas: se pueden usar los propios del día o dos o más de las siguientes.

Antiguo Testamento

Éxodo 6: 2-8 (Y os tomaré por pueblo mio)
Ezequiel 11: 17-20 (Yo os recogeré de entre los pueblos)
Ezequiel 36: 23b-30 (Entonces las naciones sabrán que you soy el Señor.)

Entre las Lecturas puede cantarse o decirse un Salmo, himno o cánntico. Los Salmos 67 y 98 son los apropiados.

From the New Testament

2 Corinthians 5:16-21 (So if anyone is in Christ, there is a new creation)
Hebrews 10:19-25 (Let us hold fast to the confession of our hope)

The Gospel

John 13:31-35 (as I have loved you, you also should love one another)
Matthew 11:2-6 (the blind receive their sight, the lame walk)

A sermon, homily or other reflection follows the readings.

Prayers of the People

Here prayers are offered, which may include

A Litany for the Mission of the Church *(page 196)*
Prayers of the People *(such as BCP pages 383-393)*
General Intercessions and Thanksgivings

At the Eucharist

Preface *The Preface for Pentecost, for Apostles and Ordinations or another preface appropriate to the occasion is used.*

Post-Communion Prayers *Prayers especially appropriate are prayers found on page 174 of the Commissioning liturgy; in Enriching Our Worship I, page 69; in the BCP, page 366*

Dismissal

Officiant/Celebrant	Let us go forth into the world, rejoicing in the power of the Spirit. [Alleluia, alleluia.]
People	Thanks be to God. [Alleluia, alleluia.]

In Lent, the alleluias are omitted. In the Easter Season, they are included.

Epístola

2 Corintios 5: 16-21 (De modo que si alguno está en Cristo, nueva criatura es.)
Hebreos 10. 19-25 (Mantengamos firme la profesión de nuestra esperanza sin vacilar.)

Evangelio

Juan 13: 31-35 (que como you os he amado, asi también os améis los unos a los oros.)
Mateo 11: 2-6 (Los ciegos reciben la vista y los cojos andan.)

A las lecturas sigue un sermón, homilía u otra reflexión.

Las oraciones

Se pueden ofrecer oraciones que pueden incluir

Una letanía por la Misión de la Iglesia (página 197)
Oraciones de los fieles (LOC páginas 305-316)
Intercesiones generales y acciones de gracias

La eucaristía

Prefacio eucarístico: *el de Pentecostés; el de los apóstoles/ordenaciones; u otro prefacio apropiado para la ocasión*

Oración después de la comunión: *son especialmente apropiadas las que se encuentran en la página 175 de la liturgia para comisionar.. en Enriqueciendo nuestra Adoración I, página 69; en el LOC, página 288*

Despedida

Oficiante/celebrante	Salgamos al mundo, gozándonos en el poder del Espíritu. [¡Aleluya, aleluya!]
Pueblo	Demos gracias a Dios [¡Aleluya, aleluya!]

En Cuaresma se omiten las aleluyas. En la época pascual se incluyen.

Concerning the Service

This rite is designed for use by a church planting team or new congregation, as it begins worship in a facility such as a school, nursing home, "storefront" or other secular space. With adaptation it could be used in a variety of other situations, such as the initial gathering of a retreat group in a hotel. It anticipates regular but not exclusive use of the room or building for worship purposes. It may be desirable to place in the room significant symbols of Christian worship, such as a cross, candles, banner, etc. before or during the service.

An Entrance Hymn may be sung, and the congregation and liturgical ministers may process to the site of dedication, if appropriate. A large cross may be placed in a location visible to all.

Lo Concerniente al Rito

Este rito se ha pensado para que lo use un equipo fundador o una congregación nueva que empieza a tener servicios en una localidad tal como una escuela, un asilo, o cualquier otro espacio secular. Adaptándolo se puede usar en otras varias situaciones, como cuando un grupo se reúne para un retiro en un hotel. Se espera que sea, pero no exclusivamente, un lugar o edificio regular con fines de adoración. Se podrían colocar en la habitación símbolos significativos cristianos, como una cruz, velas, un estandarte, etc. antes o durante el servicio.

De entrada se puede cantar un himno, y, si es apropiado, la congregación y los ministros litúrgicos pueden ir en procesión hasta el lugar que va a ser dedicado.

Setting Apart Secular Space for Sacred Use

Antiphon

You will bring them in and plant them, O Lord,
in the sanctuary you have established.

V.   All your works praise you, O God,
R.   And your faithful servants bless you.

or (especially if a cross has just been put in place)

V.   Through the Cross of Jesus,
R.   We have been brought near and reconciled to God.

Officiant   Let us pray.

Blessed are you, O God, ruler of the universe. Your gifts are many, and in wisdom you have made all things to give you glory. Be with us now and bless us as we dedicate this *space* to your praise and honor. As often as we worship you here, precede us and abide with us. Be known to us in the Word spoken and heard, in fellowship with one another, and in the breaking of bread. Give us joy in all your works, and grant that this *space* may always be a place where your will is done and your name is glorified; through Jesus Christ our Savior, in the power of the Holy Spirit, we pray. *Amen.*

At a celebration of the Eucharist the Gloria in Excelsis *or other Song of Praise may be sung, as all take their places for worship. The Collect of the Day or Collect for an Opening Liturgy would follow. At a service of Morning/Evening Prayer or similar, an appropriate Invitatory psalm or hymn may follow the dedication.*

Reservando un espacio secular para uso sagrado

Antífona

Tú, oh Señor, los traerás y los plantarás
en el santuario que has establecido.

V.   Todas tus obras te alaban, oh Dios,
R.   Y tus fieles siervos te bendicen.

O bien (especialmente si se acaba de colocar una cruz en el lugar)

V.   Mediante la cruz de Jesús,
R.   Nos hemos reunidos y reconciliado en Dios.

Oficiante   Oremos

Bendito seas, oh Dios, soberano del universo. Abundantes son tus dones y con sabiduría has creado todas las cosas para que te den gloria. Acompáñanos y bendícenos mientras dedicamos este espacio para tu gloria y honor. Siempre que te adoremos aquí, antecédenos y acompáñanos. Dátenos a conocer en la Palabra que se nos hable y que oigamos, en el compañerismo mutuo y al romper el pan. Danos alegría en todas tus obras, y concede que este espacio sea un lugar donde siempre se cumpla tu palabra y tu nombre sea glorificado. Lo pedimos por Jesucristo, nuestro salvador, en el poder del Espíritu Santo. Amén.

En una celebración de la Eucaristía se puede cantar el Gloria in Excelsis u otra canción de alabanza, mientras todos van ocupando su lugar para la adoración. Seguirá la colecta del día o la colecta una liturgia de iniciación. En un servicio de Oración de la mañana o de la tarde o semejante, puede seguir a la dedicación un salmo apropiado de invitatorio o un himno.

A Litany for the Mission of the Church

Holy God, in whom all things in heaven and earth have their being,
Have mercy on us.

Jesus the Christ, through whom the world is reconciled to the Father,
Have mercy on us.

Holy Spirit, whose glory fills the world and searches the depths of God,
Have mercy on us.

Blessed Trinity, source of both unity and diversity,
Have mercy on us.

From blind hearts and petty spirits, that refuse to see the need of all humankind for your love,
Savior, deliver us.

From pride, self-sufficiency and the unwillingness to admit our own need of your compassion,
Savior, deliver us.

From discouragement in the face of pain and disappointment, and from lack of persistence and thoroughness,
Savior, deliver us.

From ignorance, apathy, and complacency that prevent us from spreading the Gospel,
Savior, deliver us.

O God, we pray for the gifts of ministry. Inspire our minds with a vision of your kingdom in this time and place.
Hear us, O Christ.

Touch our eyes, that we may see your glory in all creation.
Hear us, O Christ.

Touch our ears, that we may hear from every mouth the hunger for hope and stories of refreshment.
Hear us, O Christ.

Touch our lips, that we may tell in every tongue and dialect the wonderful works of God.
Hear us, O Christ.

Touch our hearts, that we may discern the mission to which you call us.
Hear us, O Christ.

Letanía por la misión de la Iglesia

Dios santo, en quien todas las cosas, en el cielo y en la tierra, tienen su ser,
Ten compasión de nosotros.

Jesús el Cristo, por quien el mundo se reconcilia con el Padre,
Ten compasión de nosotros.

Santo Espíritu, cuya gloria llena el mundo y escudriña las profundidades de Dios,
Ten compasión de nosotros.

Bendita Trinidad, fuente de unidad y diversidad,
Ten compasión de nosotros.

De corazones ciegos y espíritus mezquinos, que se niegan a ver la necesidad que la humanidad tiene de tu amor,
Líbranos, Salvador.

Del orgullo, la auto-suficiencia y la falta de admisión sobre nuestra necesidad de tu compasión,
líbranos Salvador.

Del desaliento ante el dolor y la decepción, y de la falta de persistencia y esmero,
Líbranos, Salvador.

De la ignorancia, de la apatía y complacencia, que nos impiden difundir el evangelio,
Líbranos, Salvador.

Oh Dios, te rogamos por los dones del ministerio. Inspira nuestras mentes con una visión de tu reinado para este lugar y tiempo,
Escúchanos, oh Cristo.

Toca nuestros ojos para que veamos tu gloria en toda la creación,
Escúchanos, oh Cristo.

Toca nuestros oídos para que oigamos de cada voz el hambre de esperanza e historias estimulantes,
Escúchanos, oh Cristo.

Toca nuestros labios para que transmitamos en toda lengua y dialecto las maravillosas obras de Dios,
Escúchanos, oh Cristo.

Toca nuestros corazones para que podamos discernir la misión para la que nos llamas,
Escúchanos, oh Cristo.

Touch our feet, that we may take your Good News into our neighborhoods, communities, and all parts of the world.
Hear us, O Christ.

Touch our hands, that we may each accomplish the work you give us to do.
Hear us, O Christ.

Strengthen and encourage all who minister in your name in lonely, dangerous and unresponsive places.
Hear us, O Christ.

Open the hearts and hands of many to support your Church in this and every place.
Hear us, O Christ.

The Litany concludes with a collect, such as those provided in the Church Planting Liturgies or a collect for the Mission of the Church (BCP pages 257, 816).

Toca nuestros pies para que llevemos tus Buenas Nuevas a nuestros barrios, comunidades y a todas las partes del mundo,
Escúchanos, oh Cristo.

Toca nuestras manos para que podamos cumplir la obra que nos pides realizar,
Escúchanos, oh Cristo.

Fortalece y anima a todos los que ministran en tu nombre en lugares solitarios, peligrosos e ingratos,
Escúchanos, oh Cristo.

Abre los corazones y las manos de los que apoyan tu Iglesia en este y en todo lugar,
Escúchanos, oh Cristo.

La letanía concluye con una colecta, como las ofrecidas en las liturgias para fundar iglesias o una colecta por la misión de la Iglesia (LOC páginas 175, 706)

A variety of Church Planting collects, blessings and other prayers

These collects may be used and adapted for a variety of situations, such as sending forth church planters, evangelists, missioners, stewardship committee members, etc.

O God the Creator and ruler of all things,
your reign grows like a mustard seed into abundant life:
bless those who plant and tend the new life of your Church,
that it may become a place of welcome, a refuge of healing,
a school for souls, and a life-giving spring;
all of which we ask through Jesus Christ,
our strength and our salvation. *Amen.*

Blessed God, who makes all things new:
grant that this young community of Word and Sacrament may be
leaven for the world's bread, and wine of delight for hearts in need;
a gathering strong for service and glad in praise;
and a people listening and responding to your presence in their midst;
through Jesus our redeemer and steadfast companion. *Amen.*

You raise up laborers for your harvest, Holy God,
sending them out as sowers of your good news,
workers of healing, and caretakers of new life:
bless *N. (and N.)* in *their* work of planting and tending your Church *(in ____);*
equip *them* for service, enliven *them* with your joy,
and help *them* remember and trust that it is you who will bring in the harvest;
through Jesus Christ, the Savior of souls. *Amen.*

Blessed God, you call forth light from darkness:
send the power of your Spirit upon your servants *N. (and N.)*
as *they* carry your Gospel to ____.
May your light so fill *them* that *they* may shine with your radiance,
drawing all to the brightness of your love and mercy;
through Jesus, our Savior and true Light. *Amen.*

Jesus, Savior, made known to us
in broken bread and in wine poured out for reconciliation:
give us good courage for this work of mission
that as we, too, are broken, poured, and shared for the world's feeding,
we find ourselves made whole in you. *Amen.*

Varias colectas, bendiciones y oraciones, para fundaciones de iglesias.

Estas colectas se pueden usar y adaptar a diferentes situaciones, como cuando se envía en misión a fundadores de iglesias, a evangelistas, a misioneros, a miembros de un comité de mayordomía, etc.

Oh Dios, creador y soberano de todas las cosas,
tu reino crece como un grano de mostaza y se transforma en vida copiosa:
bendice a quienes fundan iglesias y cuidan de la nueva vida de tu Iglesia,
para que se convierta en un lugar acogedor, en un refugio de salvación,
en una escuela para las almas, y en manantial de vida.
Te lo pedimos por Jesucristo, nuestra fortaleza y salvación. *Amén.*

Dios bendito, que creas todas las cosas nuevas:
concede que esta joven comunidad de la Palabra y del Sacramento
pueda ser levadura para el pan del mundo y vino que alegra el corazón de los necesitados;
una asamblea vigorosa para el servicio y alegre en la alabanza;
y un pueblo que escucha y responde a tu presencia en medio de ellos.
Por Jesús, nuestro redentor y firme compañero. *Amén*

Dios santo, que escoges trabajadores para tu cosecha,
y los envías como sembradores de tus buenas nuevas,
portadores de salud, y guardianes de nueva vida:
bendice a *N. (y a N.)* en su labor de fundar y cuidar de tu Iglesia *(en_____)*;
hazlos aptos para el servicio, anímalos con tu alegría,
y ayúdalos a que se acuerden y confíen en que eres tú quien da la cosecha.
Por Jesucristo, el salvador de las almas. *Amén.*

Bendito Dios, que sacas luz de las tinieblas:
envía el poder de tu Espíritu sobre estos siervos *N. (y N.)*
que se disponen a llevar tu Evangelio a_____.
Que vayan llenos de tu luz para que brillen con tu resplandor,
y atraigan a todo el mundo al deslumbre de tu amor y compasión.
Por Jesús, nuestra luz y salvación. *Amén.*

Oh Jesús salvador,
que te nos diste a conocer al quebrar el pan
y al derramar vino para nuestra reconciliación:
danos ánimo en este trabajo misionero
para que así como nosotros también somos quebrados, derramados y compartidos,
alimentando al mundo, encontremos en ti perfección. *Amén.*

Most Holy and life-giving God:
Bless these ambassadors of the Gospel (*N. and N.*).
As the friends of Jesus carried your good news,
each to a different place according to their gifts and calling,
so may these friends carry your word of love,
making disciples for your service and building up your Church;
through the power of your Spirit and in the Name of Jesus. *Amen.*

A prayer of dedication

Christ Jesus, you go before and behind *us/me,*
you are *our* light and *our* shield;
guide *our* path, be *our* clear sight, lift *us* up in your Gospel joy,
and bless the work *we* do in your name and honor,
for you are *our* beloved, and *our* life made new. *Amen.*

Oh Dios santísimo y dador de vida:
bendice a estos embajadores de tu evangelio *(N.y N.)*.
Así como los amigos de Jesús llevaron las buenas nuevas,
cada uno a diferentes lugares según su talento y vocación,
que así estos amigos lleven tu Palabra de amor,
logrando discípulos para tu servicio y edificando tu Iglesia.
Por el poder de tu Espíritu y en el nombre de Jesús. *Amén.*

Oración de dedicación.

Cristo Jesús, que nos acompañas en el caminar,
eres nuestra luz y nuestro escudo; guía nuestro camino,
sé nuestra clara visión, elévanos con la alegría
de tu evangelio, y bendice el trabajo que hacemos en tu nombre y honor,
porque tú eres nuestro amado, y nuestra nueva vida. *Amén.*

Hymn suggestions for Church Planting liturgies

From the *Hymnal 1982*

302/303	Father, we thank thee who hast planted
304	I come with joy to meet my Lord
521	Put forth, O God, thy Spirit's might
527	Singing songs of expectation
528	Lord, you give the great commission (Rowthorn)
530	Spread, O spread thou mighty Word
537	Christ for the world we sing!
576/577	God is love, and where true love is

From *Wonder, Love and Praise*

741	Filled with the Spirit's power
752	There's a sweet, sweet Spirit
761	All who hunger gather gladly
763	As we gather at your table
778	We all are one in mission
779	The church of Christ in every age
780	Lord, you give the great commission (Abbot's Leigh)
782	Gracious Spirit, give your servants
787	We are marching in the light of God
794	Muchos resplandores
796	Unidos
811	You shall cross the barren desert
812	I, the Lord of sea and sky
819	Guide my feet Lord

From *Lift Every Voice and Sing II*

50	The angel said to Philip
120	There's a sweet, sweet Spirit in this place
159	How to reach the masses
160	This little light of mine
161	"Go preach my gospel," saith the Lord

From *El Himnario*

2	Es tiempo de que alabemos a Dios
9	Todo se hace para la gloria de Dios
14	Grandes y maravillosas son tus obras
19	Señor, ¿qué es nuestro templo?
33	Cantemos al amor de los amores
56	Hay un dulce espíritu
205	Iglesia de Cristo, tu santa misión

209	Es Cristo de su Iglesia
213	¡Suelta la alegría!
216	Muchos resplandores
223	Somos uno en espíritu
243	Una espiga
246	Te ofrecemos, Padre nuestro
252	Somos pueblo que camina
303	He decidido seguir a Cristo
306	Yo, el Dios de cielo y mar
312	A este santo templo
313	Tú has venido a la orilla (also in WLP at 758)
317	Caminenos a la luz de Dios
321	Dios hoy nos llama
322	Sois la semilla
324	Yo soy sal de mi tierra
327	Cristo te necesita
328	Criso está buscando obreros
332	¿Quieres tú seguir a Cristo?
334	Tocando a tu puerta están
341	Grande gozo hay en mi alma hoy
342	En Jesucristo, puerto de paz
386	Vienen con alegría
400	De los cuarto rincones del mundo
439	Salmo 150 - Alabad a Dios en su santuario
440	Salmo 150 - ¡Aleluya, aleluya, aleluya!

Himnos sugeridos para las liturgias relacionadas a la fundación de nuevas iglesias o misiones

De el *Hymnal 1982*

302/303	Father, we thank thee who hast planted
304	I come with joy to meet my Lord
521	Put forth, O God, thy Spirit's might
527	Singing songs of expectation
528	Lord, you give the great commission (Rowthorn)
530	Spread, O spread thou mighty Word
537	Christ for the world we sing!
576/577	God is love, and where true love is

De *Wonder, Love and Praise*

741	Filled with the Spirit's power
752	There's a sweet, sweet Spirit
761	All who hunger gather gladly
763	As we gather at your table
778	We all are one in mission
779	The church of Christ in every age
780	Lord, you give the great commission (Abbot's Leigh)
782	Gracious Spirit, give your servants
787	We are marching in the light of God
794	Muchos resplandores
796	Unidos
811	You shall cross the barren desert
812	I, the Lord of sea and sky
819	Guide my feet Lord

De *Lift Every Voice and Sing II*

50	The angel said to Philip
120	There's a sweet, sweet Spirit in this place
159	How to reach the masses
160	This little light of mine
161	"Go preach my gospel," saith the Lord

De *El Himnario*

2	Es tiempo de que alabemos a Dios
9	Todo se hace para la gloria de Dios
14	Grandes y maravillosas son tus obras

19	Señor, ¿qué es nuestro templo?
33	Cantemos al amor de los amores
56	Hay un dulce espíritu
205	Iglesia de Cristo, tu santa misión
209	Es Cristo de su Iglesia
213	¡Suelta la alegría!
216	Muchos resplandores
223	Somos uno en espíritu
243	Una espiga
246	Te ofrecemos, Padre nuestro
252	Somos pueblo que camina
303	He decidido seguir a Cristo
306	Yo, el Dios de cielo y mar
312	A este santo templo
313	Tú has venido a la orilla (also in WLP at 758)
317	Caminenos a la luz de Dios
321	Dios hoy nos llama
322	Sois la semilla
324	Yo soy sal de mi tierra
327	Cristo te necesita
328	Criso está buscando obreros
332	¿Quieres tú seguir a Cristo?
334	Tocando a tu puerta están
341	Grande gozo hay en mi alma hoy
342	En Jesucristo, puerto de paz
386	Vienen con alegría
400	De los cuarto rincones del mundo
439	Salmo 150 - Alabad a Dios en su santuario
440	Salmo 150 - ¡Aleluya, aleluya, aleluya!

Resolution A101 Church Planting Liturgies

1 *Resolved,* the House of _____ concurring, That this 74th General Convention approve for publication and
2 distribution by Church Publishing, Inc., these liturgies: Discernment for a New Church Mission; A Liturgy
3 for Commissioning a Church Planter, Missioner or Mission Team; A Liturgy for the Opening of a New
4 Congregation; Setting Apart Secular Space for Sacred Use; A Litany for the Mission of the Church; A
5 Variety of Church Planting Collects, Blessings and other Prayers; and Hymn Suggestions for Church
6 Planting Liturgies; and be it further
7 *Resolved,* that these liturgies be printed side-by-side in English and Spanish.

In addition to its work on liturgies in the context of new church starts, the committee explored a variety of multi-cultural rites. This work is in response to General Convention Resolution A066.

Resolution A102 Culturally Sensitive Rites

1 *Resolved,* the House of _____ concurring, the 74th General Convention direct the Standing Commission on
2 Liturgy and Music to prepare rites that are culturally sensitive for use in a wide range of settings, and that
3 these rites may include, but not be limited to:
4 Rites of Passage including Quinceañeras (e.g. Latin American); Naming of Elders (e.g. Korean); Day of
5 the Dead (e.g. Latin American); Honoring of Ancestors (e.g. Chinese); and Adoption Rites (e.g. Native
6 American); and be it further
7 *Resolved,* That $30,000.00 be appropriated for the next triennium for this project and be administered by
8 the Office for Liturgy and Music and that rites developed be presented to the 75th General Convention.

EXPLANATION

In light of the following: *GC Resolution 2000-A066* which asked for "the liturgical renewal and enrichment of the common worship of this…multi-cultural, multi-ethnic, multi-lingual and multi-generational Church;" the 20/20 vision to double the size of our church by the year 2020; and anti-racism resolutions that previous conventions have passed, it is imperative that there be available for use liturgical services and resources that respect the diversity of our church and allow for the new majority to feel welcomed in their new spiritual home.

Committee on Resolution A063

SCLM Member: Marcia Pruner. *Consultant:* Clay Morris. Commission meetings included this topic.

GC 2000 adopted the following resolution, which in part, read:

Resolved, That the readings and psalms of *The Revised Common Lectionary*, as distinct from the rubrics, be authorized for continued trial use during the 2001-2003 triennium; and be it further *Resolved,* That, for purposes of trial use, *The Revised Common Lectionary* be adapted in the following ways:

1. III Advent Year B: Add Canticle 3 or 15 as an alternative to the psalm appointed.
III Advent Year C: Add Canticle 9 as an alternative to the psalm appointed.
2. First Sunday after Christmas Day: Substitute readings from the lectionary in the Book of Common Prayer.
3. Second Sunday after Christmas: Substitute readings from the lectionary in the Book of Common Prayer.
4. Ash Wednesday: Substitute Psalm 103 or 103:8-14. (Psalm 51 is used as part of
the liturgy for Ash Wednesday in the BCP.)
5. II Lent Year A: Omit the option of Matthew 17:1-9.
II Lent Year B: Omit the option of Mark 9:2-9.
II Lent Year C: Omit the option of Luke 9:28-36. (These RCL options are stories of the Transfiguration, which would not be appropriate to use in II Lent after we have celebrated the Transfiguration on last Epiphany.)
6. III Lent Year C: Substitute Exodus 3:1-15. (Isaiah 55:1-9 is used at the Easter
Vigil.)
7. Weekdays in Easter Week: Insert lections for Weekdays in Easter from the Book of Common Prayer.
8. Vigil of Pentecost: Insert lections from the Book of Common Prayer.
9. Trinity Sunday: Add Canticle 2 or 13 as an alternative to the psalm appointed.
10. The Annunciation: Add Canticle 3 or 15 as an alternative to the psalm appointed.
11. Holy Cross Day: Substitute lections from the lectionary in the Book of Common Prayer.
12. Proper 8, Year B: Add verses 21 and 22 to the reading from Lamentations. (*The Revised Common Lectionary* begins at verse 23, which is in middle of a sentence and is out of context.);

Bishops were asked to designate congregations who would use the *RCL* materials and the SCLM was asked to create an evaluation process after the usage. Three hundred twenty-six congregations participated in the *Revised Common Lectionary (RCL)* trial use project. In answer to the question of whether or not the lectionary should be adopted, 22.1% said yes and 5.5% said no. 72.4% of the respondents chose not to answer the question.

The SCLM did a major survey of congregational liturgical usage in the year 2000. 1145 congregations responded to the questionnaire, which asked, among other things, what lectionaries are in use on Sunday. 83% reported always using the Prayer Book Lectionary. 17% reported always using the *RCL*. 22% reported often using the RCL and 30% report occasional use of the *RCL*.

Over the years that the Church has been considering whether or not to adopt the *Revised Common Lectionary*, the rationale for its adoption has only gotten more crucial. Fourteen denominations with whom the Church has inter-Anglican and ecumenical relations use the *RCL*. Thus, it is essential that the Episcopal Church join them. A close look at the results of various data-gathering exercises suggests a conundrum: The Church is not likely to take the *RCL* seriously until General Convention adopts it.

Resolution A103 Adopt the *Revised Common Lectionary*

1   *Resolved,* the House of _____ concurring, That this 74th General Convention authorize the *Revised*
2   *Common Lectionary,* as amended in General Convention Resolution A063, affirmed by the 73rd General
3   Convention; and be it further
4   *Resolved*, That substitution of the *Revised Common Lectionary* for the table of readings currently printed
5   in the Book of Common Prayer take effect on the first day of Advent in the year 2003; and be it further
6   *Resolved,* That the Standing Commission on Liturgy and Music make available the table of readings and
7   suggestion for its use to the congregations of the Episcopal Church.

Liturgical Studies

The SCLM intends to continue collecting articles for the series entitled *Liturgical Studies,* published by Church Publishing, Inc. The series currently consists of four volumes. The commission recognizes a need for a volume in this series exploring *Rites of Passage: Life Cycle Transition*. This volume will gather the current, ongoing conversations about such topics as rites of passage and rites in the context of divorce.

The Commission also recognizes the need for articles on musical enrichment and the Calendar of Saints (LLF) Two additional title possibilities are *Participation in the Eucharist* and *Celebration of the Eucharist*.

GC Resolution 2000- A066 In the Voices of all God's Children

Resolved, the House of Deputies concurring, That the 73rd General Convention receive the report of the Standing Commission on Liturgy and Music in response to Resolution C021s of the 72nd General Convention (*The Blue Book, 2000* pp. 232-242, 292-294); and be it further

Resolved, That the 73rd General Convention direct the Standing Commission on Liturgy and Music to implement a plan for liturgical renewal and enrichment of the common worship of this Church based on this report; and be it further

Resolved, That this implementation begin with a thorough process of data-collection involving the whole church to be reported to the 74th General Convention; and be it further

Resolved, That congregations, dioceses, provinces, and the other organizations of this Church be encouraged to be active participants in this process; and be it further

Resolved, That at every stage, this plan will support this process by the development and dissemination of educational programs and materials to deepen liturgical understanding and enhance liturgical skills; and be it further

Resolved, That this plan include liturgical forms reflective of our traditional experience of worship as well as our multi-cultural, multi-ethnic, multi-lingual, and multi-generational Church while providing for the unity and continuity of the Book of Common Prayer; and be it further

Resolved, That any new or revised rites when authorized be available for distribution in a variety of forms including multi-media, when appropriate, and electronic options; and be it further

Resolved, That the Standing Commission on Liturgy and Music be directed to prepare for publication and use supplemental liturgical materials to be presented to the 74th General Convention, and be it further

Resolved, That the sum of $180,400 be appropriated for the triennium 2000-2003 for support of this program; this appropriation to be administered by the Office for Liturgy and Music.

History

In the Voices of All God's Children was a data-collecting process undertaken to inform a plan for the *Renew and and Enrichment of the Common Worship of this Church.* The process was designed and implemented by a task force consisting of Dr. Mary Abrams; Senior Systems Administrator, Kentucky Community and Technical College System, The Rev. Bruce Jenneker; Associate Rector, Trinity Church, Copley Square, Boston, Mass., Mrs. Paula MacLean; Advertising, Communications and Stewardship Consultant, Bethesda by the Sea, Palm Beach, Fl., The Rev. John Ruder; Vicar, St. Columba's Church, Kent, Wa., The Rev. Patrick Malloy; Priest in Charge, Grace Church, Allentown, PA, The Rev. Dr. Clayton L. Morris, Liturgical Officer and Mr. Frank Tedeschi, Vice President and Managing Editor, Church Publishing Inc. Throughout the process, progress was reported to the SCLM, who assisted the Task Force in developing strategy as the process unfolded.

Implementation

The original intention of the Task Force was to recruit volunteers from every diocese who would be gathered, trained and sent into their dioceses to gather information about the church's worship life and its hope for a liturgical future. The events of September 11, 2001 forced the cancellation of the national gathering planned to launch the process. The Task Force regrouped and decided to use the internet to gather the data.

Two questionnaires were designed: one to gather low-inference data about current liturgical practices; another to gather high-inference data about hopes for the future. Invitations to participate in the low-inference survey were mailed to all the 7000+ congregations in the church. Every diocesan bishop was asked to name 10 people, representing the range of experience in the diocese, to answer high-inference questions.

The Task Force received 1143 responses to the congregational survey representing every diocese in the church. The bishops of all 106 dioceses received an invitation to participate in the diocesan survey. 58 responded. The Task Force received 251 responses to the questionnaire spread across the geography of the American church. The internet management of both instruments was developed with the assistance of The Rev. Clayton Crawley, Senior Vice President at the Church Pension Group, and Netvolution, an internet consulting company in Los Angeles.

Once the survey data was complete, the Liturgical Officer, assisted by consultant Mary O'Shaughnessy, collated the information and produced graphic representations of the statistics for review by the Task Force. The Task Force, over the course of several meetings, studied the data, in order to draw conclusions that would be useful in charting a direction for the development of liturgical resources.

These summary comments indicate something of the nature of the data gathered. More data can be viewed on the Office for Liturgy and Music page at www.episcopalchurch.org.

From the Diocesan Survey –

Episcopalians say that the most important reason for going to church is:
to take their place in the central act of the worshiping community.
The second most important reason is:
to find grace and direction for advancing the reign of God in the world, and *to minister to the other people who come to church.*
The third most important reason is:
for a personal, subjective experience of God in Holy Communion, art, music and liturgy, and *to give thanks to God.*
The fourth most important reason is:
to feel the presence of God in scripture and in preaching.

Episcopalians say that
- preaching, music and community have a very significant effect on their worship experience.

Episcopalians say that
- ceremonial, liturgical text, tradition, and connection with life and social issues have a less significant effect on their worship experience.

Episcopalians say that their experience of
- architecture, the use of silence, vesture, and engaging intergenerational and cultural diversity has the least effect on their worship experience.

From the Congregational Survey:

- When the Episcopal Church gathers, it gathers for Eucharist.
- The typical Episcopal Church is a small congregation. The typical Episcopalian worships in a large congregation.
- Most Episcopalians no longer have a regular, corporate experience of Morning Prayer as principal act of Sunday worship.
- The typical congregation has two services on Sunday morning, both eucharistic.
- Some congregations have a third morning service.
- Rite II is the norm, except early on Sunday morning.
- Services, in general, are an hour long. About 20% of that is spent in preaching.
- On weekends, congregations meet primarily on Sunday morning, but services also take place on Saturday and Sunday evenings.
- Use of the BCP 1979 is almost universal, and is widely supplemented on occasion by *Enriching our Worship* and other alternative materials. On Sunday evenings, the use of supplemental materials is more prevalent.
- While members of the Episcopal Church speak a wide variety of languages at home, most Episcopal congregations worship exclusively in English.
- Music is a very important aspect of the common worship of this church, except for early Sunday morning when there is hardly ever any music, and on Saturday and Sunday evenings where there is little music.
- Saturday and Sunday evenings, when they do include music, are the times of greatest diversity of both musical instruments and printed musical resources. Music sung at these services often comes from resources outside the Episcopal Church.
- In nearly every congregation, worshipers sing hymns. *Hymnal 1982* is all but universal, often accompanied by *Wonder, Love and Praise* and *Lift Every Voice and Sing.* Church Publishing, Inc. reports continued and significant sales of both volumes.
- In a significant majority of congregations, worshipers sing service music as well as hymns.

- The organ is the primary instrument, except on those occasions when there is music on Sunday evening, then other instruments, especially popular instruments, predominate.
- On special occasions, most congregations have special music using classical instruments along with the organ.
- Worshipers use prayer books and hymnals, and in almost every case, use a leaflet containing music, as well.
- Generally, people stand for the Opening Rite, kneel for most of the eucharistic rite, and stand for the dismissal.
- Most congregations continue to use the BCP Lectionary, rather than the Revised Common Lectionary.
- The vast majority of Congregations use of the Forms for the Prayers of the People from the BCP. There is little evidence of experimentation with other forms.
- Most Episcopal Churches are served by one full-time priest and a part-time musician.
- Few Episcopal Churches involve volunteers in their liturgy planning team.
- In the majority of Episcopal Churches lay volunteers play a vital role in the implementation of liturgical planning, serving as lay coordinators of altar guilds, acolytes, lectors and lay eucharistic ministers.
- Most clergy wear eucharistic vestments. Those who do not wear an alb and a stole.
- Most people dress casually for worship. More dress "in-between" than formally.
- On special occasions, about 2/3 of our congregations use incense, 1/3 use sanctuary bells, the sprinkling of holy water, dalmatics and copes.
- In most churches, the altar is free standing, the furniture is seldom moved, and the space is traditionally configured.
- Less than 25% of congregational membership attend Holy Days that fall on weekdays. Significant exceptions are Advent Lessons and Carols, Christmas Pageant, and especially Christmas Eve services which all draw record crowds.

Voices from the Diocesan Survey   A sampling of comments volunteered by respondents:

"PLEASE CHANGE THE PRAYER BOOK!"
"DON'T CHANGE THE PRAYER BOOK, WHATEVER YOU DO!"
"MORE MUSIC, MORE CONTEMPORARY MUSIC, MORE TRADITIONAL MUSIC, MORE MUSIC FROM MORE CULTURES"
"HELP! HOW DO I 'DO' A SEEKER SERVICE?"
"WHERE DO I FIND RESOURCES?"
"WHAT ARE OTHER PEOPLE DOING? WHAT HAS WORKED FOR THEM?"
"TEACH ME HOW, PLEASE"
"MORE PRAYERS OF THE PEOPLE, PLEASE?"
"WHY DO WE DO WHAT WE DO - WHERE CAN I GO FOR THE ANSWERS? CREATE A PROGRAM TO HELP ME"
"GET THE SEMINARIES TO TEACH PREACHING!"

"HOW DOES MY EXPERIENCE, CULTURE FIND A PLACE IN ALL THIS?"
"LAY RITE I TO REST!"
"DON'T TAKE MY CHURCH AWAY FROM ME!"
"CAN WE CREATE OUR OWN SERVICES? DO WE NEED PERMISSION?
HOW DO WE GET IT?"
"FIX THE ORDINAL - MAKE IT MATCH BAPTISM"
"MAKE A DECISION ABOUT THE REVISED COMMON LECTIONARY - DON'T MAKE US JUGGLE TWO LECTIONARIES!"
"WHAT ABOUT OPEN EUCHARIST - SHOULDN'T WE BE MORE INCLUSIVE?"
"TEACH, TEACH, TEACH!!"
"HOW DO WE REACH GEN X, Y, Z ....?"

More Voices at the Table

When the SCLM began conversation about the enrichment of the church's worship resources following the 1997 General Convention, one of their initial realizations was that the commission didn't adequately represent the diversity of the church. In order to provide more *voices at the table,* the commission agreed to meet in locations where specific communities in the larger church could be invited to meet with the SCLM, in order to explore the particular needs of people living in a variety of cultural circumstances.

Between 1998 and 2002, these gatherings occurred:

Linthicam Heights, Maryland	October 25, 1998	High School and College Students
Del Ray Beach, Florida	February 7, 199	Elders
Chicago, Illinois	June 20, 1999	The Latino Community
San Francisco, California	October, 24 1999	The Japanese, Chinese and Filipino Communities
Los Angeles, California	May 22, 2001	The Latino and Korean Communities
Wilmington, North Carolina	August 27, 2001	People ministering with and to Young People
New Orleans, Louisiana	January 29, 2002	The African American Community
Sioux Falls, South Dakota	May 21, 2002	The Lakota/Dakota Community

While these gatherings could not be expected to make up for the absence of a suitably diverse membership on the commission, the conversations were of enormous value as the commission did its work in the two triennia.

Recommendations of the A066 Task Force

SCLM Members: Mary Abrams, Bruce Jenneker, Paula MacLean, John Ruder. *Consultants:* Patrick Malloy, Clay Morris, Frank Tedeschi. *Meetings:* November 9 – 11, 2001, New York, NY; June 20 – 23, 2002, Santa Fe, New Mexico; August 8 – 11, 2002, Delray Beach, Florida

Resulting from the diocesan and congregational surveys, and from the SCLM's discussions with communities representing a variety of cultures within our church, the following recommendations are made for the next triennium, to be addressed by Resolutions A-101 – A-104:

- Launch a diversified campaign inviting the whole church to move beyond worship that is primarily shaped and bound by text into worship that is intentionally open to the renewing power of God transforming the world.
- Create and maintain curricula and resources for an integrated program of liturgical education and training for the whole church.
- Engage and create networks of partners, mentors and educators, and strategies for their deployment.
- Schedule opportunities for liturgical ministers and practitioners from different contexts and cultures to inspire and learn from one another.
- Establish a web-site for collecting, cataloguing, editing and offering locally developed materials, strategies and processes.
- Include in this program learning opportunities for lay people, bishops, priests, deacons, seminarians, musicians, vestries, etc. on local, diocesan, regional and national levels.

Resolution A104 Facilitate the Enrichment of Worship with Evangelism Focus

1   *Resolved,* the House of _____ concurring, That the 74th General Convention direct the Standing
2   Commission on Liturgy and Music, in consultation with the Committee on the State of the Church; and the
3   Standing Commissions on Domestic Mission and Evangelism (20/20); and Small Congregations, to
4   identify issues involving in evangelism in the context of a multicultural and pluralistic society and to direct
5   the Office for Liturgy and Music to offer appropriate liturgical materials and provide resources supporting
6   evangelism through worship; and be it further
7   *Resolved,* That the SCLM build on *Enriching our Worship* and *Enriching our Music,* adding additional
8   liturgical materials to support indigenous, multi-cultural and multi-generational communities and church
9   growth bearing in mind that most Episcopal congregations are small; and be it further
10 *Resolved,* That the SCLM establish a task force to explore seeker services, identify partners in developing
11 resources for seeker services, and direct the Office for Liturgy and Music to establish a network to connect
12 and support those working in this field; and be it further

13 *Resolved,* That the SCLM and the Office for Liturgy and Music be directed to integrate the spirituality of
14 GenX into all of their initiatives; and be it further
15 *Resolved,* That the SCLM direct and assist the Office for Liturgy and Music in providing resources in
16 various forms to support the development of congregational song; creating a network of partners, mentors
17 and educators involved in the ministry of music and a strategy for their deployment; and increase
18 opportunities for musicians from different contexts and cultures to inspire and learn from one another; and
19 be it further
20 *Resolved,* That the sum of $30,000.00 be appropriated to provide for the costs of consultation and
21 communication necessary in the completion of all these tasks, this appropriation to be administered by the
22 Office for Liturgy and Music.

Resolution A105 Resources for Liturgical Education

1 *Resolved,* the House of _____ concurring, That the Office for Liturgy and Music, in consultation with the
2 SCLM, be directed to develop curricula for an integrated program of liturgical education and training, for
3 persons both lay and ordained; and be it further
4 *Resolved,* That the Office for Liturgy and Music be directed to establish a web-site for collecting,
5 cataloguing, editing and offering locally developed educational and training materials, strategies and
6 processes.

Resolution A106 Liturgical Development and Episcopal Authority

1 *Resolved,* the House of _____ concurring, That the Standing Commission on Liturgy and Music direct the
2 Office of Liturgy and Music to invite bishops and the larger church into dialogue about the relation
3 between local liturgical initiatives and ordered authority; and be it further
4 *Resolved,* That the SCLM be directed to develop frameworks for resolving the theological, pastoral,
5 canonical and liturgical issues involved in the creation of new rites, and to provide facilitated
6 conversations at the meetings of Provincial Synods in which bishops and the larger church enter into
7 dialogue about the relation between liturgical initiatives and ordered authority; and be it further
8 *Resolved,* That the SCLM in consultation with the Commission on Constitution and Canons examine
9 canons and rubrics that govern the development and use of liturgical materials and propose amendments
10 authorizing appropriate local and regional liturgical initiatives; and be it further
11 *Resolved,* That the Office for Liturgy and Music be directed to establish a website for collecting,
12 cataloguing, editing and offering locally developed explanatory materials, strategies and processes; and be
13 it further
14 *Resolved,* That the sum of $15,000.00 be appropriated to provide for the costs of consultation and
15 communication necessary in the completion of these tasks, this appropriation to be administered by the
16 Office for Liturgy and Music.

Resolution A107 Renewal and Enrichment of Common Worship

1 *Resolved,* the House of _____ concurring, That the Office for Liturgy and Music be directed to implement
2 the vision for the *Renewal and Enrichment of the Common Worship of this Church* contained in this report
3 and that the Presiding Bishop add staff to the Office for Liturgy and Music to more effectively implement
4 the program initiatives of the General Convention; and be it further
5 *Resolved,* sum of $100,000.00 per year ($300,000.00 for the triennium) be appropriated for this purpose;
6 and be it further
7 *Resolved,* That the Office for Liturgy and Music formulate and maintain a reporting structure holding this
8 program accountable to the SCLM for this vision.

EXPLANATION

The previous two General Conventions have directed the Standing Commission on Liturgy and Music to
propose strategies for the *Renewal and Enrichment of the Common Worship of this Church.* The
commission's report to this 74th Convention outlines strategies that will accomplish the church's goals for
renewal and enrichment, This appropriation allows the Presiding Bishop and Liturgical Officer to develop
a staffing strategy that will facilitate the work.

Article X of the Constitution

Resolution A108 Constitution Article X, Second Reading

1   *Resolved,* the House of _____ concurring, That Article X of the Constitution be amended to include the
2   following sentence at the end of the second paragraph:
3   <u>Provide for use of other forms for the renewal and enrichment of the common worship of this church for</u>
4   <u>such periods of time and upon such terms and conditions as the General Convention may provide; and be</u>
5   <u>it further</u>
6   *Resolved,* That this resolution be sent within six months to the Secretary of the Convention of every
7   Diocese to be made known to the Diocesan Convention at its next meeting.

EXPLANATION

This resolution was adopted by the 73rd General Convention and must be affirmed at this second reading.

INTERNATIONAL ANGLICAN LITURGICAL CONSULTATION

The steering committee of the International Anglican Liturgical Consultation met in London, England on April 16 – 20, 2002. The steering committee reviewed the work of the Consultation at its meeting in Berkeley, California in August of 2001. There was representation from 32 provinces of the Anglican Communion, the largest yet for a Consultation. Alcuin/Grove Press has published the statement and papers of the Consultation on the theology of order and the liturgical rites of ordination. Supporting papers are being edited by Dr. David Holeton and will be ready for publication by the Fall of 2002. The committee is exploring publishers for these papers and a contract will probably be signed with the Anglican Book Centre, which has published previous volumes of the IALC's work.

An interim conference of the IALC will be held in conjunction with Societas Liturgica on August 6 – 9, 2003 at Ripon College outside of Oxford in England. The main topic will be the formation and education for leadership of the liturgical life of the church.

Preliminary plans were discussed for the next full Consultation in August of 2005. Societas Liturgica will meet in Germany and there is a possibility that the Consultation will meet in Prague.

One of the major concerns of the Consultation is the ongoing financial support of the works. Approximately $50,000.00 will have to be raised for a full Consultation in 2005. The majority of funding has been from the United Kingdom and the United States. There is some funding from the Anglican Consultative Council, and the Archbishop of Canterbury. Other funds have been raised from dioceses in the UK, the Presiding Bishop of the United States, and grants from churches and societies in the US.

The Rev. Sister Jean Campbell, OSH, serves as a member of the Steering Committee.

Resolution A109 International Anglican Liturgical Consultation

1   *Resolved,* the House of _____ concurring, That this 74th General Convention appropriate $25,000.00 to
2   support the church's participation in and support of the Consultation; and be it further
3   *Resolved,* that this appropriation be administered by the Office for Liturgy and Music. 1852.

Voices Found

Voices Found is a collection of hymns and spiritual songs by, for, and about women. Lisa Neufeld Thomas, a scholar and church musician from the Diocese of Pennsylvania, began collecting such music in 1995. Her engagement of others in the project resulted in the establishment of *The Women's Sacred Music Project,* an ecumenical group aided by the Diocese of Pennsylvania, Rosemont College and the Office for Congregational Ministries at the Episcopal Church Center upon the completion of the collection and evaluation of manuscripts. The possibility of publishing a collection was presented to the 72nd General Convention meeting in Philadelphia. Convention adopted a resolution calling for the development of a collection of music that would *celebrate the contributions and diversity of women in scripture, women saints and churchwomen.* The collection will be published in the summer of 2003.

CUSTODIAN OF THE STANDARD BOOK OF COMMON PRAYER

At the 73rd General Convention I was appointed by the Presiding Bishop to be the Custodian of the Book of Common Prayer. It has been a pleasure and an honor to serve him and the Church in an area that has been one of major personal interest and activity for many years. During the last triennium I have attended all meetings of the Standing Commission on Liturgy and Music as an *ex officio member*, and have assisted the Commission's work, as directed.

Also, during the previous triennium, I have granted Certificates as follows: to a fine Spanish language CD-ROM produced by the Office of Multi-Cultural Ministries of the Diocese of Los Angeles – this Hispanic version of The Rite Brain should be of significant assistance to any congregation with Hispanic ministry; to *Preghiere Comuni*, a bi-lingual English/Italian Book of Common Prayer, with some hymns, produced and published by St. James Church, Florence, Italy—on behalf of the Convocation of American Churches in Europe; and to a Chinese/English Book of Common Prayer, produced by the Office of Asiamerican Ministries, and published by Church Publishing, Inc.

Looking to the future, it is anticipated that an English/French and an English/German version of the Book of Common Prayer may be presented for Certificates in the coming triennium.

Respectfully submitted,

The Rev. Canon Gregory M. Howe
Custodian of the Standard Book of Common Prayer

STANDING COMMISSION ON MINISTRY DEVELOPMENT
www.episcopalchurch.org/gc/ccab/scmd/default.html

Membership

Appointed Members

The Rt. Rev. John P. Croneberger, *Chair*	Newark, 2006
Ms. Ellen W. Bruckner, *Vice-Chair*	Iowa, 2006
The Rev. Jennifer L. Adams	Western Michigan, 2006
Dr. R. William Franklin	Connecticut, 2003
The Rev. Warren Frelund	Iowa, 2006
The Rev. L. Ann Hallisey	Northern California, 2003
The Rev. Joyce Hardy	Arkansas, 2003
The Rt. Rev. James A. Kelsey	Northern Michigan, 2006
Mrs. Christine D. Keyser-Ball	Florida, 2006
The Very Rev. Dr. Guy F. Lytle III	Tennessee, 2003
Mrs. Judy R. Mayo	Fort Worth, 2003
The Rt. Rev. C. Wallis Ohl Jr.	Northwest Texas, 2003
Mr. Timothy D. Wittlinger	Michigan, 2006
The Rev. Brian N. Prior	*Executive Council liaison*

Provincial Represenatives

The Rev. Ellen L. Tillotson	Province I, 2003
Mrs. Janet B. Farnsworth	Province II, 2006
The Ven. Richard L. Cluett	Province III, 2006
The Rev. Howard Maltby	Province IV,2003, *resigned*
The Rev. Canon Richard A. Halladay	Province V, 2006
The Rev. Roy Walworth	Province VI, 2006
Ms. Thurma Hilton	Province VII, 2006
The Rt. Rev. Harry B. Bainbridge	Province VIII, 2003

Meeting Participants

Mrs. Stephanie Cheney	CREDO, Consultant to SCMD
The Rev. Patricia M. Coller	Church Pension Fund Representative
Mr. William Craddock	CREDO
Dr. Susanne C. Monahan	Consultant to SCMD
The Ven. Ormonde Plater	NAAD Representative
Mrs. Carol Stevenson	NNLP Representative
The Rev. Roy Tripp	NNECA Representative
The Rev. James Wilson	Church Deployment Office Representative

Staff

The Rev. Lynne A. Grifo	Office for Ministry Development
The Rev. Melford E. Holland	Office for Ministry Development
Ms. Molly A. Shaw	Office for Ministry Development

WORK SUMMARY

Introduction

The Standing Commission on Ministry Development (SCMD) was assigned the following 73rd General Convention Resolutions:

1. A073: To undertake a full review of Title III Canons, and prepare and present to the 74th General Convention any proposed revisions to Title III.

2. A074: To receive diocesan plans for continuing education of all clergy and lay professionals, present guidelines for minimum hours or days of continuing education, and make recommendations to dioceses and the 74th General Convention.

3. A103: To conduct a study of the theology of confirmation, and the relation of confirmation to evangelism, baptism, adult membership, church leadership, and eligibility for election to church office, and report to the 74th General Convention.

4. C011: In collaboration with the Standing Commission on Constitutions and Canons (SCCC), to study the system for adjudication of disputes and due process for Licensed Lay Persons, and develop appropriate canons for lay persons and their ministries.

5. C033: In collaboration with the North American Association for the Diaconate, to review the current role of deacons in the Councils of the Church, in the dioceses, and the congregations, and report to the 74th General Convention.

6. D014: To receive annual reports from seminaries about funds received from dioceses and congregations, and report on this to the 74th General Convention.

7. D080: In collaboration with the Ministries with Young People Cluster, to study the programs of youth ministry at all levels of the Church, to use this study to inform the SCMD's review of Title III, and to issue a report to the 74th General Convention that includes recommendations for the development and support of youth ministry.

GC Resolution 2000-A073
Revision of Title III Canons
The Challenge

The SCMD devoted most of its time to the Title III revision which began after the 73rd General Convention accepted *"Towards a Theology of Ministry."* A paper exploring how today's Church understands and is ordered to engage in ministry. This paper, researched and written during the 1997-2000 triennium, provided guidelines to structure the Title III revision. The SCMD also drew on the 1997 Stafford and Falkowski study of diocesan ordination practices that found: "Title III has too many committee meetings and steps and certificates; its requirements are not well integrated, and they offer too little provision for leadership, spirituality and ministerial formation" (p. 10-11).

Additionally, in conversations with various groups in the Church, the SCMD heard that the present ordination process has too many hoops for candidates and discourages young and minority aspirants. It also assumes a single model for parish ministry and fails to embrace new developments in the Church. In addition, some perceive that using two ordination Canons (Canons III.7 and 9) creates two classes of clergy.

The Process

SCMD's process to formulate the revisions: (1) drew on the wealth of available information, (2) elicited additional comment from the broader Church; (3) engaged the diversity viewpoints in the Church; and (4) considered the full range of diocesan practices.

First, SCMD identified issues to present to the Church for further comment. Included were:

- General issues, such as: a) how Canon law expresses and supports lay ministry; b) the role of faith communities in discernment, formation and call to ministry; c) the responsiveness of Canons to local context.
- Structural issues, such as: a) the possibility of separate canons for each order; and b) the possibility of integrating Canons 7 and 9 to form one Priesthood.
- Specific concerns, such as: a) the roles of Commissions on Ministry, Standing Committees and Bishops; b) direct ordination to the Priesthood; c) areas of competence for ordination; and d) the relationship between confirmation and ministry.

SCMD used a variety of methods to elicit comment from the Church: (1) An interactive survey on the Office for Ministry Development website; (2) an article in *Episcopal Life* that directed people to the website and provided text of the issues and questions; (3) focus groups at numerous provincial and other Church meetings; and (4) a mailing of the issues and questions to many organizations and groups in the church.

Second, responses were received, and subgroups of the SCMD collated, analyzed and presented their findings to the whole Commission in April 2002. Based on this comment, the foundation in the *"Towards a Theology of Ministry"* paper, Stafford and Falkowski's research, and conversations with those in and outside the SCMD, the SCMD articulated underlying values, principles and assumptions to guide its work. Ultimately the proposed revisions emerged from these premises:

- On the theology of ministry: There is a clear theology of ministry expressed in Baptism, the Eucharist and Ordination rites, but also different interpretations of that theology. Episcopalians generally share a theological starting point: God's mission drives ministry. Canonical revisions begin here, all the while respecting diversity in the Church.

- On Baptism and the Eucharist: The theological and liturgical recovery of Baptism and the Eucharist reshaped how the Church understands and practices ministry. Baptism, and its call to serve God, creates Christian identity. All the baptized are formed in the one ministry of Jesus Christ, doing the work of God's kingdom in all places and at all times. The Baptismal Covenant is fundamental to ministry, and the Canons should support this.

- On the Importance of Discernment and Formation for All the Baptized: All the baptized need support in discernment for ministry. Dioceses should provide training for effective discernment, and discernment should be viewed, first and foremost, as a process of affirmation. Formation is the foundation for the on-going transformation of persons into the likeness of Christ. The Canons should highlight and support discernment and formation, assist the Church as it recruits and equips leaders, and encourage and enable the ministry of all the baptized.

- On the Role of Christian Communities: Christian communities provide the context for mission; ministry originates in community. Discernment and formation for all ministries should, therefore, take place in community. The Canons should recognize and support the role of Christian communities in mission, ministry, discernment and formation.

- On Ministry: Our relationship with God and our relationships in the world express our Christian identity. Each calling has full and equal dignity. The Canons should reflect this vision of ministry.

Third, task groups were formed to revise specific parts of Title III. Task groups worked through the summer and Fall of 2002. Throughout the revision process, members of SCCC met with SCMD, as did representatives from a variety of groups throughout the Church.

In November 2002, the SCMD voted on the proposed changes. Because SCMD reflects the diversity of opinion in the Church, it is not in total agreement on all the proposed changes. Nonetheless, a clear and sizeable majority of members support the revisions. After the November 2002 meeting, the draft revisions were forwarded to Constitutions and Canons for its advice and recommendations. In January 2003, the SCMD finalized its proposed revisions and devised strategies for informing the broader Church of the proposed revisions before General Convention convenes.

Proposed Title III Revisions
SCMD proposes that the Church adopt the following substantive changes:

- **Expand the non-discrimination provisions in Title III** (see proposed Canon III.1.2). This provision supports the diversity of ministers in the Church by broadening the present non-discrimination provisions to encompass race, color, ethnic origin, national origin, sex, marital status, sexual orientation, disabilities and age and applying them to lay and ordained ministry.

- **Clarify the importance of discernment and formation for all the baptized, and the responsibilities of dioceses, congregations and other communities of faith to provide support for discernment and formation** (see proposed Canon III.1, Canon III.2, Canon III.3, Canon III.6.1-3, Canon III.8.2(b), Canon

III.8.2(d), Canon III.8.4). The revised Canons place discernment and formation at the center of Christian life and community.

- **Allow dioceses to establish criteria for licensed lay ministries** (see proposed Canon III.4.1(a)). This revision respects the diversity of ministry settings in the Church by permitting each diocese to develop licensing criteria that meet its specific needs.

- **Clarify the roles of licensed ministries, and modify the titles of and requirements for licensed ministries** (see proposed Canon III.4.1(a), Canon III.4.3-8). This revision recognizes that licensed ministries are the work of all the baptized, and not limited to times when clergy are not available. The revisions also remove "lay" from some of the titles, distinguish between Eucharistic Ministers and Eucharistic Visitors, and allow youth access to some licensed ministries.

- **Reorganize the ordination canons to reflect each order's distinctive call** (see proposed Canon III.6-7, Canon III.8-9). Because each calling has full and equal dignity, each order is distinct. In the revision, the Canons are grouped by order: That is, there is one set of Canons for Deacons (i.e., their ordination, life and work) and another for Priests (i.e., their ordination, life and work).

- **Replace the transitional Diaconate and subsequent ordination to the Priesthood with direct ordination to the Priesthood** (see proposed Canon III.9.8). In accord with our theology of baptism, Deacons are called to the Diaconate, and Priests to the Priesthood. Based on historical precedent and for practical reasons, this revision honors the distinct ministries of Deacons and Priests by ordaining people directly to the order to which they are called. Should they be needed, the SCMD has crafted versions of proposed Canon III.8 that retain the transitional Diaconate, or that allow dioceses to choose whether to retain the transitional Diaconate or adopt direct ordination.

- **Create a single canon for ordination to the Priesthood** (see proposed Canon III.8). This revision weaves together the existing Canons III.7 & 9, re-establishing a single canon for the selection, formation and ordination of Priests. The revised Canon is flexible enough to embrace the variety of practices now followed in dioceses regarding locally-formed and seminary-trained Priests.

- **Streamline the ordination process and clarify the roles of Bishops, Commissions on Ministry, Standing Committees, congregations, seminaries and ordinands** (see proposed Canon III.8, throughout, but especially Canon III.8.2(d)). This revision retains the basic structure of the ordination process, while simplifying its steps and providing flexibility so that each diocese can design an ordination process that best meets its needs.

- **Treat formation as an on-going process facilitated by continuing education** (see proposed Canon III.2.5, Canon III.4.1(a), Canon III.7.5, Canon III.9.1). The revised Canons incorporate expectations for continuing education for Deacons, Priests, Bishops and, in fact, all the baptized.

The complete text of the resolutions including the resolution is printed beginning on the next page of this document and available at:
http://www.episcopalchurch.org/ministry/2003convention/proposedcanons.html

Unfinished work
The SCMD did not finish its Title III revision work. Canons concerning Bishops, Religious Orders and Other Christian Communities, the General Board of Examining Chaplains, and the Church Deployment Board still need to be examined this year and in the next triennium.

Resolution A110 Complete Title III Revisions
1 *Resolved,* the House of _____ concurring, That the Standing Commission on Ministry Development
2 complete its revisions of the present Title III Canons, 10, 11, 12, and 22 – 32, and report to the 75th
3 General Convention.

PROPOSED TITLE THREE REVISIONS[1]

Resolution A111 Title III Proposed Canons

1 *Resolved,* the House of _____ concurring, That Canons III.1-9, 13-21 be deleted and replaced by the
2 following proposed Canons III.1-9:

CANON 1: Of the Ministry of All Baptized Persons

4 **Sec.1.** Each Diocese shall make provision for the affirmation and development of the ministry of all baptized
5 persons, including:

6   (a) Assistance in understanding that all baptized persons are called to minister in Christ's name, to
7   identify their gifts with the help of the Church and to serve Christ's mission at all times and in all
8   places.
9   (b) Assistance in understanding that all baptized persons are called to sustain their ministries through
10   commitment to life-long Christian formation.

11 **Sec. 2.** No person shall be denied the exercise of any ministry, lay or ordained, in this Church because of race,
12 color, ethnic origin, national origin, sex, marital status, sexual orientation, disabilities or age, except as
13 otherwise provided by these Canons. No right to licensing, ordination, or election is hereby established.

CANON 2: Commissions on Ministry

15 **Sec. 1.** In each Diocese there shall be a Commission on Ministry ("Commission") consisting of Priests,
16 Deacons, if any, and Lay Persons. The Canons of each Diocese shall provide for the number of members,
17 terms of office, and manner of selection to the Commission.

18 **Sec. 2.** The Commission shall advise and assist the Bishop:
19   (a) In the implementation of Title III of these Canons.
20   (b) In the determination of present and future opportunities and needs for the ministry of all baptized
21   persons.
22   (c) In the design and oversight of the ongoing process for discernment, formation and assessment.

23 **Sec. 3** The Commission may adopt rules for its work, subject to the approval of the Bishop; Provided that
24 they are not inconsistent with the Constitution and Canons of this Church and of the Diocese.

25 **Sec. 4** The Commission may establish committees consisting of members and other persons to report to the
26 Commission or to act on its behalf.

27 **Sec. 5** The Bishop and Commission shall ensure that the members of the Commission and its committees
28 receive ongoing education and training for their work.

CANON 3: Of Discernment

30 **Sec 1.** The Bishop and Commission shall provide encouragement, training and necessary resources to assist
31 each congregation in developing an ongoing process of community discernment appropriate to the cultural
32 background, age and life experiences of all persons seeking direction in their call to ministry.

33 **Sec. 2.** The Bishop, in consultation with the Commission, may designate college and university campus
34 ministry centers, and other communities of faith as additional discernment communities.

35 **Sec. 3.** The Bishop and Commission shall actively solicit from congregations, schools and other youth
36 organizations, college and university campus ministry centers, seminaries, and other communities of faith,

---

[1] These proposed canonical changes would replace in its entirety Canon III.1-9 and 13-21. Please refer to the *2000 Constitution and Canons of the Episcopal Church* for the original text that this text proposes to replace.

37 names of persons whose potential for leadership and vision mark them as desirable candidates for positions of
38 leadership in the Church.

39 **Sec. 4.** The Bishop, Commission, and the discernment community shall assist persons engaged in a process of
40 ministry discernment to determine appropriate avenues for the expression and support of their ministries,
41 either lay or ordained.

42 # CANON 4: Of Licensed Ministries

43 **Sec. 1**
44   (a) A confirmed communicant in good standing or, subject to guidelines established by the Bishop, a
45   communicant in good standing, may be authorized or licensed by the Ecclesiastical Authority to serve
46   as Pastoral Leader, Worship Leader, Preacher, Eucharistic Minister, Eucharistic Visitor, Catechist, or in
47   other licensed ministries. The Bishop, or Ecclesiastical authority, in consultation with the Commission
48   on Ministry, may determine other licensed ministries. Requirements and guidelines for the selection,
49   training, continuing education, and deployment of such persons shall be established by the Bishop in
50   consultation with the Commission on Ministry.
51   (b) The Presiding Bishop or the Bishop Suffragan for the Armed Services, Healthcare and Prison
52   Ministries may authorize a member of the Armed Services to exercise one or more of these ministries
53   in the Armed Services in accordance with the provisions of this Canon. Requirements and guidelines
54   for the selection, training, continuing education, and deployment of such persons shall be established
55   by the Bishop granting the license.

56 **Sec. 2**
57   (a) The Priest-in-Charge or other leader exercising oversight of the congregation or other community of
58   faith may request the Ecclesiastical Authority to license persons within that congregation to exercise
59   such ministries. The license shall be issued for a period of time to be determined under Canon
60   III.4.1(a) and may be renewed. The license may be revoked by the Ecclesiastical Authority upon
61   request of or upon notice to the Priest-in-Charge or other leader exercising oversight of the
62   congregation or other community of faith. The Ecclesiastical Authority shall communicate the reasons
63   for revocation or non-renewal to the person whose license is being revoked or not renewed.
64   (b) In renewing the license, the Ecclesiastical Authority shall consider the performance of the ministry by
65   the person licensed, continuing education in the licensed area, and the endorsement of the Priest-in-
66   Charge or other leader exercising oversight of the congregation or other community of faith in which
67   the person is serving.
68   (c) A person licensed in any Diocese under the provisions of this Canon may serve in another congregation
69   or other community of faith in the same or another Diocese only at the invitation of the Priest-in-
70   Charge or other leader exercising oversight, and with the consent of the Ecclesiastical Authority in
71   whose jurisdiction the service will occur.

72 **Sec. 3.** A Pastoral Leader is a lay person authorized to exercise pastoral or administrative responsibility in a
73 congregation under special circumstances, as defined by the Bishop.

74 **Sec. 4.** A Worship Leader is a lay person who regularly leads public worship under the direction of the Priest-
75 in-Charge or other leader exercising oversight of the congregation or other community of faith.

76 **Sec. 5.** A Preacher is a lay person authorized to preach. Persons so authorized shall only preach in
77 congregations under the direction of the Priest-in-Charge or other leader exercising oversight of the
78 congregation or other community of faith.

79 **Sec. 6.** A Eucharistic Minister is a lay person authorized to administer the Consecrated Elements at a
80 Celebration of Holy Eucharist. A Eucharistic Minister shall act under the direction of a Deacon, if any.

81 **Sec. 7.** A Eucharistic Visitor is a lay person authorized to take the Consecrated Elements in a timely manner
82 following a Celebration of Holy Eucharist to members of the congregation who, by reason of illness or

83 infirmity, were unable to be present at the Celebration. A Eucharistic Visitor shall act under the direction of a
84 Deacon, if any.

85 **Sec. 8**. A Catechist is a lay person authorized to prepare persons for Baptism, Confirmation, Reception, and
86 the Reaffirmation of Baptismal Vows.

87 CANON 5: Of General Provisions Respecting Ordination

88 **Sec. 1.**

89 (a) The canonical authority assigned to the Bishop Diocesan by this Title may be exercised by a Bishop
90 Coadjutor, when so empowered under Canon III.25, by a Bishop Suffragan when requested by the
91 Bishop Diocesan, or by any other Bishop of the Anglican Communion canonically in charge of a
92 Diocese, at the request of the ordinand's Bishop.

93 (b) The Council of Advice of the Convocation of American Churches in Europe, and the board appointed
94 by a Bishop having jurisdiction in an Area Mission in accordance with the provisions of Canon
95 I.11.2(c), shall, for the purpose of this and other Canons of Title III have the same powers as the
96 Standing Committee of a Diocese.

97 (c) In case of a vacancy in the episcopate in a Diocese, the Ecclesiastical Authority may authorize and
98 request the President of the House of Bishops of the Province to take order for an ordination.

99 **Sec. 2.**

100 (a) All certificates and testimonials required by this Title shall be in the form provided by this Title, and
101 shall be signed and dated.

102 (b) No Applicant, Postulant or Candidate for ordination shall sign any of the certificates prescribed by this
103 Title.

104 (c) Testimonials required of the Standing Committee by this Title must be signed by a majority of the
105 whole Committee, at a meeting duly convened, except that testimonials may be executed in
106 counterparts, each of which shall be deemed an original.

107 (d) Whenever the certificate of a Vestry is required, such certificate must be signed by at least two-thirds
108 of all of the members of the Vestry, at a meeting duly convened, and by the Rector or Priest-in-Charge
109 of the Parish, and attested by the Clerk of the Vestry. Should there be no Rector or Priest-in-Charge,
110 the certificate shall be signed by a Priest of the Diocese acquainted with the applicant and the Parish,
111 the reason for the substitution being stated in the attesting clause.

112 (e) If the congregation or other community of faith of which the applicant is a member is not a Parish, the
113 certification required by Canon III.6 or Canon III.8 shall be given by the Priest-in-Charge and the local
114 council of the congregation or other community of faith to which the applicant belongs, and shall be
115 attested by the secretary of the meeting at which the certification was approved. Should there be no
116 Priest-in-Charge, the certification shall be signed by a Priest of the Diocese acquainted with the
117 applicant and the congregation or other community of faith, the reason for the substitution being stated
118 in the attesting clause.

119 (f) If the applicant is a member of a Religious Order or Christian Community recognized by Canon III.30
120 the certificates referred to in Canon III.6 or Canon III.8 and any other requirements imposed on a
121 congregation or Priest-in-Charge, may be given by the Superior or person in charge, and Chapter, or
122 other comparable body of the Order or Community.

123 **Sec. 5** An application for any dispensation permitted by this Title from any of the requirements for ordination
124 must first be made to the Bishop, and if approved, referred to the Standing Committee for its advice and
125 consent.

126 CANON 6: Of the Ordination of Deacons

127 **Sec. 1**. Selection

128 The Bishop, in consultation with the Commission, shall establish procedures to identify and select persons for
129 ordination to the Diaconate.

130 (a) Nomination. A confirmed adult communicant in good standing, who has been a member of the
131   Episcopal Church for the preceding three years, may be nominated to be a Postulant for ordination to
132   the diaconate by the person's congregation or other community of faith. The nomination shall be in
133   writing, signed by the Rector or Priest-in-Charge and at least two-thirds of the Vestry or comparable
134   body, and shall be submitted to the Bishop. Upon acceptance in writing by the nominated person, the
135   Bishop may admit the person as a Postulant for ordination to the diaconate.
136 (b) Postulancy. Postulancy is a time of exploration of and decision on the Postulant's call to the diaconate.
137   (1) During Postulancy there shall be a thorough investigation of the Postulant which shall include:
138   (i) a background check, and
139   (ii) medical and psychological examinations, by professionals approved by the Bishop, using
140   forms prepared for that purpose by The Church Pension Fund. Reports of all investigations
141   and examinations shall be kept on file by the Bishop. The Bishop, with regard for
142   confidentiality, may make information from the reports available to the Commission.
143   (2) The Bishop, or the Bishop's designee, may interview the Postulant. The Commission or a
144   designated committee shall interview the Postulant, and the Commission or designated committee
145   shall submit a recommendation to the Bishop.
146   (3) The Bishop may then admit the Postulant as a Candidate, informing the Candidate and the
147   Candidate's Rector or Priest-in-Charge in writing.

148 **Sec. 2.** Candidacy
149 (a) Candidacy is a time, no less than one year in length, of formation in preparation for ordination to the
150   Diaconate.
151 (b) The Bishop may assign the Candidate to any congregation of the diocese or other community of faith
152   after consultation with the Rector or other leader exercising oversight.
153 (c) At the Bishop's sole discretion, any Candidate may be removed from the list of Candidates, with
154   reasons given to the Candidate and written notice of the removal being given to the Rector or other
155   leader exercising oversight of the nominating congregation or other community of faith and the
156   Commission.

157 **Sec. 3.** Preparation for Ordination
158 (a) The Bishop, in consultation with the Commission, shall determine the length of time and extent of
159   formation needed to prepare each Candidate for ordination. Formation shall reflect the local culture and
160   each Candidate's background, age, occupation, and ministry. Prior education and learning from life
161   experience may be considered as part of the formation required for ordination.
162 (b) Before ordination each Candidate shall be prepared in and demonstrate basic competence in five
163   general areas:
164   (1) Diakonia and the diaconate,
165   (2) Human awareness and understanding,
166   (3) Spiritual development and discipline,
167   (4) Practical training and experience,
168   (5) Academic study and education.
169 (c) Wherever possible, formation shall take place in community, including persons in preparation for the
170   diaconate, or others preparing for ministry.
171 (d) The formation process shall include sexual misconduct prevention training, training regarding Title IV
172   of these Canons, and anti-racism training.
173 (e) Each Candidate shall communicate with the Bishop in person or by letter, four times a year, in the
174   Ember Weeks, reflecting on the Candidate's diaconal, human, spiritual, practical, and academic
175   development.
176 (f) During Candidacy each Candidate's progress shall be evaluated from time to time, and there shall be a
177   written report of the evaluation. Upon certification by those in charge of the Candidate's program of
178   preparation that the Candidate has successfully completed preparation and is ready for ordination, a
179   final written assessment of readiness for ordination to the Diaconate shall be prepared as determined by

180 the Bishop in consultation with the Commission. Records shall be kept of all evaluations and
181 assessments and shall be made available to the Standing Committee.
182 (g) Upon certification in writing by the Standing Committee that all canonical requirements have been
183 met, the Bishop may ordain the Candidate a Deacon.

184 **Sec. 4.** A person previously ordained a Priest or a Bishop, and not previously ordained a Deacon, may be
185 nominated to be a Postulant for the diaconate and shall fulfill the requirements of this Canon. Upon
186 completion of these requirements, the Priest or Bishop may be ordained a Deacon.

187 CANON 7: Of the Life and Work of Deacons

188 **Sec. 1.** This canon applies only to deacons called to the diaconate as a vocation.

189 **Sec. 2.** Deacons serve directly under the authority of and are accountable to the Bishop.

190 **Sec. 3.** Deacons canonically resident in each Diocese constitute a Community of Deacons, which shall meet
191 from time to time. The Bishop may appoint one or more of such Deacons as Archdeacon(s) to assist the
192 Bishop in the formation, deployment, supervision, and support of the Deacons or those in preparation to be
193 Deacons, and in the implementation of this canon. The Bishop may establish a council to oversee, study, and
194 promote the diaconate.

195 **Sec. 4.** The Bishop, after consultation with the Rector or other leader exercising oversight, may assign a
196 Deacon to one or more congregations, other communities of faith or non-parochial ministries. Deacons
197 assigned to a congregation or other community of faith act under the authority of the Rector or other leader
198 exercising oversight in all matters concerning the congregation.
199 (a) Deacons may have a letter of agreement, subject to the Bishop's approval, setting forth mutual
200 responsibilities in the assignment.
201 (b) Deacons shall report annually to the Bishop or the Bishop's designee on their life and work.
202 (c) Deacons may serve as administrators of congregations or other communities of faith, but no Deacon
203 shall be in charge of a congregation or other community of faith.
204 (d) Deacons may accept a chaplaincy in any hospital, prison, or other institution, or serve as Deacons in
205 the Armed Services.

206 **Sec. 5.** The Bishop and Commission shall require and provide for the continuing education of Deacons and
207 keep a record of such education.

208 **Sec. 6.** (a) After consultation among all affected parties, a Bishop may license Deacons canonically resident in
209 another diocese to serve in that Bishop's diocese. A Deacon without such a written license may not serve as
210 Deacon for more than two months outside the diocese in which the Deacon is canonically resident.

211 (b) (1) A Deacon desiring to become canonically resident within a Diocese shall present to the
212 Ecclesiastical Authority a testimonial from the Ecclesiastical Authority of the Diocese in which the
213 Deacon is canonically resident, which testimonial shall be given by the Ecclesiastical Authority to the
214 applicant, and a duplicate thereof may be sent to the Ecclesiastical Authority of the Diocese to which
215 transfer is proposed. The testimonial shall be in the following words:
216 **I hereby certify that A.B., who has signified to me the desire to be transferred to the Ecclesiastical**
217 **Authority of _____, is a Deacon of _____ in good standing, and has not, so far as I**
218 **know or believe, been justly liable to evil report, for error in religion or for viciousness of life, for**
219 **the last three years.**
220 **(Date) _____**
221 **(Signed) _____**

222 (2) Such testimonial shall be called Letters Dimissory. If the Ecclesiastical Authority is moved to accept
223 the Letters Dimissory, the canonical residence of the Deacon so transferred shall date from the
224 acceptance of the Letters Dimissory, of which prompt notice shall be given both to the applicant and to
225 the Ecclesiastical Authority from which it came.

226 (3) Letters Dimissory not presented within six months from the date of their transmission to the applicant
227 shall become void.
228 (4) A statement of the record of payments to The Church Pension Fund by or on behalf of the Deacon
229 concerned shall accompany Letters Dimissory.

230 **Sec. 7.** A Deacon may retire from active service at any time mutually acceptable to the Deacon and the
231 Bishop, or at any time for reasons of health. The Bishop may assign a retired Deacon to any congregation,
232 other community of faith or non-parochial ministry, for a period not to exceed twelve months, and this period
233 may be renewed.

234 **Sec. 8.**
235 (a) A Deacon of this Church not subject to the provisions of Canon IV.8 may declare, in writing, to the
236 Ecclesiastical Authority of the Diocese of canonical residence, a renunciation of the Diaconate of this
237 Church, and a desire to be removed therefrom. Upon receipt of such declaration, the Bishop shall
238 record it. The Bishop, upon determining that the person is not subject to the provisions of Canon IV.8
239 but is acting voluntarily and for causes that do not affect the Deacon's moral character, shall present the
240 declaration to the clerical members of the Standing Committee. With the advice and consent of a
241 majority of such members, the Bishop may pronounce that such renunciation is accepted, and the
242 Deacon is released from the obligations of the office and deprived of the rights conferred in ordination.
243 The Bishop shall also declare that the renunciation was for causes that do not affect the person's moral
244 character and, if requested, shall give a certificate to this effect to the person so removed from the
245 Diaconate.
246 (b) If a Deacon making the declaration provided in the preceding section of this Canon is under
247 Presentment for any canonical Offense, or has been placed on Trial for the same, the Ecclesiastical
248 Authority to whom such declaration is made shall not consider or act upon such declaration until after
249 the Presentment is dismissed or the Trial concluded and the Deacon judged not to have committed an
250 Offense.
251 (c) If a renunciation is accepted, the Bishop shall pronounce a declaration of removal in the presence of
252 two or more Deacons or members of the Standing Committee and shall enter it in the official records of
253 the Diocese of canonical residence. The Bishop who pronounces the declaration of removal shall give
254 notice thereof in writing to every Member of the Clergy, each Vestry, the Secretary of the Convention
255 and the Standing Committee of the Diocese in which the Deacon was canonically resident; and to all
256 Bishops of this Church, the Ecclesiastical Authority of each Diocese of this Church, the Presiding
257 Bishop, the Recorder, the Secretary of the House of Bishops, the Secretary of the House of Deputies,
258 the Church Pension Fund, and the Church Deployment Board.
259 (d) In case of a vacancy in the episcopate in a Diocese, the Ecclesiastical Authority may request the
260 President of the House of Bishops of the Province, or the President's designee, to exercise the
261 canonical authority assigned to the Bishop by this section.
262 (e) A person removed from the Diaconate pursuant to this section may apply to the Bishop in writing for
263 restoration to the Diaconate, and the Bishop, with the consent of the Standing Committee, may restore
264 the person as a Deacon.

265 **CANON 8: Of the Ordination of Priests**

266 **Sec. 1.** The Bishop, in consultation with the Commission, shall establish procedures to identify and select
267 persons for ordination to the Priesthood.

268 **Sec 2.** Of General Provisions concerning Postulancy and Candidacy

269 (a) Postulancy is a time, no less than six months in length, for the exploration of and decision on the
270 Postulant's call to the Priesthood.
271 (b) Candidacy is a time of formation in preparation for ordination to the Priesthood, established by a
272 formal commitment by the Candidate, the Bishop, the Commission and the congregation or other
273 community of faith. The period of Candidacy shall be no less than six months.

274   (c) The combined period for Postulancy and Candidacy under this Canon shall last no less than 18
275   months.
276   (d) The responsibilities for the formation and preparation of Postulants and Candidates shall include the
277   following.

278   (1) Each Postulant or Candidate for ordination to the Priesthood shall communicate with the
279   Bishop in person or by letter, four times a year, in the Ember Weeks, reflecting on the
280   individual's academic experience and personal and spiritual development.
281   (2) The congregation or other community of faith shall nominate appropriate persons for the
282   ordination process, nurture them in their faith, and provide continuing support for such
283   persons through Postulancy, Candidacy, and ordination.
284   (3) The Bishop and the Commission shall work closely with the Postulant or Candidate to
285   develop and monitor a program of preparation for ordination to the Priesthood in
286   accordance with Canon III.8.4 and to ensure that pastoral guidance is provided throughout
287   the period of preparation.
288   (4)The Standing Committee shall certify that all canonical requirements for ordination have
289   been met.
290   (5) The seminary or other formation program shall provide for, monitor and report on the
291   academic performance and personal qualifications of the Candidate or Postulant for
292   ordination. These reports will be made upon request of the Bishop and Commission, but
293   at least once per year.

294   (e) Prior to ordination, the following must be accomplished:
295   (1) a thorough background check of the applicant,
296   (2) sexual misconduct prevention training, training regarding Title IV of these Canons, and
297   anti-racism training,
298   (3) consultation by the Bishop with the applicant regarding financial resources available for
299   the support of the applicant throughout preparation for ordination, and
300   (4) thorough examinations, both physical and psychological, by professionals appointed by
301   the Bishop. The appointed professionals shall use the forms for medical and
302   psychological or psychiatric reports prepared by the Church Pension Fund for this
303   purpose. These reports shall be kept on file by the Bishop. When deemed appropriate the
304   Bishop may make available information from the reports to the Commission with proper
305   regard for confidentiality.

306 **Sec. 3**. Postulancy

307   (a) A person desiring to be considered for admission as a Postulant for ordination to the Priesthood shall
308   apply to the Bishop. Such application shall include the following.
309   (1) Full name and date of birth.
310   (2) The length of time resident in the Diocese.
311   (3) Evidence of Baptism and Confirmation.
312   (4) Whether an application has been made previously for Postulancy in any diocese.
313   (5) A description of the process of discernment by which the applicant has been identified for
314   ordination to the Priesthood.
315   (6) The level of education attained and, if any, the degrees earned and areas of specialization.
316   (7) A letter of support by the applicant's congregation or other community of faith, including
317   a statement committing the congregation or other community of faith to involve itself in
318   the applicant's preparation for ordination to the Priesthood. If it be a congregation, the
319   letter shall be signed by a two-thirds majority of the Vestry or comparable body, and the
320   Rector or leader exercising oversight.
321   (b) Before granting admission as a Postulant, the Bishop:

322   (1) shall determine that the person is a confirmed adult communicant in good standing of a
323   congregation or other community of faith, and has been a member of the Episcopal
324   Church for the preceding three years, and
325   (2) shall confer in person with the applicant.
326   (c) On the basis of the application and the personal interview, the Bishop shall notify the
327   applicant and the Commission whether the application process may proceed.
328   (d) If the Bishop approves proceeding, the Commission, or a committee of the Commission,
329   shall meet with the applicant to review the application and prepare an evaluation of the
330   applicant's qualifications to pursue a course of preparation for ordination to the
331   Priesthood. The Commission shall present its evaluation and recommendations to the
332   Bishop.
333   (e) The Bishop may admit the applicant as a Postulant for ordination to the Priesthood. The
334   Bishop shall record the Postulant's name and date of admission in a Register kept for that
335   purpose. The Bishop shall inform the Postulant, the Rector or other leader exercising
336   oversight of the Postulant's congregation or other community of faith, the Commission,
337   the Standing Committee, and the Dean of the seminary the Postulant may be attending or
338   proposes to attend, or the director of Postulant's program of preparation, of the fact and
339   date of such admission.
340   (f) Any Postulant may be removed as a Postulant at the sole discretion of the Bishop, who
341   shall give the reasons to the Postulant. The Bishop shall give written notice of the
342   removal to the Rector or other leader exercising oversight of the Postulant's congregation
343   or other community of faith, the Commission, the Standing Committee, and the Dean of
344   the seminary the Postulant may be attending or the director of the program of preparation.
345   (g) No Bishop shall consider accepting as a Postulant any person who has been refused
346   admission as a Candidate for ordination to the Priesthood in any other Diocese, or who,
347   having been admitted, has afterwards ceased to be a Candidate, until receipt of a letter
348   from the Bishop of the Diocese refusing admission, or in which the person has been a
349   Candidate, declaring the cause of refusal or of cessation. If the Bishop decides to proceed
350   the Bishop shall send the letter to the Commission.

351 **Sec. 4.** Formation. Postulants shall pursue the program of preparation for ordination to the Priesthood
352 developed by the Bishop and Commission. The program shall include theological training, practical
353 experience, emotional development, and spiritual formation.

354   (a) If the Postulant has not previously obtained a baccalaureate degree, the Commission, Bishop and
355   Postulant shall, as necessary, design a program of additional academic work to prepare the Postulant to
356   undertake a program of theological education.
357   (b) Prior education and learning from life experience may be considered as part of the formation required
358   for the Priesthood.
359   (c) Whenever possible, formation for the Priesthood shall take place in community, including other
360   persons in preparation for the Priesthood, a ministry team, or others preparing for ministry.
361   (d) Formation shall take into account the local culture and each Candidate's background, age, occupation,
362   and ministry.
363   (e) Subject areas for study during this program of preparation shall include:
364   (1) The Holy Scriptures;
365   (2) Church History, including the Ecumenical Movement;
366   (3) Christian Theology, including Missionary Theology and Missiology;
367   (4) Christian Ethics and Moral Theology;
368   (5) Studies in contemporary society, including racial and minority groups;
369   (6) Liturgics and Church Music; Christian Worship and Music according to the contents and
370   use of the Book of Common Prayer and the Hymnal, respectively; and
371   (7) Theory and practice of ministry.

372 **Sec. 5.** Candidacy

373   (a) A person desiring to be considered as a Candidate for ordination to the Priesthood shall apply to the
374   Bishop. Such application shall include the following:
375   (1) the Postulant's date of admission to Postulancy, and
376   (2) a letter of support by the Postulant's congregation or an authorized representative of
377   the Postulant's congregation or other community of faith. If it be a congregation, the letter
378   shall be signed by at least two-thirds of the Vestry and the Rector or other leader exercising
379   oversight.
380   (b) Upon compliance with these requirements, and receipt of a statement from the Commission attesting to
381   the continuing formation of the Postulant, the Bishop may admit the applicant as a Candidate for
382   ordination to the Priesthood. The Bishop shall record the Candidate's name and date of admission in a
383   Register kept for that purpose. The Bishop shall inform the Candidate, the Rector or leader exercising
384   oversight of the Candidate's congregation or other community of faith, the Commission, the Standing
385   Committee, and the Dean of the seminary the Candidate may be attending or proposes to attend, or the
386   director of the Candidate's program of preparation, of the fact and date of such admission.
387   (c) A Candidate must remain in canonical relationship with the Diocese in which admission has been
388   granted until ordination to the Priesthood, except as provided in Canon III.8.5(d).
389   (d) For reasons satisfactory to the Bishop, the Candidate may be transferred to another Diocese upon
390   request, provided that the Bishop of the receiving Diocese is willing to accept the Candidate.
391   (e) Any Candidate may be removed as a Candidate at the sole discretion of the Bishop, who shall give the
392   reasons to the Candidate. The Bishop shall give written notice of the removal to the Rector or other
393   leader exercising oversight of the Candidate's congregation or other community of faith, the
394   Commission, the Standing Committee, and the Dean of the seminary the Candidate may be attending or
395   the director of the program of preparation.
396   (f) If a Bishop has removed the Candidate's name from the list of Candidates, except by transfer, or the
397   Candidate's application for ordination has been rejected, no other Bishop may ordain the person
398   without readmission to Candidacy for a period of at least twelve months.

399 **Sec. 6.** Ordination to the Priesthood

400   (a) A person may be ordained Priest
401   (1) after at least six months as a Candidate, and
402   (2) upon attainment of at least twenty-four years of age.
403   (b) The Bishop shall obtain in writing:
404   (1) an application from the Candidate requesting ordination as a Priest, including the
405   Candidate's dates of admission to Postulancy and Candidacy,
406   (2) a letter of support from the Candidate's congregation, signed by at least two-thirds of the
407   Vestry and the Rector or other leader exercising oversight, or from an authorized
408   representative of the Candidate's congregation or other community of faith,
409   (3) a certificate from the seminary or other program of preparation, showing the Candidate's
410   scholastic record in the subjects required by the Canons, and giving an evaluation with
411   recommendation as to the Candidate's other personal qualifications for ordination together
412   with a recommendation regarding ordination, and
413   (4) a statement from the Commission attesting to the successful completion of the program of
414   formation designed during Postulancy under Canon III.8.4.
415   (c) The Standing Committee shall obtain:
416   (1) the application for ordination specified in Canon III.8.6(b)(i), including the accompanying
417   letter of support by the Candidate's congregation or community of faith specified in Canon
418   III.8.6(b)(ii),
419   (2) certificates from the Bishop who admitted the Candidate to Postulancy and Candidacy,
420   giving the dates of admission, and

421 (3) a certificate from the Commission attesting to successful completion of the program of
422 formation designed during Postulancy under Canon III.8.4, and recommending the
423 Candidate for ordination to the Priesthood.
424 (d) On the receipt of such certificates, the Standing Committee shall certify that the canonical
425 requirements for ordination have been met, by a testimonial addressed to the Bishop in the form
426 specified below and signed by the President of the Standing Committee.

427 **To the Right Reverend _____, Bishop of _____ We, the Standing Committee of _____,**
428 **having been duly convened at _____, do testify that A.B., desiring to be ordained to the Priesthood,**
429 **has presented to us the certificates as required by the Canons indicating A.B.'s preparedness for**
430 **ordination; and we certify that all canonical requirements for ordination have been met. In witness**
431 **whereof, we have hereunto set our hands this _____ day of _____, in the year of our Lord _____**
432 **(Signed) _____**

433 (e) The testimonial having been presented to the Bishop, and there being no sufficient objection on
434 medical, psychological, moral, doctrinal, or spiritual grounds, the Bishop may ordain the Candidate to
435 the Priesthood; and at the time of ordination the Candidate shall subscribe publicly and make, in the
436 presence of the Bishop, the declaration required in Article VIII of the Constitution.
437 (f) No Candidate shall be ordained to the Priesthood until having been appointed to serve in a Parochial
438 Cure within the jurisdiction of this Church, or as a Missionary under the Ecclesiastical Authority of a
439 Diocese, or as an officer of a Missionary Society recognized by the General Convention, or as a
440 Chaplain of the Armed Services of the United States, or as a Chaplain in a recognized hospital or other
441 welfare institution, or as a Chaplain or instructor in a school, college, or other seminary, or with other
442 opportunity for the exercise of the office of Priest within the Church judged appropriate by the Bishop.
443 (g) A person ordained to the Diaconate who is subsequently called to the Priesthood shall fulfill the
444 Postulancy and Candidacy requirements set forth in this canon. Upon completion of these
445 requirements, the Deacon may be ordained to the Priesthood.

446 CANON 9: Of the Life and Work of Priests

447 **Sec. 1**. The Bishop and Commission shall require and provide for the continuing education of Priests and
448 keep a record of such education.

449 Of the Appointment of Priests

450 **Sec. 2**. (a) Rectors.

451 (1) When a Parish is without a Rector, the Wardens or other officers shall promptly notify the
452 Ecclesiastical Authority in writing. If the Parish shall for thirty days fail to provide services of
453 public worship, the Ecclesiastical Authority shall make provision for such worship.
454 (2) No Parish may elect a Rector until the names of the proposed nominees have been
455 forwarded to the Ecclesiastical Authority and a time, not exceeding thirty days, given to the
456 Ecclesiastical Authority to communicate with the Vestry, nor until any such communication,
457 has been considered by the Vestry at a meeting duly called and held for that purpose.
458 (3) Written notice of the election of a Rector, signed by the Wardens, shall be forwarded to the
459 Ecclesiastical Authority. If the Ecclesiastical Authority is satisfied that the person so elected is
460 a duly qualified Priest and that such Priest has accepted the office to which elected, the notice
461 shall be sent to the Secretary of the Convention, who shall record it. Race, color, ethnic origin,
462 sex, national origin, marital status, sexual orientation, disabilities or age, except as otherwise
463 specified by these Canons, shall not be a factor in the determination of the Ecclesiastical
464 Authority as to whether such person is a duly qualified Priest. The recorded notice shall be
465 sufficient evidence of the relationship between the Priest and the Parish.
466 (4) Rectors may have a letter of agreement with the Parish setting forth mutual responsibilities,
467 subject to the Bishop's approval

468   (b) Priests-in-Charge. The Bishop may appoint a Priest to serve as Priest-in-Charge of any congregation in
469   which there is no Rector. In such congregations, the Priest-in-Charge shall exercise the duties of Rector
470   outlined in Canon III.9.4 subject to the authority of the Bishop.
471   (c) Assistants. A Priest serving as an assistant in a Parish, by whatever title designated, shall be selected by
472   the Rector, and when required by the Canons of the Diocese, subject to the approval of the Vestry, and
473   shall serve under the authority and direction of the Rector. Before the selection of an assistant the name
474   of the Priest proposed for selection shall be made known to the Bishop and a time, not exceeding thirty
475   days, given for the Bishop to communicate with the Rector and Vestry on the proposed selection. Any
476   assistant shall serve at the pleasure of the Rector and may not serve beyond the period of service of the
477   Rector, except that pending the call of a new Rector, an assistant may continue in the service of the
478   Parish if requested to do so by the Vestry under such conditions as the Bishop and Vestry shall
479   determine. Assistants may have a letter of agreement with the Rector and the Vestry setting forth
480   mutual responsibilities subject to the Bishop's approval.
481   (d) Chaplains.
482   (1) A Priest may be given ecclesiastical endorsement for service as a Chaplain in the Armed Services
483   of the United States of America or as a Chaplain for the Veterans' Administration, or in any
484   Federal Correctional Institution, by the Office of the Bishop Suffragan for the Armed Services,
485   Health Care Ministries and Prison Ministries subject to the approval of the Ecclesiastical
486   Authority of the Diocese in which the Priest is canonically resident.
487   (2) Any Priest serving on active duty with the Armed Services shall retain the Priest's canonical
488   residence and shall be subject to the ecclesiastical supervision of the Bishop of the Diocese of
489   which the Priest is canonically resident, even though the Priest's work as a Chaplain shall be
490   subject to the general supervision of the Office of the Bishop Suffragan for the Armed Services,
491   Health Care Ministries and Prison Ministries, or such other Bishop as the Presiding Bishop may
492   designate.
493   (3) Any Priest serving on a military installation or at a Veterans' Administration facility or Federal
494   Correctional Institution shall not be subject to Canons III.9.2.(f)(1) or III.10.3(a). When serving
495   other than on a military installation or at a Veterans' Administration facility, or Federal
496   Correctional Institution, a Chaplain shall be subject to these Sections.
497   (e) Non-ecclesiastical or Non-parochial Employment of Priests
498   (1) Any Priest who has left a position in this Church without having received a call to a new position
499   and who desires to continue the exercise of the office of Priest shall notify the Ecclesiastical
500   Authority of the Diocese in which the Priest is canonically resident and shall advise the Bishop
501   that reasonable opportunities for the exercise of the office of Priest exist and that use will be made
502   of such opportunities. After having determined that the person will have and use opportunities for
503   the exercise of the office of Priest, the Bishop, with the advice and consent of the Standing
504   Committee, may approve the Priest's continued exercise of the office on condition that the Priest
505   report annually in writing, in a manner prescribed by the Bishop, as provided in Canon I.6.2.
506   (2) A Priest who would be permitted under Canon III.9.7 to renounce the exercise of ordained office,
507   who desires to enter into other than ecclesiastical employment, may declare in writing to the
508   Ecclesiastical Authority of the Diocese in which the Priest is canonically resident a desire to be
509   released from the obligations of the office and a desire to be released from the exercise of the
510   office of Priest. Upon receipt of such declaration, the Ecclesiastical Authority shall proceed in the
511   same manner as if the declaration was one of renunciation of the ordained Priesthood under Canon
512   III.9.7.
513   (3)   (i). A Priest not in parochial employment moving to another jurisdiction shall report to the
514   Bishop of that jurisdiction within sixty days of such move.
515   (ii). The Priest:
516   (a) May officiate or preach in that jurisdiction only under the terms of Canon III.9.5(a).
517   (b) Shall provide notice of such move, in writing and within sixty days, to the
518   Ecclesiastical Authority of the Diocese in which the Priest is canonically resident.

519 (c) Shall forward a copy of the report required by Canon I.6.2 to the Ecclesiastical
520 Authority to whose jurisdiction the Priest has moved.
521 (iii). Upon receipt of the notice required by Canon III.9.2(d)(iii)(b)(2), the Ecclesiastical
522 Authority shall provide written notice thereof to the Ecclesiastical Authority into whose
523 jurisdiction the person has moved.
524 (4) If the Priest fails to comply with the provisions of this Canon, the Bishop of the Diocese in which
525 the Priest is canonically resident may proceed in accordance with Canon IV.11.

526 *Of Letters Dimissory*
527 **Sec. 3.** (a) A Priest desiring to become canonically resident within a Diocese shall present to the Ecclesiastical
528 Authority a testimonial from the Ecclesiastical Authority of the Diocese of current canonical residence, which
529 testimonial shall be given by the Ecclesiastical Authority to the applicant, and a duplicate thereof may be sent
530 to the Ecclesiastical Authority of the Diocese to which transfer is proposed. The testimonial shall be
531 accompanied by a statement of the record of payments to The Church Pension Fund by or on behalf of the
532 Priest concerned and shall be in the following words:

533 **I hereby certify that A.B., who has signified to me the desire to be transferred to the Ecclesiastical**
534 **Authority of _____, is a Priest of _____ in good standing, and has not, so far as I know or**
535 **believe, been justly liable to evil report, for error in religion or for viciousness of life, for the last three**
536 **years.**
537 **(Date) _____**
538 **(Signed) _____**
539 (b) Such a testimonial shall be called Letters Dimissory. If the Ecclesiastical Authority accepts the Letters
540 Dimissory, the canonical residence of the Priest transferred shall date from such acceptance, and
541 prompt notice of acceptance shall be given to the applicant and to the Ecclesiastical Authority issuing
542 the Letters Dimissory.
543 (c) Letters Dimissory not presented within six months of their date of receipt by the applicant shall become
544 void.
545 (d) If a Priest has been called to a Cure in a congregation in another Diocese, the Priest shall present
546 Letters Dimissory. The Ecclesiastical Authority of the Diocese shall accept Letters Dimissory within
547 three months of their receipt unless the Bishop or Standing Committee has received credible
548 information concerning the character of the Priest concerned which would form grounds for canonical
549 inquiry and presentment. In such a case, the Ecclesiastical Authority shall notify the Ecclesiastical
550 Authority of the Diocese in which the Priest is canonically resident and need not accept the Letters
551 Dimissory unless and until the Priest shall be exculpated. The Ecclesiastical Authority shall not refuse
552 to accept Letters Dimissory based on the applicant's race, color, ethnic origin, sex, national origin,
553 marital status, sexual orientation, disabilities or age.
554 (e) A Priest shall not be in charge of any congregation in the Diocese to which the person moves until
555 obtaining from the Ecclesiastical Authority of that Diocese a certificate in the following words:
556 **I hereby certify that A.B. has been canonically transferred to my jurisdiction and is a Priest in good**
557 **standing.**
558 **(Date) _____**
559 **(Signed) _____**
560 (f) No person who has been refused ordination or reception as a Candidate in any Diocese, and is
561 thereafter ordained in another Diocese, shall be transferred to the Diocese in which such refusal has
562 occurred without the consent of its Ecclesiastical Authority.

563 *Of the Priests and Their Duties*
564 **Sec. 4.** (a)(1) The Rector shall have full authority and responsibility for the conduct of the worship
565 and the spiritual jurisdiction of the Parish, subject to the Rubrics of the Book of Common Prayer, the
566 Constitution and Canons of this Church, and the pastoral direction of the Bishop.

567   (2) For the purposes of the office and for the full and free discharge of all functions and duties
568   pertaining thereto, the Rector shall at all times be entitled to the use and control of the Church and
569   Parish buildings together with all appurtenances and furniture.
570   (b) (1) It shall be the duty of the Priest to ensure all persons in their charge receive instruction in the
571 Holy Scriptures; in the subjects contained in An Outline of the Faith, commonly called the Catechism; in
572 the doctrine, discipline and worship of this Church; and in the exercise of their ministry as baptized
573 persons.
574   (2) It shall be the duty of Priests to ensure that all persons in their charge are instructed concerning
575   Christian stewardship, including:
576   (i) reverence for the creation and the right use of God's gifts;
577   (ii). generous and consistent offering of time, talent, and treasure for the mission and ministry
578   of the Church at home and abroad;
579   (iii). the biblical standard of the tithe for financial stewardship; and
580   (iv) the responsibility of all persons to make a will as prescribed in the Book of Common
581   Prayer, page 445.
582   (3) It shall be the duty of Priests to ensure that persons be prepared for Baptism. Before baptizing
583   infants or children, Priests shall ensure that sponsors be prepared by instructing both the parents
584   and the Godparents concerning the significance of Holy Baptism, the responsibilities of parents
585   and Godparents for the Christian training of the baptized child, and how these obligations may
586   properly be discharged.
587   (4) It shall be the duty of Priests to encourage and ensure the preparation of persons for
588   Confirmation, Reception, and the Reaffirmation of Baptismal Vows, and to be ready to present
589   them to the Bishop with a list of their names.
590   (5) On notice being received of the Bishop's intention to visit any congregation, the Rector shall
591   announce the fact to the congregation. At every visitation it shall be the duty of the Rector and the
592   Wardens, Vestry or other officers, to exhibit to the Bishop the Parish Register and to give
593   information as to the state of the congregation, spiritual and temporal, in such categories as the
594   Bishop shall have previously requested in writing.
595   (6) The Alms and Contributions, not otherwise specifically designated, at the Administration of the
596   Holy Communion on one Sunday in each calendar month, and other offerings for the poor, shall
597   be deposited with the Rector or with such Church officer as the Rector shall appoint to be applied
598   to such pious and charitable uses as the Rector shall determine. When a Parish is without a Rector
599   or Priest-in-Charge, the Vestry shall designate a member of the Parish to fulfill this function.
600   (7) Whenever the House of Bishops shall publish a Pastoral Letter, it shall be the duty of the Rector to
601   read it to the congregation on some occasion of public worship on a Lord's Day, or to cause copies
602   of the same to be distributed to the members of the congregation, not later than thirty days after
603   receipt.
604   (8) Whenever the House of Bishops shall adopt a Position Paper, it may require communication of the
605   content of the Paper to the membership of the Church in the manner set forth in the preceding
606   section of this Canon.
607 (c) (1) It shall be the duty of the Rector to record in the Parish Register all Baptisms, Confirmations
608 (including the canonical equivalents in Canon I.17.1(d)), Marriages and Burials.
609   (2) The registry of each Baptism shall be signed by the officiating Member of the Clergy.
610   (3) The Rector shall record in the Parish Register all persons who have received Holy Baptism, all
611 communicants, all persons who have received Confirmation (including the canonical equivalents in
612 Canon I.17.1(d)), all persons who have died, and all persons who have been received or removed by
613 letter of transfer. The Rector shall also designate in the Parish Register the names of (1) those persons
614 whose domicile is unknown, (2) those persons whose domicile is known but are inactive, and (3)
615 those families and persons who are active within the congregation. The Parish Register shall remain
616 with the congregation at all times.

Of Licenses

Sec. 5. (a) No Priest shall preach, minister the Sacraments, or hold any public service, within the limits of any Diocese other than the Diocese in which the Priest is canonically resident for more than two months without a license from the Ecclesiastical Authority of the Diocese in which the Priest desires to so officiate. No Priest shall be denied such a license on account of the Priest's race, color, ethnic origin, sex, national origin, marital status, sexual orientation, disabilities or age, except as otherwise provided in these Canons.

(b) No Priest shall preach, read prayers in public worship, or perform any similar function, in a congregation without the consent of the Rector or Priest-in-Charge of that congregation, except as follows:

(1) In the absence or disability of the Rector or Priest-in-Charge, and if provision has not been made for the stated services of the congregation or other community of faith, a Warden may give such consent.

(2) If there be two or more congregations or Churches in one Cure, as provided by Canon I.13.3(b), consent may be given by the majority of the Priests-in-Charge of such congregations, or by the Bishop; Provided, that nothing in this Section shall prevent any Member of the Clergy of this Church from officiating, with the consent of the Rector or Priest-in-Charge, in the Church or place of public worship used by the congregation of the consenting Rector or Priest-in-Charge, or in private for members of the congregation; or in the absence of the Rector or Priest-in-Charge, with the consent of the Wardens or Trustees of the congregation; Provided further, that the license of the Ecclesiastical Authority provided in Canon III,9.5(a), if required, be obtained.

(3) This Canon shall not apply to any Church, Chapel, or Oratory, which is part of the premises of an incorporated institution created by legislative authority, provided that such place of worship is designated and set apart for the convenience and use of such institution, and not as a place for public or parochial worship.

(c) No Rector or Priest-in-Charge of any congregation of this Church, or if there be none, no Wardens, Members of the Vestry, or Trustees of any congregation, shall permit any person to officiate in the congregation without sufficient evidence that such person is duly licensed and ordained and in good standing in this Church; Provided, nothing in these Canons shall prevent:

(1) The General Convention, by Canon or otherwise, from authorizing persons to officiate in congregations in accordance with such terms as it deems appropriate; or

(2) The Bishop of any Diocese from giving permission

(i). To a Member of the Clergy of this Church, to invite Clergy of another Church to assist in the Book of Common Prayer Offices of Holy Matrimony or of the Burial of the Dead, or to read Morning or Evening Prayer, in the manner specified in Canon III.9.5; or

(ii). To Clergy of any other Church to preach the Gospel, or in ecumenical settings to assist in the administration of the sacraments; or

(iii). To godly persons who are not Clergy of this Church to address the Church on special occasions.

(iv). To the Rector or Priest-in-Charge of a congregation or if there be none, to the Wardens, to invite Clergy ordained in another Church in communion with this Church to officiate on an occasional basis, provided that such clergy are instructed to teach and act consistent with the Doctrine, Discipline, and Worship of this Church.

(d) If any Rector or Priest-in-Charge, as a result of disability or any other cause, shall neglect to perform regular services in the congregation, and refuse, without good cause, to consent to any other duly qualified Member of the Clergy to perform such services, the Wardens, Vestry, or Trustees of the congregation shall, upon providing evidence to the Ecclesiastical Authority of the Diocese of such neglect or refusal and with the written consent of the Ecclesiastical Authority, have the authority to permit any duly qualified Member of the Clergy to officiate.

(e) (1) Any Priest desiring to officiate temporarily outside the jurisdiction of this Church but in a Church in communion with this Church, shall obtain from the Ecclesiastical Authority of the Diocese

667   in which the person is canonically resident, a testimonial which shall set forth the person's official
668   standing, and which may be in the following words:
669 **I hereby certify that A.B., who has signified to me the desire to be permitted to officiate temporarily in**
670 **churches not under the jurisdiction of The Episcopal Church, yet in communion with this Church, is a**
671 **Priest of _____ in good standing, and as such is entitled to the rights and privileges of that Order.**
672 **(Date) _____**
673 **(Signed) _____**
674 Such testimonial shall be valid for one year and shall be returned to the Ecclesiastical Authority at the end of
675 that period.
676   (2) The Ecclesiastical Authority giving such testimonial shall record its issuance, the name of the
677   Priest to whom issued, its date and the date of its return.
678 *Of Disagreements Affecting Pastoral Relation*
679 **Sec. 6.** (a) Reconciliation. In a Parish, when the pastoral relationship between a Rector and the Vestry or
680 congregation is imperiled by disagreement or dissension, and the issues are deemed serious by the Rector or
681 by a majority vote of the Vestry, either party may petition the Ecclesiastical Authority, in writing, to intervene
682 and assist the parties in their efforts to resolve the disagreement. The Ecclesiastical Authority shall initiate
683 appropriate proceedings under the circumstances, which may include the appointment of a consultant. The
684 parties to the disagreement, following the recommendations of the Ecclesiastical Authority, shall labor in
685 good faith to reconcile their differences. Whenever the Standing Committee is the Ecclesiastical Authority, it
686 shall request the Bishop of a neighboring Diocese to perform the duties of the Ecclesiastical Authority under
687 this Canon.
688   (b) Dissolution
689   (1) Except upon mandatory resignation by reason of age, a Rector may not resign as Rector of a
690   Parish without the consent of its Vestry, nor may any Rector canonically or lawfully elected and in
691   charge of a Parish be removed by the Vestry without the consent of the Rector, except as
692   hereinafter provided.
693   (2) If for any urgent reason a Rector or Vestry desires a dissolution of the pastoral relation, and the
694   parties cannot agree, either party may give notice in writing to the Ecclesiastical Authority of the
695   Diocese. Whenever the Standing Committee is the Ecclesiastical Authority of the Diocese, it shall
696   request the Bishop of another Diocese to perform the duties of the Ecclesiastical Authority under
697   this Canon.
698   (3) Within sixty days of receipt of the written notice the Bishop, as chief pastor of the Diocese,
699   shall mediate the differences between Rector and Vestry in every informal way which the Bishop
700   deems proper and may appoint a committee of at least one Presbyter and one Lay Person, none of
701   whom may be members of the Parish involved, to make a report to the Bishop.
702   (4) If the differences between the parties are not resolved after completion of the mediation, the
703   Bishop shall proceed as follows:
704   (i). The Bishop shall give notice to the Rector and Vestry that a godly judgment will be
705   rendered after consultation with the Standing Committee and that either party has a right within
706   ten days to request in writing an opportunity to confer with the Standing Committee before
707   such consultation.
708   (ii). If a timely request is made, the President of the Standing Committee shall set a date for a
709   conference within thirty days of the request.
710   (iii). At the conference each party shall be entitled to representation and to present its position
711   fully.
712   (iv). Within thirty days after the conference, or after the Bishop's notice if no conference is
713   requested, the Bishop shall confer with the Standing Committee, receive its recommendation
714   and thereafter, as final arbiter and judge, render a godly judgment.
715   (v). Upon the request of either party the Bishop shall explain the reasons for the judgment. If
716   the explanation is in writing, copies shall be delivered to both parties.

717 (vi). If the pastoral relation is to be continued, the Bishop shall require the parties to agree on
718 definitions of responsibility and accountability for the Rector and the Vestry.
719 (vii) If the pastoral relation is to be dissolved:
720 (a) The Bishop shall direct the Secretary of the Convention to record the dissolution.
721 (b) The judgment shall include such terms and conditions including financial settlements as
722 shall be deemed by the Bishop to be just and compassionate.
723 (5) In either event the Bishop shall offer supportive services to the Priest and the Parish.
724 (6) In the event of the failure or refusal of either party to comply with the terms of the judgment,
725 the Bishop may impose such penalties as may be set forth in the Constitution and Canons of the
726 Diocese, and in the absence thereof, may:
727 (i). In the case of a Rector, suspend the Rector from the exercise of the priestly office until the
728 Priest shall comply with the judgment.
729 (ii). In the case of a Vestry, invoke any available sanctions including recommending to the
730 Convention of the Diocese that the Parish be placed under the supervision of the Bishop as a
731 Mission until it has complied with the judgment.
732 (7) The Bishop may extend the time periods provided by this Canon, for cause shown, provided
733 that all be done to expedite these proceedings. All parties shall be notified in writing of the length
734 of any extension.
735 (8) (a). Statements made during the course of proceedings under this Canon are not discoverable
736 nor admissible in any proceedings under Title IV, provided that such does not require the
737 exclusion of evidence in any proceeding under the Canons which is otherwise discoverable and
738 admissible.
739 (b). In the course of proceedings under this Canon, if a charge is made by the Vestry against
740 the Rector that could give rise to a disciplinary proceeding under Canon IV.1, all proceedings
741 under this Canon with respect to such charge shall be suspended until the charge has been
742 resolved or withdrawn.
743 (9) This Canon shall not apply in any Diocese which has established, by Canon, a provision on
744 this subject consistent with this Canon.

745 *Of Renunciation*

746 **Sec. 7.** (a) A Priest of this Church not subject to the provisions of Canon IV.8 may declare, in writing, to the
747 Ecclesiastical Authority of the Diocese of canonical residence, a renunciation of the Priesthood of this
748 Church, and a desire to be removed there from. Upon receipt of such declaration, the Bishop shall record it.
749 The Bishop, upon determining that the person is not subject to the provisions of Canon IV.8 but is acting
750 voluntarily and for causes that do not affect the Priest's moral character, shall present the declaration to the
751 clerical members of the Standing Committee. With the advice and consent of a majority of such members,
752 the Bishop may pronounce that such renunciation is accepted, and the Priest is released from the obligations
753 of the office and deprived of the rights conferred in ordination. The Bishop shall also declare that the
754 renunciation was for causes that do not affect the person's moral character and, if requested, shall give a
755 certificate to this effect to the person so removed from the Priesthood.
756 (b) If a Priest making the declaration provided in the preceding Section of this Canon is under Presentment
757 for any canonical Offense, or has been placed on Trial for the same, the Ecclesiastical Authority to whom
758 such declaration is made shall not consider or act upon such declaration until after the Presentment is
759 dismissed or the Trial concluded and the Priest judged not to have committed an Offense.
760 (c) If a renunciation is accepted, the Bishop shall pronounce a declaration of removal in the presence of two
761 or more Priests, and shall enter it in the official records of the Diocese of canonical residence. The Bishop
762 who pronounces the declaration of removal shall give notice thereof in writing to every Member of the
763 Clergy, each Vestry, the Secretary of the Convention and the Standing Committee of the Diocese in which
764 the Priest was canonically resident; and to all Bishops of this Church, the Ecclesiastical Authority of each
765 Diocese of this Church, the Presiding Bishop, the Recorder, the Secretary of the House of Bishops, the
766 Secretary of the House of Deputies, the Church Pension Fund, and the Church Deployment Board.

767   (d) A person removed from the Priesthood pursuant to this section may apply to the Bishop in writing for
768   restoration to the Priesthood, and the Bishop, with the consent of the Standing Committee, may restore the
769   person as a Priest.
770   (e) In case of a vacancy in the episcopate in a Diocese, the Ecclesiastical Authority may request the
771   President of the House of Bishops of the Province, or the President's designee, to exercise the canonical
772   authority assigned to the Bishop by this section.

773 *Of Retirement*

774 **Sec. 8**. Upon attaining the age of seventy-two years, a Priest occupying any position in this Church shall
775 resign that position and retire from active service, and the resignation shall be accepted. Thereafter, the Priest
776 may accept any position in this Church, except the position or positions from which resignation pursuant to
777 this Section has occurred; Provided,
778   (a) tenure in the position shall be for a period of not more than one year, which period may be renewed
779   from time to time,
780   (b) service in the position shall have the express approval of the Bishop and Standing Committee of the
781   Diocese in which the service is to be performed, acting in consultation with the Ecclesiastical Authority of
782   the Diocese in which the Priest is canonically resident.
783   Anything in this Canon to the contrary notwithstanding, a Priest who has served in a non-
784   stipendiary capacity in a position before retirement may, at the Bishop's request, serve in the same
785   position for six months thereafter, and this period may be renewed from time to time.

GC Resolution 2000-A074
Continuing Education Standards for Clergy and Lay Professionals

Resolution A074 asked the SCMD to receive plans from each diocese on continuing education requirements
and make recommendations for continuing education guidelines for clergy and lay professionals. In response,
a pilot project in trial use for the past two years was developed by the House of Bishops' Office of Pastoral
Development and Miller and Associates, Inc. The report from this task group, including recommendations
and resolutions, is found in the Theological Education Task Group section of this report.

GC Resolution 2000-A103
A Study of the Theology of Confirmation

The SCMD's Ministry in Daily Life task group studied the theology of confirmation, and produced a study
paper for the Church's use as it considers the meaning and role of confirmation in today's Church. The paper
synthesized the findings of more than fifty articles and research studies, as well as the results of a survey
distributed to all bishops in the ECUSA and a sample of bishops in other parts of the Anglican Communion.
Neither the SCMD nor the Church is in full agreement on how the practice of confirmation should be used in
the Church. For the "Theology of Confirmation" paper, see
http://www.episcopalchurch.org/ministry/2003convention/toc.html

Resolution A112 Amend Article I, Section 4 of the Constitution

1   *Resolved,* the House of _____ concurring, That Article I, Section 4 be amended to read as follows:
2   ...and not more than four Lay Persons, ~~confirmed~~ adult communicants of this Church, in good standing in
3   the Diocese...

    EXPLANATION
    This proposed revision brings this Article of the Constitution referring to members of the House of
    Deputies into conformity with the Church's understanding of baptism as full membership in the Church.
    For such positions of leadership, being an active communicant in good standing is prerequisite.

Resolution A113 Amend Canon I.1.2(a)

1   *Resolved,* the House of _____ concurring, That Canon I.1.2 (a) be amended to read as follows:
2   ...and Lay Persons, who shall be ~~confirmed~~ adult communicants of this Church in good standing....

    EXPLANATION
    This proposed revision brings this Canon referring to members of the Standing Committee into conformity

with the Church's understanding of baptism as full membership in the Church. For such positions of leadership, being an active communicant in good standing is prerequisite.

Resolution A114 Amend Canon I.2.5

1   *Resolved,* the House of _____ concurring, That Canon I.2.5 be amended to read as follows:
2   The Presiding Bishop may appoint, as Chancellor to the Presiding Bishop, an ~~confirmed~~ adult
3   communicant of the Church in good standing who is learned in both ecclesiastical and secular law,.....

EXPLANATION
This proposed revision brings this Canon referring to the Chancellor to the Presiding Bishop into conformity with the Church's understanding of baptism as full membership in the Church. For such positions of leadership, being an active communicant in good standing is prerequisite.

Resolution A115 Amend Canon I.4.1(c)

1   *Resolved,* the House of _____ concurring, That Canon I.4.1(c) be amended to read as follows:
2   ...and by one Lay Person who is ~~a confirmed~~ an adult communicant in good standing of a Diocese...

EXPLANATION
This proposed revision brings this Canon referring to the elected Provincial Representative to Executive Council into conformity with the Church's understanding of baptism as full membership in the Church. For such positions of leadership, being an active communicant in good standing is prerequisite. It also makes the requirements for a Provincial Representative consistent with the requirements for General Convention elected representatives.

Resolution A116 Amend Canon I.4.3(d)

1   *Resolved,* the House of _____ concurring, That Canon I.4.3(d) be amended to read as follows:
2   The Presiding Bishop shall appoint, with the advice and consent of a majority of the Executive Council, an
3   executive director, who shall be an adult ~~confirmed~~ communicant in good standing....

EXPLANATION
This proposed revision brings this Canon referring to an executive director into conformity with the Church's understanding of baptism as full membership in the Church. For such positions of leadership, being an active communicant in good standing is prerequisite.

Resolution A117 Amend Canon I.9.7

1   *Resolved,* the House of _____ concurring, That Canon I.9.7 be amended to read as follows:
2   ... resident in the Diocese or Area Mission, and Lay Persons, ~~confirmed~~ adult communicants of this
3   Church in good standing....

EXPLANATION
This proposed revision brings this Canon referring to members of the Provincial House of Deputies into conformity with the Church's understanding of baptism as full membership in the Church. For such positions of leadership, being an active communicant in good standing is prerequisite.

Resolution A118 Amend Canon IV.3.27

1   *Resolved,* the House of _____ concurring, That Canon IV.3.27 be amended to read: There shall be a
2   Review Committee consisting of five Bishops of this Church, two Priests, and two ~~confirmed~~ adult lay
3   communicants in good standing ....

EXPLANATION
This proposed revision brings this Canon referring to a review committee for Bishops charged with other offenses into conformity with the Church's understanding of baptism as full membership in the Church. For such positions of leadership, being an active communicant in good standing is prerequisite.

GC Resolution 2000-C011
Study the System for Adjudication of Disputes and Due Process for Licensed Lay Persons
The Commission tried to include canons dealing with this adjudication process in the Title III revision work. SCMD realized, however, that substantially more research and consultation with affected individuals and groups needs to be completed this year and in the next triennium before revisions are proposed.

GC Resolution 2000-C033
Review the Current Role of Deacons in the Councils of the Church
The North American Association for the Diaconate researched this issue. SCMD would like to review its work this year and in the next triennium as well to consider the broader question of each order's role in the Councils of the Church.

Resolution A119 Role of Deacons
1   *Resolved,* the House of _____ concurring, That the Standing Commission on Ministry Development in
2   consultation with the North American Association of the Diaconate will continue the study of the role of
3   deacons in the councils of the church, in the dioceses and in congregations. A report on this work will be
4   submitted to the 75th General Convention.

EXPLANATION
This continues the work of GC Resolution 2000-D033.

GC Resolution 2000-D014
Reaffirm the 1% Giving to Seminaries, Designate Theological Education Sunday and an Annual Seminary Report to the SCMD
This work is reported in the Theological Education Task Force report found later in this report.

GC Resolution 2000-D080
Study the Programs of Youth Ministry
This resolution directed the SCMD, in collaboration with the Ministries with Young People Cluster (MYP), to study youth programs throughout the Church, and use the findings to inform the revision of the Title III canons. Early in the triennium, SCMD met with MYP representatives to discuss the project; this collaboration did not, however, progress further during the triennium. Much research on youth programs must be completed this year and in the next triennium before the Commission can recommend canonical revisions that will support the development of youth ministries. As a first step, the SCMD removed the word "adult" from some of the licensed lay ministries, making them accessible to young ministers. In light of the 20/20 A Clear Vision program, SCMD recommends that this resolution be continued in the next triennium.

THEOLOGICAL EDUCATION TASK FORCE REPORT
Members: R. William Franklin (Chair), Molly Shaw, Thurma L. Hilton, Pat Coller and Howard Maltby.

PART ONE
PROPOSAL FOR A THEOLOGICAL EDUCATION STRATEGIC PLANNING COMMITTEE
The Conant Fund
The Conant Fund was established by John and Mary Conant for the improvement of theological education. In this triennium the Theological Task Force and then the entire SCMD, following the suggestions of a screening committee, awarded a total of $204,915 in grants to 33 faculty members at Episcopal Seminaries. The current value of the fund is approximately $2 million, with available funds of approximately $346,000.

The Theological Task Force has proposed, and the full SCMD has approved these changes in the guidelines of the Conant Fund:
- incentive grants of $5,000 for one month, $10,000 for two months, or $15,000 for three months.
- travel and subsistence grants of up to $10,000.
- preference to projects that benefit the needs of theological education in the seminary or in the wider church.

THE FOCUS OF OUR WORK DURING THE TRIENNIUM

The goal of the committee was to take the pulse of the church in the area of theological education. We have defined "theological education" as certainly the work of the seminaries, but we have broadened the definition to include what local diocesan schools, parishes, colleges, and universities are doing in the area of theological education. We have also been concerned about how the whole church is formed by theology, both the ordained and the whole people of God. We were interested in topics like the role of lay professionals, continuing education, the ordination process, non-traditional ways of doing theological education.

From the beginning of our work six years ago we had a sense that we are at a great turning point in the history of theological education which is the result of the baptismal theology and broadened understanding of ministry expressed in the American Book of Common Prayer of 1979. The goals of the ecumenical movement have changed and the nature of our cooperation with other Churches in the future is less clear to us. The future shape of at least three of our historic seminaries is unclear at the moment because of contractual shifts in their relationships to other institutions. We are at a time of financial uncertainty for all institutions. We sensed that a revolution is going on, and we wanted to find out what is working and what is not working in the theological life of the church.

Our conclusion is that we are at a time of great transition. New institutions and locations for theological education are taking up the role of education that the seminaries alone once performed. These are: dioceses, cathedrals, parishes, colleges, universities, local programs.

All that we can do here is report what we have heard. We are not making suggestions for the future. But we do suggest that the change of the terrain is so great that the national church should organize something like the Pusey Commission of the 1960's that might suggest, as the Pusey Report suggested there might be a new and even radical reconfiguration of the seminaries, and the focus of theological education, particularly for the laity, in institutions that are independent of but work in harmony with the seminaries. Possible agenda for such a new commission include n evaluation of the seminaries, an evaluation of local and diocesan programs in theological education, including continuing education in theology, and the definition of new institutions to perform some of the tasks that were once performed only by seminaries.

But above all our Task Force strongly suggests that there be visible national leadership in evaluation of where we are in theological education, and boldness and imagination in leading us to new forms of theological education which matches the life of the church which has emerged from the liturgical context of the 1979 Prayer Book, the ordination of women, and a revival of the ministry and leadership of the laity in the life of the Church, as well as transitions in the patterns of life of all the Church's institutions.

"Theological Education: A Renewed Vision" is a four-year project whose goal is to inspire all Episcopalians to think theologically and to call all congregations to places of intentional theological reflection and learning. This project responds to *GC Resolution 2000-D014* dealing with reaffirming the 1% giving to seminaries and designating a Theological Education Sunday. Sponsors of this project are the Council of Episcopal Seminary Deans and the Episcopal Church Center. The project is funded by these partners and grants from Trinity Church, Wall Street, and the Lilly Endowment. Significant aspects of this project include a video presentation of theological education in many areas of our Church's life, a discussion guide for congregations to explore the presence and potential of theological education in their settings, the visits of over 2,200 congregations by the seminaries in 2003-2005 for conversation and exploration about theological education in its many forms, and a national consultation on theological education in 2005.

METHODS, GOALS, AND QUESTIONS THAT SHAPED OUR WORK

We devised a series of five questions which we believed covered the essential areas of theological education
    that were troubling the Episcopal Church at this time.
We interviewed all SCMD members on these questions.
We surveyed bishops, interviewed seminary deans, and we raised these questions at meetings of lay
    professionals, at ecumenical dialogues, and at other meetings of the church, such as the General Board of
    Examining Chaplains, and The Presiding Bishop's Task Force on Seminaries.
We posted our questions on the web and received more than fifty thoughtful replies.

Throughout the triennium we continued to refine the questions and tabulate answers, and we began to compile conclusions at a special meeting in New York September 5-7, 2002.

SUMMARY OF FINDINGS

A. Institutions of Theological Education

1. Our most important discovery has been that the Bishops are the primary teachers of the Church and they are the principal gatekeepers of theological education in our Church. In fact, this has been the pattern since the earliest days of Christianity. No other persons or groups rival the Bishops in this historic role. The bishops of the Church, acting individually, are our Episcopal accrediting agency for the Episcopal Church. The opinion is strong that they should continue to act in this capacity.

2. The standard requirement for those seeking ordination in the Episcopal Church should be attendance at one of the 11 seminaries of the Episcopal Church.

3. The primary function of the seminaries is the education and formation of priests. This is a different task than training "ordained leaders." A standard expectation is that priests are being formed in seminaries by spiritual direction, liturgy, a rule of life, as well as by academic study. None of these activities should be diluted by any other mission or any other focus of seminary life. However, there is a strong emphasis that priests should be formed to serve the Church that exists now, not to serve a Church of the past.

4. People want the 11 seminaries to be distinct but cooperative.

5. The Church approves of the fact that there are a variety of theological perspectives made available to our Church in the spectrum of our 11 seminaries.

6. Responsibility for formation of the ordained should be shared by the diocese, the parish, and the seminary. But the principal link-person in the process is the bishop of the diocese. Bishops view the formation of priests as one of their primary tasks, not to be delegated lightly to Commissions on Ministry or the seminaries without close Episcopal oversight. We endorse the program developed by the seminaries, "*Theological Education for All,*" as the initial way to educate the Church in this broader and deeper theological mission.

7. There is wide support for other forms of non-priestly theological training and strong centers of theological education for the whole people of God at locations of theological education other than the seminaries. Therefore, the seminaries are freed from bearing the entire burden of the task of theological education for the Episcopal Church.

8. Our survey reveals that the Church values both the 11 seminaries represented by the Council of Deans and the local diocesan schools of theology. They want each to maintain its unique integrity and mission. There is little desire to merge the identity of these institutions into a common structure supervising theological education, for example, by formally admitting the heads of the local diocesan schools of theology to the Council of Deans or by creating one national commission on training for ordination.

9. The responsibility of theological education is shared by the whole Church: parishes and dioceses now must exercise their teaching mission at a more professional level, with the diocesan bishop bearing ultimate responsibility for the quality of theological education for the people under his or her care.

10. Bishops should continue to be the authority to authorize attendance of postulants at non-Episcopal seminaries, but the practice of Episcopal postulants attending non-Episcopal seminaries should not be seen as the standard practice of the Church.

B. Ordination Process

1. There is church-wide complaint about the ordination process as it currently exists.

2. There is a call for greater standardization of the process from diocese to diocese—and greater unity of experience for future priests who may potentially serve in any of the 100 dioceses of the national church.

3. We have noted an expressed need for in-depth conversation among the seminaries, the House of Bishops, and the General Board of Examining Chaplains regarding the purpose, nature, and timing of the General Ordination Examination. A coordinated and long term in-depth exploration of these issues among the

parties concerned has not taken place since the late 1960's when the current General Ordination Examination was devised by Bishop Stephen Bayne and others.

C. Total Ministry

1. In the future the whole church needs to be educated in the goals and methods of "Total Ministry." Total Ministry and its perspective on lay and ordained service should not be combined to one narrow band of dioceses.

2. In the future the seminaries should form partnerships which would allow them to integrate the insights of Total Ministry into their own preparation of men and women for priesthood and they should explore ways to link themselves and support local Total Ministry initiatives.

3. For the future ample opportunities must be made available in each diocese of the Church to explain to laity and clergy alike the goals, methods, and approach of Total Ministry, so that ways may be found to integrate its legitimate insights into the life of the Episcopal Church as a whole.

D. Life Long Learning

Ways must be found to integrate into the dioceses the recommendations of the "Summary Report of the Continuing Education Pilot Program" which forms Part II of this report.

CONCLUSION OF OUR SIX YEAR IN-DEPTH STUDY

A serious look at theological education must be at the heart of the Episcopal Church if it expects to grow and match God's call with quality, dignity, and pride. Therefore, we propose the creation of a Strategic Planning Committee which would, in a broad collaborative way, develop a vision for the theological life of the Church. This Committee will be funded by grant. It will meet from 2003-2009 in order to produce a guide for theological education through 2020. At the conclusion of its first triennium in 2006, it will issue a preliminary report to the outgoing Presiding Bishop and the General Convention for revision and commentary. In 2009 it will produce its final report to the new Presiding Bishop and General Convention to guide the Church through the tenure of the next Presiding Bishop.

This Strategic Planning Committee should be inclusive in membership, and inclusive of the breadth, scope, and perspectives of the Church. The committee will tirelessly seek to consult with the diversity of initiatives, programs, groups, and individuals that seek to provide leadership in theological education. They will seek to establish creative links between institutions and other alliances so that those groups and the Church itself might be the beneficiary of a wisdom that is larger than any one group or program.

Resolution A120 Theological Education Committee

1 *Resolved,* the House of _____ concurring, That the 74th General Convention direct the Standing
2 Commission on Ministry Development to convene a Strategic Planning Committee, consisting of three
3 groups: a) 11 Bishops appointed by the Presiding Bishop, b) the 11 Seminary Deans or their appointees,
4 and c) 18 Provincial Representatives, two to be elected from each province; and be it further
5 *Resolved,* That this Committee is to function in a broad collaborative manner for six years to prepare an in-
6 depth study that will chart the future of theological education in the Church; and be it further
7 *Resolved* That funding for the work of this Committee be sought from sources outside the General
8 Convention and administered by the Standing Commission for Ministry Development; and be it further
9 *Resolved,* That the Standing Commission on Ministry Development will report on the work of this
10 Strategic Planning Committee to the 75th General Convention and will deliver its final report to the 76th
11 General Convention.

PART TWO

THE CONTINUING EDUCATION PILOT PROGRAM

In 2000, in response to *GC Resolution 2000-D034a*, Miller & Associates, Inc., in partnership with the House of Bishops' Office of Pastoral Development, developed and administered a two-year pilot program, *Building Our Capacity for Ministry: A Pilot Program To Create A Continuing Education Program.* This program was developed by Susy Miller and Mary May.

The pilot program was modeled on the competency-based model favored by academic institutions rather than the professional development model found in the business community. The program was inclusive, covering all aspects of a viable continuing education program. It began by explaining the purposes of continuing education, and suggested ways of governing the diocesan program. Most important, it provided a process whereby a diocese could ascertain its overall goals, and then create a continuing education process that would support those aims.

To make establishing a continuing education process as easy as possible, the pilot program provided both structure and content, while allowing each diocese to adjust the content to suit their own goals, needs, and resources. Some of the topics covered in the pilot program were:

- How to establish a governing body
- How most effectively to present the continuing education process to the diocese
- How to extrapolate the continuing education goals from the overall goals of the diocese
- How to identify the competencies required to meet the continuing education goals
- How to insure balance in the continuing education program by dividing the focus between religious studies, professional development, and personal development
- How to determine the value of a continuing education unit (CEU)/credit
- How to define the ways to earn CEUs and how to assign CEU credit to events
- How to evaluate continuing education events
- How to provide the ways and means for continuing education opportunities
- How to fund continuing education
- How to assess participant accountability

This pilot program provided a suggested format to cover all these areas, as well as step-by-step handouts to assist in their creation and implementation. It also included all the necessary administrative forms/reports on computer disk so that they could be used as created or edited to suit each diocese's needs.

In October 2000, the Office of Pastoral Development provided funds to bring together the people who would be responsible for the programs in the twelve participating dioceses. This time together, and the training that each received, was to prove invaluable in the years ahead.

Pilot Program Outcomes

Of the twelve dioceses that originally participated, two dropped out quickly because of administrative changes. Over the first year, three more dioceses experienced a loss of the original personnel, and only partially participated. Six dioceses established full continuing education programs, and one created an altered version of the pilot program. For brevity, we will summarize our findings in the following areas:

Implementation

- The bishop and administration must make their full support of continuing education clear from the start.
- While finding a person to take on the additional work load of director is difficult, it is imperative to have one person, perhaps supported by an advisory board, be in charge.
- The person who presents the program must be fully informed about continuing education, and he or she benefits from using a suggested process for presenting continuing education to the participants.
- Dioceses that had some type of continuing education process already in place were far more successful than those who had none, since the expectation for continuing education was already a part of the culture.

Creating Goals

- A national and diocesan program for continuing education is related to diocesan mission. Therefore, the diocese must first make certain that it has identified its own goals and priorities before the continuing education process can proceed.
- Having a process, complete with handouts, to guide people through the tasks of identifying goals and then establishing educational competencies, was a valuable asset.
- Requiring that the overall program cover a wide range of study (religious, professional, and personal) was unanimously accepted as important.

Creating Standards
- Establishing that 1 hour of contact time equals 1 hour of credit was an easily accepted norm, but calling it a continuing education unit (CEU) rather than some other name often caused much discussion.
- The general outline of how to assign credits contained in the pilot program was usually accepted with little change.
- The pilot program suggested a requirement of 24 CEUs per year for participants. Twenty CEUs per year was the lowest requirement adopted; 30 CEUs per year was the highest. All felt twenty or above was realistic.

Participation
- Defining clergy participants presented no problems.
- Defining lay professionals proved to be one of the most difficult parts of the pilot program in every diocese. Some dioceses worked to define and include "lay professionals;" others just focused on clergy.
- In most cases, careful preparation before implementation of the pilot program was a key factor. In the case of clergy, and lay professionals where applicable, their participation in creating the goals and the curriculum of the pilot program was in direct proportion to their support of the program.
- Providing interesting, useful local continuing education events that were easily accessible and economically feasible (or free) to participants was judged a major factor in creating a viable program.

Accountability
- How to require participation and determine accountability was a difficult problem for every diocese.
- Most directors believe that it must be the task of the bishops to determine how they will hold clergy (and lay professionals) accountable. Most directors think that accountability must be tied to advancement and deployment.

Funding
- Some dioceses had funding in place. Others struggled. All found ways to continue at both the diocesan and local levels.
- It is imperative that continuing education become part of every budget.

Evaluation
- Most dioceses used the basic forms, making changes to suit their own needs.
- All dioceses reported that these forms made the process easier. Some simply changed the titles. For example, when clergy spent too much time arguing about having to fill out an "Accountability Form", the director of one such program simply changed the name to "Feedback Form," and everyone was happy.

Recommendations
As a result of the pilot program, we make the following recommendations.
- That the National Church adopt a standard for continuing education, making it an expectation of the clergy and lay professionals of the church.
- That the terms "clergy and lay professionals," as stated in the resolution, be defined, or at least clarified.
- That at least two more rounds of continuing education pilot programs be offered to individual dioceses as soon as possible, since these successfully operating programs throughout the National Church will be a key factor in the successful establishment of a national program.
- That any national program include extensive pre-training of the key persons in each diocese who will administer the program. The pilot program made it very clear that those untrained persons who took charge of programs <u>after</u> the initial training did not have a clear understanding of continuing education, and as a result, got involved in unproductive controversies that the trained directors were able to deal with effectively.

- That standards be suggestions rather than requirements for the first three years of a national program, thus providing a smoother transition from no national standards to implementation of national standards.
- That the participating bishops address the issue of accountability before a program is implemented.
- That funding for continuing education become a standard part of the budget process.

Resolution A121 Clergy and Lay Professional Continuing Education

1   *Resolved,* the House of _____ concurring, That this 74th General Convention direct each Diocese to
2   develop a plan and make provisions for the continuing education of all clergy and lay professionals in its
3   jurisdiction, such plan and its progress to be reported annually to the Standing Commission on Ministry
4   Development; and be it further
5   *Resolved,* That dioceses that do not have continuing education policies or programs be urged to participate
6   in a pilot program for the development of a diocesan continuing education policy and program sponsored
7   by the Office for Ministry Development and Miller and Associates; and be it further
8   *Resolved,* That the 74th General Convention authorize $46,000 to support the participation of up to 20
9   dioceses in the above mentioned pilot program.

EXPLANATION

This responds to *GC Resolution 2000-A074* and continues to express the Church's wish for the continuing education of clergy and lay professionals serving in the Church. Miller and Associates has worked with the Office of Pastoral Development to develop the first round of pilot programs for continuing education in ten dioceses.

PART THREE
REPORTS FROM THE EPISCOPAL SEMINARIES

The narratives from the seminaries are in response to these questions:
1. What are some of the distinct features of your seminary?
2. What were your major accomplishments in the past three years?
3. What are your major needs these next three years?

Berkeley Divinity School at Yale
1. The Berkeley Divinity School at Yale is distinguished by its affiliation with the Yale Divinity School along with the Institute of Sacred Music. All our graduates receive their degrees from Yale and may also concomitantly earn our Diploma or Certificate in Anglican Studies. Students benefit from teaching by the faculty of both Divinity Schools and the Institute (offering courses in religion and the arts) and the University. In a rich university, ecumenical and urban setting with Divinity Schools intentionally training many of their students for ordained Christian ministries, Episcopal students (over one hundred of them, with the majority planning ordination and others various lay vocations) also benefit from Berkeley's spiritual formational programs and programs designed for training for ministry in the contemporary church.
2. After some challenges and difficulties involving full compliance with the affiliation agreement with Yale, the affiliation agreement was jointly reaffirmed for a ten-year period. Berkeley finds itself yet more closely affiliated with Yale Divinity School now in the recently restored Sterling Quadrangle, rebuilt and refurbished at a cost of more than 40 million dollars. The new facilities and, we believe, the faculty, library and related resources are outstanding.
3. Our major needs are financial. We have good scholarship endowment, but tuition is high and more scholarship support will be very helpful to our students. While endowments are reasonably adequate for Berkeley's own small faculty, we would like to strengthen those resources for the future. The greatest need is for endowment for our staff and support services, funds that have been depleted by expenses over the years and the recent realignments of policies and procedures.

Bexley Hall

1. Bexley Hall is one of the oldest seminaries in the country. Originally established in 1824 as a missionary seminary in Ohio, Bexley Hall relocated to Rochester, New York in the 1960's. Bexley Hall is distinguished by its commitment to formation for ministry in the "liberal Anglo-Catholic" stream within Anglicanism as well as its ecumenical partnerships with the Evangelical Lutheran, American Baptist and Roman Catholic traditions.

2. A significant accomplishment has been the reestablishment of an Ohio campus through an extension site at Trinity Lutheran Seminary in Columbus. In a short period of time the student body has equaled that of the Rochester site. This is a return to the original seminary home, only now in tandem with the Evangelical Lutheran Church, with whom we are moving toward full communion. Bexley Hall has also developed, with assistance from a grant from the Lilly foundation, the Bexley Institute for ministry studies based in Rochester. This program supports diocesan education programs for a variety of local ministries, both lay and ordained, in New York and West Virginia. Through the efforts of its dean, Bexley Hall is also involved in the administration of the American branch of "Affirming Catholicism," an international organization devoted to promoting Scripture, Reason, and Catholic Tradition in the modern world.

3. The seminary continues to develop its endowment, expand its alumni/ae base, and recruit students for both sites. Increases in enrollment and maintaining two campuses have placed pressure on resources. Endowment growth is the immediate priority.

Church Divinity School of the Pacific

1. The Church Divinity School of the Pacific (CDSP) is located in Berkeley and is the only freestanding residential Episcopal seminary west of the Rocky Mountains. The school offers degree and certificate programs for those preparing for both ordained and lay ministries as well as a Doctor of Ministry degree for those who have already earned the M.Div. or its equivalent. CDSP is an integral part of the Graduate Theological Union, an interfaith consortium of nine seminaries and several study centers where cross registration for all programs and doctoral instruction occurs. The multicultural character of the West influences the seminary and its instructional programs greatly. The diversity of the church, its ministry and its mission in this part of the world is also a distinctive shaping factor for the school.

2. In the past triennium CDSP has continued to strengthen its special focus on worship leadership and liturgical instruction. The diversity (international students, non-Western dioceses, race, age, etc.) of the student body has increased. The Center of Anglican Learning and Life has expanded its on-line education as well as facilitating many programmatic partnerships with dioceses and other institutions. The School for Deacons, serving the dioceses of California, Northern California, and El Camino Real has moved onto the CDSP campus, offering weekend programs; and Cornerstone has moved its central office to the center of the Graduate Theological Union campus.

3. The seminary is involved in a major building project, which will eventually result in a new chapel and a modern residential center for short-term students and visitors. Major fund raising is a prerequisite for this project. The faculty has recently revised the curriculum for the M.Div. program. Special attention to the educational outcomes and goals of all our degrees and certificates is an all-important component for our future teaching. Finally, CDSP must always remain open to new ways to be partners with our ecumenical sister schools in the Graduate Theological Union as well as church, schools, and dioceses throughout the Anglican Communion.

Episcopal Divinity School

1. Episcopal Divinity School (EDS) has a curriculum that allows adult learners to take responsibility for their educational process. Working in consultation with faculty and choosing from the offerings of some 200 faculty through the Boston Theological Institute, students focus their learning in a much more effective manner than the usual "hopscotch" form of curriculum. Consequently, EDS graduates always rank at the top in the General Ordination Examinations of the Episcopal Church. EDS also has the most multi-cultural faculty in the church and the most balanced between male and female professors. Finally,

EDS is recognized as one of the outstanding centers for spiritual formation within the Boston theological consortium.

2. In the last three years EDS has completed a long-range plan to continue to grow the seminary in three major areas: technology, environmental action and spirituality. EDS learning technologies are now interfaced with Weston Jesuit School of Theology through our combined Library, placing EDS-Weston on the cutting edge of change in educational-informational-research capabilities. EDS has been recognized as one of the leaders in environmental initiatives and will continue to become a "green seminary." Worship and prayer life at the seminary continues to thrive with many new services arising spontaneously from the student community. EDS was selected by the Presiding Bishop to work with the House of Bishops in a series of learning dialogues around issues of reconciliation; EDS faculty became key resource persons for the HOB and helped the church respond to the crisis after 9/11. On the academic front, four new certificate programs for lay leadership development have been successfully launched. The shift has been made to late afternoon and evening classes to make education more accessible to a wider range of students. As a recipient of a Lilly Grant in excess of $1 million, EDS will be expanding our direct support to local congregational development, especially in areas neglected or underserved.

3. In the coming three years, EDS will concentrate on expanding our network of partnerships, especially with alumni/ae, local parishes and dioceses. With a strong priority on spiritual formation, EDS will focus on its three-fold emphasis on justice, compassion and reconciliation. Technologies at EDS will grow and more experimental forms of learning will be tested in our classrooms. In three years, the greenhouse gas emissions of the school will be significantly reduced as the seminary becomes a fully integrated ecological system.

Episcopal Theological Seminary of the Southwest

1. Equipping church leaders to relate Christ's gospel to culture was prominent in the vision of John Hines, then bishop of Texas and later presiding bishop, in founding the Episcopal Theological Seminary of the Southwest (ETSS) in 1952. Today the many and diverse cultures of the USA and the global community participate in the gospel-culture dialogue that is central at ETSS, located in Austin, Texas. How is Christ being revealed afresh through the gospel experience of diverse peoples? How can people historically oppressed and pushed to the margins be invited in to transform the church? These kinds of questions shape all studies at ETSS, whether in Bible or mission, liturgy or history, ministry or ethics, theology or history. Ministry with the Hispanic community, now the largest minority in the USA, is important in a student's course work and experience. First-year students experience a January immersion in Hispanic culture. Relationship with a seminary of Iglésia Anglicana de México is being explored. Union Téologica Hispana—a joint project of ETSS, the Lutheran Seminary Program in the Southwest (located at ETSS), and Austin Presbyterian Seminary—is developing Spanish-language theological education through the three institutions. The Province VII Center of Hispanic Ministries is located at ETSS, as are the Archives of the Episcopal Church, an important resource for exploring the church's mission.

2. Over the past three years, ETSS has implemented a new curriculum that integrates spiritual formation, academic disciplines, and ministry in a diverse world. Symposium helps students to think theologically about a major dimension of human social experience through year-long reflection in small groups; annual topics have included work, health, and art; ecology is next. With students from all parts of the country, enrollment is at an all-time high in our three degree programs: Master of Divinity, Master of Arts in Pastoral Ministry, and Master of Arts in Religion. The Very Rev'd Dr. Durstan McDonald retired as dean and president in May 2002 after 18 years of distinguished leadership and is now dean emeritus. The Very Rev'd Dr. Titus Presler, a mission scholar and parish priest with wide international experience, came as the new dean and president in June 2002. He cites spirituality, leadership and mission as three emphases in the formation we offer. A major capital campaign for endowment and facilities expansion exceeded its goal, and work on new classrooms and faculty offices began in April 2003.

3. "Embracing Difference" is the principal theme ETSS has chosen for the coming years as part of its re-accreditation process. That vision calls us to diversify our faculty, student body, and staff in racial, ethnic and linguistic make-up. As we equip leaders to participate in God's mission in the world, we must expand

our offerings in world religions, processes of globalization, and mission studies. The economy's downturn has heightened the need to examine our priorities and increase endowment. As we embark on facilities renovation and expansion, we will also be raising funds for an innovative new library-learning center. Distance learning through the internet was inaugurated in 2002 and will be expanded so that the seminary can better serve parts of the country and the world that do not have resources to support residential seminary education.

General Theological Seminary

1. "The General Theological Seminary is an Episcopal institution called to educate and form leaders for the church in a changing world." This sentence serves as General Seminary's (GTS) mission statement and emphasizes two important elements of life at GTS: education and formation. A seminary is different from a secular university school of religion. We do not seek so much to study religion as we do to live our faith. We pursue academic excellence as a means of personal growth, and at the same time we pursue personal transformation through our worship and interaction within the community of faith. Education is more than learning about God; it includes growing in our relationship with God, a maturing that involves the transformation of our minds and spirits so that our actions become an icon of Christ's love. Formation involves the integration of spiritual practice and academic study in order to equip leaders who are mature and collaborative, leaders who are responsible both to the community that has raised them up and to the wider community in which they live and serve.

2. The last three years have been a time of tremendous change at GTS. Our enrollment has increased in each of those years; total Masters of Divinity enrollment is 120, almost twice that in 1999. Continuing the trend of younger postulants, the average age of the class of 2005 is 35, and 11 seminarians are under the age of 30. The Center for Christian Spirituality rejuvenated its program and course offerings under the leadership of the Rev. Dr. Jonathan Linman. The Center offers three opportunities to complete a Masters of Sacred Theology degree: the 'Summers at General', 'January at General', and 'Thursdays at General' programs. Another major initiative is the *Programa Hispano/Latino de Teología Y Pastoral*, an alternate track to the M.Div. degree conducted in Spanish to train much-needed Hispanic clergy for the Episcopal Church. GTS has welcomed two new faculty members in addition to Dr. Linman: the Rev. Dr. James Farwell, Assistant Professor of Liturgics, and the Rev. Dr. Robert Owens, Professor of Old Testament. GTS has completed the first phase of a major stabilization of our physical plant, re-roofing and re-pointing four of the seminary's landmark buildings. GTS also commissioned several feasibility studies to explore creative ways of realizing the potential latent in the buildings and grounds of the Close.

3. General Seminary strives to meet the educational needs of the church in a world that is changing dramatically. Our M.Div. program provides excellent training for ordination; we plan to build programs that provide the same excellence for laypersons, for those whose first language is Spanish, and for commuting and nontraditional students. We intend to expand our summer course offerings and become a year-round leader in conferences and special events for the Anglican Communion. We wish to enhance our profile in New York City and to become a true center for urban ministry. To achieve these goals, we need facilities for the 21st century. A capital campaign is now underway to increase our endowment, provide funds to develop an education center, equip our classrooms with leading-edge technology, and modernize and enhance our library. Over the next three years, we will need the leadership and support of the whole church as we recreate our instructional facilities for the new century.

Nashotah House

1. Founded in 1842 as a mission to the American frontier, Nashotah House's mission today is the formation of men and women for ministries of congregational leadership, pastoral care, missions and evangelism, and church growth. Our distinct emphases are:
   - A disciplined spiritual life centered in the Anglican heritage of daily prayer, corporate worship, and the sacraments.
   - Academic discipline in the spirit of classical theological study.
   - Preparation for practical ministry as congregational leaders.
   - Active attention to contemporary social concerns in light of the Gospel.

- Support for every student and family member in the personal challenges of vocational preparation.
- Continuing education for former students and others who engage in Christian ministry.
- Cultivation of a community which embraces all members in God's love.

2. Our magnificent, contemplative setting on a 411-acre wooded lake-front campus, our attractive, modern townhouses for married students and families, and our commitment to strong community life provide an excellent environment for preparation for parish ministry. Our major accomplishments during the last three years include:
   - Transition to a new dean and administration.
   - Final ATS approval of our 2-year Master of Theological Studies (MTS) program.
   - Admission for 2002-2003 of our largest incoming class since 1986.
   - Establishment of one-week intensive January and June terms.
   - Modernization of our classroom facilities.

3. Our major goals for the next three years are:
   - To grow our enrollment through outreach to a broader cross-section of dioceses.
   - To increase our enrollment of women and minority students.
   - To build a larger base of individual and parish contributors.
   - Campus renovation.

The Protestant Episcopal Theological Seminary in Virginia

1. The Virginia Theological Seminary (VTS) is located on a spacious campus in Alexandria, just a few miles from downtown Washington, D.C. The Seminary is part of a consortium of theological schools in the greater Washington area, which includes Roman Catholic, Methodist, Lutheran, Presbyterian, and inter-denominational seminaries. The Seminary offers three Master's degrees, the Doctor of Ministry degree, and diplomas in Anglican Studies and theology. Each year our community includes between eight and twelve students from other schools who are in full-time residence on our campus. Students and faculty worship together each weekday morning and have lunch in the Refectory with staff members and with individuals and groups visiting the campus.

2. Eight new faculty members joined our faculty over the past three years, as well as a new Vice President for Institutional Advancement. The M.Div. and M.T.S. curricula were significantly revised to provide greater flexibility while maintaining a core curriculum. A new January term has provided opportunities for intensive, short courses and participation in cross-cultural immersion experiences and/or mission trips to Africa, Asia, and Latin America. The Seminary continues to welcome civic groups, local parishes, national church committees, and international consultations to our campus. In 2001 the former Continuing Education Center was renovated and converted to a dormitory named for former faculty member Charles Price. Sparrow Hall was also renovated to provide offices, classrooms, and meetings spaces for our Lifetime Theological Education and D.Min. programs and staff. New programs have been developed through our Center for LTE, increasing the number of continuing education opportunities for clergy and laity. Grants from the Lilly Endowment have enabled the Seminary to expand the use of technology in classroom teaching and learning, and to launch a new program to encourage pastoral excellence in the first three years of ordained ministry.

3. Looking ahead, we anticipate a significant renovation of Meade Hall, and expanded Library facilities. Additional scholarship funds will be sought for international students and for making cross-cultural opportunities available for all students and faculty. Consultations with the National Association of Episcopal Schools are underway to develop a new track within our D.Min. degree for those who work in school ministries. In conjunction with the Washington Theological Consortium, plans are underway for a D.Min. in Communications and Homiletics.

School of Theology, University of the South

1. Sewanee tries to portray a rich, centrist theology, not a watered-down compromise but an articulate comprehensiveness. We maintain an extensive program in homiletics and stress an awareness of worldwide Anglican Christianity (missiology, persecution, theological diversity). We have an extensive liturgical life in our new chapel.

2. When one thinks of Sewanee, one almost always thinks of the EFM (Education for Ministry) program. A full theological education, primarily for laity, which attracts almost 10,000 per year worldwide. We are focusing on preparing for the future by appointing some of the most talented young faculty members in the Church. We completed our Chapel and are developing a master plan for expansion. We have almost doubled in size and had 12 surplus budgets.

3. A certain amount of bricks and mortar are needed as we remodel a beautiful old building for the School of Theology use. Development of a Junior Fellows post-doctoral program. Continued expansion of our foreign mission efforts, our continuing education efforts, etc. We face with confidence both an accreditation process and a capital campaign. Trying to alleviate the clergy shortage and the need for lay religious/spiritual education. Addressing the issues of funding for seminary education and health insurance for seminarians.

Seabury-Western Theological Seminary

1. Seabury-Western Theological Seminary's mission is to "develop empowered and empowering leaders for Christ's Church and God's Mission" in the world. We believe that theological education and leadership development must be joined together. To that end a new curriculum has been introduced that unites tradition and theological inquiry with a focus on mission, context, congregational vitality, and leadership. Seabury is pioneering new approaches to the formation of leaders while providing a solid foundation of prayer, learning, and community life. Seabury's Evanston/Chicago location brings great benefits including access to the library and learning resources of 11 seminaries and our nearest neighbor Northwestern University. The metropolitan environment is a learning laboratory for exciting ministry. The Seabury Institute provides unparalleled learning in congregational development to laity and clergy throughout North America. There is a growing diversity in the faculty and student body.

2. Seabury has developed a new, pioneering curriculum. The student body has doubled. The faculty and student body reflect a much greater ethnic and racial diversity than was previously found. A major building project has been completed. Faculty and Administrators have published and exercised leadership in the wider Church. Cutting edge research on the characteristics of effective clergy has been undertaken in the "Toward a Higher Quality of Christian Ministry" project. College age students have been able to experience seminary life through the "Chicago Collegiate Seminarians" program. The Seabury Institute has grown and operates two extension sites, in Maryland and Arizona. Special programs have been undertaken for parish nurses, deacons, heads of Episcopal Schools, and laity. Seabury has strengthened relations with Northwestern University and other partners and is a leader in technology. Seabury's Board of Trustees continues to gain strength and leadership.

3. Seabury's major need is the continuing development of its distinct mission. To do this we must develop human and financial resources. Scholarship resources are limited requiring that we work with partners to develop church-wide financial support for seminarians. Seabury also needs to develop capital and foundation support for its expanding ministry. Some facilities renovation needs to be undertaken. The institution needs to partner with others in drawing younger candidates to seminary and leadership in the Church. Seabury will continue to foster its imaginative curriculum learning experience, research and service to the mission of the Church. It needs to develop partnerships for these endeavors inside and outside the Episcopal Church.

Trinity Episcopal School for Ministry

1. Trinity Episcopal School for Ministry, the youngest of the Church's eleven seminaries, was founded 25 years ago in order to lay a solid biblical, theological and pastoral foundation beneath the renewal movements that were touching the life of the Church at that time. It continues to provide these emphases with a full year of required Greek, a scholarly and conservative (though not fundamentalist) approach to Scripture, an academically rigorous program with 90 credit hours required for an M.Div., extensive field ministry experience, and a comprehensive approach to Anglicanism that includes the evangelical as well as traditionalist and modernist aspects of our heritage. Since our founding we have added a strong missionary dimension, linking us with those fast-growing parts of our Communion that embrace evangelism and mission as the lifeblood of the church. A full exposure to the theory and practice of

mission, as well as the practice of evangelism, is required of all M.Div. students. Every three years we endeavor to take all students and faculty to the 5-day New Wineskins for Global Missions conference in North Carolina. We will have had Canon Michael Green, the premier evangelist in the Anglican Communion, in residence for three weeks in 2002 and 2003.

2. Trinity has maintained a consistent residential population over the past three years, while expanding its delivery of ministerial training through Interterms (January, June and August), extension sites where credit courses are offered, and online courses. This has extended our reach to many more students than can live in the immediate area of the seminary. We have jointly created an Anglican/Episcopal Sunday School curriculum with David C. Cook that is now used in 800 churches. We began a Doctor of Ministry program four years ago that now includes nearly 75 students. While we have emphasized program and ministry, we have also completed the construction of a new technologically sophisticated library/academic building which was dedicated at our Silver Anniversary this past May by The Archbishop of Canterbury, Dr. George L. Carey. We have tried not to neglect our immediate area. Students have started a "Trinity Loves Ambridge" program that reaches out to the community, and have also begun a thriving Young Life Club at the local high school. A local group of African Americans use our library/academic facility weekly in a degree completion program from a nearby college.

3. Among our major needs are finances. While Trinity successfully completed a Capital Campaign that has yielded significant funds for student scholarships and for reaching out to the Two-Thirds World, we remain radically dependent upon the giving of individuals and churches to raise the $1.8 million needed to supplement other income and reach our annual budget. This is always a matter for prayer and hard work, though we have seen God's faithfulness over the years in remarkable ways. We would like to see more bishops send postulants to Trinity, and overcome the tendency of some to stereotype those expressions of Anglicanism to which we are drawn. However, we rejoice that nearly all graduates are ordained and find useful positions in the Church. We would like to endow some faculty salaries, do active recruitment among colleges and parishes, strengthen the younger, unmarried portion of our student body, continue to expand our campus with the acquisition of some large, unsightly derelict buildings to the rear, renovate our chapel, and find new ways to support our alumni who are experiencing stress in their service of God.

Minority Report on the Proposed Title III Revisions

This Minority Report focuses on the proposed revisions to the Title III Ministry Canons. The Standing Commission on Ministry Development (SCMD) has taken seriously its charge from General Convention to look at these Canons in great detail, and to present revisions where necessary. Commissioners have worked very hard on this charge the last three years, and I commend their dedication and persistence.

I feel that some positive things have come out of this revision process. There has been an honest attempt to simplify the existing Canons, to make them clearer and more understandable, and to acknowledge that a wide variety of procedures and practices do exist, throughout the dioceses of our Church, in identifying and discerning calls to ministry and in laying out tracts for ordination. Also, the revisions spell out, in greater and clearer detail, the important ministry of all baptized persons in the work of the Church, and continuing education is listed as a requirement for the laity and the clergy. Also, the need for more serious training for Commissions on Ministry and Standing Committees is found in these revisions, as is the emphasis on the more active and involved role which a parish or other faith community can and should have in discerning, identifying, and calling forth persons for specific lay ministries and for ordination. These things are all generally positive and good.

However, I do have some serious concerns about several specific areas and some recurring themes which are a part of these proposed revisions. I feel there is a general move to dismantle the traditional, centuries-old, patriarchal view of the priesthood which is a hallmark of the one, holy, catholic, apostolic Church, and to replace it with a "total ministry concept" which, a generation or so down the road could become mandatory in all dioceses throughout our Church. We have seen this same thing happen with regard to women's ordination, which at first was offered as a permissive Canon, and later was declared mandatory in every diocese.

There also seems to be a general and gradual blurring of the lines between the ministry of the clergy and that of the laity. This could well result in the resolution to have lay presidency at the Eucharist in just a few years. If carried to its extreme in years to come, one might well even ask if we needed the ministry of priests and bishops.

Also, in the proposed Canon 5, the term, "lay" has been dropped from the categories of licensed ministries; i.e., we now have simply "Preacher, Eucharistic Minister and Eucharistic Visitor" (compare with Title III, Canon 3 in the existing Canons). Also, we no longer have a Lay Reader, but rather a "Worship Leader." And note that a Lay Eucharistic Minister is no longer "a person licensed to this extra-ordinary ministry, who administers the elements at any celebration of the Holy Eucharist in the absence of a sufficient number of Priests or Deacons assisting the celebrant," as we have it laid out in the current Canons. All this tends to make "normal" that which has heretofore been listed as an "extra-ordinary" ministry, and to give more duties and privileges to lay persons which were formerly reserved for priests. I note here that I am one hundred percent **for** the concept of very active, involved, committed lay ministry, but **not** for the move to blur the lines between the ministry of the laity and that of the clergy.

And finally, I must note here that I am against the new proposed Canon 1, Sec.2, (which is also echoed in Canon 10, Sec. 5). Accordingly to this Canon, no Bishop, Standing Committee, Commission on Ministry, Rector, or Vestry could deny the exercise of any ministry, lay or ordained, to a person, either heterosexual or homosexual, whose open, public lifestyle might be immoral and contrary to Scripture, or to someone who might have severe mental or psychological disabilities or impediments. There are some cases where the godly, pastoral duty of Priests, Vestries, Bishops, Standing Committees, and Commissions on Ministry is to say "no" up front to persons who simply should not be holding leadership positions in the Church or entering a process toward licensing or ordination. To allow such persons to enter or proceed upon such a pathway, or to exercise public ministries, often of leadership, is neither kind nor loving to them or to the Church. As a Commission member I voted against the new proposed Canon 1, Sec. 2 as well as against other Canons which touch upon the general areas which I have listed above. The odds at stake here are serious and important, and for these reasons, I wish to register this Minority Report.

Respectfully submitted,
Judy Mayo
Standing Commission on Ministry Development Member

STANDING COMMISSION ON NATIONAL CONCERNS
www.episcopalchurch.org/gc/ccab/scnc/default.html

Membership

Ms. Deborah J. Stokes, *Chair*	Southern Ohio, 2003
The Rev. Dr. Eugene C. McDowell, *Vice Chair*	Western North Carolina, 2006
Ms. Pamela B. Chapman, *Secretary*	Western Michigan, 2003
Mrs. Judith Amber	Nebraska, 2003
The Rev. Canon Michael L. Barlowe	California, 2006
Dr. Cynthia B. Cohen	Washington, 2003
Mrs. Lillian Davis-Wilson	Western New York, 2006
Mrs. Georgette Forney	Pittsburgh, 2006
The Venerable Michael S. Kendall	New York, 2003
Sen. Marge Kilkelly	Maine, 2006
The Rt. Rev. John B. Lipscomb	Southwest Florida, 2003
Mrs. Karen O. Patterson	Southwest Florida, 2006
The Rt. Rev. M. Thomas Shaw, III	Massachusetts, 2006
The Rev. Carol Sims	Montana, 2003
The Rev. Dr. Richard L. Tolliver	Chicago, 2006
The Rev. Emery Washington, Sr.	Missouri, 2003
The Hon. James E. Bradberry	*Executive Council Liaison*

COMMISSION REPRESENTATIVES AT GENERAL CONVENTION
Bishop John B. Lipscomb and Deputy Deborah J. Stokes are authorized to receive non-substantive amendments to this report.

Introduction

The Standing Commission on National Concern's (SCNC) charge in Canon I.1.2(n)(8) is "to identify, study and consider general policies, priorities and concerns about the theological, ethical and pastoral issues and strategies as to the ministries of this Church serving Christ, to strive for justice and peace among all peoples through the proclamation of the Gospel and to develop and recommend to the General Convention comprehensive and coordinated policies and strategies applicable to the same."

SCNC met five times during the triennium to address its charge. We reviewed 2000 General Convention actions related to it, continued work in the areas of health care and the theology of work that was carried from the previous triennium, and devoted the balance of our efforts to the health needs of children, substance abuse among clergy and laity, the prison and criminal justice systems, "at risk" youth, racial profiling, a living wage, and issues of violence and war. Health care for children was the area with the greatest need.

This report comes from a diverse group of people who found unity in faith, love, and concern for others. In our hearts, we sought justice, peace, and respect for every human being in light of the Gospel. We trust this goal is evident in this report and the accompanying resolutions.

The Church and Children's Health

The Gospel of Matthew reminds us that the Episcopal Church needs to be an advocate for children and for their parents as they struggle to meet children's needs in a world whose powerful social and economic forces can overwhelm a family (Mt. 2:18). The care and treatment of children is a measure of faith.

A. Children Who Need Access to Medical Care and Adequate Nutrition

Children are our greatest resource. Yet currently 16% of children in the United States live in poverty and 40% of children less than six years of age (9 million children) live in homes with incomes less than 200% of poverty level. Moreover, nearly 11 million children lack basic health care insurance, even though nine out of ten of them live in families where at least one parent works and more than half live in families where both work.

Many children are uninsured because their parents cannot afford the rising costs of health insurance. Many parents who work part-time or on a contract basis do not receive health insurance. Some small businesses health care insurance premiums include high deductibles to minimize the cost, which threatens to put them out of business. Out-of-pocket expenses may deter parents from obtaining health insurance for their families.

Children who lack basic health care and adequate nutrition need assistance from our society and the Church. The Church and its dioceses and congregations can assist several ways.

1. **Under-enrollment in Medicaid, in the State Children's Health Insurance Program (SCHIP), and in the Special Supplemental Nutrition Program for Women, Infants, and Children (WIC)**

The federal government has funded two programs designed to provide health care for children who are without it: Medicaid and the State Children's Health Insurance Program (SCHIP).

Medicaid is a program administered by states that provides health care coverage to children in families with low incomes, including the working poor. The State Children's Health Insurance (SCHIP) assists children up to the age of nineteen in families with incomes too high for Medicaid but too low to purchase health care insurance. Currently, 38 states and the District of Columbia have developed SCHIP programs.

In addition, the federal Special Supplemental Nutrition Program for Women, Infants, and Children (WIC) provides short-term intervention for the nutritional needs of lower-income infants, children up to the age of five, and pregnant women. For every dollar invested in WIC, over three dollars is saved in Medicaid health costs for pregnant mothers and their infants.

Five million children who are eligible for Medicaid or SCHIP are not enrolled. The WIC program has also been under-enrolled. Reasons these programs are not used, include lack of awareness, lack of trust in those administering them, and perceived or real barriers to service.

2. **How Episcopal Church dioceses can help increase SCHIP and WIC enrollment**

Many states provide grants helping local groups reach out to eligible parents and improve enrollment in Medicaid, SCHIP, and WIC. Religious organizations are eligible for these grants. Dioceses and congregations can encourage parents to register by:
- Making Medicaid, SCHIP, and WIC enrollment part of their outreach, using materials from Ministries with Young People Office at the Episcopal Church Center, among others.
- Partnering with other local organizations involved in outreach to eligible families.
- Planning health activities for a Children's Day.
- Working with state and local agency service providers to coordinate outreach activities.
- Providing volunteers for Medicaid, SCHIP, and WIC local agency service providers, e.g., Church WIC.

B. The Mental Health Needs of Children

A report by the National Council on Disability, a 15-member independent federal panel, found that children who get caught in the public mental health system are under-served and have a much higher dependence on the adult system later in life. A National Alliance for the Mentally Ill survey of parents of children with serious emotional disturbance found that nearly one fourth had been advised to give up custody to ensure that their children would receive mental health services. One in five very reluctantly did so for the child's sake.

The Episcopal Church can respond by:
- Urging federal and state legislators to provide adequate mental health care that enables children to remain within the family unit.
- Advocating that mental health systems develop the expertise to deliver not just medication and counseling to the children who need it, but housing and transportation as well.
- Encouraging licensed therapists in congregations to offer *pro bono* or affordable therapy to under-served children.

- Encouraging congregations to assist financially with the high cost of psychotropic medications for children in need of these.

C. The Impact of Trauma and Violence on Children

Many children in this country are victims of violence -- physical, mental, or emotional -- which traumatizes, slows, or inhibits healthy development. The Children's Bureau of the U. S. Department of Human Services reported in 2000, three million referrals of approximately five million children were made to Child Protective Service agencies in the USA. Whether a child witnesses violence or experiences it personally, we are called to help prevent any further harm to the child. Clergy and congregations can assist by knowing the local, state, and federal resources for children who are subjected to trauma and violence. The Episcopal Church, clergy and lay, has a responsibility to protect children where they are in danger of physical or mental abuse.

D. Palliative Care for Dying Children

About 28,000 children die every year from chronic illnesses such as cancer, heart disease, congenital anomalies, and degenerative disorders. Fewer than 10% of dying children receive hospice care, according to the National Hospice and Palliative Care Organizations. A 2001 report of the Institute of Medicine on end-of-life cancer care declared that dying children should receive better relief of their pain and suffering, their doctors need more education, and their families need better support services. The American Academy of Pediatrics called for regulatory changes in Medicaid, Medicare, and private health plans to improve access to end-of-life care for children.

Children nearing the end of life who are in pain should receive narcotic levels that are carefully monitored as well as other forms of palliative care that ease difficulties they may have with swallowing, nausea, and vomiting. Families need support as they grapple with losing a child whose life had previously seemed to stretch out far into the future.

Resolution A122 Improving Health Care for Children

1   *Resolved,* the House of _____ concurring, That the 74th General Convention of the Episcopal Church
2   encourage dioceses and congregations to establish programs to assist parents to apply for services for
3   eligible children offered by Medicaid, the State Children's Health Insurance Program (SCHIP), and the
4   Special Supplemental Nutrition Program for Women, Infants, and Children (WIC); and be it further
5   *Resolved,* That the Office of Government Relations of the Episcopal Church work with the Office of the
6   Secretary of Health and Human Services and the Office of the Secretary of Agriculture, the White House,
7   and Congress to ensure that these programs are adequately funded to meet the needs of the participants
8   they serve; and be it further
9   *Resolved,* That the Office of Government Relations urge the Office of the Secretary of Health and Human
10   Services, the White House, the United States Congress and state legislatures to provide more adequate
11   access to mental health services for children in a form that does not require the separation of children from
12   their families; and be it further
13   *Resolved,* That the Episcopal Church encourage congregations to become educated about and involved in
14   the prevention of violence and maltreatment perpetrated upon children; and be it further
15   *Resolved,* That the Office of Government Relations of the Episcopal Church request the Office of the
16   Secretary of Health and Human Services to make regulatory changes in Medicare and Medicaid health
17   plans to enable terminally ill children to receive more adequate palliative care and pain relief services and
18   their families to receive appropriate supportive services.

EXPLANATION

The Episcopal Church, as a caring Christian community, has a call to help parents find resources to meet the health needs of their children, including basic medical care, nutritional supplementation, mental health care, and palliative care for children who are terminally ill. The church can carry out this responsibility by encouraging dioceses and congregations to assist families with children who are eligible for Medicaid, the State Children's Health Insurance Program (SCHIP), or the Special Supplemental Nutrition Program for Women, Infants, and Children (WIC) to enroll in these programs.

The Church can also urge the Congress to pass a mental health treatment act that mandates better coverage for children who need mental health care and that does not require parents to give up their children in order to receive such care. Children enduring physical and/or mental abuse are in urgent need of attention by congregations that can alert proper local, state, or federal authorities to their plight. Finally, the Church can assist children who are dying by urging the Secretary of Health and Human Services to modify Medicare and Medicaid regulations in order to provide greater medical and social support for children who are terminally ill and also for their families.

Dependence on Alcohol and/or Drugs

Alcohol and/or drug dependency is a life-threatening disease that affects millions of Americans and their families. It is a serious public health problem today. Ten to fifteen per cent of drinkers become alcoholics and about 7.5 percent of Americans are dependent on drugs. The social costs of drug and alcohol dependence have been estimated at $277 billion. This includes lost productivity, accident-related costs, damaged health, and law enforcement expenses. (National Drug Control Strategy. Washington, D.C. Office of National Drug Control Policy, 1999, pg. 14-15.) An Episcopal bishop stated, "The devastation of substance abuse, particularly alcoholism, is perhaps the single most pressing problem in the life of congregations today."

Almost twenty years ago General Convention reaffirmed the 1979 General Convention call to address alcohol and drug dependency (*GC Resolution 1985-A083*). Since then new information and more effective treatment for these diseases have been developed and issues related to the care of affected clergy have arisen. The Church needs to take these advances into account today to help restore lost lives, families, and ministries.

A. Developing Constructive Ways of Responding to Alcoholism and Drug Dependency

Dependence on alcohol or drugs is marked by signs such as inability to control the frequency or amount of alcohol or drugs used, mood swings, slurred speech, blackouts, memory loss, and personality changes. Yet it is a treatable condition. Affected individuals often are in denial and unable to comprehend the serious threat alcohol or drugs present to their health. Friends and colleagues may also deny that they should take action to assist. Appropriate care is essential and may be life-saving for those who are dependent on alcohol or drugs.

An intervention may be necessary and these are steps for carrying out an intervention and obtaining treatment for the affected person:

- Make confidential inquiries of the spouse or close friend about whether there is a problem of alcohol or drug dependency.
- Obtain information about alcohol and drug dependency from an addiction counselor, physician, clergyperson, someone in recovery, and church and national organizations devoted to this problem, such as Recovery Ministries of the Episcopal Church, Recovering Addicted Clergy Association, Alcoholics Anonymous, and National Council on Alcoholism and Drug Dependence.
- Consider other reasons for the symptoms.
- Plan an intervention with the assistance of a qualified professional addiction counselor.
- Plan ahead for treatment in a specific program after the intervention.
- Address the person involved and persuade him or her to enter into treatment.
- Care for that person after the intervention and treatment.

B. Special Issues Relevant to Clergy and Staff of the Episcopal Church

The Episcopal Church has a responsibility to address circumstances in which clergy and church staff appear to be dependent on alcohol or drugs. A major problem is that those identified as alcohol or drug dependent often risk losing their positions without access to treatment. They are caught between two choices: reporting themselves and possibly losing their jobs or else remaining at their posts and harming themselves and those around them.

To remedy this situation, several barriers to treatment that clergy and church staff currently face should be addressed. These include:

1. Few clergy and employee assistance programs exist. Committees within each diocese of the Episcopal Church are needed to help clergy and church staff to recognize alcohol and drug dependence and to assist them to enter treatment. Yet many dioceses have no such committees.

2. Resources for assistance and education are inadequately used including those from Recovery Ministries of the Episcopal Church and the Recovering Addicted Clergy Association. These organizations can provide information and education.

3. Health care insurance coverage for clergy and church staff is inadequate. There is a pressing need for adequate insurance coverage for those who are dependent on alcohol or drugs. Such insurance should include inpatient or outpatient treatment by a certified addiction counselor and follow-up care.

C. Forming a Diocesan Alcoholism and Drug Dependency Committee

Diocesan committees are needed to address situations in which clergy and church staff are thought to be dependent on alcohol or drugs and, when requested, to assist laypersons believed to be dependent on such substances. One possible model for a committee would:

- Include clergy and laity on the committee and, when possible, those recovering from alcohol or drug dependency.
- Be trained by a qualified professional addiction counselor about the disease of addiction and about carrying out interventions for those who are alcohol or drug dependent.
- Provide educational programs to congregations on the nature, prevention and treatment of alcohol and drug dependency, and pastoral care for those who are substance dependent and their families.
- Develop a diocesan written policy on treatment and appropriate pastoral responses to alcohol and drug dependency among clergy and church staff. This policy would include intervention procedures, entry into treatment, post-treatment monitoring, and future employment.
- Be available for consultation about possible substance dependency in a clergy person, church staff member, or a layperson with symptoms of concern.
- Arrange for interventions, with the assistance of a professional addiction counselor, for clergy persons or church staff who exhibit signs and symptoms of addiction and, when appropriate, for laypersons with symptoms of concern.
- Whenever possible give assurance to alcohol or drug dependent clergy and church staff, that upon completion of a recognized treatment regimen and entry into a monitoring program they will be able to return in a capacity identical or similar to that before diagnosis and treatment.
- Inform those clergy or church staff diagnosed as alcohol or drug dependent by a qualified professional addiction counselor but refusing to undergo treatment, that their position is not protected and that poor job performance due to alcohol or drug dependency will provide grounds for removal with cause.

The costs of not funding diocesan programs to address alcohol and drug dependence among clergy, church staff, and laypersons include personal costs, ecclesiastical and pastoral costs, financial costs and legal costs.

Resolution A123 Diocesan Alcohol and Drug Dependency Policies

1 *Resolved,* the House of _____ concurring, That this 74th General Convention call on all dioceses to
2 establish Diocesan Committees on Alcoholism and Drug Dependency to provide educational programs for
3 clergy, church staff, and congregations that take account of recent advances in treatment of alcohol and
4 drug dependency, and that such committees address problems related to alcohol or drug dependency in
5 clergy, church staff, and, when requested, laypersons, and be it further
6 *Resolved,* That dioceses make strong efforts to develop policies concerning treatment and future
7 employment for diocesan clergy and church staff who are dependent on alcohol or drugs, and be it further
8 *Resolved,* That dioceses make strong efforts to ensure that health care insurance for diocesan clergy and
9 church staff includes coverage for mental health and addiction, particularly inpatient treatment for
10 dependency on alcohol or drugs.

EXPLANATION

Alcohol or drug dependency is a treatable disease that should be addressed both medically and pastorally. Christians seek transformation and redemption for those who are addicted, not stigmatization and abandonment. The Episcopal Church needs to affirm that care for those who are dependent on alcohol or drugs should be directed toward rehabilitation rather than punishment, treatment rather than condemnation. Moreover, it should urge its members to address outright the problems of those who are alcohol or drug dependent, rather than deny or ignore them, as this disease can be life-threatening and life-destroying.

The General Convention of 1985 reaffirmed the call of the General Convention of 1979 to all dioceses to appoint a Diocesan Committee on Alcoholism and Drug Dependency to develop a diocesan policy for educational and treatment programs regarding alcohol and drug dependency. However, many dioceses have no such committees. Further, new information and more effective treatment programs have been developed for these diseases since then that need to be taken into account. Special questions have arisen regarding the treatment, insurance coverage, and future employment of clergy and church staff who are dependent on alcohol and/or drugs. Therefore, an updated set of recommendations regarding the treatment of those who are considered to be dependent on alcohol and/or drugs, particularly of clergy and church staff, is needed and is provided in this resolution.

RESTORING THE STANDING COMMISSION ON HEALTH AND A STAFF POSITION IN HEALTH CARE TO THE CHURCH

The Episcopal Church has long been a strong voice calling for a health care system in which those who need health care and healing can receive adequate appropriate treatment. This is in keeping with the mission of the early Church, which established ways to address the spiritual and the physical needs of the sick and dying.

In recent times, the Episcopal Church has had a Standing Commission on Health (SCH) and a staff person at the Episcopal Church Center (ECC) to carry on the Christian moral vision of seeking a decent health care system for those who are ill and dying. Currently, neither a SCH or a staff officer exist. Although the Suffragan Bishop for Chaplaincies (former title was Bishop for the Armed Services, Healthcare, and Prison Ministries) and his staff have devoted considerable time and effort to filling this gap, it has been difficult for them to do so amid their other obligations. The Episcopal Church is called upon to continue the tradition set by previous General Conventions and to address the health care needs of the people of this country by restoring a SCH and a corresponding staff position in health care.

Resolution A124 Standing Commission on Health and a Staff Position in Health Care

1   *Resolved,* the House of _____ concurring, That this 74th General Convention reaffirm the commitment of
2   the Episcopal Church in providing a Christian response to the health care needs of those within our nation,
3   as expressed in the 1991 and 1994 Blue Book reports of the Standing Commission on Health and the 2000
4   Blue Book Report of the Standing Commission on National Concerns, and be it further
5   *Resolved*, That this 74th General Convention reestablish a Standing Commission on Health and that it
6   direct Executive Council to appoint a person to the staff at the Episcopal Church Center with background
7   in and knowledge about health care policy to assist this commission, and that their joint duties include:
8   • Articulating and communicating positions adopted by the Episcopal Church on health care policy to
9   Episcopalians, the public, and public policy makers;
10   • Advocating, in cooperation with the Office of Government Relations, for a health care system in
11   which all may be guaranteed decent and appropriate primary health care during their lives and as they
12   approach death;
13   • Bringing together those within the Episcopal Church who develop, provide and/or teach health care
14   and health care policy to continue to develop a Christian approach to pressing issues that affect the
15   health care system of this nation;
16   • Understanding and keeping abreast of the rapidly changing health care market and developments in
17   biomedical research that affect health policy;

18   •   Collecting and developing resources and teaching materials related to access to health care for the use
19   of dioceses, congregations, and individuals;
20   •   Advocating health ministry in and through local Episcopal congregations; and be it further
21   *Resolved,* That this 74th General Convention direct the Executive Council to report to the 75th General
22   Convention about this appointment; and be it further
23   *Resolved*, that $200,000 be appropriated from the budget for the triennium.

EXPLANATION

This resolution restores the Standing Commission on Health and a position in health care to the Episcopal Church Center and dedicates them to addressing together the health care needs of persons in this country and to improving the health care system. They will articulate the positions of the Episcopal Church related to health care policy; advocate for a decent and accessible health care system in cooperation with the Office of Government Relations; continue efforts begun by the Bishop for the Armed Forces, Healthcare, and Prison Ministries to bring together those within the Episcopal Church involved in health care and health care policy to develop further recommendations regarding health care; and assist those carrying out health ministry in congregations. Moreover, the staff person will have sufficient background to keep track of new developments in the health care system and biomedical research and will take steps to develop resources and teaching materials related to access to health care that can be used throughout the Church.

Prison Ministry, Prisoners' Families, and Mandatory Sentencing

Ministry to Prisoners and Their Families

Jesus sent his disciples to visit those in prison. This ministry has always been foundational to the work of the church. SCNC calls upon dioceses and congregations to serve our incarcerated neighbors and their families.

Alternative Facilities for Youths Charged and Convicted as Adults

Juveniles do not have the same rights and protections as adult offenders. There are no facilities or a way for youths charged as adults to be kept from hard-core criminals in federal prisons. Recent acts of violence by youths have brought awareness of the need to develop theological, psychological, and sociological understanding and methodology for addressing juveniles in our justice system. We recommend that the Peace and Justice Office study and make available resources to dioceses and congregations for ministering to families and youth heading toward or in our criminal justice system.

Reviewing Mandatory Sentencing Guidelines for Effectiveness

In 1951, Congress passed a law providing for mandatory minimum criminal sentences in certain areas. By the 1970s, these were considered unworkable and were repealed. In 1984, they were reinstated. Congress passed the Sentencing Reform Act (SRA) to eliminate inequities in federal sentencing in different parts of the country. SRA established mandatory minimum sentences for over 40 crimes. Its primary focus was on drug use and sale, as well as on the use of firearms during a crime.

Current mandatory sentencing guidelines severely limit judicial discretion and have had a disparate impact on people of color. Approximately 85% of federal judges have called for abolishing mandatory sentencing because it is not helping win the war on drugs, and results in long sentences for minor drug offenders at great financial and social cost to the public.

Resolution A125 Ministry to Prisoners and Their Families

1   *Resolved,* the House of _____ concurring, That the 74th General Convention of the Episcopal Church,
2   through the Executive Council, urge dioceses and congregations to become familiar with the criminal
3   justice system and form ministries which assist prisoners and their families during sentencing, while in
4   prison, and during their readjustment period; and be it further
5   *Resolved,* That the 74th General Convention support the establishment and/or expansion of occupational
6   and academic programs in prisons where prisoners may be prepared for re-entry into society; and be it
7   further
8   *Resolved*, That the 74th General Convention ask the Suffragan Bishop for Chaplaincies to identify training
9   programs that will help dioceses and congregations support the post-release employment of convicted
10   felons.

EXPLANATION

This resolution calls upon the dioceses and congregations of the Episcopal Church to know and serve our neighbors who are incarcerated and to care for their families. This is in fulfillment of our Baptismal Covenant: "to seek and serve Christ in all persons, loving our neighbors as ourselves, and to respect the dignity of every human being." The formation of ministries to those who are incarcerated is essential to our Christian witness. Such ministries include assistance before, during, and after prison.

Resolution A126 Youth Charged and Convicted as Adults

1 *Resolved,* the House of _____ concurring, That the 74th General Convention of the Episcopal Church
2 direct the Office of Government Relations to work for legislation that provides alternatives to sentencing
3 for juveniles and establishes intermediary facilities for incarceration (between farm schools and adult
4 prisons) for serious juvenile offenders; and be it further
5 *Resolved,* That the Peace and Justice Office explore, study, and make available to dioceses and
6 congregations resources for ministering to families and juveniles who are heading toward or caught up in
7 the U.S. criminal justice system.

EXPLANATION

There are no intermediary facilities or system to sequester youths charged as adults from the hard-core adult criminals in federal prisons. The recent school killings and other acts of violence perpetrated by youths have heightened awareness of our need to develop theological, psychological, and sociological understanding and methodology for addressing juveniles who are caught up in our justice system. The Peace and Justice Office should explore, study and make available to our dioceses and congregations resources for ministering to families and juveniles who are heading toward or caught up in our criminal justice system and the Office of Government Relations should work for legislation to accomplish these goals.

Resolution A127 Mandatory Sentencing Guidelines

1 *Resolved*, the House of _____ concurring, That the 74th General Convention direct the Office of
2 Government Relations to work for legislation to eliminate or significantly revise mandatory sentencing
3 guidelines to give federal judges more discretion in sentencing offenders, and to overcome the current
4 racially discriminatory impact of these guidelines.

EXPLANATION

Mandatory sentencing guidelines were meant to establish uniformity in sentencing. However, they are not helping us to win the war on drugs and are resulting in long sentences for minor drug offenders at great financial and social cost to the public. Moreover, they have had a discriminatory impact on people of color and they severely limit judicial discretion. Mandatory minimum sentencing guidelines should either be eliminated or else revised to provide a sentencing pattern that avoids racial discrimination and sends appropriate signals about the sale and use of drugs, enabling judges to consider the seriousness of the offense, the underlying criminal conduct and the offender's past.

Recognizing and Helping "At-Risk" Youth

Years ago it was common to describe "at risk" youth as those lacking support, empowerment, and boundaries in low-income urban communities. At times this description included rural areas. Programs reached out to youth in these communities to prevent substance abuse, victimization, violence and dysfunctional behavior.

Then came the tragic events of youth killing youth in Moses Lake, Washington (February 1996); Bethel, Alaska (February 1997); Pearl, Mississippi (October 1997); Paducah, Kentucky (December 1997); Jonesboro, Arkansas (March 1998); Edinboro, Pennsylvania (April 1998); Springfield, Oregon (May 1998); Columbine, Colorado (April 1999); Conyers, Georgia (May 1999); Mount Morris Township, Michigan (February 2000); and the recent events in Fort Worth, Texas and Santee, California. These events revealed that violence, threats to persons and dysfunctional behavior exist in urban, suburban and rural communities in this country.

Churches must find ways to offer hope and meaning to all youth, helping them to form a Christian worldview that challenges them to consider who they are in Christ. Youth should be encouraged to living a life conscious of the needs of others, rather than one devoted solely to self. Churches and dioceses can offer youth ways to manage anger and show them the value of forgiveness. They can also develop partnerships with community-based agencies, institutions, and schools to build an infrastructure that will permit outreach to "at risk" youth.

Resolution A128 Ministering to "At Risk" Youth

1   *Resolved*, the House of _____ concurring, That the 74th General Convention of the Episcopal Church
2   recognize the value of young people and the problem of violence that pervades our society making all of
3   our youth "at risk" youth; and be it further
4   *Resolved,* That the 74th General Convention of the Episcopal Church reaffirm the commitment of the
5   Church to support the development of caring, competent and loving young people; encourage dioceses and
6   churches to offer ways to manage anger and teach the value of forgiveness to our young people; and
7   recommend to dioceses and churches development of partnerships with community-based agencies,
8   institutions, and schools to build an infrastructure that will permit outreach to "at risk" youth in every
9   community.

EXPLANATION

Churches must reach out to all youth, especially those "at risk" of becoming involved in violence. The Church is called to offer a foundation of hope to our young people based upon a striving for the Kingdom of God "on earth as it is in heaven." It is called to be proactive in helping our youth form a Christian worldview that challenges them to consider who they are in Christ. Rather than living a life devoted to themselves, youth should be encouraged to become aware of the needs of others, to manage anger responsively and learn the value of forgiveness. Churches and dioceses can also develop partnerships with community-based agencies, institutions, and schools to help build an infrastructure that will permit outreach to "at risk" youth.

Racial Profiling

Racism has been addressed by the Episcopal Church in several ways. The Office of Peace and Justice has a Social Justice Officer who works with the Executive Council Anti-Racism Committee. We specifically commend the committee's blue book report and resolution to this 74th General Convention. Further, diversity training seminars are held in all dioceses in the Episcopal Church. We applaud the work and commitment with regard to the problem of racism by the Church. While anti-racism training has provided much needed awareness and training to eradicate racism, the issue of profiling has not been the focus of any specific group.

SCNC defines racial profiling as: "The discriminatory practice of suspecting, detaining, investigating and/or interrogating individuals as suspects of criminal behavior because of the color of their skin or their race." The use of profiling against a specific group of people deeply concerns this commission. This type of profiling is influenced by prejudices or pre-determined judgments. It is unjustly influenced by a perceived threat to one's safety or position. The practice of racial profiling is reprehensible.

Resolution A129 Dismantling Racial Profiling

1   *Resolved,* the House of _____ concurring, That the 74th General Convention deplore the immoral use of
2   racial profiling unjustly to identify certain behaviors, and call for the Episcopal Church to re-commit itself to
3   being vigilant in speaking out against all negative profiling but especially racial profiling wherever it happens;
4   and be it further
5   *Resolved,* That we renew our commitment to treat all people of color with honor and dignity, modeling the
6   behavior that we commit to in our Baptismal Covenant: to strive for justice and peace among all people and
7   respect the dignity of every human being; and be it further
8   *Resolved,* That each diocese be urged to commit funds specifically to help those who take action against racial
9   profiling in their community; and be it further
10   *Resolved,* That the Anti-Racism Committee's diversity training be adjusted to include teaching about racial
11   profiling, how to identify it, and various methods to end it.

EXPLANATION

Racial profiling, or the discriminatory practice of detaining, investigating and/or interrogating individuals as suspects of criminal behavior because of the color of their skin or race, is based on an inherent bias against a specific group of people. The vast majority of all discriminatory racial profiling focuses on African-American people. In the recent past, however, other persons have increasingly come under suspicion: Muslims, Native Americans, Hispanics, and Asians. In each instance, the practice of racial profiling is reprehensible and should be eliminated.

Theology of Work and A Living Wage

The Episcopal Church has long explored the Christian meaning of work to both labor and management. In 1901, the church established a Commission on Capital and Labor to study the labor movement, as well as conflicts between labor and management, and to offer itself as arbitrator when appropriate. Today, the Episcopal Church continues its support by calling for passage of laws establishing a "living wage." The Church should embrace this policy for itself, its contractors and its investments.

Resolution A130 Establish Living Wage

1   *Resolved,* the House of _____ concurring, That this 74th General Convention of the Episcopal Church,
2   through the Secretary of the Convention, call upon the President of the United States and members of
3   Congress to establish a living wage as the standard of compensation for all workers in the United States;
4   and be it further
5   *Resolved,* That it is the policy of the Episcopal Church and its dioceses and congregations to provide
6   employees with a living wage and be a model for ethical labor practices; and be it further
7   *Resolved,* That it is the policy of the Episcopal Church to insist that companies in which the Church
8   invests or with which it contracts provide their employees with a living wage and serve as a model for
9   ethical labor practices.

EXPLANATION

Everyone should be able to support his or her family adequately. Therefore, it is important that the Episcopal Church support laws establishing a "living wage," which is defined as "a wage that allows and enables full-time workers to raise their families outside poverty, apart from government subsidies." In asking this of others, the Episcopal Church should also embrace this policy for itself, its contractors and its investments.

Resolution A131 Worker's Prayer

1   *Resolved,* the House of _____ concurring, That the 74th General Convention recommend to the Standing
2   Commission on Liturgy and Music to include the prayer, "A Worker's Prayer" in the *Book of Common*
3   *Prayer* in the *Prayers for the Social Order* section.
4   Lord, we pray today for all who work and all who are seeking work.
5   As You looked at the work You had done and saw that it was good, help us to value all work performed
6   with diligence, care and honesty.
7   Help us to seek rewards for our work not only in the wages we receive, but also in stewardship of Your
8   creation and justice toward all persons. Help us to recognize that we cannot do our work alone, but depend
9   upon the work of many others, some of whom we do not even know. Help us to remember that it is Your
10 gift to find, even in the inevitable routine, occasions of interest and joy. Help us to remember that laborers
11 are worthy not only of their hire, but of their rest. Help us to say "Well done" to others, as we hope to hear
12 the same.
13 Finally, when we cannot see the direction to go, give us faith that you can always work for good through
14 us.
15 We ask these things in the name of Him who promised to be with us always. Amen.

EXPLANATION

The Standing Commission on National Concerns extends its appreciation to Celeste Parsons, Diocese of Southern Ohio, for allowing it to use the above prayer that she prepared in connection with the work of the Diocese of Southern Ohio on the Theology of Work.

Christian Response to Warfare

The Christian tradition has historically embraced two responses to warfare: just war theory and pacifism. The Episcopal Church has long studied and acted on issues of war and peace, as in the 1982 Blue Book Report

"To Make Peace" and the *GC Resolution 2000-A058* "The Pledge of Non-Violence." Today, the actions taken and planned by the government of the United States, as well as the many armed conflicts around the world, call for a response by all Christians and people of faith that promote peace, justice, and reconciliation, taking into account these traditional responses to warfare.

Resolution A132 Christian Responses to Warfare

1   *Resolved,* the House of _____ concurring, That the 74th General Convention urge dioceses and
2   congregations to study and better understand just war theory and pacifism as they apply to the situation of
3   the United States in responding to contemporary international conflicts.

EXPLANATION

It is important at this time to return to foundational Christian approaches to national involvement in warfare. The Christian tradition has historically embraced two responses to warfare: just war theory and pacifism. The commission recommends that dioceses and congregations study just war theory and pacifism as they apply to the actions taken and planned by the government of the United States, as well as the many armed conflicts around the world.

Financial Report

The Commission was budgeted for $99,000 for the 2001-2003 Triennium. At the time of this report, SCNC had expended $47,594 of its budget.

The Standing Commission on National Concerns will meet approximately five times during the 2004-2006 Triennium. This will require $25,000 in 2004, $26,000 in 2005 and $28,000 in 2006 for a total of $79,000.

Conclusion

The Book of Common Prayer's Baptismal Covenant, page 305 asks, "Will you strive for justice and peace among all people, and respect the dignity of every human being?" Our response is, "I will, with God's help." This report concludes with confidence that this commission sought to fulfill this covenant and trusts that the 74th General Convention will affirm it by passing the submitted resolutions.

STANDING COMMISSION FOR SMALL CONGREGATIONS
www.episcopalchurch.org/congdev/Rural/Rural.htm

Membership

Ms. Ramona Burroughs, *Co-chair*	South Dakota, 2006
Ms. Judith W. Fleener, *Co-chair*	Western Michigan, 2003
Mrs. Karen DuPlantier, *Secretary*	Louisiana, 2006
The Rt. Rev. Bruce Caldwell	Wyoming, 2003
The Rt. Rev. Thomas Clark Ely	Vermont, 2003
The Very Rev. Marilyn J. Engstrom	Wyoming, 2003
The Very Rev. Canon H. W. Herrmann, SSC	Quincy, 2006
The Rt. Rev. F. Neff Powell, Southern	Virginia, 2003
Mr. Richard H. Snyder	Nevada, 2003
Ms. Bonnie Studdiford	Maine, 2006
Staff	
The Rev. Ben E. Helmer	Missioner for Rural and Small Communities
	Office of Congregational Development

WORK SUMMARY

The Standing Commission for Small Congregations (SCSC) canonical mandate is to concern itself with plans for directions for small congregations. SCSC met three times and held one telephone conference. We have:

- Examined vitality in small congregations. Our work during the triennium leads us to propose *"Expanding Mission and Vitality in Small Congregations: A Framework for Affirming and Strengthening the Ministry of Small Churches"* as a strategy that would be available to small congregations.
- Reviewed available demographic material on small churches. It is posted on our web-site.
- Continued our conversations with seminaries regarding their offerings for small congregations.
- Met with the Evangelical Lutheran Church in America (ECLA) to investigate the possibility of ecumenical activities.
- Met with members of the Commission on Domestic Missions and Evangelism, the 20/20 Task Force, and the Standing Commission for Ministry Development.
- Collaborated with networks and organizations involved with ministry development.
- Compiled a list of resources for small congregations as part of our report, and posted on our web-site.

Report of Our Findings: "Expanding Mission and Vitality in Small Congregations: A Framework for Affirming and Strengthening the Ministry of Small Churches"

Introduction

The Commission's discussions have been shaped by the Episcopal Church's teaching about the primacy of mission and the centrality of baptismal ministry. As stated in the Catechism, "the mission of the Church is to restore all people to unity with God and each other in Christ" and "The Church pursues its mission as it prays and worships, proclaims the Gospel, and promotes justice, peace and love." (p. 855, BCP) The Baptismal Covenant gives expression to the Church's understanding of the ministry of all the baptized.

Principles informing our work about small congregations (those with 150 or less average Sunday attendance)
- Vitality in small congregations is achieved when abundance is claimed.
- Vitality in small congregations is a sign that God is transforming those faith communities and the wider community of which those congregations are a part.
- Incarnation and Resurrection are manifested as all members of a congregation claim new life and engage in mission and ministry individually and together, in the church and in every part of their lives.

- The gifts of the Holy Spirit are present in every congregation for the work God desires to be done in and through that faith community.
- Learning that equips every member for full participation in the mission and ministry of Christ is a life-long process.
- Vitality can be sustained by a variety of ministry development strategies.
- Congregational viability is assessed locally, in partnership with the Bishop.

Characteristics of a Vital Small Church in the Episcopal Tradition

- The Eucharist and other sacraments are available as needed and desired, no matter the size, location, or wealth of the congregation.
- Worship is participatory, mediates a sense of God's presence and helps transform people for baptismal living.
- There is full local engagement in determining strategies for mission and ministry in partnership with the Bishop.
- Members understand and support mission direction and priorities.
- Members are open to possibilities and willing to embrace new opportunities for mission.
- Members engage in broad-based, collaborative-decision making in which issues and agenda are discerned by the community, which takes ownership of decisions.
- There is collegiality and collaboration between local leaders--who provide sustainability, continuity, and local wisdom--and leaders from beyond the local community--who provide additional knowledge, experience, and expertise in ministry development.
- Members display a clear capacity to do the hard work of reconciliation with one another, keep faith with one another and speak the truth in love.
- The ministry priorities of pastoral care, liturgy, and administration are well provided by leaders local to the community.
- The congregation is organized for ministry and mission as is appropriate to its circumstances.
- Members participate in on-going engagement with the Gospel through theological education and reflection; prayer and worship; and the nurturing of each person's gifts as a minister.
- Effective support of the ministry of all members in daily life is ongoing. The unique perspective and contribution of every member is valued.
- Were a vital congregation to disappear from its community, it would truly be missed by others in that community, even those who had never been its members.

A Strategy

A strategy for expanding and sustaining vitality in small congregations involves equipping those congregations for self-assessment, discernment, local ownership and development.

Self-assessment is an honest evaluation by a congregation of its history, resources, strengths, challenges, opportunities and organizational structure.

As discernment this process is prayerful, patient, imaginative, collaborative, hopeful, flexible, attentive to God's intention, and leads to clear shared vision of the unique calling of that particular faith community, including the effect its life and work will have beyond itself. Outside resources can be helpful in facilitating this step.

Local ownership or commitment can be seen as the congregation as a whole steps forward to embrace that calling, to claim its responsibility and authority to become what God intends it to be. It includes the discovery of gifts and resources, claiming of abundance and embracing the power unleashed by interdependence. It involves a decision on the part of the congregation to commit itself to a time of planning and development of its capacity to extend its participation in the mission of God in Christ, and readiness to collaborate with others in the diocese and beyond as it engages in its life and work.

Congregational development involves training and theological education, using the variety of resources available to identify and develop ministry, as well as establish appropriate structures for mission and decision making. It results in total, confident engagement of the full membership in life-long spiritual formation, theological learning, and work for justice and peace.

Resources for Small Congregations to Expand Mission and Vitality

There is an impressive amount and quality of resources available for small congregations. We have found that there are organizations within the Church that can provide information, materials and assistance. Available resources include: books; web-sites; consultants available to work with parishes and with dioceses and conferences and workshops.

We urge congregations seeking any assistance to check the Rural/Small Community Ministries web-page of the Episcopal Church's web site. All available resources from SCSC are on the web-page, and we urge its use both by those seeking information and those offering it.

RESOURCES FOR SMALL CONGREGATIONS FROM THE CHURCH'S SEMINARIES

SCSC began conversations with the Episcopal Church's seminaries during the last triennium. We believe these conversations have been helpful in identifying ways in which the seminaries are working with small congregations, and in which the seminaries are preparing their graduates to work in small congregations. We believe that it is valuable for both the Standing Commission and for the seminaries to continue these conversations so that the needs and concerns of small congregations are addressed.

Church Divinity School of the Pacific *2451 Ridge Rd., Berkeley, CA 94709; (510) 204-0700. info@cdsp.edu.*

Church Divinity School of the Pacific (CDSP) has a record of involvement with and for small congregations. Classes available on site for MDiv students include ministry development and congregational development classes, some of which are taught in coordination with members of the Ministry Developers' Collaborative. A variety of classes designed to prepare clergy for working in small congregations is available through the Graduate Theological Union, a consortium of seminaries in Berkeley, Calif., of which CDSP is a member.

CDSP has pioneered efforts at providing on-line education, including classes for credit that are available to people throughout the country. Several such classes are available now.

The Seminary's Center for Anglican Learning and Life (CALL) collaborates with dioceses of Province 8 to assist in meeting their program needs, including a variety of workshops and assistance for educational programs within the dioceses. CALL's two-year program "Anglican Studies On-Line" offers other on-line courses and opportunities for continuing education workshops both at the seminary and at other sites, many of them designed to meet the needs of small congregations.

Episcopal Divinity School *99 Brattle, Cambridge, MA 02138; (617) 868-3450. info@episdivschool.org*

EDS offers Congregational Studies programs which focus on aspects of training and support for laity and clergy in small congregations, especially those in the region. Topics offered have included lay pastoral teams, preaching and teaching the lectionary, anti-racism training and stewardship. There are also annual workshops and resources for Christian Education and leadership development. Costs for the programs are kept low through subsidies from the seminary.

Students at EDS take a course in "congregational contexts," half of which is devoted to ministry in small congregations. Many of the field education sites are in small congregations, and course offerings in pastoral theology focus on the small congregation. The seminary is exploring several partnerships with dioceses that will provide additional support to congregations. Also being developed is an on-line education component.

Episcopal Theological Seminary of the Southwest *PO Box 2247, Austin, TX 78768; (512) 472-4133. seminary@etss.edu*

Certificate Programs in Youth Ministry and Christian Education are offered by Episcopal Seminary of the Southwest. The programs offer basic theological education which includes scripture, theology and practical skills of ministry on basic, associate and advanced levels. Distance learning courses began in the fall of 2002. Courses are offered each semester on a non-credit basis. The seminary's statement of purpose defines mission comprehensively in terms of living out the Baptismal Covenant in a multicultural context.

Nashotah House 2777 Mission Road, Nashotah, Wisconsin 53058-9793; 1-800-Nashotah

There are two summer programs that would benefit small congregations. The School of Evangelization is designed to equip laity and clergy intellectually, spiritually and practically for evangelization. The school explores spirituality and evangelization in different congregational settings. Participants develop a strategic plan for their home congregations.

The Boone Porter Institute for local ministry is designed to strengthen the already existing network of Christians working in local and regional ministries. Education, training and support are offered for both lay and ordained leadership. Epiphany Term, offered between the fall and spring terms, offers graduate-level, intensive classes.

The Protestant Episcopal Theological Seminary in Virginia Seminary Post Office, 3737 Seminary Road, Alexandria, Virginia 22304; www.vts.edu

Small congregation issues are included as part of virtually every pastoral theology and pastoral care course offered at Virginia Theological Seminary. In addition, there are courses explicitly for small congregation ministry. A small church ministry course is planned for the January 2004 term. The bishops of West Virginia and Easton led classes exploring alternative models for church organization and leadership in areas with many small congregations. Students may also take courses in Appalachian ministry, which include on-site study and reflection.

The Leadership Program in Music in sponsored and hosted by VTS. It concentrates on musical ministry in small congregations. The seminary participated in a program with a nearby diocese to offer concentrated workshops on homiletics and liturgics for small congregations, taught by the regular faculty.

The Center for the Ministry of Teaching provides resources, materials and consultation for Christian education in small congregation settings, and the Lifetime Theological Education program invites clergy and lay leaders of small congregations for workshops and courses.

The School of Theology, The University of the South, Sewanee, TN 37383; (800) 722-1974. theology@sewanee.edu

The Center for Ministry in Small Churches is associated with the seminary and offers workshops, retreats and consultations to small congregations. It also hosts an annual conference on themes of interest to a small congregation. Several dioceses formerly helped fund CMSC, which is now completely under the School of Theology.

The seminary offers a small church ministry elective, and classes have covered specific areas of ministry such as ministry in Appalachia and small-church lay ministry training. Seminarians take part in field education in a number of smaller parishes near the seminary.

A five-church regional ministry, located in churches near the seminary, has been started to model mutual ministry in a program that was coordinated with CMSC. This has provided students with a practical knowledge in the creating of a regional ministry with the seminary as a resource for their training.

A quarterly journal, "Tuesday Morning," offers articles on ecumenical ministry and liturgical preaching. There is a focus on articles and material for small congregations which may not have access to the resources that are more easily accessed in larger congregations. Subscription rate is $20 annually.

Trinity Episcopal School for Ministry, 311 Eleventh St., Ambridge, PA 15003. 1-800-874-8754. tesm@tesm.edu

Second year students in the ordination track participate in Field Based Placement. The liturgical expectation for these students encourages many to do their work in rural and small community parishes. The course also has a critical issues seminar to prepare students for small as well as larger church ministries.

The pastoral theology department has several offerings that recognize that "most of the churches in America are small churches." The needs of small churches, as contrasted with those of larger churches, are noted and addressed in the classes.

Trinity offers a professional doctoral degree that affords clergy in small churches the opportunity to address the skills they identify as needed in their ministry.

Resolution A133 Adopt *"Expanding Mission and Vitality in Small Congregations"*

1   *Resolved,* the House of _____ concurring, That the 74th General Convention adopt *"Expanding Mission*
2   *and Vitality in Small Congregations: A Framework Affirming and Strengthening the Ministry of Small*
3   *Churches"* offered by the Standing Commission for Small Congregations; and be it further
4   *Resolved,* That the Office of Congregational Development and the Missioner for Rural and Small
5   Communities be directed to print and distribute this document throughout the Episcopal Church.

EXPLANATION

There are many valid measures for determining congregational vitality. This document offers ways for dioceses and small congregations to determine their vitality and to develop plans for enhancing their ability to do Christ's work in the world.

Financial Report

The Standing Commission for Small Congregations was budgeted $31,000 for the 2001-2003 Triennium. At the time of this report, SCSC had expended $15,699 of its budget.

The Standing Commission for Small Congregations will meet approximately three times during the 2004-2006 Triennium. This will require $8,000 in 2004, $17,000 in 2005, and $10,000 in 2005 for a total of $35,000 for the Triennium.

STANDING COMMISSION ON STEWARDSHIP AND DEVELOPMENT
www.episcopalchurch.org/gc/ccab/scsd/default.html

Membership

Mr. Thomas R. Gossen, *Co-Chair*	Kansas, 2003
The Rt. Rev. Henry N. Parsley, Jr., *Co-Chair*	Alabama, 2003,
Ms. Susan T. Erdey, *Secretary*	New York, 2006
The Rev. Richard J. Aguilar	West Texas, 2003
Mr. Eugene T. Chrostowski	West Missouri, 2003
Canon Sharon L. Davenport	Northwestern Pennsylvania, 2006
The Very Rev. Dr. W. Richard Hamlin	Central New York, 2006
Ms. Marissa Jennings	North Carolina, 2006
Mrs. Joan O. Kline	Southwest Florida, 2003
Ms. Blanca Rivera	Milwaukee, 2006
The Rt. Rev. Gordon Paul Scruton	Western Massachusetts, 2006
Mr. Walter Virden III	Fort Worth, 2003
The Rev. Barnum McCarty	*Executive Council liaison*
Ms. Terry Parsons	*Staff liaison, Stewardship and Discipleship Missioner* *Episcopal Church Center*

CHARGE

Title I, Canon 1.2 (n) (9) calls for:

A Standing Commission on Stewardship and Development (SCSD), consisting of 12 members (2 Bishops, 2 Priests and/or Deacons, and 8 Lay Persons). It shall be the duty of the Commission to hold up before the Church the responsibility of faithful stewardship of time, talent and treasure in grateful thanksgiving for God's gifts. It shall recommend strategies for stewardship education throughout the Church with special sensitivity to the cultural and linguistic diversity of our Church. It shall recommend programs for long-range planning and development, ensuring that other Church bodies, including the Executive Council, are part of the process. It shall assure that there is an official, periodic gathering, interpretation, evaluation and reporting of stewardship from throughout the Church. It shall help coordinate all church-wide fund-raising activities.

MEETINGS

The Commission met four times during the triennium: March 22-24, 2001, Episcopal Church Center, New York, NY; November 12-14, 2001, Dallas, TX; March 19-22, 2002, Ellenton, FL; November 14-16, 2002, Virginia Theological Seminary, Alexandria, VA.

RESPONSE TO 2000 GENERAL CONVENTION RESOLUTIONS

The full commission made the following disposition of the work committed to it by the action of the 73rd General Convention:

1. *A106:* Affirmation of the Tithe and Stewardship Statement. The commission notes that God has been working on this at least since the time of Jacob (Genesis 28:22) and Malachi (Malachi 3:8-10), and so shall we. We continue to develop ways to hold up for our church the tithe (10%) as the minimum standard for Christian giving.

2. *A111:* Legacy Stewardship. See our comments on the teaching and development of Legacy Stewardship below.

3. *A112:* Christian Stewardship Curriculum in Seminaries. A survey of the seminaries is in process and our work in this area will continue into the next Triennium.

4. *A113:* 1% Support to Seminaries by Congregations. We ask all deputies to affirm this important funding stream for our Episcopal seminaries in your annual diocesan conventions.

WORK SUMMARY

Introduction

The Standing Commission on Stewardship and Development (SCSD) believes the ministry of Christian stewardship is about the joyful transformation of hearts, minds, and spirits. In the Gospel, Christ issues an urgent call to turn ourselves from a life of sinful self-centeredness so that we might begin life renewed as people of God. This call is to a life of on-going conversion, transformation, and challenge as we seek to be stewards of the Gospel of Jesus Christ, stewards of God's gifts, and stewards of all creation.

A lay participant in a regional stewardship event once said, "I used to give so that I would be saved, but through my journey toward tithing I have learned that I have been saved so that I can give." We believe that stewardship so understood lies at the core of our corporate call as Christ's Body, the Church, to become *missio Dei*, God's missional church. God's mission has a church. We are it. The Biblical discipline of the tithe, returning to God 10% of all God gives us from the first fruits of our labors, is an important way of becoming and sustaining God's missional church. According to the gifts we are given, we are called to continue Christ's work of reconciliation in the world.

We recognize a deep chasm between our stated norms and our corporate and individual practice. The average pledge (Year 2000) throughout all 100 dioceses is $1,564, with the lowest diocesan average $895, and the highest $2,406. (Please see charts posted at www.tens.org/SCSD/Parochial-Report.html for full details.) Further, between 1969 and 1998, giving in American churches has not kept pace with increases in income. While U.S. per capita disposable income increased during that period by 91% (from $11,864 to $22,637), giving as a percentage of income declined 19% (from 3.1% to 2.42%). These statistics suggest we have a long way to go to becoming a missional church that tithes. Similarly, 37 of 100 Episcopal dioceses still give less than the full asking to support the mission and ministry of the whole church. In response to these trends we must remain vigilant in our canonical task to invite the whole church to enter into a life of continued and joyful transformation of hearts, minds, and spirits so that together we might build God's church.

Stewardship Defined

The theology of Christian stewardship concerns our core belief that God has created us *imago Dei,* in God's image, and that as such "God has given the whole world into our care so that we might rule and serve all God's creatures," the world and everything therein.

Our Christian understanding of what it means to be *imago Dei* is informed in part by our Lord's own words in John 3:16: "God so loved the world that God gave…" That is, our God is a God who loves and who gives. What God loves is "the world." We are created to be like God in our loving and in our giving. Christ Jesus lived among us, died, and was raised from the dead to draw us away from a life of sinful self-centeredness and deeper into a discovery of what it means to be *imago Dei.*

"And, that we might live no longer for ourselves, but for him who died and rose for us, Christ sent the Holy Spirit, his own first gift for those who believe, to complete his work in the world, and to bring to fulfillment the sanctification of all." The Spirit is Christ's own tithe, his own first gift from the first fruits of his incarnation, which embodies the life-giving essence to sustain our new life as *imago Dei.*

William Countryman in his Good News of Jesus (Cowley, 1993: p. 105) reminds us that since the earliest witness, the church has always believed that the Spirit provides for all its needs. The Spirit does so, however, in a peculiar manner. The gifts you need, the Spirit gives to someone else. The gifts you are given are meant for others. The Christian community can live only by the sharing of these gifts (I Corinthians 12-14).

Christian stewardship is our **joyful** response to the magnitude of God's love revealed in this most intrinsic aspect of human nature: the giving and sharing of gifts.

Stewardship is the **intentional** choice to shape our lives, both individually and corporately as his Body, the church, in such ways so as to be **transformed** into people of God who daily take the **risk** to live lives of loving and giving for the spread of God's kingdom. Such shaping of our lives comes from our **intentional** living-out of the promises we make and continually renew in our Baptism.

It is our experience, and the witness of all the saints who have come before us, that a life of stewardship so understood has the power to **transform** the life of the giver as well as the lives of the recipients of our gifts.

And it is our experience that those congregations and dioceses where an **intentional** choice is made to live such an understanding of Christian stewardship become centers transformed into a **missional** church which indeed lives no longer for itself, but for him who died and rose for us.

There can be no doubt that after the events that have transpired in our national life and the life of the world since this church last met in General Convention, there is a fresh *urgency* for us, as a people of God, to embrace such an understanding of Christian stewardship. For our sake, and for the sake of the world our Lord loved and for which he gave his life, we need to continually find new ways to respond to our call to be a missional church.

The Alleluia Fund – Build My Church

Living in this new post-September 11, 2001, world, the SCSD recognizes the urgency for the church to awaken as a major agency for God's transforming love and giving that we might be a witness to a greater sense of security than the world can give. In its 73rd General Convention, the Episcopal Church affirmed the Alleluia Fund initiative. In partnership with the 20/20 movement, the SCSD offers the Alleluia Fund initiative as a significant funding stream for the realization of the goals and objectives of 20/20.

In December 2002, every bishop in the church received a copy of Alleluia Fund: A Guide for Dioceses and Congregations. The Alleluia Fund is designed as an annual diocesan campaign during the Great Fifty Days of Easter. Each household in the church is invited to make daily contributions to the Alleluia Fund for fifty days to be used by the diocese to fund new mission initiatives.

The guide outlines a four phase process to initiate the Alleluia Fund in your diocese: 1) Create the Vision (four methods of doing this are outlined), 2) Live into the Vision (What will we do with the money?), 3) Fund the Vision (Inviting gifts) and 4) Ways to Give. The guide also includes appendices suggesting resources and computer software to facilitate running the annual Alleluia Fund campaign in your diocese.

Running the Alleluia Fund for a period of 20 years gives it the capacity to be a cornerstone funding stream for 20/20. The Alleluia Fund also possesses the potential to be creative and fun in building our funding structures for 20/20 and all special diocesan mission initiatives. Although the money ordinarily is to remain in the diocese, exciting possibilities exist to partner with other domestic and foreign dioceses.

As of this report, several dioceses have already started Alleluia Funds during the Great Fifty Days of Easter. They bear witness to the fact that the Alleluia Fund is already building God's Church and reaching beyond the church and into the world. The Office of Stewardship is the source for more information and support materials to initiate your diocese's own Alleluia Fund.

Stewardship Stories and Prayers

During the past triennium the Commission collected stewardship stories and prayers from throughout the church. These have been published as Faces of Faith: A Steward's Book of Prayers, available to bishops and deputies at this convention. More copies can be obtained through Episcopal Parish Services or the Office of Stewardship.

Holy Habits

We understand God's invitation to be faithful stewards as a call to a lifelong journey of repentance, conversion, and renewed life. God calls us to grow into the *imago Dei* that we are created to be. Often, faithful response will require us to make choices that challenge our culture's obsessions with scarcity, self-sufficiency, and acquisitiveness.

We are called to be stewards of our faith, of creation, of civil society, and of our lives. None of this comes naturally; it requires both faith and commitment, and so the church has developed a number of practices and disciplines—or holy habits—to help us on our journey. All of these find expression in our baptismal vows.

At the center of our individual and corporate lives is the call to be stewards of the Gospel. We are called not just to live our faith in Jesus Christ, but also to proclaim that faith by word and example. This finds expression in the way we work, pray, and give.

We are entrusted with the stewardship of creation. This means we must reflect on our use of resources and on what it means to have been given the care of the whole world and charged to rule and serve all God's creatures. The baptismal promise to strive for justice and peace impels us to be actively involved as citizens of our communities, nation, and world.

To live as Christian stewards is to be intentional in our use of all that God has given us. Certainly that includes the first-fruits tithing of our material wealth as a reminder and symbol of our thankful acknowledgement of God as the gracious source of all and as a way to begin dealing with our addiction to money. It also includes the discernment, cultivation and use of our skills and abilities to further God's work in the world, the *missio Dei*. Because our gifts differ, and because we sometime find it difficult to recognize and develop our own God-given giftedness, our baptism grafts us into the body of Christ. We are to recognize the *imago Dei* within ourselves and within every human being.

One of the great stewardship challenges of our age is our stewardship of time. We live in a culture that offers nearly infinite diversions and demands that we fill every moment with activity. There is no greater need, and nothing more counter-cultural, than for us to reclaim Sabbath time. Not only is the commandment for Sabbath time the second-longest of the ten; Sabbath is part of the order of Creation—it is the very culmination of Creation. As the church—and as dioceses, parishes, and individuals—it is imperative that we find ways to teach the absolute necessity of Sabbath as part of individual spiritual life, and that we encourage and enable our bishops and clergy to model the balance of activity and Sabbath.

Theology of Legacy Stewardship
Christian stewardship is rooted in the conviction of faith that all we are and all we have is God's gracious gift. Christians believe, as Archbishop Michael Ramsey once wrote, that "I come from God, I belong to God, I go to God."

We are stewards of the whole of our lives. The joyful work of Christian stewardship is to be applied not only to our annual giving, but also to giving at the end of our lives. It is important that God's people offer a faithful portion of our accumulated resources for the work of the church and the mission of God. Giving a faithful percentage of our resources through our wills or living trusts, through planned gifts such as charitable remainder trusts, and other special gifts from our abundance are ways to accomplish such "legacy stewardship." Such legacy giving bears final witness to our Christian faith and helps strengthen the church's future mission. Gifts at the end of our lives express our gratitude for the whole of our lives.

It is imperative the dioceses and parishes of this church teach legacy stewardship and provide ways and means for the receiving and securing of such gifts. The Episcopal Church Foundation is an excellent resource, providing teaching and a secure trust for legacy gifts. Endowments can be a vital source for mission, but should be structured in a way that prevents dependence on their income for annual operations. Further, it is incumbent upon the clergy and lay leaders of our parishes to encourage all faithful people to make wills and offer a percentage of their accumulated resources for the church's mission from generation to generation.

EFT and Online Giving
Time was spent investigating forms of Electronic Funds Transfer (EFT) as a method for paying one's pledge. The principal methods would be a direct transfer arranged from one's bank account to the parish account (including online services), or the use of credit cards. Denominations and parishes that offer EFT as a pledge payment option report more predictable and even cash flow throughout the year, as well as an increase in giving (since most people who give by EFT also put cash in the plate on Sunday morning). Possible negative issues revolve around the use of credit cards, which could be seen as encouraging debt to pay one's pledge. Both EFT and credit card payments involve some sort of service fee that may be incurred by the church or passed on to the individual. The Commission stresses that this is simply one of a variety of collection methods and is not related to any theology of giving. Although we are not prepared to make any recommendation at

this time, we encourage parishes and dioceses that may use EFT as a method of collection to send this Commission detailed reports of your experiences.

GOALS AND OBJECTIVES FOR THE NEXT THREE YEARS AND BEYOND

During the next triennium the Commission will:

- Continue to urge dioceses to implement The Alleluia Fund.
- Look into new models of mission funding.
- Continue our research into the role of stewardship education in clergy formation at our church's seminaries, and seek to determine effective models for preparing future clergy to fulfill their canonical duty to teach the Biblical standard of the tithe for financial stewardship (Title III, Canon 14, Sec. 2 (a)).
- Seek to hold several of our five meetings at seminaries of this church to engage students in conversation about clergy, money and stewardship.
- Encourage the development of teaching materials and opportunities for stewardship education, which appropriately reflect the diversity of this church.
- Continue to encourage the teaching of holy habits (tithing, prayer, Sabbath time), the development of stewardship statements at all dimensions of our church's life, and the telling of our stewardship stories.

RESOLUTIONS

Resolution A134 Implement Alleluia Fund

1   *Resolved,* the House of _____ concurring, That this 74th General Convention commend those dioceses
2   that have already implemented Resolution A036 of the 73rd General Convention, The Alleluia Fund —
3   Build My Church; and be it further
4   *Resolved,* That all dioceses be encouraged to engage in this process of planning, giving, and spiritual
5   transformation as a part of their 20/20 initiative in order to develop and maintain relationships with
6   individual members of their dioceses and to fund new mission opportunities; and be it further
7   *Resolved,* That all dioceses are encouraged to designate a tithe of their Alleluia Fund offerings to mission
8   beyond the diocese.

Resolution A135 Holy Habits

1   *Resolved,* the House of _____ concurring, That in recognition of the church's tradition of calling us to
2   work, pray, and give for the spread of God's kingdom, all members of the Episcopal Church be
3   encouraged to develop a personal spiritual discipline that includes, at a minimum, the holy habits of
4   tithing, daily personal prayer and study, Sabbath time, and regular corporate worship; and be it further
5   *Resolved,* That the Bishops and Deputies of this 74th General Convention be given an opportunity to sign
6   the following declaration:
7   As Christian stewards and leaders of the Episcopal Church, we affirm that we are tithing, or have
8   adopted a plan to work toward tithing; and that, if we are not already doing so, we are committed to
9   give priority to corporate worship, personal daily prayer and study, and Sabbath time in our own lives;
10   and we invite all members of the Episcopal Church to join us in these holy habits;
11   and be it further
12   *Resolved,* That the Secretary publish a list of these signatories in the Journal of the 74th General
13   Convention and provide the same to *Episcopal Life* for publication of the statement and the list of
14   signatories.

Resolution A136 National Mission Narrative/Annual Report

1   *Resolved,* the House of _____ concurring, That this 74th General Convention direct the Episcopal Church
2   Center staff to develop, produce, publish, and distribute to the Episcopal Church at large an annual report
3   that describes, in word and image, the good works that are being accomplished throughout our church in
4   this country and in the world.

EXPLANATION

The Episcopal Church has a powerful story and witness that should be shared widely. The Journal of General Convention, while comprehensive, does not effectively convey the vibrancy of the ministries that are being accomplished every day; furthermore, it is published only once every three years. Too few Episcopalians are aware of the breadth and scope of churchwide mission and ministry opportunities and accomplishments. An annual report that presents facts, figures, and information in a visual and compelling form will help tell the story of the Episcopal Church in a way that will engage and excite our own members and those who do not yet know about the Church. Such a report can be a powerful tool for evangelism and outreach. The ELCA department of stewardship provides an excellent model for this report.

Resolution A137 Accountability Of Mission Partners

1 *Resolved,* the House of _____ concurring, That the 74th General Convention require that recipients of
2 grants or gifts from the Domestic and Foreign Missionary Society maintain appropriate accounting records
3 and controls over such grants and gifts.

EXPLANATION

Incidents of irregularities and abuses in administration of certain gifts have been reported in recent years. Good stewardship requires that we be accountable for all God's gifts.

Resolution A138 50/50 Outreach for Congregations

1 *Resolved,* the House of _____ concurring, That the 74th General Convention urge congregations to adopt
2 the principle of devoting as much of their resources of time, talent, and treasure outside of the
3 congregation as on itself. Part of the 50/50 sharing should include adoption of the 1% giving to seminaries,
4 the .7% giving to international development programs that address root causes of ill health, illiteracy, and
5 economic justice, and other worthwhile causes.

EXPLANATION

We are the children of God, and we are invited to respond to God's abundance by being joyful givers. In every aspect of our life, we are entrusted to be stewards of God's creation. God invites us to give freely and to exercise joyfully our gifts through mission and ministries. Adoption of the 50/50 principle is a means of demonstrating our commitment to engaging in God's mission to reconcile, restore, rebuild, and reconnect.

Resolution A139 Affirm the Work of TENS

1 *Resolved,* the House of _____ concurring, That this 74th General Convention commend the transforming
2 ministry of The Episcopal Network for Stewardship (TENS), a ministry that invites individuals,
3 congregations, and dioceses to grow into a new understanding of Christian stewardship theology that
4 transforms us from selfishness and fear to love and giving, and we invite all dioceses and congregations to
5 become members of TENS not only to support this important ministry but also to receive the many
6 resources TENS is developing and making available to the church.

EXPLANATION

The Episcopal Network for Stewardship is a voluntary network of people who understand the important role of leadership in calling the Church to a faithful response to God's call to share generously of our time, talents, and treasures to provide for God's work in the world. The purpose of TENS is to lead in the growth of a network of dedicated stewardship ministers serving congregations and dioceses; and to support each other with personal consultations and fellowship opportunities, as well as print, video, and electronic resources.

For further information, contact The Episcopal Network for Stewardship by telephone at 800.699.2669 or 316.686.0470; FAX to 316.686.9201; or e-mail to tens@tens.org. Information is also available online at http://www.tens.org.

Resolution A140 Mission Funding

1   *Resolved,* the House of _____ concurring, That the 74th General Convention direct:

2   • the beginning of a discernment process for a church-wide major mission funding effort; and

3   • the immediate creation of a Mission Funding Office for the Episcopal Church, grounded in the

4   stewardship theology of this church.

EXPLANATION

The Episcopal Church can and needs to raise large sums of money for mission. We believe there are major gifts for mission that parish and diocesan funding efforts do not challenge. We recognize that in addition to the missional initiatives emerging from the 20/20 movement, there are many efforts within the church that need to be coordinated in seeking new funds, such as an Episcopal Relief and Development endowment, Episcopal Church Foundation planned giving initiatives, Alleluia Fund — Build My Church, overseas mission, and diocesan and congregational capital fund drives. We know that this effort requires professional expertise.

BUDGET APPROPRIATION FOR SCSD

The Standing Commission for Stewardship and Development will hold five (5) meetings in the next triennium (Jan 21-24, 2004, June 2004, November 2004, March 2005, November 2005) for a cost of $67,500.

SUMMARY

The Standing Commission on Stewardship and Development submits this report to the 74th General Convention to encourage the joyful transformation of hearts, minds, and spirits, to discover and embrace what it means individually to be created *imago Dei*, and as congregations and dioceses to become intentional centers for *missio Dei*, recognizing that God's mission has a church. This is what we are called to be: God's missional church.

STANDING COMMISSION ON THE STRUCTURE OF THE CHURCH
www.episcopalchurch.org/gc/ccab/scs/default.html

Membership

Mrs. Patricia B. Kilpatrick, *Chair*	Ohio, V, 2003
The Rev. Canon Gene Robinson, *Vice-Chair*	New Hampshire, I, 2006
Mrs. Mary S. Kimball, *Secretary*	California, VIII, 2003
The Very Rev. H. Jay Atwood	Fort Worth, VII, 2006
Mrs. Kit T. Caffey	Central Gulf Coat, IV, 2003
Mr. Justin Chapman	Minnesota, VI, 2006
John Wood Goldsack, Esq.	New Jersey, II, 2006
Hon. Maggie N. Tinsman	Iowa, VI, 2006
Mr. David R. Pitts, *Special Representative*	Louisiana, IV, 2003
The Rev. John David Lane	Southwestern Virginia, III, 2006
The Rt. Rev. Dorsey F. Henderson	Upper South Carolina, IV, 2003
The Rt. Rev. D. Bruce MacPherson	Western Louisiana, VII, 2006
The Rt. Rev. R. Stewart Wood	Vermont, I, 2003
The Rev. Canon Stephen T. Lane	Rochester, II, Executive Council liaison*

*Canon Lane was transferred to act as liaison to the Anglican Church in Canada
The Very Rev. Cynthia Black (Western Michigan, V) replaced him as Council liaison.

COMMISSION REPRESENTATIVES AT GENERAL CONVENTION

The Rt. Rev. D. Bruce MacPherson for the House of Bishops and John Wood Goldsack, Esq. for the House of Deputies to accept or reject, on behalf of the Commission, any non-substantial amendments in such House to any Resolution contained in this Report.

MEETING OF THE COMMISSION

The Standing Commission on the Structure of the Church (the Commission or SCSC) met three times during the triennium: at Duncan Center, DelRay Beach, FL, March 19-21, 2001, at The Episcopal Church Center, New York, NY, December 3-5, 2001, and Bishop Mason Conference Center, Flower Mound, TX, April 28-30, 2002. These General Principles adopted in 1995 have guided the Commission:

- This church is a national church participating fully in the Anglican Communion.
- This church is one diverse community of Christ's reconciling ministry in the world.
- This church will commit to the dioceses and provinces only that mission and ministry which cannot be accomplished effectively by parishes and congregations.
- This church will commit to national structures only that mission and ministry which cannot be accomplished effectively by dioceses and provinces.
- The form of this church will follow function, and the structure of this church will follow ministry and mission.
- This church must be structured at all levels so that structures do not inhibit deliberate change.

The Future of Province IX

GC Resolution 2000-B005 in part resolved "that the Standing Commission on the Structure of the Church be directed to work with the Executive Council and the provincial leadership to study and make recommendations to the 74th General Convention" on "the future of Province IX, working with the Standing Commission on World Mission and the individual dioceses."

Early in the triennium, the desire of three extra-provincial dioceses (Puerto Rico, Venezuela, and Cuba) to join or re-join ECUSA was made known to the two Standing Commissions named in the resolution. The matter of their possible incorporation was folded into the work of the two Commissions, with the Standing Commission on World Mission (SCWM) asking the theological and missiological questions, and the Standing

Commission on the Structure of the Church focusing on the structural issues raised by such an incorporation, in the context of the overall future of Province IX. This report should be read in tandem with SCWM's Blue Book Report.

Pursuant to the question of the future of Province IX and the incorporation of these three extra-provincial dioceses, the Standing Commission on Structure convened a meeting in the Dominican Republic in April, 2002. Participants at the meeting included: all the bishops of the dioceses remaining in Province IX (Dominican Republic, Honduras, Central Diocese of Ecuador, Litoral Diocese of Ecuador, Colombia); the bishops of the three extra-provincial dioceses seeking incorporation (Puerto Rico, Cuba, Venezuela); representatives of the Standing Commission on Structure, the Standing Commission on World Mission, the House of Bishops Office of Pastoral Development, the Presiding Bishop's staff, and the Church Pension Fund. The following questions/issues were raised, with the following results:

Should the dioceses which remain in Province IX, following the autonomy processes of Mexico and IARCA, be divided up and assigned to provinces in the continental United States? There is NO support from any of the remaining dioceses of Province IX to be divided up and distributed among the eight continental dioceses of ECUSA. All agreed that such an alternative would divide and weaken the voice and witness of our Spanish-speaking brothers and sisters in Christ at all levels of the Church's life and ministry. Such a "non-future" was resoundingly abandoned.

What are the intentions of the extra-provincial dioceses about their own future in and with Province IX? The Bishops of these three dioceses expressed their intention to ask to be incorporated into ECUSA, to place themselves under the metropolitical authority of the Presiding Bishop of the Episcopal Church, and to become part of Province IX. Each bishop reported that appropriate resolutions requesting such incorporation had been passed by their respective Diocesan Conventions. [This may have been a bit of a stretch with regard to the resolution passed by Cuba. Please see note at the end of this report.] The bishops of the dioceses of Province IX were unanimously supportive of such an application for incorporation and excited about what their joining might mean for the future of Province IX. A resolution expressing that support read, in part: "That the Committees on Structure and World Mission present to the 74th General Convention of the Episcopal Church in the United States of America in 2003, the formal request for the incorporation of the Diocese of Venezuela and the re-incorporation of the dioceses of Cuba and Puerto Rico as members of the General Convention of the United States of America." And "That the Bishops of the IX Province fully support the initiatives by the diocesan conventions of Cuba, Puerto Rico and Venezuela requesting that the 74th General Convention of the Episcopal Church in the United States of America accepts these dioceses as members in good standing with this Church."

What does all this mean for the process of autonomy, which has been central to ECUSA's approach to mission and ministry in this region? While the autonomy process has guided our relationships in the past (resulting in the new Anglican provinces of Mexico and Central America), there seems to be NO support for or movement toward autonomy from ECUSA for the remaining Province IX dioceses. Indeed, after frank and open discussions about the past and present, the group expressed its belief that the unintended effect of assuming that all the dioceses of Province IX would one day exist in their own autonomous provinces was a gradual pulling back – from both sides – by ECUSA and by these Province IX dioceses. Sadness was expressed by all for this state of affairs, and there was great interest in reversing this trend. The incorporation of the three extra-provincial dioceses and the revitalization of Province IX was seen to be a timely opportunity for reinvigorating the relationship between Province IX and the rest of ECUSA.

What does all this mean for the regionalization process within Province IX and the Caribbean? During the past few years, several attempts have been made to gather dioceses of the Caribbean in regions ("the Caribbean region" and ARENSA). Such a division of these dioceses not only left out Honduras, but contributed to the notion that all of these dioceses were headed toward autonomy. This meeting unanimously made clear that such a "regionalization" in Province IX is counterproductive and undesirable.

Who will lead the newly-reorganized and revitalized Province IX? In recent years, there has been no duly constituted Synod meeting in Province IX. Therefore, the leadership had been irregularly elected by an Executive Committee. Plans were put in place for an interim period of leadership, until a duly constituted Synod could meet and elect Synod officers. That transition has now occurred, and Province IX is now functioning according to the same canons and guidelines as the other eight provinces of ECUSA.

It is important to note here that it is Province IX's hope to operate much as the other eight provinces do and be accorded the same rights and bear the same responsibilities. Rather than being regarded as a "missionary" province, with exceptional staffing, funding and program, they hope to be one of nine equal provinces of the church, all the while recognizing the special circumstances which exist in that region. In June, 2002, the Provincial Leadership Conference (the presidents, vice presidents and program coordinators) met in San Juan, Puerto Rico, and spent considerable time with the people and staff of the Diocese of Puerto Rico. Bishop Allen, of Honduras, also attended that meeting, and for the first time in several years, the voice of Province IX was present. They were warmly welcomed and heard. Province IX was also a full participant in the December meeting of the Provincial Leadership Conference, and the PLC welcomed its "return to the table."

What work needs to be done regarding the Church Pension Fund and these three dioceses which seek reincorporation into ECUSA? Church Pension Fund Vice President Linda Curtiss, and her new assistant, The Rev. Efrain Huerta, newly named Director of Companion Pension Relations (who had not yet begun his job with CPG), were present to discuss the ramifications of the three extra-provincial dioceses' incorporation into ECUSA. The very complicated issue of how to incorporate the new dioceses into the Church Pension Fund was discussed. One of the issues brought to light in these discussions – which is true for ALL the dioceses of Province IX – is that the church pension compensation formula for clergy is based upon the notion that a base amount of compensation is provided by Social Security – an assumption that is not true for the dioceses of Province IX, since they are obviously not part of the United States' Social Security system. Ms. Curtiss noted that some different formula may need to be developed for these non-U.S. dioceses, based on different assumptions and realities. The calculations which will need to be done to explore pension fund options will largely depend on the three dioceses' provision of relevant data. Church Pension seems very willing and eager to serve the church in this incorporation process, but cannot proceed without sufficient data from the dioceses themselves (not always easy to obtain).

It is important to note that the subject of pensions for the clergy of the three dioceses seeking incorporation was the LAST topic to be undertaken. We are aware that some people in the Church hold the opinion that the application for reincorporation into ECUSA by these three dioceses is being driven by the need for adequate pensions. As a result of this meeting, it seems clear to the Standing Commission on Structure that the issue of pensions is NOT the driving force, but rather one of several issues and needs addressed by the application for incorporation. Such a narrow accusation, in our view, underestimates the mission and ministry of our brothers and sisters in Christ and trivializes their appropriate and faithful aspirations for incorporation into ECUSA.

NOTE: Subsequent to the meeting and conclusions denoted above, the Standing Commission on World Mission encountered some further developments with the Diocese of Cuba which seemed to indicate a less-than-enthusiastic support in the Diocese of Cuba for the proposed incorporation. Indeed, a closer look at the "enabling" legislation passed by the Diocesan Convention indicated that a formal application for incorporation into ECUSA had not been completed. (Also, see the SCWM Blue Book report.)

Therefore, the following TWO resolutions are presented jointly by the Standing Commission on the Structure of the Church and the Standing Commission on World Mission. They are based on clear and well supported resolutions for incorporation from the Diocesan Conventions of Puerto Rico and Venezuela. While we support the incorporation of the Diocese of Cuba into ECUSA, a resolution to that effect will await a formal and well supported petition from the Diocese of Cuba – which, if received, will be prepared as a supplementary resolution.

Resolution A141 Admit Diocese of Puerto Rico

1   *Resolved,* the House of _____ concurring, That the 2003 General Convention admit the Diocese of Puerto
2   Rico to the Episcopal Church USA and recognize it as a diocese in union with General Convention; and be
3   it further
4   Resolved, That the General Convention designate the Diocese of Puerto Rico as a member diocese of
5   Province IX of the Episcopal Church; and be it further
6   *Resolved,* That the Diocese of Puerto Rico be entitled to all rights pertaining to membership in the
7   Episcopal Church as provided in the Constitution and Canons, including, but not limited to, voice and vote
8   in the House of Bishops and House of Deputies, in accordance with the rules of those houses; and be it
9   further
10   *Resolved*, That the Diocese of Puerto Rico be obligated to undertake all responsibilities pertaining to
11   diocesan membership in the Episcopal Church as provided in the Constitution and Canons, including, but
12   not limited to, conforming its constitution and canons to the provisions of the Constitution and Canons of
13   the Episcopal Church; submitting annual diocesan and parochial reports to the General Convention Office;
14   contributing annually to the apportionment budget of the Domestic and Foreign Missionary Society; and
15   reporting fully on any financial assistance it receives from the General Convention budget; and be it
16   further
17   *Resolved,* That this convention affirm that the clergy and lay employees of the Diocese of Puerto Rico will
18   be eligible to participate in companion pension plans administered by the Church Pension Fund, with
19   benefits adapted to the particular needs of the Diocese and consistent with applicable law; and be it further
20   *Resolved,* That this convention urge the Church Pension Fund to work with the Diocese of Puerto Rico to
21   develop a plan to cover the unfunded period of time for those of its clergy who previously participated in
22   the Church Pension Fund when the Diocese was a member of the Episcopal Church; and be it further
23   *Resolved,* That the portion of this resolution accepting the Diocese of Puerto Rico into union with the
24   General Convention become effective by written directive by the Presiding Bishop to the Bishop of the
25   Diocese on such date after January 1, 2004 on which the Secretary of the General Convention certifies to
26   the Presiding Bishop that the Secretary has received from the Diocese written evidence that the Diocese
27   has successfully undertaken all the foregoing responsibilities pertaining to membership in the Episcopal
28   Church as provided in the Constitution and Canons; and be it further
29   *Resolved,* That this convention re-affirm the principle that dioceses of this church that are not located
30   within the United States may seek autonomy according to the procedures set forth in Resolution 235a of
31   the 1991 General Convention or may join other provinces of the Anglican Communion.

EXPLANATION

On Jan. 14, 2003, the Rt. Rev. David Andres Alvares, Bishop of Puerto Rico wrote to the Commission chair: "This is to inform you that in a special Convention of the Diocese of Puerto Rico, held on the 11th of January at the Diocesan Center in Saint Just, a Resolution was approved to ask for Incorporation into the Episcopal Church in the United States. The Convention dealt with the ecclesiological, canonical, financial and administrative aspects. After receiving reports on them, the Resolution was presented as follows: 'Resolved by this Special Convention to ask the Standing Commission on Structure and the Standing Commission on World Mission of the Episcopal Church in the United States to present to the General Convention to meet in the city of Minneapolis in July of 2003, our request for Incorporation and Canonical Conformity in that Province of the Anglican Communion with all the responsibilities, rights and privileges it conveys.' In a secret vote by orders, the results for the clergy were 54 in favor to 11 against. For the laity the results were 63 in favor to 22 against, for a total of 117 in favor and 33 against."

The Standing Commission on World Mission regards this as a well supported resolution from the Diocese of Puerto Rico and supports incorporation for reasons set forth in its Blue Book Report.

Resolution A142 Admit Diocese of Venezuela

1   *Resolved,* the House of _____ concurring, That the 74th General Convention admit the Diocese of
2   Venezuela to the Episcopal Church USA and recognize it as a diocese in union with General Convention;
3   and be it further

4 *Resolved*, That the General Convention designate the Diocese of Venezuela as a member diocese of
5 Province IX of the Episcopal Church; and be further
6 *Resolved*, That the Diocese of Venezuela be entitled to all rights pertaining to membership in Episcopal
7 Church as provided in the Constitution and Canons, including, but not limited to, voice and vote in the
8 House of Bishops and House of Deputies, in accordance with the rules of those houses; and be it further
9 *Resolved*, That the Diocese of Venezuela be obligated to undertake all responsibilities pertaining to
10 diocesan membership in the Episcopal Church as provided in the Constitution and Canons, including, but
11 not limited to, conforming its constitution and canons to the provisions of the Constitution and Canons of
12 the Episcopal Church; submitting annual diocesan and parochial reports to the General Convention Office;
13 contributing annually to the apportionment budget of the Domestic and Foreign Missionary Society; and
14 reporting fully on any financial assistance it receives from the General Convention budget; and be it
15 further
16 *Resolved*, That this convention affirm that the clergy and lay employees of the Diocese of Venezuela will
17 be eligible to participate in the Church Pension Fund, subject to the rules of the Church Pension Fund; and
18 be it further
19 *Resolved*, That this convention urge the Church Pension Fund to work with the Diocese of Venezuela to
20 develop a plan to cover the unfunded period of time for those of its clergy who previously participated in
21 the Church Pension Fund when the diocese was a member of the Episcopal Church; and be it further
22 *Resolved*, That this convention re-affirm the principle that dioceses of this church that are not located
23 within the United States may seek autonomy according to the procedures set forth in Resolution 235a of
24 the 1991 General Convention or may join other provinces of the Anglican Communion.

EXPLANATION
The Standing Commission on World Mission regards this as a well supported resolution from the Diocese
of Venezuela and supports incorporation for reasons set forth in its Blue Book Report.

The General Convention

Resolution A143 Constitution Article I, Section 7

1 *Resolved,* the House of _____ concurring, That Article I, Section 7 of the Constitution is amended to read:
2 Section 7. The General Convention shall meet not less than once in each three years, at a time and place
3 appointed by ~~a preceding Convention; but if there shall appear to the Presiding Bishop, acting with the~~
4 ~~advice and consent of the Executive Council of the Church or of a successor canonical body having~~
5 ~~substantially the powers now vested in the Executive Council, sufficient cause for changing the place or~~
6 ~~date so appointed, the Presiding Bishop, with the advice and consent of such body, shall appoint another~~
7 ~~place or date, or both, for such meeting.~~ the Joint Standing Committee on Planning and Arrangements.
8 Special meetings may be provided by Canon.

Resolution A144 Canon I.1.14(a)

1 *Resolved,* the House of _____ concurring, That Canon I.1.14 is amended to read as follows:

2 (a) At each meeting of the General Convention the Joint Standing Committee on Planning and
3   Arrangements shall submit to the General Convention its recommendations for sites for the meeting of
4   the General Convention to be held as the ~~second~~ third succeeding General Convention following the
5   General Convention at which the report is made…

6 (c)From the sites approved by the General Convention, the Joint Committee, with the advice and consent
7   of a majority vote of the following: The Presidents and the Vice-Presidents of both Houses of
8   Convention, the Presidents of the Provinces and the Executive Council, shall determine the site for
9   such General Convention and proceed to make all reasonable and necessary arrangements and
10   commitments for that meeting of the General Convention. ~~The site shall be recommended before the~~
11   ~~meeting of the General Convention next preceding that Convention.~~

12 ~~(d)Subject to the Constitution, the General Convention shall appoint a site at the General Convention next~~
13   ~~preceding such Convention.~~

14 ~~(e)~~ (d)Upon the final selection of and the arrangements for the site for that General Convention, the Joint
15 Committee shall advise the Secretary of General Convention, who shall communicate the
16 determination to the Dioceses.

17 ~~(f) In the event of a change of circumstances indicating the necessity or advisability of changing the site of~~
18 ~~a future meeting of the General Convention previously determined by action of the General~~
19 ~~Convention, the Joint Committee shall investigate and make recommendations to the Presiding Bishop,~~
20 ~~to the President of the House of Deputies, and to the Executive Council if such Convention is the next~~
21 ~~succeeding meeting or to the General Convention with respect to any later meeting of the Convention.~~

22 ~~(g)~~ (e) Within such guidelines as may have been established by the General Convention regarding the date
23 and length of future General Conventions, and pursuant to the reasonable and necessary arrangements
24 and commitments with the Dioceses and operators of facilities within the Diocese in which the next
25 General Convention will be held, the Joint Committee shall fix the date and the length of the next
26 succeeding Convention, report the same to the Secretary of the General Convention and include the
27 same in its report to the Convention. In the event of a change of circumstances indicating the necessity
28 or advisability of changing the date or length previously fixed, the Joint Committee shall investigate
29 and make recommendations to the Presiding Bishop and the President of the House of Deputies, who,
30 with the advice and consent of the Executive Council, may fix a different date or length or both.

EXPLANATION

The economic realities and competitive market for large conventions requires that the Joint Committee on Planning and Arrangements be able to enter into binding contracts for Convention sites more than three years before the scheduled event. Inability to act earlier and decisively has already resulted in key sites becoming unavailable as General Convention sites.

The proposed changes are both constitutional, requiring passage at two consecutive conventions, and Canonical which can be perfected at a single convention.

General Convention will still be able to select those cities to be considered as potential sites for future Conventions but the Joint Committee on Planning and Arrangements will be able to choose from among the potential sites without further action on the part of General Convention.

Resolution A145 General Convention Model

1 *Resolved,* the House of _____ concurring, That the Presiding Bishop and the President of the House of
2 Deputies appoint a Joint Task Force consisting of members of the Standing Commission on Structure of
3 the Church and the Joint Standing Committee on Planning and Arrangements to prepare a comprehensive
4 model for General Convention with respect to the Structure of General Convention and the General
5 Convention Agenda to be considered for implementation by the 75th General Convention.

EXPLANATION

GC Resolution 2003-C020 charged the Standing Commission on Structure of the Church "to review the structure of General Convention that considers ways to establish greater efficiency, ensure the diversity of representation, make use of all available technology, and shorten the duration of Convention.

The Commission believes the goals set forth in C020 are imperative but cannot be addressed by SCSC without the benefit of discussion with the Joint Standing Committee on Planning and Arrangements. Working together and with the assistance of the Presiding Bishop and the President of the House of Deputies, the Commission believes in resolving the competing needs of "gathering the family" and shortening the length of Convention to make it more accessible to people who are unable to commit themselves to two weeks away from their families and their business lives. The Church must commit itself to thinking seriously about finding ways to allow people from all backgrounds to participate in the General Convention process.

Provincial Coordinators

Resolution A146 Provincial Coordinators Funding

1   *Resolved,* the House of _____ concurring, That the 74th General Convention continue to appropriate
2   sufficient funds to ensure the continuation of Provincial Coordinators.

EXPLANATION

During the past triennium General Convention provided $200,000.00 each year to compensate a paid
Provincial Coordinator in each of the eight Provinces. As a result, the Provinces were able to become more
pro-active in the mission and ministry of the church and experienced widespread growth in Provincial
Program Ministries. The investment in funding Provincial Coordinators has generated the results intended.
(See also the report of the Provincial Leadership Conference.)

Legislative Committees

Resolution A147 Legislative Committee Membership

1   *Resolved,* the House of _____ concurring, That all Legislative Committees be appointed in such a manner
2   to include a sufficient number of the members of the Standing Commission or Committee for such area of
3   concern, together with a sufficient number of deputies not serving on the Standing Commission or
4   Committee.

EXPLANATION

At the 73rd General Convention, the Standing Commission on the Structure of the Church had very few
members assigned to the Legislative Committee on Structure. As a result, the Legislative Committee often
lacked a clear understanding of the work performed by the Standing Commission. The Commission
believes every Legislative Committee will benefit by having a sufficient number of members from the
respective Standing Commission/ Committee to ensure continuity in the work being pursued.

Resolution A148 Filing Resolutions

1   *Resolved,* the House of _____ concurring, That Article VI, Resolutions and Memorials, Rule 21(e)
2   of the Rules of Order, House of Deputies be amended to read:
3   (e) Any such Resolution received by the Secretary of the House of Deputies at least ~~ninety (90)~~ thirty (30)
4   days prior to the opening date of the Convention shall be referred to the proper Legislative Committee or
5   Special Committee Chair at least ~~sixty (60)~~ fifteen (15) days prior to the opening date of Convention. The
6   Secretary shall acknowledge receipt of all such Resolutions to the proposer.

EXPLANATION

With the wide use of technology and with most resolutions being submitted electronically the Commission
believes the shortened time frame suggested will be reasonable and will ensure that Legislative
Committees will receive the materials they need prior to the opening of Convention.

Resolution A149 Special Legislative Committees

1   *Resolved,* the House of _____ concurring, That Special Legislative Committees appointed to handle "hot
2   button" issues be appointed sufficiently in advance of General Convention to ensure that existing
3   Legislative Committees not lose vital members, and to allow scheduling of Special Hearings at times when
4   members of Legislative Committees can attend.

EXPLANATION

At the 73rd General Convention a Special Legislative Committee was formed to deal with Human
Sexuality issues. While no one disputes the wisdom of such special committees to handle "hot button"
issues, the Commission is concerned that such committees be appointed sufficiently in advance of
Convention so as not to remove vital members of other Standing Committees or Commissions.

The Commission is also concerned that the hearings of such special committees be held so that members
of existing legislative committees can attend without neglecting their own legislative responsibilities.

Budget

The Standing Commission on the Structure of the Church will meet three times in the next triennium. This
will require $15,000 in 2004, $24,000 in 2005 and $10,000 in 2006 for a total of $49,000 for the triennium.

STANDING COMMISSION ON WORLD MISSION
www.episcopalchurch.org/gc/ccab/scwm/default.html

Membership

The Very Rev. Dr. Titus Presler, *Chair*	Texas *(previously Massachusetts),* 2003
The Rev. Canon Kathleen J. Cullinane, *Vice-Chair*	Indianapolis, 2003
Ms. Nancy W. Broadwell, *Secretary and Treasurer*	East Carolina, 2003,
Mr. Dennis G. Case	Southwestern Virginia, 2003
Dr. Diana Dillenberger-Frade	Southeast Florida, 2006
The Rt. Rev. James E. Folts	West Texas, 2006
Ms. Joan Hermon,	Virgin Islands, 2003
Mr. Willis Jenkins	Oklahoma, 2006
The Rev. Dr. Harold Lewis	Pittsburgh, 2006, resigned December 2002
Ms. Helena Mbele-Mbong	Churches in Europe, 2006
The Rt. Rev. Wilfrido Ramos-Orench	Connecticut, 2006
The Rt. Rev. William J. Skilton	South Carolina, 2003
Ms. Carole Jan Lee	*Executive Council liaison*
The Rev. Canon Patrick Mauney	*Episcopal Church Center staff liaison*

WORK SUMMARY

Mandate: "It shall be the duty of the Commission, as to all mission outside the United States, to review and evaluate existing policies, priorities and strategies, and to promote partnership for global mission among the various groups within the church, to plan and propose policy on overseas mission, and to make recommendations pertaining to the Executive Council and the General Convention." (Canon I.1.2(n)(9)

Introduction

During this triennium the work of the Standing Commission on World Mission (SCWM) has been guided by the following priorities:

- Develop a vision statement for the church's world mission
- Convene a consultation on roles of race, money, and power in mission
- Assist in processes related to autonomy of international dioceses
- Assist in processes related to incorporation of international dioceses
- Monitor and collaborate with Episcopal Partnership for Global Mission
- Support development of the Convocation of American Churches in Europe

The Commission met at St. Christopher's Conference Center, South Carolina, in January 2001; at St. Margaret's Convent, Boston in October 2001; at St. Christopher's Conference Center, South Carolina, in April 2002; in Havana, Cuba, in October 2002; and in Miami in January 2003. The meeting at St. Christopher's in April 2002 was held jointly to coincide with the annual general meeting of the Episcopal Partnership for Global Mission (EPGM). The Boston meeting included the Consultation on Race, Money and Power. The meeting in Havana included the Consultation on Incorporation with the Dioceses of Cuba, Puerto Rico, and Venezuela. Members visited the Convocation of American Churches in Europe three times.

The commission's work in helping develop the Standards for Sending Long-Term Missionaries was presented at the Jacksonville meeting of Executive Council. The Vision Subcommittee met with the staff of Anglican and Global Relations in New York in September 2001, with the Seminary Consultation on Mission in Berkeley in October 2001, and in Austin in June 2002 to work on the Vision Statement.

The chair represented the Commission and presented at the Conference of Anglican Mission Organizations in Cyprus in February 2003. A member presented the Vision Statement at the New Wineskins for Global Mission Conference in Ridgecrest, NC, in April 2003. Members of the Autonomy Subcommittee met with representatives of dioceses in the Caribbean region at the Episcopal Church Center in New York, at Camp

Washington in Connecticut, and in Boca Chica, Dominican Republic. One member visited the Diocese of Venezuela in preparation for the 2003 General Convention.

Vision Statement
Companions in Transformation: The Episcopal Church's World Mission in a New Century

The Standing Commission on World Mission offers to the people of the Episcopal Church, through the General Convention of 2003, a vision for the church's world mission in the future. Turmoil and change in the church and on the planet make it imperative that world mission, one of the church's most extensive engagements with the wider world, be guided by reflection on the past, discernment in the present, and vision for the future. The future we realistically anticipate is the next six triennia, to the year 2020.

The vision statement is entitled "Companions in Transformation: The Episcopal Church's World Mission in a New Century." It includes a theological basis for world mission, an ethos of world mission, reflection on world crises that form the environment for world mission, proposed modes of mission, and a specific plan for gathering resources and carrying out world mission. The entire statement, is available on our web-site and will be provided to bishops and deputies at the Convention, as required for legislative action.

Consultation with many individuals and groups occurred throughout the triennium to produce a document with as wide a scope of input at possible. Those consulted included the Episcopal Partnership for Global Mission (EPGM) and its member organizations in the areas of sending, receiving, education, funding and networking; the Seminary Consultation on Mission; international mission companions in Africa, Asia, Europe, Latin America, and Oceania; mission agencies in other Anglican provinces; ecumenical companions; and missionaries of the church serving through various agencies.

Resolution A150 World Mission Vision

1 *Resolved,* the House of _____ concurring, That the 2003 General Convention call the church to study,
2 during the 2004–2006 triennium, the vision for world mission contained in the document, "Companions in
3 Transformation: The Episcopal Church's World Mission in a New Century," prepared by the Standing
4 Commission on World Mission; and be it further
5 *Resolved,* That this Convention call on parishes, dioceses, voluntary mission agencies, seminaries, mission
6 networks, and Episcopal Church Center agencies to consider the statement's proposals and reflect on the
7 feasibility of initiating their implementation during the 2007–2009 triennium; and be it further
8 *Resolved,* That this Convention request the Standing Commission on World Mission to gather and
9 interpret responses from around the church and make specific programmatic and budgetary proposals to
10 the 2006 General Convention.

EXPLANATION

The Commission initially envisioned implementation of "Companions in Transformation: The Episcopal Church's World Mission in a New Century" as commencing during the 2004–2006 triennium. The scope of the proposals, however, requires a triennium of study so that church members can explore and appropriate the mission understandings that the statement sets forth. The church also needs time to consider the statement's deployment and financial proposals, develop consensus, and plan for the implementation of these or other proposals during the 2007–2009 triennium. The economic slow-down and its effect of restricting the church's income are supporting reasons to call for a triennium of study and planning.

Resolution A151 World Mission Funds

1 *Resolved,* the House of _____ concurring, That the 2003 General Convention adopt the principle that
2 world mission funds historically committed to the church's global engagement through financial covenants
3 to former international jurisdictions of the church be re-deployed in other areas of the church's global
4 engagement, and especially to world mission, as such funds become available through incrementally
5 diminishing levels of support to the autonomous jurisdictions; and be it further
6 *Resolved,* That a detailed financial plan for the re-deployment of such funds be presented by the Standing
7 Commission on World Mission to the 2006 General Convention.

EXPLANATION

The vision statement prepared by the Standing Commission on World Mission, "Companions in Transformation: The Episcopal Church's World Mission in a New Century," proposes that the vision be implemented through substantial increases in the church's global mission engagement. In particular, the commission proposes energetic development of mission education; an increase in the number of missionaries sent and received, including a larger Young Adult Service Corps (YASC) and more minority missionaries; an increase in seminarian internships; better-prepared short-term mission pilgrimages; and expanded mission networking.

Greater allocations within the program budget of General Convention are necessary to implement this plan. The Commission proposes that such allocations be funded from the resources that are being released, beginning in the 1990s, as the Episcopal Church's financial obligations decrease incrementally to former Episcopal jurisdictions that are now autonomous Anglican provinces, such as the Episcopal Church in the Philippines, La Iglésia Anglicana de México, and La Iglésia Anglicana de la Région Centrale de America.

The Commission recommends that these funds continue to be used in the church's global engagement. Using them to support specific world mission initiatives will continue the Episcopal Church's historic commitment to the wider world. The proposed re-allocation is more in keeping with companionship and mutuality in mission than generalized subsidies have proved to be. Simply re-absorbing the funds into the general and undifferentiated revenues of the church — as has been the practice from the inauguration of the covenants — impairs our church's global vision of God and diminishes our church's global discipleship. Further details are set forth in the vision statement itself.

Consultation on the Intersection of Race, Money and Power in the World Mission of the Episcopal Church

The Commission met at St. Margaret's Convent, Boston, October 3–5, 2001 for a consultation on the role of race, money and power in the world mission of the Episcopal Church, one of the Commission's priorities. The consultation examined the intersection of these complex realities with world mission both historically and in the present. Presenters were: speaking on race, the Rev. Canon Burgess Carr, Candler School of Theology, Emory University, Atlanta; speaking on money, the Rev. Dr. Jonathan J. Bonk, Overseas Ministries Study Center, New Haven, Connecticut; and, speaking on power, the Rev. Canon Edmundo Desueza, Church of the Good Shepherd, Newberg, New York. Present also were eight representatives of various mission agencies working within the Episcopal Church.

A colloquy followed each presentation. The substance of the consultation is to be published by Cowley Publications and made available to the wider church. Minutes of the Consultation are available at www.episcopalchurch.org. We commend continued examination and discussion of these realities, too complex to be summarized within this report, as a means of mitigating their negative effects on the mission of the church. The discussions of the Consultation have been integral to the development of the vision statement, "Companions in Transformation: The Episcopal Church's World Mission in a New Century."

Autonomy Matters
Relationships with Autonomy Processes and Autonomous Churches

Matters related to the process by which international jurisdictions of the Episcopal Church become autonomous provinces of the Anglican Communion are overseen by this Commission, because historically autonomy has been one major outcome of the church's world mission.

SCWM maintains concern for the nurture of international dioceses that continue to be part of the Episcopal Church, which include Colombia, the Convocation of American Churches in Europe, Dominican Republic, Ecuador Central, Ecuador Litoral, Haiti, Honduras, Taiwan, and Virgin Islands. *GC Resolution 2000-129a* called on the Executive Council to tend to relationships with those dioceses in a variety of ways. It also called on Executive Council to tend to the church's relationships with jurisdictions that formerly were members of the Episcopal Church and that now are part of autonomous Anglican provinces, namely, La Igreja Episcopal Anglicana do Brasil, the Episcopal Diocese of Liberia (now part of the Province of West Africa), the

Episcopal Church in the Philippines, La Iglésia Anglicana de México, and La Iglésia Anglicana de la Region Centrale de America.

Each Covenant Committee has met at least once during the 2002–2003 triennium, and reports have been received. The financial difficulties experienced in La Iglésia Anglicana de México (IAM) as a result of the misappropriations of church funds by the Bishop of the Diocese of Western Mexico and the Bishop of the Diocese of Northern Mexico, together with the inability of the Diocese of Ecuador Central to answer auditing questions, point to the need for a relationship that assists and requires accountability for funds received from the Episcopal Church. The statement issued by the ECUSA/IAM Covenant Committee in November 2002 was an important first step toward such accountability.

Proposals for Incorporation into the Episcopal Church

Arising out of its oversight of autonomy processes, the Commission was closely involved during the 2001–2003 triennium with proposals from the Diocese of Cuba, the Diocese of Puerto Rico, and the Diocese of Venezuela to be incorporated into the Episcopal Church. It is unprecedented for a fully developed and autonomous diocese to seek membership in the Episcopal Church. Historically, the movement has been a progression from missionary district to missionary diocese to Episcopal diocese to autonomy in the Anglican Communion. These proposals represent a reverse movement and have required extensive consultation and careful reflection.

ECUSA's overall mission strategy after mid-century was for Province IX, which included Episcopal dioceses in Latin America and the Caribbean, to become one autonomous province. In 1984, the autonomy movement was differentiated regionally. Mexico proceeded to autonomy in 1995 and Central America in 1998.

During the 2001–2003 triennium the Commission participated actively in the conversations held by the Caribbean Province in Formation, which included four dioceses. Two of the four, Dominican Republic and Haiti, are dioceses of the Episcopal Church. Two of the four, Cuba and Puerto Rico, are extra-provincial, which means that they are members of no Anglican province. The Diocese of Cuba, previously an Episcopal missionary diocese under the jurisdiction of the House of Bishops, was designated extra-provincial in 1967. Metropolitical authority for it was transferred to the Metropolitan Council of Cuba, which consists of the Archbishop of the Anglican Church of Canada, the Primate of the Province of the West Indies, and the President of Province IX of ECUSA. The Diocese of Puerto Rico, also previously an Episcopal missionary diocese, became extra-provincial in 1979, with the Synod of Province IX designated as its metropolitical authority. In both cases, extra-provincial status was anticipated to be brief and transitional, with a Caribbean province to be formed imminently. In fact, Cuba's status has persisted for 36 years, and Puerto Rico's for 24 years.

With forward movement toward Caribbean autonomy difficult to achieve, Cuba and Puerto Rico initiated discussions in 2001 concerning incorporation into the Episcopal Church. In 2002, the Caribbean Covenant Committee decided to go into "recess," pending the outcome of these initiatives by Cuba and Puerto Rico. Meanwhile, the Diocese of Venezuela, also an extra-provincial diocese, initiated discussion concerning incorporation into ECUSA. Previously part of the Province of the West Indies, Venezuela became extra-provincial in 1982 and anticipated joining a projected province of the Andes that never materialized.

Theological and Missiological Basis for Incorporation

Unity and universality are fundamental to the catholic nature of the church. Catholicity involves parts of the church being in vital relationship with one another as the church is extended over time and geographical space. The Anglican Communion is a global fellowship of church families. Each church family consists of dioceses that join together to constitute one provincial church.

In this Anglican understanding of what it means to be the church, fulfilling the church's unity and universality is incompatible with the three dioceses' present situation as extra-provincial dioceses. While they are members of the Anglican Communion, they are organic members of no particular province of the communion. Thus they have no fully developed legislative, judicial or executive links with other dioceses with which they share membership in a province. The links they do have, as with the Metropolitan Council established for Cuba or with the Synod of Province IX of ECUSA, are unusual, attenuated, and anomalous. Indeed, extra-provincial status is no longer an organizational practice in the Anglican Communion. The present situation poses practical problems of governance and suffuses the identity of these dioceses with ambiguity. In Anglican polity, a diocese alone cannot function fully as a diocese.

Equally important is the rooting of the church's mission in particular contexts. In this dynamic of enculturation and indigenization the gospel takes flesh in the lifeways of peoples. Such movement in the life of a healthy church highlights the local and the particular, in contrast to the shared and the universal. Complementing the unity of the Body of Christ, its model is the particularity of God's incarnation in Jesus.

From this standpoint, the three dioceses have excelled in carrying out God's mission faithfully and vitally in their respective contexts of Cuba, Puerto Rico, and Venezuela. Separation from particular Anglican provinces has encouraged them to develop forms of gospel life that are authentic to their contexts and are not imported from the shared life of a large and powerful province such as ECUSA, or from a smaller trans-national province. The experience of true enculturation and ownership in their church life has been inspiring for them. The Commission heard of and witnessed work that confirmed that these dioceses are vigorous and strong. At the same time, their isolation from wider church conversations has been discouraging and has hampered their mission.

Supporting mission is an essential criterion for incorporating international dioceses into the Episcopal Church. At the Commission's consultation held in Cuba in October 2002, leaders of the three dioceses stated that the need for catholicity must take priority over autonomy at this historical moment. They stated that seeking an organic relationship with a viable Anglican province is essential to enabling them to carry out the fullness of God's mission among them. To the question whether incorporation would be a regressive mission strategy, the dioceses responded that incorporation will advance, not retard, their mission. To the question whether incorporation would invite neo-colonial domination, the dioceses responded that they originated these initiatives and that their experience of colonialism enables them to avoid repeating the patterns of the past. To the question whether incorporation is anachronistic in a "national church," the Commission responds that the Episcopal Church has long been international. To the question whether incorporation of mainly Hispanic dioceses is anomalous for an "Anglo church," the Commission responds that Hispanics are now the largest USA minority and that the Episcopal Church is increasingly multi-cultural. Indeed, the Commission suggests that a larger international Hispanic presence will help the Episcopal Church in its growing Hispanic mission in the USA. Additional dioceses will also strengthen Province IX.

"As a Commission, we are clear that an ECUSA diocese outside the U.S. is welcome in our church and under no obligation to become autonomous or join another Anglican province," the Commission stated in its 2000 Blue Book report. "At the same time, our church remains committed to assisting with the autonomy process of non-U.S. dioceses that do wish to become autonomous" (p. 491). While the incorporation proposals we support are not framed as interim or temporary, dioceses incorporated will be free to pursue autonomy in the future under the terms of Resolution 235a of the 1991 General Convention.

Pension Concerns

A concern of the three dioceses has been to provide a pension system that assures the well-being and security of their clergy and lay employees. The complexity of the issue requires that the Church Pension Fund be sensitive and fair to the particular needs and dynamics of each diocese. The Commission understands that clergy will be eligible to join these plans from their diocese's time of entry as long as pension premiums are being paid. The Commission hopes that the unfunded liability, i.e., coverage for the period during which dioceses previously part of ECUSA dioceses were not contributing, will be resolved by the time of General Convention.

Political Environments

Having considered the political environments of the three dioceses, the Commission believes that fulfilling God's mission is the primary consideration that should occupy General Convention's attention. The long-standing independence movement in Puerto Rico, the ongoing enmity between the United States of America and Cuba, and the current turmoil in Venezuela are important ongoing conditions in the countries concerned.

Companionship in mission, however, and the unity of the body of Christ must be our guiding principles as a church. Political challenges should not determine whether to proceed with incorporation. Practically, the mutual support that membership in Province IX will offer may mitigate the effects of adverse political conditions.

Structural Matters

Congregational and diocesan structures in dioceses being incorporated should be based on local models, not necessarily on models in the USA. On the basis of their regional location, dioceses being incorporated would be a part of Province IX, which would also help to strengthen Province IX, a concern of the 2000 General Convention. Dioceses being incorporated would be full and regular dioceses of ECUSA, not missionary dioceses (of which there are none in ECUSA at this time). The Commission consulted with the Standing Commission on Structure during the 2001-2003 triennium concerning the advisability of incorporation and the form it would take in the church's structure.

Resolutions

Clear and well supported resolutions for incorporation have been received from the Diocese of Puerto Rico and the Diocese of Venezuela. In concert with the Standing Commission on Structure, the Commission offers resolutions supporting the incorporation of these two dioceses. The Commission supports the Diocese of Cuba in its discussions regarding incorporation into ECUSA. As of the date of this report a formal petition from the Diocese of Cuba had not been received, but the Commission was prepared to offer a supplementary resolution should a well supported petition be forthcoming.

Resolution A141 Admit Diocese of Puerto Rico

1 *Resolved,* the House of _____ concurring, That the 2003 General Convention admit the Diocese of Puerto
2 Rico to the Episcopal Church USA and recognize it as a diocese in union with General Convention; and be
3 it further
4 Resolved, That the General Convention designate the Diocese of Puerto Rico as a member diocese of
5 Province IX of the Episcopal Church; and be it further
6 *Resolved,* That the Diocese of Puerto Rico be entitled to all rights pertaining to membership in the
7 Episcopal Church as provided in the Constitution and Canons, including, but not limited to, voice and vote
8 in the House of Bishops and House of Deputies, in accordance with the rules of those houses; and be it
9 further
10 *Resolved*, That the Diocese of Puerto Rico be obligated to undertake all responsibilities pertaining to
11 diocesan membership in the Episcopal Church as provided in the Constitution and Canons, including, but
12 not limited to, conforming its constitution and canons to the provisions of the Constitution and Canons of
13 the Episcopal Church; submitting annual diocesan and parochial reports to the General Convention Office;
14 contributing annually to the apportionment budget of the Domestic and Foreign Missionary Society; and
15 reporting fully on any financial assistance it receives from the General Convention budget; and be it
16 further
17 *Resolved,* That this convention affirm that the clergy and lay employees of the Diocese of Puerto Rico will
18 be eligible to participate in companion pension plans administered by the Church Pension Fund, with
19 benefits adapted to the particular needs of the Diocese and consistent with applicable law; and be it further
20 *Resolved,* That this convention urge the Church Pension Fund to work with the Diocese of Puerto Rico to
21 develop a plan to cover the unfunded period of time for those of its clergy who previously participated in
22 the Church Pension Fund when the Diocese was a member of the Episcopal Church; and be it further
23 *Resolved,* That the portion of this resolution accepting the Diocese of Puerto Rico into union with the
24 General Convention become effective by written directive by the Presiding Bishop to the Bishop of the
25 Diocese on such date after January 1, 2004 on which the Secretary of the General Convention certifies to
26 the Presiding Bishop that the Secretary has received from the Diocese written evidence that the Diocese
27 has successfully undertaken all the foregoing responsibilities pertaining to membership in the Episcopal
28 Church as provided in the Constitution and Canons; and be it further
29 *Resolved,* That this convention re-affirm the principle that dioceses of this church that are not located

30 within the United States may seek autonomy according to the procedures set forth in Resolution 235a of
31 the 1991 General Convention or may join other provinces of the Anglican Communion.

EXPLANATION

On January 14, 2003, the Rt. Rev. David Andres Alvares, Bishop of Puerto Rico wrote to the Commission: "This is to inform you that in a special Convention of the Diocese of Puerto Rico, held on the 11th of January at the Diocesan Center in Saint Just, a Resolution was approved to ask for Incorporation into the Episcopal Church in the United States. The Convention dealt with the ecclesiological, canonical, financial and administrative aspects. After receiving reports on them, the Resolution was presented as follows: 'Resolved by this Special Convention to ask the Standing Commission on Structure and the Standing Commission on World Mission of the Episcopal Church in the United States to present to the General Convention to meet in the city of Minneapolis in July of 2003, our request for Incorporation and Canonical Conformity in that Province of the Anglican Communion with all the responsibilities, rights and privileges it conveys.' In a secret vote by orders, the results for the clergy were 54 in favor to 11 against. For the laity the results were 63 in favor to 22 against, for a total of 117 in favor and 33 against."

The Standing Commission on World Mission regards this as a clear and well supported resolution from the Diocese of Puerto Rico and supports incorporation for reasons set forth in its Blue Book Report.

Resolution A142 Admit Diocese of Venezuela

1   *Resolved,* the House of _____ concurring, That the 74th General Convention admit the Diocese of
2   Venezuela to the Episcopal Church USA and recognizes it as a diocese in union with General Convention;
3   and be it further
4   *Resolved,* That the General Convention designate the Diocese of Venezuela as a member diocese of
5   Province IX of the Episcopal Church; and be it further
6   *Resolved,* That the Diocese of Venezuela be entitled to all rights pertaining to membership in the
7   Episcopal Church as provided in the Constitution and Canons, including, but not limited to, voice and vote
8   in the House of Bishops and House of Deputies, in accordance with the rules of those houses; and be it
9   further
10 *Resolved,* That the Diocese of Venezuela be obligated to undertake all responsibilities pertaining to
11 diocesan membership in the Episcopal Church as provided in the Constitution and Canons, including, but
12 not limited to, conforming its constitution and canons to the provisions of the Constitution and Canons of
13 the Episcopal Church; submitting annual diocesan and parochial reports to the General Convention Office;
14 contributing annually to the apportionment budget of the Domestic and Foreign Missionary Society; and
15 reporting fully on any financial assistance it receives from the General Convention budget; and be it
16 further
17 *Resolved,* That this convention affirm that the clergy and lay employees of the Diocese of Venezuela will
18 be eligible to participate in companion pension plans administered by the Church Pension Fund, with
19 benefits adapted to the particular needs of the Diocese and consistent with applicable law; and be it further
20 *Resolved,* That the portion of this resolution accepting the Diocese of Venezuela into union with the
21 General Convention become effective by written directive by the Presiding Bishop to the Bishop of the
22 Diocese on such date after January 1, 2004 on which the Secretary of the General Convention certifies to
23 the Presiding Bishop that the Secretary has received from the Diocese written evidence that the Diocese
24 has successfully undertaken all the foregoing responsibilities pertaining to membership in the Episcopal
25 Church as provided in the Constitution and Canons; and be it further
26 *Resolved,* That this convention re-affirm the principle that dioceses of this church that are not located
27 within the United States may seek autonomy according to the procedures set forth in Resolution 235a of
28 the 1991 General Convention or may join other provinces of the Anglican Communion.

EXPLANATION

At a meeting that the Standing Commission on the Structure of the Church convened with representatives of Province IX in Boca Chica, Dominican Republic, on April 18, 2002, the Rt. Rev. Orlando Guerrero, Bishop of Venezuela, presented documentation of the actions of the convention of the Diocese of Venezuela in Caracas on April 9, 2002, when it resolved: " I. To request that the Episcopal Church of the

United States incorporate us as full members, joining in this process with the dioceses of Puerto Rico and Cuba. II. To seek the support of Province IX as our metropolitical authority to initiate the process to enter our petition as an agenda item in the General Convention of 2003. III. To present this communication to the Restructuring Committee of Province IX meeting in Boca Chica, Dominican Republic on the 18th of April of this year [2002]. IV. To send a copy of this communication to the Executive Council of Province IX and to the dioceses of Puerto Rico and Cuba so that they will be informed of our actions." The vote was reported to be unanimous, and signatures were presented indicating the affirmative votes of 11 clergypersons and 18 laypersons.

The Diocese of Venezuela is small. The unprecedented nature of requests from dioceses to enter the Episcopal Church means that precise requirements for such incorporation are not set forth in the Constitution and Canons. However, for comparision, the Commission notes that the Diocese of Venezuela exceeds the minimum size required for the formation of a new diocese (which the Diocese of Venezuela is not), as defined in Article V, Section 5, of the Constitution of the Episcopal Church, which specifies at least six parishes and at least six presbyters.

The Standing Commission on World Mission regards the Diocese of Venezuela's resolution as clear and well supported. The Commission supports incorporation for reasons set forth in its Blue Book Report.

Episcopal Partnership for Global Mission

EPGM is a partnership of mission organizations of the Episcopal Church, including the Domestic and Foreign Missionary Society, that was formally recognized by Resolution A128 of the 2000 General Convention. Agencies sending missionaries, receiving missionaries, funding mission, educating for mission or advancing mission strategies may belong to EPGM. Members of EPGM commit to covenants that set forth guidelines for the conduct of world mission.

During the 2001–2003 triennium, EPGM worked with Executive Council to develop the Standards for Sending Long-Term Missionaries. In accord with the EPGM Plan approved by the 2000 General Convention, these comprehensive standards, unique in the Anglican Communion, enable Executive Council to recognize missionaries sent by any member organization of EPGM as missionaries of the Episcopal Church. Thus, such recognition is extended beyond the missionaries sent by the Domestic and Foreign Missionary Society. Executive Council offered its first such recognitions at its meeting held in the Dominican Republic, January 27-30, 2003.

Resolution A152 Episcopal Partnership for Global Mission

1   *Resolved,* the House of _____ concurring, That the 74th General Convention commend the Executive
2   Council of the Episcopal Church for its collaboration with the Episcopal Partnership for Global Mission
3   (EPGM) and for its recognition of missionaries from EPGM agencies at its January 2003 meeting in the
4   Dominican Republic.

Emerging Anglicanism in Europe

A continuing priority of the SCWM over the past triennium was to continue its supportive consultation with the Convocation of American Churches in Europe. The Convocation is a collection of churches, mission congregations and specialized ministries spread geographically over five countries in continental Europe. A network of mission congregations has grown from the existing eight parishes, providing ministry to indigenous communities in Europe. Members of the Commission have been present in the conventions held during 2000–2002 and have participated in key events.

On Sunday, November 18, 2001, the Convention and guests gathered at St. Paul's Within-the-Walls, Rome, to consecrate the Rt. Rev. Pierre Welté Whalon as Bishop to serve in the Convocation of American Churches in Europe. Electing their own Bishop-in-Charge with the Presiding Bishop's approval was an important step and one fully supported and endorsed by the SCWM. On Saturday, November 17, members of the Convention, together with Bishop-elect Whalon and the Presiding Bishop, were granted an audience with Pope John Paul II. Joining the Pontifical Council for the Promotion of Christian Unity, a warm welcome was extended and personal greetings were exchanged during this historic occasion.

The 2002 Annual Convention, held at Emmanuel Church in Geneva, Switzerland, offered a time of regional discussions regarding the goals and achievements of the Convocation's vision of mission in Europe. This was part of the European Anglican Partners in Mission (PIM) process begun in 2001, which will culminate in a continent-wide consultation in May 2003. Two presenters in this discussion were members of the Commission: Helena Mbele-Mbong and Bp. William Skilton.

Specialized ministries continue to flourish, including a Taiwanese Ministry in Paris, a French congregation in Bordeaux, a refugee Center in Rome, and a Spanish congregation in Rome. The developing convocation-wide emphasis on youth and the full-time employment of a youth minister for this work affirm the Convocation's continuing spirit of mission. A European Institute for Christian Studies was established in 2002, and a full-time director was appointed.

During this triennium, a second and expanded Italian/English Book of Common Prayer has been published, and a German/English version was presented at the 2001 Convention. A Spanish/English and a French/English Book of Common Prayer are also in preparation.

The Convocation of American Churches in Europe provides a model of ministry in changing cultures for sharing the gospel and responding to the needs within these communities. A new Anglican identity is being born from an international English-speaking population. This new identity is in the process of becoming a new voice in Europe.

SCWM PRIORITIES FOR THE NEXT TRIENNIUM
World Mission
- Serve as a focal point for the study of and planning for the implementation of the vision statement, "Companions in Transformation: The Episcopal Church's World Mission in a New Century," presented to the 2003 General Convention, and make specific programmatic and budgetary proposals to the 2006 General Convention.
- Continue collaboration with the Episcopal Partnership for Global Mission, particularly in the formulation of guidelines for short-term missions, and in developing the above proposals; and hold one Commission meeting jointly with EPGM during the triennium.
- Discern greater opportunities for world mission cooperation with our Anglican and ecumenical companions.

International Dioceses
- Monitor developments in the Dioceses of Cuba, Puerto Rico and Venezuela; monitor the effectiveness of those incorporated as members of the Episcopal Church; and assure at least one visit of Commission members to each of the three dioceses during the triennium.
- Continue the Commission's involvement in the Convocation of American Churches in Europe and monitor cooperative developments with the Anglican jurisdictions in continental Europe.
- Monitor and encourage the participation of ECUSA's international dioceses in the full life of the church, while encouraging the dynamic enculturation of Christ's mission in the particular context of each.

Autonomy Process
- Continue to review the autonomy process, particularly in light of previous covenants and of the incorporation resolutions of this General Convention.
- Continue to receive and review covenant committee reports that have been directed to Executive Council.

PROPOSED BUDGET FOR THE 2004–2006 TRIENNIUM

The Standing Commission on World Mission will meet at least five times during the triennium, with three to four meetings to be held in the USA and at least two meetings outside the continental USA. SCWM's engagement with Anglican partners and the global church makes it imperative to meet from time to time outside the continental USA. Funding for consultations or sub-groups with our companions is also needed, including the Episcopal Partnership for Global Mission and the international dioceses, especially those that may be incorporated into ECUSA. This will require $38,000 in 2004; $49,000 in 2005 and $39,000 in 2006 for a total of $126,000 for the triennium.

OTHER REPORTS

THE JOINT STANDING COMMITTEE ON NOMINATIONS

Membership

Mr. Matthew K. Chew, *Chair*	Arizona
Ms. Cynthia S. Schwab, *Vice Chair*	West Missouri
The Rev. Can. David E. Bailey, *Secretary*	Utah
Ms. Marjorie L. Christie	Newark, *resigned*
Ms. Margaret Ann Delaplane	Delaware
The Rt. Rev. Barbara C. Harris	Massachusetts
The Rev. Carolyn S. Keil-Kuhr	Montana
The Rt. Rev. Edward S. Little II	Northern Indiana, *appointed to fill vacancy*
Mr. Lance Nielsen	Idaho
The Rev. David S. Pollock	Washington
The Rt. Rev. Hays H. Rockwell	Missouri, *resigned*
Mr. Lee Davis Thames	Mississippi
The Rt. Rev. Don A. Wimberly	Texas

Committee Representatives at General Convention

Bishop Don A. Wimberly and Deputies Matthew K. Chew and Cynthia H. Schwab are authorized to receive non-substantive amendments to this report.

WORK SUMMARY

The Joint Standing Committee on Nominations (the Committee) held three meetings. The first was held in Hendersonville, NC, March 6-8, 2001. The next was held at the Church Center in New York City, in conjunction with a meeting of the CCAB chairs, May 9-10, 2001. The final meeting was held at Trinity Cathedral in Phoenix, AZ, February 20-21, 2002. At the first meeting officers were elected and we addressed many housekeeping matters involved with carrying out our duties. In addition the Committee:

- Decided to cast the widest possible net for candidates. We placed ads and articles in various church publications, sent letters to all Bishops and to other individuals and groups in the Church. This included accepting names from interested persons without requiring someone else to nominate them.
- Expressed its desire to attract younger people and those who have not had the opportunity to be active participants in the committees, commissions and other organized groups in the Church.
- Began work on various forms and letters required for our operations.
- Considered ways to communicate with the CCABs to ensure they had the opportunity to provide potential nominees.
- Scheduled our next meeting and drafted a proposed agenda.
- Planned to invite representatives of the four groups we provide nominations to meet with us for the purpose of obtaining information about their requirements.

At the second meeting, the Committee met with representatives from the three bodies it provides with nominations. The committee gained information concerning their needs and especially the talents and experiences needed. The fourth group provided us written information.

At this meeting we also received information concerning our need to nominate the secretary and the treasurer of the General Convention. We also met with Tom Chu to explore ways to attract candidates from the younger adults within the church. We broke into small groups to work on various matters including completing development of our communications forms and evaluation procedures.

At our final meeting we learned that of the approximately 225 persons that responded to our original appeals by expressing interest in a position, only some 130 had followed up with the necessary detail information.

This compares with 173 persons available to the 2000 Committee. Considering our efforts to attract interested people the committee is extremely disappointed that more Episcopalians had not answered the call to serve.

Breaking up into four groups, one for each entity for which we were nominating, we proceeded with our selections. Each small group's results were presented to the entire committee for final confirmation.

At the completion of our meeting there were a number of unfilled positions requiring bishops. Bishop Little agreed to consult with the other two bishops on the Committee and to recruit the additional bishops needed to complete the slate. In lieu of a fourth meeting the Committee decided to finish the rest of its work by email, FAX, telephone and mail with the help of General Convention Office staff.

The Committee wishes to thank the General Convention Office staff especially Jennifer Seltzer, Anne Karoly, Lucy Lacovara and Tony Jewiss, for their help and support without which it would have been much more difficult to complete our work.

The Joint Standing Committee on Nominations is pleased to place in nomination for balloting at the 74th General Convention, the names which follow this report. The list of nominees including their biographical information is available on the web, www.episcopalchurch.org. The statistics regarding the nominees are as follows:

Total Nominations	Gender	Ethnicity
93 nominations	31 female	7 African American
	62 male	2 Asian
		2 Hispanic
		1 Korean American
		1 Latin American

Triennium Financial Report

The Joint Standing Committee was budgeted $29,000 for the 2000-2003 triennium. At the time of this report, the Committee had expended $21,059 of its budget. It must be noted that expenses were lower because there was one less committee meeting; one member did not seek expense reimbursement, one meeting was near a member's home and, where possible, special hotel rates were used.

The Joint Standing Committee on Nominations will require $16,000 in 2004, $12,000 in 2005 and $5,000 in 2006 for meeting and other expenses, for a total of $33,000 during the triennium.

Goals and Objectives for the Upcoming Triennium

Despite the concerns expressed by the Committee for the 2000 General Convention and the changes we instituted in attracting candidates, the pool of interested persons was less than for the 73rd General Convention. Like previous committees we believe that it is critical to attract wider representation in the elected leadership of our church. While there is no question that the talents needed and the time requirements for these positions limit the persons available, it seems that of our million-plus members there should be more than 125-150 interested in these positions. Each of us involved in the work of our church should do our utmost to recruit others. In particular, present and past members of the four bodies which are elected by The General Convention should be interested in attracting qualified persons to carry on this important work.

The Episcopal Church elects its leaders. This is a distinctive and traditional feature of our common life. It is a vital function of the General Convention. This report shares biographical information and a photograph of each nominee. A description of each office and the qualifications for election are provided by representatives of the Church Pension Fund Board of Trustees, the Executive Council, the General Board of Examining Chaplains and the General Theological Seminary Board of Trustees. The report also includes nominees for Secretary of General Convention and Treasurer of the General Convention. Nominees responded to the following statement and their answers compose each individual biographical sketch. At the end of this report there is a balloting tally sheet for tracking elections during General Convention.

Each person of faith engages in many forms of ministry. We assume your convictions of faithfulness are in place and your faithfulness is not in question! The question is: What special competencies, skills, church or life experiences do you have that you believe are relevant to serving in the position for which you are being nominated? Please give particular focus to the last five years.

NOMINEES FOR ELECTION

OFFICES OF THE GENERAL CONVENTION

SECRETARY OF THE GENERAL CONVENTION

THREE-YEAR TERM
House of Deputies elects; House of Bishops confirms.

The Rev. Rosemari G. Sullivan
Alexandria, VA
Virginia, III

I was elected Secretary of the Executive Council and Interim Secretary of the General Convention at its November 1998 meeting following my appointment as Executive Officer of The General Convention by our Presiding Bishop, The Most Rev. Frank T. Griswold and the President of the House of Deputies, Mrs. Pamela Chinnis. Prior to this appointment I served as the Rector of The Church of St. Clement in Alexandria, Virginia for eleven years. During that time, I served as deputy to the 70th, 71st and 72nd General Conventions and as chair of the legislative committee on Prayer Book and Liturgy for the 71st and 72nd General Conventions.

TREASURER OF THE GENERAL CONVENTION

THREE-YEAR TERM
House of Deputies elects; House of Bishops confirms.

Mr. Ralph O'Hara
Winnetka, IL
Chicago, V

Ralph O'Hara, hired as the Chief Financial Officer in January 2002, is accountable to the Presiding Bishop for the operating budget and endowment of the national church, including international financial operations. He provides leadership supporting DFMS's mission and strategic initiatives. Previously, he was controller of GATX Corp. and Senior Manager with Price Waterhouse. At GATX, he was responsible for corporate governance and compliance, in addition to accounting and control. At Price Waterhouse he led a major audit and internal control reviews for clients. His community and church work has included vestry member, Trustee of two major social service agencies and town caucus and planning commission officer. Mr. O'Hara has a BS from Wharton School of Penn, a MBA from Washington Univ., is a CPA and attended Harvard Business School's Corporate Financial Management program. He is married with three grown children.

TRUSTEES OF THE CHURCH PENSION FUND

Position Description: The Trustees of the Church Pension Fund (CPF) play a critical role in the governance and management of the multi-billion dollar Church Pension Fund and its affiliated companies: Church Life Insurance Corporation, The Church Insurance Companies, The Medical Trust, and Church Publishing Incorporated. They make significant policy decisions affecting investment policies, pension benefits, and services CPF provides with an appropriate concern for sometimes conflicting social and fiduciary responsibilities.

Other Information: Trustees serve on committees of the board such as the Audit Committee, the Benefits Policy Committee, the Board Review and Compensation Committee, the Budget and Finance Committee, the Investment Committee, and the Social and Fiduciary Responsibility in Investments Committee, or other special committees. Trustees may also serve on the boards of the Church Insurance Companies, Church Life Insurance Corporation, Church Publishing Incorporated, and the Medical Trust.

Special Qualifications: Nominees should have a broad, compassionate understanding of the needs of the Episcopal Church, its clergy and lay employees. In addition, the Board needs expertise in a wide range of financial, legal and business areas. Five critical needs are: a) experience in the management of multi-billion-dollar investment portfolios and evaluation of specific investment opportunities; b) experience with the financial and regulatory requirements of insurance companies; c) a sensitivity to the critical need for balancing social responsibility with fiduciary responsibility; d) sensitivity to the needs of the clergy and their families; and e) sensitivity to the needs of church institutions.

Time Expectations: Historically, there have been 3 Full Board meetings per year (2 days each) and 3 Executive Committee meetings per year (2 days each). Currently, the board is contemplating a change to 4 Full Board meetings per year (2 days each), with the Executive Committee meeting only as necessary. Other Committee meetings: 3 or more days (usually in conjunction with board meetings)

THREE-YEAR TERMS
House of Deputies elects two; House of Bishops confirms.

Mrs. Barbara B. Creed
Hillsborough, CA
El Camino Real, VIII
St. Francis Episcopal Church

As a former Senior Warden, member of Diocesan Council, member of Diocesan Board of Directors and chair of Diocesan Personnel Practices Committee, I have learned the importance of maintaining the well-being of clergy and lay employees serving our Church. As a clergy spouse I am aware of the tremendous demands placed on our clergy and the importance of helping them maintain sound financial, physical and spiritual health. As a practicing lawyer for over 33 years, specializing in employee benefits law, I am very familiar with the legal and tax requirements which govern the CPF. My brief service as Trustee since February, 2002 has shown me - and, I believe, has shown the other CPF Trustees and Staff – that my expertise in the employee benefits field can be a productive resource for the CPF. I thank God for this opportunity and pray that Convention will allow me to continue to serve in this capacity.

The Rev. Mark Stevens Nestlehutt
Chicago, IL
Chicago, V
St. Chrysostom's

As a new Trustee, I would bring a unique and varied set of competencies and life experiences to the CPF. For six years prior to seminary in 1994, I worked in employee benefits and corporate trust, specifically in the area of qualified retirement plans for defined contribution and defined benefit plans. At FirstNBC (now BankOne), Manufacturers, and at Bolton Offutt Donovan (now Wm M. Mercer), I was responsible for helping clients match investment policy statements with money managers. As a seminarian, I served on the Finance Subcommittee of the Board of Trustees, and during the past five years of full-time parish ministry I have continued to use my background in finance by serving on the board of two Episcopal schools, and working with the CPF on its "Stewardship of Abundance" study. Lastly, as a GenX priest (married to another GenX priest), I offer a unique perspective as an active priest with almost three decades of ordained ministry ahead of him.

Mr. Theodore B. "Tim" Sloan
Covington, TN
West Tennessee, IV
St. Matthew's - Covington

Minister's son. Rhodes College, graduate LSU School of Banking. 40 years with First State Bank Covington, then Union Planters Bank, retired Chairman-CEO, presently Chairman of advisory board. Married former Thirza Mobley. 2 children and 3 grandchildren. Past president Tipton Co. Chamber of Commerce, still a director. Past president Rotary Club, still member. Five years TN Arts Commission. Mason and Shriner. 10 years County Commissioner, mainly Chairman. 9 years alderman Covington. Foundation trustee Dyersburg State Community College serving as Chairman of College's County Advisory board. Organized the Tipton County Historical Society and served as treasurer since. Member, chaplain, and past President of the Memphis Ch. of the Sons of American Revolution. VP of the West TN Hist. Society, a director of TN Preservation Trust affiliate of the National Trust. Life long Episcopalian serving all capacities local church, on the Bishop and Council, alternate deputy 1997, 2000 GC, GC 2003 deputy, served as Chair Committee to elect Bishop of West Tennessee.

Mr. Cecil Wray
New York, NY
New York, II
St. James

A lawyer by training and vocation (senior partner in large firm; now retired from active practice), I have long been active in the Episcopal Church, including years of service as Senior Warden of a large parish, founding President of Episcopal Charities of New York (supporting outreach parish programs in the Diocese of New York), and a trustee of the Board of Foreign Parishes (which gives me a perspective on

the mission of the church abroad). At the time of my election to the CPF Board, I had been serving as special legal counsel to CPF and was the board's only lawyer; my background in law and finance has provided a useful resource for the board. I serve on the Advisory Committee on Pension Fund Abundance and the Church Life Insurance Corporation board. I'm active in civic and community endeavors and serve on boards of other non-profit organizations.

SIX-YEAR TERMS
House of Deputies elects twelve; House of Bishops confirms.

The Very Rev. M.L. Agnew Jr
Shreveport, LA
Western Louisiana, VII
St. Mark's Cathedral

I have served the Episcopal Church well as an elected member of the CPF Trustees since 1997. It would be an honor to continue. I am privileged to serve on the Investment Committee, the Social and Fiduciary Responsibility in Investments Committees, the Budget and Finance Committee, the Committee on Ecclesiastical Offices Held by Beneficiaries and the Board of the Church Insurance Company. As Dean of St. Mark's Cathedral and Cathedral School, I manage with others budgets totaling 3.5 million dollars. Recently elected to the Board of Regents of the University of the South, Sewanee, I serve on the Property and Finance Committee, University Relations Committee, School of Theology Committee and the Investment Committee. I was six years on ECUSA's Executive Council ('94-'00), chairing the A&F Committee. Other administrative and financial responsibilities in the Episcopal Church are diocesan Executive Committee (MS, TX, and Western LA), the Executive Committee of Province VII and diocesan finance committees. I am interested in the financial well-being of the laity and clergy and will serve with loyalty and enthusiasm.

The Rt. Rev. David C. Bane Jr
Norfolk, VA
Southern Virginia, III

I have been Bishop of the Diocese of Southern VA since 1997. Before entering seminary at 40, I spent fifteen years in secular management positions including experience as an agent with a major life insurance/pension company. I had already seen the incredible impact the CPF has on clergy families. My father was an Episcopal priest who died in 1980 at the age of 64. My mother, who is now 85, has been one of many whose life has been deeply affected by the CPF in a very positive and pastoral way. I would truly love to be given the charge by the Church to help the CPF continue and even improve its effective, responsive, and faithful ministry to clergy families for many years to come. With a BA in Economics, a MBA in Management, business experience, and deep love of the Episcopal Church I believe I could be a helpful presence.

Mr. James E. Bayne
Dallas, TX
Dallas, VII
Church of the Incarnation

For four years, I have been privileged to be a CPF trustee, and on its diversity committee (co-chair), Benefits Policy Committee and Advisory Committee on Pension Fund Abundance. I would be honored to be elected to a full term. Fourteen years with global responsibility for ExxonMobil's pension and benefit funds has allowed me to make a meaningful impact as a trustee. Previously, I held various international management and finance positions mostly in Europe and Latin America. Before, I worked for Bankers Trust, studied history at Yale (BA) and finance at Columbia (MBA). Currently, I am a consultant. As a life-long Episcopalian, I have been on vestries on three continents, various parish and diocesan committees, and chaired the Episcopal Renewal Center. I am active in mission work in Honduras. I serve on the boards and finance/investment committees of a number of non-profit charitable, professional and church related foundations and organizations.

Mr. Sheridan C. Biggs
Quaker Street, NY
Albany, II
Christ Church - Duanesburg

I presently serve as a CPF trustee and on several Boards of its subsidiaries. I am Chairman of the Group's Audit Committee. Substantial progress has been made under my leadership. I am a graduate of Lehigh University and served in the US Navy for seven years. My business career was with Price Waterhouse, the accounting firm. I was responsible for auditing services to major companies and prior to my retirement became a Vice Chairman of the firm. I am a member of Christ Church, Duanesburg in the Diocese of Albany where I am a Church School teacher of teenagers. I have served as Chairman of our Diocese' Finance Committee and as a Trustee. I would be pleased to continue to serve as a CPF Trustee.

Mr. Jon Bancroft Boss
Cincinnati, OH
Southern Ohio, V
Ch. of Ascen. & Holy Trin. - Wyoming OH

Discussing difficulties maintaining medical insurance continuity "between positions" with an early 60's interim rector during a Search Team interview; evaluating the Lay Employees' Benefit Survey responses to understand trends and suggest improvements; considering the pros and cons for a $4.5 million dollar expansion of a Presbyterian Church as a City Planning Commissioner; evaluating managers and strategies for an Episcopal retirement corporation's investments; developing strategies for presenting the next triennial budget as a member of PB&F; serving as Province V's ER&D Fund Coordinator; or analyzing clergy compensation against diocesan guidelines and discussing how, when and what assistance is appropriate, are the skills and experiences I offer the CPF - and 14 years as the Diocese of Southern Ohio's Director of Administration; 23 years as a Kroger Co. executive; a Denison University AB in Economics; and a Harvard Business School MBA.

Mr. David L. Brigham
Weston, VT
Vermont, I
Zion Episcopal Church

My association with the CPF dates back to 1965. It includes serving as portfolio manager for stocks and bonds, informal advisor to two presidents of the CPF and now as trustee. I have chaired the Investment Committee the past five years as a CPF trustee. My work experience and service on the Investment Committee are identical. For over 38 years, I have managed financial assets for institutions and individuals. The last ten years of my career were spent managing a large world-wide investment management firm. It included directing investment policy, reviewing new services, and the general administration and supervision of several hundred professionals. At retirement in 1998, I joined an investment management firm in VT on a part time basis, continuing my constant familiarity with our capital market and financial asset classes. I hope that my contributions will help our clergy's retiredment years, those who have cared for us all for so long.

Ms. Theresa M. Brion
Lexington, VA
Southwestern Virginia, III
Emmanuel Episcopal - Staunton

I am a tax/ERISA sole practitioner lawyer, a CFP® certificant, and a part-time tax/ERISA editor of Thomson Corporation. A 1985 law graduate, I earlier practiced within the tax, employee benefits, and trusts/estates departments of several law firms with sophisticated practices. Through that work and consulting work for the CFP Board of Standards, I developed essential financial, tax, and fiduciary skills. I have served in many capacities in parishes and the community since childhood. In 2001, I completed EFM and earned a pastoral care certificate; in 2002, I completed a CPE unit in 2002. I recently established a LEM program and researched restoring a healing service in my current parish. Recent parish responsibilities include performing church audits, advising on church tax matters, and assisting with ongoing service duties. Diocesan activities include serving as annual council delegate and attending Church Development Institute. I have attended CREDO and Planning for Tomorrow events. I would be honored to serve as CPF trustee.

The Very Rev. Samuel Glenn Candler
Atlanta, GA
Atlanta, IV
The Cathedral of St. Philip

I have been a priest for twenty years, serving very small and very large congregations in three different dioceses. Presently Dean of the Cathedral of St. Philip, Atlanta, I have also served rural parishes; and I have led by honoring God's diverse expressions of faith. I am honored to offer that leadership to CPF, and I would help it care for an ever-changing Church. I enjoy that change. I am committed to social justice in South Carolina, I was a member of the Governor's Commission on Race Relations, education (Vice-chair of the Episcopal Media Center, on the boards of the Berkeley Divinity School at Yale, LaGrange College in Georgia, and The Westminster Schools in Atlanta), and the city I serve on the boards of the Atlanta YMCA and the Interfaith Alliance of Metro Atlanta. I graduated Occidental College, cum laude, and Yale Divinity School, magna cum laude.

The Rev. Peter F. Casparian
Florence, Italy,
Churches in Europe, II
St. James

I have been Rector of St. James Church, Florence, Italy, since 1995. I went to Rhodes College, Memphis, TN, then Sewanee (M. Div, D. Min). I've been elected six times to GC from the Dioceses of KS, Lexington, and the Churches in Europe. I've served on finance and/or investment committees of church and community agencies and administered several trusts and endowments. In Florence I'm deeply involved in raising, maintaining and spending endowments for ministry and historical building preservation. My main interest in serving is my hope that I'll be among the longer term "end users" of the fund's benefits to retired clergy. I was ordained at 23 and in the pension system since 1974. By this convention I'll have "paid in" for 29 years and be 52. I'll probably use the "early retirement" option soon after age 55 with 32 years of service. As one hoping to be "supported" by the CPF for many more years of "creative ministry" or foreign mission, I offer my longevity in the priesthood and financial experience as a willing possibility to serve as a CPF trustee.

Mrs. Carla M. Cooper PhD
Houston, TX
Texas, VII
Palmer Memorial Episcopal Church

I serve as senior vice president of St Luke's Episcopal Health System (SLEHS) and as executive director of St Luke's Episcopal Health Charities (www.slehc.org.). Created in 1997 and devoted to Advancing Community Health: Body, Mind, and Spirit, the Charities is supported by a $150 million endowment and has invested $45 million to date throughout the 57-county Diocese. After earning a Ph.D. in literature from Purdue University in1980, I spent 14 years in higher education, joining SLEHS in 1994 and welcoming the opportunity to become part of a community of faith in action. I currently chair the Guiding Board of The World Community for Christian Meditation, lead a weekly meditation group at Palmer, as well as give talks and retreats on contemplative prayer. I would be most honored to serve on the CPF and hope that my experiences might lend both creativity and mindfulness to the work at hand.

The Rev. Donald Allston Fishburne
Sanibel, FL
Southwest Florida, IV
St. Michael & All Angels

I seek to contribute to the work of the CPF out of my abiding interest in its ministry, and as a part of my care for clergy and lay people, young and old, active and retired, as well as members of their households. I have experience as trustee of several trusts and as director of several foundations. I participated in an early CREDO pilot project. I have attended several Pension Fund programs and was a panel speaker at a CPF regional event. In 23 years of parish ministry in four dioceses, I have served congregations from the small to the large. Relevant interest areas include diocesan Standing Committee, Conference Center boards, Stewardship Commissions, Congregational Development, Christian Education, Youth and College Ministries. I am a graduate of The University of the South (Sewanee), from which I hold a D.Min. and have a M.Div. from VTS. My wife and I have a son, 16, and a daughter, 13.

The Rev. Canon Carlson Gerdau
New York, NY
Chicago, V
All Saints

For the past five years, I have served as Canon to the Presiding Bishop and Primate. I am also up for my second term as a member of the Pension Group. During my present term on the Pension Group, I have served on the Audit Committee, The Social Responsibilities for Investments Committee as well as the Board of the Church Insurance Company. I also have been on the Advisory Board for the Medical Trust. Previously, I also served on the BRACE Committee. Before my appointment as Canon to the Presiding Bishop, I was Canon of the Ordinary in Chicago, Archdeacon of Missouri and served parishes in the Diocese of Northern Michigan. A long-term interest has been issues affecting the clergy. I was also the first member of the Diocesan Trust in Northern Michigan, as well as the first member of the Diocesan Trust in the Diocese of Chicago.

The Rt. Rev. Gayle Elizabeth Harris
Boston, MA
Massachusetts, I

It has been an honor to serve the Church as a Trustee of the Church Pension Group for the past 5 years, and as a member of several board subcommittees (Social and Fiduciary Responsibility in Investment, Budget and Finance, Benefits Policy). As a trustee, I feel it is vital to maintain the stability of the Fund, and ensure the investment strategy is informed by values to enhance life and protects creation. I have strongly supported the increase benefits for those who have served the church faithfully and their survivors but find themselves in financial distress. I have also supported the new enhancements for wellness as developed in CREDO and full retirement after 30 years of work. In these challenging times for our economy and our common life in faith, I wish to continue to address the needs of the people of God, and celebrate the blessing of diversity given to us.

The Rev. Scott B. Hayashi
Menlo Park, CA
California, VIII
Christ Church - Portola Valley

I am the Rector of Christ Church Portola Valley in the Diocese of California. I have served in Parishes and Missions in three dioceses, many Diocesan committees, a General Convention Deputy, and on the national level with programs that work with Young Adults, Family Ministries, and presently with the CREDO Institute. I am a third generation Japanese American. Since 1986 I have worked diligently for health and wellness of Clergy and their families. Through this work I have been privileged to know many Clergy from across athe United States. My experience has given me a conviction for enhancing the lives of the clergy in the present so they are fulfilled and healthy in their professional and personal lives and to maintain that wellness throughout their careers in order that they are able to enjoy many strong and happy years when they retire. I would be honored to serve as trustee of the CPF.

The Rev. Canon Lynn Jay
Valencia, CA
Los Angeles, VIII
St. Stephen's - Santa Clarita

A parish priest for over 20 years, I am currently the vicar of a mission of over 700 people. Prior to ordination I was a full-time mother of three then an elementary school teacher. As Deputy to the last four General Conventions I was a member of the Joint CPF group. I am not a person of finance but, rather, a grassroots voice for clergy needs, and providing for the clergy provides for the church as a whole. As a member of the Pension Fund's Abundance Committee I see clergy and laity working together to bring Biblical imparities to bear on the business of providing for clergy. The work of the Abundance Committee is a model of justice and mercy for the whole Church. Locally, I initiated the founding of the Interfaith Council, Food Pantry and Homeless Shelter Coalition. I would be honored to serve on the Board.

The Rt. Rev. Robert Hodges Johnson
Asheville, NC
Western North Carolina, IV

In 15 years as bishop I've served on the Total Ministry Task Force, the Committee on the Status of Women, the Church Deployment Board, and ECUSA's Executive Council chairing the National Concerns Committee and the Congregations in Ministry Committee. Executive Council service has broadened my perspective on ministry. As Province IV's House of Bishops President, I am on the Presiding Bishop's Council of Advice. In twelve years on House of Bishops Pastoral Development Committee, I have served on the leadership team for New Bishops/Spouses Conference. This has strengthened my commitment to justice ministries and support of clergy and laity in their call to ministry. I have served small congregations, been on Cathedral staff, and served as a large parish rector. My Business Administration degree and background in finance have been useful and helpful.. With this background and lengthy pastoral ministry and service, CPF Trustee service would be an honor.

The Rev. Caryl Ann Marsh
Salt Lake City, UT
Utah, VIII
St. Paul's

I was born in England, where I worked for the Guaranty Trust Company; Coutts Bank, and Trans World Airlines as an internal auditor. Institute of Bankers Diploma, London; B.A. cum laude; MDiv. Ordained1977. Parish priest and Director of Christian Growth and Development, Diocese of Spokane. As Rector of St. Paul's, Salt Lake City, Utah, I have just completed a $4.3 million restoration and addition project. Deputy to General Convention 1982 - 2000; State of the Church Committee, Advisory Council of the President of the House of Deputies; Nominating Committee to Elect a Presiding Bishop; Young Adult Ministry; Commission on Ministry; President of the Standing Committee; United Way, Legal Aid Society, Partnership for End of Life Care; Governor of Utah's Health 2000 Committee. I will retire soon and would like to continue to serve the church in this capacity.

Ms. Joon D. Matsumura
Yorba Linda, CA
Los Angeles, VIII
Church of the Resurrection

I have served on various commissions and committees for the National Church and Province, including Comptroller of the Diocese of Los Angeles for 21 years. I am currently the Treasurer of Province 8. I've been fortunate to serve as a trustee and contribute to the CPF for the last 6 years. It has been an exciting and wonderful experience to participate in the enhancement of clergy pension using my knowledge and skills in finance and diversity. Re-election would allow me to continue to serve congregations, priests, laity and families for their future financial security and well being after retirement. As an Asian American woman, I bring an important perspective for balanced dialogue with my background, multi-cultural knowledge, and for diversified experience. I would love to continue to serve God as a reflection of our changing society through this special ministry. I would be honored to be your choice.

Mrs. Virginia A. Norman
Santo Domingo, Dominican Republic
Dominican Republic, IX
Epiphany

I have been a CPF trustee since 1997, with a business background. I have worked for many years as a Diocesan Treasurer of the Church in the Dominican Republic, also for Province Nine and the Caribbean Region, of which I have been a part of their finance and Investments Committees, and invalued in their pension and retirement plans, for clergy and lay employees, the experience gained is valuable and helpful to the CPF. As an incumbent CPF trustee, I have served on the social and fiduciary responsibility on investments committee, medical trust and the executive committee. I am an active member of the Episcopal Church in the Dominican Republic, and have served on many diocesan committees, a member of ECUSA's Executive Council, Standing Commission of world mission, Church in Metropolitan Areas, United Thank Offering, Companion Dioceses, have attended several General Conventions as a deputy, and also ECW treasurer.

The Rt. Rev. Henry N. Parsley Jr
Birmingham, AL
Alabama, IV

I view the CPF as one of the foundational institutions of the Episcopal Church. Its services are essential for the wellness of the clergy and their families throughout their lives, as well as for many lay professionals. As a bishop I see its ministry at work daily. As a clergy child I experienced its service to my parents. As a member of the Abundance Committee I have become aware of how critical careful stewardship of the Fund's financial resources is for the well being of our leaders and how we must continually seek to enhance the effectiveness of our benefits and services for all beneficiaries. The Fund has been graced with visionary leadership and has demonstrated its capacity to contribute significantly to the health of the church. I would be privileged to assist the Fund in continuing this tradition of excellence and insuring its future strength.

Mr. David R. Pitts
St. Francisville, LA
Louisiana, IV
St. Lukes - Baton Rouge

I am an Incumbent Trustee of the CPF currently serving as Co-Chair of the Search Committee for the new President, as Chair of the Medical Trust Board and on the Audit, Executive,and Investment Committees. These responsibilities are the most important in a long career of service to the Episcopal Church. I would be honored to serve a second term. In private life I am Chair and CEO of PMA, one of the largest hospital and healthcare firms in the nation. Other business interests include serving on serveral firm's Boards of Directors; publicly traded, privately held and not-for-profit. Industries served as Director include: banking, electrical power. rice, timber. construction, hospitals insurance, technology, home healthcare broadcasting, and executive compensation. Involved my entire life in the Episcopal Church, 1 have served as Senior Warden, on the Standing Committee, as Trustee of two seminaries, Diocesan Capital Campaign Chair, as General Convention deputy for five terms. Thank you for considering me for a second term.

The Rev. Canon V. Gene Robinson
Concord, NH
New Hampshire, I
St. Paul's - Concord

As Canon to the Ordinary, Diocese of New Hampshire since 1988, I assist the bishop with the pastoral care of clergy and congregations, and as Executive Secretary for the seven dioceses of the Province of New England since 1983, I have served and observed large and small dioceses. I have served on the CPF legislative committee of the General Convention and am currently a member of the Pension Fund's Committee on Abundance. Clergy health and well-being has been a focus during my 30 years of ordained ministry – leading The Cornerstone Project's "Being Well in Christ" program on clergy health in some twenty dioceses and co-authoring "Fresh Start: A Resource for Clergy and Congregations in Transition," now used across the church. I currently serve as Trustee of GTS and Trustee of the New Hampshire Endowment for Health. An $80 million fund working to promote health care accessibility for all. Business experience includes being founding director of a retreat center and professional camp owner/director of a girl's summer riding camp. I would like to continue the important work explored and begun by the Committee on Abundance as a Trustee of CPF.

The Rev. Robert L. Sessum
Lexington, KY
Lexington, IV
Good Shepherd Episcopal Church

Rector of Good Shepherd Church. Member of ECUSA's Executive Council serving as Chair of International Concerns Committee and on Executive Committee; ECUSA Clergy Representative to the Anglican Consultative Council. Deputy at five General Conventions; during thirty-three (33) years of ministry has served churches in the Dioceses of TN, NC and Lexington (KY). M. Div. from VTS and BA from Rhodes College. Served nine years as Treasurer of the North American Regional Committee of St. George's College, Jerusalem. Founding member and Treasurer of Greater Lexington Faith Housing Inc. which provides affordable and low income housing. Founding catalyst for two HUD Housing projects. Having worked with many congregations, clergy, lay employees and spouses, I have extensive knowledge about their retirement and medical needs. I would bring that experience to CPF as the Board continues to reach out to those who have given of their lives to God's ministry in the Episcopal Church.

The Rt. Rev. Wayne P. Wright
Wilmington, DE
Delaware, III

Since 1998 I have served as bishop of Delaware. My goal is to support and encourage the ministry of laity and clergy who serve in our congregations, schools, and community ministries. I was a leader in diocesan and national clergy associations before becoming bishop. I have grass roots knowledge of the pastoral and economic needs of congregations, clergy, and laity who serve the Episcopal Church. As a parish priest I served a pastoral-sized rural congregation and a multi-ethnic urban parish. I have a personal appreciation for the remarkable variety of congregations and ministries in our church. I am a fluent Spanish-speaker. I want the Episcopal Church to be a just and good place for everyone to work and serve. As a trustee I will seek to be an effective listener, communicator, and coalition builder. I will advocate for policies that reflect the wisdom, compassion, and justice of Christ.

THE EXECUTIVE COUNCIL

Position Description: The members of Executive Council carry out the program and policies adopted by the General Convention and have charge of the coordination, development, and implementation of the ministry and mission of the Church. The Executive Council is required to manage the budget of the church, submit to General Convention a budget for the next triennium, and make annual reports to the church of receipts and disbursements and a statement of all trust funds and properties. They also serve as the Board of Directors of the Domestic and Foreign Missionary Society.

Other information: Bishops (by Presiding Bishop) and other members (by President of the House of Deputies) may be appointed as liaison persons to the Standing Commissions of General Convention. Such service involves attending meetings lasting from 1 to 5 days per year. Standing Committees of the Council may meet in the interim between Council's regular meetings for 2 or 3 days with additional travel time.

Time expectations: Regular Meetings (3 per year - 5 days each), Standing Committee meetings (8 days per year), CCAB meetings (6 days per year), Special Appointments (5 days per year), General Convention (14 days every three years)

BISHOPS

House of Bishops elects two for six-year terms; House of Deputies confirms.

The Rt. Rev. John W. Howe
Orlando, FL
Central Florida, IV

The great adventure of being a private school chaplain for five years was seeing hundreds of teenagers come to a life-changing faith in Christ. At least a dozen of them have gone into full-time Christian service. The great adventure of seventeen years of parish ministry was seeing a parish live into the vision of "spending as much on others as we do on ourselves". More than half of our income was devoted to outreach and there was no endowment. We were successful in integrating the several streams of tradition and renewal, evangelical and catholic, structure and freedom. The great adventure in being a bishop for fourteen years has been building trust and camaraderie among clergy and people who are across the spectrum of "issues" but who share a common commitment to the Lordship of Christ. It has been my privilege to travel to some 45 countries for preaching and teaching missions and of late to sit on the Theology Committee of the House of Bishops where I am committed to building bridges between those of different points of view. I would be greatly honored to serve on the ECUSA's Executive Council.

The Rt. Rev. Wilfrido Ramos-Orench
Bloomfield, CT
Connecticut, I

During the past two years I have served as Bishop Suffragan of Connecticut. I see my ministry in the diocese and in the Church at large primarily as a bridge builder. The Episcopal Church is increasingly becoming a culturally diverse, multi-ethnic entity. Thus, the importance for us as Church leaders to reach out to those who are in and to those who are out with due respect and sensitivity as reconciling and empowering agents of Christ. In the process barriers and boundaries of ethnicity, culture, language, gender, age and class can be transcended and overcome. I come from Puerto Rican-Latino descent. I am fully bilingual: English and Spanish. I trained in systems theory and practice as a marriage and family therapist. Currently I serve on the Standing Commission on World Mission. Also I am very involved in the development and strengthening of Hispanic ministry in my diocese and in the national Church. If elected, it shall be a privilege to serve in the Executive Council of ECUSA. I currently serve on the GTS Board of Trustees as an Alumnae representative.

The Rt. Rev. Stacy F. Sauls
Lexington, KY
Lexington, IV

I believe I would have two things to offer on the Executive Council: First, I try to tell the truth as I see it and be open to the truth as others see it. Second, I never give up on relationships. As the bishop of a small and largely rural diocese, including the heart of Appalachia, I would like to see that particular experience represented on Executive Council. We are working to represent the Gospel creatively amidst rural as well as urban poverty, both of which are challenges for us. We are trying hard as a diocese, and with some success, to maintain unity by concentrating on building trust and fostering hospitality. Finally, my background as a lawyer and work as a member of the Standing Commission on Constitution and Canons might be useful in this office.

The Rt. Rev. James E. Waggoner Jr
Spokane, WA
Spokane, VIII

I began as Bishop of Spokane in October 2000, following more than 20 years ordained ministry in West Virginia as a parish priest and then as Canon to the Ordinary (9 years). I have exercised leadership at regional and national levels, having served as President of the Conference of Diocesan Executives and President of the Deployment Ministry Conference. In recent years I have focused increasingly on leadership development and congregational development, in preparation for which I studied family systems theory with Rabbi Edwin Friedman and Dr. Peter Steinke. My doctoral thesis was on discernment of call at the congregational level and I continue to be energized by the challenge to develop creative models of ministry to carry out Christ's mission boldly. I have been a five-time Deputy to General Convention, and am currently a member of PB&F. I would be honored to serve on the Executive Council.

LAY PERSONS
House of Deputies elects six for six-year terms; House of Bishops confirms.

Mr. R. P. M. Bowden Sr
Atlanta, GA
Atlanta, IV
St. Luke's - Atlanta

It would be an honor to serve on The Executive Council and a continuation of a lifetime of church service. I serve on the Stewardship, Congregational Growth and Development, Anti-Racism, and Ministry commissions; the Executive Board; Finance, and Budget committees for my diocese. National leadership roles include the Union of Black Episcopalians and the Episcopal Urban Caucus. Currently, I am on ECUSA's Board of Archives. My professional educator experiences adds to my understanding of church issues in today's world. I have been involved professionally, nationally and internationally in education organizations. This will be my tenth General Convention, deputy nine times and alternate once. My experience affords me an understanding of the time and responsibility required. It is my pleasure to serve in God's church.

Ms. Dorothy J. Fuller
Salinas, CA
El Camino Real, VIII
Church of the Good Shepherd

I have a strong belief in people and in the Episcopal Church. My organizational and diplomatic skills will help move us toward reconciling our differences. My ability to see all sides of a question is recognized in city and rural parishes (Lay reader, LEM, vestry, choir, altar guild, convention delegate) and in the diocese where I served on Council, Department of Intercultural Education and Ministry and founding member of Integrity El Camino Real. I am a member of the Standing Committee and liaison to the Commission on Ministry. I am deputation Chair for General Convention 2003; Deputy in 1997/2000, Alternate 1991/1994, Integrity volunteer 1985/1998. My experiences give me a working knowledge of church polity. Professionally I am a nurse practitioner working with minority immigrants. Justice issues and full inclusion of all people are my passions.

Mr. Thomas R. Gossen
Wichita, KS
Kansas, VII
St. James - Wichita

I am currently Executive Director of The Episcopal Network for Stewardship (TENS), a 501(c)(3) organization. I was called to lead for networking like-minded persons concerned with providing resources for stewardship formation and leadership development. Since 1998 I have devoted my energies full-time to stewardship ministry, retiring early from an architecture firm I co-founded and a 30-year career managing projects, $60 million plus in cost. TENS' newsletter circulation exceeds 4,000. Membership includes 45 dioceses, 100's parishes, and individuals. I have served as Board Member and President of Episcopal Social Services of SW KS; diocesan/parish Stewardship and Planned Giving commissions, 15+ years; LEM and Vestry member, 20+ years, Sr. Warden 3 times; and General Convention deputy three times. Current Co-chair of SCSD and 12th year as EFM mentor. My ministries and work experience qualify me to serve on Executive Council. I would be honored to be elected.

Mr. F. Rick Harrell
Sarasota, FL
Southwest Florida, IV
St. Bonifare - Sarasota

I am director of Open Heart Recovery and Respiratory Services at a community owned hospital, responsible for $10M and 175 employees in 6 distinct areas; celebrating 15 years in leadership and as volunteer chaplain. I represent these services and patients on many councils and committees. At St. Boniface church, vestry member, assisting others in the pledge campaign and special events. Active as acolyte, lay reader, verger, LEM, choir and church representative for Consortium of Endowed Episcopal Parishes focusing on vestry development. Diocesen facilitator in the discernment program for lay and ordain ministry; serving on an ad-hoc committee to redesign the school of ministry programs. In the community selected for a pilot project on diversity leadership focused on creating a forum for selection of diverse membership on community boards. I am an experienced public speaker, leader, and educator who sees improving life around me as a gift. It would be my privilege to serve on the Executive Council.

Ms. Josephine H. Hicks
Charlotte, NC
North Carolina, IV
St. Peter's

I am a litigation lawyer. I have served as an advisor to two Ecclesiastical Courts, one for the trial of the Bishop of Montana, and one for the trial of a priest in the Diocese of North Carolina. I am a life-long Episcopalian and daughter of an Episcopal priest. I graduated from Sewanee in 1983 and Vanderbilt Law School in 1986. I have been active in many areas of lay ministry, including youth ministry, Christian education, evangelism, and stewardship. I have co-chaired an every member canvas. I am currently a Vestry member at St. Peter's in Charlotte, NC, where I am creating and advising an evangelism committee. I am a delegate to the Diocesan Convention. I have demonstrated leadership skills and am a consensus-builder. I would be honored to bring these skills and experiences to bear as a member of the Executive Council.

Mr. Edward Wilson Jones
Fredericksburg, VA
Virginia, III
St. George's

In my professional and church life, I have taken on a number of leadership challenges. A theme of my work has been an effort to bring diverse people together to support a common mission. In my hometown of Fredericksburg, VA, I have been editor of a newspaper recognized by Time magazine as representative of the best of grass-roots journalism; as president of three national editors' groups and my state press association; as a Pulitzer Prize juror; as senior warden and LEM in my parish; as chair of my diocese's Resolutions Committee; and as editor of Center Aisle, a daily newspaper for the 2000 General Convention published by the Diocese of VA. Whether it was uniting editors for more credibility, reconciling a parish after an embezzlement scandal, or speaking as a centrist at General Convention, I try to balance my strong opinions with a tolerance for others. My academic training at Harvard in the late '60s, my legal training at the University of VA leaves me with an appreciation for advocacy and tolerance. As a believer in the healing power of effective communications, I would be honored to serve on the Executive Council.

Ms. Sandra Ferguson McPhee
Evanston, IL
Chicago, V
St. Matthew's - Evanston

As a life long Episcopalian, I believe everyone's contribution must be valued.The church, Christ's body includes the parish, the diocese, the national church and the Anglican Communion. I have worked with the American Committee for KEEP, who supports mission projects in the Phillipines and Japan for 25 years. My Episcopal Partnership for Global Mission work and past convener has let me know people with different views, each a brother or a sister in Christ. My passion for mission is grounded at St. Matthew's, Evanston, where I grew up. I have been Chancellor, Treasurer, and Vestry Member. For the Diocese of Chicago, I am on the diocesan real estate board, chair the Commission on Global Ministry and the Episcopal Church Council at Northwestern University, and a 2000/2003 General Convention alternate deputy. I have practiced law since 1976 and own a marketing/public relations firm. I would bring my professional expertise and participation in all church levels to the Executive Council.

Mrs. Deborah Dalton Melnyk
Jacksonville, FL
Florida, IV
St. Mark's - Jacksonville

I live in Jacksonville, FL where I have served my church and community in leadership roles. Most recently I served as a Trustee for the Cummer Museum of Art and on the Board of the Wolfson Children's Hospital. I am a founding member of the Women's Giving Alliance, an organization to benefit women and children in northeast Florida through grants, education and research. I serve the Diocese of FL as a elected Deputy and other committees. I recently served five years on St. Mark's Vestry. At the Bishop's request I was Senior Warden for 3 years during an uncertain transition time in a 2200 parish. I was involved in conflict management, working with clergy and lay to ensure a successful interim tenure. My service as Senior Warden furthered my skills as a listener, negotiator and conflict manager. These skills would serve me well as a Executive Council member. If this is God's calling, I am capable and qualified to serve. It would be my privilege so to do.

Mr. Albert Theodore Mollegen Jr
Glastonbury, CT
Connecticut, I
St. James' - Glastonbury

I have extensive senior level leadership experience in many organizations: ECUSA parish, diocese and national levels; three publicly-held companies, three not-for-profits, and a town finance committee. I influence groups consciously to define key issues, examine alternative approaches, and choose the best plan for a situation. Since 1993, Founder/president, engineering and factory safety company. Chair /president, defense engineering company, employee growth 56 to 1500+, 1976-92. ECUSA roles: Secretary, 2020 Task Force, 2000-01, SCDME, since 1998; SCSD, 1988-94, Co-Chair, 1991-94. General Convention committees: Evangelism, 2000; Stewardship/Development, 91, 94, 97; Environment, 1991. Founder/Convenor, Ep. Network for Evangelism, since 1998. New Commandment Task Force, 1999-2000, building bridges among church leaders who disagree on sexuality issues. CT Diocesan Executive Council 1980-96. Chair, Mystic, CT Area Ecumenical Council, 1969-71. Lay Reader, Chalicist since 1965. Vestry, 65-68; 70-73; 96-98.

Mrs. Jamel K. Shimpfky
Monteray, CA
El Camino Real, VIII
St. Dunstan's - Carmel Valley

The Episcopal Church expects leadership that is deeply grounded in Anglican ethos, committed to diversity and with experience in deploying human resources. My Mexican Godmother brought me as a child of Lebanese parents to the Church in Mexico City. At age eleven, my family moved to VA, at the time marked by prejudice, segregation and racism. The situation served to guide, direct and motivate my spiritual involvement in the life of the Church. I am a practicing psychotherapist, disaster relief worker with the Red Cross, Salvation Army Board member, chair of several allocations committees of the United Way, CREDO faculty member, House of Bishops Spouse Planning Group; and have represented the Episcopal Church/National Council of Churches in initiatives for peace in the Middle East. I am well informed of the challenges facing us and know that the Church can best serve the Good News of Jesus Christ.

Mr. John Bennet Waters
Austin, TX
Texas, VII
St. David's - Austin

As Vice President for Administration at the Episcopal Theological Seminary of the Southwest I use acquired skills from my executive management career in life insurance and vending/food service companies. Educated in business/finance at Tulane, I was a licensed CPA. I have been actively involved in the Episcopal Church my entire life. I was Senior Warden of the Tulane chapel, an EYC sponsor, and have served vestries in three states including treasurer, junior warden twice and recently as senior warden at a resource sized parish. I chair the search committee and have chaired two building committees. My ministries include LEM, Christian education chair, small group leader, DOCC facilitator, J2A sponsor. I served recently as volunteer coordinator and Vice President of Province VII for six years and was involved in re-energizing of the PLC. I am a Diocese of TX deputy. My broad experience in the church is a strong foundation for a clear vision on the Executive Council.

Mr. Harris G. Willman
Jacksonville, FL
Florida, IV
St. Mark's & Nativity

I am president and CEO of a Jacksonville, FL business employing twenty-six people with a degree in Finance. I have skills in general business and management as owner for 25 years. I want to serve on the Executive Council because I see the Episcopal Church heading to a split as a denomination due to heretical teaching and misguided leadership. If it is God's will that I am elected, I will represent the traditional values revealed in Holy Scripture and passed by apostolic succession. Does doctrine matter in the Episcopal Church today? From my pew seat it seems many ancient heresies are re-appearing. I am not a scholar in church history or doctrine, but represent the faithful remnant clinging to the truth revealed by the triune God. A true faith can be known. The Holy Spirit who once inspired that faith and scripture want to show the way. When truth's light shines on contemporary culture we see her real grotesque and disfigured form.

PRIESTS/DEACONS
House of Deputies elects two for six-year terms;
House of Bishops confirms.

The Rev. Canon Patrick P. Augustine
Waynesboro, VA
Southwestern Virginia, III
St. John's Episcopal Church

In my ministry I have gained rich experience of the national, ecumenical and global Anglican Communion. In 1998 I served as an advisor at the Lambeth Conference on Interfaith and International issues. I was a General Convention deputy in 2000, Chair of the Companions for World Mission and on my diocesan Executive Board. Understanding world faiths and cultures is important to me. August 2002 I went to Pakistan as the Presiding Bishop's emissary and met with the Islamic leaders to share a message of reconciliation. I spoke on religious persecution before Congressional hearings in Washington, D.C. The Archbishop of Sudan has appointed me his Canon and Commissary in the USA because of my commitment to peace and justice. My vision to serve on the Executive Council is to help to build a church that will break down the walls of homogeneity and encourage welcoming all God's children.

The Rev. Robert G. Certain
Palm Desert, CA
San Diego, VIII
St. Margaret's - Palm Desert

I am the rector of a resource-sized parish with a parochial school and the founding president of the Unchained Eagle Memorial Society, a charity that funds POW/MIA memorials. My church and civic experience includes leadership in all size congregations, broad experience in diocesan, provincial and national church ministries, chairty board membership and significant involvement in local, national, and international goodwill ministries. The last five years my efforts have focused on corporate stewardship, particularly church funds management and accountability and communication. Committed to the 20/20 goals my parish is organized for growth in numbers and depth. I have laid the groundwork for major increase in evangelistic, outreach and social ministries. I consult with other parishes seeking the same.

The Rev. Hayden G. Crawford
St. Petersburg, FL
Southwest Florida, IV
St. Augustine's Episcopal Church

I am the Rev. Hayden Green Crawford of the Diocese of Southwest FL. I was ordained for Alabama by the Rt. Rev. Stough more than 22 years ago. I serve on the Standing Committee and forabout seven years, a family type parish in St. Petersburg, FL. With prayer we have developed a ministry for our older adult citizens and an at-risk youth day-shelter ministry, Youth Overcoming Unemployment and Rejection Place (YOUR). The administrative and interpersonal skills for serving this parish and the Standing Committee are always present. I wish to share my listening with a non-judgmental ear and being a voice for those who hesitant in sharing their thoughts. Seeking not so much answers, but making the question heard, then coming to a resolve with the information. Finally, my being present, as family, sacramental and pastoral duties allow, when there is need for physical support. To use these experiences and skills, that are natural is what I offer as your clergy representative on the Executive Council.

The Rev. Kathleen Cullinane
Indianapolis, IN
Indianapolis, V
Christ Church Cathedral

My gifts are cultural sensitivity, global vision and a heart for mission. I am the Associate Dean and Canon Missioner of Christ Church Cathedral , responsible for its outreach, mission and ecumenical efforts. I was the Rector of a multi-cultural parish with Japanese roots in Los Angeles. I have been an Episcopal missionary to Uganda. I have leadership experience with the homeless, refugee resettlement with Church World Service and ERD, HIV/AIDS education programs and Campus ministry. I have served as President of the St. Committee in Los Angeles and finance committee chair of the St. Committee in Indianapolis. I was elected General Convention deputy for 1997, 2000 and 2003 . I am Vice-Chair, SCWM. Incarnation Deanery Dean, Convenor of the Japanese Convocation of Episcopal Asiamerica Ministry, West Coast Field Officer for Migration Affair for ERD. I would appreciate the opportunity to offer my gifts and skills to Executive Council.

The Rev. SaraLouise C. Krantz
Massapequa, NY
Long Island, II
Grace Episcopal - Massapequa

As a teenager trying to decide between a nursing or math career, I did not anticipate that my interests would combine in a vocation as a parish priest in the church! As a skilled administrator, I have had little trouble establishing practices in accord with church guidelines. On the diocesan level I served on the budget department for several years. During a six year term on the Family Consultation Board, I served as chair of the Ad Hoc Administrative Committee that was responsible for addressing crucial financial issues for the organization. Our plan for re-organization was accepted by the board and aided the social service agency in remaining solvent. I really enjoy using the gifts named above to improve the credibility of the church and diocese and believe that they can be used on the Executive Committee to further the church's mission.

The Very Rev. Titus L. Presler ThD
Austin, TX
Texas, VII
Christ Chapel - Austin

A mission activist and theological educator with long parish ministry experience, I want to contribute to Executive Council's work in guiding the church's future in a diverse USA, with our dioceses in Latin America and the Caribbean, and in mission companionships in the Anglican Communion. As secretary, then chair, of the SCWM 1997-2003, I helped frame the EPGM, the proposals for adding Cuba, Puerto Rico and Venezula dioceses and the vision statement for world mission. Since 2002, dean and president of the ETS of the Southwest, I teach mission and world Christianity with a commitment to form church leaders for the multicultural 21st century. As I learn Spanish, I serve on Union Teologico Hispano and the Province VII Hispanic Ministries Center boards. I was rector of St. Peter's in Cambridge, MA 1991-2002, and as an Episcopal missionary in Zimbabwe, with experience in India. As deputy to five General Conventions 1988-2000, I was active in Jubilee 2000 and global mission resolutions. I studied at Harvard and GTS and hold a doctorate in mission from Boston University.

The Rev. James Burdette Simons
Ligonier, PA
Pittsburgh, III
St. Michael's of the Valley

I have been the rector of St. Michael's church since 1988 during that time the church has seen such growth that we are in the process of exploring building a new facility. In addition to the central act of worship the, parish has focused on outreach and education. Currently we give away 17% of our budget to outreach projects. This focus has enabled me to have a wide a contact with the church both domestically and abroad. We have been involved with relief work in the diocese of West Virginia and I have had the opportunity to visit the church and missionary projects in such places as Nepal, Uganda, Rwanda, Guatemala, Pakistan, and India. These trips have allowed me to grow in my understanding of Anglicanism as well as other major world religions especially Islam. I have been a deputy to convention five times and have served on communication, have been the vice chair of Dispatch, and sit on the Presidents council of advice.

GENERAL BOARD OF EXAMINING CHAPLAINS

Position Description: The members of the General Board of Examining Chaplains (GBEC) compose the annual General Ordination Examination (GOE) administered to Candidates for Holy Orders. They also produce background material for readers of the examination papers, read and supervise teams of readers at reading stations, and review written evaluations of all responses to GOE questions. Board meetings entail evaluation and planning for the next year's work.

Computer literacy is important. Especially needed in the year 2003 will be persons with high degrees of competency in these canonical areas: (a) Church history; (b) Christian theology; and (c) Christian ethics and moral theology. Board members should be able to work comfortably in teams and task groups. The GBEC assignments demand ability to concentrate intently on tasks at hand.

Time expectations: Regular meetings (6 days per year), Reading exams (varies up to 15 exams, 4 hours each), Individual projects (time requirements vary), Planning meetings (5 days per term), Members are expected twice during term to attend a 2½ day planning meeting in Washington in June.

BISHOPS

House of Bishops elects one for a three-year term; House of Deputies confirms.

The Rt. Rev. Philip M. Duncan
Pensacola, FL
Central Gulf Coast, IV

Philip Duncan is the Bishop of the Diocese of the Central Coast, consecrated May 12, 2001. Previously dean and rector of Saint Matthew's Cathedral in Dallas (1993-3/2001); an urban congregation in the inner city of Dallas with 2,100 baptized members and 1,500 communicants. He was rector of St. John's Church, Clearwater, FL, from 1972 to 1993 and associate rector of Christ Church, Ridgewood, NJ, from 1970 to 1972. His bachelor's in history is from Baldwin Wallace College in Berea, OH. He received the Bachelor of Sacred Theology and M.Div. degrees from GTS and the D.Min. in Evangelism from VTS. In the Diocese of Dallas he has been a deputy and an alternate to GC. He is a member of the board of directors of The Children's Foundation of the Episcopal Diocese of Dallas and the East Dallas Community Organization. He is an author, chaplain, and a member of the General Board of Examining Chaplains (rotated of December 2001). He is an associate of the Society of Saint John the Evangelist, a religious order for men focusing on Spirituality, and a member of the Order of Saint John of Jerusalem. Born in 1944; he has been married to Kathlyn Anne, since 1970. They have two sons, Andrew Gray and Ian James.

BISHOPS

House of Bishops elects two for six-year terms; House of Deputies confirms.

The Rt. Rev. Mark Andrus
Birmingham, AL
Alabama, IV
Cathedral Church of the Advent

I am currently actively engaged in graduate study, and have stayed close to school ministry during the past 15 years of ordained ministry, having served as a school chaplain, and a board member of two schools. Since being called to serve as a bishop, it has been my privilege to be involved in the ordination process, interviewing aspirants, and working with the Commission on Ministry. Further, as a bishop in one of the "owning dioceses", I have been added to the trustees of the seminary at the University of the South. It has been my experience that our culture emphasizes "life above the shoulders" to the detriment of the essential consciousnesses of body and soul. Still I have found that regular engagement in intellectually stimulating, challenging learning is vital for my ministry. I am committed to the academic quality of our clergy's education.

The Rt. Rev. William O. Gregg
The Dalles, OR
Eastern Oregon, VIII

I bring to the GBEC a broad range of experience, interest , and knowledge from academia (Associate Professor of Theology, 1991-66; Ph.D. (Theology) University of Notre Dame; school chaplain; college work), parish/diocesan ministries (Rector, Interim, supply, COM (SWVa & IN], Examining Chaplains [CT], designing and implementing education programs/events, continuing education), and as Bishop directly involved in both the formation, education, and training of persons for ordained and licensed ministries, and deployment. The preparation of persons for ordained and non-ordained ministries is a major focus and commitment as a Bishop. I bring skills and knowledge for determining effective, substantive preparation for ministry; openness to think in new and different ways; willingness to work with dioceses, seminaries, and persons in preparation to design and implement appropriate instruments for testing, preparedness for ministry. I am committed to equipping all the saints for the ministries by which we live out our Baptism.

The Rt. Rev. Barry R. Howe
Kansas City, MO
West Missouri, VII

In my thirty-six years of ordained ministry, the discernment of and preparation for the ordained ministry in the church has been a priority for me. I have served as a faculty member for two Diocesan Schools for Ministry, where the primary focus is on diaconal and lay ministry. I have been a member of the Commission on Ministry in two dioceses, serving as the chairperson in one diocese. I have also served on the Standing Committee in two dioceses, serving as chairperson in each of those instances. The interfacing of the Commission on Ministry and the Standing Committee in the discernment roles has been a very important aspect of that work. In the years of my parish ministry, I sought to discern and to nurture from within the congregations I served a dozen persons who have been ordained. I have also served as an Examining Chaplain, helping to plan programs for post-GOEs. In my ministry as a bishop

I am intimately involved with all details of the ordination process. I retain a strong desire to work with the educational institutions that prepare the clergy for ordained ministry, and also hear first-hand from those who are attending seminaries from the diocese their perceptions of how they are being prepared. I serve as a Trustee of ETSS. I would be grateful to have the opportunity to use my experience and my gifts as a member of the GBEC.

The Rt. Rev. Katharine Jefferts Schori
Henderson, NV
Nevada, VIII

My adult years have been largely devoted to ministry in the academic environment. I was trained as an oceanographer (Ph.D. 1983), have taught in the university setting in several disciplines (fisheries, philosophy, religious studies), and served as the Dean of the Diocese of Oregon's School of Theology and Ministry. Following ordination, my focus in ministry has been on adult education, preaching, and formation of those called to a variety of forms of ministry, including those ordained under Title III, Canon 9. I also bring experience in Hispanic ministry and hospice chaplaincy. I currently serve a diocese distinguished by immense geographical challenges and a coincident hunger for excellent educational offerings. As a member of the Board of Examining Chaplains, I would bring a passion for baptismal ministry and excellence in education in a variety of settings.

LAY PERSONS
House of Bishops elects three for six-year terms; House of Deputies confirms.

Dr. Mary Chilton Callaway
New York, NY
New York, II
Parish of Trinity Church

Active member of the GBEC since 1997; Scripture consultant to the Board 1995-96. Ph.D. in Biblical Studies from Columbia University, 1979; Associate Professor of Old Testament at Fordham University 1980-present; Chairman of the Theology Department, Fordham University, 1995-1999. Contributor to two most recent editions of the

Oxford Annotated Bible; author of "The Apocrypha in the Episcopal/Anglican Tradition" in The Parallel Apocrypha. Special interest in the relation between the Old and New Testaments. Member, Anglican Association of Biblical Scholars; teacher of Scripture classes and lecturer for churches in the Episcopal Dioceses of New York, Newark, Connecticut and Massachusetts; visits to partner churches in the Anglican dioceses of Central Zambia and Capetown. Married to the Rev. James G. Callaway, Jr. (1972).

Ms. Maggie Alston Claud
Hartford, CT
Connecticut, I
Church of the Good Shepherd

Currently, I work with a Chaplain at Seabury Retirement Community in Bloomfield. My ministry includes Lay Eucharistic Minister, Lay Reader, Minister of Communion and officiating at Morning Prayer. At the diocesan level, I have served on the Standing Committee (5 years) including Secretary for one year; a developer of Ministry Exploration and Education Program (MEEP) for people desiring to go in the ordained ministry; on the Board of Managers for Camp Washington where I helped identify Chaplains for camp; served on the diocesan Social Concerns committee and was a member of the support team for Bishop Andrew Donnan Smith. I presently serve as the Diocesan Jubilee Officer. Other related work: member of the Hartford Board of Education (1971-75); Commissioner on the Connecticut Real Estate Commission; Commissioner on the Permanent Commission on the Status of Hartford Women; member of the Episcopal Urban Caucus Board of Directors. Received Bishops Award for Distinguished Service in 1998. I am Ms Senior Connecticut 2002 and was a Finalist in the Ms Senior America pageant.

Ms. Josephine R. Giannini
Indianapolis, IN
Indianapolis, V
Christ Church Cathedral

I am a life long Episcopal lay woman whose current positions as EFM mentor for deacons-in-training in Episcopal Diocese of Indianapolis and lay woman on GBEC would support my re-election to Examining Chaplains.

Mr. Hershel R. Hartford
Fayetteville, AR
West Missouri, VII
Christ Episcopal Church

I am 38 years old married with one child, four step-children and two grand children. I reside in Fayetteville, Arkansas; attend St. Paul's Church in Fayetteville. I came to the Episcopal Church 22 years ago, a young person seeking a spiritual home. I found it in the Episcopal Church with its rich history, liturgical, social and theological diversity. I serve as Director of Youth Ministry for St. Paul's in Fayetteville Arkansas as well as the Adult representative from the Diocese of Arkansas to the Province VII Youth Network. Previous church service includes: 5 years as Director of Youth Ministry & Camps, Diocese of West Missouri, 5 years as Director of Youth Ministry, Christ Church Springfield Missouri; work with interdenominational youth programs in Missouri, and service at St. Stephen's, Longmont Colorado. I have served at the local, convocation, diocesan, and provincial levels of the church in various capacities.

Mr. Leonard Wilkie Johnson
Oakland, CA
California, VIII
St. Mark's - Berkeley

During my career as professor at the University of California, Berkeley, I was also a consultant for Educational Testing Service, as a member of the committee charged with composing the national Advanced Placement examinations in French, and for four years as Chief Reader, in charge of the assessment of those examinations. Active in the church over many years, I have served several terms as Senior Warden of my parish, and I continue to chair the congregational Vocations Committee. Among other diocesan responsibilities, I have been president of the Standing Committee. I am presently on the Commission on Ministry and chair the Diocesan Board of Examining Chaplains. Elected two years ago Vice-Chair of the GBEC, I hope to be able to continue for a second term to work with the administrator and the other members of the board to improve the quality and usefulness of the examination and its evaluation.

Mrs. Cynthia McFarland
Ithaca, NY
Central New York, II
Saints Peter and John, Auburn

A.B. Wells College, Greek and Latin, magna cum laude, Phi Beta Kappa. Doctoral candidate, University of Virginia, Webb Fellowship in Greek. Archivist and historian of Central New York since 1994 and an independent scholar in Episcopal history. Documented the William White library in Philadelphia and in the Diocese of Western New York assessed the papers of Bishop AC Coxe. Most recent article, in 'Anglican and Episcopal History' (March 2001), concerned my discovery of a long-lost, important manuscript of William White. My interest is the early American high-church circle, particularly Bishop GW Doane. Managing Editor, Anglicans Online, with more than 200,000 weekly readers. Vice-president of the Society of Archbishop Justus, devoted to using the Internet to further unity among Anglicans. Manager, Bishops and Deputies email list. Principal of McFarland and Associates. Clients include Indiana, Pittsburgh, Oregon, and Cornell universities. Professional church work includes diocesan profiles for New Jersey and Central New York and websites for the Archbishop of Canterbury, the Diocese in Europe, and Bexley Hall seminary.

PRIESTS WITH PASTORAL CURES OR IN SPECIALIZED MINISTRIES
House of Bishops elects three for six-year terms; House of Deputies confirms.

The Rev. Ronald L. Baird
Westerville, OH
Southern Ohio, V
St. Matthew's - Westerville

During my ordained ministry I have held a passion to bring relevance and excellence to the ordained ministry. I read GOE's for eight years and served on the Commission on Ministry in two dioceses. In Southern Ohio, I served as Chair of the COM and assisted in rewriting our diocesan canons to make the COM an enabling commission rather than a gatekeeping one. In West Virginia I served as Chair of the Board of Examining Chaplains and Chair of the Committee on the Diaconate developing and implementing the vocational diaconate for that diocese as well as establishing standards for ordination. I currently serve on the Standing Committee in Southern Ohio. My goal has been to bring relevance, practicality and ease of use to the systems we utilize. I would be honored to bring this experience and expertise to serve the broader church on the GBEC.

The Rev. Dr. Mark T. Crawford
Alvin, TX
Texas, VII
Grace Episcopal Church

I have served a number of years as a reader of the GOEs and the last six years as an active member of the GBEC . I studied theology at Oxford and have recently completed a doctorate specializing in spiritual formation. I have over 20 years of experience in the parish ministry and have been active in many Diocesan Committees such as Hispanic Ministry, Evangelism and Renewal, Spiritual Formation and World Mission. I have also served as a University Chaplain in two positions in the Diocese of Texas. I would be willing to serve a second term on the GBEC as I consider it to be an important ministry of our church.

The Rev. Harry A. Elliott III
Manchester, CT
Connecticut, I
St. Mary's

I am the rector of St. Mary's Episcopal Church, a large, urban parish in Manchester, Connecticut. This parish, as well as my previous parish, has given me the blessing to recruit, hire, train and minister to/with recent seminary graduates and newly ordained persons. I have helped guide numerous persons through the ordination process. I have also served on many Diocesan committees and commissions. I have served the National Church as a G.O.E. reader. Before entering the priesthood I was a high school teacher as well as a corporate education coordinator. My parish, diocesan and life experiences have given me valuable learning and insight into the ordination process. I believe this learning would serve me well as a member of the GBEC. I would be honored to be elected to serve our Church as a member of the GBEC.

The Rev. Kurt J. Gerhard
Austin, TX
Texas, VII
St. Andrew's Episcopal School

I am the chaplain at St. Andrew's Episcopal School in Austin, TX. This work offers me the opportunity to develop relationships and foster deep spiritual growth in the young people of the church. I also have the opportunity to read and comment on the work of students and give them incite on improving their writing and their arguments. My first ordained call was to serve Holy Trinity Parish in Lincoln, NE as the assistant rector giving me a parish perspective. Before attending seminary, I used my undergraduate degree in Finance to serve as a Financial Analyst at Ameritrade, Inc. As one of the few priests in the thirty and under category, I would bring a different perspective to the board. I can express my deep regard for the importance of the GOE, but also bring a recent memory of the consternation involved in its process.

The Rev. Stephen E. Moore
Edmonds, WA
Olympia, VIII
All Saint's Church - Bellevue

I am happily blessed to do two things I love to earn a living -- as the Vicar of All Saints' Church in Bellevue, Washington, and the Judge of the Lynnwood (Washington) Municipal Court. I also love to teach: judicial ethics (recently for the National Conference of Chief Justices) and moral theology (in our Diocesan School of Ministry and Theology). I've been a Reader for the GBEC for almost a decade. My little book "Church Words: Origins and Meanings" was published by Forward Movement in 1996, the same year I was a Fellow-in-Residence at Sewanee. I am a second-time deputy to General Convention 2003. I married Dede, a member of the Bishop's staff, in 2001, having been widowed in 1998 after almost 29 years of marriage. She is occasionally well fed in that I was named a Chef of the West by Sunset Magazine in 1987.

The Rev. Caroline M. Stacey
East Lansing, MI
Michigan, V
All Saints - E. Lansing

Since 1996, I have been Rector of All Saints, East Lansing, MI, which also houses the Chaplaincy to Michigan State University. I previously served at Trinity, Wall Street; and Trinity-on-the-Green, New Haven, CT. I have tried to stay alert to emerging theological trends and new directions in seminary education. I have a strong commitment to the formation of new clergy, having hired and supervised several seminarians and two curates. Currently, I serve on several committees, including the Trustees of the Episcopal Ministry at Michigan State University, the Standing Committee and the Examining Chaplains of the Diocese of Michigan. I am also a Reader for the GOE. I would welcome the opportunity to be involved more deeply in the formation of the next generation of clergy, and see GOEs as a significant process of reflection and learning for seminarians.

The Rev. Mary Catherine Miller Sulerud
Silver Spring, MD
Washington, III
Church of the Ascension - Sligo

As Canon for Ministry and Resource Development for the Diocese of Washington and, as a former rector in the diocese, I have supervised a dozen seminarians from the Virginia Theological Seminary in field education, served 5 years as a chaplain to those being screened for postulancy in the diocese, served 6 years as a spiritual director for seminarians at VTS, and for 5 years have been a co-trainer of field education supervisors. Prior to being appointed to fill an unexpired term on the GBEC I was a GOE reader for 4 years. I understand the ministry of the GBEC through the development and evaluation of the GOE to be part of the formation of clergy for the church. It would be a great privilege to be elected to serve as a member of the GBEC.

The Rev. Nancy Van Dyke Platt
Augusta, ME
Maine, I
St. Matthew's

I have been rector of St. Matthew's, Hallowell, Maine for 18 years, adding small church experience to urban ministry in Chicago after my ordination in 1980. My BA is in English History, an MT ASCP in Chemistry, and an M. Div. focussed on Pastoral Care. Continuing Education courses include 7 units of Clinical Pastoral Education, 4 courses at St. George's College in Jerusalem, 3 courses at the College of Preachers and certification as a substance abuse counselor. I have numerous publications in the field of pastoral care. I have been a Field Education Supervisor at Seabury Theological Seminary, a member of the Diocesan Examining Chaplains, participated in vocational discernment groups and presented four people for ordination. I am currently a mentor in Fresh Start, a program for clergy entering new pastorates. I think that my broad ministry experience would be helpful in assisting and evaluating students who are preparing for ordination.

MEMBERS OF ACCREDITED SEMINARY FACULTIES OR OTHER EDUCATIONAL INSTITUTIONS

House of Bishops elects three for six-year terms; House of Deputies confirms.

The Rev. Susan M. Dolan-Henderson
Austin, TX
Texas, VII
St. Mark's

I was raised in New York on Long Island. I was first a nurse, and I attended Boston College School of Nursing. I graduated and three years later, I attended Yale Divinity School. After graduating with a Master's in Divinity, I remained a lay person for a time as I pursued graduate studies in Ethics at Emory University in Atlanta. While still a student, I applied for and received the job of instructor of Ethics at the Seminary of the Southwest. I finished my graduate degree in 1994, was ordained to the priesthood in 1995, received tenure in 1996 and I am currently Associate Professor of Christian Ethics and Moral Theology at ETSS. I have published numerous articles and I am currently working on a book. I am married and have a seven-year old son.

The Rev. Theodore W. Edwards Jr
Ledyard, CT
Florida, IV
US Navy Chaplain

I serve the Church as a Navy Chaplain with 26 years ordained service including 20 in naval chaplaincy -- currently the Command Chaplain of Naval

Submarine School with additional service on the Humanities Faculty of the Coast Guard Academy and as Assisting Priest at Bishop Seabury Church, Groton, CT. Professional credentials consist of formation at VTS (M.Div. 1977), management degree from Webster University (M.A. 1985), and theological studies at Yale University (S.T.M. 2001). I currently engage the transition of young people into adulthood, development into highly skilled citizens, and entry into arduous careers as qualified submarine sailors in the Navy and commissioned officers in the Coast Guard. Similarly, we need to actively recruit and prepare young adults for vocations of ordained leadership and certify their strong character and mature faith to exercise fiduciary responsibility. I welcome the privilege of share in raising up strong leaders for the mission of the Church.

The Rev. Robert Davis Hughes PhD
Sewanee, TN
Southern Ohio, V
Otey Memorial Parish - Sewanee

I am the Norma and Olan Mills Professor of Divinity and Professor of Systematic Theology at the School of Theology, University of the South, where I have taught for over twenty-five years. I am a publishing scholar, active in the Society of Anglican and Lutheran Theologians and the theology sections of the American Academy of Religion, as well as with the Seminary Consultation on Mission and, as a graduate Fellow, with the Episcopal Church Foundation Fellows' Forum and other programs. I have experience of the GOE's as a diocesan canonical examiner (Southern Ohio for a number of years before graduate school) and 25 years as a professor preparing students to take them. I have recently served on the GBEC, fulfilling the unexpired term of a colleague who had to resign, and have recently been appointed by the Chair as convenor of the Christian Theology team. I bring to the table three passions: the good of the Church, a deep love for sound and relevant theology, and fairness and compassion for those taking the test. In addition to systematic theology proper, I have both research and practical interests in Christian Spirituality and Missiology, which are adjunct disciplines assigned to be evaluated by the Christian theology section. I have enjoyed my brief service on the GBEC and would be privileged to serve a full term of my own.

The Rev. Canon Elizabeth Kaeton

Chatham, NJ
Newark, II
St. Paul's - Chatham

The last five years experience as GC deputy, Core Team member, New Commandment Task Force, Adjunct Faculty at Drew University and Canon Missioner to The Oasis has blessed me with several gifts: (1) the capacity to be in dialogue with the liberal, progressive, moderate, conservative and orthodox voices in the Episcopal church and Anglican Communion – especially on the tensions between the struggle for justice and the desire for holiness; (2) an experience of the depth of the work of truth-telling, repentance, forgiveness and reconciliation; (3) the ability to develop and implement parish-based curricula, especially on the issues of scripture, human sexuality and the spirit and spirituality of Anglicanism. These gifts will be an asset to the GBEC in terms of (1) the capacity to hear and appreciate various positions of belief; (2) the facility to incorporate the ethical implications of a life in Christ; and (3) the ability to develop questions for and assess responses to GOE exams.

The Rev. Frank G. Kirkpatrick

Wethersfield, CT
Connecticut, I
Trinity - Hartford

For the past 32 years I have been a professor of Religion at Trinity College (Hartford) where I've taught in the fields of philosophical and historical theology, and Christian ethics. I've served my church as supply priest and as Diocesan Commission on Ministry Chair as well as chair of its sub-committee of Examining Chaplains. My most recent scholarly work includes books on The Ethics of Community - Blackwells), a study of comparative concepts of God (Together Bound - Oxford), an upcoming book on religious and secular ethics (A Moral Ontology for a Theistic Ethic - Ashgate) and a contracted book on the political and religious philosophy of John Macmurray. Given my expertise in teaching and scholarship in the fields of Christian religious thought, I would bring much to the GBEC and would be honored to do so.

The Rev. Nayan V. McNeill

Los Gatos, CA
El Camino Real, VIII
St. Luke's - Los Gatos

A retired professor of literature, linguistics, and history, for over 20 years, a member of the teaching faculty and Dean of Language Arts and Humanities at Foothill College in Los Altos Hills, CA and ctive in the college's and a state-wide committee on curriculum and evaluation. During this time, I served on eight accrediting teams for The Accrediting Commission of Western Schools and Colleges. I hold a English and History undergraduate degree, an M.A. in English and an M.A. in Rhetoric, and a Ph.D. in Educational Philosophy, all from UC, Berkeley. After years of lay ministry, I was encouraged by my Bishop to seek ordination. My work as a priest non-stipendiary parish work, service as the diocesan Vocations Secretary, and Rector elect of a diocesan wide Cathedral School; to be devoted to post ordination education for clergy, training for Canon 9 clergy, and short courses for lay ministry. I am an examining chaplain for El Camino Real and have served as a GOE Reader. I would be honored to apply my training and experience to this service.

The Rev. Frederick W. Schmidt

Garland, TX
Washington, III
St. Michael's & All Angels - Dallas

I am Director of Spiritual Life and Formation and Assoc. Professor of Christian Spirituality at Perkins School of Theology, Southern. Methodist University, Dallas, TX; for over two years. From 1997-2000 I served as Canon Educator and Director of Programs in Spirituality and Religious Ed. at Washington National Cathedral. These experiences, and with a Doctor of Philosophy in New Testament Studies (Oxford, 1986) and extensive parish experience— full-time and part-time—has been an opportunity to observe and listen to the lives of students, priests and deacons. As a writer (65 books and articles), retreat facilitator and advisor to Epis. students at Perkins I am fortunate to have experiences in academic and ecclesiastical settings that broaden, deepen and provoke me to think the theological education's shape. I would bring careful listening and reflective leadership to the GBEC board, if elected. I am honored to be nominated.

TRUSTEES OF THE GENERAL THEOLOGICAL SEMINARY

Position Description: The Trustees of The General Theological Seminary (GTS) manage the Seminary, including: constituting professorships, electing the Dean and members of the faculty, prescribing the course of study, and establishing rules and regulations for the governance of the Seminary. Of the 42 Trustees, two are Bishops elected by the House of Bishops and four (two Presbyters or Deacons and two lay persons) are elected by the House of Deputies.

Time expectations: Regular meetings (3 meetings - 3-5 days per year), Committee meetings (3 meetings - at least one day prior to each board meeting), Executive Committee meetings (1-3 days, several times a year)

BISHOPS
House of Bishops elects two for three-year terms; House of Deputies confirms.

The Rt. Rev. J. Neil Alexander
Atlanta, GA
Atlanta, IV

For more than twenty years my ministry has been focused on theological education. I have served on the faculties of three of our seminaries, GTS, Sewanee, and Berkeley at Yale, and know our seminary system quite well. At GTS I undertook a variety of administrative assignments which enabled me to get good picture of the institution from the business and financial perspectives. I have also seen GTS from the perspective of a student, having earned my doctorate there as well. Lynn and I raised our family on Chelsea Square and our children will always consider it home. As a bishop, I deal with issues related to seminaries and theological education on an almost daily basis. I serve at the pleasure of the Presiding Bishop on his task force on seminaries that is charged with improving communication between seminaries and dioceses around issues such as canonical evaluations of seminarians, GOEs, and a variety of other issues that require effective working relationships in order to better serve the needs of the church and fulfill our canonical processes. I am pleased to be nominated to the Board of Trustees of GTS and to offer service to the national church by serving in this way.

The Rt. Rev. Michael Bruce Curry
Raleigh, NC
North Carolina, IV

For virtually all of my ordained ministry I have lived and worked in the urban context or in a context in which God 's people must struggle with the systems that disenfranchise and oppress. The Gospel of our Lord Jesus Christ is a loving, life giving God and a liberating reality which frees and saves all who will hear. GTS, set in the context of New York City, represents a place of theological education in which the gospel engages the world in such a way that the world can be transformed by it. I trust that my experience in urban ministry, in which social and evangelical tasks of the gospel are seen as one, can be of some assistance in the great work of preparing men and women for the ordained ministry.

The Rt. Rev. James Jelinek

Photograph and biographical data unavailable at time of publication.

The Rt. Rev. William Klusmeyer
Charleston, WV
West Virginia, III

I have always had a passion for education and formation, whether inside the Church or outside. One of the most basic aspects of who we are as Christians, and as Episcopalians, specifically, is to educate and form People of God. I have been called to work at all levels in this task: Commission on Ministry; Standing Committee; various Task Forces – some to work with Search Committees, and others to work with evaluating existing curricula, and now as I work with my Diocese to explore the future of education and formation for our leadership. I would find it a great joy to serve the Church by serving on the Board of GTS, to work for the future of our Church, and the formation of all our People. In a new generation, new approaches must be adopted, to better do the mission of God.

LAY PERSONS

House of Deputies elects two for three-year terms; House of Bishops confirms.

Mr. Bradford Warren Agry
New York, NY
New York, II
St. Thomas - 5th Avenue

I am co-founder of CareerTeam Partners, an executive coaching and career development firm and president of Agry Communications, a marketing consulting firm - both located in New York City. As a career counselor, I conceive and develop curriculum as well as deliver training to a variety of private clients and corporate audiences. I would enjoy utilizing this skill to help determine educational policy and the future of spiritual formation for students at GTS. In my capacity as a marketing/public relations consultant, I have over 25 years experience in developing business plans and managing their implementation. I would look forward to applying this knowledge to board activities at GTS. I hold an M.B.A in Marketing from Columbia University and a B.A. from Dartmouth College. I also serve on The Board of Directors for the American Society of Training and Development and The Huguenot Society of America. My parish is St. Thomas Fifth Avenue-where I serve as a Lector, Licensed Lay Reader and a member of the Music Committee.

Mrs. Marjorie Christie
Mahwah, NJ
Newark, II
Christ Church - Ridgewood

My experience related to the position of seminary trustee includes a dozen years as a member of the Standing Committee and five on the Commission on Ministry, during which years I was a participant in most aspirant conferences. Two terms of service on search committees for rector and for bishop coadjutor have added to my understanding of the church's ministry needs from its clergy. Concern for urban ministry and for full inclusion of women in the Church's life provide background for my interest in seminary preparation. As an incumbent trustee, I particularly value my service on the subcommittee to oversee the preparation of a Memorandum of Intent between the Seminary and the Church Center for its projected joint mission and ministry in Chelsea Square. I have also served GTS as a member of its budget and enrollment committees. As a Deputy to nine General Conventions I have served on Program, Budget & Finance, Social & Urban Affairs and Dispatch of Business. I am currently consultant to the Executive Council Committee on the Status of Women.

Mr. Douglas A. Olsen PhD
Minneapolis, MN
Minnesota, VI
St. John the Baptist

In my forty years as a member of the Episcopal Church I have served my parish as a warden and vestryman and the diocese as a trustee. I can further offer experience that is both academic and financial. I have an earned doctorate which allowed me to pursue scholarly studies in thoughtful research settings. I have taught at the Universities of Iowa and Minnesota and at the Technical University of Denmark. As an undergraduate I had a strong minor in philosophy and religion. Thus, I have some insight into the academic mission of a seminary, i.e., to produce well educated clergy. I was a co-founder of a successful biomedical device company which became a division of Medtronic. Later I went into the investment community where I continue to deal with securities of all types. I served as a Trustee of the Diocese of Minnesota with responsibilities for oversight of diocesan endowments and real property. I was later treasurer of the University Episcopal Center. Thus, I appreciate the "bricks and mortar" needs of the church. I would be honored to be elected a Trustee of The GTS.

Mrs. Joan Jennings Scalfani
Williamsville, NY
Western New York, II
Calvary - Williamsville

Joan Jennings Scalfani possesses special competencies and skills in public relations, marketing and broadcasting. As the Episcopal Representative on the Radio & Television Board of the Greater Buffalo Council of Churches, she developed new programs to highlight church in society. As producer/host of a television program airing on the local ABD affiliate, she brought together church and community leaders to discuss tough issues. Her interviewing skills, ability to put her guests at ease and intuitive questioning style made for fast paced and exciting broadcasts. "I have been blessed with opportunities for ministry in broadcasting and am grateful to the individuals interviewed over the years who helped me view the world in new ways that give deeper meaning to my own faith." The gifts of understanding, tolerance and compassion along with her technical skills would serve her well as a board member of GTS.

Mr. Edward P. Seibert
Guilford, CT
Connecticut, I
Christ Church - Guilford

I have over 25 years experience in financial and strategic planning leadership in not-for-profit and church-related organizations. As a Trustee of the Diocese of NY from 1990-2000, I served on the Budget, Investment, Strategic Planning, Congregational Support Plan and Mission Strategy committees. I initiated a program to provide financial and administrative training for parish clergy. As a Trustee of the Futures Industry Institute from 1989-1998, I helped develop interactive ethics training and other educational programs. I was Treasurer, Vestry person and Warden of my church in NY and am currently chair of the Finance Committee of Christ Church, Guilford, CT. For the past 12 years, I have consulted with parishes in the dioceses of NY, CT and Western MA, assisting them with issues such as governance, parish administration, finance, real estate and investment management. Currently, I am Treasurer of the Episcopal Housing Corp., in NY and the Mutual Housing Association of South Central CT in New Haven. I am a trustee of the Overseas Ministries Study Center in New Haven and will become its Treasurer in December 2002. I am also a Hearing Committee (disciplinary) member and Arbitrator for the National Futures Association in Chicago.

Mr. Robert E. Wright
Chapel Hill, NC
North Carolina, IV
Chapel of the Cross - Chapel Hill

Since the 72nd General Convention, I have served as a Trustee of The GTS, where I am a member of the Strategic Planning and Development Committees. Previous national Church involvement included experience as a GOE Reader in 1996 and 1997. Within the Diocese of North Carolina, I currently serve as Treasurer and delegate to our annual Diocesan Convention, and previously served a three-year term on Diocesan Council, where I chaired the Department of Finance and the Department of Christian Formation and was an ex officio member of the Committee on the State of the Church. I was also a founding member of the Triangle Institute for Anglican Studies and a member and convenor of the Advisory Board of St. John's House (Society of St. John the Evangelist) in Durham. In my parish, I am now serving my second term on the Vestry, am a member of the Finance Committee, and am an acolyte advisor and lay reader. I have also chaired the Personnel and Development Committees. I am currently Vice President for Institutional Planning and Development at the National Humanities Center in Research Triangle Park, North Carolina. Prior appointments included Associate Director, Capital Campaign for the Arts & Sciences and Engineering, Duke University; Director, Program on Preparing Minorities for Academic Careers, Duke University; and teaching positions at Duke University, Washington College, Baylor University, and Houghton College. I received my Ph.D. in English and medieval studies from Duke University in 1986, with my dissertation, "Art and the Incarnate Word: Medieval Christologies and the Problem of Literary Inexpressibility."

PRIESTS/DEACONS

House of Deputies elects two for three-year
terms; House of Bishops confirms.

The Rev. Kempton D. Baldridge

1410 Waterloo, Belgium
Churches in Europe, II
All Saints Episcopal Church

Before becoming rector in 1999, I was privileged to
be in full-time ministry with, to and for young people
for 11 years. As youth minister, navy chaplain and
university vicar, I appreciated the amazing gifts
offered by this current generation. It is a joy to
participate in and witness how our church, for all its
tradition, could still excite, inspire, inform and equip
the most "untraditional" and progressive of our
young. I want to help a great seminary attract more
of this talented and forward looking tide of
humanity, and identify effective and faithful means
of adapting ministry to those largely unreached by
the Gospel. I believe links between campus
ministries and seminaries need strengthening, and
better training in and for youth ministry by
seminarians has great potential for future clergy and
parishes they serve. As a "flagship" seminary, GTS
sets the mood and pace for the entire church. As
trustee, I would hope to bring to GTS some of the
excitement, energy and passion this latest crop of
God's children bring. Relevant experience:
Commission on the Ministry of the Baptized (Conv.
Of Amer. Ch. In Europe), 1999 - present; Prov. III
Coordinator for Ministry in Higher Education, 1998 -
1999; Gospel Music Association (professional
member), 1994 - present; Clerical Deputy - 1,
General Convention 2003; capital campaign and
annual fund executive (in higher education), 1979 -
1985.

The Rev. Yamily Bass-Choate

Jackson, MS
Mississippi, IV
St. Andrew's Cathedral - Jackson

I am Canon for Hispanic Ministries for the Diocese
of Mississippi and a graduate of GTS. While at GTS
I was a member of the seminary's Hispanic Lutheran
Episcopal Task Force and worked for the Instituto
Pastoral Hispano. In my Senior year, I was selected
to attend the World Council of Churches 'Decade
Festival: Visions Beyond 1998' held in Harare,
Zimbabwe. After graduation, I was appointed to the
Anti-racism Commission for the National Church.
Currently, I am a member of the National Church's
Trust Fund for Hispanic Theological Education and I
am Chaplain for Hispanic Women United in
Leadership (MUEL). I am a board member for
Mississippi Immigrant Rights Alliance and
CONTACT, the emergency crisis line for
Mississippi. I initiated and organized a statewide
Spanish language crisis line, AYUDA. At GTS I was
a student, spouse, mother, and a member of the
minority Hispanic community. Through my years at
seminary and my experiences gained from day to day
life as a priest, working with multicultural
communities in New York and Mississippi, and with
seminarians across this country, I have learned a lot
about the countless issues facing our church. My
experience gained in the active multicultural ministry
of the Episcopal Church enables me to bring a
distinct perspective to the ministry and the mission
of GTS. I will be honored to serve as a board
member of the GTS.

The Rev. Jessica Ann Hatch

Salt Lake City, UT
Utah, VIII
All Saints

I serve as Director of Episcopal Community Services
for the Diocese of Utah. I have also served as parish
priest for 12 years. I am a Director for Centro de la
Familia, assisting Hispanic families toward self-
sufficiency and a leader in Community Churches of
Utah. From 1996-2000 I served at GTS as Director
of Alumni/ae and Church Relations, as Deployment
Officer and as Associate Dean for Planning and
Program Development. Exercising these
responsibilities for four years gave me a substantive
and compassionate grasp of the challenges and
choices facing theological education and this premier
church institution. I am also a GTS graduate. I
believe my direct, hands-on experience and
enthusiasm as student, as occasional lecturer, as one
involved with students and alumni/ae for institutional
development, and as a recent member of the senior
management team could be particularly useful to the
Board of Trustees. I would feel privileged to serve.

The Rev. Paula Lawrence Wehmiller
Lewes, DE
Pennsylvania, III

In 1998, following a long and fruitful career as an educator, author and churchwoman, I answered a lifelong call to ordination to the priesthood. After graduating from GTS, I served the Diocese of Pennsylvania, shepherding seminarians through the ordination process and overseeing liturgical planning. In due time, I was led to combine my teaching and priestly vocations, traveling nationally and internationally as a full time spiritual director and consultant to educators, clergy, and the communities they serve. As an African-American woman priest formed in a family steeped for three generations in the work of the National Episcopal Church and the concerns of theological education, I am called to help the People of God to wrestle with the seen and unseen hurts that separate us from God in one another. I welcome the opportunity to encourage the GTS community to include, honor and nourish the variety and diversity of gifts of the women and men called to this transformative work.

TALLY SHEET FOR BALLOTING
CHURCH PENSION FUND

	BALLOTS						ELECTED	CONFIRMED
	1	2	3	4	5	6		
THREE-YEAR TERMS House of Deputies elects two; House of Bishops confirms.								
Creed, Mrs. Barbara B.								
Nestlehutt, Rev. Mark Stevens								
Sloan, Mr. Theodore B. "Tim"								
Wray, Mr. Cecil								
SIX-YEAR TERMS House of Deputies elects twelve; House of Bishops confirms.								
Agnew Jr, V. Rev. M.L.								
Bane Jr, Rt. Rev. David C.								
Bayne, Mr. James E.								
Biggs, Mr. Sheridan C.								
Boss, Mr. Jon Bancroft								
Brigham, Mr. David L.								
Brion, Ms. Theresa M.								
Candler, V. Rev. Samuel Glenn								
Casparian, Rev. Peter F.								
Cooper PhD, Mrs. Carla M.								
Fishburne, Rev. Donald Allston								
Gerdau, Rev. Cn. Carlson								
Harris, Rt. Rev. Gayle Elizabeth								
Hayashi, Rev. Scott B.								
Jay, Rev. Cn. Lynn								
Johnson, Rt. Rev. Robert Hodges								
Marsh, Rev. Caryl Ann								
Matsumura, Ms. Joon D.								
Norman, Mrs. Virginia A.								
Parsley Jr, Rt. Rev. Henry N.								
Pitts, Mr. David R.								
Robinson, Rev. Cn. V. Gene								
Sessum, Rev. Robert L.								
Wright, Rt. Rev. Wayne P.								

TALLY SHEET FOR BALLOTING
EXECUTIVE COUNCIL

	BALLOTS						ELECTED	CONFIRMED
	1	**2**	**3**	**4**	**5**	**6**		
BISHOPS House of Bishops elects two for six-year terms; House of Deputies confirms.								
Howe, Rt. Rev. John W.								
Ramos-Orench, Rt. Rev. Wilfrido								
Sauls, Rt. Rev. Stacy F.								
Waggoner Jr, Rt. Rev. James E.								
LAY PERSONS House of Deputies elects six for six-year terms; House of Bishops confirms.								
Bowden Sr, Mr. R. P. M.								
Fuller, Ms. Dorothy J.								
Gossen, Mr. Thomas R.								
Harrell, Mr. F. Rick								
Hicks, Ms. Josephine H.								
Jones, Mr. Edward Wilson								
McPhee, Ms. Sandra Ferguson								
Melnyk, Mrs. Deborah Dalton								
Mollegen Jr, Mr. Albert Theodore								
Shimpfky, Mrs. Jamel K.								
Waters, Mr. John Bennet								
Willman, Mr. Harris G.								
PRIESTS/DEACONS House of Deputies elects two for six-year terms; House of Bishops confirms.								
Augustine, Rev. Cn. Patrick P.								
Certain, Rev. Robert G.								
Crawford, Rev. Hayden G.								
Cullinane, Rev. Kathleen								
Krantz, Rev. SaraLouise C.								
Presler ThD, V. Rev. Titus L.								
Simons, Rev. James Burdette								

TALLY SHEET FOR BALLOTING
GENERAL BOARD OF EXAMINING CHAPLAINS

	BALLOTS						ELECTED	CONFIRMED
	1	2	3	4	5	6		
BISHOPS House of Bishops elects one for a three-year term; House of Deputies confirms.								
Duncan II, Rt. Rev. Philip M.								
House of Bishops elects two for six-year terms; House of Deputies confirms.								
Andrus, Rt. Rev. Mark								
Gregg, Rt. Rev. William O.								
Howe, Rt. Rev. Barry R.								
Jefferts Schori, Rt. Rev. Katharine								
LAY PERSONS House of Bishops elects three for six-year terms; House of Deputies confirms.								
Callaway, Dr. Mary Chilton								
Claud, Ms. Maggie Alston								
Giannini, Ms. Josephine R.								
Hartford, Mr. Hershel R.								
Johnson, Mr. Leonard Wilkie								
McFarland, Mrs. Cynthia								
PRIESTS WITH PASTORAL CURES OR IN SPECIALIZED MINISTRIES House of Bishops elects three for six-year terms; House of Deputies confirms.								
Baird, Rev. Ronald L.								
Crawford, Rev. Dr. Mark T.								
Elliott III, Rev. Harry A.								
Gerhard, Rev. Kurt J.								
Moore, Rev. Stephen E.								
Stacey, Rev. Caroline M.								
Sulerud, Rev. Mary Catherine Miller								
Van Dyke Platt, Rev. Nancy								
MEMBERS OF ACCREDITED SEMINARY FACULTIES OR OTHER EDUCATIONAL INSTITUTIONS House of Bishops elects three for six-year terms; House of Deputies confirms.								
Dolan-Henderson, Rev. Susan M.								
Edwards Jr, Rev. Theodore W.								
Hughes PhD, Rev. Robert Davis								
Kaeton, Rev. Cn. Elizabeth								
Kirkpatrick, Rev. Frank G.								
McNeill, Rev. Nayan V.								
Schmidt, Rev. Frederick W.								

TALLY SHEET FOR BALLOTING
GENERAL THEOLOGICAL SEMINARY

	BALLOTS						ELECTED	CONFIRMED
	1	**2**	**3**	**4**	**5**	**6**		
BISHOPS House of Bishops elects two for three-year terms; House of Deputies confirms.								
Alexander, Rt. Rev. J. Neil								
Curry, Rt. Rev. Michael Bruce								
Jelinek, Rt. Rev. James								
Klusmeyer, Rt. Rev. William								
LAY PERSONS House of Deputies elects two for three-year terms; House of Bishops confirms.								
Agry, Mr. Bradford Warren								
Christie, Mrs. Marjorie								
Olsen PhD, Mr. Douglas A.								
Scalfani, Mrs. Joan Jennings								
Seibert, Mr. Edward P.								
Wright, Mr. Robert E.								
PRIESTS/DEACONS House of Deputies elects two for three-year terms; House of Bishops confirms.								
Baldridge, Rev. Kempton D.								
Bass-Choate, Rev. Yamily								
Hatch, Rev. Jessica Ann								
Wehmiller, Rev. Paula Lawrence								

HOUSE OF BISHOPS COMMITTEE ON PASTORAL DEVELOPMENT

Membership

The Rt. Rev. Vincent W. Warner, *Chair*	Olympia
The Rt. Rev. Bruce Caldwell	Wyoming
The Rt. Rev. Clarence Coleridge	Connecticut
Mrs. Betty Creighton	Central Pennsylvania
The Rt. Rev Theodore Daniels	Virgin Islands
The Rt. Rev. Gary Gloster	North Carolina
The Rt. Rev. Clark Grew	Ohio, *resigned*
The Rt. Rev. Robert H. Johnson	Western North Carolina
Mrs. Ira Leidel	Western Michigan
The Rt. Rev. Mary Adelia McLeod	Vermont, *resigned*
The Rt. Rev. Jack McKelvey	Rochester
The Rt. Rev. Larry Maze	Arkansas
The Rt. Rev. Don A. Wimberly	Texas
The Rt. Rev. F. Clayton Matthews	*Bishop for the Office of Pastoral Development*

SUMMARY OF THE COMMITTEE'S WORK

The Committee met twice a year during the Triennium in November and April respectively. The primary function of the Committee was to serve as a council of advice to the Bishop of the Office of Pastoral Development, as well as to oversee pastoral programs for the House of Bishops including providing input to the Planning Committees of the House and the Spouses.

During the triennium the Committee worked in partnership with other Committees as designated in responding to Resolutions A045 (Ordination of Women) and X018 (Human Sexuality). The Rt. Rev. Gary Gloster was appointed to represent the Committee on the Theology Committee which was assigned the responsibility of Resolution A045.

In response to the provision to "provide pastoral care for all in our Communion, as we grow in Christ's wisdom," from the Anglican Communion Primate's Pastoral Address, the Committee established, *"Pastoral Dimensions Of Our Shared Lives,"* through which the following initiatives were carried out:
- "members of the Committee will be intentional about contacting bishops and spouses who are less involved for whatever reason in the life of the communities of the House and the Spouses Group;
- members of the Committee will communicate to the Planning Committees the need to be sensitive in creating programs and obtaining speakers that will better insure that we are not isolating each other or particular groups;
- the Committee will monitor the work being done on Resolutions A045 (Women's Ordination) and X018 (Human Sexuality) through the Executive Council, and any special committees created for the purpose of examining the pastoral implications;
- through the Council of Advice, each Provincial President will be encouraged to make special efforts to invite those who are not attending meetings regularly to attend; and
- working with the Office of the Presiding Bishop, the Committee will seek to be attentive to committee and commission appointments for the House, and for General Convention to assure as broad and as varied leadership as is feasible."

The following initiatives were adopted for the Triennium:
- take seriously the systemic and individual importance of the pastoral dimensions of our shared life;
- continue as a council of advice and support to the Bishop for the Office of Pastoral Development;
- provide direct attention to the pastoral care of bishops and spouses;
- monitor the work on Resolutions A045 and X-18 from a pastoral perspective;
- find increased funding for Episcopal formation, development and education courses and programs;

- respond to specific needs raised by the House and the Spouses Group.

During the course of the Triennium, each member was given oversight of specific programs being offered by the Office of Pastoral Development under the heading of Formation and Development as well as Pastoral Care. The Office of Pastoral Development offers seven annual programs to support and inform bishops as they exercise episcopé. In addition, the Office supports all Dioceses conducting Episcopal Elections. Since 1998 through the upcoming General Convention of the Church, we will have elected 65 new bishops, and 10 bishops-elect will be presented to the General Convention for the necessary consents of election from both Houses.

The Committee offered advice on the selection of new leaders for the New Bishops' and Spouses' Retreat, The Orderly Transitions Conference, The New Bishops' Research Project, and the Reorganization of The College for Bishops. In addition, the Committee offered advice and support on the notion of creating a national network (Nathan Network) to support, educate, train, and advocate for diocesan personnel directly responsible for handling responses to boundary violations and reported misconduct.

In direct response to a Mind of the House Resolution adopted in the Fall of 2002, the Committee devised a process to be used by the House to respond to "breaches of collegiality, church order, or previously agreed upon covenants." This process, which has been positively received by the Presiding Bishop and the Council of Advice, will be presented to the House of Bishops at the March 2003 meeting at Kanuga Conference Center in the Diocese of Western North Carolina.

BUDGET APPROPRIATION

Income	2004	2005	2006	TOTAL
	$15,000	$15,000	$15,000	$45,000

Resolution A153 House of Bishops Committee on Pastoral Development Budget Appropriation

1   *Resolved,* the House of _____ concurring, That there be appropriated from the Budget of the General
2   Convention, the sum of $45,000 for the expenses of the Committee on Pastoral Development for the
3   Triennium

THE JOINT STANDING COMMITTEE ON PLANNING AND ARRANGEMENTS

Membership

The Most Rev. Frank T. Griswold III, *Chair*	Presiding Bishop
Mr. J. P. Causey, Jr.	Dispatch of Business Chair, House of Deputies
The Rt. Rev. Richard S.O. Chang	Secretary, House of Bishops
The Rev. Bernice Coleman	Presbyter or Deacon Representative
Charles M. Crump, Esq.	Lay Representative
Mr. Vincent Currie, Jr.	Vice President, House of Deputies
Ms. Janet Farmer	Vice President, Episcopal Church Women
Mr. Gary F. Gleason	Host Diocese Representative
Ms. Lori M. Ionnitu	General Convention Manager
The Rt. Rev. James L. Jelinek	Bishop of Host Diocese
Mr. Ralph L. O'Hara	Treasurer, Domestic and Foreign Missionary Society
The Rt. Rev. Kenneth L. Price, Jr.	Dispatch of Business Chair, House of Bishops
Ms. Pamela Steward	President, Episcopal Church Women
The Rev. Rosemari G. Sullivan	Executive Officer & Secretary, General Convention
The Very Rev. George L.W. Werner	President, House of Deputies
The Rt. Rev. Arthur B. Williams, Jr.,	Vice President, House of Bishops
Mrs. Nancy Caparulo	*Staff Assistant*

WORK SUMMARY

The task of the Joint Standing Committee on Planning and Arrangements is to arrange for the meeting of the next General Convention and to propose an agenda which the Convention may accept or reject, with or without amendments. The Committee also investigates sites for future meetings of the General Convention and makes recommendations to the General Convention.

The full committee held its first meeting in Minneapolis, Minnesota on January 10th and 11th of 2001. The first order of business was a tour of the Minneapolis Convention Center, site of the 74th General Convention. The group then reviewed learnings from the 73rd General Convention around orientation, worship, facilities, secretariats, legislative process, communications, exhibits, and related events. All of these areas were examined for applicability towards making the 74th General Convention even better than the 73rd. An initial draft calendar was distributed.

Looking forward to the 75th General Convention, Lori Ionnitiu reported that the sites for 2006 had been narrowed to Baltimore, MD, Charlotte, NC, Columbus, OH, and San Antonio, TX. The Executive Committee agreed to travel to these sites in May of 2002.

The second meeting took place in San Antonio, Texas on February 21, 2002. The theme of the 74th General Convention was discussed in terms of "new confidence" expressing itself in an outward-looking stance toward the world, which one might capture in the word "mission." The ECW reported that their theme will be "A New Light is Shining." The calendar was reviewed again, and further refined.

Columbus and Charlotte were selected as primary possibilities for the 75th General Convention, with Baltimore as a back-up if Charlotte were to fall through for any reason. In May, site visits were conducted, and the visiting group voted to recommend Columbus because of the configuration of the Convention Center, its technology infrastructure, and the 50% break in the price which was offered for the Convention Center. This recommendation was then forwarded to the Provincial Presidents and the Executive Council, with the proposed dates of June 12-21, 2006.

The third meeting of the full committee was conducted via conference call. The draft GC Calendar was again reviewed and refined. The theme for General Convention, "Engage God's Mission," was discussed. It was agreed that the ECW schedule would be added as a link on the ECUSA website.

Columbus has been approved by the Provincial Presidents and the Executive Council, and a resolution will be presented to Convention for final approval.

The site selection process for the 76th General Convention has begun. The group agreed to propose that the 76th Convention be nine days in length. The sites proposed for 2009 include Salt Lake City, UT; Reno, NV, Portland, OR, Charlotte, NC and Anaheim, CA.

Resolution A154 75th General Convention Site

1   *Resolved,* the House of _____ concurring, That Columbus, Ohio be selected as the site for the 75th
2   General Convention in 2006.

Resolution A155 76th General Convention Site

1   *Resolved,* the House of _____ concurring, That the following five sites be considered for the 76th General
2   Convention and that no less than three be selected for final consideration. The five sites are: Salt Lake
3   City, Utah, Reno, Nevada, Portland, Oregon, Anaheim, California, and Charlotte, North Carolina.

Resolution A156 2003 General Convention Daily Agenda

1   *Resolved,* the House of _____ concurring, That the 2003 General Convention function through the following
2   activities:
3   1. formal legislative sessions of the two Houses;
4   2. a joint session for presentation of the budget proposal;
5   3. meetings of the legislative committees of the two Houses; and
6   4. open hearings to be conducted as needed by all legislative committees; and be it further
7   *Resolved,* That the schedule and the daily timetable of the 74th General Convention held in Minneapolis, Minnesota be:

8   Sunday, July 27
9   11:00 -1:30pm   Volunteer Supervisors Gathering
10 4:00 - 6:00pm   HD Secretariat & Dispatch Orientation

11 Monday, July 28
12 9:30am - 5:00pm   Registration
13 9:30am - 5:00pm   Deputy Certification
14 2:00 - 6:00pm   Legislative Committee Officers Orientation

15 Tuesday, July 29
16 9:30am - 5:30pm   Registration
17 9:00am - 12:00pm   Legislative Committee Meetings
18 9:30am - 1:45pm   Deputy Certification
19 2:00 - 3:00pm   PB/Pres HD Presentation to GC
20 3:00 - 5:00pm   Orientation
21 3:30 - 5:30pm   Deputy Certification
22 8:00pm   Legislative Committee Meetings

23 Wednesday, July 30
24 7:30 - 9:00am   Legislative Committee Meetings
25 8:00am - 5:00pm   Registration
26 8:30 - 9:30am   Deputy Certification
27 9:30am - 10:45pm   Eucharist & Scripture Reflection
28 11:00am - 12:30pm   Legislative Session
29 1:00 - 1:30pm   Deputy Certification
30 2:00 - 4:00pm   Legislative Committee Meetings
31 4:15 - 6:00pm   Legislative Session
32 8:00pm   Conversations

33 Thursday, July 31
34 7:30 - 9:00am   Legislative Committee Meetings
35 8:00am - 5:00pm   Registration
36 8:30 - 9:30am   Deputy Certification
37 9:30 - 10:45am   Eucharist & Scripture Reflection
38 11:00am - 12:30pm   Legislative Session

39	1:00 - 1:30pm	Deputy Certification
40	2:00 - 3:30pm	Legislative Committee Hearings
41	3:45 - 6:00pm	Legislative Session
42	5:00pm	Resolution Filing Deadline
43	8:00pm	PB&F & Hearing

44 Friday, August 1

45	7:00 – 8:30am	Legislative Committee Meetings
46	9:00am – 1:00pm	Morning of Prayer
47	12noon – 5:00pm	Registration
48	1:00 – 1:30pm	Deputy Certification
49	2:30 – 6:00pm	Legislative Session
50	8:00pm	PB&F Hearing

51 Saturday, August 2

52	7:30 - 9:00am	Legislative Committee Meetings
53	8:00am - 1:00pm	Registration
54	8:30 - 9:30am	Deputy Certification
55	9:30 - 10:45am	Eucharist & Scripture Reflection
56	11:00am - 1:00pm	Legislative Session

57 Sunday, August 3

58	10:00am	UTO Ingathering & Eucharist
59	12:30 - 5:00pm	Registration
60	1:00 - 1:30pm	Deputy Certification
61	2:30 - 6:00pm	Legislative Session
62	8:00pm	Anti-Racism Program

63 Monday, August 4

64	7:30 - 9:00am	Legislative Committee Meetings
65	8:00am - 5:00pm	Registration
66	8:30 - 9:30am	Deputy Certification
67	9:30 - 10:45am	Eucharist & Scripture Reflection
68	11:00am - 1:00pm	Legislative Session (Provincial Caucuses)
69	1:00 - 1:30pm	Deputy Certification
70	2:30 - 6:00pm	Legislative Session

71 Tuesday, August 5

72	7:30 - 9:00am	Legislative Committee Meetings
73	8:00am - 5:00pm	Registration
74	8:30 - 9:30am	Deputy Certification
75	9:30am - 10:45am	Eucharist & Scripture Reflection
76	11:00am - 1:00pm	Legislative Session
77	1:00 - 1:30pm	Deputy Certification
78	2:30 - 6:00pm	Legislative Session

79 Wednesday, August 6

80	7:30 - 9:00am	Legislative Committee Meetings
81	8:00am - 5:00pm	Registration
82	8:30 - 9:30am	Deputy Certification
83	9:30 - 10:45am	Eucharist & Scripture Reflection
84	11:00am - 1:00pm	Legislative Session (Provincial Caucuses)
85	1:00 - 1:30pm	Deputy Certification
86	2:30 - 6:00pm	Legislative Session (Includes Joint Session: PB&F Budget)
87	8:00pm	Reserved for Legislation

88 Thursday, August 7

89	7:30 - 9:00am	Legislative Committee Meetings
90	8:00am - 5:00pm	Registration
91	8:30 - 9:30am	Deputy Certification
92	9:30 - 10:45am	Eucharist & Scripture Reflection

93	11:00am - 1:00pm	Legislative Session
94	1:00 - 1:30pm	Deputy Certification
95	2:30 - 6:00pm	Legislative Session
96	8:00pm	Reserved for Legislation
97	Friday, August 8	
98	9:00 - 10:15am	Eucharist & Scripture Reflection
99	8:00am - 2:00pm	Registration
100	8:30 – 9:30pm	Deputy Certification
101	10:30am - 1:00pm	Legislative Session
102	1:00 - 1:30pm	Deputy Certification
103	2:30 - 6:00pm	Legislative Session

THE JOINT STANDING COMMITTEE ON PROGRAM, BUDGET AND FINANCE

Membership

Ms. Bonnie Anderson, *Chair*	Michigan
The Rt. Rev. Russell E. Jacobus, *Vice-Chair*	Fond du Lac
The Rev. William D. Nix, Jr., *Secretary*	Northwest Texas
Mr. Stephen C. Duggan	Treasurer, *ex officio, resigned*
Mr. Ralph L. O'Hara	Treasurer, ex officio
The Rev. Rosemari G. Sullivan	Secretary of the General Convention, *ex officio*
The Rev. Wilifred S. N. Allen-Faiella	Pennsylvania, *resigned*
Mr. Donald W. Bushyager	Pittsburgh
Ms. Anne Bardol	Northwestern Pennsylvania
The Rev. Canon Ernest L. Bennett	Central Florida
The Rt. Rev. Charles E. Bennison	Pennsylvania
Mr. Arthur M. Bjontegard, Jr.	Upper South Carolina
Mr. Jon B. Boss	Southern Ohio
The Rev. James T. Boston	Oregon, *replaced*
The Rev. Altagracia Perez	Los Angeles
The Rev. Canon Anthony F. Buquor	South Dakota, *resigned*
The Rev. Willa M. Goodfellow	Iowa
The Rev. Alan C. French	New Jersey, *replaced*
Ms. Lyn Headley-Moore	Newark
The Rev. Gayle E. Harris	Rochester, *resigned*
The Rev. Canon Dr. Johncy Itty	Long Island
The Rt. Rev. Julio Cesar Holguin	Dominican Republic
The Rt. Rev. David B. Joslin	New Jersey
The Rt. Rev. James B. Krotz	Nebraska
Senor Roy Lara	Honduras
The Rt. Rev. Alfred C. Marble, Jr.	Mississippi, *resigned*
The Rt. Rev. Charles G. von-Rosenberg	East Tennessee
Canon Holly McAlpen	California
The Rev. Kathleen S. Milligan	Iowa
The Rt. Rev. Claude E. Payne	Texas, *resigned and replacement to be announced*
The Rev. Gregory H. Rickel	Texas, *replaced*
The Rev. Janie L. Kirt Morris	Oklahoma, *replaced*
Ms. Pan Adams	Arkansas
Mr. Byron Rushing	Massachusetts
The Rev. Sandino Augusto Sanchez	Dominican Republic
The Rt. Rev. Andrew D. Smith	Connecticut
Mr. Dennis Stark	Rhode Island
The Rt. Rev. James Edward Waggoner	Spokane

The Presiding Bishop and the President of the House of Deputies appointed the Rt. Rev. Russell Jacobus to propose and present a slate of officers for the Program, Budget and Finance (PB&F) Committee for the Triennium. The following were approved by a mail poll of the entire Committee: Ms. Bonnie Anderson, *Chair*: The Rt. Rev. Russell Jacobus, *Vice-Chair;* The Rev. William Nix, *Secretary;* The Rev. Gayle E. Harris (resigned) and The Rt. Rev. Andrew Smith, *Canonical and Administrative Support Section;* The Rt. Rev. Russell E. Jacobus, *Funding Section*; Mr. Byron Rushing, *Program/Mission Section* and Canon Holly McAlpen, *Presentation Section.*

The Executive Committee, which also serves as the Funding Section, was composed of the following members: Ms. Anderson, Bishop Jacobus, the Rev. Mr. Nix, Canon McAlpen, Mr. Rushing, and the Rev. Harris, resigned.

WORK SUMMARY

The primary responsibilities of the Joint Standing Committee on Program, Budget and Finance (PB&F or the Committee) are to recommend funding and spending policies to each General Convention for the succeeding triennium, i.e. mission (program), expense and budgets; and between Conventions, to (a) maintain the balanced budget policies, assuring that income is equal to proposed expenditures each year and (b) monitor the priorities established by General Convention and give advice to Executive Council with regard to any adjustments in priorities.

Early in the triennium a letter was sent to the Executive Council's Standing Committee on Administration and Finance (A&F) by the chair and vice chair of PB&F outlining specific areas of follow-up from the General Convention. The areas were:
- The importance of budget priorities.
- Suggestions for following up on funding issues identified at the General Convention.
- Expense items including the Alleluia Fund, Congregational Ministries, ERD, and accountability procedures for institutions/organizations that receive "block grant type" funds from the Episcopal Church budget.

PB&F unanimously resolved to ask the Executive Council to be explicit to PB&F and the General Convention about the priorities used to establish the budget for the next triennium.

During this triennium, PB&F's primary concern was to continue to evaluate and improve the current budget-making process. In addition, the Committee continued to encourage and work with the staff and the Standing Committee on Administration and Finance of the Executive Council (A&F) to identify clear budget priorities. The underlying motivation for initiating this work during the last triennium and continuing it through this triennium was the belief that the Episcopal Church budget is a theological statement of what we believe and value. The Budget for the Episcopal Church should follow the Church's vision.

Throughout the triennium the Committee continued to maintain that a clear vision of mission/ministry priorities and subsequent allocation of monetary resources to enable their implementation is important. In order to maintain regular communication and collaboration in the budget process, PB&F's chair or vice-chair attended A&F and Executive Council meetings during the triennium.

To support PB&F's quest for General Convention to understand the budget process, PB&F requested that the draft budget developed by the Executive Council should be in a plain paper format that will clearly indicate its status as a work in progress, to be finalized by the General Convention.

The Committee acknowledged that the funding formula approved by the 73rd General Convention is working well and should remain in place during the next triennium. The funding formula will be discussed again at PB&F's meeting in March 2003, prior to the General Convention.

EXECUTIVE COMMITTEE
For the purpose of proposing section chairs, the Committee officers met by conference call on January 29, 2001. The Executive Committee met by conference call on August 1, 2001, January 27, 2002, June 7, 2002, and gathered as part of the committee of the whole on March 4, 2002. A meeting is scheduled for March 31, 2003 in Minneapolis.

The August 1, 2001 conference call included these items:
- Update of PB&F appointments
- DFMS/General Convention Treasurer search (Bonnie Anderson, PB&F chair, served on the search committee.)
- Budget priorities

- Response to PB&F's resolution asking Executive Council for a priority based budget
- Update by A&F Chair on priorities development
- Request to A&F that the Executive Council survey be sent to all bishops and deputies

The February 27, 2002 conference call included these items:
- Development of agenda and tasks for the upcoming meeting of the committee of the whole

The June 7, 2002 conference call included a review of the draft list of budget priorities identified by Executive Council.

Subsequent discussion regarding PB&F's ability to insure that the mission priorities reflected in the Budget accurately express the priorities embraced by the General Convention:
- Disclosure of the alleged misuse of diocesan funds by bishops in Northern and Western Mexico
- Financial accountability for funds disbursed to supported dioceses and domestic block grants
- Committee membership appointments
- Telephone orientation of new committee members including chair's conference with members appointed after March 2002

COMMITTEE OF THE WHOLE
The whole PB&F Committee met at Camp Allen, Texas, on March 4-6, 2002. The Committee will meet again in Minneapolis on March 31-April 3, 2003. The 2002 meeting held at Camp Allen was an orientation session for new members. The responsibilities of PB&F and its role at General Convention were discussed, as were the state of the finances of the Domestic & Foreign Missionary Society. Orientation included:
- Background of financial statements, including differentiating between budgetary and statutory financials
- Current forecasts for the trust funds and the triennial budget for the General Convention
- Budget elements, categories, and time frame for budget development
- Anticipated 2002 diocesan commitments
- Configuration of the management team and programmatic heads at the Church Center
- Report and update on mission/program
- Review by staff of the major issues identified in the survey conducted by Executive Council designed to assist them in developing budget priorities

The Committee examined the interconnectedness of PB&F with other financial areas, thoroughly reviewed the budget-making process including PB&F's role with A&F and Executive Council in requesting budget priorities. A General Convention overview and preparation for resolution tracking was presented. PB&F requested that the open hearing on spending occur after the funding hearing at General Convention.

Because PB&F would like to be prepared to adequately discuss budget allocations for supported dioceses and domestic block grants, the need for a clear process of accountability for the use of funds disbursed to supported dioceses and domestic block grants was re-emphasized.

FUNDING SECTION
At the meeting of the PB&F Committee of the whole in 2002, the Funding Section discussed the 21% asking and ascertained that it is still appropriate. The Section reviewed the procedures in place during the last triennium for letters to the dioceses urging those under 21% to raise their pledge, and thanking those responding at 21% or above. The proposed funding formula will be reviewed and discussed at the March, 2003 meeting of the committee of the whole.

As of September 30, 2002 the diocesan pledged income was:
> 51 dioceses at the asking of 21%
> 3 dioceses slightly above 21%
> 7 dioceses significantly above 21%
> 37 dioceses below 21%

AUDIT

In compliance with Joint Rule II.11, two members, Art Bjontegard and Bonnie Anderson, of the Joint Standing Committee on PB&F, serve on the Audit Committee of the Executive Council. In compliance with Joint Rule II.11, it is the responsibility of the Audit Committee of the Executive Council to report annually to PB&F, who then reports to the General Convention.

The 2000 and 2001 audits (Arthur Andersen and Company) yielded no reportable conditions or material weaknesses. Audits were conducted for each of the years (2000 and 2001) with no exceptions or qualifications noted.

In order to select a CPA firm to conduct the 2002 audit of the Domestic & Foreign Missionary Society (DFMS), requests for proposals were sent by the Audit Committee to Ernst & Young, KPMG, and Grant Thornton. These three firms presented proposals and entered into discussion with the Audit Committee and staff. Grant Thornton was selected by a unanimous vote of the Audit Committee and accepted by the Executive Council at its meeting in October 2002. The 2002 audit completion is expected by July 2003.

The Audit Committee recommended the implementation of "best practices" techniques offered to all Province IX dioceses at periodic Business Management Institute sessions. These sessions have been well-attended and will be continued. Reportable findings have been or are in the process of being corrected.

In some instances, the Audit Committee has recommended temporarily suspending grant payments into affected dioceses and making adjustments to ensure that clergy in these dioceses are paid and that their pensions are protected. The Audit Committee continues to monitor closely the situations in the assisted dioceses of Ecuador-Central and Ecuador-Litoral as well as the northern and western dioceses within the autonomous Province of the Anglican Church of Mexico.

PRESENTATION SECTION

The Presentation Section does the majority of its work on site during the General Convention. PB&F budget presentation is governed by I.4.6 (c). Consideration is being given to a budget format that can be easily interpreted by the General Convention bishops and deputies. Graphic illustrations and language translations, and availability on the web are all under consideration. Presentation planning will continue at the 2003 meeting of the committee of the whole.

Budget Report
FINANCIAL REPORT FOR THE 2001-2003 TRIENNIUM

	2001	2002	2003
Allocation	$30,000	$35,000	$55.000
Expenses			
Budget	$1,380.00 (actual)	$17,771 (actual 9/30/02)	$55,000

BUDGET APPROPRIATION

	2004	2005	2006
Budget	$6,000	$35,000	$65,000

Resolution A157 Joint Standing Committee on Program, Budget and Finance Budget Appropriation

1   Resolved, the House of _____ concurring, That $106,000 be appropriated for the work of the Joint
2   Standing Committee on Program, Budget and Finance for the 2004-2006 triennium.

HOUSE OF DEPUTIES COMMITTEE ON THE STATE OF THE CHURCH

Membership

The Rev. Reynolds S. Cheney II, *Chair*	West Tennessee
The Rev. Cecily P. Broderick y Guerra, *Vice-Chair*	Long Island
The Rev. Canon Augusta R. Anderson	North Carolina, *Appointed 2002*
Mr. Wesley Baldwin	Washington
Ms. Anne C. Brown	Vermont
Mr. Richard Carroll, Jr.	Albany, *Resigned*
The Rev. Kelly M. Demo	Kansas, *Resigned*
The Rev. Canon Mark Dunnam	Central Gulf Coast
The Rev. Susan Hansell	Central Florida
The Rev. Canon Paul E. Lambert	Dallas
Mr. John McCann	Lexington
The Rev. Canon Antonio Munoz	El Camino Real
Mr. Alfred D. Price	*Executive Council liaison, appointed 2002*
Ms. Terry Roberts	Minnesota
Mrs. Tabitha M.L. Secretario	Hawaii, *Resigned*
The Rev. Susan Skinner	Missouri

Mr. Lee Clark, *Office of the General Convention, Manager of Parochial Report Systems*
Ms. Verlyn Hinds, *Episcopal Church Center Staff liaison*
Mr. Ray Duncan, *Episcopal Church Center Staff liaison, deceased*

SUMMARY OF WORK: KNOWING WHO WE ARE

The Committee on the State of the Church is a committee of the House of Deputies charged with preparing and presenting to the House of Deputies "a report on the State of the Church" (I.6.5(b)). The committee is also responsible for the form of the Parochial Report.

The committee met five times during the triennium and offers the following "snapshot" of the Episcopal Church in the opening years of the new millennium. A primary resource is the annual Parochial Report. We also met with representatives of the Church Pension Group, the Office of Congregational Development, the Episcopal Church Foundation and the General Convention Office. We used studies produced by some of those groups as additional resources.

A New Millennium, a New Context

The ministry of reconciliation is the primary mission of the Episcopal Church. As part of the Body of Christ, the church responds to its calling in many and diverse ways. At the close of the twentieth century and the opening of the third millennium, we find ourselves at an important crossroads.

The modern era as we have known it is giving way to a post-modern era characterized by greater diversity, pluralism and globalism. The church's life within this global community (now a "village"), our relationship with the environment and integrity of creation, our response to third world debt and first world consumerism, issues of business, medical/bio-ethics, science and religion, deep conversation between the religions of the world, war, peace and justice, sexuality and racism—all these and more create the arena within which we do ministry. The implications are immense, the opportunities challenging. What occurs in our country affects others around the world, and vice versa. Now more than ever, the state of the church is intimately entwined with the state of the world.

In looking toward the future, we often find ourselves caught in a tension between the ways we have always done things and the call to find new ways of being the church in order to do ministry and mission. How much do we allow the culture of our time and place to influence the direction of the church, and how much do we stand against that culture? The Anglican Communion and the Episcopal Church have a heritage of dealing with such tensions, a heritage of living with diversity and ambiguity that we can offer as a gift to a diverse and uncertain world. That heritage challenges us to hold on to the good that has been passed down to us and to step out in hope and in faith, offering a ministry of reconciliation to a world torn by violence and fear of difference.

Our Anglican heritage also challenges us within the church to seek a kind of unity—or reconciled communion with one another—that at the same time celebrates and affirms our diversity. The Committee on the State of the Church quickly discovered that we faced that challenge as a group, for we reflect at least some of the diversity of the Episcopal Church. We come from California to Vermont, from Minnesota to Florida, and places in between. We are black, brown and white; conservative, moderate and progressive; male and female; clergy and lay; straight and gay. And we have built relationships that bridge the distance of our differences to become a community of reconciliation.

Response to September 11

We held our second meeting at the Church Center in New York City barely two weeks after the attacks of September 11, 2001. We believe the response of the Episcopal Church, at all levels, made manifest what it means to make the hope of the gospel concrete, what it means to be a reconciling presence in the midst of chaos and fear. We commend the ministry of the institutions and individuals who responded to the tragic events of that day with love, generosity and both practical and pastoral assistance.

We note particularly the work of St. Paul's Chapel of Trinity Church, Wall Street; the Seamen's Church Institute of New York and New Jersey; the General Theological Seminary; the Episcopal Church Center; the Office of the Bishop Suffragan for the Armed Services, Healthcare and Prison Ministries; and the many individuals who offered themselves as volunteers.

Congregations all across the country opened their doors to a population suddenly finding itself in need of connection to a praying community. They ministered to those who lost friends and family members; they sent volunteers and messages of encouragement; they contributed clothing and other material items needed by rescue and recovery workers and by those who lost their homes; they raised funds for the work of Episcopal Relief and Development; and many embraced the challenge to reach out to people of other faiths, particularly those who were experiencing discrimination.

History of the Parochial Report

The General Convention from its earliest days has sought information to measure the church's relative well being, even then referred to as "the State of the Church." As we continue to face the challenges of a mission of reconciliation in a complex context, having a sense of who we are is vital. Data obtained from the annual parochial reports and other carefully constructed studies allows us to move beyond assumptions and perceptions to a more accurate picture of many aspects of the life and health of the church.

Staff at the Archives of the Episcopal Church informed us that during the General Convention held in 1792, the House of Deputies went into a "Committee of the Whole on the State of the Church" to review the constitution that had been completed by the previous General Convention. By canon adopted in 1804, the House of Deputies was directed to prepare a triennial report on the "State of the Church" that would be based on diocesan reports and other papers such as, "Episcopal charges, addresses, and pastoral letters as may tend to throw light on the State of the Church in each diocese." The General Convention was concerned about the dramatic decline in the number of clergy and communicants following the Revolutionary War, when perhaps only 10,000 Episcopalians inhabited the new republic, and only some 3,000 would have been able to attend worship services. By 1820, the church had gone from being the third largest denomination in the colonies before the Revolutionary War to being the smallest relative to the mainline churches. By 1830, the Episcopal Church had grown to about 30,000 members.

Two centuries ago, the House of Deputies understood the value of systematically gathering intelligence, a process that creates its own interconnections, in order to evaluate and restore the church's vitality. Concerned about decline, they began gathering data in order to plan for growth.

In more recent years, the Committee on the State of the Church has focused on the characteristics, attitudes and needs of various segments of the church community. It conducted a census in 1950, and has initiated studies of the needs of minorities (1985 – A141), the demographics of working class and membership (1988 –

A159), and the demographic characteristics of students and staff of Episcopal Day Schools (1991 – A182). In 1991 (A178), the committee promoted the use of parochial and diocesan reports as planning and development tools for the Presiding Bishop and his staff, a continuing reflection of the 1804 canon. In 1994, the committee was directed to analyze church growth trends (D044). In 2000, the General Convention, on the recommendation of the committee, called for a census by 2005 (A101).

In the present triennium, the General Convention Office has addressed the need to improve the accuracy of the data it receives and has made an effort both to subject the data to more in-depth statistical analysis and to provide reports that are better suited for the planning needs of the church. The previous Committee on the State of the Church recommended revisions to the parochial report form that were approved by Executive Council in February, 1999. The review process continues, with the assistance of Church Center staff.

Current Data and Trends

As the Episcopal Church embraces "20/20: A Clear Vision," a commitment to double the church's baptized membership between the years 2000 and 2020, the analysis of key parochial report data can provide a periodic progress report. Current data tell us about:

Attendance and Membership: The number of "active baptized members" in the Episcopal Church has decreased over the last decade, but the number of "communicants in good standing" has increased. Many consider "average Sunday attendance" to be the best indicator of vitality in the church, and that figure has increased in the last decade, especially in 2000 and 2001.

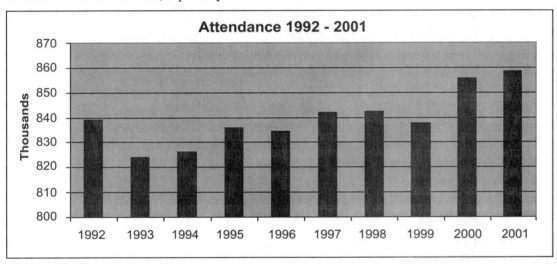

	Year 2001	1 year change	3 year change	9 year change
Attendance	858,510	0.32 %	1.92 %	2.30 %
Membership	2,330,283	-0.14 %	-0.07 %	-4.06 %
Communicants	1,807,280	-3.55 %	0.59 %	9.78 %

A chart at the end of this report shows membership, communicants, and average attendance for years 2001 and 1997 by diocese and province. The number of active baptized members decreased in six domestic provinces and increased in two, Province IV (2.5%) and Province VII (3%). The population of the United States grew in the decade of the 90s in all provinces, with the greatest percentage growth occurring in Provinces IV (15%), VII and VIII (16% each).

Stewardship: The number of pledging units has decreased, but the average pledge showed a steady increase until 2001. The downturn in the national economy is reflected in a drop of nearly $460 in the average pledge between 2000 and 2001, and a significant drop in the value of invested assets over the same period. The proportional percentage (average pledge divided by household income) is 3.8%, a long way, we note, from the tithe.

	Year 2001	1 year change	3 year change	9 year change
Pledge Units	567,569	-4.01 %	-3.94 %	-8.26 %
Pledge and Plate	$1,118,923,904	1.62 %	17.46 %	51.24 %
Average Pledge	$1,667.63	-21.63 %	13.81 %	59.41 %
Value of Invested Assets	$3,371,193,005	-14.75 %	35.00 %	134.38 %

A chart at the end of this report, "Congregations' Revenues and Expenses used for Operations from 1997-2001," shows trends in the total operating income and expenses for the domestic Episcopal Church. A final chart compares "Normal Operating Income and Expenses for Episcopal Parishes 1997-2001," by diocese and province (Provinces I-VII).

Sunday Attendance by Church Size: Seventy-two percent of Episcopal congregations account for twenty-seven percent of Episcopalians who attend church on a given Sunday. These are the family or pastoral size congregations with an average Sunday attendance of 140 or fewer persons. The remaining seventy-three percent of Episcopalians attend the twenty-eight percent of congregations with an average Sunday attendance above 140, and these are the growing churches. The rate of growth is greatest in the largest congregations. The categories below are those used by the Diocese of Texas.

	Family <75	Pastoral 75 ->140	Transitional 141->225	Program 226->400	Resource >400
1999	128,258	195,630	194,375	179,120	137,893
2001	127,827	191,180	199,799	186,798	152,906
% Change	-0.34 %-2.27 %	2.79 %	4.28 %	10.88 %	

Total Attendance by Church Size Category

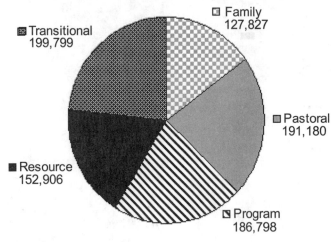

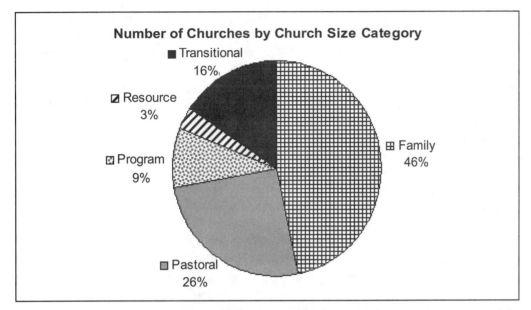

Number of Churches by Church Size Category

- Transitional 16%
- Resource 3%
- Program 9%
- Pastoral 26%
- Family 46%

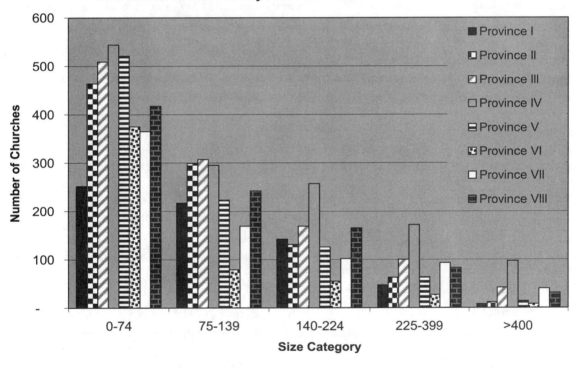

Distribution of Churches by Province and Size of Attendance - 2001

Legend: Province I, Province II, Province III, Province IV, Province V, Province VI, Province VII, Province VIII

Y-axis: Number of Churches

X-axis (Size Category): 0-74, 75-139, 140-224, 225-399, >400

Church School Enrollment: Enrollment (288,819 in 2001) has declined by 14.08% over the past nine years. We do not have figures for actual church school participation, so it is not possible to tell if the relationship between church school enrollment and attendance bears any similarity to the relationship between baptized members and average Sunday attendance. That is, is attendance increasing while the number of those who merely enroll declines, or are both declining? The apparent decline does lend support to the claim that the Episcopal Church has an aging membership.

Parochial Report Issues and Limitations

Awareness of the importance of effective data gathering and dissemination is growing. Compliance with the canonical requirement to file the parochial report is 96%, an all time high. Unfortunately, too many churches file long after the required date for submission, thus delaying timely use and analysis of the data.

Reports are now being made available to all levels of church governance. For example, the 2002 Parochial Report package mailed to each congregation included a chart showing their average Sunday attendance pattern since 1991. The Office of Congregational Development sponsored the preparation and inclusion of the attendance charts.

The parochial report data goes back only to 1990 in electronic form, and we do not have reliable parochial report data from the non-domestic dioceses. Recent efforts to improve the quality of the database from the early part of the decade, and that of the new data collected annually, have made it more useful. We believe that as reports are made available to parish clergy and vestries, they will be motivated to produce parochial report data on their individual churches that is accurate. Personnel in the General Convention Office are working to improve the rate of compliance with submission requirements from its current level of 96% to as close to 100% as possible. In addition, parochial report workshops are being given around the country to improve the accuracy of data submitted.

The committee is acutely aware that the parochial reports only begin to give a picture of the "state of the church" as we enter a new millennium. It cannot tell us, for example, about:
- What we believe and why we believe.
- Who our members, visitors, and program participants are in terms of age, race, nationality, ethnicity, income, education, work, etc.
- The character and effectiveness of ministry in and by congregations.
- How many people, lay and clergy, actively perform the ministries of our congregations, dioceses, and church institutions.
- Our many outreach ministries and how they express our mission of reconciliation.

In other words, we cannot draw adequate conclusions about the viability of our mission, the quality of our congregations, and the productivity of our lay and ordained ministers solely from data about size, income, attendance, membership, and expenses. Such conclusions, to be accurate, require other forms of data, some of which are available to us.

Other Resources

The Zacchaeus Project: Discerning Episcopal Identity at the Dawn of the New Millennium (June 1999): The committee met with the Rev. Dr. William L. Sachs, co-director of the national research project conducted by the Episcopal Church Foundation, in which interviewers spoke with some 2000 Episcopalians in nine dioceses selected to reflect the diversity of the whole church. Their goal was to investigate "how Episcopalians at the grassroots level currently view themselves and their Church," and their focus was qualitative rather than quantitative. Key findings of the survey are:

A. Episcopalians are committed to worship and an Anglican tradition that binds them in Christian community and forms a spiritual framework for personal growth and ministry.

B. Creative ferment and vitality characterizes Episcopal life in local congregations.

C. Profound tensions are impacting the life and relationship among congregations and judicatories.

D. Episcopalians are successfully embracing diversity and changes in the life of their congregations (p. 15).

Dr. Sachs told the committee that no congregation had escaped conflict—the largest source of which is diversity—but that nearly all had found ways to heal. He also pointed to a shift in attitude from a sense of belonging to a religious institution to one of being on a shared spiritual journey, and to a sense of disconnection with wider church structures. However, he also said that the sense of purpose among the laity is "very solid and strong."

A Report on Episcopal Churches in the United States (April 2002): C. Kirk Hadaway prepared this report for the Office of Congregational Development, using Episcopal Church data collected for a large study of religious life in America (Faith Communities Today or FACT) conducted in the spring of 2000. Data are from 726 churches responding to a stratified random sample questionnaire.

According to the report, "The survey … provides a profile of Episcopal congregations and also speaks to sources of vitality and growth" (p. 1). Findings include:

- Episcopal churches tend to be located in towns and cities, but those in newer suburbs tend to be stronger (pp. 10-11).
- Larger churches tend to be stronger, and those with a "presence" in their communities are more likely to be strong congregations (pp. 13-14).
- The Episcopal Church is a "destination denomination" for non-Episcopalians who join as adults, attracted by the liturgy, identity and status (p. 18).
- Churches that are open to change tend to be strong (p. 31).
- Churches that are spiritually alive and justice oriented tend to be the strongest congregations (p. 49), and those that are clear about their mission and purpose are more likely to be growing congregations (p. 66).

The report concludes, "The Episcopal Church is unique among Protestant denominations in that is has a clear identity which is celebrated by almost all its churches and a large number of healthy, growing congregations" (p. 83). It notes that, "…certain problems or 'serious realities' are also apparent.…Specifically, the Episcopal Church has many small, weak congregations that are attended and supported by an aging (and largely female) membership.…The aging of the Episcopal Church and the weakening of smaller congregations in small towns and older urban neighborhoods can only be expected to worsen, given the demographics of the population, the minimal evangelism efforts of most Episcopal congregations, and the small numbers of new churches being started in expanding suburban areas" (p. 83).

The conclusions also state, "The Episcopal Church has an advantage in that it could respond to its serious realities by expanding on its strong points, rather than trying to somehow turn weaknesses into strengths" (p. 83). And finally, "The challenge facing the churches is to find balance between doing things in new ways and retaining the distinctive gifts of the Anglican Communion" (p. 83)

Will There be a Clergy Shortage? Analysis and Predictions for Uncertain Times (September 2001): The Committee met with Matthew J. Price, Director of Analytical Research, Service Strategies and Development, the Church Pension Group, who shared his report analyzing concerns about a clergy shortage. The report (available at www.cpg.org/home/research/index.html) states:

> "Most Episcopalians are used to more than just a purely liturgical celebrant, whose sole point of contact with the congregation is a sacramental functionary. Despite the increasing importance of lay ministry, the clergy have not reduced the number of roles they play within the life of the parish. Rather, the succession of models of ministry that have evolved since World War II have overlain, rather than displaced each other.… Rightly or wrongly, the priest still stands at the center of parish life. The separation between the sacramental and communal leadership would be, to say the least, a difficult change. It is precisely this shortage of parish priests, rather than priests per se, that is the looming cloud on the clergy supply horizon" (pp. 2-3).

Price's report looks at trends that could lead to "an absolute shortage of clergy," and it acknowledges a "relative" clergy shortage arising from a set of "'mismatches,' both in terms of geography and in the expectations of churches and candidates" (pg. 4). The report recommends establishing an internship program for college students and the formation of a blue ribbon commission on young people and the ministry.

The 2001 Clergy Compensation Report Addendum: Additional Salary Statistics and Analysis: This report for the Church Pension Group makes clear the modest level of clergy compensation. Clergy rely upon the income of spouses or significant others for their 'daily bread.' The findings of this report left us wondering how single and widowed or divorced clergy (especially those with children or elderly dependents) are managing. It is urgent that deployment officers and others responsible for determining clergy compensation 'read mark and inwardly digest' this report.

The State of the Clergy

The Committee sees reason in the above studies for continued concern about a "clergy shortage" occurring in the near future. *Will There be a Clergy Shortage?* presents some troubling statistics:

1. The average age of active congregational priests is 52 (p. 6).
2. Fewer young persons, both male and female, are offering themselves for the ordination process (pp. 7-11).
3. The number of congregations in which regularly employed clergy will retire within the next 10 years nears 40%, or 2,500 existing congregations with vacancies. Thus we can expect a shortage of clergy available to take their place (pp. 13-16).

The problems of low morale and burn-out reported to exist among one-quarter to one-third of active clergy indicate the need to attend to the crucial issue of clergy wellness. These problems appear to result from mismatched priests and congregations, low levels of compensation, and unrealistic demands and expectations on the part of both clergy and congregations.

The compensation issue is particularly acute in the many small congregations, most of which are carrying on important ministries in rural, small town and urban settings, and many of which can afford only to employ part-time clergy.

The need to be pro-active in raising up and supporting clergy in the numerous places around the country where multicultural congregations are emerging will present an economic challenge as well as a challenge to the present ordination process.

Programs like CREDO, sponsored by the Church Pension Fund, the Clergy Leadership Project, sponsored by the Episcopal Church Foundation through Cornerstone, and Fresh Start, sponsored by the Office of Congregational Development, are positive ways the church is attending to clergy wellness. In addition, both clergy and congregations need to be intentional about scheduling sabbatical leaves and opportunities for clergy retreats and about clarifying roles and expectations.

Tensions in the Church

Controversy within the church is not new. Perhaps that is why St. Paul emphasized that the work of the church is reconciliation. To comment on the state of the church without acknowledging that controversies continue to swirl around us is to live in denial. Controversies in the past fifty years over General Convention Special Programs, Prayer Book revision, ordination of women, and human sexuality have, from time to time, played a role in shaping who we are as we attempt to discern God's will for our beloved church. At present there may be no definitive resolution to any one of these tensions, yet we are still called to move forward as a community of faith reconciling one to another and to God in the name of Jesus Christ.

One of the chief tensions at this time in the life of our church is related to issues of authority. While few dispute the traditional Anglican understanding that authority is vested in scripture, tradition, and reason, some give much greater weight to Holy Scripture and prefer less latitude in its interpretation, while others believe more balanced weight should be given to scripture, tradition, and reason. Thus, some in the church urge that scripture, tradition, and reason support the blessing of same sex unions, while other Episcopalians understand the same authorities to rule out such blessing.

Another focus of energy and attention is on how our canons define authority, and how and through whom such authority may be exercised. For example, we live with creative tensions between, on the one hand, the authority of the canons and the rubrics of the Book of Common Prayer and, on the other hand, the practices of our churches. Departure from recognized ways of making decisions adds to tensions in our common life.

Yet another manifestation of the issue of authority is the question of how much variation in the exercise of autonomy our concept of episcopal authority is willing to tolerate. To what extent are bishops accountable to an expression of "the mind of the church"? How this tension is resolved is related to the concept of order within our denomination and within the Anglican Communion. This aspect of the authority issue is also reflected at the diocesan level, where practices in local parishes sometimes challenge the local bishop and where the bishop sometimes challenges practices in the parishes. Continued use of the 1928 Prayer Book is an example of a lingering, unresolved issue of authority that contributes to the tensions with which we live.

The speed of change presents an additional challenge. The way the institutional church is constituted is intended to protect the sacred mystery that is the church. Yet the pace of contemporary social change, technological advance, and the speed at which old forms of ministry are challenged and new ways of being the church emerge can sometimes seem unrelated, indeed out of touch with one another. Many Episcopalians are frustrated by what they see as an unresponsive church structure, while others are unsettled by what they perceive as a threat to the order and discipline of an institution to which they have devoted their lives.

These issues of authority, and the controversies through which they are manifest, challenge our diverse community to be faithful simultaneously to the movement of the Holy Spirit doing new things and to the traditional faith and order of the church. In the midst of the whirlwind, we rejoice that God is present among us, that we continue to live in communion with one another, and that, in response to God's call to us, exciting new ministries continue to emerge.

Multiculturalism
Dioceses that have taken seriously the anti-racism training recommended by the 73rd General Convention report that they are making great progress in inter-cultural understanding. We urge dioceses and congregations that have not yet undertaken such programs of education and training to commence doing so at the earliest possible time.

We note that we are *already* a multi-cultural church (although more so in some places than others). For example, in some dioceses numerical growth in membership in the last ten years has been largely comprised of Hispanic persons. One diocese now reports its overall membership to be nearly fifty percent Hispanic. Two dioceses report regularly celebrating the Sunday Eucharist in numerous languages or dialects. The spiritual strength of our denomination is vastly increased by this cultural richness, even in geographic areas where numerical growth is absent.

Our church's efforts should be re-doubled in order to insure that greater numbers of bi-lingual and multi-lingual clergy are available to serve and support our ministries; that more sensitive and respectful incorporation of differing traditions of liturgical expression are made possible; and that greater efforts are made to raise up lay leadership for training opportunities.

Other Issues
The committee observes other areas of church life that deserve attention and study, namely the current state of communication at all levels of the church's institutions, the activity of mission and outreach, and the "aging" demographics of church membership.

Communication among national interim committees and organizations is inconsistent and haphazard. We encourage committee leaders at the national level to be intentional about sharing their work to foster better communication. Likewise, we encourage leaders at the local level to be more informed on church ministry by taking advantage of existing resources and information.

The committee recognizes that the church desires to know about the state of its mission and outreach ministries at the diocesan and congregational levels. The parochial report does not currently provide such information.

Statistics reveal the character of national church membership to be "aging," and the church should address ways to respond proactively to the needs of these members.

Finally, the committee did not have time to address a question concerning our polity raised by the fact that voting practices in many diocesan conventions give congregations of a variety of sizes equal voting power. Because of our many small churches, it may be that a majority of the members is represented by a minority of delegates. Does this comport with concepts of fairness as understood by our members? Should a high-level commission be charged with the responsibility of considering this matter?

Conclusions and Recommendations for the Next Triennium

1. The Episcopal Church cannot make reasonable decisions about future mission and ministry without sound data and information about the past and present. In the fall of 2001, RoperASW conducted a survey, commissioned by Executive Council, that asked congregation members, clergy, bishops, national leadership and General Convention deputies about what mission priorities should drive budget considerations for the Episcopal Church. The council used the results to inform their selection of six "areas of energy in the life of the church which need to be expanded" and which should "inform our mission and budget over the next triennium" (see the Executive Council report). Virtually all of these "areas of energy," but most particularly the commitment to inclusion of youth, the commitment to diversity, and the commitment to outreach, require information and data collection, both to aid in planning and to evaluate effectiveness.

2. The 73rd General Convention approved a resolution (A101) calling for a "comprehensive demographic census" of the church by 2005. We urge the Executive Council to ensure that funding and a procedure are in place to accomplish this goal. The church has, on numerous occasions, affirmed and encouraged diversity—including race, ethnicity, class and age—in its membership. Without such a census, we have no way of knowing how diverse we actually are or what geographical areas of the church exhibit the greatest diversity.

3. Information and data are collected and analyzed by a variety of groups, as we have noted above. The committee encourages cooperation and regular interaction among those responsible for data gathering and analysis.

4. Changes in the nature of the data collected by the Parochial Report (addition or deletion of data categories) affect the ability to do long-term comparisons. We believe any future changes should be made with care and in consultation with experts in social science and statistics as well as in Episcopal Church congregational development and clergy deployment. Also involved in the decision process should be representatives of the various racial, ethnic and age constituencies in the church.

5. We believe the congregations providing data through the Parochial Report will be more invested in submitting timely and accurate information if they are provided feedback. With the 2002 Parochial Report forms, they did receive a chart showing trends in average Sunday attendance. We believe this should be continued and expanded. In addition, congregations and dioceses need to be educated about the utilization of the data collected from the parochial reports.

6. The Committee on the State of the Church should not operate in isolation, and it should have some continuity in membership. We believe that a member of Executive Council should be appointed to serve on the committee, and we encourage the next committee to assign members to be in regular communication with other standing committees and organizations.

7. Finally, the Committee on the State of the Church offers a positive assessment of the "state of the church." We have our tensions and our conflicts, but some degree of tension and conflict will always characterize an institution that is alive, that is attempting to meet the many challenges of a complex world. This is not to minimize the tensions, but it is to say, in the words of one of our members, that we are busy doing ministry "in the cutting middle." Most important are the story we have to tell and the gifts we have to offer. At the level where ministry is being done—in our congregations—we *are* bringing hope to a struggling world, we *are* proclaiming the joy of the Gospel. Can we do better? Of course, for we have seen a church with the vitality, the talents and the commitment to do the ministry of Jesus Christ.

Expenditures

The House of Deputies Committee on the State of the Church will meet five times during the next triennium. This will require a total of $71,000.

NOTE: The data used in this report is based on a different record of open and closed churches than that used for The Episcopal Church Annual. For this reason, totals in membership, communicants, and attendance will vary somewhat.

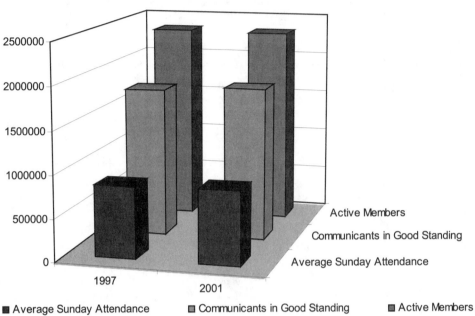

Membership, Communicants in Good Standing and Average Sunday Attendance

Diocese	Active Members Reported in 1997	Communicants in Good Standing as % of Members	Average Sunday Attendance as % of Members	Active Members Reported in 2001	Communicants in Good Standing as % of Members	Average Sunday Attendance as % of Members
Connecticut	75,121	68%	31%	71,413	65%	33%
Maine	16,176	69%	34%	14,931	78%	37%
Massachusetts	83,372	70%	28%	77,487	69%	31%
New Hampshire	17,281	73%	29%	16,628	79%	32%
Rhode Island	29,551	62%	28%	26,659	71%	29%
Vermont	9,416	71%	35%	8,859	81%	38%
Western Massachusetts	22,585	62%	33%	20,058	69%	35%
Province 1 Subtotals	*253,502*	*68%*	*30%*	*236,035*	*70%*	*32%*
Albany	23,342	65%	35%	21,055	67%	38%
Central New York	24,030	67%	32%	22,994	69%	31%
Long Island	62,699	69%	32%	59,366	77%	32%
New Jersey	54,442	70%	34%	54,427	70%	34%
New York	62,521	70%	36%	64,966	72%	36%
Newark	37,065	73%	32%	36,092	74%	30%
Rochester	15,706	65%	32%	13,762	78%	34%
Western New York	19,969	70%	33%	17,618	72%	36%
Province 2 Subtotals	*299,774*	*69%*	*34%*	*290,280*	*73%*	*34%*
Bethlehem	16,775	71%	31%	17,206	75%	32%
Central Pennsylvania	17,546	75%	37%	16,870	78%	37%
Delaware	13,046	74%	34%	12,962	78%	34%
Easton	10,497	72%	33%	9,892	75%	37%

Diocese	Active Members Reported in 1997	Communicants in Good Standing as % of Members	Average Sunday Attendance as % of Members	Active Members Reported in 2001	Communicants in Good Standing as % of Members	Average Sunday Attendance as % of Members
Maryland	45,515	71%	33%	47,390	78%	32%
Northwestern Pennsylvania	5,977	78%	42%	5,745	72%	40%
Pennsylvania	61,751	70%	31%	57,815	73%	34%
Pittsburgh	20,888	79%	39%	20,584	81%	42%
Southern Virginia	33,192	76%	39%	33,573	81%	41%
Southwestern Virginia	13,821	77%	38%	12,558	88%	38%
Virginia	81,045	70%	37%	83,652	74%	36%
Washington	40,803	76%	41%	41,175	81%	44%
West Virginia	11,186	76%	39%	10,323	80%	41%
Province 3 Subtotals	*372,042*	*73%*	*36%*	*369,745*	*77%*	*37%*
Alabama	32,234	83%	36%	34,602	49%	35%
Atlanta	53,968	73%	33%	54,694	81%	35%
Central Florida	38,270	81%	44%	38,147	86%	43%
Central Gulf Coast	20,784	81%	40%	20,745	81%	39%
East Carolina	18,535	84%	40%	18,348	80%	39%
East Tennessee	17,191	85%	37%	16,713	85%	39%
Florida	32,041	83%	37%	32,566	89%	40%
Georgia	17,303	83%	42%	18,464	83%	41%
Kentucky	10,500	83%	38%	10,157	85%	41%
Lexington	8,949	87%	44%	8,884	85%	42%
Louisiana	19,351	71%	33%	20,233	76%	32%
Mississippi	21,305	84%	38%	20,482	85%	39%
North Carolina	44,752	79%	35%	47,208	87%	36%
South Carolina	25,869	76%	46%	27,370	81%	48%
Southeast Florida	36,476	78%	42%	38,722	76%	39%
Southwest Florida	37,609	79%	47%	37,970	86%	46%
Tennessee	13,752	74%	37%	15,005	81%	41%
Upper South Carolina	25,569	85%	36%	26,666	84%	34%
West Tennessee	12,618	85%	37%	12,146	67%	37%
Western North Carolina	15,334	84%	45%	15,861	84%	47%
Province 4 Subtotals	*502,410*	*80%*	*39%*	*514,983*	*80%*	*39%*
Chicago	43,538	76%	37%	43,966	83%	37%
Eastern Michigan	10,963	69%	36%	9,998	84%	40%
Eau Claire	2,389	87%	47%	2,388	90%	46%
Fond Du Lac	8,012	65%	33%	6,485	78%	42%
Indianapolis	12,619	76%	41%	12,280	82%	41%
Michigan	33,510	74%	31%	37,384	83%	41%
Milwaukee	13,577	84%	42%	13,991	86%	42%
Missouri	14,597	81%	35%	14,710	79%	34%
Northern Indiana	7,610	77%	42%	7,180	85%	43%
Northern Michigan	2,768	66%	34%	2,182	66%	42%
Ohio	35,360	70%	33%	32,975	76%	34%
Quincy	3,062	84%	45%	3,020	82%	42%

Diocese	Active Members Reported in 1997	Communicants in Good Standing as % of Members	Average Sunday Attendance as % of Members	Active Members Reported in 2001	Communicants in Good Standing as % of Members	Average Sunday Attendance as % of Members
Southern Ohio	26,210	74%	37%	25,617	79%	39%
Springfield	6,833	77%	43%	6,494	86%	45%
Western Michigan	14,243	83%	38%	13,759	76%	40%
Province 5 Subtotals	*235,291*	*75%*	*36%*	*232,429*	*81%*	*39%*
Colorado	36,870	71%	38%	33,097	82%	41%
Iowa	12,600	76%	34%	11,966	74%	34%
Minnesota	30,139	73%	31%	28,495	86%	34%
Montana	6,411	77%	35%	6,756	82%	35%
Nebraska	9,945	88%	39%	10,206	78%	41%
North Dakota	3,235	54%	23%	2,903	64%	28%
South Dakota	12,616	52%	22%	11,784	53%	24%
Wyoming	8,443	71%	33%	8,803	78%	30%
Province 6 Subtotals	*120,259*	*71%*	*34%*	*114,010*	*78%*	*35%*
Arkansas	13,804	81%	39%	14,668	83%	38%
Dallas	36,453	82%	36%	39,365	90%	38%
Fort Worth	17,546	81%	41%	18,120	70%	41%
Kansas	14,360	81%	40%	14,127	87%	43%
Northwest Texas	8,779	80%	37%	8,550	88%	35%
Oklahoma	19,611	81%	38%	18,240	84%	41%
Rio Grande	14,240	87%	39%	14,983	83%	41%
Texas	79,510	78%	37%	84,942	82%	36%
West Missouri	12,355	81%	42%	12,663	86%	40%
West Texas	28,787	79%	38%	27,837	83%	40%
Western Kansas	2,617	78%	40%	2,507	89%	39%
Western Louisiana	13,808	78%	35%	13,746	80%	35%
Province 7 Subtotals	*261,870*	*80%*	*38%*	*269,748*	*83%*	*38%*
Alaska	6,283	72%	29%	6,958	41%	28%
Arizona	29,653	78%	37%	29,224	80%	39%
California	29,433	79%	37%	29,687	80%	40%
Eastern Oregon	3,555	68%	30%	3,687	74%	36%
El Camino Real	15,891	81%	40%	16,193	79%	38%
Hawaii	11,721	73%	33%	10,753	70%	34%
Idaho	5,952	70%	38%	6,401	83%	34%
Los Angeles	73,381	71%	32%	71,387	71%	33%
Navaho Missions	1,462	52%	20%	924	41%	23%
Nevada	5,781	75%	40%	5,687	81%	45%
Northern California	19,337	79%	40%	19,150	81%	40%
Olympia	33,682	80%	38%	34,188	76%	39%
Oregon	21,545	78%	36%	21,023	82%	37%
San Diego	19,501	84%	41%	21,672	82%	40%
San Joaquin	10,180	78%	43%	10,658	74%	43%
Spokane	9,330	79%	34%	8,585	77%	35%
Utah	6,570	89%	30%	6,876	80%	29%
Province 8 Subtotals	*303,257*	*77%*	*36%*	*303,053*	*76%*	*37%*
National Totals:	*2,348,405*	*75%*	*36%*	*2,330,283*	*78%*	*37%*

Congregations' Revenues and Expenses used for Operations
from 1997 - 2001

Domestic Totals	1997	1998	1999	2000	2001
Operating Expenses	$ 1,157,467,093	$1,227,613,323	$1,299,018,058	$1,403,811,814	$1,453,323,540
Operating Income*	$1,174,623,594	$1,239,895,942	$1,300,387,623	$1,401,791,241	$1,414,557,218
Plate & Pledge	$907,544,094	$958,757,981	$1,018,218,550	$1,102,849,843	$1,118,923,904

* Includes Investment Income available for operations. Does not include unrestricted bequests or Assistance from the dioceses

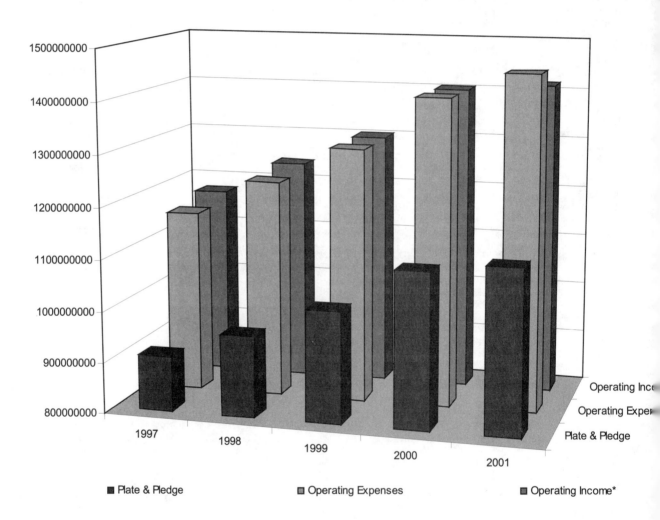

**% Increase between 1997-2001

Operating Expenses	26%
Operating Income*	20%
Plate & Pledge	23%

** Dollars reported are not adjusted for inflation. Inflation for the same period was 10.1%,
based on CPI changes posted by the bureau of Labor and Statistics.

Normal Operating Income and Expenses for Episcopal Congregations 1997-2001

Diocese	1997 Plate & Pledge	1997 Operating Income	1997 Operating Expense	2001 Plate & Pledge	2001 Operating Income	2001 Operating Expense	**5 Yr Change In Op Income
Connecticut	$ 23,607,044	$ 35,843,531	$ 36,518,974	$ 25,998,275	$ 38,299,862	$ 40,782,917	6.9%
Maine	$ 4,774,734	$ 6,590,579	$ 6,540,782	$ 6,088,881	$ 8,008,295	$ 8,192,678	21.5%
Massachusetts	$ 20,779,435	$ 30,424,600	$ 31,937,388	$ 26,031,605	$ 34,985,516	$ 37,146,827	15.0%
New Hampshire	$ 4,369,515	$ 6,027,926	$ 5,659,272	$ 5,775,694	$ 7,772,012	$ 7,851,178	28.9%
Rhode Island	$ 5,830,764	$ 8,185,499	$ 8,490,003	$ 7,230,035	$ 10,526,716	$ 10,886,107	28.6%
Vermont	$ 2,581,757	$ 3,926,890	$ 3,982,366	$ 3,315,317	$ 4,904,476	$ 4,879,079	24.9%
Western Massachusetts	$ 5,727,281	$ 8,722,491	$ 8,152,469	$ 6,961,682	$ 10,074,001	$ 10,427,513	15.5%
Province 1 Subtotals	$ 67,670,530	$ 99,721,516	$ 101,281,254	$ 81,401,489	$ 114,570,878	$ 120,166,299	14.9%
Albany	$ 5,868,552	$ 8,387,179	$ 8,585,348	$ 6,462,647	$ 9,813,224	$ 10,165,557	17.0%
Central New York	$ 6,184,583	$ 9,363,040	$ 9,454,842	$ 8,615,430	$ 12,193,574	$ 10,691,062	30.2%
Long Island	$ 14,941,976	$ 25,230,226	$ 24,057,952	$ 18,422,403	$ 28,593,126	$ 26,838,957	13.3%
New Jersey	$ 16,139,321	$ 22,127,460	$ 22,309,003	$ 18,969,430	$ 25,291,006	$ 25,662,263	14.3%
New York	$ 19,621,767	$ 42,618,922	$ 49,745,290	$ 28,552,970	$ 52,418,940	$ 74,740,152	23.0%
Newark	$ 12,879,112	$ 18,958,855	$ 18,081,659	$ 14,288,926	$ 19,558,424	$ 20,446,455	3.2%
Rochester	$ 4,749,254	$ 6,601,740	$ 6,432,637	$ 5,329,742	$ 7,292,916	$ 7,464,437	10.5%
Western New York	$ 5,355,338	$ 7,259,760	$ 7,352,022	$ 5,843,880	$ 7,979,594	$ 8,144,785	9.9%
Province 2 Subtotals	$ 85,739,903	$ 140,547,182	$ 146,018,753	$ 106,485,428	$ 163,140,804	$ 184,153,668	16.1%
Bethlehem	$ 4,595,911	$ 6,883,505	$ 6,769,871	$ 5,841,275	$ 8,921,109	$ 8,975,630	29.6%
Central Pennsylvania	$ 5,839,125	$ 7,726,733	$ 7,383,732	$ 6,981,474	$ 9,514,350	$ 9,380,991	23.1%
Delaware	$ 4,878,391	$ 6,963,555	$ 7,128,672	$ 5,707,687	$ 9,626,262	$ 9,444,782	38.2%
Easton	$ 3,195,851	$ 4,269,872	$ 4,112,799	$ 3,874,066	$ 5,057,079	$ 5,021,922	18.4%
Maryland	$ 15,030,485	$ 20,456,950	$ 20,206,833	$ 17,604,219	$ 25,913,804	$ 24,273,156	26.7%
Northwestern Pennsylvania	$ 1,975,528	$ 3,200,851	$ 3,292,333	$ 2,185,461	$ 3,765,367	$ 3,743,555	17.6%
Pennsylvania	$ 20,109,690	$ 33,113,473	$ 32,535,359	$ 24,433,183	$ 38,400,212	$ 37,885,304	16.0%
Pittsburgh	$ 9,236,473	$ 12,228,740	$ 11,230,121	$ 11,156,425	$ 14,590,394	$ 15,126,729	19.3%
Southern Virginia	$ 14,623,571	$ 17,726,062	$ 15,960,326	$ 18,267,952	$ 21,609,869	$ 21,290,160	21.9%
Southwestern Virginia	$ 6,615,633	$ 7,606,505	$ 6,798,714	$ 7,057,010	$ 7,924,025	$ 7,778,338	4.2%
Virginia	$ 38,257,382	$ 45,864,515	$ 41,030,767	$ 45,963,341	$ 55,165,199	$ 51,862,574	20.3%
Washington	$ 18,867,284	$ 33,916,400	$ 35,894,896	$ 25,210,567	$ 45,682,331	$ 49,304,550	34.7%
West Virginia	$ 4,921,292	$ 6,126,997	$ 5,667,255	$ 5,487,422	$ 7,302,069	$ 7,088,120	19.2%

Province 3 Subtotals	$ 148,146,616	$ 206,084,158	$ 198,011,678	$ 179,770,082	$ 253,472,070	$ 251,175,811	23.0%
Alabama	$ 17,508,540	$ 19,611,145	$ 17,819,179	$ 13,447,898	$ 15,138,053	$ 14,662,980	-22.8%
Atlanta	$ 25,903,530	$ 29,118,461	$ 27,105,619	$ 31,314,650	$ 34,982,184	$ 33,481,904	20.1%
Central Florida	$ 17,760,562	$ 19,823,757	$ 18,759,668	$ 21,200,800	$ 24,549,731	$ 24,442,615	23.8%
Central Gulf Coast	$ 10,663,650	$ 11,945,767	$ 11,556,006	$ 10,915,050	$ 12,966,023	$ 12,198,198	8.5%
East Carolina	$ 8,738,063	$ 10,029,814	$ 9,861,585	$ 9,866,934	$ 10,918,887	$ 10,965,744	8.9%
East Tennessee	$ 8,857,719	$ 10,224,572	$ 9,981,647	$ 10,967,673	$ 11,958,529	$ 11,649,271	17.0%
Florida	$ 14,949,074	$ 16,699,214	$ 15,832,997	$ 19,743,269	$ 21,363,951	$ 20,833,580	27.9%
Georgia	$ 9,098,822	$ 10,134,991	$ 9,939,779	$ 11,257,258	$ 12,613,824	$ 12,180,234	24.5%
Kentucky	$ 4,649,391	$ 5,797,864	$ 5,594,971	$ 5,584,463	$ 6,486,456	$ 6,931,512	11.9%
Lexington	$ 4,598,175	$ 5,839,851	$ 5,533,405	$ 5,366,614	$ 7,037,747	$ 6,380,292	20.5%
Louisiana	$ 7,338,388	$ 9,265,255	$ 9,171,565	$ 8,070,162	$ 9,551,135	$ 9,882,082	3.1%
Mississippi	$ 10,531,754	$ 12,024,068	$ 11,321,652	$ 12,616,860	$ 14,126,664	$ 14,286,947	17.5%
North Carolina	$ 21,586,550	$ 24,549,793	$ 21,960,395	$ 29,123,155	$ 31,571,270	$ 31,586,493	28.6%
South Carolina	$ 15,778,652	$ 17,560,015	$ 16,573,079	$ 21,026,803	$ 23,759,130	$ 23,617,573	35.3%
Southeast Florida	$ 13,501,863	$ 16,644,506	$ 16,709,200	$ 16,836,650	$ 19,555,051	$ 19,661,724	17.5%
Southwest Florida	$ 17,466,003	$ 20,854,564	$ 19,174,098	$ 21,194,720	$ 24,079,151	$ 33,810,695	15.5%
Tennessee	$ 6,343,264	$ 7,080,092	$ 6,340,557	$ 9,416,318	$ 10,460,523	$ 10,193,864	47.7%
Upper South Carolina	$ 12,766,968	$ 13,852,466	$ 13,478,905	$ 16,447,681	$ 17,447,777	$ 17,294,662	26.0%
West Tennessee	$ 7,086,851	$ 8,565,858	$ 8,235,818	$ 6,758,987	$ 7,855,749	$ 7,253,595	-8.3%
Western North Carolina	$ 7,478,197	$ 9,084,096	$ 8,316,020	$ 9,650,624	$ 10,649,275	$ 10,456,468	17.2%
Province 4 Subtotals	$ 242,606,016	$ 278,706,149	$ 263,266,145	$ 290,806,569	$ 327,071,110	$ 331,770,433	17.4%
Chicago	$ 19,595,737	$ 25,420,101	$ 24,208,861	$ 24,239,862	$ 30,096,206	$ 30,246,570	18.4%
Eastern Michigan	$ 3,671,502	$ 4,713,509	$ 4,433,263	$ 4,279,039	$ 5,389,017	$ 5,617,045	14.3%
Eau Claire	$ 1,079,433	$ 1,296,157	$ 1,256,610	$ 1,217,457	$ 1,504,316	$ 1,573,826	16.1%
Fond Du Lac	$ 2,286,867	$ 3,035,516	$ 3,015,721	$ 3,057,789	$ 3,890,761	$ 3,902,065	28.2%
Indianapolis	$ 5,072,122	$ 9,382,044	$ 8,683,978	$ 5,951,596	$ 15,038,291	$ 14,215,856	60.3%
Michigan	$ 11,633,425	$ 15,800,673	$ 14,975,414	$ 21,973,545	$ 27,095,740	$ 26,950,131	71.5%
Milwaukee	$ 5,826,750	$ 8,153,562	$ 7,586,764	$ 7,532,729	$ 9,649,445	$ 9,687,006	18.3%
Missouri	$ 6,590,164	$ 8,127,637	$ 9,042,567	$ 7,588,429	$ 9,481,991	$ 10,144,870	16.7%
Northern Indiana	$ 3,403,531	$ 3,867,654	$ 3,937,411	$ 3,860,789	$ 4,472,545	$ 4,610,449	15.6%
Northern Michigan	$ 653,972	$ 900,237	$ 888,552	$ 581,559	$ 872,008	$ 896,648	-3.1%
Ohio	$ 12,840,193	$ 17,746,583	$ 17,557,164	$ 14,515,323	$ 19,663,388	$ 20,353,338	10.8%
Quincy	$ 1,164,711	$ 1,963,539	$ 1,809,528	$ 1,295,593	$ 2,048,733	$ 1,879,582	4.3%
Southern Ohio	$ 10,835,035	$ 14,770,301	$ 14,755,135	$ 13,761,612	$ 18,790,409	$ 19,184,231	27.2%
Springfield	$ 2,783,241	$ 4,093,382	$ 3,735,972	$ 3,261,574	$ 4,494,038	$ 4,542,487	9.8%

Western Michigan	$ 5,657,319	$ 6,717,148	$ 6,521,284	$ 6,177,997	$ 7,244,626	$ 7,120,629	7.9%
Province 5 Subtotals	$ 93,094,002	$ 125,988,043	$ 122,408,224	$ 119,294,893	$ 159,731,514	$ 160,924,733	26.8%
Colorado	$ 13,575,374	$ 16,982,018	$ 16,816,426	$ 16,431,564	$ 19,818,010	$ 20,470,870	16.7%
Iowa	$ 4,705,543	$ 6,062,688	$ 5,902,650	$ 5,279,322	$ 6,594,198	$ 6,576,453	8.8%
Minnesota	$ 9,384,296	$ 11,250,158	$ 11,916,365	$ 11,985,314	$ 14,145,902	$ 15,244,466	25.7%
Montana	$ 1,855,228	$ 2,218,708	$ 2,199,954	$ 2,286,649	$ 2,829,529	$ 2,936,938	27.5%
Nebraska	$ 3,719,416	$ 4,219,446	$ 4,842,325	$ 4,197,336	$ 4,895,555	$ 5,241,263	16.0%
North Dakota	$ 774,792	$ 1,020,203	$ 1,164,780	$ 848,158	$ 1,081,040	$ 1,114,990	6.0%
South Dakota	$ 1,531,016	$ 1,965,776	$ 1,881,520	$ 1,741,418	$ 2,196,352	$ 2,093,386	11.7%
Wyoming	$ 2,549,776	$ 2,980,121	$ 2,844,024	$ 3,084,190	$ 3,516,474	$ 2,984,718	18.0%
Province 6 Subtotals	$ 38,095,441	$ 46,699,118	$ 47,568,044	$ 45,853,951	$ 55,077,060	$ 56,663,084	17.9%
Arkansas	$ 7,011,804	$ 8,258,351	$ 8,204,237	$ 8,486,968	$ 9,608,669	$ 9,806,637	16.4%
Dallas	$ 17,076,860	$ 18,893,765	$ 18,280,023	$ 25,092,116	$ 26,674,174	$ 26,384,808	41.2%
Fort Worth	$ 6,919,902	$ 7,396,694	$ 8,099,218	$ 9,135,639	$ 10,260,716	$ 11,042,105	38.7%
Kansas	$ 5,880,397	$ 6,919,422	$ 6,813,247	$ 7,574,255	$ 8,503,980	$ 8,779,803	22.9%
Northwest Texas	$ 4,516,814	$ 5,020,849	$ 5,077,607	$ 4,882,059	$ 5,387,627.00	$ 5,589,954	7.3%
Oklahoma	$ 9,044,554	$ 9,921,026	$ 10,242,192	$ 10,697,531	$ 12,134,878	$ 12,035,917	22.3%
Rio Grande	$ 6,532,892	$ 7,465,882	$ 7,494,142	$ 8,197,269	$ 8,892,250	$ 10,452,101	19.1%
Texas	$ 36,712,869	$ 41,200,514	$ 40,396,760	$ 49,140,781	$ 54,946,129	$ 54,841,388	33.4%
West Missouri	$ 6,127,365	$ 7,749,801	$ 7,654,166	$ 7,010,195	$ 9,127,985	$ 9,966,249	17.8%
West Texas	$ 14,102,910	$ 15,551,023	$ 16,098,187	$ 18,076,701	$ 19,704,070	$ 20,068,580	26.7%
Western Kansas	$ 1,101,137	$ 1,295,534	$ 1,209,744	$ 1,125,876	$ 1,283,994	$ 1,320,393	-0.9%
Western Louisiana	$ 6,453,770	$ 7,298,269	$ 7,442,215	$ 7,451,779	$ 8,234,925	$ 8,131,903	12.8%
Province 7 Subtotals	$ 121,481,274	$ 136,971,130	$ 137,011,738	$ 156,871,169	$ 174,759,397	$ 178,419,838	27.6%
Alaska	$ 1,802,410	$ 2,229,594	$ 1,945,938	$ 1,176,732	$ 1,406,116	$ 1,227,327	-36.9%
Arizona	$ 10,044,447	$ 11,384,980	$ 11,688,313	$ 12,094,303	$ 13,711,464	$ 13,761,958	20.4%
California	$ 13,385,507	$ 17,616,496	$ 17,256,493	$ 19,338,385	$ 23,219,358	$ 24,090,979	31.8%
Eastern Oregon	$ 1,109,083	$ 1,164,565	$ 1,291,844	$ 1,383,234	$ 1,606,519	$ 1,534,910	38.0%
El Camino Real	$ 6,042,075	$ 7,381,264	$ 7,230,158	$ 8,160,659	$ 9,749,362	$ 10,181,285	32.1%
Hawaii	$ 3,309,952	$ 5,786,671	$ 5,757,915	$ 3,472,011	$ 6,651,986	$ 6,513,917	15.0%
Idaho	$ 1,874,404	$ 2,170,142	$ 2,288,404	$ 2,399,138	$ 2,789,504	$ 2,821,413	28.5%
Los Angeles	$ 25,131,228	$ 33,099,577	$ 37,426,807	$ 30,710,349	$ 37,775,243	$ 39,376,977	14.1%
Navaho Missions	$ 23,015	$ 400,330	$ 390,801	$ 24,384	$ 61,609	$ 57,048	-84.6%
Nevada	$ 1,984,888	$ 2,266,348	$ 2,192,254	$ 2,470,709	$ 2,606,090	$ 2,306,867	15.0%
Northern California	$ 7,491,700	$ 8,811,989	$ 8,165,901	$ 9,398,869	$ 10,783,495	$ 10,726,679	22.4%

Olympia	$	13,708,173	$	16,282,418	$	15,588,077	$	17,244,255	$	20,115,059	$	19,888,007	23.5%
Oregon	$	7,756,777	$	9,677,550	$	9,256,214	$	9,399,788	$	10,688,015	$	10,672,275	10.4%
San Diego	$	7,677,711	$	9,487,623	$	9,676,871	$	10,171,924	$	11,821,460	$	13,247,496	24.6%
San Joaquin	$	4,789,636	$	5,759,900	$	5,486,355	$	5,972,049	$	6,701,957	$	6,696,461	16.4%
Spokane	$	3,044,114	$	3,679,939	$	3,711,206	$	3,237,221	$	3,851,196	$	3,729,004	4.7%
Utah	$	1,535,192	$	2,706,912	$	2,547,706	$	1,786,313	$	3,195,952	$	3,217,071	18.1%
Province 8 Subtotals	$	110,710,312	$	139,906,298	$	141,901,257	$	138,440,323	$	166,734,385	$	170,049,674	19.2%
National Totals:	$	907,544,094	$	1,174,623,594	$	1,157,467,093	$	1,118,923,904	$	1,414,557,218	$	1,453,323,540	20.4%

** Dollars reported are not adjusted for inflation. Inflation for the same period was 10.1%, based on CPI changes posted by the bureau of Labor and Statistics.

THE TASK FORCE ON DISCIPLINARY POLICY AND PROCEDURES
(TASK FORCE ON TITLE IV REVISIONS)

Membership

The Rt. Rev. Catherine Waynick, *Chair*	Indianapolis
Stephen F. Hutchinson, Esq., *Secretary*	Utah
Timothy D. Wittlinger, Esq., *Treasurer*	Michigan
Les Alvis, Esq.	Mississippi
Duncan A. Bayne, Esq.	Olympia
The Rev. Dr. George W. Brandt, Jr	New York
The Rev. Virginia Herring	North Carolina
Very Rev. Dr. Guy F. Lytle III	Tennessee
The Rev. Margo Maris	Minnesota
The Rt. Rev. Wallis Ohl	Northwest Texas
Ms. Woodi Sprinkel, LCSW	Virginia

Consultants

The Rt. Rev. F. Clayton Matthews   *Bishop for the Office of Pastoral Development*
Sally Johnson, Esq.

TASK FORCE REPRESENTATIVES AT GENERAL CONVENTION

The Rt. Rev. Catherine Waynick, the Rt. Rev. Wallis Ohl, and Deputies Duncan Bayne (Olympia), Stephen Hutchinson (Utah) and Timothy Wittlinger (Michigan) expect to be present and are authorized to receive comments on this report.

SUMMARY OF THE COMMITTEE'S WORK

The 73rd General Convention, spurred by commentary and concerns from a variety of sources on the appropriateness and ongoing effectiveness of the 1994 Title IV revisions, adopted Resolution A028, as follows:

> *Resolved*, The House of Bishops concurring, That the General Convention establish, pursuant to Joint Rule 23, a Task Force of not less than 6 or more than 12 persons, of whom one-half shall be appointed by the Standing Commission on Ministry Development and one-half shall be appointed by the Standing Commission on Constitution and Canons; and, that in light of the Church's theology and the Church's experience, the TaskForce: (1) assess the present models of church discipline, as reflected both in the policies and procedures addressing allegations of clergy misconduct and in Title IV of the national canons of the Episcopal Church; (2) study and explore other models for addressing misconduct, such as the disciplinary models used by physicians, professors, lawyers and other professionals, and (3) at or before the 74th General Convention, deliver a report of its findings and recommendations to the Standing Commission on Ministry Development, The Standing Commission on Constitution and Canons, and the Committee on Sexual Exploitation, and the 74th General Convention: and (4) at or before the 75th General Convention, deliver its final report of such findings and recommendations to the same bodies; and be it further
> *Resolved*, That the sum of $60,000 be appropriated for the work of the Task Force.

At its meeting in February, 2001, the Standing Commission on Constitution and Canons appointed the Rt. Rev. Catherine M. Waynick, Duncan Bayne, Stephen Hutchinson and the Rev. Dr. Harold Lewis to represent that Commission on the Task Force. The Rev. Dr. Harold Lewis subsequently resigned and the Rev. Canon George Brandt, Jr. joined the Task Force as a representative from SCCC.

The Standing Commission on Ministry Development appointed as its representatives the Rt. Rev. Wallis Ohl, the Very Rev. Dr Guy F. Lytle III, and Timothy Wittlinger.

In consultation with the Committee on Sexual Exploitation, the two Standing Commissions appointed the Rev. Virginia Herring, the Rev. Margo Maris, Ms. Woodi Sprinkel, and Les Alvis, to represent COSE on the Task Force.

In addition, the Task Force has invited the participation of the Rt. Rev. Clay Matthews, Bishop of the Office of Pastoral Development, and Ms. Sally Johnson, as consultants.

The Task Force met during the triennium in Chicago, Illinois in November, 2001, Memphis, Tennessee in March, 2002, Salt Lake City in June of 2002, Kansas City, Missouri in October, 2002, and Albuquerque, New Mexico in January, 2003. At its first meeting The Rt. Rev. Catherine Waynick was selected as Chair, Stephen Hutchinson as Secretary, and Timothy Wittlinger as Treasurer.

Discussion

There was consensus early on that our work would be guided by theological reflection and prayerful conversation. Our hope was to come to some clarity about what we believe the Church is called to be and do in response to failure or wrongdoing on the part of our leaders. Given that our mission is "the reconciliation of all persons to God and each other in Christ" how can our canons include that essential note and still hold offenders accountable in meaningful ways? How can all involved be encouraged to enter into a process which can lead to healing for themselves and the whole Church? How can we facilitate both honesty and compassion, both confession and forgiveness? How can we become the graced community in which reconciliation can actually occur?

A second point of early agreement was that the ECUSA must begin anew with Title IV. It will not be possible to accomplish what we hope for ourselves by making even major adjustments to Title IV as it presently exists.

Our own conversations helped us decide to invite one or more theologians to enter into the next phase of our work: crafting a statement which would honor our sense of direction and be used as a catalyst for a broad based conversation about the purposes of disciplinary provisions in the canons and our most faithful expression of those purposes.

The Rev. Pamela Cooper-White Ph.D., an Episcopal priest who is Associate Professor of Pastoral Theology at the Lutheran Theological Seminary at Philadelphia, was invited to draft the theological statement which is attached to this report. (Biographical detail on Dr. Cooper-White can be found at www.ltsp.edu.) The Task Force conversed at length with Dr. Cooper-White on the substance of this statement, and unanimously supports it. It is the hope of the Task Force that this statement will serve as a catalyst for further conversation in the Church on the theology of discipline. The Task Force presently expects that this paper, together with others on the same topic, will be published in the Sewanee Theological Review, prior to the convening of the 74th General Convention, further enhancing the richness of this discussion. We also hope to conduct at least one listening session during the Convention. The Task Force further plans to engage various bodies and groups within the Church, communicating our work and obtaining the broadest possible range of feedback and input. In addition, we hope to make electronic feedback possible via a web site linked to the General Convention web site.

As work on this theological statement was progressing we began to acquaint ourselves with the processes of other denominations and professional organizations. These investigations will continue as the conversation about our theology of discipline and reconciliation widens and takes further shape to guide our work.

Given the scope of our work, and the conviction we carry that we cannot recommend refinements to the existing canon, we must also report that it may not be possible to complete our task within the next triennium. The Task Force is also sensitive to how any future changes to Title III will impact the disciplinary process.

Budget Report

For the triennium the Task Force's budget allocation was $52,000. We expect to finish our work in this triennium within this budget allocation.

For the coming triennium, an increased number of meetings will be required. In addition, it is expected that Task Force members will be participating in meetings with constituent groups within the Church on the issues in its charge, and will incur expenses for other services which need support. A minimum allocation of $75,000 will be required for these purposes.

Resolution A158 Title IV Budget Appropriation

1   *Resolved,* the House of _____ concurring, That the sum of $75,000 be appropriated for the work of the
2   Task Force on Disciplinary Policy and Procedures during the next triennium, pursuant to Resolution A028
3   of the 73rd General Convention.

SOME THOUGHTS TOWARD CANON REVISION:
CANONS AS GIFT OF GRACE AND DANCE OF LOVE
The Rev. Pamela Cooper-White, Ph.D.

This paper was written at the request of the Episcopal Church's national Task Force on Title IV Revisions (Task Force on Disciplinary Policy and Procedures) during the fall of 2002.[1] Its purpose is to serve as a catalyst for further discussion of the theological grounds and rationale for understanding the underlying purposes of disciplinary canons, and in particular, addressing continuing concerns about sexual abuse in the church and "keeping God's people safe."[2] The intent here is not to present *the* single, definitive theological statement on this subject, but rather, to offer some constructive theological and ethical "food for thought" as our church, among many, moves toward deeper formulations of our the theological foundations and rationale for canon revision.

<u>What is the ultimate purpose of disciplinary canons?</u>

In my view, the canons of the church represent "law" in its highest sense--as a God given expression of care for the ordering of the church that is grounded not merely in restraint of evil (as often is the case in secular law)[3], but focused on creating a community in which every member is supported in living a life grounded in desire for God, and the joy of being in harmony with the original goodness of God's creation. This is the church's earthly vocation, and the vocation of its ministers--who ultimately include *all* the baptized, "lay persons, bishops, priests and deacons" (BCP p. 855). There is, as well, a distinctive vocation to serve within this community, among those who hold ordained and other professional leadership roles within the church's earthly organization: to "equip the saints for the work of ministry" (Eph. 4:12), assisting each and every child of God to discern more and more fully his or her own unique vocation from God toward the living of God's own Realm of peace, justice and freedom, encapsulated in Jesus' summary of the law: "You shall love the Lord your God with all your heart, and with all your soul, and with all your mind.' This is the greatest and first commandment. And a second is like it: You shall love your neighbor as yourself.' On these two commandments hang all the law and the prophets." (Matt. 22:37-40; also in Mk. 12:28-34, Lk. 10:25-28).

Perhaps in an ideal world, there would be no need for canons at all. Yet the church, like all earthly, human institutions, participates in the paradox of God's Realm: the mystery of the already-not yet character of God's final redemption of the world. Jesus came to proclaim that God's Realm of peace and justice is already here, now, and it is up to us to live daily into that already given reality, which exists now in *kairos* time, God's time-in-eternity; yet the fallenness of creation persists in the daily tick tock *chronos* time of our creaturely existence. Thus the church both participates in the Church Eternal in which all human community is perfected and made at one with one another and with God; and at the same time is an earthly creature.

This duality mirrors the mystery of Christ's own incarnation, at once divine and human. The church, as the Body of Christ in the world, is at once divinely ordained, and bound by earthly limitations. The canons, and in particular those canons that govern the relations among persons in community including matters of *professional*[4] conduct and accountability, at their best serve as a bridge between these two dialectical poles of the church's earthly existence. Canons are thus both an expression of God's gracious gift of law to aid human persons in governance that is loving, merciful and just: "Oh, how I love your law! It is my meditation all day long." (Ps. 119:97)--and also an expression of the just and peaceful vision of the Church Eternal toward which the church on earth aspires and awaits in the final day of God's coming.[5]

As this gift of God, the canons participate in a vision of just and peaceful relationality that dwells at the heart of the church's Trinitarian faith. In the words of the "Virginia Report" of 1997 by the Inter-Anglican Theological and Doctrinal Commission in response to a call from the Lambeth Conference of 1988:[6]

> ...*The unity of the Anglican Communion derives form the unity given in the triune God, whose inner personal and relational nature is communion. This is our center. This mystery of God's life calls us to communion in visible form. This is why the Church is called again and again to review and reform the structures of its life together so that they nurture and enable the life of communion in God and serve God's mission in the world.*

In practice, this means that the canons must be congruent with the church's moral theology.[7] As Episcopalians and members of the Anglican Communion, the church's moral consensus is not derived only from magisterial authority, and is not implemented through a top-down hierarchy. We draw, rather, on the oft cited "tricycle" of scripture, tradition, and reason/experience, which had its classical 16th century articulation at the time of the Elizabethan Settlement in the writings of Richard Hooker, and has been a continuing theme in the works of other Anglican divines throughout the centuries.[8]

Scripture (the large wheel of the tricycle), as in all Protestant traditions, is primary. Rich in general guidelines for Christian community and the moral life of the baptized, Scripture grounds the community of faith both in Christ's teachings, rooted in turn in the Jewish commandment of love of God and neighbor, and in the example of Christ's own *kenosis*, his freely self-giving love (Phil. 2:6-7). Scripture provides general rubrics for the conduct of Christian community as well, especially in the Epistles, e.g., to seek the fruits of the Spirit: love, joy, peace, patience, kindness, goodness, faithfulness, gentleness, and self control (Gal. 5:22-23).

Scripture is often mute or contradictory, however, when it comes to the *specific* ways in which particular communities bound by their own chronological, cultural, racial, ethnic, and other aspects of social location, work out the time and context bound problems and conflicts that arise in the course of living out their particular vocations. Canons, therefore, must also draw on both *tradition* and *God-given reason and experience* to interpret Scripture contextually for the sake of the church's sense of vocation in its own unique time and social location.

Tradition is embodied in the history of the church catholic, and the deposit of canon and interpretation that has come down to us through time. The explicit recognition of the importance of culture and context as a dimension of both tradition and reason has emerged in the discourse of Anglican churches worldwide especially in recent decades: "Anglicanism sees reason in the sense of the 'mind' of the culture in which the Church lives and the Gospel is proclaimed, as a legitimate and necessary instrument for the interpretation of God's message in the Scriptures."[9]

Reason, valued in Anglicanism following the long tradition of natural law back to Aristotle and through the Thomist Catholic tradition, is the God-given human ability to interpret and make moral decisions—not only based on rational thought, but also sense, feeling, and experience. In Hooker's words:[10]

> *Whatsoever either men on earth, or the Angels of heaven do know, it is as a drop of that unemptiable fountaine of wisdom, which wisdom hath diversely imparted her treasures unto the world. As her waies are of sundry , so her maner of teaching is not merely one and the same. Some things she openeth by the sacred bookes of Scripture; some things by the glorious works of nature: with some things she inspireth them from above by spirituall influence, in some thinges she leadeth and trayneth them onely by worldly experience and practise. We may not so in any one speciall ind admire her that we disgrace her in any other, but let all her wayes be according unto their place and degree adored.*

Reason and experience also need not be narrowly defined as drawing only on theological discourse narrowly defined as such, but may draw equally and be informed in a mutual dialogical relationship with the secular disciplines of sociology, psychology, law, medicine, and others, in a relationship of "critical correlation."[11] In fact, following Hooker, Anglicans in our incarnational approach find that the Holy Spirit can speak to us freely through the signs and practices of our embodied contemporary world, and the best recorded wisdom of thoughtful people from a variety of traditions, cultures, and disciplines. "The Word of God is addressed to the Church as it is part of the world..."[12]

The following therefore assumes that canon law is not a static body of legislation and ecclesiastical jurisprudence which is changed in order to "perfect" it, but, rather, a living, breathing, dynamic document that represents the best wisdom of God's people in a particular time and place, "*leges ecclesiae semper reformandae*,"[13] even as the church on earth is *semper reformanda*. As Hooker asserted, Christ has not forbidden change: "Christ hath not deprived his church so far of all liberty in making orders and laws for itself..."[14]

To summarize, then, if the canons are to be understood as an incarnational, dynamic gift of God, they may even further be understood sacramentally, as a means of grace by which the visible church is given the power to order its common life for holy purpose-- to promote human communion that reflects as closely as is humanly possible the unity and relationality of God.

What form of governance, and in particular, ecclesiastical discipline, then, does our present time and context call forth from us, as the Protestant Episcopal Church in America in the first decade of the 21st century? Different eras in church history have focused on different aspects of ecclesiology and clerical conduct. Most recently, much of the focus has been on uncovering formerly hidden practices surrounding clergy sexual misconduct, on disputes over human sexuality more generally, and concerns about the boundaries of intra-Anglican church collegiality and intrusions between ecclesiastical jurisdictions. In addition, financial misconduct, other forms of abuse of authority, and refusals of local Episcopal oversight have harmed the church's trust and unity.[15]

In particular, our North American experience in just the last decade has included a growing, painful awareness of sexual abuse and exploitation in the home, in public institutions, and in the church. Sexual misconduct, including sexual harassment, abuse, and exploitation, have been identified in recent years as constituting a serious problem affecting the integrity of the ministry, and the capacity of the church to be a safe and just place for all people. Research studies have estimated that up to 20% or more of clergy have violated sexual boundaries with parishioners (a higher percentage than any other professional group).[16] This problem, once cloaked in secrecy, is now being addressed in healthy ways by our church denominations and by individuals and groups within the church who are committed to promoting positive professional sexual ethics and models of self-care, boundaries and wellness among church workers. However, while important strides have been made to address this issue, serious problems persist, as demonstrated by the recent vividly painful disclosures of the Roman Catholic Church, and continuing devastating cases of misconduct in our own communion.

The ultimate goal of the canons in such a context, it seems to me, must be directed toward the *restoration of right relation in community*, through truth telling, healing of the wounds in this part of the Body of Christ, and reconciliation--not in the sense of cheap or premature forgiveness, but in the sense of the whole community, the whole church.[17] It is important to note that such reconciliation is not an end-in-itself. The goal of reconciliation is not solipsistic, but missional. As I have written in *The Cry of Tamar*, to "reconcile" translates the Greek words *apokatallatto, katallasso/katallage*, and *diallattomai*, all of which mean a thorough change: "To be reconciled is to be changed through and through. This is the precise meaning of the passage in Paul's second letter to the church in Corinth, entreating Christians to be ambassadors for Christ's reconciling love for the world, and themselves to be reconciled to God. (2 Cor. 5:18-19). It is in this sense of thoroughgoing change that Paul promises unity and peace between Jew and Greek (Eph. 2:14-16), humanity and God (Rom 5:10; Col. 1:19-23). We are called by the gospel to *restore right relation*,[18] not just between individual men and women, and not in the sense of premature or cheap forgiveness, but in the sense of the whole community, the whole church. We are called by baptism to be re-*concilers*, that is, restorers of the *concilium*--the whole community of God, called and blessed as God's children, and equally precious in God's sight."[19] This, then, empowers the church in turn for its mission—to proclaim and live out the Good News of justice, peace, and reconciliation in the wider world.

How do we do this? I would propose that, if the canons are to provide us with a bridge between the needs of the earthly church for healing and justice, and the vision of the Church Eternal to live into the re-establishment of right relation that is finally the Realm of God, they must then address at least four areas of both moral theology (vision) and ecclesiastical polity (*praxis*): 1) safety; 2) truth-telling; 3) healing; and 4) reconciliation.

1. Safety:

In all areas of discipline, the most fundamental ethical/theological principle is one of safety. In secular ethics, particularly the ethics of allied helping and healing professions, this is made plain in the classical dictum: *Primum non nocere*--first do no harm. But in the church, again, we are guided not only by the negative avoidance of evil, but the positive vocation to love and justice. In our Baptismal Covenant, we are called to "seek and serve Christ in all persons, loving our neighbor as ourselves," and to "strive for justice and peace among all people, and respect the dignity and freedom of every human being." (BCP, p. 305). Safety within the church, paradoxically, is the necessary pre-condition for the missional goal of taking risks for the Gospel. Risks taken for the sake of the Gospel are never imposed or coerced. Safety within the Body of Christ is what nurtures and empowers Christians to take up the cross, not submitting passively to involuntary suffering, but having the courage to confront evil and injustice as they encounter it in both the church and the wider world.[20]

Sanctuary is at the heart of Christian ecclesiological tradition: "Throughout history, the Church has been understood to be a 'sanctuary,' a place of safety for all who enter. This has been profoundly demonstrated in times of strife, war, plague, tragedy, oppression, and chaos. The Church with all its ministers is both sign and symbol of the Divine Reality of Christ's compassion and justice."[21]

This raises an important definitional question: *who constitute the ministers of the church, who, for the purpose of canon law are accountable to canonical discipline?* As stated above, our catechism makes explicit that the ministers of the church are comprised of *all* the baptized, "lay persons, bishops, priests and deacons," with the laity in first place (BCP p. 855). While Paul makes it clear that there is a variety of gifts and forms of service which are all interdependent in the Body of Christ (Rom. 12:3-8; I Cor. 12:4-11, 27-31), there is an over-arching call to right relation that is incumbent upon all baptized Christians as the "priesthood of all believers." The canons should offer a process that recognizes the responsibilities and accountability of the ministry of the baptized in our relations with one another at all levels of the church's earthly organization (in practical terms, encompassing both "paid" and "volunteer" workers). This means guidelines not only for ethical, non-exploitative behavior by all Christians toward those whom we serve in our communities (again, the negative imperative), but for the faithful living out of our baptismal call to love and justice, and means to call one another to account when we fall short. In the words of the Diocese of Virginia, "Christians have a high calling. Christ invites and empowers us to live out our lives in the love he shows us. Our identity as Christians is both gift and demand. Promised fullness of life, we are called to the self-giving of the cross, to faithfulness, compassion and justice. Our faith is framed between acknowledgement of our arrogance, sinfulness and brokenness, and commitment to the renewal of human life through dying to self. That renewal encompasses 'the healing, wholeness and liberation promised by God's grace to every facet of human life' which is the task of ministry."[22]

While ordained clergy are not to be understood, then, as having a "higher" calling, they have historically been understood as "set apart" for specialized service to the church and the world. This is true across a spectrum of understandings of ordination within the Anglican tradition, from the more Catholic or sacramental understanding of ordination as an "indelible mark" (Hooker's view[23]) or ontological status, to the more Protestant or functional understanding of ordination as a vocation or profession with a unique authority and status within the church.[24] This is equally true across the spectrum of ordained ministries of deacons, priests, and bishops, and therefore the canons should reflect a parallelism in disciplinary processes among all three Holy Orders.

Ordained clergy in all three Holy Orders are called to particular forms of equipping ministry, whether service (*diakonia*), sacramental leadership (*presbyteros*), or oversight (*episkope*). Such ministry is set apart always for the sake of others, by preaching the Word, administering the Sacraments "to equip the saints for the work of ministry, for building up the body of Christ." (Eph. 4:12) This vowed responsibility creates an asymmetry of power and authority that is at once both spiritual and temporal in the involvement of clergy with the lives of those whom they serve (both in the church and the wider community).[25] In both biblical and traditional sources, this asymmetry has been recognized in the form of a particular responsibility, as stated in the ordinal of the 1979 BCP, "to do your best to pattern your life in accordance with the teachings of Christ, so that you may be a wholesome example to your people" (BCP p. 532), and that candidates for both the diaconate and the priesthood must be certified before ordination as having a "manner of life…suitable to the exercise of this ministry." (BCP pp. 526, 538).[26] In the words of the pastoral epistles: "Train yourself in godliness, for while physical training is of some value, godliness is valuable in every way…" (2 Timothy 3:7b-8a).

2. Truth-telling:

"For nothing is hidden that will not be disclosed, nor is anything secret that will not become known and come to light. Then pay attention to how you listen." (Luke 8:17-18a). The canons should offer an ecclesiastical process that creates a safe space for disclosure of the truth, and strives to eliminate a climate of toxic secrecy and shame, for victims in cases of personal harm, and for those accused of offending, alike. Such processes should not threaten victims with re-traumatization by forcing disclosures for which they are not sufficiently healed or encounters with (alleged or admitted) offenders. Similarly, processes should not confuse assignment of responsibility with shaming offenders. In the words of one policy from another communion, "A church that balances the needs of individuals with the comfort and admonition of a caring community will be in a better position to exercise discipline without harshness or resentment. The sharing of burdens and failures can be such a regular part of church life that correction and comfort from others will be expected. The speaking of truth in a spirit of love and self-control helps build a climate that counters the worldly practice of concealment and defense. If a congregation (church body/structure) is accustomed to confrontation alongside forgiveness and acceptance, the secular practices of concealment and contempt will be given up."[27]

Another perhaps more distinctly Anglican way of thinking about this truth telling might be to connect it sacramentally to the Eucharist, as *anamnesis*. The central feature of the Eucharist itself is the *anamnesis*, the recalling of God's saving acts in history and in the lives of believer. In the words of Marion Hatchett, "Anamnesis is the antithesis of amnesia. A person with amnesia has lost identity and purpose. To know who you are, to whom you belong, and where you are headed, you must remember."[28] Especially in situations of trauma, the importance of remembering and telling are crucial for healing of both individuals and communities. The participation of the community as witnesses to the truth is a crucial element in healing and justice. As Elie Wiesel has written, "Let us remember: What hurts the victim most is not the cruelty of the oppressor, but the silence of the bystander."[29] Those not directly involved in the traumatic events have an equally important role to play in the work of truth-telling and remembering The Greek word for witness is *martys*, martyr. The work of faithful listening and witnessing is, indeed, wrenching and sacrificial. The canons must continue to offer a process to support the community's willingness to know painful truths in the face of prevailing cultural denial.[30]

Given the continued prevailing disbelief about abuse (which has not suddenly gone away in the wake of two decades of disclosures) and the natural tendency toward minimization and denial,[31] the church must not retrench on mechanisms designed to maximize and protect a fair hearing of the most vulnerable, i.e., as in the "reasonable woman standard" established in secular law,[32] those alleging abuse, and more generally, the laity, women, persons of color, and children, and other groups who have experienced systematic and institutional oppression both in the secular society and in the church.[33] Grounded in Christ's own teachings that the last shall be first, the canons need to reflect a "preferential option" for the vulnerable, in order to apply the necessary counter-cultural strength needed to resist the prevailing preferential option in society for those traditionally endowed with institutional power and cultural privilege. This does not mean denial of due process, but does call for preserving canonical safeguards and protections that take into consideration the courage required for victims to come forward with complaints, their fear of disbelief, ostracism, retaliation, even spiritual harm[34], and the prevailing societal tendency toward denial.

Processes should also be refined in order to…

a) assist those who (in a very small minority of painful cases)[35] are falsely accused in being restored to their community without stigma, and

b) assist those against whom complaints are founded to own their responsibility for the impact of their behaviors and to take appropriate steps toward both healing and restitution. Canons should offer mechanisms by which the church can rightfully enforce appropriate consequences aimed toward the protection of potential future victims and the safety of the community, without shaming the offender or implying a level of personal or spiritual condemnation that is not within the purview of humanity to impose.

Existing canons have too often focused only on individual clergy and complainants, however. Canons should further offer a process by which the *full community* also takes responsibility for systemic sources of abuse, and in specific instances, for corporate responsibility *via* silence, or even unwitting collusion, with abusive dynamics, patterns, and behaviors on the part of clergy and other church leaders. While confidentiality and safety must take first precedence, the effort of any ecclesiastical process should always be to help safely move all affected parties--not only victims and offenders, but secondary victims such as family members, friends, and ultimately the whole congregation and wider community--toward greater transparency, honesty, and as appropriate, ownership of responsibility for the next steps toward healing and restoration of trust, justice and safety.

This greater accountability of the wider community may further be understood as a call to every ecclesiastical level, from national church, to province, to diocese, to local parish and mission. In the words of Roman Paur, churches must confront an underlying "ecclesial culture of abuse: The fundamental challenge of religious leaders across faith systems is to examine how abuse of power through the sexual misconduct of clerics is reinforced by their interpretive documents and traditions. Such an examination is formidable because it goes to the core of structural and institutional identity as evolved over time, claims on originating sources, understanding of ordained and lay leadership, and mandates of mission and purpose."[36]

3. Healing

The word healing corresponds with the Teutonic root word *haelen/helen*, linking it with "health" and "wholeness." The Latin parallel is *salvare*, from which we get both "salve" and "salvation." Thus, healing and salvation belong together.[37] For most Anglicans, salvation is ultimately understood as the reconciliation between humanity and God, a healing or re-whole-ing of humanity's original turning away from the inherent desire for God. Sin is therefore understood most deeply as a condition of alienation,[38] of separation, or isolation, both from God and from others in creation. For Hooker, *participation* was a central theological theme.[39] Baptism is the sacrament of incorporation into the Body of Christ, the initiation into full participation which is then renewed in the sacrament of Holy Communion. The "Real Presence" of Christ in the Eucharist was not for Hooker a technical change in the elements of bread and wine themselves, but rather, the transforming presence of Christ in the hearts of the believers who receive them, through "our participation of his body and blood"[40]—echoing Cranmer's eucharistic prayer, "that we may be made one body with him, that he may dwell in us, and we in him" (BCP 336).[41]

While only God can bring about the ultimate salvation of reconciliation between humanity and God's own self, the church through its long tradition of "cure of souls" has worked in more humble ways toward healing and wholeness for individuals within their particular communities. The traditional functions of pastoral care have always involved healing, sustaining, guiding, and reconciling,[42] and more recently have also been understood to include nurturing, empowering, and liberating.[43] If sin is the ultimate condition of alienation, then human illness, injury and hunger may also be understood not merely as wounds to be physically treated, or problems to be fixed, but rather as manifestations of alienation and isolation to be healed, i.e., "re-wholed." Examples in the Gospels of Jesus' own healing ministry frequently addressed not only an individual's need for physical healing, but restored that person to community.

The healing that is facilitated through canonical processes will not, and possibly should not, take away the realities of pain and injury. But the memory and experience of that injury can be transformed, by God's grace, through processes that both honor the truth, and restore wounded individuals to community. Episcopal ethicist David H. Smith has written, "The salvation that is made possible by the incarnation does not fundamentally consist of bringing suffering to an end. Rather, salvation involves God's participation in suffering, to establish community between suffering humankind and himself. Salvation does not mean an end to suffering; it means an end to *isolated* suffering."[44] Perhaps paradoxically, experience has shown that those ecclesiastical processes that do not rush to cover over truth or prematurely seek an end to pain, usually result—over time—in more lasting and profound healing from pain and suffering for all involved. The truth-telling involved is also, in and of itself, one crucial dimension of justice. Truth-telling, healing and reconciliation are all intimately intertwined with justice.

Some might want to argue for a separate category at this point, entitled "Justice." While I agree with others who have written extensively on the healing of the trauma of exploitation and misconduct by church leaders, that there can be no complete healing without justice,[45] I have also come to believe that there is a false dichotomy between the two. This begins with the error of separating God's own love from God's judgment. God's judgment *is* a loving word. As Phillip Bennett has written, "How can we reconcile God's love with God's judgment? The most satisfying answer I have found is that God's judgment is God's love, in its penetrating, unremitting power. God's judgment is never divorced from God's love; it is not some angry part of God which is split off from God's mercy and gentleness. Instead, God's judgment is the way we experience pure and constant love which sees and knows us to our core…our layers of self-deception and avoidance of intimacy must be unwound until love can touch us to our core."[46]

While all judgment ultimately belongs to God, the church's discipline should be a mirror of that all-knowing, all-compassionate loving judgment of God. The healing functions of pastoral care have often been considered incompatible with justice. However, we are enjoined to do both together: "What does the Lord require of you but to do justice, *and* to love kindness, and to walk humbly with your God?" (Mic. 6:8). The canons offer an opportunity to effect both in a process that integrates healing mercy with appropriate discipline. The canons should facilitate a process in which the very process of truth telling itself, this *anamnesis*, is so safely and compassionately facilitated that it has the potential to bring all parties alike to their knees, not in shame, but in awe of the mystery of being so truly and deeply known. In such a process, consequences and responsibility may come to be experienced by offenders not as punishment, but as part of the healing process itself, a means by which those who have caused injury can begin a process of repentance in its true sense, re-turning to align oneself again with God's will. Note that this is not the same as relieving offenders of consequences for past behavior, nor does it assume reinstatement to the office and practice of ordained ministry, because the safety of the whole community must take priority over the privilege of clergy. But this orientation to discipline as healing recognizes the intrinsic human worth and dignity of all participants in any ecclesiastical process, including those who have caused great harm.

Much has already been written and need not be duplicated here about the specific ways in which healing can best be effected for victims, offenders, family members, and congregations, particularly in cases of sexual and/or financial misconduct where clergy misconduct has caused personal injury.[47] The canons should continue to make these distinctions. In brief: victims require intensive healing in the realm of treatment for post-traumatic stress. Offenders require long-term healing to address issues of narcissistic wounding, together with appropriate containment. Family members of both victims and offenders often require assistance in the form of family therapy. The community also requires healing in the form of traumatic debriefing and the normalization of a wide variety of reactions and feelings. In every case, "It is absolutely necessary for discipline to be seen as a part of pastoral care. Discipline and consolation, reformation and reconciliation, fellowship and guidance are all part of the practice of discipline. It is difficult to bring all these elements to bear upon the case of a problem individual, but it is also clear that we have a greater problem when any of these elements are missing."[48]

4. Reconciliation

The final purpose of the canons is to establish processes by which conditions are created in which God can bring about reconciliation in the wounded community, so that the church is freed and strengthened for mission in the world. I am defining "reconciliation" in the biblical sense of thoroughgoing change or transformation described above. The marks of such reconciliation would include a felt sense of restoration of safety, trust, and justice--all precursors to a communal praxis of *agapic* love that is "unstuck," spontaneous, free and fruitful. Reconciliation is, ultimately, the work of the Holy Spirit, not the earthly church or its agents. However, in the sense described above in which canons offer a bridge between the earthly church and the Church Eternal, the canons can help facilitate the conditions in which this work of the Spirit can occur.

Furthermore, reconciliation must be understood a *process*, not an event. The canons can offer a spacious process in which the ongoing support for both healing and ownership of responsibility can be given the time they need, with enough flexibility to recognize that timelines for healing will vary from individual to individual, parish to parish, and diocese to diocese.

The ultimate goal of reconciliation and restoration of the community is not an end in itself, and does not stop at the goal of attempting to satisfy immediately affected individuals or groups, but is finally always directed toward the restoration of mission. Mission is disabled by fractures in trust and safety. Reconciliation is not only meant to reinstate good feeling among believers, although this is a welcome outcome. In its fullest sense, reconciliation, transformation, enables the community to move again from a preoccupation with internal concerns to an outward focus, even evangelism, bringing once again the good news (*evangelio*) of God's undying compassion, passionate mercy, love and justice to the rest of the world.

Conclusion

Finally, all canons must be grounded in an *imago Dei*.[49] The canons of the church help us in our earthly pilgrimage to create right relation. Right relation depends not solely upon rules for behavior, or categories of virtues that can enhance civility (as in secular ethics), but more fundamentally upon an understanding of our identity as children of God--to know who we are, as human beings created in the image and likeness of God. I believe a Trinitarian understanding of God is most helpful in underpinning all our relational practices,[50] including those guided by canonical process, because in the Trinity, we comprehend God as Being-in-Relation in God's own essence. Taking the Rublev icon of the Trinity as her exemplar, Elizabeth Johnson has written about a trinitarian image of God as fluid, multiple, and profoundly relational. Johnson finds support for this idea in Aquinas: "...relation really existing in God is really the same as His essence, and only differs in intelligibility. In God relation and essence do not differ from each other but are one in the same."[51]

Quoting Catherine LaCugna, "To be God is to-be-relationally."[52] Johnson concludes with the following Johannine-inspired statement, which perhaps offers us a summary of the theology that should undergird all efforts at canonical revision: "At its most basic the symbol of the Trinity evokes a livingness in God, a dynamic coming and going with the world that points to an inner divine circling around in unimaginable relation. God's relatedness to the world in creating, redeeming, and renewing activity suggests to the Christian mind that God's own being is somehow similarly differentiated. Not an isolated, static, ruling monarch but a relational, dynamic, tripersonal mystery of love--who would not opt for the latter?"[53]

Canons, like all human products, are not infallible. I have hoped to show in this paper that they are, nevertheless, gifts of grace from God, and though we have them "in earthen vessels," we are called to continue to discern how God would ask us to shape them anew for our own time and context. If we are faithful in our discernment, our canon revisions may indeed help us to approximate more closely in our church on earth that Realm of human community which is God's *perichoresis*, the divine relational dance of peace and justice, safety and freedom for all people, now, and until the Time to come.

[1] I am grateful for the feedback in response to an earlier draft of this manuscript by the members of this Task Force in conversation at their meeting in Kansas City, October, 2002, and for detailed input from Les Alvis, Margo Maris, and especially Timothy Sedgwick for his careful reading of an earlier draft. I am also grateful to Guy Lytle and Timothy Sedgwick for encouraging a wider dissemination of the paper to promote further theological discussion on the subject of canon law in the Episcopal Church.

[2] Episcopal Diocese of Chicago, *Keeping God's People Safe: Sexual Misconduct: Policies, Procedures, Prevention,* August 1, 1994.

[3] I was delighted to discover a parallel formulation of this distinction between secular law and canon law as grounded first in theology in Jesuit theologian Ladislas Orsy, *Theology and Canon Law: New Horizons for Legislation and Interpretation* (Collegeville, MN: Liturgical Press, 1992). While Orsy's project focuses on the interpretation, implementation and reception of Roman Catholic canonical revisions since Vatican II, (especially the latest revision of law in the Code of 1983), and therefore must contend with arguments concerning magisterial authority that do not apply in the Anglican context, his fundamental thesis of grounding canon first in theology is relevant to this committee's project: "Since the church is…the continuation of the incarnation, we may say that it exists for the sake of redeeming human persons. To understand canon law as having a function in our redemption is to distinguish it sharply from civil law, and to collocate it in a spiritual order which is never purely juridical." (p. 29.)

[4] The Rev. Dr.Francis Bridger of Trinity College, Bristol, (also citing Roman Catholic moral theologian Richard Gula) has argued convincingly for the reappropriation of the term "professional," not in the sense of secular occupation, but as "standing for (*professio*) a set of transcendent values and principles which derive from a theology of vocation," being called as Christians to be "signs and agents of God's love." Francis Bridger, "A Theological Reflection," in *Guidelines for the Professional Conduct of the Clergy*, The Convocations of Canterbury and York, February, 2002, pp. 1-8.

[5] Analogies to this eschatological approach can be found in both Catholic and Lutheran understandings. Orsy, op. cit., writes: "On the level of ideals the next revision of canon law should begin by examining all our institutions, one by one, in order to determine the theological values which the law must uphold and serve. Then it should assess how far the existing norms measure up to the theological demands. If they do not, they should be duly amended. Obviously a dream; although this was the historical process by which our laws were conceived and established in the first place. On the level of our fallen world (by which I mean a world affected by original sin and its consequences) we can take many small steps toward the ideal. By upholding the organic relationship between theological concepts and practical norms, we can in our daily work defend and promote the integrity of the church. By integrity I mean an internal harmony and unity, where all norms of action flow from a vision. In this, obviously, we shall never achieve perfection; it ought to be an on-going process." (pp. 117-18). In Lutheran theology, this mirrors Luther's emphasis on the distinction between law and Gospel, and the later doctrine, derived from Melanchthon, known as the "two kingdoms doctrine," in which there is a recognition that in the kingdom on earth, governed by law, human agents are divinely ordained to approximate divine justice, but the fullness of salvation and grace is only reached in the heavenly kingdom, when in the fullness of time God redeems all creation through the lovingkindness of God's grace.

[6] Robert Eames, "The Report of the Inter-Anglican Theological and Doctrinal Commission," Anglican Consultative Council, 1997, 1.11.

[7] Orsy, pp. 119ff.

[8] Richard Hooker, *The Lawes of Ecclesiastical Polity* (Cambridge, MA: Harvard University Press, 1977-1981).

[9] Eames, op. cit., 3.10.

[10] Hookes, *Lawes*, II.1.4. "Hooker based his insistence on the role of reason in church polity on the idea of reasonable law, which he took to be manifest in the workings of God and the various orders of creation." A.S. McGrade, "Reason," in Stephen Sykes and John Booty, Eds. *The Study of Anglicanism*, (Minneapolis: Fortress, 1998), p. 108.

[11] This concept of correlation is found first in the work of Paul Tillich, *Systematic Theology*, I (Chicago: University of Chicago Press, 1951), 18-28, and elaborated as a discipline of mutual dialogue in David Tracy, *Blessed Rage for Order: The New Pluralism in Theology* (New York: Seabury, 1975), especially pp. 45ff.

[12] Eames, op. cit., 3.10.

[13] Orsy, p. 18.

[14] Hooker, *Lawes*, III.11.13.

[15] More subtle forms of unethical practices by clergy that often do not rise to the level of ecclesiastical discipline have also caused harm to the church's trust and unity. These involve breaches in such areas as truth-telling, use of discretionary funds, confidentiality, plagiarism, authority in teaching and preaching, representation of credentials, role in society, representation of personal piety, ignoring the power inherent in the clergy role and the related requirement of nonmaleficence, the need to be liked, and ministering only to certain groups or persons, outlined by Phillip Cato in

"Beyond Sex: A Broader Look at Clergy Ethics," *Leaven: A Journal of the National Network of Episcopal Clergy Association*, Oct.-Nov. 2002, pp. 1ff.

[16] A range of 12-20.7% can be extrapolated from a *Christianity Today* survey, reported in "How Common is Pastoral Indiscretion?" *Leadership* (Winter 1988), 1. A doctoral study at Fuller Seminary shows fully 38.6% of respondents having had sexual contact with a parishioner. Richard Allen Blackmon, "The Hazards of the Ministry" (unpublished Ph.D. dissertation, Fuller Seminary, 1984). In my own most recent research among pastoral counselors and clinical social workers, respondents estimated a mean prevalence of sexual misconduct of 14.5% among pastoral counselors; and 82% had heard a client report of a clergyperson crossing a sexual boundary with him or her, with a mean of over 4 incidents told to each therapist. Cooper-White, "The Use of the Self in Psychotherapy: A Comparative Study of Pastoral Counselors and Clinical Social Workers," *American Journal of Pastoral Counseling* 4/4 (2001), 14.

[17] I have written more extensively about this distinction between individual forgiveness and reconciliation as a communal activity in the Conclusion to *The Cry of Tamar: Violence Against Women and the Church's Response* (Minneapolis: Fortress Press, 1995), pp. 253-62. (See especially pp. 261-62). The theologial method of *The Cry of Tamar* is one of critical correlation, in which social and psychological knowledge and in particular the insights of traumatology are brought into fruitful engagement with constructive ethical and theological reflection in a more classical mode.

[18] Carter Heyward has written extensively about the call to right relation, with perhaps the most systematic elaboration in her first book, *The Redemption of God: A Theology of Mutual Relation* (Lanham, MD: University Press of America, 1982.

[19] Cooper-White, *The Cry of Tamar*, pp. 262-63.

[20] Feminist theologians have rightly challenged a reading of the cross as a justification for involuntary suffering by the oppressed and a glorification of suffering as "divine child abuse." E.g., Joanne Carlson Brown and Rebecca Parker, "For God So Loved the World?" in Joanne Carlson Brown and Carole Bohn, Eds., *Christianity, Patriarchy and Abuse* (New York: Pilgrim Press, 1989), 26; and Rita Nakashima Brock, "And a Little Child Will Lead Us: Christology and Child Abuse," in *Christianity, Patriarchy and Abuse*, 42-61. In my view, Christ's surrender to the cross is not redemptive because of his suffering, which is never redemptive in itself, but rather because of his choice to remain faithful even in the face of death, against the oppressive powers and principalities of his day. (*The Cry of Tamar*, p.94) God does not cause suffering, but rather, as Latin American Liberation theologians have powerfully asserted, God stands in solidarity with those who suffer. E.g., Jon Sobrino, *Christology at the Crossroads* (Maryknoll, NY: Orbis, 1978); and Jon Sobrino and Juan Hernandez Pico, *Theology of Christian Solidarity*, trans. P. Berryman (Maryknoll, NY: Orbis, 1985). See also Sally B. Purvis, *The Power of the Cross: Foundations for a Christian Feminist Ethic of Community* (Nashville: Abindon, 1993).

[21] Episcopal Diocese of Chicago, *Keeping God's People Safe*, p. 5.

[22] Diocese of Virginia, "Theological Basis: For All Christians," in *Policy and Procedures on Sexual Misconduct in Pastoral Care*, November, 1998, p. 1. Available on the internet at http://www.thediocese.net/Diocese/cpsm/policies.htm or from The Mayo Memorial Church House of the Diocese of Virginia, 110 W. Franklin St., Richmond, VA 23220-5095.

[23] Hooker, *Lawes*, V.1.

[24] For a discussion of this question, see Owen Thomas, "Ministry: Is There a Theological Difference Between a Lay Person and an Ordained Person?" in *Theological Questions: Analysis and Argument* (Wilton, CT: Morehouse-Barlow, 1983), pp. 119-123. See also Timothy Sedgwick, *The Making of Ministry* (Cambridge, MA: Cowley, 1993).

[25] Roman Paur, OSB, Executive Director of the Interfaith Sexual Trauma Institute, has written: "Clergy and religious frequently, if not typically, are quite unaware of their relational 'power,' and often do not appreciate how they are perceived by the faithful within their congregations or, for that matter, by people at large. They can express genuine surprise and consider themselves even powerless and ineffective toward achieving their pastoral goals. Such lack of awareness can jeopardize relational integrity by minimizing appropriate differences in wanting to be perceived as just another guy or crossing lines of professional propriety with indifference or distortions of transference and countertransference. Power is more a matter of how clergy are perceived by others than how they perceive themselves. In any case it is imperative that clergy be clear about who they are in their various roles and the relational requirements those roles impose on them. Power derived from the authority of pastoral appointment is rooted in the community of the faithful and in the service of their safety, freedom, and growth." In "Recommendations of the Executive Director: The Humanity of Belief Systems, Twelve Critical Issues," Interfaith Sexual Trauma Institute web site, http://www.csbsju.edu/isti/recommendations/english/dir_rec.htm

[26] Cranmer's words from the ordinal in the first Book of Common Prayer carried even more solemn warning: "Have always printed in your remembrance, how great a treasure is committed to your charge. For they are the sheep of Christ,

which he bought with his death, and for whom he shed his blood. The Church and Congregation whom you must serve, is his Spouse, and his body. And if it shall chance the same Church, or any Member thereof to take any hurt or hindrance by reason of your negligence, ye know the greatness of the fault, and also the horrible punishment which will ensue."

[27] New York Conference, United Church or Christ, Syracuse, NY, 1990, "Guidelines for Responding to Allegations of Professional Misconduct by Authorized Ministers…," also citing Malony, Needham, Southard, Eds., *Clergy Malpractice*, Westminister Press, pp. 86-87), reprinted in M. Fortune et al., Eds., *Clergy Misconduct: Sexual Abuse in the Ministerial Relationship: Workshop Manual*, 1992 (Seattle, WA: Center for the Prevention of Sexual and Domestic Violence, 1914 N. 34th St. Ste. 105, Seattle, WA 98103), Appendix I, p. 11.

[28] Marion J. Hatchett, *Commentary on the American Prayer Book* (New York: Seabury Press, 1981), p. 366. For a discussion of *anamnesis* in the context of Anglican views on healing and suffering, see also David H. Smith, *Health and Medicine in the Anglican Tradition* (New York: Crossroad, 1986), pp.21ff. Smith is an Episcopal medical ethicist, Professor of Religious Studies at Indiana University, Bloomington, and Director of the Poynter Center for the Study of Ethics & American Institutions.

[29] Themes of remembering, knowing vs. not-knowing, and breaking silence are pervasive in the writings of Holocaust survivor Elie Wiesel, e.g., "We Must Remember," in *Against Silence: The Voice and Vision* of Elie Wiesel, Ed. I Abrahamson (New York: Holocaust Library, 1985), 3:192-3; and "The Call to Remember" in *Against Silence*, 1:112-14.

[30] For more on the importance of a community of witnesses and a social context that values justice, see Judith Herman, *Trauma and Recovery* (New York: Basic Books, 1992) 8-9.

[31] For more on the psychological mechanism of denial as a group phenomenon in the face of human-caused trauma, see Judith Herman, *Trauma and Recovery* (New York: Basic Books, 1992), pp. 8-9; *The Cry of Tamar,* pp. vii-ix.

[32] In the landmark case Ellison v. Brady, (U.S. Court of Appeals, 9th Circuit, No. 89-15248, 1991, 878ff.), two nominally conservative, male federal appellate court judges established the "reasonable woman" standard, with the following historic statement: "We believe that in evaluating the severity and pervasiveness of sexual harassment we should focus on the perspective of the victim. If we only examined whether a reasonable *person* would engage in allegedly harassing conduct, we would run the risk of reinforcing the prevailing level of discrimination. Harassers could continue to harass merely because a particular discriminatory practice was common, and victims of harassment would have no remedy." A more lengthy excerpt and discussion is given in *The Cry of Tamar*, pp. 71-72.

[33] For a list of basic principles necessary to safeguard victims and prevent further harm, see *The Cry of Tamar*, pp. 143-4.

[34] For survivor testimonies and a discussion of the spiritual damage of clergy sexual misconduct, see Cooper-White, "Soul-Stealing: Power Relations in Pastoral Sexual Abuse," *The Christian Century*, February 20, 1991, pp. 196-99; and *The Cry of Tamar*, pp. 136-39..

[35] See "The Clergy Nightmare: False Allegations," in *The Cry of Tamar*, pp. 139-40).

[36] In "Recommendations of the Executive Director," op. cit., p. 1.

[37] For a more detailed discussion of pastoral understandings of healing, see Larry Kent Graham, "Healing," *Dictionary of Pastoral Care and Counseling*, ed. R.J. Hunter (Nashville: Abingdon, 1990), 497-501.

[38] John Macquarrie, *Principles of Christian Theology*, 2nd ed. (New York: Scribner's, 1977), pp. 71-72.

[39] Hooker, *Lawes*, V.57.

[40] Hooker, *Lawes*, V.67.5.

[41] Cf., Hooker's statement, "that mutual inward hold which Christ hath of us and we of him, in such sort that each possesses the other by way of special interest, property or inherent copulation." (*Lawes*, V.56.1)

[42] William Clebsch and Charles Jaekle, *Pastoral Care in Historical Perspective* (Englewood Cliffs, NJ: Prentice Hall, 1964).

[43] Carroll Watkins Ali, *Survival and Liberation: Pastoral Theology in African American Context* (St. Louis: Chalice Press, 1999), p. 9.

[44] Smith, op. cit., p. 8.

[45] For a thoughtful discussion of the relationship between justice and mercy and the importance of remediating injustice as part of the healing process, see Marie Fortune, *Is Nothing Sacred?: When Sex Invades the Pastoral Relationship* (San Francisco: Harper & Row, 1989), pp. 108-29.

[46] Phillip Bennett, *Let Yourself Be Loved*, Illumination Books, (New York: Paulist Press, 1997), p. 25. Bennett is an Episcopal priest, spiritual director and psychoanalyst in the Diocese of Pennsylvania.

[47] For example, for resources on healing for victims, see, e.g., *The Cry of Tamar*, pp. 126-44 and 229-51. For healing for offenders, see *The Cry of Tamar*, pp. 195-228; Gary Schoener et al., "The Betrayal of the Pastoral Relationship," "Sexual Exploitation by Clergy," and "Intervention," Chs. 9, 20 and 32 in *Psychotherapists' Sexual Involvement with Clients: Intervention and Prevention*, 1990 (Walk-In Counseling Center, 2421 Chicago Ave. So., Minneapolis, MN 55404); some useful considerations of treatment and institutional responses are also found in Glen O. Gabbard, "Sexual misconduct,"

Annual Review of Psychiatry, 1994, 433-56 and Glen O. Gabbard and Eva P. Lester, *Boundaries and Boundary Violations in Psychoanalysis*, (Washington, DC: American Psychiatric Press, 1995), 87-121 and 175-196. For resources for congregational healing, see Larry Kent Graham, "Healing the Congregation," *MCS Conciliation Quarterly*, (Spring, 1991), pp. 2-4, 15; Chilton Knudsen, "Trauma Debriefing: A Congregational Model," *MCS Conciliation Quarterly* (Spring, 1991), pp. 12-13; Nancy Myer Hopkins, "Symbolic Church Fights: The Hidden Agenda When Clerical Trust Has Been Betrayed," *Congregations: The Alban Journal* (May/June, 1993), pp. 15-18; and Hopkins and Mark Laaser, Eds., *Restoring the Soul of a Church: Healing Congregations Wounded by Clergy Sexual Misconduct* (Collegeville, MN: Alban Institute and Interfaith Sexual Trauma Institute, 1995). For an overview from a systems perspective, see also Candace Benyei, *Understanding Clergy Misconduct in Religious Systems* (New York: Haworth Pastoral Press, 1998).

[48] New York Conference, United Church or Christ, Syracuse, NY, 1990, "Guidelines," op. cit., p. 14.

[49] Orsy, 29-30. While Orsy makes this assertion, he does not go further in proposing a specific *imago Dei*.

[50] Cooper-White, "Higher Powers and Infernal Regions..." *Pastoral Psychology* 50/5 (2002), 319-43.

[51] Elizabeth Johnson, *She Who Is* (New York: Crossroad, 1994), pp. 227-28.

[52] Cited in Johnson, p. 228.

[53] Ibid., p. 192.

RESOLUTION INDEX

ABBREVIATION LIST

DFMS, PECUSA .... The Domestic and Foreign Missionary Society of the Protestant Episcopal Church in America
ECC .... Episcopal Church Center
CCABs .... Commissions, Committees, Agencies and Boards
GC .... General Convention
HB .... House of Bishops
HD .... House of Deputies
ELCA .... Evangelical Lutheran Church of America

AGENCIES AND BOARDS

AEC, Archives .... Board of the Archives of the Episcopal Church
BCD .... Board for Church Deployment
CPF .... Church Pension Fund
AEC .... Association of Episcopal Colleges
ECBF .... Episcopal Church Building Fund
ERD .... Episcopal Relief and Development
GBEC .... General Board of Examining Chaplains
FM .... Forward Movement Publications
GTS .... General Theological Seminary
HSEC .... Historical Society of the Episcopal Church

EC, COUNCIL — EXECUTIVE COUNCIL

A&F .... Administration and Finance
CIM .... Congregations in Ministry
INC .... International Concerns
NAC .... National Concerns
AR .... Anti-Racism Committee
EJLC .... Economic Justice Loan Committee
ENGTF, Genetics .... Ethics and the New Genetics Task Force
ECIM .... Episcopal Council of Indigenous Ministries
JMAC .... Jubilee Ministries Advisory Committee
ST&F .... Committee on Science, Technology and Faith
SRI .... Social Responsibilities in Investments Committee
HIV/AIDS .... Standing Committee on HIV/AIDS
COSE .... Committee on Sexual Exploitation
CSW .... Committee on the Status of Women

STANDING COMMISSIONS

SCAIPJC .... Anglican and International Peace with Justice Concerns
SCCC .... Constitution and Canons
SCDME .... Domestic Mission and Evangelism
SCER .... Ecumenical Relations
SCLM .... Liturgy and Music
SCMD .... Ministry Development
SCNC .... National Concerns
SCSC .... Small Congregations
SCSD .... Stewardship and Development
Structure .... Structure of the Church
SCWM .... World Mission

OTHERS

PB&F .... Joint Standing Committee on Program, Budget and Finance